Managing Change

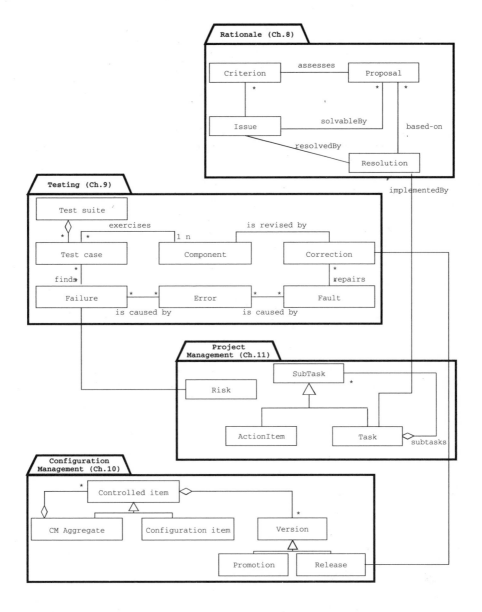

Object-Oriented Software Engineering

Conquering Complex and Changing Systems

Bernd Bruegge & Allen H. Dutoit

Technical University of Munich
Department of Computer Science
Munich, Germany

Carnegie Mellon University
School of Computer Science
Pittsburgh, PA, United States

An Alan R. Apt Book

Prentice Hall
Upper Saddle River, NJ 07458
http://www.prenhall.com

Library of Congress Cataloging-in-Publication Data

Object-Oriented Software Engineering: Conquering Complex and Changing
    Systems / Bernd Bruegge, Allen H. Dutoit
        p.   cm,
    Includes bibliographical references and index.
    ISBN 0-13-489725-0
    1. Software engineering. 2. Object-oriented programming.
    I. Dutoit, Allen H. II. Title
    QA76.758.B785 2000   99-42746
    005.1'17--dc21   CIP

Publisher: *Alan Apt*
Project Manager: *Ana Arias Terry*
Editorial Assistant: *Toni Holm*
Editorial/production supervision: *Ann Marie Kalajian and Scott Disanno*
Editor-in-Chief: *Marcia Horton*
Executive Managing Editor: *Vince O'Brien*
Cover Design: *Amy Rosen*
Art Director: *Heather Scott*
Assistant to Art Director: *John Christiana*
Cover Image: ©Superstock, Tamserky, A Himalayan Peak, Khumbu Nepal
Book Photos: Bernd Bruegge and Blake Ward
Manufacturing Buyer: *Pat Brown*

©2000 Prentice Hall
Prentice-Hall, Inc.
Upper Saddle River, New Jersey 07458

Prentice Hall books are widely used by corporations and government agencies for training, marketing, and resale.
The publisher offers discounts on this book when ordered in bulk quantities.
For more information, contact Corporate Sales Department, Phone: 800-382-3419;
Fax: 201-236-7141; E-mail: corpsales@prenhall.com
Or write: Prentice Hall PTR, Corp. Sales Dept., One Lake Street, Upper Saddle River, NJ 07458.

Product names mentioned herein are the trademarks or registered trademarks of their respective owners.

Printed in the United States of America
10 9 8 7 6 5 4 3 2 1

ISBN 0-13-489725-0

Prentice-Hall International (UK) Limited, *London*
Prentice-Hall of Australia Pty. Limited, *Sydney*
Prentice-Hall Canada Inc., *Toronto*
Prentice-Hall Hispanoamericana, S.A., *Mexico*
Prentice-Hall of India Private Limited, *New Delhi*
Prentice-Hall of Japan, Inc., *Tokyo*
Prentice-Hall (Singapore). Pte., *Singapore*
Editora Prentice-Hall do Brasil, Ltda., *Rio de Janeiro*

Preface

The K2 towers at 8,611 meters in the Karakorum range of the western Himalayas. It is the second highest peak of the world and is considered the most difficult 8000er to climb. An expedition to the K2 typically lasts several months in the summer, when the weather is most favorable. Even in summer, snow storms are frequent. An expedition requires thousands of pounds of equipment, including climbing gear, severe weather protection gear, tents, food, communication equipment, and pay and shoes for hundreds of porters. Planning such an expedition takes a significant amount of time in the life of a climber and requires dozens of participants in supporting roles. Once on site, many unexpected events, such as avalanches, porter strikes, or equipment failures, will force the climbers to adapt, find new solutions, or retreat. The success rate for expeditions to the K2 is currently less than 40%.

The United States National Airspace System (NAS) monitors and controls air traffic in the United States. The NAS includes more than 18,300 airports, 21 air route traffic control centers, and over 460 control towers. This adds up to more than 34,000 pieces of equipment, including radars, communication switches, radios, computer systems, and displays. The current infrastructure is aging rapidly. The computers supporting the 21 air route traffic control centers, for example, are IBM 3083 mainframes that date back to the early 1980s. In 1996, the United States government initiated a program to modernize the NAS infrastructure, including improvements such as satellite navigation, digital controller/pilot communications, and a higher degree of automation in controlling the air routes, the order in which aircraft land, and control of ground traffic as aircraft move from and to the runways. Modernizing such a complex infrastructure, however, can only be done incrementally. Consequently, while new components offering new functionality are introduced, older components still need to be supported. For example, during the transition period, a controller will have to be able to use both analog and digital voice channels to communicate with pilots. Finally, the modernization of the NAS coincides with a dramatic increase in global air traffic, predicted to double within the next 10–15 years. The previous modernizing effort of the NAS, called the Advanced Automation System (AAS), was suspended in 1994 because of software-related problems, after missing its initial deadline by several years and exceeding its budget by several billions of dollars.

Both of the above examples discuss complex systems, where external conditions can trigger unexpected changes. Complexity puts the problem beyond the control of any single individual. Change forces participants to move away from well-known solutions and to invent new ones. In both examples, several participants need to cooperate and develop new techniques to address these challenges. Failure to do so results in the failure to reach the goal.

This book is about conquering complex and changing software systems.

The theme

The application domain (mountain expedition planning, air traffic control, financial systems, word processing) usually includes many concepts that software developers are not familiar with. The solution domain (user interface toolkits, wireless communication, middleware, database management systems, transaction processing systems, wearable computers, etc.) is often immature and provides developers with many competing implementation technologies. Consequently, the system and the development project are complex, involving many different components, tools, methods, and people.

As developers learn more about the application domain from their users, they update the requirements of the system. As developers learn more about emerging technologies or about the limitations of current technologies, they adapt the system design and implementation. As quality control finds defects in the system and users request new features, developers modify the system and its associated work products, resulting in continuous change.

Complexity and change represent challenges that make it impossible for any single person to control the system and its evolution. If controlled improperly, complexity and change defeat the solution before its release, even if the goal is in sight. Too many mistakes in the interpretation of the application domain make the solution useless for the users, forcing a retreat from the route or the market. Immature or incompatible implementation technologies result in poor reliability and delays. Failure to handle change introduces new defects in the system and degrades performance beyond usability.

This book reflects more than 10 years of building systems and of teaching software engineering project courses. We have observed that students are taught programming and software engineering techniques in isolation, often using small problems as examples. As a result, they are able to solve well-defined problems efficiently, but are overwhelmed by the complexity of their first real development experience, when many different techniques and tools need to be used and different people need to collaborate. Reacting to this state of affairs, the typical undergraduate curriculum now often includes a software engineering project course, organized as a single development project.

The tools: UML, Java, and Design Patterns

We wrote this book with a project course in mind. This book can be used, however, in other situations as well, such as short and intensive workshops or short-term R&D projects. We use examples from real systems and examine the interaction between state-of-the art techniques, such as UML (Unified Modeling Language), Java-based technologies, design patterns, design rationale, configuration management, and quality control. Moreover, we discuss project management related issues that are related to these techniques and their impact on complexity and change.

The principles

We teach software engineering following five principles:

Practical experience. We believe that software engineering education must be linked with practical experience. Understanding complexity can only be gained by working with a complex system; that is, a system that no single student can completely understand.

Problem solving. We believe that software engineering education must be based on problem solving. Consequently, there are no right or wrong solutions, only solutions that are better or worse relative to stated criteria. Although we survey existing solutions to real problems and encourage their reuse, we also encourage criticism and the improvement of standard solutions.

Limited resources. If we have sufficient time and resources, we could perhaps build the ideal system. There are several problems with such a situation. First, it is not realistic. Second, even if we had sufficient resources, if the original problem rapidly changes during the development, we would eventually deliver a system solving the wrong problem. As a result, we assume that our problem-solving process is limited in terms of resources. Moreover, the acute awareness of scarce resources encourages a component-based approach, reuse of knowledge, design, and code. In other words, we support an engineering approach to software development.

Interdisciplinarity. Software engineering is an interdisciplinary field. It requires contributions from areas spanning electrical and computer engineering, computer science, business administration, graphic design, industrial design, architecture, theater, and writing. Software engineering is an applied field. When trying to understand and model the application domain, developers interact regularly with others, including users and clients, some of whom know little about software development. This requires viewing and approaching the system from multiple perspectives and terminologies.

Communication. Even if developers build software for developers only, they would still need to communicate among themselves. As developers, we cannot afford the luxury of being able to communicate only with our peers. We need to communicate alternatives, articulate solutions, negotiate trade-offs, and review and criticize others' work. A large number of failures in software engineering projects can be traced to the communication of inaccurate information or to missing information. We must learn to communicate with all project participants, including, most importantly, the client and the end users.

These five principles are the basis for this book. They encourage and enable the reader to address complex and changing problems with practical and state-of-the-art solutions.

The book

This book is based on object-oriented techniques applied to software engineering. It is neither a general software engineering book that surveys all available methods nor a programming book about algorithms and data structures. Instead, we focus on a limited set of techniques and explain their application in a reasonably complex environment, such as a multiteam development project that includes 20–60 participants. Consequently, this book also reflects our biases, our strengths, and our weaknesses. We hope, nevertheless, that all readers will find something they can use. The book is structured into 12 chapters organized into four parts, which can be taught as a semester-long course.

Part I, *Getting Started*, includes three chapters. In this part, we focus on the basic skills necessary for a developer to function in a software engineering context.

- In Chapter 1, *Introduction to Software Engineering*, we describe the difference between programming and software engineering, the current challenges in our discipline, and basic definitions of concepts we use throughout the book.

- In Chapter 2, *Modeling with UML*, we describe the basic elements of a modeling language, UML (Unified Modeling Language), used in object-oriented techniques. We present modeling as a technique for dealing with complexity. This chapter teaches the reader how to read and understand UML diagrams. Subsequent chapters teach the reader how to build UML diagrams to model various aspects of the system. We use UML throughout the book to model a variety of artifacts, from software systems to processes and work products.

- In Chapter 3, *Project Communication*, we discuss the single most critical activity that developers perform. Developers and managers spend more than half of their time communicating with others, either face-to-face or via E-mail, groupware, video conference, or written documents. While modeling deals with complexity, communication deals with change. We describe the main means of communications, their application, and discuss what constitutes effective communication.

In Part II, *Dealing with Complexity*, we focus on methods and technologies that enable developers to specify, design, and implement complex systems.

- In Chapter 4, *Requirements Elicitation*, and Chapter 5, *Analysis*, we describe the definition of the system from the users' point of view. During requirements elicitation, developers determine the functionality users need and a usable way of delivering it. During analysis, developers formalize this knowledge and ensure its completeness and consistency. We focus on how UML is used to deal with application domain complexity.

- In Chapter 6, *System Design*, we describe the definition of the system from the developers' point of view. During this phase, developers define the architecture of the system in terms of design goals and a subsystem decomposition. They address global issues, such as the mapping of the system onto hardware, the storage of persistent data, and global control flow. We focus on how developers can use design patterns, components, and UML to deal with solution domain complexity.
- In Chapter 7, *Object Design*, we describe the detailed modeling and construction activities related to the solution domain. We refine the requirements and system models and specify precisely the classes that constitute the system and define the boundary of existing class libraries and frameworks. For the specification of class interfaces we use UML's Object Constraint Language.

In Part III, *Managing Change*, we focus on methods and technologies that support the control, assessment, and implementation of changes throughout the life cycle.

- In Chapter 8, *Rationale Management*, we describe the capture of design decisions and their justifications. The models we develop during requirements elicitation, analysis, and system design help us deal with complexity, by providing us with different perspectives on *what* the system should be doing and *how* it should do it. To be able to deal with change, we need also to know *why* the system is the way it is. Capturing design decisions, the evaluated alternatives, and their argumentation enables us to access the rationale of the system.
- In Chapter 9, *Testing*, we describe the validation of system behavior against the system models. Testing detects faults in the system, including those introduced during changes to the system or its requirements. Testing activities include unit testing, integration testing, and system testing. We describe several testing techniques such as whitebox, blackbox, path testing, state-based testing, and inspections.
- In Chapter 10, *Software Configuration Management*, we describe techniques and tools for modeling the project history. Configuration management complements rationale in helping us deal with change. Version management records the evolution of the system. Release management ensures consistency and quality across the components of a release. Change management ensures that modifications to the system are consistent with project goals.
- In Chapter 11, *Project Management*, we describe techniques necessary for initiating a software development project, tracking its progress, and dealing with risks and unplanned events. We focus on organizations, roles, and management activities that allow a large number of participants to collaborate and deliver a high-quality system within planned constraints.

In Part IV, *Starting Over*, we revisit the concepts we described in the previous chapters from a process perspective. In Chapter 12, *Software Life Cycle*, we describe software life cycles, such as Boehm's Spiral Model and the Unified Software Development Process, which provide an abstract model of development activities. In this chapter, we also describe the Capability Maturity Model, which is used for assessing the maturity of organizations. We conclude with two examples of software life cycles, which can be applied in a class project.

The topics above are strongly interrelated. To emphasize their relationships, we selected an iterative approach. Each chapter consists of five sections. In the first section, we introduce the issues relevant to the topic with an illustrative example. In the second section, we describe briefly the activities of the topic. In the third section, we explain the basic concepts of the topic with simple examples. In the fourth section, we detail the technical activities with examples from real systems. Finally, we describe management activities and discuss typical trade-offs. By repeating and elaborating on the same concepts by using increasingly complex examples, we hope to provide the reader with an operational knowledge of object-oriented software engineering.

The courses

We wrote this book for a semester-long, software engineering project course for senior or graduate students. We assume that students have experience with a programming language such as C, C++, Ada, or Java. We expect that students have the necessary problem-solving skills to attack technical problems, but we do not expect that they have been exposed to complex or changing situations typical of system development. This book, however, can also be used for other types of courses, such as short intensive professional courses.

Project and senior level courses.   A project course should include all the chapters of the book, roughly in the same order. An instructor may consider teaching early in the course introductory project management concepts from Chapter 11, *Project Management*, such that students become familiar with planning and status reporting.

Introductory level course.   An introductory course with homework should focus on the first three sections of each chapter. The fourth section can be used as material for homework and can simulate the building of a minisystem using paper for UML diagrams, documents, and code.

Short technical course.   This book can also be used for a short, intensive course geared towards professionals. A technical course focusing on UML and object-oriented methods could use the chapter sequence 1, 2, 4, 5, 6, 7, 8, 9, covering all development phases from requirements elicitation to testing. An advanced course would also include Chapter 10, *Software Configuration Management*.

Short management course.   This book can also be used for a short intensive course geared towards managers. A management course focusing on managerial aspects such as communication, risk management, rationale, maturity models, and UML could use the chapter sequence 1, 2, 11, 3, 4, 8, 10, 12.

About the authors

Dr. Bernd Bruegge has been studying and teaching Software Engineering at Carnegie Mellon University for 20 years, where he received his masters and doctorate degrees. He received his Diplom from the University of Hamburg. He is now a university professor of Computer Science with a chair for Applied Software Engineering at the Technische Universität München and an adjunct faculty member of Carnegie Mellon University. He has taught object-oriented software engineering project courses on the text materials and Website described in this book for 10 years. He won the Herbert A. Simon Excellence in Teaching Award at Carnegie Mellon University in 1995. Bruegge is also an international consultant and has used the techniques in this book to design and implement many real systems including: an engineering feedback system for DaimlerChrysler, an environmental modeling system for the E.P.A., and an accident management system for a municipal police department, to name just a few.

Dr. Allen Dutoit is a Research Scientist at the Technische Universität München. He received his M.S. and Ph.D. from Carnegie Mellon University and his Diplôme d'Ingénieur from the Swiss Federal Institute of Technology in Lausanne. He has been teaching software engineering project courses with Professor Bruegge since 1993, both at Carnegie Mellon University and the Technische Universität München, where they used and refined the methods described in this book. Dutoit's research covers several areas of software engineering and object-oriented systems, including knowledge management, rationale management, distributed decision support, and prototype-based systems. He was previously affiliated with the Software Engineering Institute and the Institute for Complex Engineered Systems at Carnegie Mellon University.

Contents

Acknowledgments

This book has witnessed much complexity and change during its development. In 1989, the first author originally set out to teach software engineering in a single-project course format. The goal was to expose students to the important issues in software engineering by solving real problems described by real clients with real tools under real constraints. The first course, listed as 15-413 in the Carnegie Mellon catalog of courses, had 19 students, used SA/SD as a development methodology, and produced 4000 lines of code. Since then, we have successively tried many methods, tools, and notations (e.g., OMT, OOSE, UML). We are currently teaching a distributed version of the course involving up to 80 students from Carnegie Mellon and Technische Universität München, resulting into systems with up to 500 pages of documentation and 50,000 lines of code.

The drawback of project courses is that instructors do not escape the complexity and change that their students experience. Instructors quickly become themselves participants in the development, often acting as a project manager. We hope that this book will help both instructors and students conquer this level of complexity and change.

Somehow, in spite of much energy spent on the course, we found time to write and complete this textbook, thanks to the help and patience of numerous students, clients, teaching assistants, support staff, coinstructors, reviewers, Prentice Hall staff, and, most of all, our families. Some have contributed to improving the course, others have provided constructive feedback on successive drafts, and yet others were simply there when the going got tough. Over the past 10 years, we have indebted ourselves to many people who we acknowledge here.

The participants of Workstation Fax (1989)   Mark Sherman (client). Keys Botzum, Keith Chapman, Curt Equi, Chris Fulmer, Dave Fulmer, James Gilbert, Matt Jacobus, John Kalucki, David Kosmal, Jay Libove, Chris Maloney, Stephen Mahoney, Bryan Schmersal, Rich Segal, Jeff Shufelt, Stephen Smith, Marco Urbanic, Chris Warner, and Tammy White.

The participants of Interactive Maps (1991)   David Garlan (client). Jeff Alexander, Philip Bronner, Tony Brusseau, Seraq Eldin, Peter French, Doug Ghormley, David Gillen, Mike Ginsberg, Mario Goertzel, Tim Gottschalk, Susan Knight, Bin Luo, Mike Mantarro, Troy Roysedorph, and Stephen Sadowski.

The participants of Interactive Pittsburgh (1991)   Charles Baclawski, Ed Wells and David Wild (clients). Jason Barshay, Jon Bennett, Jim Blythe, Brian Bresnahan, John Butare, Jon Caron, Michael Cham, Ross Comer, Eric Ewanco, Karen Fabrizius, Kevin Gallo, Ekard Ginting, Stephen Gifford, Kevin Goldsmith, Jeff Jackson, Gray Jones, Chris Kirby, Brian Kircher, Susan Knight, Jonathan Levy, Nathan Loofbourrow, Matthew Lucas, Benjamin McCurtain, Adam Nemitoff, Lisa Nush, Sean O'Brien, Chris Paris, David Patrick, Victoria Pickard, Jeon Rezvani, Erik Riedel, Rob Ryan, Andy Segal, and David VanRyzin.

The participants of FRIEND (1992, 1993, 1994)   Chief Michael Bookser (client). Soma Agarwal, Eric Anderson, Matt Bamberger, Joe Beck, Scott Berkun, Ashish Bisarya, Henry Borysewicz, Kevin Boyd, Douglas Brashear, Andrew Breen, James Brown, Kevin Chen, Li-Kang Chen, Daniel Cohn, Karl Crary, Dan Dalal, Laurie Damianos, Mark Delsesto, Court Demas, Carl Dockham, Ezra Dreisbach, Jeff Duprey, Tom Evans, Anja Feldman, Daniel Ferrel, Steve Fink, Matt Flatt, Pepe Galmes, Zafrir Gan, Steven Gemma, Dave Gillespe, Jon Gillaspie, Shali Goradia, Rudolf Halac, John Henderson, Brian Hixon, Mike Holling, Zach Hraber, Thomas Hui, Asad Iqbal, Sergey Iskotz, Isam Ismail, Seth Kadesh, Parlin Kang, George Kao, Paul Karlin, Shuntaro Kawakami, Dexter Kobayashi, Todd Kulick, Stephen Lacy, Jay Laefer, Anna Lederman, Bryan Lewis, Wendy Liau, Ray Lieu, Josephene Lim, Edward Liu, Kenneth Magnes, Patrick Magruder, Stephanie Masumura, Jeff Mishler, Manish Modh, Thomas Mon, Bill Nagy, Timothy Nali, Erikas Napjus, Cuong Nguyen, Kevin O'Toole, Jared Oberhaus, Han Ming Ong, David Pascua, David Pierce, Asaf Ronen, David Rothenberger, Sven Schiller, Jessica Schmidt, Hollis Schuller, Stefan Sherwood, Eric Snider, Paul Sonier, Naris Siamwalla, Art Sierzputowski, Patrick Soo Hoo, David Stager, Wilson Swee, Phil Syme, Chris Taylor, James Uzmack, Kathryn van Stone, Rahul Verma, Minh Vo, John Wiedey, Betty Wu, Bobby Yee, Amit Zavery, and Jim Zelenka.

The participants of JEWEL, GEMS (1991, 1994, 1995)   Greg McRay, Joan Novak, Ted Russel and James Wilkinson (clients). William Adelman, Robert Agustin, Ed Allard, Syon Bhattacharya, Dan Bothell, Kin Chan, Huifen Chan, Yuzong Chang, Zack Charmoy, Kevin Chea, Kuo Chiang Chiang, Peter Chow, Lily Chow, Joe Concelman, Gustavo Corral, Christopher Ekberg, David Fogel, Bill Frank, Matthew Goldberg, Michael Halperin, Samuel Helwig, Ben Holz, Jonathan Homer, Sang Hong, Andrew Houghton, Dave Irvin, James Ivers, Christopher Jones, Harry Karatassos, Kevin Keck, Drew Kompanek, Jen Kirstein, Jeff Kurtz,

Heidi Lee, Jose Madriz, Juan Mata, Paul McEwan, Sergio Mendiola, David Mickelson, Paul Mitchell, Jonathan Moore, Sintha Nainggolan, Donald Nelson, Philip Nemec, Bill Ommert, Joe Pekny, Adrian Perrig, Mark Pollard, Erik Riedel, Wasinee Rungsarityotin, Michael Sarnowski, Rick Shehady, Hendrick Sin, Brian Solganick, Anish Srivastava, Jordan Tsvetkoff, Gabriel Underwood, Kip Walker, Alex Wetmore, Peter Wieland, Marullus Williams, Yau Sheng, Mark Werner, and David Yu.

The participants of DIAMOND (1995, 1996) Bob DiSilvestro and Dieter Hege (clients). Tito Benitez, Bartos Blacha, John Chen, Seth Covitz, Chana Damarla, Dmitry Dakhnovsky, Sunanda Dasai, Xiao Gao, Murali Haran, Srinivas Inguva, Joyce Johnstone, Chang Kim, Emile Litvak, Kris McQueen, Michael Peck, Allon Rauer, Stephan Schoenig, Ian Schreiber, Erik Siegel, Ryan Thomas, Hong Tong, Todd Turco, A. J. Whitney, and Hiyung Yu.

The participants of OWL (1996, 1997) Volker Hartkopf (client). Paige Angstadt, Ali Aydar, David Babbitt, Neeraj Bansal, Jim Buck, Austin Bye, Seongju Chang, Adam Chase, Roberto De Feo, Ravi Desai, Kelly DeYoe, John Dorsey, Christopher Esko, Benedict Fernandes, Truman Fenton, Ross Fubini, Brian Gallew, Samuel Gerstein, John Gillies, Asli Gulcur, Brian Hutsell, Craig Johnson, Tim Kniveton, John Kuhns, Danny Kwong, DeWitt Latimer, Daniel List, Brian Long, Gregory Mattes, Ceri Morgan, Jeff Mueller, Michael Nonemacher, Chris O'Rourke, Iroro Orife, Victor Ortega, Philipp Oser, Hunter Payne, Justus Pendleton, Ricardo Pravia, Robert Raposa, Tony Rippy, Misha Rutman, Trevor Schadt, Aseem Sharma, Mark Shieh, Caleb Sidel, Mark Silverman, Eric Stein, Eric Stuckey, Syahrul Syahabuddin, Robert Trace, Nick Vallidis, Randon Warner, Andrew Willis, Laurence Wong, and Jack Wu.

The participants of JAMES (1997, 1998) Brigitte Pihulak (client). Malcolm Bauer, Klaus Bergner, Reinhold Biedermann, Brian Cavalier, Gordon Cheng, Li-Lun Cheng, Christopher Chiappa, Arjun Cholkar, Uhyon Chung, Oliver Creighton, Aveek Datta, John Doe, Phillip Ezolt, Eric Farng, William Ferry, Maximilian Fischer, Luca Girardo, Thomas Gozolits, Alfonso Guerrero-Galan, Sang Won Ham, Kevin Hamlen, Martin Hans, Pradip Hari, Russel Heywood, Max Hoefner, Michael Karas, Yenni Kwek, Thomas Letsch, Tze Bin Loh, Alexander Lozupone, Christopher Lumb, Vincent Mak, Darren Mauro, Adam Miklaszewicz, Hoda Moustapha, Gerhard Mueller, Venkatesh Natarajan, Dick Orgass, Sam Perman, Stan Pavlik, Ralf Pfleghar, Marek Polrolniczak, Michael Poole, Wolfgang Popp, Bob Poydence, Kalyana Prattipati, Luis Rico-Gutierrez, Andreas Rausch, Thomas Reicher, Michael Samuel, Michael Scheinholtz, Marc Sihling, Joel Slovacek, Ann Sluzhevsky, Marc Snyder, Steve Sprang, Paul Stadler, Herbert Stiel, Martin Stumpf, Patrick Toole, Isabel Torres-Yebra, Christoph Vilsmeier, Idan Waisman, Aaron Wald, Andrew Wang, Zhongtao Wang, Ricarda Weber, Pawel Wiktorza, Nathaniel Woods, Jaewoo You, and Bin Zhou.

The participants of PAID (1998, 1999) Helmut Ritzer and Richard Russ (clients). Ralf Acker, Luis Alonso, Keith Arner, Bekim Bajraktari, Elizabeth Bigelow, Götz Bock, Henning Burdack, Orly Canlas, Igor Chernyavskiy, Jörg Dolak, Osman Durrani, John Feist, Burkhard Fischer, David Garmire, Johannes Gramsch, Swati Gupta, Sameer Hafez, Tom Hawley, Klaas

Hermanns, Thomas Hertz, Jonathan Hsieh, Elaine Hyder, Florian Klaschka, Jürgen Knauth, Guido Kraus, Stefan Krause, James Lampe, Robin Loh, Dietmar Matzke, Florian Michahelles, Jack Moffett, Yun-Ching Lee, Wing Ling Leung, Andreas Löhr, Fabian Loschek, Michael Luber, Kent Ma, Asa MacWilliams, Georgios Markakis, Richard Markwart, Dan McCarriar, Istvan Nagy, Reynald Ong, Stefan Oprea, Adam Phelps, Arnaldo Piccinelli, Euijung Ra, Qiang Rao, Stefan Riss, William Ross, Pooja Saksena, Christian Sandor, Johannes Schmid, Ingo Schneider, Oliver Schnier, Florian Schönherr, Gregor Schraegle, Rudy Setiawan, Timothy Shirley, Michael Smith, Eric Stein, Daniel Stodden, Anton Tichatschek, Markus Tönnis, Ender Tortop, Barrett Trask, Ivan Tumanov, Martin Uhl, Bert van Heukelkom, Anthony Watkins, Tobias Weishäupl, Marko Werner, Jonathan Wildstrom, Michael Winter, Brian Woo, Bernhard Zaun, Alexander Zeilner, Stephane Zermatten, and Andrew Zimdars.

The people who supported the projects for their commitment, for their kindness, and for getting us out of trouble when we needed it: Catherine Copetas, Oliver Creighton, Ava Cruse, Barry Eisel, Dieter Hege, Joyce Johnstone, Luca Girardo, Monika Markl, Pat Miller, Ralf Pfleghar, Barbara Sandling, Ralph Schiessl, Arno Schmackpfeffer, and Stephan Schoenig.

The colleges, coinstructors, and friends who influenced us with ideas and countless hours of support: Mario Barbacci, Len Bass, Ben Bennington, Elizabeth Bigelow, Roberto Bisiani, Harry Q Bovik, Sharon Burks, Marvin Carr, Mike Collins, Robert Coyne, Douglas Cunningham, Michael Ehrenberger, Kim Faught, Peter Feiler, Allen Fisher, Laura Forsyth, Eric Gardner, Helen Granger, Thomas Gross, Volker Hartkopf, Bruce Horn, David Kauffer, Kalyka Konda, Suresh Konda, Rich Korf, Birgitte Krogh, Sean Levy, K. C. Marshall, Dick Martin ("Tang Soo"), Horst Mauersberg, Roy Maxion, Russ Milliken, Ira Monarch, Rhonda Moyer, Robert Patrick, Mark Pollard, Martin Purvis, Raj Reddy, Yoram Reich, James Rumbaugh, Johann Schlichter, Mary Shaw, Jane Siegel, Daniel Siewiorek, Asim Smailagic, Mark Stehlik, Eswaran Subrahmanian, Stephanie Szakal, Tara Taylor, Michael Terk, Günter Teubner, Marc Thomas, Jim Tomayko, Blake Ward, Alex Waibel, Art Westerberg, and Jeannette Wing.

Reviewers who gave us constructive feedback and who helped us get many details right: Martin Barrett, Thomas Eichhorn, Henry Etlinger, Ray Ford, Gerhard Mueller, Barbara Paech, Joan Peckham, Ingo Schneider, and Eswaran Subrahmanian. All remaining errors are ours.

Everybody at Prentice Hall who helped us making this book a reality, in particular Alan Apt, our publisher, for never losing faith; Sondra Scott and Ana Terry, our project managers, for tracking and facilitating the million or so questions associated with this project; Eileen Clark, our production manager, Ann Marie Kalajian and Scott Disanno, our production editors, and Heather Scott, our art director, for designing elegant and attractive book cover and chapter openers and for making many wonderful and impossible things happen on schedule; Joel Berman, Toni Holm, Eric Weisser, and many others who worked hard toward the completion of this book but whom we did not have the opportunity and pleasure to meet personally.

And finally our families to whom we dedicate this book and without whose infinite love and patience this enterprise would never have been possible.

PART I
Getting Started

1

Introduction to Software Engineering

The amateur software engineer is always in search of magic, some sensational method or tool whose application promises to render software development trivial. It is the mark of the professional software engineer to know that no such panacea exists.

—Grady Booch, *in Object-Oriented Analysis and Design*

The term software engineering was coined in 1968 as a response to the desolate state of the art of developing quality software on time and within budget. Software developers were not able to set concrete objectives, predict the resources necessary to attain those objectives, and manage the customers' expectations. More often than not, the moon was promised, a lunar rover built, and a pair of square wheels delivered.

The emphasis in software engineering is on both words, *software* and *engineering.* An engineer is able to build a high-quality product using off-the-shelf components and integrating them under time and budget constraints. The engineer is often faced with ill-defined problems, partial solutions, and has to rely on empirical methods to evaluate solutions. Engineers working on application domains such as passenger aircraft design and bridge construction have met successfully similar challenges. Software engineers have not been as successful.

The problem of building and delivering complex software systems on time has been actively investigated and researched. Everything has been blamed, from the customer ("What do you mean I can't get the moon for $50?") to the "soft" in software ("If I could add that one last feature ...") to the youth of this discipline. What is the problem?

Complexity and change.

Useful software systems are complex. To remain useful they need to evolve with the end users' need and the target environment. In this book, we describe object-oriented techniques for conquering complex and changing software systems. In this chapter, we provide a motivation for object-oriented techniques and define the basic concepts used throughout this book.

1.1 Introduction: Software Engineering Failures

Consider the following examples [Neumann, 1995]:

Year 1900 bug

In 1992, Mary from Winona, Minnesota, received an invitation to attend a kindergarten. Mary was 104 at the time.

Leap-year bug

A supermarket was fined $1000 for having meat around 1 day too long, on February 29, 1988. The computer program printing the expiration date on the meat labels did not take into account that 1988 was a leap year.

Interface misuse

On April 10, 1990, in London, an underground train left the station without its driver. The driver had taped the button that started the train, relying on the system that prevented the train from moving when doors were open. The train operator had left his train to close a door which was stuck. When the door was finally shut, the train simply left.

Security

On November 2, 1988, a self-propagating program, subsequently called the Internet Worm, was released into the Internet. The program exploited vulnerabilities in network services, such as the sendmail Unix program, to replicate itself from one computer to another. Unfortunately, the Internet Worm, upon arriving at a machine, consumed all available computing resources and took the infected machine down. An estimated 10% of all Internet nodes were affected. The infection took several days to eradicate.

Late and over budget

In 1995, bugs in the automated luggage system of the new Denver International Airport caused suitcases to be chewed up. The airport opened 16 months late, $3.2 billion over-budget, with a mostly manual luggage system.

On-time delivery

After 18 months of development, a $200 million system was delivered to a health insurance company in Wisconsin in 1984. However, the system did not work correctly: $60 million in overpayments were issued. The system took 3 years to fix.

Unnecessary complexity

The C-17 cargo plane by McDonnell Douglas ran $500 million over budget because of problems with its avionics software. The C-17 included 19 onboard computers, 80 microprocessors, and 6 different programming languages.

Each of the failures described above was due to a software-related problem. In some cases, developers did not anticipate seldom-occurring situations (a person living more than 100 years, leap years impacting expiration dates). In other cases, developers did not anticipate the user actively misusing the system (taping down a button, exploiting sendmail's debugging facilities). In yet other cases, system failures resulted from management failures (late and over-budget delivery, on-time delivery of an incorrect system, unnecessary complexity).

Software systems are complex creations: They perform many functions; they are built to achieve many different, and often conflicting, objectives; they comprise many components; many of their components are custom made and complex themselves; many participants, from different disciplines, take part in the development of these components; the development process and the software life cycle often spans many years; finally, complex systems are difficult to understand completely by any single person. Many systems are so hard to understand, even during their development phase, that they are never finished: These are called vaporware.

Software development projects are subject to constant change. Because requirements are complex, they need to be updated when errors are discovered and when the developers have a better understanding of the application. If the project lasts many years, the staff turn-around is high, requiring constant training. The time between technological changes is often shorter than the duration of the project. The widespread assumption of a software project manager that all changes have been dealt with and that the requirements can be frozen lead to an irrelevant system being deployed.

In the next section, we present a high-level view of software engineering. We describe software engineering in the perspective of science, engineering, and knowledge acquisition and formalization. In Section 1.3, we describe in more detail the main terms and concepts we use in this book. In Section 1.4, we provide an overview of the development activities of software engineering. In Section 1.5, we give an overview of the managerial activities of software engineering.

1.2 What is Software Engineering?

Software engineering is a **modeling** activity. Software engineers deal with complexity through modeling, by focusing at any one time on only the relevant details and ignoring everything else. In the course of development, software engineers build many different models of the system and of the application domain.

Software engineering is a **problem-solving** activity. Models are used to search for an acceptable solution. This search is driven by experimentation. Software engineers do not have infinite resources and are constrained by budget and deadlines. Given the lack of a fundamental theory, they often have to rely empirical methods to evaluate the benefits of different alternatives.

Software engineering is a **knowledge acquisition** activity. In modeling the application and solution domain, software engineers collect data, organize it into information, and formalize it into knowledge. Knowledge acquisition is nonlinear, as a single piece of data can invalidate complete models.

Software engineering is a **rationale-driven** activity. When acquiring knowledge and making decisions about the system or its application domain, software engineers also need to capture the context in which decisions were made and the rationale behind these decisions. Rationale information, represented as a set of issue models, enables software engineers to understand the implication of a proposed change when revisiting a decision.

In this section, we describe in more detail software engineering from the perspectives of modeling, problem solving, knowledge acquisition, and rationale. For each of these activities, software engineers have to work under people, time, and budget constraints. In addition, we assume that change can occur at any time.

1.2.1   Modeling

The purpose of science is to describe and understand complex systems, such as a system of atoms, a society of human beings, or a solar system. Traditionally, a distinction is made between *natural sciences* and *social sciences* to distinguish between two major types of systems. The purpose of natural sciences is to understand nature and its subsystems. Natural sciences include, for example, biology, chemistry, physics, and paleontology. The purpose of the social sciences is to understand human beings. Social sciences include psychology and sociology.

There is another type of system that we call an artificial system. Examples of artificial systems include the space shuttle, airline reservation systems, and stock trading systems. Herbert Simon coined the term *sciences of the artificial* to describe the sciences that deal with artificial systems [Simon, 1970]. Whereas natural and social sciences have been around for centuries, the sciences of the artificial are recent. Computer science, for example, the science dealing with understanding computer systems, is a child of this century.

Many methods that have been successfully applied in the natural sciences and humanities can be applied to the sciences of the artificial as well. By looking at the other sciences, we can learn quite a bit. One of the basic methods of science is modeling. A model is an abstract representation of a system that enables us to answer questions about the system. Models are useful when dealing with systems that are too large, too small, too complicated, or too expensive to experience firsthand. Models also allow us to visualize and understand systems that either no longer exist or that are only claimed to exist.

Fossil biologists unearth a few bones and teeth preserved from some dinosaur that no one has ever seen. From the bone fragments, they reconstruct a model of the animal, following rules of anatomy. The more bones they find, the clearer their idea of how the pieces fit together and the higher the confidence that their model matches the original dinosaur. If they find a sufficient number of bones, teeth, and claws, they can almost be sure that their model reflects reality accurately, and they can guess the missing parts. Legs, for example, usually come in pairs. If the left leg is found, but the right leg is missing, the fossil biologists have a fairly good idea what the missing leg should look like and where it fits in the model. This is an example of a model of a system that no longer exists.

Today's high-energy physicists are in a similar position to that of a fossil biologist who has found most of the bones. Physicists are building a model of matter and energy and how they fit together at the most basic subatomic level. Their tool is the high-energy particle accelerator. Many years of experiments with particle accelerators have given high-energy physicists enough confidence that their models reflect reality and that the remaining pieces that are not yet found will fit into the so-called standard model. This is an example of a model for a system that is claimed to exist.

Both system modelers, fossil biologists and high-energy physicists, deal with two types of entities: the real-world system, observed in terms of a set of phenomena, and the problem domain model, represented as a set of interdependent concepts. The system in the real world is a dinosaur or subatomic particles. The problem domain model is a description of those aspects of the real-world system that are relevant to the problem under consideration.

Software engineers face similar challenges as fossil biologists and high-energy physicists. First, software engineers need to understand the environment in which the system is to operate. For a train traffic control system, software engineers need to know train signaling procedures. For a stock trading system, software engineers need to know trading rules. Software engineers do not need to become a fully certified train dispatcher or a stock broker; they only need to learn the problem domain concepts that are *relevant* to the system. In other terms, they need to build a model of the problem domain.

Second, software engineers need to understand the systems they could build, to evaluate different solutions and trade-offs. Most systems are too complex to be understood by any one person and are expensive to build. To address these challenges, software engineers describe important aspects of the alternative systems they investigate. In other terms, they need to build a model of the solution domain.

Object-oriented methods combine the problem and solution domain modeling activities into one. The problem domain is first modeled as a set of objects and relationships. This model is then used by the system to represent the real-world concepts it manipulates. A train traffic control system includes train objects representing the trains it monitors. A stock trading system includes transaction objects representing the buying and selling of commodities. Then, solution domain concepts are also modeled as objects. The set of lines used to depict a train or a transaction are objects that are part of the solution domain. The idea of object-oriented methods is that the solution domain model is an extension of the problem domain model. Developing software translates into the activities necessary to identify and describe a system as a set of models that addresses the end user's problem. We describe in more detail modeling and the concepts of objects in Chapter 2, *Modeling with UML*.

1.2.2   Problem Solving

Engineering is a problem-solving activity. Engineers search for an appropriate solution, often by trial and error, evaluating alternatives empirically, with limited resources and incomplete knowledge. In its simplest form, the engineering method includes five steps:

1. formulate the problem
2. analyze the problem
3. search for solutions

4. decide on the appropriate solution

5. specify the solution

Software engineering is an engineering activity. It is not algorithmic. It requires experimentation, the reuse of pattern solutions, and the incremental evolution of the system toward a
solution that is acceptable to the client.

Software development typically includes five development activities: requirements
elicitation, analysis, system design, object design, and implementation. During requirements
elicitation and analysis, software engineers formulate the problem with the client and build the
problem domain model. Requirements elicitation and analysis correspond to steps 1 and 2 of the
engineering method. During system design, software engineers analyze the problem, break it
down into smaller pieces, and select general strategies for designing the system. During object
design, they select detail solutions for each piece and decide on the most appropriate solution.
System design and object design result in the solution domain model. System and object design
correspond to steps 3 and 4 of the engineering method. During implementation, software
engineers realize the system by translating the solution domain model into an executable
representation. Implementation corresponds to step 5 of the engineering method. What makes
software engineering different from problem solving in other sciences is that change occurs
while the problem is being solved.

Software development also includes activities whose purpose is to evaluate the
appropriateness of the respective models. During the analysis review, the application domain
model is compared with the client's reality, which in turn might change as a result of modeling.
During the design review, the solution domain model is evaluated against project goals. During
testing, the system is validated against the solution domain model, which might change due to
the introduction of new technologies. During project management, managers compare their
model of the development process (i.e., the project schedule and budget) against reality (i.e., the
delivered work products and expended resources).

1.2.3   Knowledge Acquisition

A common mistake that software engineers and managers make is to assume that the
acquisition of knowledge needed to develop a system is linear. This mistake is not made by
software managers alone. It can be found in other areas as well. In the seventeenth century, a
book was published that offered to teach all the German poems by pouring them into the
student's head in 6 hours with a funnel.[1] The idea of using a funnel for learning is based on the
widespread assumption that our mind is a bucket that is initially empty and can be filled in a
linear fashion. Material enters through our senses, accumulates, and is digested. Popper calls
this linear acquisition model for knowledge "the bucket theory of the mind." Among the many

---

1. G. P. Harsdoerfer (1607–1658) "Poetischer Trichter, die teutsche Dicht- und Reimkunst, ohn Behuf der lateinischen
    Sprache, in 6 Stunden einzugießen," Nuernberg, 1630.

other things that are wrong with this theory (described in [Popper, 1992]) is the assumption that knowledge is conceived as consisting of things that can fill a bucket; that is, the fuller the bucket is, the more we know.

Knowledge acquisition is a nonlinear process. The addition of a new piece of information may invalidate all the knowledge we have acquired for the understanding of a system. Even if we had already documented this understanding in documents and code ("The system is 90% coded, we will be done next week"), we must be mentally prepared to start from scratch. This has important implications on the set of activities and their interactions we define to develop the software system. The equivalent of the bucket theory of the mind is the linear waterfall model for software development, in which all steps of the engineering method are accomplished sequentially.

The nonlinearity of the knowledge acquisition process has severe implications on system development. There are several software processes that deal with this problem by avoiding the linear dependencies inherent in the waterfall model. *Risk-based development* attempts to anticipate surprises late in a project by identifying the high-risk components. *Issue-based development* attempts to remove the linearity altogether. Any development activity, be it analysis, system design, object design, implementation, testing, or delivery, can influence any other activity. In issue-based development, all these activities are executed in parallel. The difficulty with nonlinear development models, however, is that they are hard to manage.

1.2.4 Rationale Management

When describing the acquisition or evolution of knowledge, we are even less well equipped than when describing the knowledge of an existing system. How does a mathematician derive a proof? Mathematical textbooks are full of proofs but rarely provide hints about the proof derivation. This is because mathematicians do not think of it as being important. Once the axioms and the rules of deduction have been stated, the proof is timeless. It will only have to be revisited when the basic assumptions or deduction rules change. In mathematics, this happens quite rarely. The appearance of non-Euclidean geometries 2000 years after Euclid is an example. Non-Euclidean geometries are based on the first four axioms of Euclid but assume an alternative axiom in place of the fifth axiom of Euclid (given a line l and a point p not part of l, there is exactly one line l' parallel to l including point p). A non-Euclidean geometry was later used by Einstein in his general relativity theory. In astronomy, change is also not a daily event. It took 1500 years to move from Ptolemy's geocentric model of the universe to the Copernican heliocentric model of the universe.

For software engineers, the situation is different. Assumptions that developers make about a system change constantly. Even though the application domain models eventually stabilize once developers acquire an adequate understanding of the problem, the solution domain models are in constant flux. Design and implementation faults discovered during testing and usability problems discovered during user evaluation trigger changes to the solution models. Changes can also be caused by new technology. The availability of a long-life battery and of high-bandwidth wireless communication, for example, can trigger revisions to the concept of a portable terminal. Change introduced by new technology often allows the formulation of new functional or nonfunctional requirements. A typical task to be done by software engineers is to change a currently operational software system to incorporate this new enabling technology. To change the system, it is not enough to understand its current components and behavior. It is also necessary to capture and understand the context in which each design decision was made. This additional knowledge is called the **rationale** of the system.

Capturing and accessing the rationale of a system is nontrivial. First, for every decision made, several alternatives may have been considered, evaluated, and argued. Consequently, rationale represents a much larger amount of information than the solution models do. Second, rationale information is often not explicit. Developers make many decisions based on their experience and their intuition, without explicitly evaluating different alternatives. When asked to explain a decision, developers may have to spend a substantial amount of time recovering its rationale. In order to deal with changing systems, however, software engineers must address the challenges of capturing and accessing rationale.

So far, we have presented a high-level view of software engineering, from the perspectives of modeling, problem solving, knowledge acquisition, and rationale. In the next section, we define the main terms and concepts we use in the book.

1.3 Software Engineering Concepts

In this section, we describe the main concepts we use throughout the book.[2] A `Project`, whose purpose is to develop a software system, is composed of a number of `Activities`. Each `Activity` is in turn composed of a number of `Tasks`. A `Task` consumes `Resources` and produces a `WorkProduct`. A `WorkProduct` can be either a `System`, a `Model`, or a `Document`. `Resources` are either `Participants`, `Time`, or `Equipment`. A graphical representation of these concepts is shown in Figure 1-1. This figure is represented in the Unified Modeling Language (UML) notation. We use UML throughout the book to represent models of software and other systems. Intuitively, you should be able to understand this diagram without full knowledge of the UML semantics. Similarly, you can also use UML diagrams when interacting with a client or a user, even though they may not have any knowledge of UML. We describe the semantics of these diagrams in detail in Chapter 2, *Modeling with UML*.

---

2. As much as possible, we follow the definitions of the IEEE standards on Software Engineering [IEEE, 1997].

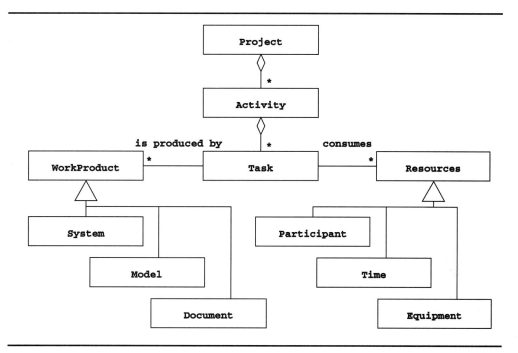

Figure 1-1   Software engineering concepts, depicted as a UML class diagram (OMG, 1998).

1.3.1   Participants and Roles

Developing a software system requires the collaboration of many people with different backgrounds and interests. The client orders and pays for the system. The developers construct the system. The project manager plans and budgets the project and coordinates the developers and the client. The end users are supported by the system. We refer to all the persons involved in the project as **participants**. We refer to a set of responsibilities in the project or the system as a **role**. A role is associated with a set of tasks and is assigned to a participant. The same participant can fill multiple roles.

Consider a machine that distributes tickets for a train. Travelers have the option of selecting a ticket for a single trip, for multiple trips, or a time card for a day or a week. The ticket distributor computes the price of the requested ticket based on the area in which the trip will take place and whether the traveler is a child or an adult. In this example, travelers purchasing tickets are end users. The train company, contracting the development of the ticket distributor, is the client of the project. The engineers realizing the system (and the software), John, Marc, and Zoe, are developers. Their boss, Alice, coordinating the work and the communication with the client, is the project manager. End user, client, developer, and project manager are roles. Alice, John, Marc, Zoe, the train company and the travelers are participants.

1.3.2   Systems and Models

We use the term **system** to refer to the underlying reality and the term **model** to refer to any abstraction of the reality. A ticket distributor for an underground train is a system. Blueprints for the ticket distributor, schematics of its electrical wiring, and object models of its software are models of the ticket distributor. Note that a development project is itself a system that can be modeled. The project schedule, its budget, and its planned deadlines are models of the development project.

1.3.3   Work Products

A **work product** is an artifact that is produced during the development, such as a document or a piece of software for other developers or for the client. We refer to a work product for the project's internal consumption as an **internal work product**. We refer to a work product for a client as a **deliverable**. Deliverables are generally defined prior to the start of the project and specified by a contract binding the developers with the client.

In the ticket distributor example, the operation and maintenance manuals needed by the train company are deliverables. The ticket distributors and its software are also deliverables. Demonstration prototypes, test scenarios, and test results produced by the developers for the project manager are internal work products, unless they are specified by the contract as items to be delivered to the client.

1.3.4   Activities, Tasks, and Resources

An **activity** is a set of tasks that is performed toward a specific purpose. For example, requirements elicitation is an activity whose purpose is to define with the client what the system will do. Delivery is an activity whose purpose is to install the system at an operational location. Management is an activity whose purpose is to monitor and control the project such that it meets its goals (e.g., deadline, quality, budget). Activities can be composed of other activities. The delivery activity includes a software installation activity and an operator training activity. Activities are also sometimes called **phases**.

A **task** represents an atomic unit of work that can be managed: A manager assigns it to a developer, the developer carries it out, and the manager monitors the progress and completion of the task. Tasks consume resources, result in work products, and depend on work products produced by other tasks.

Resources are assets that are used to accomplish work. Resources include time, equipment, and labor. When planning a project, a manager breaks down the work into tasks and assigns them to resources.

1.3.5   Goals, Requirements, and Constraints

A **goal** is a high-level principle that is used to guide the project. Goals define the attributes of the system that are important. Different projects have different goals. The primary goal of the development of the space shuttle guidance software is to produce a system that is safe (i.e., which does not put human life in danger). The primary goal for a ticket distributor is to produce a system that is highly available (i.e., which functions correctly most of the time).

Goals often conflict; that is, they are difficult to achieve simultaneously. For example, producing a safe system such as a passenger aircraft is expensive. Aircraft manufacturers, however, also need to pay attention to the retail cost of the aircraft, that is, to produce an aircraft that is cheaper than the competition. Safety and low cost are conflicting goals. A substantial amount of complexity in software development comes from ill-defined or conflicting goals.

Requirements are features that the system must have. A **functional requirement** is an area of functionality that the system must support, whereas a **nonfunctional requirement** is a constraint on the operation of the system.

For example, *Provide the user with ticketing information* is a functional requirement. *Providing feedback in less than one second* is a nonfunctional requirement. *Providing a reliable system* is a design goal. *Producing a system at low cost* is a managerial goal. Other constraints include requiring a specific hardware platform for the system or requiring backward compatibility with a legacy system that the client is unwilling to retire.

1.3.6 Notations, Methods, and Methodologies

A **notation** is a graphical or textual set of rules for representing a model. The Roman alphabet is a notation for representing words. UML (Unified Modeling Language [OMG, 1998]), the notation we use throughout this book, is an object-oriented notation for representing models. Z [Spivey, 1989] is a notation for representing systems based on set theory.

A **method** is a repeatable technique for solving a specific problem. A recipe is a method for cooking a specific dish. A sorting algorithm is a method for ordering elements of a list. Rationale management is a method for justifying change. Configuration management is a method for tracking change.

A **methodology** is a collection of methods for solving a class of problems. A seafood cookbook is a methodology for preparing seafood. The Unified Software Development Process [Jacobson et al., 1999], the Object Modeling Technique (OMT [Rumbaugh et al., 1991]), the Booch methodology [Booch, 1994], and Catalysis [D'Souza & Wills, 1999], are object-oriented methodologies for developing software.

Software development methodologies decompose the process into activities. OMT provides methods for three activities: *Analysis*, which focuses on formalizing the system requirements into an object model, *System Design*, which focuses on strategic decisions, and *Object Design*, which transforms the analysis model into an object model that can be implemented. The OMT methodology assumes that requirements have already been defined and does not provide methods for eliciting requirements. The Unified Software Development Process also includes an *Analysis* activity and treats *System Design* and *Object Design* as a single activity called *Design*. The Unified Process, unlike OMT, includes a *Requirements Capture* activity for eliciting and modeling requirements. Catalysis, while using the same notations as the Unified Process, focuses more on reuse of design and code using patterns and frameworks. All of these methodologies focus on dealing with complex systems.

In this book, we present a methodology for developing complex as well as changing systems. During the course of our teaching and research ([Bruegge, 1992], [Bruegge & Coyne, 1993], [Bruegge & Coyne, 1994], [Coyne et al., 1995]), we have adapted and refined methods from a variety of sources. For activities modeling the application domain, such as requirements elicitation and analysis, we describe methods similar to those of OOSE [Jacobson et al., 1992]. For solution domain modeling activities, such as system design and object design, we describe object-oriented activities similar to those of OMT. For change-related activities, we focus on rationale management, which originated from the design rationale research [Moran & Carroll, 1996], and configuration management, which originated from the maintenance of large systems [Babich, 1986].

1.4 Software Engineering Development Activities

In this section, we give an overview of the technical activities associated with software engineering. Development activities deal with the complexity by constructing models of the problem domain or the system. Development activities include:

- requirements elicitation (Section 1.4.1)

- analysis (Section 1.4.2)

- system design (Section 1.4.3)

- object design (Section 1.4.4)

- implementation (Section 1.4.5)

In Section 1.5, we give an overview of the managerial activities associated with software engineering.

1.4.1   Requirements Elicitation

During requirements elicitation, the client and developers define the purpose of the system. The result of this activity is a description of the system in terms of actors and use cases. Actors represent the external entities that interact with the system. Actors include roles such as end users, other computers the system needs to deal with (e.g., a central bank computer, a network), and the environment (e.g., a chemical process). Use cases are general sequences of events that describe all the possible actions between an actor and the system for a given piece of functionality. Figure 1-2 depicts a use case for the ticket distributor example we discussed previously.

Use case name	`PurchaseOneWayTicket`
Participating actor	Initiated by `Traveler`
Entry condition	1. The `Traveler` stands in front of the ticket distributor, which may be located at the station of origin or at another station.
Flow of events	2. The `Traveler` selects the source and destination stations.
	3. The `TicketDistributor` displays the price of the ticket.
	4. The `Traveler` inserts an amount of money that is at least as much as the price of the ticket.
	5. The `TicketDistributor` issues the specified ticket to the `Traveler` and returns any excess change.
Exit condition	6. The `Traveler` holds a valid ticket and any excess change.
Special requirements	If the transaction is not completed after 1 minute of inactivity, the `TicketDistributor` returns all inserted change.

Figure 1-2 An example of use case: `PurchaseOneWayTicket`.

During requirements elicitation, the client and developers also agree on a set of nonfunctional requirements. The following are examples of nonfunctional requirements:

• The ticket distributor should be available to travelers at least 95% of the time.

• The ticket distributor should provide feedback to the traveler (e.g., display the ticket price, return excess change) within 1 second after the transaction has been selected.

We describe requirements elicitation, including use cases and nonfunctional requirements, in detail in Chapter 4, *Requirements Elicitation*.

1.4.2 Analysis

During analysis, developers aim to produce a model of the system that is correct, complete, consistent, unambiguous, realistic, and verifiable. Developers transform the use cases produced during requirements elicitation into an object model that completely describes the system. During this activity, developers discover ambiguities and inconsistencies in the use case model that they resolve with the client. The result of analysis is an object model annotated with attributes, operations, and associations. Figure 1-3 depicts an example of object model for the `TicketDistributor`.

We describe analysis, including object models, in detail in Chapter 5, *Analysis*. We describe in detail the UML notation for representing models in Chapter 2, *Modeling with UML*.

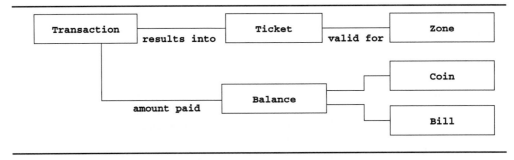

Figure 1-3 An object model for the ticket distributor (UML class diagram). In the `PurchaseOneWayTicket` use case, a `Traveler` initiates a transaction that will result in a `Ticket`. A `Ticket` is valid only for a specified `Zone`. During the `Transaction`, the system tracks the `Balance` due by counting the `Coins` and `Bills` inserted.

1.4.3   System Design

During system design, developers define the design goals of the project and decompose the system into smaller subsystems that can be realized by individual teams. Developers also select strategies for building the system, such as the hardware/software platform on which the system will run, the persistent data management strategy, the global control flow, the access control policy, and the handling of boundary conditions. The result of system design is a clear description of each of these strategies, a subsystem decomposition, and a deployment diagram representing the hardware/software mapping of the system. Figure 1-4 depicts an example of system decomposition for the ticket distributor.

We describe system design and its related concepts in detail in Chapter 6, *System Design*.

1.4.4   Object Design

During object design, developers define custom objects to bridge the gap between the analysis model and the hardware/software platform defined during system design. This includes precisely describing object and subsystem interfaces, selecting off-the-shelf components, restructuring the object model to attain design goals such as extensibility or understandability, and optimizing the object model for performance. The result of the object design activity is a detailed object model annotated with constraints and precise descriptions for each element. We describe object design and its related concepts in detail in Chapter 7, *Object Design*.

1.4.5   Implementation

During implementation, developers translate the object model into source code. This includes implementing the attributes and methods of each object and integrating all the objects such that they function as a single system. The implementation activity spans the gap between the detailed object design model and a complete set of source code files that can be compiled

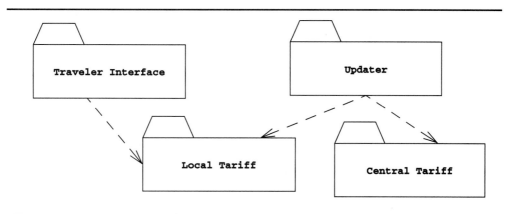

Figure 1-4   A subsystem decomposition for the `TicketDistributor` (UML class diagram, folders represent subsystems, dashed lines represent dependencies). The `Traveler Interface` subsystem is responsible for collecting input from the `Traveler` and providing feedback (e.g., display ticket price, returning change). The `Local Tariff` subsystem computes the price of different tickets based on a local database. The `Central Tariff` subsystem, located on a central computer, maintains a reference copy of the tariff database. An `Updater` subsystem is responsible for updating the local databases at each `TicketDistributor` through a network when ticket prices change.

together. We do not cover any implementation activity in this book, as we assume the reader is already familiar with programming concepts.

1.5 Managing Software Development

In this section, we briefly describe the activities related with managing a software engineering project. Management activities focus on planning the project, monitoring its status, tracking changes, and coordinating resources such that a high-quality product is delivered on time and within budget. Management activities not only involve managers but also most of the other project participants as well. Management activities include:

- communication (Section 1.5.1)
- rationale management (Section 1.5.2)
- testing (Section 1.5.3)
- software configuration management (Section 1.5.4)
- project management (Section 1.5.5)
- software life cycle modeling activities (Section 1.5.6)

1.5.1   Communication

Communication is the most critical and time-consuming activity in software engineering. Misunderstandings and omissions often lead to faults and delays that are expensive to correct later in the development. Communication includes the exchange of models and documents about the system and its application domain, reporting the status of work products, providing feedback on the quality of work products, raising and negotiating issues, and communicating decisions. Communication is made difficult by the diversity of participants' backgrounds, by their geographic distribution, and by the volume, complexity, and evolution of the information exchanged.

To deal with communication issues, project participants have many tools available. The most effective one is conventions: When participants agree on notations for representing information, on tools for manipulating information, and on procedures for raising and resolving issues, they already have eliminated substantial sources of misunderstanding. Examples of notations include UML diagrams, templates for writing documents and meeting minutes, and identification schemes for naming software components. Examples of tools include Computer Aided Software Engineering (CASE) tools for maintaining models, word processors for generating documents, and interchange formats for publishing information. Examples of procedures include meeting procedures for organizing, conducting, and capturing a meeting, review procedures for reviewing documents and providing feedback, and inspection procedures for detecting defects in models or source code. The selected conventions do not need to be the best available; they only need to be shared and agreed on by everybody. We describe communication issues in detail in Chapter 3, *Project Communication*.

1.5.2   Rationale Management

Rationale is the justification of decisions. Given a decision, its rationale includes the problem that it addresses, the alternatives that developers considered, the criteria that developers used to evaluate the alternatives, the debate developers went through to achieve consensus, and the decision. Rationale is the most important information developers need when changing the system. If a criterion changes, developers can reevaluate all decisions that depend on this criterion. If a new alternative becomes available, it can be compared with all the other alternatives that were already evaluated. If a decision is questioned, they can recover its rationale to justify it.

Unfortunately, rationale is also the most complex information developers deal with during development, and thus, the most difficult to update and maintain. To deal with this challenge, developers capture rationale during meetings and on-line discussions, represent rationale with issue models, and access rationale during changes. We describe these issues in detail in Chapter 8, *Rationale Management*.

1.5.3   Testing

During testing, developers find differences between the system and its models by executing the system (or parts of it) with sample input data sets. Although testing is not usually thought of as a management activity, we describe it here because it aims at determining the quality of the system and its related models. During unit testing, developers compare the object design model with each object and subsystem. During integration testing, combinations of subsystems are integrated together and compared with the system design model. During system testing, typical and exception cases are run through the system and compared with the requirements model. The goal of testing is to discover as many faults as possible such that they can be repaired before the delivery of the system. We describe these issues in more detail in Chapter 9, *Testing*.

1.5.4   Software Configuration Management

Software configuration management is the process that monitors and controls changes in work products. Change pervades software development. Requirements change as the client requests new features and as developers improve their understanding of the application domain. The hardware/software platform on which the system is built changes as new technology becomes available. The system changes as faults are discovered during testing and are repaired. Software configuration management used to be in the realm of maintenance, when improvements are incrementally introduced in the system. In modern development processes, however, changes occur much earlier than maintenance does. As the distinction between development and maintenance is blurred, changes can be dealt with using configuration management at all stages.

Configuration management enables developers to track changes. The system is represented as a number of configuration items that can be independently revised. For each configuration item, its evolution is tracked as a series of versions. Examining and selecting versions enables developers to rollback to a well-defined state of the system when a change fails.

Configuration management also enables developers to control change. After a baseline has been defined, any change needs to be assessed and approved before being implemented. This enables management to ensure that the system is evolving according to project goals and that the number of problems introduced into the system is limited. We describe these issues in detail in Chapter 10, *Software Configuration Management*.

1.5.5   Project Management

Project management does not produce any artifact of its own. Instead, project management includes the oversight activities that ensure the delivery of a high-quality system on time and within budget. This includes planning and budgeting the project during negotiations with the client, hiring developers and organizing them into teams, monitoring the status of the project, and intervening when deviations occur. Most project management activities are beyond the scope of this book. We describe, however, the project management activities that are visible to the developers and techniques that make the development/management communication more effective. We describe these issues in detail in Chapter 11, *Project Management*.

1.5.6   Software Life Cycle

In Section 1.2, we described software engineering as a modeling activity. Developers build models of the application and solution domains to deal with their complexity. By ignoring irrelevant details and focusing only on what is relevant to a specific issue, developers can more effectively resolve issues and answer questions. The process of developing software can also be viewed as a complex system with inputs, outputs, activities, and resources. It is then not surprising, then, that the same modeling techniques applied to software artifacts can be used for modeling software processes. A general model of the software development process is called a software life cycle. We describe software life cycles in the concluding chapter of this book, Chapter 12, *Software Life Cycle*.

1.6 Exercises

1. What is the purpose of modeling?
2. A programming language is a notation for representing algorithms and data structures. List two advantages and two disadvantages of using a programming language as sole notation throughout the development process.
3. Consider a task you are not familiar with, such as designing a zero-emissions car. How would you attack the problem?
4. What is meant by "knowledge acquisition is nonlinear"? Provide a concrete example of knowledge acquisition that illustrates this.
5. Hypothesize a rationale for the following design decisions:
   - "The ticket distributor will be at most one and a half meters tall."
   - "The ticket distributor will include two redundant computer systems."
   - "The ticket distributor will include a touch screen for displaying instructions and inputing commands. The only other control will be a cancel button for aborting a transaction."
6. Specify which of the following statements are functional requirements and which are nonfunctional requirements:
   - "The ticket distributor must enable a traveler to buy weekly passes."
   - "The ticket distributor must be written in Java."
   - "The ticket distributor must be easy to use."
7. Specify which of the following decisions were made during requirements or system design:
   - "The ticket distributor is composed of a user interface subsystem, a subsystem for computing tariff, and a network subsystem managing communication with the central computer."
   - "The ticket distributor will use PowerPC processor chips."
   - "The ticket distributor provides the traveler with an on-line help."
8. What is the difference between a task and an activity?
9. A passenger aircraft is composed of several millions of individual parts and requires thousands of persons to assemble. A four-lane highway bridge is another example of complexity. The first version of Word for Windows, a word processor released by

Microsoft in November 1989, required 55 person-years, resulted into 249,000 lines of source code, and was delivered 4 years late. Aircraft and highway bridges are usually delivered on time and below budget, whereas software is often not. Discuss what are, in your opinion, the differences between developing an aircraft, a bridge, and a word processor, which would cause this situation.

References

[Babich, 1986]   W. A. Babich, *Software Configuration Management.* Addison-Wesley, Reading, MA, 1986.

[Booch, 1994]   G. Booch, *Object-Oriented Analysis and Design with Applications,* 2nd ed. Benjamin/Cummings, Redwood City, CA, 1994.

[Bruegge, 1992]   B. Bruegge, "Teaching an industry-oriented software engineering course," *Software Engineering Education,* SEI Conference, Lecture Notes in Computer Sciences, Vol. 640, pp. 65–87, Springer Verlag, Oct. 1992 .

[Bruegge & Coyne, 1993]   B. Bruegge & R. Coyne, "Model-based software engineering in larger scale project courses," *IFIP Transactions on Computer Science and Technology,* vol. A-40, pp. 273–287, (Elsevier Science, Netherlands), 1993.

[Bruegge & Coyne, 1994]   B. Bruegge & R. Coyne, "Teaching iterative object-oriented development: Lessons and directions," *7th Conference on Software Engineering Education,* Lecture Notes in Computer, Science Jorge L. Diaz-Herrera (ed.), Vol. 750, pp. 413–427, (Springer Verlag), Jan. 1994.

[Coyne et al., 1995]   R. Coyne, B. Bruegge, A. Dutoit, & D. Rothenberger, "Teaching more comprehensive model-based software engineering: Experience with Objectory's use case approach," *8th Conference on Software Engineering Education,* Lecture Notes in Computer Science, Linda Ibraham (ed.), pp. 339–374, Springer Verlag, Apr. 1995.

[D'Souza & Wills, 1999]   D. F. D'Souza & A. C. Wills, *Objects, Components, and Frameworks with UML: The Catalysis Approach.* Addison-Wesley, Reading, MA, 1999.

[IEEE, 1997]   *IEEE Standards Collection Software Engineering.* IEEE, Piscataway, NJ, 1997.

[Jacobson et al., 1992]   I. Jacobson, M. Christerson, P. Jonsson, & G. Overgaard, *Object-Oriented Software Engineering—A Use Case Driven Approach.* Addison-Wesley, Reading, MA, 1992.

[Jacobson et al., 1999]   I Jacobson, G. Booch, & J. Rumbaugh, *The Unified Software Development Process.* Addison-Wesley, Reading, MA, 1999.

[Moran & Carroll, 1996]   T. P. Moran & J. M. Carroll (eds.), *Design Rationale: Concepts, Techniques, and Use.* Lawrence Erlbaum Associates, Mahwah, NJ, 1996.

[Neumann, 1995]   P. G. Neumann, *Computer-Related Risks.* Addison-Wesley, Reading, MA, 1995.

[OMG, 1998]   Object Management Group, *OMG Unified Modeling Language Specification.* Framingham, MA, 1998. http://www.omg.org.

[Popper, 1992]   K. Popper, *Objective Knowledge: An Evolutionary Approach.* Clarendon, Oxford, 1992.

[Rumbaugh et al., 1991]   J. Rumbaugh, M. Blaha, W. Premerlani, F. Eddy, & W. Lorensen, *Object-Oriented Modeling and Design.* Prentice Hall, Englewood Cliffs, NJ, 1991.

[Simon, 1970]   H. A. Simon, *The Sciences of the Artificial.* MIT Press, Cambridge, MA, 1970.

[Spivey, 1989]   J. M. Spivey, *The Z Notation, A Reference Manual.* Prentice Hall Int., Hertfordshire, U.K. 1989.

2

2

Modeling with UML

*"Every mechanic is familiar with the problem of the part
you can't buy because you can't find it because the
manufacturer considers it a part of something else. "*

—Robert Pirsig, in Zen and the Art of Motorcycle
Maintenance

Notations enable us to articulate complex ideas succinctly and precisely. In projects involving many participants, often of different technical and cultural backgrounds, accuracy and clarity are critical as the cost of miscommunication increases rapidly.

For a notation to enable accurate communication, it must come with a *well-defined* semantics, it must be *well suited* for representing a given aspect of a system, and it must be *well understood* among project participants. In the latter lies the strength of standards and conventions: When a notation is used by a large number of participants, there is little room for misinterpretation and ambiguity. Conversely, when many dialects of a notation exists, or when a very specialized notation is used, the notation users are prone to misunderstandings as each user imposes its own interpretation. We selected UML (Unified Modeling Language, [OMG, 1998]) as a primary notation for this book, given that it has a well-defined semantics, provides a spectrum of notations for representing different aspects of a system, and has been accepted as a standard notation in the industry.

In this chapter, we first describe the concepts of modeling in general and object-oriented modeling in particular. We then describe five fundamental notations of UML that we use throughout the book: use case diagrams, class diagrams, sequence diagrams, statechart diagrams, and activity diagrams. For each of these notations, we describe its basic semantics and provide examples. We revisit these notations in detail in later chapters as we describe the activities that use them. Specialized notations that we use in only one chapter are introduced later, such as PERT charts in Chapter 11, *Project Management*, and UML component and deployment diagrams in Chapter 6, *System Design*.

2.1 Introduction

UML is a notation that resulted from the unification of OMT (Object Modeling Technique, [Rumbaugh et al., 1991]), Booch [Booch, 1994], and OOSE (Object-Oriented Software Engineering, [Jacobson et al., 1992]). UML has also been influenced by other object-oriented notations, such as those introduced by Shlaer/Mellor [Mellor & Shlaer, 1998], Coad/Yourdon [Coad et al., 1995], Wirfs-Brock [Wirfs-Brock et al., 1990], and Martin/Odell [Martin & Odell, 1992]. UML has been designed for a broad range of applications. Hence, it provides constructs for a broad range of systems and activities (e.g., real-time systems, distributed systems, analysis, system design, deployment). System development focuses on three different models of the system:

- The **functional model**, represented in UML with use case diagrams, describes the functionality of the system from the user's point of view.
- The **object model**, represented in UML with class diagrams, describes the structure of a system in terms of objects, attributes, associations, and operations.
- The **dynamic model**, represented in UML with sequence diagrams, statechart diagrams, and activity diagrams, describes the internal behavior of the system. Sequence diagrams describe behavior as a sequence of messages exchanged among a *set of objects*, whereas statechart diagrams describe behavior in terms of states of an *individual object* and the possible transitions between states.

In this chapter, we describe UML diagrams for representing these models. Introducing these notations represents an interesting challenge. On the one hand, understanding the purpose of a notation requires some familiarity with the activities that use it. On the other hand, it is necessary to understand the notation before describing the activities. To address this issue, we introduce UML iteratively. In the next section, we first provide an overview of the five basic notations of UML. In Section 2.3, we introduce the fundamental ideas of modeling. In Section 2.4, we revisit the five basic notations of UML in light of modeling concepts. In subsequent chapters, we examine these notations in detail when we introduce the activities that use them.

2.2 An Overview of UML

In this section, we briefly introduce five UML notations:

- use case diagrams (Section 2.2.1)
- class diagrams (Section 2.2.2)
- sequence diagrams (Section 2.2.3)
- statechart diagrams (Section 2.2.4)
- activity diagrams (Section 2.2.5)

2.2.1   Use Case Diagrams

Use cases are used during requirements elicitation and analysis to represent the functionality of the system. Use cases focus on the behavior of the system from an external point of view. A use case describes a function provided by the system that yields a visible result for an actor. An actor describes any entity that interacts with the system (e.g., a user, another system, the system's physical environment). The identification of actors and use cases results in the definition of the boundary of the system, that is, in differentiating the tasks accomplished by the system and the tasks accomplished by its environment. The actors are outside the boundary of the system, whereas the use cases are inside the boundary of the system.

For example, Figure 2-1 depicts a use case diagram for a simple watch. The WatchUser actor may either consult the time on their watch (with the ReadTime use case) or set the time (with the SetTime use case). However, only the WatchRepairPerson actor may change the battery of the watch (with the ChangeBattery use case).

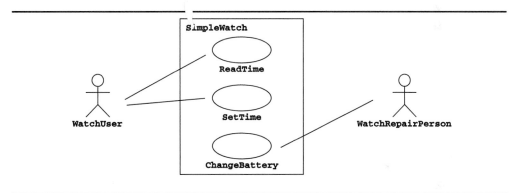

Figure 2-1   A UML use case diagram describing the functionality of a simple watch. The WatchUser actor may either consult the time on her watch (with the ReadTime use case) or set the time (with the SetTime use case). However, only the WatchRepairPerson actor may change the battery of the watch (with the ChangeBattery use case). Actors are represented with stick figures, use cases with ovals, and the boundary of the system with a box enclosing the use cases.

2.2.2   Class Diagrams

We use class diagrams to describe the structure of the system. Classes are abstractions that specify the common structure and behavior of a set of objects. Objects are instances of classes that are created, modified, and destroyed during the execution of the system. Objects have state that includes the values of its attributes and its relationships with other objects.

Class diagrams describe the system in terms of objects, classes, attributes, operations, and their associations. For example, Figure 2-2 is a class diagram describing the elements of all the watches of the SimpleWatch class. These watch objects all have an association to an object of the PushButton class, an object of the Display class, an object of the Time class, and an object of the Battery class. The numbers on the ends of associations denote the number of

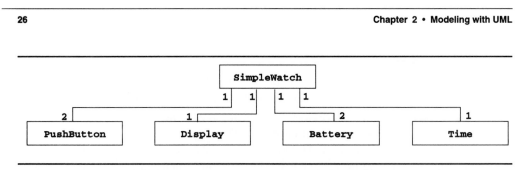

Figure 2-2   A UML class diagram describing the elements of a simple watch.

links each `SimpleWatch` object can have with an object of a given class. For example, a `SimpleWatch` has exactly two `PushButtons`, one `Display`, two `Batteries`, and one `Time`. Similarly, all `PushButton`, `Display`, `Time`, and `Battery` objects are associated to exactly one `SimpleWatch` object.

2.2.3   Sequence Diagrams

Sequence diagrams are used to formalize the behavior of the system and to visualize the communication among objects. They are useful for identifying additional objects that participate in the use cases. We call objects involved in a use case **participating objects**. A sequence diagram represents the interactions that take place among these objects. For example, Figure 2-3 is a sequence diagram for the `SetTime` use case of our simple watch. The leftmost column represents the `WatchUser` actor who initiates the use case. Labeled arrows represent stimuli that an actor or an object sends to other objects. In this case, the `WatchUser` presses button 1 twice and button 2 once to set her watch a minute ahead. The `SetTime` use case terminates when the `WatchUser` presses both buttons simultaneously.

2.2.4   Statechart Diagrams

Statechart diagrams describe the behavior of an individual object as a number of states and transitions between these states. A state represents a particular set of values for an object. Given a state, a transition represents a future state the object can move to and the conditions associated with the change of state. For example, Figure 2-4 is a statechart diagram for the `SimpleWatch`. Note that this diagram represents different information than the sequence diagram of Figure 2-3 does. The sequence diagram focuses on the messages exchanged between objects as a result of external events created by actors. The statechart diagram focuses on the transitions between states as a result of external events for an individual object.

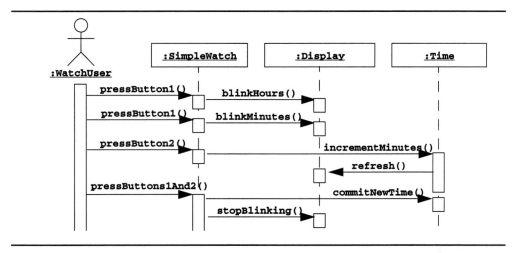

Figure 2-3   A UML sequence diagram for the SimpleWatch. The leftmost column represents the timeline of the WatchUser actor who initiates the use case. The other columns represent the timeline of the objects that participate in this use case. Object names are <u>underlined</u> to denote that they are instances (as opposed to classes). Labeled arrows are stimuli that an actor or an object sends to other objects.

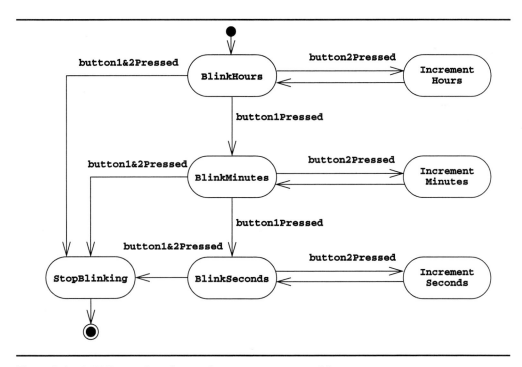

Figure 2-4   A UML statechart diagram for SetTime use case of the SimpleWatch.

2.2.5   Activity Diagrams

An activity diagram describes a system in terms of activities. Activities are states that represent the execution of a set of operations. The completion of these operations triggers a transition to another activity. Activity diagrams are similar to flowchart diagrams in that they can be used to represent control flow (i.e., the order in which operations occur) and data flow (i.e., the objects that are exchanged among operations). For example, Figure 2-5 is an activity diagram representing activities related to managing an `Incident` in FRIEND. Rounded rectangles represent activities; arrows represent transitions between activities; thick bars represent the synchronization of the control flow. The activity diagram of Figure 2-5 depicts that the `AllocateResources`, `CoordinateResources`, and `DocumentIncident` can be initiated only after the `OpenIncident` activity has been completed. Similarly, the `ArchiveIncident` activity can be initiated only after the completion of `AllocateResources`, `CoordinateResources`, and `DocumentIncident`. These latter three activities, however, can occur concurrently.

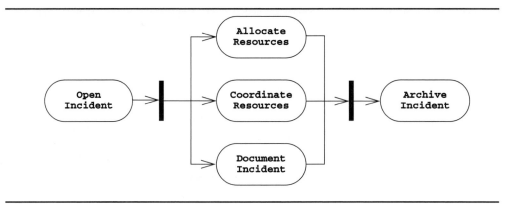

Figure 2-5   An example of a UML activity diagram. Activity diagrams represent behavior in terms of activities and their precedence constraints. The completion of an activity triggers an outgoing transition, which in turn may initiate another activity.

This concludes our first walkthrough of the five basic notations of UML. Now, we go into more detail: In Section 2.3, we introduce basic modeling concepts, including the definition of systems, models, types, and instances, abstraction, and falsification. In Sections 2.4.1–2.4.5, we describe in detail use case diagrams, class diagrams, sequence diagrams, statechart diagrams, and activity diagrams. We illustrate their use with a simple example. Section 2.4.6 describes miscellaneous constructs, such as packages and notes, that are used in all types of diagrams. We use these five notations throughout the book to describe software systems, work products, activities, and organizations. By the consistent and systematic use of a small set of notations, we hope to provide the reader with an operational knowledge of UML.

2.3 Modeling Concepts

In this section, we describe the basic concepts of modeling. We first define the terms **system** and **model** and discuss the purpose of **modeling**. We then define the terms **concept** and **phenomenon**. We explain their relationship to programming languages and terms such as **types**, **classes**, **instances**, and **objects**. Finally, we describe how object-oriented modeling focuses on building an abstraction of the system environment as a basis for the system model.

2.3.1   Systems, Models, and Views

A **system** is an organized set of communicating parts designed for a specific purpose. A car, composed of four wheels, a chassis, a body, and an engine, is designed to transport people. A watch, composed of a battery, a circuit, wheels, and hands, is designed to measure time. A payroll system, composed of a mainframe computer, printers, disks, software, and the payroll staff, is designed to issue salary checks for employees of a company. Parts of a system can in turn be considered as simpler systems called **subsystems**. The engine of a car, composed of cylinders, pistons, an injection module, and many other parts, is a subsystem of the car. Similarly, the integrated circuit of a watch and the mainframe computer of the payroll system are subsystems. This subsystem decomposition can be recursively applied to subsystems. Objects represent the end of this recursion, when each piece is simple enough that we can fully comprehend it without further decomposition.

Many systems are made of numerous subsystems interconnected in complicated ways, often so complex that no single developer can manage its entirety. **Modeling** is a means for dealing with this complexity. Complex systems are generally described by more than one model, each focusing on a different aspect or level of accuracy. Modeling means constructing an abstraction of a system that focuses on interesting aspects and ignores irrelevant details. What is interesting or irrelevant varies with the task at hand. For example, assume we want to build an airplane. Even with the help of field experts, we cannot build an airplane from scratch and hope that it will function correctly on its maiden flight. Instead, we first build a scale model of the air frame to test its aerodynamic properties. In this scale model, we only need to represent the exterior surface of the airplane. We can ignore details such as the instrument panel or the engine. In order to train pilots for this new airplane, we also build a flight simulator. The flight simulator needs to accurately represent the layout and behavior of flight instruments. In this case, however, details about the exterior of the plane can be ignored. Both the flight simulator and the scale model are much less complex than the airplane they represent. Modeling allows us to deal with complexity through a divide-and-conquer approach: For each type of problem we want to solve (e.g., testing aerodynamic properties, training pilots), we build a model that only focuses on the issues relevant to the problem. Generally, modeling focuses on building a model that is simple enough for a person to grasp completely. A rule of thumb is that each entity should contain at most 7 ± 2 parts [Miller, 1956].

Unfortunately, even a model may become so complex that it is not easily understandable. As with systems, we apply the same divide-and-conquer approach to deal with the complexity of

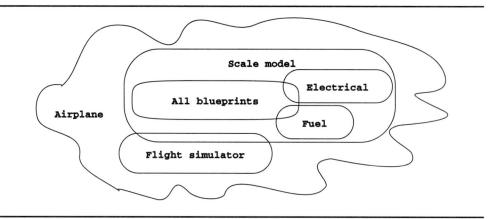

Figure 2-6   A model is an abstraction describing a subset of a system. A view depicts selected aspects of a model. Views and models of a single system may overlap each other.

models. A **view** focuses on a subset of a model to make it understandable (Figure 2-6). For example, all the blueprints necessary to construct an airplane constitute a model. Excerpts necessary to explain the functioning of the fuel system constitute the fuel system view. Views may overlap: A view of the airplane representing the electrical wiring also includes the wiring for the fuel system.

   Notations are graphical or textual rules for representing views. A UML class diagram is a graphical view of the object model. In wiring diagrams, each connected line represents a different wire or bundle of wires. In UML class diagrams, a rectangle with a title represents a class. A line between two rectangles represents a relationship between the two corresponding classes. Note that different notations can be used to represent the same view (Figures 2-7 and 2-8).

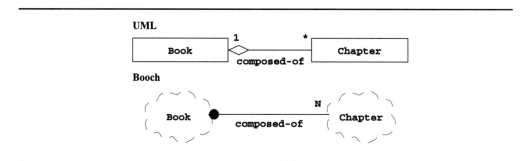

Figure 2-7   Example of describing a model with two different notations. The model includes two classes, Book and Chapter, with the relationship, Book is composed of Chapters. In UML, classes are depicted by rectangles and aggregation associations by a line terminated with a diamond. In the Booch notation, classes are depicted by clouds, and aggregation associations are depicted with a line terminated with a solid circle.

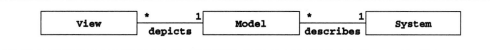

Figure 2-8   Example of describing the same model with two different notations. This UML diagram represents the information of Figure 2-6: A `System` can be described by many different `Model`s that can be depicted by many different `View`s.

In software development, there are also many other notations for modeling systems. UML describes a system in terms of classes, events, states, interactions, and activities. Data flow diagrams [De Marco, 1978] depict how data is retrieved, processed, and stored. Each notation is tailored for a different problem.

In the next sections, we focus in more detail on the process of modeling. We examine the definitions of **concept** and **phenomenon** and their relationship to the programming concepts of **type**, **variable**, **class**, and **object**.

2.3.2   Concepts and Phenomena

A **phenomenon** is an object of the world as it is perceived. The following are phenomena:

- this book
- the current savings interest rate is 3%
- my black watch
- Valley Fishermen's Club

A **concept** is an abstraction describing a set of phenomena. The following are concepts:

- textbooks on object-oriented software engineering
- savings interest rates
- black watches
- fishermen's clubs

A concept describes the properties that are common across a set of phenomena. For example, the concept *black watches* is only concerned with the color of watches, not their origin or their quality. A concept is defined as a three-tuple: its **name** (to distinguish it from other concepts), its **purpose** (the properties that determine if a phenomenon is part of the concept or not), and its **members** (the set of phenomena that are part of the concept).[1] Figure 2-9 illustrates the concept of clock. *Clock* is the name of the concept. *Measure time* is the purpose of a clock. *My wrist watch* and *the wall clock above my desk* are members of the clock concept. A club has a name (e.g.,

---

1. The three components of a concept are also referred as the name, the intension, and the extension.

Name	Purpose	Members
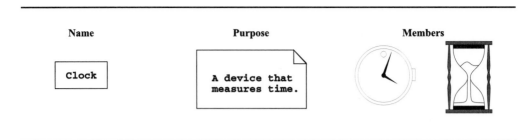		

Figure 2-9   The three components of the Clock concept: name, purpose, and members.

"Valley Fishermen's club"), attributes that members must satisfy to be part of the club (e.g., "fishermen who live in the Valley"), and actual members (e.g., "John Smith," "James Doe").

Abstraction is the classification of phenomena into concepts. **Modeling** is the development of abstractions that can be used to answer specific questions about a set of phenomena. An abstraction is simpler to manipulate and to examine than its corresponding set of phenomena because it contains less information: Irrelevant details are abstracted away. In chemistry, the table of elements summarizes the different types of atoms based on their atomic weight and number of electron pairs. Details such as the availability of each substance, its participation in different molecules, are not represented. In biology, species are classified into family trees based on significant features (e.g., species that are warm blooded, species that have vertebrae). A tree of species ignores issues related to behavior or habitat. In astronomy, stars are classified into different types based on their spectrum and dissipated energy. In this classification, the location of the stars, their detailed composition, and dimensions are ignored.

In engineering, a model may exist prior to the phenomena it represents. For example, a UML model may describe a system that has not yet been implemented. In science, the model may state the existence of systems and lead to the experiments that show their existence. For example, the theory behind the top quark was developed before accelerator experiments in CERN demonstrated the existence of the top quark.

In summary, modeling is the activity that software engineers perform when they design a system. The purpose of modeling is to construct an abstraction of the system that leaves out irrelevant details. Software engineers abstract concepts from the application domain (i.e., the environment in which the system is operating) and from the solution domain (i.e., the technologies for building a system). The resulting model is simpler than the environment or the system and thus is easier to manipulate. During the development of the model or its validation, software engineers need to communicate about the system with other engineers, clients, or users. They can represent the model in their imagination, on a napkin, with a CASE tool, using different notations. In doing so, they construct views of the model for supporting their specific communication need.

2.3.3   Data Types, Abstract Data Types, and Instances

A **data type** is an abstraction in the context of a programming language. A data type has a unique name that distinguishes it from other data types, it has a purpose (i.e., the structure and the operations valid on all members of the data type), and it has members (i.e., the members of the data type). Data types are used in typed languages to ensure that only valid operations are applied to specific data members.

For example, the name int in Java corresponds to all the signed integers between -2^{32} and $2^{32} - 1$. The valid operations on the members of this type are all the integer arithmetic operations (e.g., addition, subtraction, multiplication, division) and all the functions and methods that have parameters of type int (e.g., mod). The Java run-time environment throws an exception if a floating point operation is applied to a member of the int data type (e.g., trunc or floor).

An **abstract data type** is a special data type whose structure is hidden from the rest of the system. This allows the developer to revise the internal structure and the implementation of the abstract data type without impacting the rest of the system.

For example, the abstract data type Person may define the operations getName(),[2] getSocialSecurityNumber(), and getAddress(). The fact that the social security number of the person is stored as a number or as a string is not visible to the rest of the system. Such decisions are called **implementation decisions**.

An **instance** is any member of a specific data type. For example, 1291 is an instance of the type int, and 3.14 is an instance of the type float. An instance of a data type can be manipulated with the operations defined by the data type.

The relationship between data type and instance is similar to the relationship between concept and phenomenon: A data type is an abstraction that describes a set of instances that share common characteristics. For example, the operation for renaming an instance of Person need only be defined once in the Person data type but will be applicable to all instances of Person.

2.3.4   Classes, Abstract Classes, and Objects

A **class** is an abstraction in object-oriented programming languages. Like abstract data types, a class encapsulates both structure and behavior. Unlike abstract data types, classes can be defined in terms of other classes by using generalization. Assume we have a watch that also can function as a calculator. The class CalculatorWatch can then be seen as a refinement of the class Watch. This type of relationship between a base class and a refined class is called **generalization**. The base class (e.g., Watch) is called the **superclass**, the refined class is called the **subclass** (e.g., CalculatorWatch). In a generalization relationship, the subclass refines the superclass by defining new attributes and operations. In Figure 2-10, CalculatorWatch defines functionality for performing simple arithmetic that regular Watches do not have.

---

2. We refer to an operation by its name followed by its arguments in parentheses. If the arguments are not specified, we suffix the name of the operation by a pair of empty parentheses. We describe operations in detail in the next section.

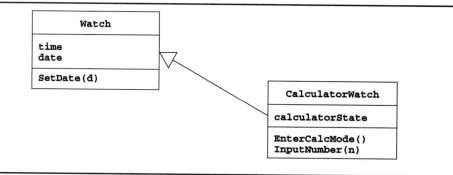

Figure 2-10 A UML class diagram depicting two classes: `Watch` and `CalculatorWatch`. `CalculatorWatch` is a refinement of `Watch`, providing calculator functionality normally not found in normal watches. In a UML class diagram, classes and objects are represented as boxes with three compartments: The first compartment depicts the name of the class, the second depicts its attributes, the third its operations. The second and third compartments can be omitted for brevity. An inheritance relationship is displayed by a line terminated with a triangle. The triangle points to the superclass, and the other end is attached to the subclass.

When a generalization serves only the purpose of modeling shared attributes and operations, that is, if the generalization is never instantiated, it is called an **abstract class**. Abstract classes often represent generalized concepts in the application domain. Whenever we classify phenomena into concepts, they often create generalizations to manage the complexity of the classification. For example, in chemistry, `Benzene` can be considered a class of molecules that belongs to the abstract class *OrganicCompound* (Figure 2-11). Note that *OrganicCompound* is a generalization and does not correspond to any one molecule, that is, it does not have any instances. When modeling software systems, abstract classes sometimes do not correspond to an existing application domain concept, but rather are introduced to reduce complexity in the model or to promote reuse.

A class defines the **operations** that can be applied to its instances. Operations of a superclass can be inherited and applied to the objects of the subclass as well. For example, in Figure 2-10, the operation `SetDate(d)`, setting the current date of a `Watch`, is also applicable for `CalculatorWatches`. The operation `EnterCalcMode()`, however, defined in the `CalculatorWatch` class, is not applicable in the `Watch` class.

A class defines the **attributes** that apply to all its instances. An attribute is a named slot in the instance where a value is stored. Attributes have a unique name within the class and a type. `Watches` have a `time` and a `date` attribute. `CalculatorWatches` have a `calculatorState` attribute.

An **object** is an instance of a class. An object has an identity and stores attribute values. Each object belongs to exactly one class. In UML, an instance is depicted by a rectangle with its name underlined. This convention is used throughout UML to distinguish between instances and types.[3] In Figure 2-12, `simpleWatch1291` is an instance of `Watch` and `calculator-Watch1515` is an instance of `CalculatorWatch`. Note that, although the operations of `Watch`

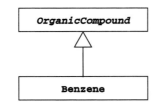

Figure 2-11 An example of abstract class (UML class diagram). *OrganicCompound* is never instantiated and only serves as a generalization.

are applicable to `calculatorWatch1515`, `calculatorWatch1515` is not an instance of the class `Watch`. Unlike abstract data types, the attributes of an object can be visible to other parts of the system in some programming languages. For example, Java allows the implementer to specify in great detail which attributes are visible and which are not.

2.3.5   Event Classes, Events, and Messages

Event classes are abstractions representing a kind of event for which the system has a common response. An **event**, an instance of an event class, is a relevant occurrence in the system. For example, an event can be a stimuli from an actor (e.g., "the `WatchUser` presses the left button"), a time-out (e.g., "after 2 minutes"), or the sending of a message between two objects. Sending a **message** is the mechanism by which the sending object requests the execution of an operation in the receiving object. The message is composed of a name and a number of arguments.

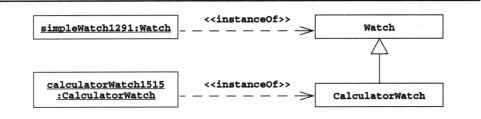

Figure 2-12 A UML class diagram depicting instances of two classes. `simpleWatch1291` is an instance of `Watch`. `calculatorWatch1515` is an instance of `CalculatorWatch`. Although the operations of `Watch` are also applicable to `calculatorWatch1515`, the latter is not an instance of the former.

---

3. Underlined strings are also used for representing Uniform Resource Locators (URLs). To improve readability, we do not use an underlined font in the text, but rather, use the same font to denote instances and classes. In general, this ambiguity can be resolved by examining the context. In UML diagrams, however, we always use an underlined font to distinguish instances from classes.

The receiving object matches the name of the message to one of its operation and passes the arguments to the operation. Any results are returned to the sending object.

For example, in Figure 2-13, the Watch object computes the current time by getting the Greenwich time from the Time object and the time difference from the TimeZone object by sending the getTime() and the getTimeDelta() messages, respectively.

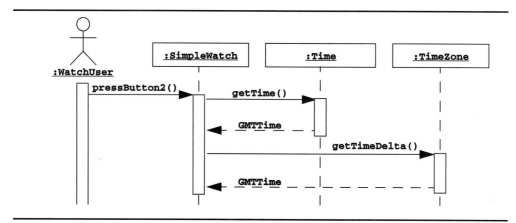

Figure 2-13 Examples of message sends (UML sequence diagram). The Watch object sends the getTime() message to a Time object to query the current Greenwich time. It then sends the getTimeDelta() message to a TimeZone objects to query the difference to add to the Greenwich time. The dashed arrows represent the results that are sent back to the message sender.

Events and messages are instances: They represent concrete occurrences in the system. Event classes are abstractions describing groups of events for which the system has a common response. In practice, the term "event" can refer to instances or classes. This ambiguity is resolved by examining the context in which the term is used.

2.3.6 Object-Oriented Modeling

The **application domain** represents all aspects of the user's problem. This includes the physical environment, the users and other people, their work processes, and so on. It is critical for analysts and developers to understand the application domain for a system to accomplish its intended task effectively. Note that the application domain changes over time, as work processes and people change.[4]

---

4. The application domain is sometimes further divided into a user domain and a client domain. The client domain includes the issues relevant to the client, such as, operation cost of the system, impact of the system on the rest of the organization. The user domain includes the issues relevant to the end user, such as, functionality, ease of learning and of use.

The **solution domain** is the space of all possible systems. The solution domain is much richer and more volatile than the application domain. This is due to emerging technologies (also called technology enablers), to changes as the implementation technology matures, or better understanding of implementation technology by the developers when they build the system. Modeling the solution domain represents the system design and object design activities of the development process. Note that the deployment of the system can change the application domain, as users develop new work processes to accommodate the system.

    Object-oriented analysis is concerned with modeling the application domain. **Object-oriented design** is concerned with modeling the solution domain. Both modeling activities use the same representations (i.e., classes and objects). In object-oriented analysis and design, the application domain model is also part of the system model. For example, an air traffic control system has a `TrafficController` class to represent individual users, their preferences, and log information. The system also has an `Aircraft` class to represent information associated with the tracked aircraft. `TrafficController` and `Aircraft` are application domain concepts that are encoded into the system (Figure 2-14).

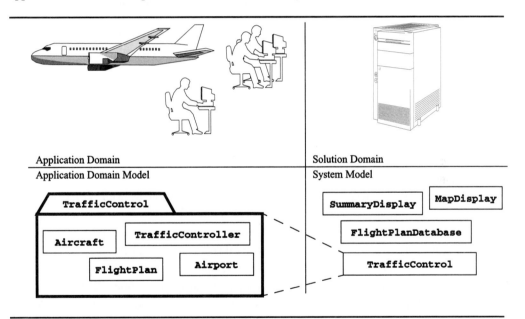

Figure 2-14   The application domain model represents entities of the environment which are relevant to an air traffic control system (e.g., aircraft, traffic controllers). The system model represents entities that are part of the system (e.g., map display, flight plan database). In object-oriented analysis and design, the application domain model is also part of the system model. An example in this figure is the `TrafficControl` package that appears in both models. (For more details, see Chapter 5, *Analysis*).

Modeling the application domain and the solution domain with a single notation has advantages and disadvantages. On the one hand, it can be powerful: Solution domain classes that represent application concepts can be traced back to the application domain. Moreover, these classes can be encapsulated into subsystems independent of other implementation concepts (e.g., user interface and database technology) and be packaged into a reusable toolkit of domain classes. On the other hand, using a single notation can introduce confusion because it removes the distinction between the real world and the model of it. The system domain is bound to be simpler and biased toward the solution. To address this issue, we use a single notation and, in cases of ambiguity, we distinguish between the two domains. In most cases, we are referring to the model (e.g., "an `Aircraft` is composed of `Manifest` and a `FlightPlan`" is a statement about the model).

2.3.7   Falsification and Prototyping

A model is a simplification of reality in the sense that irrelevant details are ignored. Relevant details, however, need to be represented. **Falsification** [Popper, 1992] is the process of demonstrating that relevant details have been incorrectly represented or not represented at all; that is, the model does not correspond to the reality it is supposed to represent.

The process of falsification is well known in other sciences: Researchers propose different models of a reality, which are gradually accepted as an increasing amount of data supports the model, but which are rejected once a counterexample is found. Ptolemy's earth-centric model of the universe was (eventually) falsified in favor of the Copernican solar-centric model once Galileo's data were accepted. The Copernican solar-centric model was then falsified once other galaxies were discovered and the concept of galaxy was added to the model.

We can apply falsification to software system development as well. For example, a technique for developing a system is **prototyping**: When designing the user interface, developers construct a prototype that only simulates the user interface of a system. The prototype is then presented to potential users for evaluation, that is, falsification, and modified subsequently. In the first iterations of this process, developers are likely to throw away the initial prototype as a result of feedback from the users. In other terms, users falsify the initial prototype, a model of the future system, because it does not represent accurately relevant details.

Note that it is only possible to demonstrate that a model is incorrect. Although, in some cases, it is possible to show mathematically that two models are equivalent, it is not possible to show that either of them correctly represents reality. For example, formal verification techniques can enable developers to show that a specific software implementation is consistent with a formal specification. However, only field testing and extended use can indicate that a system meets the needs of the client. At any time, system models can be falsified due to changes in the requirements, in the implementation technology, or in the environment.

2.4 A Deeper View into UML

We now describe in detail the five main UML diagrams we use in this book.

- **Use case diagrams** represent the functionality of the system from a user's point of view. They define the boundaries of the system (Section 2.4.1).

- **Class diagrams** are used to represent the structure of a system in terms of objects, their attributes, and relationships (Section 2.4.2).

- **Sequence diagrams** represent the system's behavior in terms of interactions among a set of objects. They are used to identify objects in the application and implementation domains (Section 2.4.3).

- **Statechart diagrams** are used to represent the behavior of nontrivial objects (Section 2.4.4).

- **Activity diagrams** are flow diagrams used to represent the data flow or the control flow through a system (Section 2.4.5).

2.4.1   Use Case Diagrams

Use cases and actors

Actors are external entities that interact with the system. Examples of actors include a user role (e.g., a system administrator, a bank customer, a bank teller) or another system (e.g., a central database, a fabrication line). Actors have unique names and descriptions.

Use cases describe the behavior of the system as seen from an actor's point of view. Behavior described by the use case model is also called **external behavior**. A use case describes a function provided by the system as a set of events that yields a visible result for the actors. Actors initiate a use case to access the system functionality. The use case can then initiate other use cases and gather more information from the actors. When actors and use cases exchange information, they are said to **communicate**. We will see later that we represent these exchanges with communication relationships.

For example, in an accident management system [FRIEND, 1994], field officers, such as a police officer or a fireman, have access to a wireless computer that enables them to interact with a dispatcher. The dispatcher in turn can visualize the current status of all its resources, such as, police cars or trucks, on a computer screen and dispatch a resource by issuing commands from a workstation. In this example, `FieldOfficer` and `Dispatcher` are actors.

Figure 2-15 depicts the actor `FieldOfficer` who invokes the use case `ReportEmergency` to notify the actor `Dispatcher` of a new emergency. As a response, the `Dispatcher` invokes the `OpenIncident` use case to create an incident report and initiate the incident handling. The `Dispatcher` enters preliminary information from the `FieldOfficer` in the incident database and orders additional units to the scene with the `AllocateResources` use case.

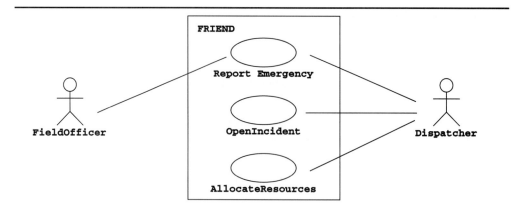

Figure 2-15 An example of a UML use case diagram: Incident initiation in an accident management system. Associations between actors and use cases represent information flows. In UML, these associations are bidirectional: They can represent the actor initiating a use case (e.g., `FieldOfficer` initiates `ReportEmergency`) or a use case providing information to an actor (e.g., `ReportEmergency` notifies `Dispatcher`).

To describe a use case, we use a template composed of six fields (see also Figure 2-16):

- The **name** of the use case is unique across the system so that developers (and project participants) can unambiguously refer to the use case.
- **Participating actors** are actors interacting with the use case.
- **Entry conditions** describe the conditions that need to be satisfied before the use case is initiated.
- The **flow of events** describes the sequence of actions of the use case, which are be numbered for reference. The common case (i.e., cases that occur frequently) and the exceptional cases (i.e., cases that seldom occur, such as errors and unusual conditions) are described separately in different use cases for clarity.
- **Exit conditions** describe the conditions that are satisfied after the completion of the use case.
- **Special requirements** are requirements that are not related to the functionality of the system. These include constraints on the performance of the system, its implementation, the hardware platforms it runs on, and so on. Special requirements are described in detail in Chapter 4, *Requirements Elicitation*.

Use cases are written in natural language. This enables developers to use them for communicating with the client and the users, who generally do not have an extensive knowledge of software engineering notations. The use of natural language also enables participants from other disciplines to understand the requirements of the system.

Use case name	ReportEmergency
Participating actor	Invoked by FieldOfficer Communicates with Dispatcher
Entry condition	1. The FieldOfficer activates the "Report Emergency" function of her terminal. FRIEND responds by presenting a form to the officer.
Flow of events	2. The FieldOfficer fills the form by selecting the emergency level, type, location, and brief description of the situation. The FieldOfficer also describes possible responses to the emergency situation. Once the form is completed, the FieldOfficer submits the form, at which point the Dispatcher is notified. 3. The Dispatcher reviews the submitted information and creates an Incident in the database by invoking the OpenIncident use case. The Dispatcher selects a response and acknowledges the emergency report.
Exit condition	4. The FieldOfficer receives the acknowledgment and the selected response.
Special requirements	The FieldOfficer's report is acknowledged within 30 seconds. The selected response arrives no later than 30 seconds after it is sent by the Dispatcher.

Figure 2-16   An example of a use case: the ReportEmergency use case.

Scenarios

A use case is an abstraction that describes all possible scenarios involving the described functionality. A **scenario** is an instance of a use case describing a concrete set of actions. Scenarios are used as examples for illustrating common cases. Their focus is on understandability. Use cases are used to describe all possible cases. Their focus is on completeness. We describe a scenario using a template with three fields:

- The **name** of the scenario enables us to refer to it unambiguously. The name of a scenario is <u>underlined</u> to indicate that it is an instance.
- The **participating actor instances** field indicates which actor instances are involved in this scenario. Actor instances also have <u>underlined</u> names.
- The **flow of events** of a scenario describes the sequence of events step by step.

Note that, there is no need for entry or exit conditions in scenarios. Entry and exit conditions are abstractions that enable developers to describe a range of conditions under which a use case is invoked. Given that a scenario only describes a single flow of events, such conditions are unnecessary (Figure 2-17).

Use case diagrams can include four types of relationships: communication, inclusion, extension, and generalization. We describe these relationships in detail next.

Scenario name	<u>warehouseOnFire</u>
Participating actor instances	<u>bob, alice: FieldOfficer</u> <u>john: Dispatcher</u>
Flow of events	1. Bob, driving down main street in his patrol car, notices smoke coming out of a warehouse. His partner, Alice, activates the "Report Emergency" function from her FRIEND laptop. 2. Alice enters the address of the building, a brief description of its location (i.e., northwest corner), and an emergency level. In addition to a fire unit, she requests several paramedic units on the scene given that area appears to be relatively busy. She confirms her input and waits for an acknowledgment. 3. John, the Dispatcher, is alerted to the emergency by a beep of his workstation. He reviews the information submitted by Alice and acknowledges the report. He allocates a fire unit and two paramedic units to the Incident site and sends their estimated arrival time (ETA) to Alice. 4. Alice receives the acknowledgment and the ETA.

Figure 2-17   The warehouseOnFire scenario for the ReportEmergency use case.

Communication relationships

Actors and use cases **communicate** when information is exchanged between them. Communication relationships are depicted by a solid line between the actor and use case symbol. In Figure 2-15, the actors FieldOfficer and Dispatcher communicate with the ReportEmergency use case. Only the actor Dispatcher communicates with the use cases OpenIncident and AllocateResources. Communication relationships between actors and use cases can be used to denote access to functionality. In the case of our example, a FieldOfficer and a Dispatcher are provided with different interfaces to the system and have access to different functionalities.

Include relationships

When describing a complex system, its use case model can become quite complex and can contain redundancy. We reduce the complexity of the model by identifying commonalities in different use cases. For example, assume that the Dispatcher can press at any time a key to access Help. This can be modeled by a use case HelpDispatcher that is included by the use cases OpenIncident and AllocateResources (and any other use cases accessible by the Dispatcher). The resulting model only describes the HelpDispatcher functionality once, thus reducing complexity. Two use cases are related by an include relationship if one of them includes the second one in its flow of events. In UML, **include relationships** are depicted by a dashed arrow originating from the including use case (see Figure 2-18). Include relationships are labeled with the string <<include>>.

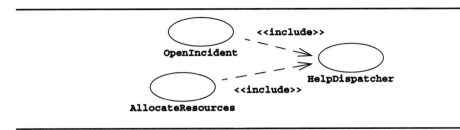

Figure 2-18   An example of an <<include>> relationship (UML use case diagram).

We represent include relationships in the use case itself with one of two ways. If the included use case can be included at any point in the flow of events (e.g., the HelpDispatcher use case), we indicate the inclusion in the *Special requirements* section of the use case. If the included use case is explicitly invoked during an event, we indicate the inclusion in the flow of events.

Extend relationships

Extend relationships are an alternate means for reducing complexity in the use case model. A use case can extend another use case by adding events. An extend relationship indicates that an instance of an extended use case may include (under certain conditions) the behavior specified by the extending use case. A typical application of extend relationships is the specification of exceptional behavior. For example (Figure 2-19), assume that the network connection between the Dispatcher and the FieldOfficer can be interrupted at any time. (e.g., if the FieldOfficer enters a tunnel). The use case ConnectionDown describes the set of events taken by the system and the actors while the connection is lost. ConnectionDown extends the use cases OpenIncident and AllocateResources. Separating exceptional behavior from common behavior enables us to write shorter and more focused use cases.

In the textual representation of a use case, we represent extend relationships as entry conditions of the extending use case. For example, the extend relationships depicted in Figure 2-19 are represented as an entry condition of the ConnectionDown use case (Figure 2-20).

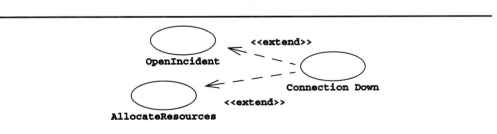

Figure 2-19   An example of an <<extend>> relationship (UML use case diagram).

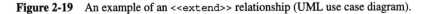

Use case name	ConnectionDown
Participating actor	Communicates with FieldOfficer and Dispatcher.
Entry condition	This use case extends the OpenIncident and the AllocateResources use cases. It is initiated by the system whenever the network connection between the FieldOfficer and Dispatcher is lost.
Flow of events	1. ...

Figure 2-20   Textual representation of extend relationships of Figure 2-19.

The difference between the include and extend relationships is the location of the dependency. Assume that we add several new use cases for the actor Dispatcher. If we modeled the HelpDispatcher function with include relationships, every new use case will need to include the HelpDispatcher use case. If we used extend relationships instead, only the HelpDispatcher use case needs to be modified to extend the additional use cases. In general, exception cases, such as help, errors, and other unexpected conditions, are modeled with extend relationships. Use cases that describe behavior commonly shared by a fixed set of use cases are modeled with include relationships.

Generalization relationships

Generalization/specialization relationships are a third mechanism for reducing the complexity of a model. A use case can specialize a more general one by adding more detail. For example, FieldOfficers are required to authenticate before they can use FRIEND. During early stages of requirements elicitation, authentication is modeled as a high-level Authenticate use case. Later, developers describe the Authenticate use case in more detail and allow for several different hardware platforms. This refinement activity results in two more use cases, AuthenticateWithPassword, which enables FieldOfficers to login without any specific hardware, and AuthenticateWithCard, which enables FieldOfficers to login using a smart card. The two new use cases are represented as specializations of the Authenticate use case (Figure 2-21).

Applying use case diagrams

Use cases and actors define the boundaries of the system. They are developed during requirements elicitation, often with the client and the users. During analysis, use cases are refined and corrected as they are reviewed by a broader audience that includes developers and validated against real situations.

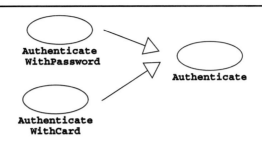

Figure 2-21 An example of a generalization relationship (UML use case diagram). The `Authenticate` use case is a high-level use case describing, in general terms, the process of authentication. `AuthenticateWithPassword` and `AuthenticateWithCard` are two specializations of `Authenticate`.

2.4.2 Class Diagrams

Classes and objects

Class diagrams describe the structure of the system in terms of classes and objects. **Classes** are abstractions that specify the attributes and behavior of a set of objects. **Objects** are entities that encapsulate state and behavior. Each object has an identity: It can be referred individually and is distinguishable from other objects.

In UML, classes and objects are depicted by boxes including three compartments. The top compartment displays the name of the class or object. The center compartment displays its attributes, and the bottom compartment displays its operations. The attribute and operation compartment can be omitted for clarity. Object names are <u>underlined</u> to indicate that they are instances. By convention, class names start with an uppercase letter. Objects in object diagrams may be given names (followed by their class) for ease of reference. In that case, their name starts with a lowercase letter. In the FRIEND example (Figures 2-22 and 2-23), Bob and Alice are field officers, represented in the system as `FieldOfficer` objects called `bob:FieldOfficer` and `alice:FieldOfficer`. `FieldOfficer` is a class describing all `FieldOfficer` objects, whereas Bob and Alice are represented by two individual `FieldOfficer` objects.

In Figure 2-22, the `FieldOfficer` class has two attributes: a `name` and a `badgeNumber`. This indicates that all `FieldOfficer` objects have these two attributes. In Figure 2-23, the `bob:FieldOfficer` and `alice:FieldOfficer` objects have specific values for these attributes: "Bob. D." and "Alice W.", respectively. In Figure 2-22, the `FieldOfficer.name` attribute is of type `String`, which indicates that only instances of `String` can be assigned to the `FieldOfficer.name` attribute. The type of an attribute is used to specify the valid range of values the attribute can take. Note that when attribute types are not essential to the definition of the system, attribute type decisions can be delayed until object design. This allows the developers to concentrate on the functionality of the system and to minimize the number of trivial changes when the functionality of the system is revised.

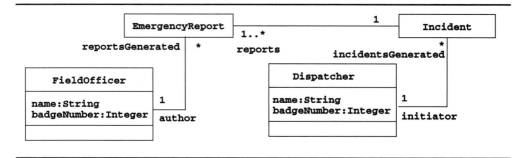

Figure 2-22   An example of a UML class diagram: classes that participate in the ReportEmergency use case. Detailed type information is usually omitted until object design (see Chapter 7, *Object Design*).

Associations and links

A **link** represents a connection between two objects. **Associations** are relationships between classes and represent groups of links. Each FieldOfficer object also has a list of EmergencyReports that has been written by the FieldOfficer. In Figure 2-22, the line between the FieldOfficer class and the EmergencyReport class is an association. In Figure 2-23, the line between the alice:FieldOfficer object and the report_1291:EmergencyReport object is a link. This link represents a state that is kept in the system to denote that alice:FieldOfficer generated report_1291:EmergencyReport.

Roles

Each end of an association can be labeled by a string called **role**. In Figure 2-22, the roles of the association between the EmergencyReport and FieldOfficer classes are author and reportsGenerated. Labeling the end of associations with roles allows us to distinguish multiple associations originating from a class. Moreover, roles clarify the purpose of the association.

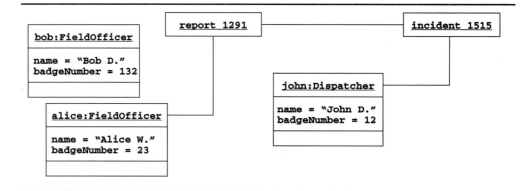

Figure 2-23   An example of a UML object diagram: objects that participate in the warehouseOnFire scenario.

Multiplicity

Each end of an association can be labeled by a set of integers indicating the number of links that can legitimately originate from an instance of the class connected to the association end. The association end `author` has a multiplicity of 1. This means that all `EmergencyReports` are written by exactly one `FieldOfficer`. In other terms, each `EmergencyReport` object has exactly one link to an object of class `FieldOfficer`. The multiplicity of the association end `reportsGenerated` role is "many," shown as a star. The "many" multiplicity is shorthand for `0..n`. This means that any given `FieldOfficer` may be the author of zero or more `EmergencyReports`.

Association class

Associations are similar to classes, in that they can have attributes and operations attached to them. Such an association is called an **association class** and is depicted by a class symbol, containing the attributes and operations, connected to the association symbol with a dashed line. For example, in Figure 2-24, the allocation of `FieldOfficers` to an `Incident` is modeled as an association class with attributes `role` and `notificationTime`.

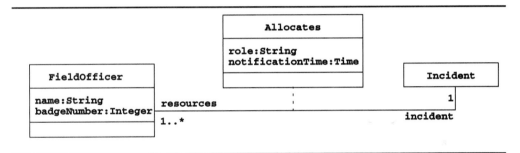

Figure 2-24   An example of an association class (UML class diagram).

Any association class can be transformed into a class and simple associations as shown in Figure 2-25. Although both representations are similar, the association class representation is clearer: An association cannot exist without the classes it links. Similarly, the `Allocation` object cannot exist without a `FieldOfficer` and an `Incident` object. Although Figure 2-25 carries the same information, this diagram requires careful examination of the association multiplicity. We examine such modeling trade-offs in Chapter 5, *Analysis*.

Aggregation

Associations are used to represent a wide range of connections among a set of objects. In practice, a special case of association occurs frequently: composition. For example, a `State` contains many `Counties`, which in turn contains many `Townships`. A `PoliceStation` is composed of `PoliceOfficers`. Another example is a `Directory` that contains a number of `Files`. Such relationships could be modeled using a one-to-many association. Instead, UML provides the concept of an **aggregation** to denote composition. An aggregation is denoted by a

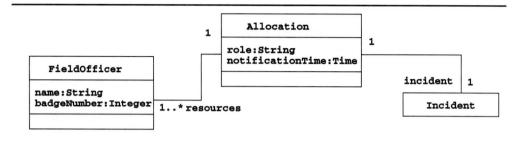

Figure 2-25   Alternative model for `Allocation` (UML class diagram).

simple line with a diamond at the container end of the association (see Figure 2-26). Although one-to-many associations and aggregations can be used alternatively, aggregations are preferable because they emphasize the hierarchical aspects of the relationship. For example, in Figure 2-26, the `PoliceOfficers` are part of the `PoliceStation`.

Generalization

Generalization is the relationship between a general class and one or more specialized classes. Generalization enables us to describe all the attributes and operations that are common to a set of classes. For example, `FieldOfficer` and `Dispatcher` both have `name` and `badgeNumber` attributes. However, `FieldOfficer` has an association with `EmergencyReport`, whereas `Dispatcher` has an association with `Incident`. The common attributes of `FieldOfficer` and `Dispatcher` can be modeled by introducing a *PoliceOfficer* class that is specialized by the `FieldOfficer` and the `Dispatcher` classes (see Figure 2-27). *PoliceOfficer*, the generalization, is called a **superclass.** `FieldOfficer` and `Dispatcher`, the specializations, are called the **subclasses**. The subclasses **inherit** the attributes and operations from their parent class. Abstract classes (defined in Section 2.3.4) are distinguished from concrete classes by *italicizing* the name of abstract classes. In Figure 2-27, *PoliceOfficer* is an abstract class. Abstract classes are used in object-oriented modeling to classify related concepts, thus reducing the overall complexity of the model.

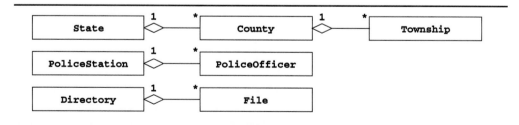

Figure 2-26   Examples of aggregations (UML class diagram). A `State` contains many `Counties`, which in turn contains many `Townships`. A `PoliceStation` has many `PoliceOfficers`. A file system `Directory` contains many `Files`.

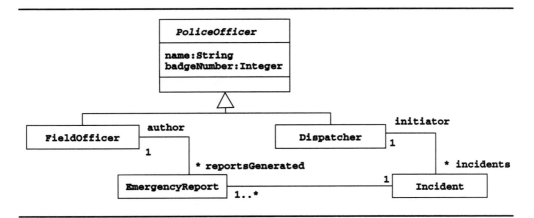

Figure 2-27   An example of a generalization (UML class diagram). *PoliceOfficer* is an abstract class which defines the common attributes and operations of the `FieldOfficer` and `Dispatcher` classes.

Object behavior is specified by **operations**. A set of operations represents a **service** offered by a particular class. An object requests the execution of an operation from another object by sending it a **message**. The message is matched up with a **method** defined by the class to which the receiving object belongs or by any of its superclasses. The operations of a class are the public services that the class offers. The methods of its class are the implementations of these operations.

The distinction between operations and methods allows for a cleaner separation between the mechanism to request a service and the location where it is provided. For example, the class `Incident` in Figure 2-28 defines an operation, called `assignResource()`, which, given a `FieldOfficer`, creates an association between the receiving `Incident` and the specified `Resource`. The `assignResource()` operation may also have a side effect such as sending a notification to the newly assigned `Resource`. The `close()` operation of `Incident` is responsible for closing the `Incident`. This includes going over all the resources that have been assigned to the incident over time and collecting their reports.

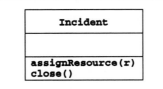

Figure 2-28   Examples of operations provided by the `Incident` class (UML class diagram).

Applying class diagrams

Class diagrams are used for describing the structure of a system. During analysis, software engineers build class diagrams to formalize application domain knowledge. Classes represent participating objects found in use cases and sequence diagrams and describe their attributes and operations. The purpose of analysis models is to describe the scope of the system and discover its boundaries. For example, using the class diagram pictured in Figure 2-22, an analyst could examine the multiplicity of the association between `FieldOfficer` and `EmergencyReport` (i.e., one `FieldOfficer` can write zero or more `EmergencyReports`, but each `EmergencyReport` is written by exactly one `FieldOfficer`) and ask the user whether this is correct. Can there be more than one author given an `EmergencyReport`? Can there be anonymous reports? Depending on the answer from the user, the analyst would then change the model to reflect the application domain. The development of analysis models is described in Chapter 5, *Analysis*.

Analysis models do not focus on implementation. Concepts such as interface details, network communication, and database storage are not represented. Class diagrams are refined during system design and object design to include classes representing the solution domain. For example, the developer adds classes representing databases, user interface windows, adapters around legacy code, optimizations, and so on. The classes are also grouped into subsystems with well-defined interfaces. The development of design models is described in Chapter 6, *System Design*, and Chapter 7, *Object Design*.

2.4.3   Sequence Diagrams

Sequence diagrams describe patterns of communication among a set of interacting objects. An object interacts with another object by sending **messages**. The reception of a message by an object triggers the execution of an operation, which in turn may send messages to other objects. **Arguments** may be passed along with a message and are bound to the parameters of the executing operation in the receiving object.

For example, consider a watch with two buttons (hereafter called 2Bwatch). Setting the time on 2Bwatch requires the actor `2BWatchOwner` to first press both buttons simultaneously, after which 2Bwatch enters the set time mode. In the set time mode, 2Bwatch blinks the number being changed (e.g., the hours, the minutes, or the seconds, day, month, year). Initially, when the `2BWatchOwner` enters the set time mode, the hours blink. If the actor presses the first button, the next number blinks (e.g, if the hours are blinking and the actor presses the first button, the hours stop blinking and the minutes start blinking. If the actor presses the second button, the blinking number is incremented by one unit. If the blinking number reaches the end of its range, it is reset to the beginning of its range (e.g., assume the minutes are blinking and its current value is 59, its new value is set to 0 if the actor presses the second button). The actor exits the set time mode by pressing both buttons simultaneously. Figure 2-29 depicts a sequence diagram for an actor setting his 2Bwatch one minute ahead.

Each column represents an object that participates in the interaction. The vertical axis represents time from top to bottom. Messages are shown by arrows. Labels on arrows represent

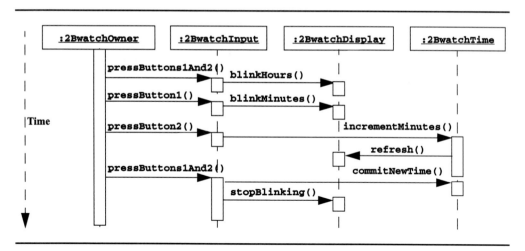

Figure 2-29 Example of a sequence diagram: setting the time on 2Bwatch.

message names and may contain arguments. Activations (i.e., executing methods) are depicted by vertical rectangles. Actors are shown as the leftmost column.

Sequence diagrams can be used to describe either an abstract sequence (i.e., all possible interactions) or concrete sequences (i.e., one possible interaction, as in Figure 2-29). When describing all possible interactions, sequence diagrams also provide notations for conditionals and iterators. A condition on a message is denoted by an expression in brackets before the message name (see `[i>0] op1()` and `[i<=0] op2()` in Figure 2-30). If the expression is true, the message is sent. Repetitive invocation of a message is denoted by a "*" before the message name (see `*op3` in Figure 2-30).

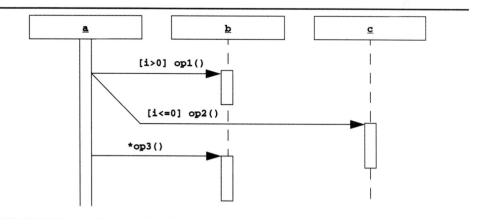

Figure 2-30 Examples of conditions and iterators in sequence diagrams.

Applying sequence diagrams

Sequence diagrams describe interactions among several objects. Typically, we use a sequence diagram to describe the event flow of a use case, identify the objects that participate in the use case, and assign pieces of the use case behavior to the objects in the form of services. This process often leads to refinements in the use case (e.g., correcting ambiguous descriptions, adding missing behavior) and consequently, the discovery of more objects and more services. We describe in detail the use of sequence diagrams in Chapter 5, *Analysis*.

2.4.4   Statechart Diagrams

A **UML statechart** is a notation for describing the sequence of states an object goes through in response to external events. Statecharts are extensions of the finite state machine model. On the one hand, statecharts provide notation for nesting states and state machines (i.e., a state can be described by a state machine). On the other hand, statecharts provide notation for binding transitions with message sends and conditions on objects. UML statecharts are based on Harel's statecharts [Harel, 1987]. A UML statechart is equivalent to a Mealy or Moore state machine.

A **state** is a condition that an object satisfies. A state can be thought of as an abstraction of the attribute values of a class. For example, an Incident object in FRIEND can be in four states: Active, Inactive, Closed, and Archived (see Figure 2-31). An active Incident denotes a situation that requires a response (e.g., an ongoing fire, a traffic accident). An inactive Incident denotes a situation that was handled but for which reports still need to be written (e.g., the fire has been put out but damage estimates have not yet been performed). A closed Incident denotes a situation that has been handled and documented. An archived Incident is a closed Incident whose documentation has been moved to off-site storage.

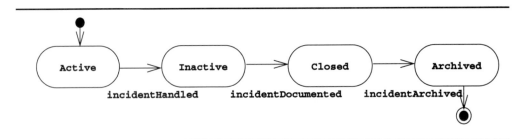

Figure 2-31   A UML statechart diagram for the Incident class.

A **transition** represents changes of state triggered by events, conditions, or time. For example, in Figure 2-31, there are three transitions: from the Active state into the Inactive state, from the Inactive state to the Closed state, and from the Closed state to the Archived state.

A state is depicted by a rounded rectangle. A transition is depicted by arrows connecting two states. States are labeled with their name. A small solid black circle indicates the initial state. A circle surrounding a small solid black circle indicates a final state.

Figure 2-32 displays another example, a statechart for the 2Bwatch (for which we constructed a sequence diagram in Figure 2-29). At the highest level of abstraction, 2Bwatch has two states, MeasureTime and SetTime. 2Bwatch changes states when the user presses and releases both buttons simultaneously. When 2Bwatch is first powered on, it is in the SetTime state. This is indicated by the small solid black circle, which represents the initial state. When the battery of the watch runs out, the 2Bwatch is permanently out of order. This is indicated with a final state. In this example, transitions can be triggered by an event (e.g., pressButtonsLAndR) or by the passage of time (e.g., after 2 min.). Actions can be associated with a transition (e.g., beep when the transition between SetTime and MeasureTime is fired on the pressButtonsLAndR event).

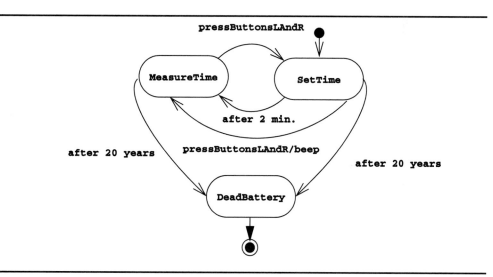

Figure 2-32   Statechart diagram for 2Bwatch set time function.

The statechart diagram in Figure 2-32 does not represent the details of measuring or setting the time. These details have been abstracted away from the statechart diagram and can be modeled separately using either internal transitions or a nested statechart. Internal transitions (Figure 2-33) are transitions that remain within a single state. They can also have actions associated with them. Entry and exit are displayed as an internal transition, given that their actions do not depend on the originating and destination states.

Nested statecharts reduce complexity. They can be used instead of internal transitions. In Figure 2-34, the current number is modeled as nested state, whereas actions corresponding to modifying the current number are modeled using internal transitions. Note that each state could

```
                    ╭──────────────────────────────────────────╮
                    │              SetTime                      │
                    ├──────────────────────────────────────────┤
                    │  entry/blink hours                        │
                    │  pressButton1/blink next number           │
                    │  pressButton2/increment current number    │
                    │  exit/stop blinking                       │
                    ╰──────────────────────────────────────────╯
```

Figure 2-33   Internal transitions associated with the `SetTime` state (UML statechart diagram).

be modeled as a nested statechart (e.g., the `BlinkHours` statechart would have 24 substates that correspond to the hours in the day; transitions between these states would correspond to pressing the second button).

Applying statechart diagrams

Statechart diagrams are used to represent nontrivial behavior of a subsystem or an object. Unlike sequence diagrams that focus on the events impacting the behavior of a set of objects, statechart diagrams make explicit which attribute or set of attributes have an impact on the behavior of a single object. Statecharts are used to identify object attributes and to refine the behavior description of an object, and sequence diagrams are used to identify participating objects and the services they provide. Statechart diagrams can also be used during system and object design to describe solution domain objects with interesting behavior. We describe the use of statechart diagrams in detail in Chapter 5, *Analysis*, and Chapter 6, *System Design*.

2.4.5   Activity Diagrams

The outgoing transitions are triggered by the completion of an action associated with the state. This is called an **action state**. By convention, the name of a state denotes a condition, whereas the name of an action state denotes an action. **Activity diagrams** are statechart

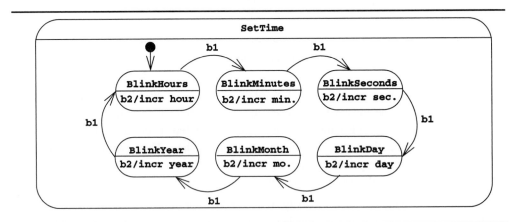

Figure 2-34   Refined statechart associated with the `SetTime` state (UML statechart diagram).

Figure 2-35 A UML activity diagram for `Incident`. During the action state `HandleIncident`, the `Dispatcher` receives reports and allocates resources. Once the `Incident` is closed, the `Incident` moves to the `DocumentIncident` activity during which all participating `FieldOfficers` and `Dispatchers` document the `Incident`. Finally, the `ArchiveIncident` activity represents the archival of the `Incident` related information onto slow access medium.

diagrams whose states are action states. Figure 2-35 is an activity diagram corresponding to the state diagram in Figure 2-31. An alternate and equivalent view of activity diagrams is to interpret action states as control flow between activities and transitions; that is, the arrows are interpreted as sequential constraints between activities.

Decisions are branches in the control flow. They denote alternative transitions based on a condition of the state of an object or a set of objects. Decisions are depicted by a diamond with one or more incoming arrows and two or more outgoing arrows. The outgoing arrows are labeled with the conditions that select a branch in the control flow. The set of all outgoing transitions from a decision represents the set of all possible outcomes. In Figure 2-36, a decision after the `OpenIncident` action selects between three branches: If the incident is of high priority and if it is a fire, the `FireChief` is notified. If the incident is of high priority and is not a fire, the `ChiefOfPolice` is notified. Finally, if neither condition is satisfied, that is, if the `Incident` is of low priority, no superior is notified and the resource allocation proceeds.

Complex transitions are transitions with multiple source states or multiple target states. Complex transitions denote the synchronization of multiple activities (in the case of multiple sources) or the splitting of the flow of control into multiple threads (in the case of multiple targets). For example, in Figure 2-37, the action states `AllocateResources`, `CoordinateResources`,

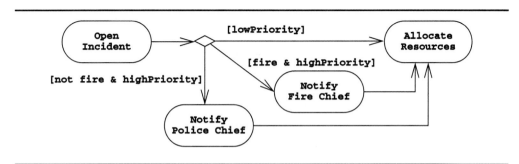

Figure 2-36 Example of decision in the `OpenIncident` process. If the `Incident` is a fire and is of high priority, the `Dispatcher` notifies the `FireChief`. If it is a high-priority `Incident` that is not a fire, the `PoliceChief` is notified. In all cases, the `Dispatcher` allocates resources to deal with the `Incident`.

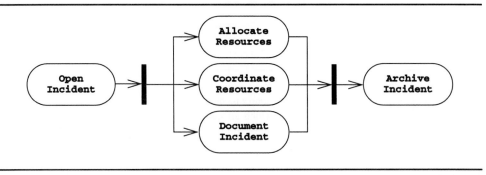

Figure 2-37   An example of complex transitions in a UML activity diagram.

and `DocumentIncident` may all occur in parallel. However, they can only be initiated after the `OpenIncident` action, and the `ArchiveIncident` action may only be initiated after all other activities have been completed.

Actions may be grouped into **swimlanes** to denote the object or subsystem that implements the actions. Swimlanes are represented as rectangles enclosing a group of actions. Transitions may cross swimlanes. In Figure 2-38, the `Dispatcher` swimlane groups all the actions that are performed by the `Dispatcher` object. The `FieldOfficer` swimlane denotes that the `FieldOfficer` object is responsible for the `DocumentIncident` action.

Applying activity diagrams

Activity diagrams provide a task-centric view of the behavior of an object. They can be used, for example, to describe sequencing constraints among use cases, sequential activities among a group of objects, or the tasks of a project. In this book, we use activity diagrams to describe the activities of software development in Chapter 11, *Project Management*, and Chapter 12, *Software Life Cycle*.

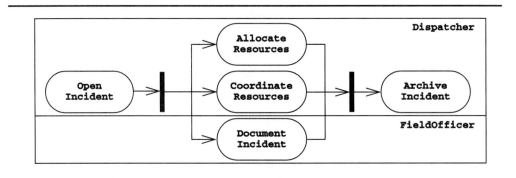

Figure 2-38   An example of swimlanes in a UML activity diagram.

2.4.6   Diagram Organization

Models of complex systems quickly become complex as developers refine them. The complexity of models can be dealt with by grouping related elements into **packages**. A package is a grouping of model elements, such as use cases, classes, or activities, defining scopes of understanding.

For example, Figure 2-39 depicts use cases of the FRIEND system, grouped by actors. Packages are displayed as rectangles with a tab attached to their upper-left corner. Use cases dealing with incident management (e.g., creating, resource allocation, documentation) are grouped in the IncidentManagement package. Use cases dealing with incident archive (e.g., archiving an incident, generating reports from archived incidents) are grouped in the IncidentArchive package. Use cases dealing with system administration (e.g., adding users, registering end stations) are grouped in the SysAdministration package. This enables the client and the developers to organize use cases into related groups and to focus on only a limited set of use cases at a time.

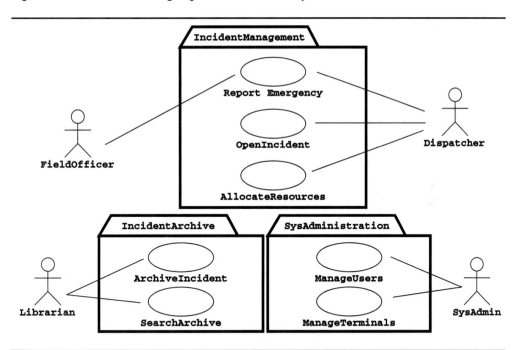

Figure 2-39   Example of packages: use cases of FRIEND organized by actors (UML use case diagram).

Figures 2-39 and 2-40 are examples of class diagrams using packages. Classes from the ReportEmergency use case are organized according to the site where objects are created. FieldOfficer and EmergencyReport are part of the FieldStation package, and Dispatcher and Incident are part of the DispatcherStation. Figure 2-39 displays the packages with the model elements they contain and Figure 2-40 displays the same information

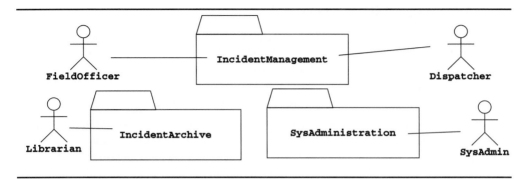

Figure 2-40   Example of packages: This figure displays the same packages as Figure 2-39 except that the details of each packages are suppressed (UML use case diagram).

without the contents of each package. Figure 2-40 is a higher level picture of the system and can be used for discussing system-level issues, whereas Figure 2-39 is a more detailed view, which can be used to discuss the content of specific packages.

Packages (Figure 2-41) are used to deal with complexity the same way a user organizes files and subdirectories into directories. However, packages are not necessarily hierarchical: The same class may appear in more than one package. To reduce inconsistencies, classes (more generally model elements) are owned by exactly one package, whereas the other packages are said to refer to the modeling element. Note that packages are organizing constructs, not objects. They have no behavior associated with them and cannot send and receive messages.

A **note** is a comment attached to a diagram. Notes are used by developers for attaching information to models and model elements. This is an ideal mechanism for recording outstanding issues relevant to a model, clarifying a complex point, or recording to-dos or reminders. Although notes have no semantics per se, they are sometimes used to express constraints that cannot otherwise be expressed in UML. Figure 2-42 provides an example of a note.

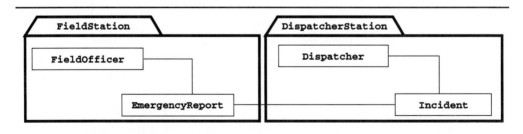

Figure 2-41   Example of packages. The `FieldOfficer` and `EmergencyReport` classes are located in the `FieldStation` package, and the `Dispatcher` and `Incident` classes are located on the `DispatcherStation` package.

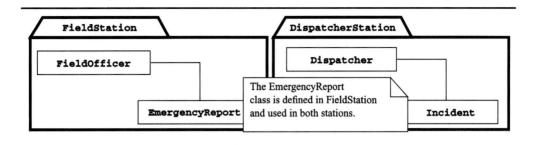

Figure 2-42   An example of a note. Notes can be attached to a specific element in a diagram.

2.4.7   Diagram Extensions

The goal of the UML designers is to provide a set of notations to model a broad class of software systems. They also recognized that a fixed set of notations could not achieve this goal, because it is impossible to anticipate the needs encountered in all application and solution domains. For this reason, UML provides a number of extension mechanisms enabling the modeler to extend the language. In this section, we describe two such mechanisms, **stereotypes** and **constraints**.

A **stereotype** is a string enclosed by angle brackets (e.g., <<subsystem>>), which is attached to a UML element, such as a class or an association. This enables modelers to create new kinds of building blocks that are needed in their domain. For example, during analysis, we classify objects into three types: entity, boundary, and control. The base UML language knows only objects. To introduce these three additional types, we use three stereotypes, <<entity>>, <<boundary>>, and <<control>> to represent the object type (Figure 2-43). Another example is the relationships among use cases. As we saw in Section 2.4.1, include relationships in use case diagrams are denoted with a dashed arrow and the <<include>> stereotype. In this book, we will define the meaning of each stereotype as we introduce them. The <<entity>>, <<boundary>>, and <<control>> stereotypes are described in Chapter 5, *Analysis*.

A **constraint** is a rule that is attached to a UML building block. This allows to represent phenomena that cannot otherwise be expressed with UML. For example, in Figure 2-44, an Incident may be associated with one or more EmergencyReports from the field. From the Dispatchers' perspective, however, it is important that they are able to view the reports chronologically. We represent the chronological ordering of EmergencyReport to Incident

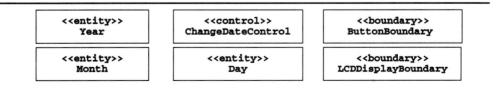

Figure 2-43   Examples of stereotypes (UML class diagram).

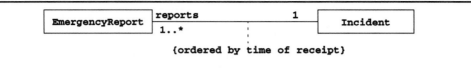

Figure 2-44   An example of constraint (UML class diagram).

associates with the constraint {ordered by time of receipt}. Constraints can be expressed as an informal string or by using a formal language such as OCL (Object Constraint Language, [OMG, 1998]). We describe OCL and the use of constraints in Chapter 7, *Object Design*.

2.5 Exercises

1. Draw a use case diagram for a ticket distributor for a train system. The system includes two actors: a traveler, who purchases different types of tickets, and a central computer system, which maintains a reference database for the tariff. Use cases should include: BuyOneWayTicket, BuyWeeklyCard, BuyMonthlyCard, UpdateTariff. Also include the following exceptional cases: Time-Out (i.e., traveler took too long to insert the right amount), TransactionAborted (i.e., traveler selected the cancel button without completing the transaction), DistributorOutOfChange, and DistributorOutOfPaper.

2. Draw a class diagram representing a book defined by the following statement: "A book is composed of a number of parts, which in turn are composed of a number of chapters. Chapters are composed of sections." Focus only on classes and relationships.

3. Draw an object diagram representing the first part of this book (i.e., Part I, *Getting Started*). Make sure that the object diagram you draw is consistent with the class diagram of Exercise 2.

4. Extend the class diagram of Exercise 2 to include the following attributes:
    • a book includes a publisher, publication date, and an ISBN
    • a part includes a title and a number
    • a chapter includes a title, a number, and an abstract
    • a section includes a title and a number

5. Consider the class diagram of Exercise 4. Note that the Part, Chapter, and Section classes all include a title and a number attribute. Add an abstract class and a generalization relationship to factor out these two attributes into the abstract class.

6. Draw a sequence diagram for the warehouseOnFire scenario of Figure 2-17. Include the objects bob, alice, john, FRIEND, and instances of other classes you may need. Draw only the first five message sends.

7. Draw a sequence diagram for the ReportIncident use case of Figure 2-16. Draw only the first five message sends. Make sure it is consistent with the sequence diagram of Exercise 6.

8. Consider the software development activities which we described in Section 1.4 in Chapter 1, *Introduction to Software Engineering*. Draw an activity diagram depicting these activities, assuming they are executed strictly sequentially. Draw a second activity diagram depicting the same activities occurring incrementally (i.e., one part of the system is analyzed, designed, implemented, and tested completely before the next part of the system is developed). Draw a third activity diagram depicting the same activities occurring concurrently.

References

[Booch, 1994]   G. Booch, *Object-Oriented Analysis and Design with Applications,* 2nd ed. Benjamin/Cummings, Redwood City, CA, 1994.

[Coad et al., 1995]   P. Coad, D. North, & M. Mayfield, *Object Models: Strategies, Patterns, & Applications.* Prentice Hall, Englewood Cliffs, NJ, 1995.

[De Marco, 1978]   T. De Marco, *Structured Analysis and System Specification.* Yourdon, New York, 1978.

[FRIEND, 1994]   *FRIEND Project Documentation*, School of Computer Science, Carnegie Mellon Univ., Pittsburgh, PA, 1994.

[Harel, 1987]   D. Harel, "Statecharts: A visual formalism for complex systems," *Science of Computer Programming*, pp. 231–274, 1987.

[Jacobson et al., 1992] I. Jacobson, M. Christerson, P. Jonsson, & G. Overgaard, *Object-Oriented Software Engineering—A Use Case Driven Approach.* Addison-Wesley, Reading, MA, 1992.

[Martin & Odell, 1992] J. Martin & J. J. Odell, *Object-Oriented Analysis and Design.* Prentice Hall, Englewood Cliffs, NJ, 1992.

[Mellor & Shlaer, 1998] S. Mellor & S. Shlaer, *Recursive Design Approach.* Prentice Hall, Upper Saddle River, NJ, 1998.

[Miller, 1956]   G.A. Miller, "The magical number seven, plus or minus two: Some limits on our capacity for processing information," *Psychological Review*, Vol. 63, pp. 81–97, 1956.

[OMG, 1998]   Object Management Group, *OMG Unified Modeling Language Specification.* Framingham, MA, 1998. http://www.omg.org.

[Popper, 1992]   K. Popper, *Objective Knowledge: An Evolutionary Approach.* Clarendon, Oxford, 1992.

[Rumbaugh et al., 1991] J. Rumbaugh, M. Blaha, W. Premerlani, F. Eddy, and W. Lorensen. *Object-Oriented Modeling and Design.* Prentice Hall, Englewood Cliffs, NJ, 1991.

[Wirfs-Brock et al., 1990] R. Wirfs-Brock, B. Wilkerson, & L. Wiener, *Designing Object-Oriented Software.* Prentice Hall, Englewood Cliffs, NJ, 1990.

3

Project Communication

Two electrical boxes for a rocket, manufactured by different contractors, were connected by a pair of wires. Thanks to a thorough preflight check, it was discovered that the wires had been reversed. After the rocket crashed, the inquiry board revealed that the contractors had indeed corrected the reversed wires as instructed.

In fact, both of them had.

Software engineering is a collaborative activity. The development of software brings together participants from different backgrounds, such as domain experts, analysts, designers, programmers, managers, technical writers, graphic designers, and users. No single participant can understand or control all aspects of the system under development, and thus, all participants depend on others to accomplish their work. Moreover, any change in the system or the application domain requires participants to update their understanding of the system. These dependencies make it critical to share information in an accurate and timely manner.

Communication can take many forms depending on the type of activity it is supporting. Participants communicate their status during weekly or bimonthly meetings and record it into meeting minutes. Participants communicate project status to the client during client reviews. The communication of requirements and design alternatives is supported by models and their corresponding documents. Crises and misunderstandings are handled through spontaneous information exchanges such as telephone calls, E-mail messages, hallway conversations, or ad hoc meetings.

In this chapter, we first motivate the need and importance of communication in software engineering. Next, we describe different aspects of project communication and their relationship with different tasks. Next, we survey a number of tools for supporting project communication. Finally, we describe an example of communication infrastructure.

3.1 Introduction: A Rocket Example

When realizing a system, developers focus on constructing a system that behaves according to specification. When interacting with other project participants, developers focus on communicating information accurately and efficiently. Even if communication may not appear to be a creative or challenging activity, it contributes as much to the success of the project as a good design or efficient implementation, as illustrated by the following example [Lions, 1996].

Ariane 501

June 4, 1996, 30 seconds into lift-off, Ariane 501, the first prototype of the Ariane 5 series, exploded. The main navigational computer experienced an arithmetic overflow, shut down, and handed control over to its twin backup, as it was designed to do. The backup computer, having experienced the same exception a few hundredths of a second earlier, had already shut down. The rocket, without a navigation system, took a fatal sharp turn to correct a deviation that had not occurred.

An independent board of inquiry took less than 2 months to document how a software error resulted into the massive failure. The navigational system of the Ariane 5 design was one of the few components of Ariane 4 that was reused. It had been flight tested and had not yet failed for Ariane 4.

The navigation system is responsible for calculating course corrections from a specified trajectory based on input from the inertial reference system. An inertial reference system allows a moving vehicle (e.g., a rocket) to compute its position solely based on sensor data from accelerometers and gyroscopes, that is, without reference to the outside world. The inertial system must first be initialized with the starting coordinates and align its axis with the initial orientation of the rocket. The alignment calculations are done by the navigation system before launch and need to be continuously updated to take into account the rotation of the Earth. Alignment calculations are complex and take approximately 45 minutes to complete. Once the rocket is launched, the alignment data are transferred to the flight navigational system. By design, the alignment calculations continue for another 50 seconds after the transfer of data to the navigation system. The decision enables the countdown to be stopped after the transfer of alignment data takes place but before the engines are ignited without having to restart the alignment calculations (that is, without having to restart a 45-minute calculation cycle). In the event the launch succeeds, the alignment module just generates unused data for another 40 seconds after lift-off.

The computer system of Ariane 5 differed from Ariane 4. The electronics was doubled: two inertial reference systems to compute the position of the rocket, two computers to compare the planned trajectory with the actual trajectory, and two sets of control electronics to steer the rocket. If any component would fail, the backup system would take over.

The alignment system, designed for onground calculations only, used 16-bit words to store horizontal velocity (more than enough for displacements due to the wind and to the rotation of the earth). Thirty seconds into flight, the horizontal velocity of Ariane 5 caused an overflow, raised an exception that was handled by shutting down the onboard computer and handing control to the backup system.

Discussion

There had not been adequate test coverage of the alignment software. It had been subjected to thousands of tests, but not one of them included an actual trajectory. The navigation system was tested individually. Tests were specified by the system team and executed by the builders of the navigation system. The system team did not realize that the alignment module could cause the main processor to shut down, especially not in flight. There had been a failure to communicate between the component team and the system team.

In this chapter, we discuss project communication within a software development project. This topic is not specific to software engineering. Communication is, however, pervasive throughout a software development project. The cost of communication failure can have a high, and sometimes fatal, impact on the project and the quality of the delivered system.

3.2 An Overview of Project Communication

Communication needs and tools that support communication are numerous and diverse. To facilitate our discussion, we introduce the following classification and definitions (Figure 3-1):

- A **communication mode** refers to a type of information exchange that has defined objectives and scope. A client review is an example of a communication mode during which the client reviews the content and quality of a project deliverable. Problem reporting is another example of a communication mode during which a user reports a bug to the developers. A communication mode can be **scheduled** if it is a planned event or **event-driven** if it occurs nondeterministically. Client reviews are usually scheduled, whereas problem reports are event driven.
- A **communication mechanism** refers to a tool or procedure that can be used to transmit and receive information and support a communication mode. Smoke signals and fax machines are communication mechanisms. Communication mechanisms are **synchronous** if they require both sender and receivers to be available at the same time. Otherwise, communication mechanisms are called **asynchronous**. Smoke signals are synchronous, whereas fax machines are asynchronous.

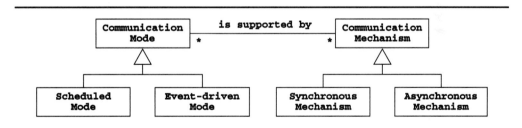

Figure 3-1   Classification of communication modes and mechanisms (UML class diagram).

Both synchronous and asynchronous communication mechanisms can be used to support a scheduled mode of communication. For example, in Figure 3-2, either smoke signals or a fax machine can be used for a client review. On the other hand, only asynchronous communication mechanisms can be used for supporting event-driven modes (reporting a problem with smoke signals may lead to loss of information if nobody was scheduled to watch the smoke. Note that a communication mode can be supported by many different communication mechanisms: The requirements analysis document can be faxed to the client, and the client sends back her comments

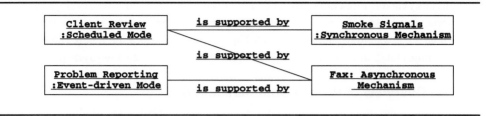

Figure 3-2   Examples of modes and mechanisms (UML class diagram). Both scheduled modes and event-driven modes can be supported by asynchronous mechanisms. Event-driven modes, however, can only be supported by asynchronous mechanisms.

using smoke signals. Similarly, the same mechanism can support many communication modes: The fax machine can receive either problem reports or comments from a client review.

In Section 3.3, we review the different communication modes that communication can be used in a project. The scheduled modes reviewed include client reviews, status reports, and system releases. Event-driven modes include requests for changes, clarifications, and issue resolution. In Section 3.4, we survey a number of communication mechanisms available to project participants. In particular, we focus on meetings, reviews, report forms, questionnaires, electronic mail, newsgroups, and groupware. In Section 3.5, we examine a specific combination of communication modes and mechanisms in an example project.

3.3 Modes of Communication

Scheduled communication occurs according to a periodic process (Table 3-1). For example, a team reviews its status every week, a client reviews the project status every month. These are focused, well-organized, and usually face-to-face points of communication directed at discovering and addressing a broad range of issues.

Event-driven communication is caused by a specific event (Table 3-2), such as the discovery of an incompatibility between two subsystems, the need for a new feature, or the necessity for resolving different interpretations before a formal review. These are spontaneous, ad hoc, and possibly asynchronous points of communication directed at resolving a single issue quickly.

Software projects require support for periodic and event-driven communication. Not all communication needs can be addressed through scheduled events and formal processes, whereas exchanging information only when needed or required results in additional crises due to miscommunications and omissions. In this section, we describe both types of modes.

Table 3-1 Scheduled modes of communication

Mode	Objectives	Scope
Problem definition (Section 3.3.1)	• Extract requirements knowledge from client and user • Extract domain knowledge from client and user	• Application domain • Functional and nonfunctional requirements • Delivery schedule
Client reviews (Section 3.3.2)	• Ensure that the system under construction is the one the client wants • Review feasibility of nonfunctional requirements (e.g, platform, performance) • Review the delivery schedule	• Functional and nonfunctional requirements • Delivery schedule
Project reviews (Section 3.3.3)	• Ensure that dependent subsystems can communicate • Anticipate late completion of critical subsystems • Disseminate operational knowledge across teams	• System design • Object design • Tests
Inspections/ Walkthroughs (Section 3.3.4)	• Ensure correctness of subsystem implementation • Improve quality of subsystem implementation • Disseminate operational knowledge across participants.	• Implementation
Status reviews (Section 3.3.5)	• Ensure adherence to the task plan • Ensure timely completion of planned deliverables • Dissemination of potential issues	• Tasks • Action items • Issues
Brainstorming (Section 3.3.6)	• Generate and evaluate solutions	• A single issue
Releases (Section 3.3.7)	• Dissemination of large volume of information (e.g., document, subsystem code)	• Project organization • Task plan • System, documents, and models
Postmortem review (Section 3.3.8)	• Capture and organization of lessons learned	• Project organization • Task plan • System and models

Table 3-2   Event-driven modes of communication

Mode	Objectives	Scope
Requests for clarification (Section 3.3.9)	• Clarification • Report an ambiguity in documentation or code	• Any
Requests for change (Section 3.3.10)	• Report a problem or a possible improvement	• Any
Issue resolution (Section 3.3.11)	• Reaching consensus • Formalizing chosen solution	• A single issue

3.3.1   Problem Definition

The goal of **problem definition** is for the project manager and the client to agree on the scope of the system under construction. The project definition activity produces a problem definition document that outlines the domain and the functionality of the system. It also contains nonfunctional requirements such as platform specification or speed constraints. Consider the following example [FRIEND, 1994].

FRIEND Problem Statement

Weaknesses of today's emergency handling. Most local government emergency handling systems are established for normal call loads and are immediately overloaded when an unusual event or multiple events occur. During an emergency, responders may acquire useful information for the decision makers. This information is not transmitted by radio, unless asked for, due to limited air time.

Government services possess a wealth of information that is invaluable during emergencies. Fire, police, emergency medical services, public works, and building inspection departments compile large amounts of paper-based information. During an emergency, this paper-based information is extremely hard to use and is rarely used.

Crucial information is not always immediately available during emergencies. Incident location information, such as hazardous materials, gas line locations, etc., are not available or do not exist. There is a need for a system that would speed up response time to emergencies and provide information to make better decisions.

Functional requirements. The objective of the FRIEND project is to build a system that handles multiple emergency incidents at one time under unusual call loads. The system must be prepared for a worst case scenario of an emergency. The system must allow quick and remote response between police officers, fire fighters, maintenance workers, and the headquarters' dispatcher. A wide bandwidth will be used, so that the need for acknowledgment before transmission will not be a constraint.

The system would provide instant use of information, such as:

• geographic information—such as city maps, including above and underground utilities
• hazardous materials information (Hazmat)
• building specific information —such as gas and water lines, fire hydrants location, floor maps, etc.
• available government resources—such as the Emergency Operations Plan (EOP)

Following guidelines and the Emergency Operations Plan, the system will automatically notify personnel in the appropriate department, create task lists to follow, and allocate resources, as well as any other tasks that would save time during an emergency.

Every command post vehicle interacting with the FRIEND system will have a mobile computer that uses wireless communication to report to the headquarter dispatcher. The goal is to replace the first responders reporting input mechanism by an easy input and responsive user interface, voice recognition, a touch screen, or a pen-based system. All transactions on the system must be archived for future analysis.

Nonfunctional requirements. The FRIEND system will first be used by the Bellevue Police Department as a standalone product. Also, FRIEND is to be later used by a group of municipalities, with the ability to provide higher levels of government with local information. The hardware used by field service personnel will be exposed to weather and rough duty. FRIEND should be portable to existing hardware available in local governments. The prototype is expected to be scalable. System design should, therefore, be engineered to be expandable to deal with accidents on the state and federal levels.

Acceptance Criteria. The client considers this problem statement to be a broad definition and does not expect all functionality to be delivered in the first release. During the Requirement Engineering phase of the project, the client will negotiate with the software engineers an acceptable prototype for delivery. After the negotiation phase, the specific requirements for the client acceptance test will be frozen. The client expects to sign off on the negotiated deliverable within 4–6 weeks of the client presentation. As a minimum, the client expects the delivered prototype to be expandable in a future course. As a minimum acceptable test, the client expects the negotiated prototype to be successfully demonstrated on the Andrew system with a wireless component. As a desired acceptable test, the client expects the prototype to be successfully demonstrated in a field trial at the Bellevue Police Department.

The problem definition does not produce a complete specification of the statement. It is merely a preliminary requirements activity that establishes common ground between the client and the project. We discuss requirements activities in Chapter 4, *Requirements Elicitation* and Chapter 5, *Analysis*.

3.3.2   Client Reviews

The goal of **client reviews** is for the client to assess the progress of the development and for the developers to confirm or change the requirements of the system. The client review can be used to manage expectations on both sides and to increase the shared understanding among participants. The focus of the review is on what the system does and what constraints are relevant to the client (e.g., performance, platform). In most cases, the review should not focus on the design or implementation of the system unless they impact the client or the user. Exceptions include software contracts that impose constraints on the development process, such as software system with safety requirements.

A client review is usually conducted as a formal presentation during which the developers focus on specific functionality with client. The review is preceded by the release of a work product, such as a specification document, an interface mock-up, or an evaluation prototype. At the outcome of the review, the client provides feedback to the developers. This feedback may

---

OWL Client acceptance test agenda
Date: 12/5/1997
Time: 3- 4:30pm
Location: Forest Hall
Goal: review of the system by the client and identification of open issues
Overview:
- problem statement
- design goals
- system architecture
- Demo 1: Remote user interface and control
- Demo 2: Site editor
- Demo 3: 3D Visualization and speech user interface
- questions and answers
- review wrap up

Figure 3-3   An example of an agenda for a client review.

consist of a general approval or a request of detailed changes in functionality or schedule. Figure 3-3 depicts an example of an agenda for a client review.

3.3.3   Project Reviews

The goal of a **project review** is for the project manager to assess status and for teams to review subsystem interfaces. Project reviews can also encourage the exchange of operational knowledge across teams, such as common problems encountered with tools or the system. The focus of the review depends on the deliverable under review. For system design, the decomposition and high-level subsystem interfaces are reviewed. For object design, the object interfaces are reviewed. For integration and test, the tests and their results are reviewed. The focus of project reviews should not be on functionality unless it impacts the feasibility or the status of the system.

A project review is typically conducted as a formal presentation during which each team presents its subsystem to the management or to teams that depend on the subsystem. The review is usually preceded by the release of a document (e.g, system design document) describing the aspects of the system under review (e.g., the subsystems interfaces). At the outcome of the review, the developers may negotiate changes in the interfaces and changes in schedule.

3.3.4   Inspections and Walkthroughs

The objective of code **inspections** and **walkthroughs** is to increase the quality of a subsystem through peer review. In the case of a walkthrough, a developer presents to the other members of her team line-by-line the code she has written. The other team members challenge any suspicious code and attempt to discover as many errors as possible. The role of the developer is to facilitate the presentation and answer the team's questions. In the case of an inspection, the members of the team focus on the compliance of the code with a predefined list of criteria (e.g., Does the code implement the specified algorithm? Does the code correctly use dependent subsystem interfaces?). In the case of inspections, the team leads the discussion, and the developer answers questions. The focus of the inspection or walkthrough is on the code, not on the programmer or the design.

Communication among participants is code based. The actual code is used as a common frame of reference. Inspections are similar to project reviews in their objective to increase quality and disseminate operational information. They differ from reviews in their formality, their limited audience, and their extended duration. Inspections and walkthroughs are widely used and have been effective at detecting defects early [Fagan, 1976], [Seaman & Basili, 1997]. We describe walkthroughs in Chapter 9, *Testing*.

3.3.5 Status Reviews

Unlike client and project reviews that focus on the system, **status reviews** focus on tasks. Status reviews are primarily conducted in a team (e.g., weekly) and occasionally conducted in a project (e.g., monthly). The objective of status reviews is to detect deviations from the task plan and to correct them. Status reviews also encourages developers to achieve closure on pending tasks. The review of task status encourages the discussion of open issues and unanticipated problems, and, thus, encourage informal communication among team members. Often, solutions to common issues can be shared more effectively and operational knowledge disseminated when discussed within the scope of a team (as opposed to within the scope of the project).

Status reviews represent an investment in person power. Increasing the effectiveness of reviews has a global impact on the team performance. Status meetings should have an agenda available prior to the meeting describing the tasks and issues to be reviewed. This enables meeting participants to prepare for the meeting and redirect the agenda if an urgent issue needs to be discussed. Minutes for each meeting should be taken by a designated participant in order to capture as much information (mainly status and decisions) as possible. Minutes are made available to the participants for review as early as possible after the meeting. This encourages the minute taker to complete the minutes and for team members who missed the meeting to catch up with team status. Meeting minutes are subsequently referenced when related tasks are discussed or when clarification is needed. Moreover, meeting minutes represent a portion of the project history that can be analyzed after the project is completed.

3.3.6 Brainstorming

The goal of **brainstorming** is to generate and evaluate a large number of solutions for a problem. Brainstorming is usually done in face-to-face meetings but can also be done via E-mail or groupware. The fundamental idea behind brainstorming is that solutions proposed by one participant, however invalid, can trigger additional ideas and proposals from other participants. Similarly, the evaluation of proposals within a group leads to more explicit evaluation criteria and to a more consistent evaluation. In situations where no clear solutions exist, the brainstorming process can be facilitated by separating the generation and evaluation. Brainstorming has also the side effect of building consensus for the chosen solution.

3.3.7   Releases

The goal of a **release** is to make available a document or a subsystem to other project participants, often replacing an older version of the artifact. A release can be as simple as a two-line electronic message (see Figure 3-4) or can consist of several pieces of information: the new version of the artifact, a list of changes made since the last release of the artifact, a list of problems or issues yet to be addressed, and an author.

```
From: Al
Newsgroups: cs413.f96.architecture.discuss
Subject: SDD
Date: Thu, 25 Nov 03:39:12 -0500
Lines: 6
Message-ID: <3299B30.3507@andrew.cmu.edu>
MimeVersion: 1.0
Content-Type: text/plain; charset=us-ascii
Content-Transfer-Encoding: 7bit

An updated version of the API document for the Notification Subsystem can be
found here: http: //decaf/~al/FRIEND/notifapi.html

--Al
Notification Group Leader
```

Figure 3-4   An example of a release announcement.

Releases are used to make a large amount of information available in a controlled manner, by batching, documenting, and reviewing many changes together. Project and client reviews are typically preceded by a release of one or more deliverables.

The management of versions of documents, models, and subsystems is described in Chapter 10, *Software Configuration Management*.

3.3.8   Postmortem Review

Postmortem reviews focus on extracting lessons from the development once the software is delivered. Postmortem reviews need to be conducted shortly after the end of the project so that minimal information is lost or distorted by subsequent experience. The end of the project is usually a good time to assess which techniques, methods, and tools have worked and have been critical to the success (or failure) of the system.

A postmortem can be conducted as a brainstorming session, a structured questionnaire followed by interviews, or individual reports written by teams (or participants). In all cases, the

Question about problems that occurred	What kinds of communication and negotiation problems have emerged in the development of the system?
Question eliciting possible solutions to those problems	Speculate on what kind of information structure is needed for team-based design in conjunction with a model-based object-oriented software engineering methodology. Do you feel the forums provided (Discuss, Issues, Documents, Announce, etc.) solved this challenge? Identify issues with the information structure and propose solutions.
Question eliciting other aspects of the project that were either perceived as positive or could be improved	What observations and comments do you have about the project concerning: • your expectations at the beginning of the project and how they evolved • the goals of this project • the use of use cases • the life cycle used in the project • the project management (meetings, communication, etc.) • the documentation process
Open-ended catch-all question	In addition to the above questions, please feel free to discuss any other issues and proposed solutions that you feel are relevant.

Figure 3-5   An example of questions for a postmortem review.

areas covered should include the tools, methods, organization, and procedures used by the project. Figure 3-5 is an example of questions that can be used during a postmortem.

Even if the results of post mortems are not disseminated through the organization via formal channels (e.g., technical reports), they can still be disseminated indirectly through the project participants. Project participants are frequently reassigned to different projects or functions and often disseminate the lessons learned from the old project to other parts of the organization.

3.3.9   Request for Clarification

Requests for clarification represent the bulk of the communication among developers, clients, and users. Requests for clarification are event driven. A participant may request clarification about any aspect of the system that may be ambiguous. Requests for clarification may occur during informal meetings, phone calls, E-mail, a form, or most other communication mechanism available to the project. Situations in which most information needs are handled through this mode are symptoms of a defective communication infrastructure. Such projects often face serious failures downstream resulting from misunderstandings and missing and misplaced information. Figure 3-6 depicts an example of request for clarification.

```
From: Alice
Newsgroups: cs413.architecture.discuss
Subject: SDD
Date: Thu, 10 Oct 23:12:48 -0400
Message-ID: <325DBB30.4380@andrew.cmu.edu>
MimeVersion: 1.0
Content-Type: text/plain; charset=us-ascii

When exactly would you like the System Design Document? There is some confusion
over the actual deadline: the schedule claims it to be October 22, while the
template says we have until November 7.
Thanks,
    Alice
```

Figure 3-6   An example of a request for clarification.

3.3.10 Request for Change

Request for change is an event-driven mode of communication. A participant reports a problem and, in some cases, proposes solutions. The participant reports a problem with the system itself, its documentation, the development process, or the project organization. Requests for change are often formalized when the number of participants and the system size is substantial. Change requests contain a classification (e.g., severe defect, feature request, comment), a description of the problem, a description of the context in which it occurs, and any amount of supporting material. Change request forms have been popularized by defects-tracking software. They can be applied to other aspects of the project (e.g., task plan, development process, testing procedures). Figure 3-7 depicts an example of change request form.

3.3.11 Issue Resolution

Once problems have been reported and solutions proposed and evaluated, a single solution needs to be selected, communicated, and implemented. A flat organization may select a solution as part of the brainstorming process. A hierarchical organization or a crisis situation may require a single individual to select and impose a solution. In all cases, the decision needs to be documented and communicated to the relevant participants. Documentation of the resolution allows participants to refer back to the decision later in the project, in case of a misunderstanding. Effective communication of the decision enables participants to remain synchronized.

An issue base can serve as a communication mechanism for supporting problem tracking, brainstorming, and **issue resolution**. The issue base displayed in Figure 3-8 displays a list of messages exchanged as a result of issue resolutions. The message captions preceded by I: denote issues, those preceded by P: (for proposal) suggested solutions, A+ and A- denote arguments supporting and arguing against a solution. Finally, once issues are resolved, a single message, called a resolution, is posted to document the decision that was taken on the issue. We describe issue bases and issue modeling in Chapter 8, *Rationale Management*.

Header information for identifying the change	Report number: 1291 Date: 5/3 Author: Dave Synopsis: The FRIEND client crashes when empty forms are submitted.
Context information for locating the problem	Subsystem: User interface Version: 3.4.1 Classification: • missing/incorrect functionality • convention violation • **bug** • documentation error Severity: • **severe** • moderate • annoying
Description of the problem and the rationale for change	Description: Rationale:
Description of desired change	Proposed solution:

Figure 3-7   An example of a change request form.

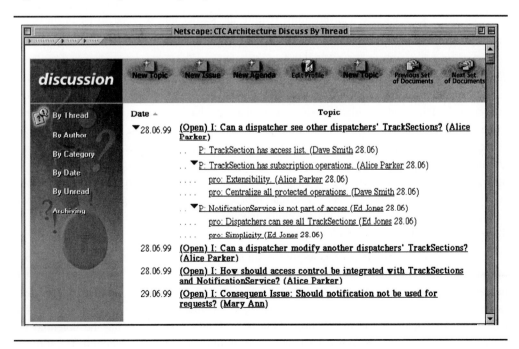

Figure 3-8   An example of an issue base (Domino Lotus Notes database).

3.3.12 Discussion

In this section, we presented a broad range of modes of communication. Not all projects put the same emphasis on all modes of communication. Projects producing shrink-wrapped software may not have client reviews but may have sophisticated change report procedures. Other projects put more emphasis on testing than on code inspections and walkthroughs.

The modes of communication used in a project are usually dictated by the application domain of the system and the activities of the project. These modes are often made explicit and formalized into procedures to address critical communication paths. For example, project reviews make it easier for all participants to synchronize their state and confront issues that pertain to more than one or two subsystems. Project reviews become especially critical when the size of the project increases to the point that few participants have a global view of the system.

3.4 Mechanisms of Communication

In this section, we describe several communication mechanisms that support information exchanges. We classify communication mechanisms in two broad categories. **Synchronous mechanisms**, such as telephone or video conference, require sender and receiver to be available at the same time, whereas **asynchronous mechanisms**, such as E-mail or fax, do not. We further classify synchronous mechanisms into same-place and different-place mechanisms. Same-place mechanisms (e.g., a hallway conversation) require the sender and receiver to be in the same location (e.g., a hallway), whereas different-place mechanisms do not.

Informal face-to-face, interviews, and meetings are synchronous, same-place mechanisms. These mechanisms are characterized by a low content of technical information. However, same-place mechanisms allow for the transfer of nonverbal information that is critical during consensus building and negotiation. Also, same-place mechanisms allow for clarifications and, more generally, a higher degree of flexibility. The cost of synchronous mechanisms is high, especially when many participants are involved. Synchronous different-place groupware attempts to reduce the cost of synchronous communication by not requiring all participants to be at the same location. Also, groupware promises to make a variety of information available (e.g., running code, editable documents, hyperlink structures), thus increasing the communication bandwidth among participants. Synchronous mechanisms of communication are listed in Table 3-3 and described in the following sections.

Questionnaires, fax, E-mail, newsgroups, and different-time groupware are asynchronous mechanisms of communication. They allow a large number of details to be communicated quickly. Moreover, they allow for a much larger number of receivers, which makes these mechanisms ideal for document and code releases. Asynchronous communication has the disadvantage of making nonverbal information inaccessible, thus increasing the potential for misunderstandings. Asynchronous mechanisms of communication are described in Table 3-4 and described in Sections 3.4.6–3.4.9.

Table 3-3   Synchronous mechanisms of communication

Mechanism	Supported modes
Hallway conversations (Section 3.4.1)	Request for clarification Request for change
Questionnaires and structured interviews (Section 3.4.2)	Application domain knowledge elicitation Postmortem review
Meetings (face-to-face, telephone, video) (Section 3.4.3)	Client review Project review Inspection Status review Postmortem review Brainstorm Issue resolution
Same-time, different-place groupware (Section 3.4.5)	Client review Project review Inspection Brainstorm Issue resolution

Table 3-4   Asynchronous mechanisms of communication

Mechanism	Supported modes
Electronic mail (Section 3.4.6)	Release Change request Brainstorm
Newsgroups (Section 3.4.7)	Release Change request Brainstorm
World Wide Web (Section 3.4.8)	Release Asynchronous code inspections Change request Brainstorm
Lotus Notes (Section 3.4.9)	Release Change request Brainstorm

3.4.1   Hallway Conversations

Hallway conversations are event-driven, informal exchanges of information based on opportunity. Two participants meet by accident and take advantage of the situation to exchange information.

Example. Two project participants, Sally and Bob, meet at the coffee machine. Sally, member of the user interface team, remembers that Bob is a member of the notification team, which is responsible for the communication between the client subsystems and the server. All morning Sally has been experiencing random failures when receiving packets from the server. She is not sure if the problem comes from the server, the communication subsystem, or her code. Bob answers that he was not aware that the server was being used at this time and that he had been testing a new revision of the communication system, explaining the behavior that Sally had observed. Bob had bypassed configuration management policy to save time.

Hallway conversations represent a substantial part in the overall project communication. They are cheap and effective for resolving simple problems that are caused by a lack of coordination between project members. In addition, they are also effective in supporting the exchange of operational knowledge, such as frequently asked questions about tools, procedures, or the location of project information. The drawbacks of hallway conversations include their small audience and lack of history: Important information can be lost and misunderstandings may occur when the content of the conversation is relayed to other participants. Moreover, no document, database, or electronic message can be accessed when referring to a decision that was made and communicated during a hallway conversation.

3.4.2   Questionnaires and Structured Interviews

The objective of a **questionnaire** is to elicit information from one or more persons in a structured manner. Questionnaires are typically used for eliciting domain knowledge from users and experts, understanding user requirements and priorities. They can also be used for extracting lessons learned during a postmortem review. Questionnaires can include both multiple choice questions and open-ended questions.

Questionnaires have the advantage of eliciting reliable information at minimal cost to the user. Questionnaires can be answered by users independently, then reviewed and analyzed by the analyst or developer. Clarifications of ambiguous or incomplete answers are then obtained during a **structured interview**. The drawback of questionnaires is that they are difficult to design. However, the cost of requirements errors and misunderstandings between the client and the developer often justify their cost. Subsequently, sufficient information is gathered about the domain and a requirements analysis document is written, so that most revisions to the systems and additional issues are addressed in client reviews.

3.4.3   Meetings

Face-to-face **meetings**[1] enable a number of participants to share, review, and negotiate issues and solutions. To date, meetings are the only mechanism that allow effective resolution of issues and the building of consensus. The drawback of meetings is their cost in resources and the difficulty in managing them. In order to increase the information transfer and the number of decisions made during a meeting, roles are assigned to selected participants:

- The **primary facilitator** is responsible for organizing the meeting and guiding its execution. The facilitator writes an agenda describing the objective and the scope of the meeting. The agenda is generally released before the meeting for preview by its participants. This allows participants to decide whether the meeting is relevant to them and to allow preparation of support material for the meeting.

- The **minute taker** is responsible for recording the meeting. The minute taker may take notes on paper or on a laptop computer, organize them after the meeting, and release them shortly after the meeting for review by the meeting participants. This enables the participants to reiterate their commitment to the outcome of the meeting. The written record of the meeting makes it also easier for participants to share information with members that were not present to the meeting.

- The **time keeper** is responsible for keeping track of time and notifying the facilitator if a discussion consumes more time than is allocated by the agenda.

A **meeting agenda** consists of at least three sections: a header identifying the planned meeting location, time, and participants; a list of items participants will report on; and a list of issues that need to be discussed and resolved in the meeting. Each information-sharing and discussion item is also assigned a time that allows the timekeeper to ensure that the meeting ends on time. Figure 3-9 is an example of a meeting agenda.

A set of **meeting minutes** consists of three sections that correspond to the sections of the agenda. In addition, meeting minutes include a section describing the action items resulting from the meeting (i.e., items describing actions to be taken by the meeting participants as a consequence of the meeting). The header section contains the actual meeting location, time, and participants. The information-sharing item section contains the information that was shared during the meeting. The decision-item section contains a record of the decisions that were made (and not made). Figure 3-10 is an example of meeting minutes.

Although meetings conducted in a single location are most efficient, it is possible to conduct meetings when participants are distributed geographically by using teleconferencing or video conferencing. This reduces costs at the expense of a lower bandwidth and lower reliability. A well-structured agenda available prior to the meeting becomes crucial as floor control

---

1. Meeting procedures described in this section are derived from [Kayser, 1990].

Header information identifying the meeting and audience	**When and Where** **Date**: 1/30 **Start**: 4:30pm **End**: 5:30pm **Building**: Wean Hall **Room**: 3420	**Role** **Primary Facilitator**: Peter **Timekeeper**: Dave **Minute Taker**: Ed
Desired outcome of the meeting	**1. Objective** Resolve any requirements issues that prevent us from starting prototyping.	
Action items to be reported on	**2. Status [Allocated Time: 15 minutes]** Dave: State of command parsing code	
Issues scheduled to be discussed (and resolved) during the meeting	**3. Discussion items [Allocated Time: 35 minutes]** 3.1 How to deal with arbitrarily formatted input data sets? 3.2 How to deal with output data? 3.3 Command parsing code (modifiability, backward compatibility)	
The wrap-up period is the same for all meetings	**4. Wrap up [Allocated Time: 5 minutes]** 4.1 Review and assign new action items 4.2 Meeting critique	

Figure 3-9   An example of a meeting agenda.

becomes difficult with lower audio and visual quality. Also, knowledge of the individual voices and particularities improves communication among participants.

When writing a meeting agenda, the facilitator should be as concrete as possible without adding to the length of the agenda. It is often tempting to develop a generic template agenda and reuse it systematically without modifications. This has the drawback of taking the substance out of the meeting process, turning it into a bureaucratic procedure. Figure 3-11 is an example of contentless agenda. By only modifying the header, this agenda could apply to most subsystem meetings, and thus, does not convey any new information to the participants are not aware of.

3.4.4   Reviews

Reviews are formal meetings during which the quality of an artifact (e.g., document or code) is evaluated by an external party. They are typically conducted as formal presentations, preceded by a release, and followed by a number of requests for change. Reviews are more costly than regular meetings, given that they often require travel for the client or the developers. As with regular meetings, an agenda is posted and sent to the external party prior to the review. Minutes of the review are carefully recorded and includes requests for changes and other comments and issues that the external party may have.

Header information identifying the meeting and audience	**When and Where** **Date**: 1/30 **Start**: 4:30pm **End**: 6:00pm **Building**: Wean Hall **Room**: 3420	**Role** **Primary Facilitator**: Peter **Timekeeper**: Dave **Minute Taker**: Ed **Attending**: Ed, Dave, Mary, Peter, Alice
Verbatim from agenda	**1. Objective** ...	
Summary of the information that was exchanged	**2. Status** ...	
Record of issue discussion and resolution	**3. Discussion** 3.1 Command parsing code is a 1200–1300 line if statement. This makes it fairly hard to add new commands or to modify existing commands without breaking backward compatibility with existing clients. Proposals: 1) Restructure the command parsing code by assigning one object per kind of command. 2) Pass all command arguments by name. The latter would make it easier to maintain backward compatibility. On the other hand, this would increase the size of the commands, thus increasing the size of the command file. Resolution: Restructure code for now. Revisit this issue if backward compatibility is really an issue (the calling code might be rewritten anyway). See AI[1]. ... *Discussion of the other issues omitted for brevity*	
Additions and modifications to the task plan	**4. Wrap up** AI[1] For: Dave. Revisit command parsing code. Emphasis on modularity. Coordinate with Bill from the database group (who might assume backward compatibility). ... *Other action items and meeting critique omitted for brevity* ...	

Figure 3-10   An example of meeting minutes.

The scope of a review (e.g., a client review) may require the review to be organized long before its execution. Flexibility should be left in the organization, however, such that the object of the review (e.g., the requirements document) can evolve as late as possible (e.g., a few days or a few hours before the review). This flexibility can enable the developers to discover more issues, points of clarification, or alternative solutions and minimize the time during which the state of the deliverable needs to be frozen.

Header information identifying the meeting and audience	**When and Where** **Date**: 1/30 **Start**: 4:30pm **End**: 5:30pm **Building**: Wean Hall **Room**: 3420	**Role** **Primary Facilitator**: Peter **Timekeeper**: Dave **Minute Taker**: Ed
Desired outcome of the meeting	**1. Objective** Resolve open issues	
Action items to be reported on	**2. Status [Allocated Time: 15 minutes]** Dave: Dave's action items	
Issues scheduled to be discussed (and resolved) during the meeting	**3. Discussion items [Allocated Time: 35 minutes]** 3.1 Requirements issues 3.2 Design issues 3.3 Implementation issues	
The wrap-up period is the same for all meetings	**4. Wrap up [Allocated Time: 5 minutes]** 4.1 Review and assign new action items 4.2 Meeting critique	

Figure 3-11   An example of poor meeting agenda.

3.4.5   Same-Time, Different-Place Groupware

Same time, different place groupware are tools that allow distributed users to collaborate synchronously. While, for a long time, these tools were only available in the realm of research [Grudin, 1988], they have been moving slowly into the commercial world with the recent popularization of Internet-based chatrooms and forums. Tools such as Teamwave [Teamwave, 1997] or Netmeeting enable a group of participants to collaborate synchronously over a shared workspace. They provide a meeting metaphor: Users "enter" a chat room, which then allows them to view a graphic or a text under consideration. All users see the same state. Usually only one can modify it at any one time. Floor control can be anarchic (whoever takes the floor has it) or sequential (whoever has the floor relinquishes it to the next user).

A weakness of same-time groupware is the difficulty in coordinating users. Typing takes more time than users are prepared to invest. Written words need to be chosen more carefully, given that nonverbal information is lost. Moreover, slight glitches in the network connection may represent enough interference for user coordination to be lost.

Same-time groupware, however, can become a useful substitute for video conferencing when combined with an audio channel: Users can view the same document and discuss it normally while scrolling and pointing to specific areas of the document. In all cases, different-place collaboration is still a nontrivial exercise that needs to be scripted and planned in advance.

Collaborative development of procedures for supporting collaboration is an challenging task when proximity and nonverbal communication are not available.

3.4.6   Electronic Mail

E-mail enables a sender to transmit an arbitrary text message to one or more recipients. The actual transmission of the message takes anywhere from a few seconds to a few hours or days. The message is received in a mailbox and kept until the receiver reads it and archives it. E-mail, in a development project, is often used in place of office memos or telephone. Participants can exchange with this mechanism a broad range of artifacts, from short informal notices to large documents. Finally, E-mail is standardized by a number of Internet Request for Comments (RFCs) that are widely implemented and used. As a consequence, E-mail is used across different organizations and platforms.

Because of its asynchronous nature and short latency, E-mail is ideal for supporting event-driven communication modes, such as requests for clarification, requests for change, and brainstorms. E-mail is also often used for announcing releases and exchanging intermediate versions of documents. Unlike the phone, E-mail enables participants to receive E-mail when they are available without introducing constraints on the sender.

A drawback of E-mail is that communication can be perceived as a trivial task. Typing a one-line message and sending it takes only a few seconds. But the same one-line message can be taken out of context and misunderstood, sent to the wrong person, or, most often, lost or unread. Because of the asynchronous nature of E-mail, potential for information loss is more likely. Project participants usually adjust to these drawbacks quickly after several serious misunderstandings have occurred.

3.4.7   Newsgroups

Newsgroups offer a similar metaphor to E-mail. However, instead of sending a message to a number of recipients, the sender posts a message to a newsgroup (often also referred to as a forum). Recipients subscribe to the newsgroups they want to read. Post and read accesses to a specific newsgroup can be controlled. Newsgroups follow a similar set of widespread standards as E-mail. There are many public domain and commercial tools available for managing a news server. Often, software for reading and sending E-mail is integrated with newsgroup readers, which facilitates the integration between E-mail and newsgroups.

Newsgroups are suited for notification and discussion among people who share a common interest. In a software project, teams may have a number of newsgroups; for example, in Figure 3-12, one for posting meeting agendas and minutes, another one for requests for clarification, yet another one for issues. Instead of enumerating the addresses of the team members every time a message is posted, the sender only has to name the targeted newsgroup. Typical modes that can be supported via newsgroups include requests for clarification, requests for change, releases, and brainstorms.

Newsgroup for communication with client	`cmu.academic.15-413.client`

Global newsgroups read by all developers	`cmu.academic.15-413.announce`
	`cmu.academic.15-413.discuss`
	`cmu.academic.15-413.issues`
	`cmu.academic.15-413.equipment`

Team newsgroups read mostly by the members of a single team (e.g., user interface team)	`...`
	`cmu.academic.15-413.ui.announce`
	`cmu.academic.15-413.ui.discuss`
	`cmu.academic.15-413.ui.minutes`

Special purpose newsgroups	`...` `cmu.academic.15-413.integration-tests`

Figure 3-12   An example of a newsgroup structure.

3.4.8   World Wide Web

The **World Wide Web** (WWW, also referred to as the "Web") provides the user with a hypertext metaphor. A WWW browser displays a document to the user that may contain hyperlinks to other documents. A Universal Resource Locator (URL) is associated with each link and describes to the browser the location of the target document and its method of retrieval. The WWW has growing popularity as hypertext documents are extended to contain embedded images, animations, and executable scripts.

In a software development project, the WWW is ideal for organizing and providing access to released information, such as preliminary and final versions of the deliverable documents, code, references (e.g., vendor home pages), and tool documentation.

Although the type of documents and functionality of WWW browsers evolves rapidly, the Web does not support in an equally straightforward manner the exchange of rapidly changing information such as newsgroup messages. However, with the integration of newsgroups into Netscape and other browsers, the WWW can play a significant part in a project's communication infrastructure.

Figure 3-13 displays the home page of the OWL project [OWL, 1996]. It contains references to the most important parts of the Web site such as the latest version of the project documents and review presentations, newsgroups, team organization charts, team Web pages, and references. The project Web site is managed by a single Web master. The pages associated with each team are administered by the teams with guidance from the project Web master.

3.4.9   Lotus Notes

Lotus Notes is a commercial tool (as opposed to a set of standards, as in the case of E-mail, newsgroups, and WWW) that provides functionality comparable to that of the Web. It provides a metaphor, however, that is closer to an database management system than to an

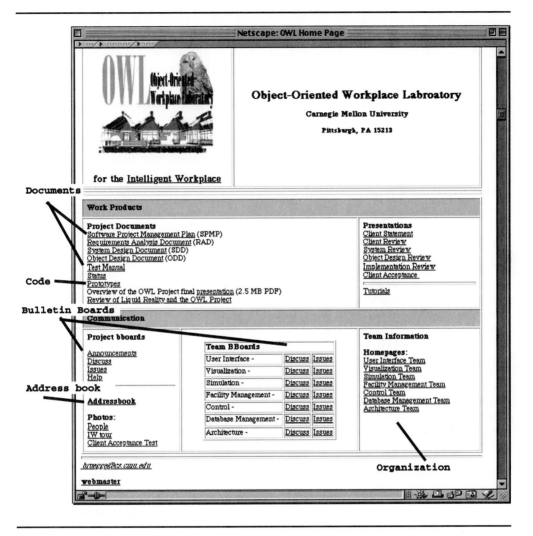

Figure 3-13   An example of a project home page for the OWL project.

E-mail system. Each user sees the information space as a set of databases. Databases contain documents composed of a set of fields. Documents are created and modified through a set of forms. Users collaborate by creating, sharing, and modifying documents. Each database can follow different templates and support application-specific functionality. For example, one database can support discussions (see Figure 3-8), in which case its documents are messages and replies. Another database can support a change request tracking system, in which case documents can be change request forms, revision logs, or release notes.

Lotus Notes differs from the Web by addressing well two additional aspects of information management: access control and replication. Access can be controlled at the level of a database (e.g., deny developers access to a management database), a document (e.g, disallow a developer to modify a change request posted by a user), or a field (e.g., allow only an administrator to modify the author field of a document). Access control can also be set in terms of groups of users. The concept of groups enables the administrator to express access control in terms of the organization of the project rather than of its individuals.

The main difference between Lotus Notes and the Web has been that Notes is a proprietary standard: Both client and server programs need to be purchased from IBM. The Web, on the other hand, is so ubiquitous because it relies on a set of public standards. It is possible to construct a Web application, accessible by users with different browsers, entirely out of public domain software (at the cost of reliability, support, and some functionality). In order to hedge the competition by the Web and to take advantage of the widespread use of the Web browsers, Lotus Notes introduced Domino, a product enabling Web browsers to access Lotus Notes databases through a standard browser.

Example. Each team may have a database for team announcements. Documents in the announcement databases are either announcements or replies. Only team members can post announcements, whereas anybody can read announcements and post replies. A Lotus Notes administrator is elected to organize project participants into access groups. Each access group corresponds to a team. Furthermore, the administrator set up the access of each announce database such that only members of the team who owns the database may post announcements. Assume Sally, a member of the user interface team, is reassigned to the notification team. The administrator needs only to remove Sally from the user interface access group and add her to the notification access group to reflect the organizational change. In the event the administrator did not organize access by group, he would have had to review and change the access to all the databases to which Sally had access.

3.4.10 Discussion

Project communication is pervasive. It occurs at many levels under different forms and can be supported by different tools. Communication is also a fundamental skill for project participants. Not all participants may be familiar with the latest development technology used by the project, but they all should have some idea of how information is disseminated through the project. For example, participants who have been using E-mail every day for previous projects may be reluctant to switch to an alternate infrastructure, such as newsgroups or Lotus Notes. For these reasons, the communication infrastructure, including the collection of tools used to support communication, needs to be carefully designed and put in place before the start of the project. The following criteria can be used in order to facilitate this:

- *Completeness.* Are all modes present in the project supported by one or more tools?
- *Complexity.* Are too many tools used to support communication? Can the information be duplicated or fragmented to the point that it is hard to find?

- *Reliability.* Is the primary communication tool reliable? What is the impact on the project if it fails?
- *Maintenance.* Does the infrastructure need a full-time administrator? Are the resources available for such a role? Are the skills available for such a role?
- *Ease of transition.* Is the metaphor presented by the infrastructure familiar enough to the users?

Transition is a critical step in setting up the communication infrastructure, even more than for other tools: The infrastructure will be used only if a majority of participants use it effectively. Otherwise, communication will occur through alternate ad hoc channels, such as hallway conversation, and the dissemination of information will be inconsistent and unreliable. In the next section, we provide an example of project communication infrastructure and of its transition.

3.5 Project Communication Activities

In this section, we examine the communication needs of an example project, select communication modes and mechanisms to support them, and describe their integration and their transition of the infrastructure into the project.

3.5.1 Identifying Communication Needs

This example project is a greenfield engineering effort with all new developers. The first phases of problem definition and preliminary design are handled directly by management in face-to-face meetings. Developers have little or no direct access to the client during these phases. Teams are also not expected to conduct inspections or walkthroughs until their level of expertise has sufficiently matured.

The preliminary design enables the management to define the initial decomposition of the system into subsystems (see Chapter 11, *Project Management*). Each subsystem is assigned to a team of developers. Additionally, cross-functional teams (e.g., documentation team, integration team) are formed to support the subsystem teams. Finally, each team has liaisons to the cross-functional teams to facilitate information transfer among teams. The initial project organization is displayed in Figure 3-14.

When defining subsystems, management attempts to identify groups of functionality that can be easily decoupled in order to reduce dependencies across subsystem teams. As a consequence, most asynchronous communication is expected to occur within teams and liaisons, whereas project-level communication is expected to happen at well-defined scheduled events, such as, project reviews and releases. A priori, management views the following modes as critical for cross-team communication:

- Client review—quarterly
- Project review—monthly

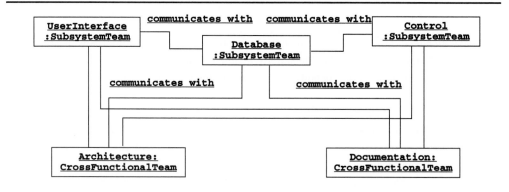

Figure 3-14 An example of a project organization, used as the basis for the communication infrastructure (UML object diagram). Associations represent communication channels via liaisons.

- Releases—weekly
- Requests for clarification—as needed
- Requests for change—as needed
- Project issue resolution—as needed

Similarly, management views the following modes as critical for intrateam communication:

- Status review—weekly
- Brainstorming—weekly
- Team issue resolution—as needed
- Request for clarification—as needed
- Request for change—as needed

Given the increasing importance of reviews in management's perspective of communication, management decides to select formal meetings for conducting client and project reviews until more expertise in the use of synchronous groupware tools is acquired. Team status and brainstorming is handled in a weekly team meeting. Management selects a forum-based groupware tool for supporting releases and the bulk of the asynchronous communication. Finally, management expects informal hallway conversations and liaisons to handle communication during crises, in case the formal communication channels break down.

3.5.2   Setting Up an Infrastructure

Two sets of forums are created to support project and team communication, respectively. Members subscribe to all project forums and to their team's forums. Project forums include:

- *Announce*. Major events (e.g., review agendas, releases) are announced by management by posting to this forum. Only management can post announcements to this forum; project members can post replies and read all documents.

- *Discuss*. Project-level requests for clarifications and requests for change are posted in this forum. Discussion about the requests (e.g., arguments and alternate solutions) are posted as replies to the original messages. All project members can post to this forum and read its documents.

- *Issues*. Open issues and their current state are posted in this forum. All project members can post to this forum and read its documents.

- *Documents*. The latest versions of the project deliverables (e.g., Requirements Analysis Document, System Design Document) and other internal project documents (e.g., Software Project Management Plan) are posted in this forum. Only the documentation team can post documents to this forum. All project members can post replies (i.e., annotations to the documents) and read the documents.

- *Equipment list*. This forum contains descriptions of available equipment and its status (e.g., availability, current borrower). Only the equipment manager can post to this forum.

The team forums are similar to the project forums, except that they support team communication. Team forums include:

- *team discussion*

- *team issues*

- *team documents*

Each project member may read any other team's forum. Team members can post only to their own team's forums. Note that the forums can be created as soon as the subsystem decomposition is relatively stable. Once forums and group accesses are set up, accounts for individual members can be created as the project is staffed.

3.5.3   Organizing Client and Project Reviews

Client reviews are conducted after the release of the requirements analysis document and after the delivery of the system. Project reviews are conducted to review the system design documents, the detailed object design, and the test. A project review may also be conducted before delivery as a dry run for the client acceptance test.

The project management decides to schedule all reviews during the planning phase (see Table 3-5).

Table 3-5   An example of a review schedule

Review	Date	Deliverable (release due 1 week before review)
Client review	week 7	Requirements Analysis Document
System design review	week 9	System Design Document
Object design review	week 13 (2 sessions)	Object Design Document
Internal review	week 16	Unit and integration tests
Client acceptance test dry run	week 17	All project deliverables
Client acceptance test	week 17	All project deliverables

The management also introduces procedures for organizing reviews:

1. The deliverables being reviewed are released 1 week[2] prior to the review.

2. Shortly after the release, the management publishes a draft agenda listing presentation topics for each team. The initial draft of the agenda is posted as a Lotus Notes document in the project *Announce* forum.

3. Candidate presenters replies to the original agendas and refine the presentation topic. The management modifies the agenda based on the replies.

4. Presenters submit their slides by replying to the agenda and including the slides in the reply. The management collates the slides before the presentation and updates the agenda.

The management also assigns the responsibility of minute taker, using the same procedure, to a project member, who will be briefed on how to take minutes by the management. During the review, the minute taker is using a laptop and carefully records all the questions from the audience and the answers. Finally, within a day of the review, the minute taker and management merge their notes and generate a list of action items to be completed as a result of the review and a list of open issues that could not be resolved during the review. The postprocessed minutes are posted on the *Announce* forum.

The emphasis on using the communication infrastructure for coordinating the organization of the review and the submission of slides enables more information to be captured, and thus, accessible in the information space of the project.

---

2. This leaves slack time for late documents. Realistically, some deliverables are often delivered as late as 1 day before the review. The critical issue here is: 1) Can the deliverable be made available to all review participants and 2) Do they have enough time to review them?

3.5.4 Organizing Weekly Team Meetings

Management decides to institute a weekly team meeting for all teams in order to support status reviews, brainstorming, and issue resolution. The weekly team meeting is organized and captured as described in Section 3.4.3. Given that the example project is a first-time development with a flat staffing, few members know each other socially and technically. Moreover, few of them are familiar with formal meeting roles and procedures. Management takes the opportunity of the first weekly team meeting to introduce meeting procedures, explain the importance of these procedures, and motivate team members in their use. Figure 3-15 displays the agenda posted by the management for the first meeting.

The goal of the first meeting is to train participants by example. Discussion about the procedures is encouraged. The meeting and group roles are explained to the participants and assigned by the team for the rest of the project. The role of facilitator is emphasized in that its purpose is to increase the efficiency of the meeting, not to impose decisions. Team members are taught that any meeting participant can take the role of secondary facilitator; that is, any participant can intervene in the discussion in order to put the meeting back within the scope of the agenda. Participants are taught keyword phrases for standard situations. (e.g., *Let me play the role of secondary facilitator* stands for "The scope of the current discussion is outside the agenda. Let us get back on track"; *Can we pop up a level?* stands for "The discussion has delved into a level of detail that is unnecessary for this audience. Actually, most of us have already gotten lost.") More generally, team members are taught that it is easy to waste time during a meeting, and that the primary goal of any meeting is to communicate efficiently and accurately such that they can go back to their respective tasks.

Management decides to have roles be rotated on a regular basis so that all participants have the opportunity to fill every role. This has the advantage of creating redundant skills across participants and better sharing of information. The drawback is that, in the short term, participants will not have time to mature into their role and thus become highly effective at a given task. Requiring early role assignment, role rotation, and more generally, meeting procedures to be in place early may introduce turbulences at the beginning of the project but represents a healthy investment in the long term. Management takes the position that everyday meeting and communication skills should be in place well before crisis-driven communication needs surface during the implementation and code activities.

The teams are responsible for assigning meeting roles and posting them in their respective team *Announce* forum. The meeting facilitator is required to post the initial draft of the agenda, composed of action items taken from the previous meeting's minutes and issues taken from the *Issues* forum.

In the team *Announce* forum 1 day before the status meeting: The minute taker is required to post the minutes within a day from the meeting, as a reply to the corresponding agenda. Other team members may comment on the agenda and minutes by posting replies. The facilitator or the minute taker may then amend the corresponding document.

When and Where	Role
Date: 1/9	**Primary Facilitator**: Alice
Start: 4:30pm	**Timekeeper**: Dave
End: 5:30pm	**Minute Taker**: Ed
Building: Wean Hall	
Room: 3420	

1. Objective

Become familiar with project management roles for a medium-scale project with a two-level hierarchy. In particular:

- Understand the difference between a role and a person
- Group roles are assigned to people
- Meeting times are finalized
- First set of action items for next meeting

2. Status and information sharing [Allocated time: 40 minutes]

2.1. How to organize a meeting
Meeting ground rules

- Active listening
- Active participating
- Punctual attendance
- No one-on-one or side meetings
- Respect the agenda
- Keep time
- Willingness to reach consensus
- Freedom to check process and ground rules

Meeting Roles

- Primary Facilitator
- Timekeeper
- Minute taker
- Scribe

2.2 Following the Agenda
Omitted for brevity

3. Discussion items [Allocated time: 15 minutes]

3.1 Team address book
3.2 Meeting roles assignments
3.3 Group roles assignment

4. Wrap up [Allocated time: 5 minutes]

4.1 Review and assign new action items
4.2 Meeting critique

Figure 3-15   First weekly team meeting agenda.

Meeting roles and procedures are often perceived as overhead. Management is aware of that perception and invests time in the beginning of the project to illustrate the benefits of the meeting procedures. In the first weeks of the project, management systematically reviews the agendas and minutes of the first few weekly meetings, suggests time-saving improvements to the facilitators (e.g., keeping an active document containing open issues and active action items from which the agenda can be cut and pasted), and to the minute takers (e.g., focusing on capturing the action items and unresolved issues first, then focusing on the discussion).

3.5.5 Transition Issues Revisited

Learning to use a new communication infrastructure in a project can be difficult [Orlikowski, 1992]. As mentioned earlier, it is critical that the transition of the communication infrastructure occur early in the project. On the one hand, once a critical mass of information and users is attained, the other users and more information will make its way into the communication infrastructure. On the other hand, if critical mass is not attained early, alternate informal channels will be set in place and solidify, making it difficult to correct them later.

Management can encourage the transition by making available a maximum of structured information up front (e.g., the problem statement, the Software Management Plan, agenda and document templates), require project participants to accomplish simple tasks using the infrastructure (e.g., posting their team roles in their *Announce* forum), and providing feedback using the communication infrastructure.

3.6 Exercises

1. You are a member of the user interface team. You are responsible for designing and implementing forms collecting information about users of the system (e.g., first name, last name, address, E-mail address, level of expertise). The information you are collecting is stored in the database and used by the reporting subsystem. You are not sure which fields are required information and which are optional.

   How do you find out?

2. You have been reassigned from the user interface team to the database team due to staff shortages and replanning. The implementation phase is well underway.

   In which role would you be most proficient given your knowledge of the user interface design and implementation?

3. Assume the development environment is Unix workstations, and the documentation team uses the Macintosh platform for writing documentation. The client requires the documents to be available on Windows platforms. Developers produce the design documentation using FrameMaker. The documentation team uses Microsoft Word for the user-level documentation. The client submits corrections on hardcopies and does not need to modify the delivered documents.

How could the information flow between the developers, the technical writers, and the client be set up (e.g., format, tools, etc.) such that duplication of files is minimized while everybody's tool preferences and platform requirements are still satisfied?

4. Which changes in the organization and communication infrastructure would you recommend for a successor of the Ariane 5 project as a consequence of the Ariane 501 failure described at the beginning of this chapter?

References

[FRIEND, 1994]   *FRIEND Project Documentation*, School of Computer Science, Carnegie Mellon Univ., Pittsburgh, PA, 1994.

[Grudin, 1988]   J. Grudin, "Why CSCW applications fail: Problems in design and evaluation of organization interfaces," *Proceedings CSCW '88,* (Portland, OR), 1988.

[Kayser, 1990]   T. A. Kayser, *Mining Group Gold*. Serif, El Segundo, CA, 1990.

[Lions, 1996]   J.-L. Lions, *ARIANE 5 Flight 501 Failure: Report by the Inquiry Board*, http://www.esrin.esa.it/htdocs/tidc/Press/Press96/ariane5rep.html, 1996.

[Orlikowski, 1992]   W. J. Orlikowski, "Learning from Notes: Organizational issues in groupware implementation," *Conference on Computer-Supported Cooperative Work Proceedings*, (Toronto, Canada) 1992.

[OWL, 1996]   *OWL Project Documentation,* School of Computer Science, Carnegie Mellon Univ., (Pittsburgh, PA) 1996.

[Reeves & Shipman, 1992] B. Reeves & F. Shipman, "Supporting communication between designers with artifact-centered evolving information spaces," *Conference on Computer-Supported Cooperative Work Proceedings*, (Toronto, Canada) 1992.

[Saeki, 1995]   M. Saeki, "Communication, collaboration, and cooperation in software development—How should we support group work in software development?" in *Asia-Pacific Software Engineering Conference Proceedings,* (Brisbane, Australia) 1995.

[Seaman & Basili, 1997] C. B. Seaman & V. R. Basili, "An empirical study of communication in code inspections," *Proceedings of the 19th International Conference on Software Engineering,* Boston, MA, 1997.

[Subrahmanian et al., 1997] E. Subrahmanian, Y. Reich, S. L. Konda, A. Dutoit, D. Cunningham, R. Patrick, M. Thomas, & A. W. Westerberg, "The *n*–dim approach to building design support systems," *Proceedings of ASME Design Theory and Methodology DTM '97* (ASME, New York) 1997.

[Teamwave, 1997]   Teamwave Inc., http://www.teamwave.com, 1997.

PART II
Dealing with
Complexity

4

Requirements Elicitation

Nobody is exempt from making mistakes.
The great thing is to learn from them.

—Karl Popper, in Objective Knowledge: An Evolutionary
    Approach

A *requirement* is a feature that the system must have or a constraint that it must satisfy to be accepted by the client. *Requirements engineering* aims at defining the requirements of the system under construction. Requirements engineering includes two main activities; *requirements elicitation*, which results in the specification of the system that the client understands, and *analysis*, which results in an analysis model that the developers can unambiguously interpret. Requirements elicitation is the more challenging of the two because it requires the collaboration of several groups of participants with different backgrounds. On the one hand, the client and the users are experts in their domain and have a general idea of what the system should do. However, they often have little experience in software development. On the other hand, the developers have experience in building systems but often have little knowledge of the everyday environment of the users.

Scenarios and use cases provide tools for bridging this gap. A *scenario* describes an example of system use in terms of a series of interactions between the user and the system. A *use case* is an abstraction that describes a class of scenarios. Both scenarios and use cases are written in natural language, a form that is understandable to the user.

In this chapter, we focus on scenario-based requirements elicitation. Developers elicit requirements by observing and interviewing users. Developers first represent the user's current work processes as as-is scenarios and then develop visionary scenarios describing the functionality provided by the future system. The client and users validate the system description by reviewing the scenarios and by testing small prototypes provided by the developers. As the definition of the system matures and stabilizes, developers and the client agree on a system specification in the form of use cases.

4.1 Introduction: Usability Examples

Consider the following examples[1]:

Feet or miles?

During a laser experiment, a laser beam was directed at a mirror on the Space Shuttle Discovery. The test called for the laser beam to be reflected back toward a mountain top. The user entered the elevation of the mountain as "10,023", assuming the units of the input were in feet. The computer interpreted the number in miles and the laser beam was reflected away from Earth, toward a hypothetical mountain 10,023 miles high.

Decimal point versus thousand separator

In the United States, decimal points are represented by a period (".") and thousand separators are represented by a comma (","). In Germany, the decimal point is represented by a comma and the thousand separator by a period. Assume a user in Germany, aware of both conventions, is viewing an on-line catalog with prices listed in dollars. Which convention should be used to avoid confusion?

Standard patterns

In the Emacs text editor, the command binding `<Control-x><Control-q>` exits the program. If any files need to be saved, the editor will ask the user, "Save file myDocument.txt? (y or n)". If the user answers y, the editor saves the file prior to exiting. Many users rely on this pattern and systematically type the sequence `<Control-x><Control-q>y` when exiting an editor. Other editors, however, ask when exiting the question: "Are you sure you want to exit? (y or n)". When users switch from Emacs to such an editor, they will fail to save their work until they manage to break this pattern.

Requirements elicitation is about communication among developers, clients, and users for defining a new system. Failure to communicate and understand each others' domain results in a system that is difficult to use or that simply fails to support the user's work. Errors introduced during requirements elicitation are expensive to correct, as they are usually discovered late in the process, often as late as delivery. Such errors include missing functionality that the system should have supported, functionality that was incorrectly specified, user interfaces that are misleading or unusable, and functionality that is obsolete. Requirements elicitation methods aim at improving communication among developers, clients, and users. Developers construct a model of the application domain by observing users in their environment (e.g., task analysis). Developers select a representation that is understandable by the clients and users (e.g., scenarios and use cases). Developers validate the application domain model by constructing simple prototypes of the user interface and collecting feedback from potential users (e.g., rapid prototyping, usability testing).

In the next section, we provide an overview of requirements elicitation and its relationship to the other software development activities. In Section 4.3, we define the main concepts used in this chapter. In Section 4.4, we discuss the activities of requirements elicitation. In Section 4.5, we discuss the management activities related to requirements elicitation.

---

1. Examples taken and adapted from [Nielsen, 1993] and from the RISK forum.

4.2 An Overview of Requirements Elicitation

Requirements elicitation focuses on describing the purpose of the system. The client, the developers, and the users identify a problem area and define a system that addresses the problem. Such a definition is called a **system specification** and serves as a contract between the client and the developers. The system specification is structured and formalized during analysis (Chapter 5, *Analysis*) to produce an analysis model (see Figure 4-1). Both system specification and analysis model represent the same information. They differ only in the language and notation they use. The system specification is written in natural language, whereas the analysis model is usually expressed in a formal or semiformal notation. The system specification supports the communication with the client and users. The analysis model supports the communication among developers. They are both models of the system in the sense that they attempt to accurately represent the external aspects of the system. Given that both models represent the same aspects of the system, requirements elicitation and analysis occur concurrently and iteratively.

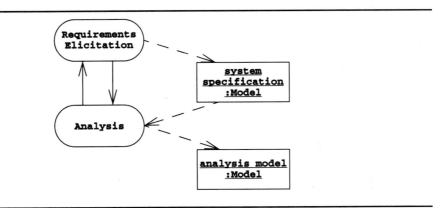

Figure 4-1 Products of requirements elicitation and analysis (UML activity diagram).

Requirements elicitation and analysis focus only on the user's view of the system. For example, the system functionality, the interaction between the user and the system, the errors that the system can detect and handle, and the environmental conditions in which the system functions, are part of the requirements. The system structure, the implementation technology selected to build the system, the system design, the development methodology, and other aspects not directly visible to the user are not part of the requirements.

Requirements elicitation includes the following activities.

- **Identifying actors**. During this activity, developers identify the different types of users the future system will support.
- **Identifying scenarios**. During this activity, developers observe users and develop a set of detailed scenarios for typical functionality provided by the future system. Scenarios are

concrete examples of the future system in use. Developers use these scenarios to communicate with the user and deepen their understanding of the application domain.

- **Identifying use cases**. Once developers and users agree on a set of scenarios, developers derive from the scenarios a set of use cases that completely represent the future system. Whereas scenarios are concrete examples illustrating a single case, use cases are abstractions describing all possible cases. When describing use cases, developers determine the scope of the system.

- **Refining use cases**. During this activity, developers ensure that the system specification is complete, by detailing each use case and describing the behavior of the system in the presence of errors and exceptional conditions.

- **Identifying relationships among use cases**. During this activity, developers consolidate the use case model by eliminating redundancies. This ensures that the system specification is consistent.

- **Identifying nonfunctional requirements**. During this activity, developers, users, and clients agree on aspects that are visible to the user but not directly related to functionality. These include constraints on the performance of the system, its documentation, the resources it consumes, its security, and its quality.

During requirements elicitation, developers access many different sources of information, including client-supplied documents about the application domain, manuals and technical documentation of legacy systems that the future system will replace, and, most important, the users and clients themselves. Developers interact the most with users and clients during requirements elicitation. We focus on three methods for eliciting information and making decisions with users and clients:

- **Joint Application Design** (JAD) focuses on building consensus among developers, users, and clients by jointly developing the system specification.

- **Knowledge Analysis of Tasks** (KAT) focuses on eliciting information from users through observation.

- **Usability testing** focuses on validating the requirements elicitation model with the user through a variety of methods.

4.3 Requirements Elicitation Concepts

In this section, we describe the main requirements elicitation concepts we use in this chapter. In particular, we describe:

- functional requirements (Section 4.3.1)
- nonfunctional and pseudo requirements (Section 4.3.2)
- levels of descriptions (Section 4.3.3)
- correctness, completeness, consistency, clarity, and realism (Section 4.3.4)

• verifiability and traceability (Section 4.3.5)

• greenfield engineering, reengineering, and interface engineering (Section 4.3.6)

We describe the requirements elicitation activities in Section 4.4.

4.3.1 Functional Requirements

Functional requirements describe the interactions between the system and its environment independent of its implementation. The environment includes the user and any other external system with which the system interacts. For example, the following is an example of functional requirements for SatWatch, a watch that resets itself without user intervention:

Functional requirements for SatWatch

SatWatch is a wrist watch that displays the time based on its current location. SatWatch uses GPS satellites (Global Positioning System) to determine its location and internal data structures to convert this location into a time zone. The information stored in the watch and its accuracy measuring time (one hundredth of second uncertainty over five years) is such that the watch owner never needs to reset the time. SatWatch adjusts the time and date displayed as the watch owner crosses time zones and political boundaries (e.g., standard time vs. daylight savings time). For this reason, SatWatch has no buttons or controls available to the user.

SatWatch has a two-line display showing, on the top line, the time (hour, minute, second, time zone) and, on the bottom line, the date (day of the week, day, month, year). The display technology used is such that the watch owner can see the time and date even under poor light conditions.

When a new country or state institutes different rules for daylight savings time, the watch owner may upgrade the software of the watch using the WebifyWatch serial device (provided when the watch is purchased) and a personal computer connected to the Internet. SatWatch complies with the physical, electrical, and software interfaces defined by WebifyWatch API 2.0.

The above functional requirements focus only on the possible interactions between SatWatch and its external world (i.e., the watch owner, GPS, and WebifyWatch). The above description does not focus on any of the implementation details (e.g., processor, language, display technology).

4.3.2 Nonfunctional and Pseudo Requirements

Nonfunctional requirements describe user-visible aspects of the system that are not directly related with the functional behavior of the system. Nonfunctional requirements include quantitative constraints, such as response time (i.e., how fast the system reacts to user commands) or accuracy (i.e., how precise are the system's numerical answers). The following are the nonfunctional requirements for SatWatch:

Nonfunctional requirements for SatWatch

SatWatch determines its location using GPS satellites, and as such, suffers from the same limitations as all other GPS devices (e.g., ~100 feet accuracy, inability to determine location at certain times of the day in mountainous regions). During blackout periods, SatWatch assumes that it does not cross a time zone or a political boundary. SatWatch corrects its time zone as soon as a blackout period ends.

The battery life of SatWatch is limited to 5 years, which is the estimated life cycle of the housing of SatWatch. The SatWatch housing is not designed to be opened once manufactured, preventing battery replacement and repairs. Instead, SatWatch is priced such that the watch owner is expected to buy a new SatWatch to replace a defective or old SatWatch.

Pseudo requirements are requirements imposed by the client that restrict the implementation of the system. Typical pseudo requirements are the implementation language and the platform on which the system is to be implemented. For life-critical developments, pseudo requirements often include process and documentation requirements (e.g., the use of a formal specification method, the complete release of all work products). Pseudo requirements have usually no direct effect on the users' view of the system. The following are the pseudo requirements for SatWatch:

Pseudorequirement for SatWatch

All related software associated with SatWatch, including the onboard software, will be written using Java, to comply with current company policy.

Analysis is a modeling activity. The developer constructs a model describing the reality as seen from a user's point of view. Modeling consists of identifying and classifying real-world phenomena (e.g., aspects of the system under construction) into concepts. Figure 4-2 is a UML class diagram representing the relationships between models and reality. In this diagram, a model is said to be correct if each concept in the model corresponds to a relevant phenomenon. The model is complete if all relevant phenomena are represented by at least one concept. The model is consistent if all concepts represent phenomena of the same reality (i.e., if a model is inconsistent, it must represent aspects of two different realities).

4.3.3   Levels of Description

Requirements describe a system and its interaction with the surrounding environment, such as the users, their work processes, and other systems. Most requirements analysis methods have focused on describing the system. When using use cases and scenarios, it becomes apparent, however, that it is also necessary to describe the environment in which the system will operate. First, developers usually do not initially know and understand the operating environment and need to check their understanding with the users. Second, the environment is likely to change, and thus, developers should capture all the assumptions they make about the environment. In general, there are four levels of description, which can uniformly be described with use cases [Paech, 1998]. We list them below from most general to most specific:

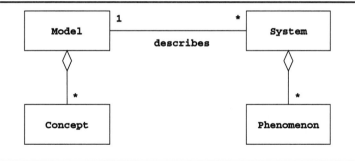

Figure 4-2 A System is a collection of real world Phenomena. A model is a collection of concepts that represent the system's phenomena. Many models can represent different aspects of the same system. An unambiguous model corresponds to only one system.

- **Work division**. This set of use cases describes the work processes of the users that are relevant to the system. The part of the process supported by the system is also described, but the focus is on defining the boundaries between the users and the system.

- **Application-specific system functions**. This set of use cases describes the functions that the system provides that are related to the application domain.

- **Work-specific system functions**. This set of use cases describes the supporting functions of the system that are not directly related with the application domain. These include file management functions, grouping functions, undo functions, and so on. These use cases will be extended during system design, when we are discussing known boundary conditions, such as system initialization, shutdown, and exception handling policies.

- **Dialog**. This set of use cases describes the interactions between the users and the user interface of the system. The focus is on designing resolving control flow and layout issues.

4.3.4   Correctness, Completeness, Consistency, Clarity, and Realism

Requirements are continuously validated with the client and the user. Validation is a critical step in the development process, given that both the client and the developer are dependent on the system specification. Requirement validation involves checking if the specification is correct, complete, consistent, unambiguous, and realistic. A specification is **correct** if it represents the client's view of the system (i.e., everything in the requirements model accurately represents an aspect of the system). It is **complete** if all possible scenarios through the system are described, including exceptional behavior (i.e., all aspects of the system are represented in the requirements model). The system specification is **consistent** if it does not contradict itself. The system specification is **unambiguous** if exactly one system is defined (i.e., it is not possible to interpret the specification two or more different ways). Finally, it is **realistic** if the system can be implemented within constraints. These properties are illustrated with UML instance diagrams in Table 4-1.

Table 4-1   Specification properties checked during validation

Correct—The model describes the reality of interest to the client, not another reality	
Complete—Every phenomenon of interest is described in the model by a concept	
Consistent—All concepts in the model correspond to phenomena of the same reality	
Unambiguous—All concepts in the model correspond to exactly one phenomenon	
Realistic—The model describes a reality that can exist	

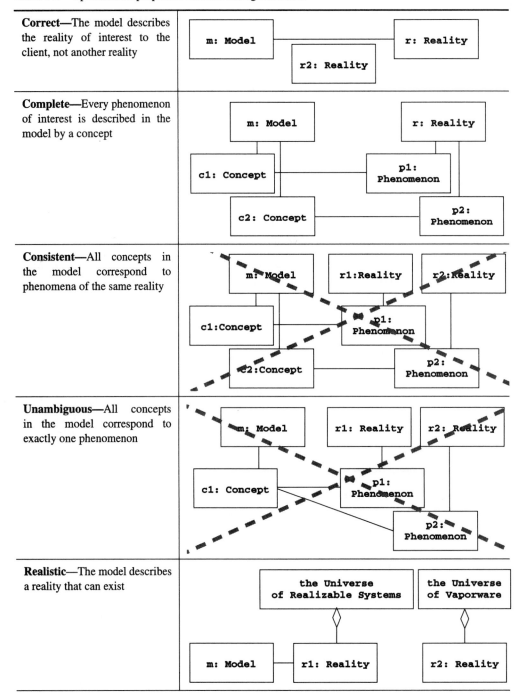

The correctness and completeness of a system specification are often difficult to establish, especially before the system exists. Given that the system specification serves as a contractual basis between the client and the developers, the system specification must be carefully reviewed by both parties. Additionally, parts of the system that present a high risk should be prototyped or simulated to demonstrate their feasibility or to obtain feedback from the user. In the case of SatWatch described above, a mock-up of the watch would be built using a traditional watch and users surveyed to gather their initial impressions. A user may remark that she wants the watch to be able to display both American and European date formats.

4.3.5 Verifiability and Traceability

Two more desirable properties of a system specification are that it be verifiable and traceable. The specification is **verifiable** if, once the system is built, a repeatable test can be designed to demonstrate that the system fulfills the requirement. For example, a mean time to failure of a hundred years for SatWatch would be difficult to achieve (assuming it is realistic in the first place). The following requirements are additional examples of nonverifiable requirements:

- *The product shall have a good user interface* (good is not defined).
- *The product shall be error free* (requires large amount of resources to establish).
- *The product shall respond to the user with 1 second for most cases* ("most cases" is not defined).

A system specification is **traceable** if each system function can be traced to its corresponding set of requirements. Traceability is not a constraint on the content of the specification, but rather, on its organization. Traceability facilitates the development of tests and the systematic validation of the design against the requirements.

4.3.6 Greenfield Engineering, Reengineering, and Interface Engineering

Requirements elicitation activities can be classified into three categories, depending on the source of the requirements. In **greenfield engineering**, the development starts from scratch, no prior system exists, the requirements are extracted from the users and the client. A greenfield engineering project is triggered by a user need or the creation of a new market. SatWatch is a greenfield engineering project.

A **reengineering** project is the redesign and reimplementation of an existing system triggered by technology enablers or by new information flow [Hammer & Champy, 1993]. Sometimes, the functionality of the new system is extended; however, the essential purpose of the system remains the same. The requirements of the new system are extracted from an existing system.

An **interface engineering** project is the redesign of the user interface of an existing system. The legacy system is left untouched except for its interface, which is redesigned and reimplemented. This type of project is a reengineering project in which the legacy system cannot be discarded without entailing high costs. In this section, we examine how requirements elicitation is performed in all three situations.

In both reengineering and greenfield engineering, the developers need to gather as much information as possible from the application domain. This information can be found in procedures manuals, documentation distributed to new employees, the previous system's manual, glossaries, cheat sheets and notes developed by the users, and user and client interviews. Note that although interviews with users are an invaluable tool, they fail to gather the necessary information if the relevant questions are not asked. Developers must first gain a solid knowledge of the application domain before the direct approach can be used.

Next, we describe the activities of requirements elicitation that result in a system specification.

4.4 Requirements Elicitation Activities

In this section, we describe the requirements elicitation activities. These map a problem statement into a system specification that we represent as a set of actors, scenarios, and use cases (see Chapter 2, *Modeling with UML*). We discuss heuristics and methods for extracting requirements from users and modeling the system in terms of these concepts. Requirements elicitation activities include:

- identifying actors (Section 4.4.1)
- identifying scenarios (Section 4.4.2)
- identifying use cases (Section 4.4.3)
- refining use cases (Section 4.4.4)
- identifying relationships among use cases (Section 4.4.5)
- identifying participating objects (Section 4.4.6)
- identifying nonfunctional requirements (Section 4.4.7)

The methods described in this section are adapted from OOSE [Jacobson et al., 1992], the Unified Software Development Process [Jacobson et al., 1999], and Responsibility-driven design [Wirfs-Brock et al., 1990].

4.4.1 Identifying Actors

Actors represent external entities that interact with the system. An actor can be human or an external system. In the SatWatch example, the watch owner, the GPS satellites, and the WebifyWatch serial device are actors (see Figure 4-3). They all interact and exchange information with the SatWatch. Note, however, they all have specific interactions with the SatWatch: the watch owner wears and looks at her watch; the watch monitors the signal from the GPS satellites; the WebifyWatch downloads new data into the watch. Actors define classes of functionality.

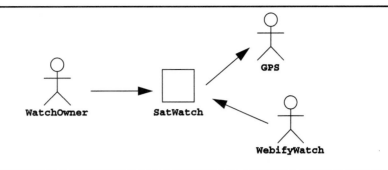

Figure 4-3 Actors for the SatWatch system. WatchOwner moves the watch (possibly across time zones) and consults it to know what time it is. SatWatch interacts with GPS to compute its position. WebifyWatch upgrades the data contained in the watch to reflect changes in time policy (e.g., changes in daylight savings time start and end dates).

Consider a more-complex example, FRIEND, a distributed information system for accident management [FRIEND, 1994], [Bruegge et al., 1994]. It includes many actors, such as FieldOfficer, who represents the police and fire officers who are responding to an incident, and Dispatcher, the police officer responsible for answering 911 calls and dispatching resources to an incident. FRIEND supports both actors by keeping track of incidents, resources, and task plans. It also has access to multiple databases, such as a hazardous materials database and emergency operations procedures. The FieldOfficer and the Dispatcher actors interact through different interfaces: FieldOfficers access FRIEND through a mobile personal assistant, Dispatchers access FRIEND through a workstation (see Figure 4-4).

Actors are role abstractions and do not necessarily directly map to persons. The same person can fill the role of FieldOfficer or Dispatcher at different times. However, the functionality they access is substantially different. For that reason, these two roles are modeled as two different actors.

The first step of requirements elicitation is the identification of actors. This serves both to define the boundaries of the system and to find all the perspectives from which the developers need to consider the system. When the system is deployed into an existing organization (such as a company), most actors usually exist before the system is developed: they correspond to roles in the organization.

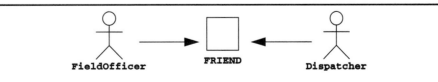

Figure 4-4 Actors of the FRIEND system. FieldOfficers not only have access to different functionality, they use different computers to access the system.

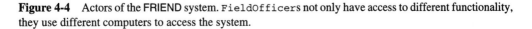

When identifying actors, developers can ask the following questions:

Questions for identifying actors
- Which user groups are supported by the system to perform their work?
- Which user groups execute the system's main functions?
- Which user groups perform secondary functions, such as maintenance and administration?
- Will the system interact with any external hardware or software system?

In the FRIEND example, these questions lead to a long list of potential actors: Fire Fighter, Police Officer, Dispatcher, Investigator, Mayor, Governor, an EPA hazardous material database, System Administrator, and so on. We then need to consolidate this list into a small number of actors, who are different from the point of view of the usage of the system. For example, a Fire Fighter and a Police Officer may share the same interface to the system as they are both involved with a single incident in the field. A Dispatcher, on the other hand, manages multiple concurrent incidents and requires access to a larger amount of information. The Mayor and the Governor will not likely interact directly with the system and will use the services of a trained Operator instead.

Once the actors are identified, the next step in the requirements elicitation activity is to determine the functionality that is accessible to each actor. This information can be extracted using scenarios and formalized using use cases.

4.4.2   Identifying Scenarios

A scenario is "a narrative description of what people do and experience as they try to make use of computer systems and applications" [Carroll, 1995]. A scenario is a concrete, focused, informal description of a single feature of the system from the viewpoint of a single actor. The use of scenarios in requirements elicitation is a conceptual departure from the traditional representations, which are generic and abstract. Traditional representations are centered around the system as opposed to the work that the system supports. Finally, their focus is on completeness, consistency, and accuracy, whereas scenarios are open ended and informal. A scenario-based approach cannot (and is not intended to) completely replace traditional approaches. It does, however, enhance requirements elicitation by providing a tool that is readily understandable to users and clients.

Figure 4-5 is an example of scenario for the FRIEND system [FRIEND, 1994], an information system for incident response. In this scenario, a police officer reports a fire and a Dispatcher initiates the incident response. Note that this scenario is concrete, in the sense that it describes a single instance. It does not attempt to describe all possible situations in which a fire incident is reported.

Scenario name	warehouseOnFire
Participating actor instances	bob, alice: FieldOfficer john: Dispatcher
Flow of events	1. Bob, driving down main street in his patrol car notices smoke coming out of a warehouse. His partner, Alice, activates the "Report Emergency" function from her FRIEND laptop. 2. Alice enters the address of the building, a brief description of its location (i.e., northwest corner), and an emergency level. In addition to a fire unit, she requests several paramedic units on the scene, given that the area appears to be relatively busy. She confirms her input and waits for an acknowledgment. 3. John, the Dispatcher, is alerted to the emergency by a beep of his workstation. He reviews the information submitted by Alice and acknowledges the report. He creates allocates a fire unit and two paramedic units to the Incident site and sends their estimated arrival time (ETA) to Alice. 4. Alice receives the acknowledgment and the ETA.

Figure 4-5 warehouseOnFire scenario for the ReportEmergency use case.

Scenarios can have many different uses during requirements elicitation and during other activities of the life cycle. Below is a selected number of scenario types taken from [Carroll, 1995]:

- *As-is scenarios* describe a current situation. During reengineering, for example, the current system is understood by observing users and describing their actions as scenarios. These scenarios can then be validated for correctness and accuracy with the users.

- *Visionary scenarios* describe a future system, either reengineered or designed from scratch. Visionary scenarios are used both as a design representation by developers as they refine their idea of the future system and as a communication medium to elicit requirements from users. Visionary scenarios can be viewed as an inexpensive prototype.

- *Evaluation scenarios* describe user tasks against which the system is to be evaluated. The collaborative development of evaluation scenarios by users and developers also improves the definition of the functionality tested by these scenarios.

- *Training scenarios* are tutorials used for introducing new users to the system. These are step-by-step instructions designed to hand-hold the user through common tasks.

In requirements elicitation, developers and users write and refine a series of scenarios in order to gain a shared understanding of what the system should be. Initially, each scenario may be high level and incomplete, as the warehouseOnFire scenario is. The following questions can be used for identifying scenarios.

Questions for identifying scenarios
- What are the tasks that the actor wants the system to perform?
- What information does the actor access? Who creates that data? Can it be modified or removed? By whom?
- Which external changes does the actor need to inform the system about? How often? When?
- Which events does the actor need to be informed by the system about? With what latency?

Developers use existing documents about the application domain to answer these questions. These documents include user manuals of previous systems, procedures manuals, company standards, user notes and cheat sheets, user and client interviews. Developers should always write scenarios using application domain terms, as opposed to their own terms. As developers gain further insight in the application domain and the possibilities of the available technology, they iteratively and incrementally refine scenarios to include increasing amounts of detail. Drawing user interface mock-ups often helps to find omissions in the specification and help the users build a more concrete picture of the system.

In the FRIEND example, we may identify four scenarios that span the type of tasks the system is expected to support:

- warehouseOnFire (Figure 4-5): A fire is detected in a warehouse; two field officers arrive at the scene and request resources.
- fenderBender. A car accident without casualties occurs on the highway. Police officers document the incident and manage traffic while the damaged vehicles are towed away.
- catInATree. A cat is stuck in a tree. A fire truck is called to retrieve the cat. Because the incident is low priority, the fire truck takes time to arrive at the scene. In the meantime, the impatient cat owner climbs the tree, falls, and breaks a leg, requiring an ambulance to be dispatched.
- earthQuake. An unprecedented earthquake seriously damages buildings and roads, spanning multiple incidents and triggering the activation of a statewide emergency operations plan. The governor is notified. Road damage hampers incident response.

The emphasis of actor identification and scenario identification is for developers to understand the application domain and to define the right system. This results in a shared understanding of the user work processes that need to be supported and of the scope of the system. Once developers identified and described actors and scenarios, developers formalize scenarios into use cases.

4.4.3   Identifying Use Cases

A scenario is an instance of a use case, that is, a use case specifies all possible scenarios for a given piece of functionality. A use case is initiated by an actor. After its initiation, a use case may interact with other actors as well. A use case represents a complete flow of events

Use case name	ReportEmergency
Participating actor	Initiated by FieldOfficer Communicates with Dispatcher
Entry condition	1. The FieldOfficer activates the "Report Emergency" function of her terminal.
Flow of events	2. FRIEND responds by presenting a form to the officer. 3. The FieldOfficer fills the form, by selecting the emergency level, type, location, and brief description of the situation. The FieldOfficer also describes possible responses to the emergency situation. Once the form is completed, the FieldOfficer submits the form, at which point the Dispatcher is notified. 4. The Dispatcher reviews the submitted information and creates an Incident in the database by invoking the OpenIncident use case. The Dispatcher selects a response and acknowledges the emergency report.
Exit condition	5. The FieldOfficer receives the acknowledgment and the selected response.
Special requirements	The FieldOfficer's report is acknowledged within 30 seconds. The selected response arrives no later than 30 seconds after it is sent by the Dispatcher.

Figure 4-6   An example of use case: ReportEmergency.

through the system in the sense that it describes a series of related interactions that result from the initiation of the use case.

Figure 4-6 depicts the use case ReportEmergency of which the scenario warehouseOnFire (see Figure 4-5) is an instance. The FieldOfficer actor initiates this use case by activating the "Report Emergency" function of FRIEND. The use case completes when the FieldOfficer actor receives an acknowledgment that an incident has been created. This use case is general and encompasses a range of scenarios. For example, the ReportEmergency use case could also apply to the fenderBender scenario. Use cases can be written at varying levels of detail as in the case of scenarios. The ReportEmergency use case may be illustrative enough to describe how FRIEND supports reporting emergencies and to obtain general feedback from the user, but it does not provide sufficient detail for a system specification.

4.4.4   Refining Use Cases

Figure 4-7 is a refined version of the ReportEmergency use case. It has been extended to include details about the type of incidents that are known to FRIEND, detailed interactions indicating how the Dispatcher acknowledges the FieldOfficer.

Location	Use case description
Field Officer station	1. The FieldOfficer activates the "Report Emergency" function of her terminal. 2. FRIEND responds by presenting a form to the officer. The form includes an emergency type menu (general emergency, fire, transportation), a location, incident description, resource request, and hazardous material fields. 3. The FieldOfficer fills the form by specifying minimally the emergency type and description fields. The FieldOfficer may also describe possible responses to the emergency situation and request specific resources. Once the form is completed, the FieldOfficer submits the form by pressing the "Send Report" button, at which point the Dispatcher is notified.
Dispatcher station	4. The Dispatcher is notified of a new incident report by a popup dialog. The Dispatcher reviews the submitted information and creates an Incident in the database by invoking the OpenIncident use case. All the information contained in the FieldOfficer's form is automatically included in the Incident. The Dispatcher selects a response by allocating resources to the Incident (with the AllocateResources use case) and acknowledges the emergency report by sending a short message to the FieldOfficer.
Field Officer station	5. The FieldOfficer receives the acknowledgment and the selected response.

Figure 4-7   Refined description for the ReportEmergency use case.

The use of scenarios and use cases to define the functionality of the system aims at creating requirements that are validated by the user early in the development. As the design and implementation of the system starts, the cost of changing the system specification and adding new unforeseen functionality increases. Although requirements change until late in the development, developers and users should strive to address most requirements issues early. This entails lots of changes and experimentation during requirements elicitation. Note that many use cases are rewritten several times, others substantially refined, and yet others completely dropped. In order to save time, a lot of the exploration work can be done using scenarios and user interface mock-ups. The following heuristics can be used for writing scenarios and use cases.

Heuristics for writing scenarios and use cases
- Use scenarios to communicate with users and to validate functionality.
- First, refine a narrow vertical slice (i.e., one scenario) to understand the user's preferred style of interaction.
- Next, define a horizontal slice (i.e., many not-very-detailed scenarios) to define the scope of the system. Validate with the user.
- Use mock-ups as a visual support only; user interface design should occur as a separate task once the functionality is sufficiently stable.
- Present the user with multiple alternatives (as opposed to extracting a single alternative from the user).
- Detail a broad vertical slice when the scope of the system and the user preferences are well understood. Validate with the user.

The focus of this activity is on completeness and correctness. Developers identify functionality not covered by scenarios and document it with new use cases. Developers describe rarely occurring cases and exception handling as seen by the actors. If actors require an on-line help support system, developers describe it with use cases during this activity.

Once the system specification becomes stable, traceability and redundancy issues can be addressed by consolidating and reorganizing the actors and use cases.

4.4.5   Identifying Relationships Among Actors and Use Cases

Even medium-sized systems have many use cases. Relationships among actors and use cases enable the developers and users to reduce the complexity of the model and increase its understandability. We use communication relationships between actors and use cases to describe the system in layers of functionality. We use extend relationships to separate exceptional and common flows of events. We use include relationships to reduce redundancy among use cases.

Communication relationships between actors and use cases

Communication relationships between actors and use cases represent the flow of information during the use case. The actor who initiates the use case should be distinguished from the other actors with whom the use case communicates. Thus, access control (i.e., which actor has access to which class functionality) can be represented at this level. The relationships between actors and use cases are identified when use cases are identified. Figure 4-8 depicts an example of communication relationships in the case of the FRIEND system.

Extend relationships between use cases

A use case extends another use case if the extended use case may include the behavior of the extension under certain conditions. In the FRIEND example, assume that the connection between the FieldOfficer station and the Dispatcher station is broken while the FieldOfficer is filling the form (e.g., the FieldOfficer's car enters a tunnel). The FieldOfficer station needs to notify the FieldOfficer that his form was not delivered and what measures he should take. The ConnectionDown use case is modeled as an extension of

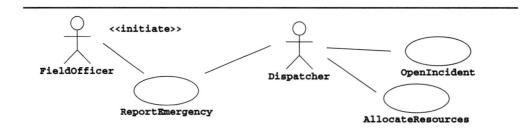

Figure 4-8 Example of communication relationships among actors and use cases in FRIEND (UML use case diagram). The `FieldOfficer` initiates the `ReportEmergency` use case and the `Dispatcher` initiates the `OpenIncident` and `AllocateResources` use cases. `FieldOfficers` cannot directly open an incident or allocate resources on their own.

`ReportEmergency` (see Figure 4-9). The conditions under which the `ConnectionDown` use case is initiated are described in `ConnectionDown` as opposed to `ReportEmergency`. Separating exceptional and optional flow of events from the base use case has two advantages. First, the base use case becomes shorter and easier to understand. Second, the common case is distinguished from the exceptional case, which enables the developers to treat each type of functionality differently (e.g., optimize the common case for response time, optimize the exceptional case for clarity). Both the extended use case and the extensions are complete use cases of their own. They must have an entry and an end condition and be understandable by the user as an independent whole.

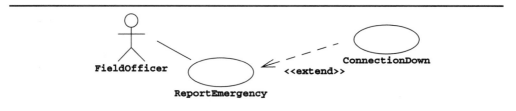

Figure 4-9 Example of use of extend relationship (UML use case diagram). `ConnectionDown` extends the `ReportEmergency` use case. The `ReportEmergency` use case becomes shorter and solely focused on emergency reporting.

Include relationships between use cases

Redundancies among use cases can be factored out using include relationships. Assume, for example, that a `Dispatcher` needs to consult the city map when opening an incident (e.g, in order to assess which areas are at risk during a fire) and when allocating resources (e.g., to find which resources are closer to the incident). In this case, the `ViewMap` use case describes the flow of events required when viewing the city map and is used by both the `OpenIncident` and the `AllocateResources` use cases (Figure 4-10).

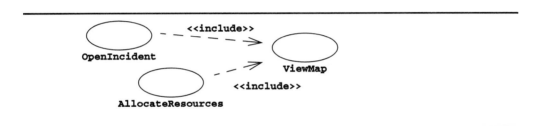

Figure 4-10   Example of include relationships among use cases. ViewMap describes the flow of events for viewing a city map (e.g., scrolling, zooming, query by street name) and is used by both OpenIncident and AllocateResources use cases.

Factoring out shared behavior from use cases has many benefits, including shorter descriptions and fewer redundancies. Behavior should *only* be factored out into a separate use case if it is shared across two or more use cases. Excessive fragmentation of the system specification across a large number of use cases makes the specification confusing to users and clients.

Extend versus include relationships

Include and extend are similar constructs, and initially it may not be clear to the developer when to use each construct [Jacobson et al., 1992]. The main distinction between these constructs is the direction of the relationship. In the case of an include relationship, the conditions under which the target use case is initiated are described in the initiating use case, as an event in the flow of events. In the case of an extend relationship, the conditions under which the extension is initiated are described in the extension as an entry condition. Figure 4-11 shows the ConnectionDown example described with an include relationship (left column) and with an extend relationship (right column). In the left column, we need to insert text in two places in the event flow where the ConnectionDown use case can be invoked. Also, if additional exceptional situations are described (e.g., a Help function on the FieldOfficer station), the ReportEmergency use case will have to be modified and will become cluttered with conditions. In the right column, we only need to describe the conditions under which the use case is invoked. Moreover, additional exceptional situations can be added with modifying the base use case (e.g., ReportEmergency). The ability to extend the system without modifying existing parts is critical, as it allows us to ensure that the original behavior is left untouched.

In summary, the following heuristics can be used for selecting an extend or an include relationship.

Heuristics for extend and include relationships
- Use extends for exceptional, optional, or seldom-occurring behavior.
- Use includes uses for behavior that is shared across two or more use cases.

ReportEmergency (include relationship)	ReportEmergency (extend relationship)
1. ...	1. ...
2. ...	2. ...
3. The FieldOfficer fills the form, by selecting the emergency level, type, location, and brief description of the situation. The FieldOfficer also describes possible responses to the emergency situation. Once the form is completed, the FieldOfficer submits the form, at which point, the Dispatcher is notified. *If the connection with the Dispatcher is broken, the ConnectionDown use case is used.*	3. The FieldOfficer fills the form, by selecting the emergency level, type, location, and brief description of the situation. The FieldOfficer also describes possible responses to the emergency situation. Once the form is completed, the FieldOfficer submits the form, at which point, the Dispatcher is notified.
4. If the connection is still alive, the Dispatcher reviews the submitted information and creates an Incident in the database by invoking the OpenIncident use case. The Dispatcher selects a response and acknowledges the emergency report. *If the connection is broken, the ConnectionDown use case is used.*	4. The Dispatcher reviews the submitted information and creates an Incident in the database by invoking the OpenIncident use case. The Dispatcher selects a response and acknowledges the emergency report.
5. ...	5. ...
ConnectionDown (include relationship)	ConnectionDown (extend relationship)
	The ConnectionDown use case extends ReportEmergency when the connection between the FieldOfficer and the Dispatcher is lost.
1. The FieldOfficer and the Dispatcher are notified that the connection is broken. They are advised of the possible reasons why such an event would occur (e.g., "Is the FieldOfficer station in a tunnel?").	1. The FieldOfficer and the Dispatcher are notified that the connection is broken. They are advised of the possible reasons why such an event would occur (e.g., "Is the FieldOfficer station in a tunnel?").
2. The situation is logged by the system and recovered when the connection is reestablished.	2. The situation is logged by the system and recovered when the connection is reestablished.
3. The FieldOfficer and the Dispatcher enter in contact through other means and the Dispatcher initiates ReportEmergency from the Dispatcher station.	3. The FieldOfficer and the Dispatcher enter in contact through other means and the Dispatcher initiates ReportEmergency from the Dispatcher station.

Figure 4-11   Addition of ConnectionDown exceptional condition to ReportEmergency. An extend relationship is used for exceptional and optional flow of events as its yields a more modular description.

In all cases, the purpose of adding include and extend relationships is to reduce or remove redundancies from the use case model, thus eliminating potential inconsistencies.

4.4.6 Identifying Initial Analysis Objects

One of the first obstacles developers and users encounter when collaborating is differing terminology. Misunderstandings result from the same terms being used in different context and with different meanings. Although developers eventually learn the users' terminology, this problem is likely to be encountered again when new developers are added to the project.

Once use cases have been consolidated, developers identify the **participating objects** for each use case. The participating objects correspond to the main concepts in the application domain. Developers identify, name, and describe them unambiguously and collate them into a glossary.

This glossary is included in the system specification and, later, in the user manuals. Developers keep this glossary up to date as the system specification evolves. The benefits of the glossary are many: New developers are exposed to a consistent set of definitions, a single term is used for each concept (instead of a developer term and a user term), and each term has a precise and clear official meaning.

The identification of participating objects results in the initial analysis model. The identification of participating objects during requirements elicitation only constitute a first step toward the complete analysis model. The complete analysis model is usually not used as means of communication between users and developers, as users are often unfamiliar with object-oriented concepts. However, the description of the objects (i.e., the definitions of the terms in the glossary) and their attributes are visible to the users and reviewed. We describe in detail the further refinement of the analysis model in Chapter 5, *Analysis*.

Many heuristics have been proposed in the literature for identifying objects. Here are a selected few:

Heuristics for identifying initial analysis objects

- terms that developers or users need to clarify in order to understand the use case
- recurring nouns in the use cases (e.g., `Incident`)
- real-world entities that the system needs to keep track of (e.g., `FieldOfficer`, `Resource`)
- real-world processes that the system needs to keep track of (e.g., `EmergencyOperationsPlan`)
- use cases (e.g., `ReportEmergency`)
- data sources or sinks (e.g., `Printer`)
- interface artifacts (e.g., `Station`)
- *Always* use application domain terms.

During requirements elicitation, participating objects are generated for each use case. If two use cases refer to the same concept, the corresponding object should be the same. If two objects share the same name and do not correspond to the same concept, one or both concepts are renamed to acknowledge and emphasize their difference. This consolidation eliminates any ambiguity in the terminology used. For example, Table 4-2 depicts the initial participating objects we identified for the `ReportEmergency` use case.

Table 4-2   Participating objects for the `ReportEmergency` use case

`Dispatcher`	Police officer who manages `Incidents`. A `Dispatcher` opens, documents, and closes incidents in response to emergency reports and other communication with `FieldOfficers`. `Dispatchers` are identified by badge numbers.
`EmergencyReport`	Initial report about an `Incident` from a `FieldOfficer` to a `Dispatcher`. An `EmergencyReport` usually triggers the creation of an `Incident` by the `Dispatcher`. An `EmergencyReport` is composed of a emergency level, a type (fire, road accident, or other), a location, and a description.
`FieldOfficer`	Police or fire officer on duty. A `FieldOfficer` can be allocated to at most one `Incident` at a time. `FieldOfficers` are identified by badge numbers.
`Incident`	Situation requiring attention from a `FieldOfficer`. An `Incident` may be reported in the system by a `FieldOfficer` or anybody else external to the system. An `Incident` is composed of a description, a response, a status (open, closed, documented), a location, and a number of `FieldOfficers`.

Once participating objects are identified and consolidated, the developers can use them as a checklist for ensuring the set of identified use cases is complete.

Heuristics for cross-checking use cases and participating objects
- Which use cases create this object (i.e., during which use cases are the values of the object attributes entered in the system)? Which actors can access this information?
- Which use cases modify and destroy this object (i.e., which use cases edit or remove this information from the system)? Which actor can initiate these use cases?
- Is this object needed (i.e., is there at least one use case that depends on this information?)

When developers identify new use cases, they describe and integrate the new use case into the model, following the process we described before. Often, in the requirements elicitation activity, shifting perspectives introduces modifications in the system specification (e.g., finding new participating objects triggers the addition of new use cases; the addition of new use cases triggers the addition or refinement of new participating objects). This instability should be anticipated and encourage shifting perspectives. For the same reasons, time-consuming tasks, such as the description of exceptional cases and refinements of the user interfaces, should be postponed until the set of use cases is stable.

4.4.7   Identifying Nonfunctional Requirements

Nonfunctional requirements describe user-visible aspects of the system that are not directly related to the functional behavior of the system. Nonfunctional requirements span a number of issues, from user interface look and feel to response time requirements to security issues. Nonfunctional requirements are defined at the same time as functional requirements are, because they have as much impact on the development and cost of the system.

For example, consider a mosaic display that an air traffic controller uses to track planes. A mosaic display system compiles data from a series of radar and databases (hence the term "mosaic") into a summary display indicating all aircraft in a certain area, including their identification, speed, and altitude. The number of aircraft such a system can display constrains the performance of the air traffic controller and the cost of the system. If the system can only handle a few aircraft simultaneously, the system cannot be used at busy airports. On the other hand, a system able to handle a large number of aircraft is more costly and more complex to build.

Nonfunctional requirements can be elicited by investigating the following issues.

- **User interface and human factors**. What kind of interface should the system provide? What is the level of expertise of the users?

- **Documentation**. What level of document is required? Should only user documentation be provided? Should there be technical documentation for maintainers? Should the development process be documented?

- **Hardware considerations**. Are there hardware compatibility requirements? Will the system interact with other hardware systems?

- **Performance characteristics**. How responsive should the system be? How many concurrent users should it support? What is a typical or extreme load?

- **Error handling and extreme conditions**. How should the system handle exceptions? Which exceptions should the system handle? What is the worse environment in which the system is expected to perform? Are there safety requirements on the system?

- **Quality issues**. How reliable/available/robust should the system be? What is the client's involvement in assessing the quality of the system or the development process?

- **System modifications**. What is the anticipated scope of future changes? Who will perform the changes?

- **Physical environment**. Where will the system be deployed? Are there external factors such as weather conditions that the system should withstand?

- **Security issues**. Should the system be protected against external intrusions or against malicious users? To what level?

- **Resource issues**. What are the constraints on the resources consumed by the system?

Once all nonfunctional requirements are identified and described, they are prioritized by importance. Although most nonfunctional requirements are highly desirable, some of them need to be met in order for the system to operate correctly.

4.5 Managing Requirements Elicitation

In the previous section, we described the technical issues of modeling a system in terms of use cases. Use case modeling by itself, however, does not constitute requirements elicitation. Even after they become expert use case modelers, developers still need to elicit requirements from the users and converge onto an agreement with the client. In this section, we describe methods for eliciting information from the users and negotiating an agreement with a client. In particular, we describe:

- eliciting requirements from users: Knowledge Analysis of Tasks (KAT) (Section 4.5.1)
- negotiating a specification with clients: Joint Application Design (JAD) (Section 4.5.2)
- validating requirements: usability testing (Section 4.5.3)
- documenting requirements elicitation (Section 4.5.4)

4.5.1 Eliciting Information From Users: Knowledge Analysis of Tasks

Task analysis originated in the United States and the United Kingdom in the 1950s and 1960s [Johnson, 1992]. Initially, task analysis was not concerned with requirements or system design. Task analysis was used to identify how people should be trained. In the United States, the military was primarily interested in task analysis to decrease the cost of training. In the United Kingdom, the Department of Trade and Industry was interested in task analysis for developing methods to enable people to move across industries. More recently, task analysis has become important in the field of Human Computer Interaction (HCI) for identifying and describing the user tasks that a system should support.

Task analysis is based on the assumption that it is inefficient to ask users to describe what they do and how they do it. Users usually do not think explicitly about the sequence of tasks that are required to accomplish their work as they have often repeated these tasks many times. Users, when ask how they accomplish their work, would describe, at best, how they are supposed to accomplish it, which may be far from reality. Consequently, task analysis uses observation as an alternative to build an initial task model. This initial task model is then refined by asking the users *why* they accomplish a task a certain way.

The **Knowledge Analysis of Tasks** (KAT) is a task analysis method proposed by Johnson [Johnson, 1992]. It is concerned with collecting data from a variety of sources (e.g., protocol analysis, standard procedures, textbooks, interviews), analyzing these data to identify individual elements involved in the task (e.g., objects, actions, procedures, goals, and subgoals), and constructing a model of the overall knowledge used by people accomplishing the task of interest. KAT is an object-oriented analysis technique in that it represents the application domain in terms of objects and actions.

KAT can be summarized by the five following steps:

1. **Identifying objects and actions.** Object and actions associated with objects are identified using similar techniques as object identification in object-oriented analysis, such as

analyzing textbooks, manuals, rule books, reports, interviewing the task performer, observing the task performer.

2. **Identifying procedures.** A procedure is a set of actions, a precondition necessary to triggering the procedure, and a postcondition. Actions may be partially ordered. Procedures are identified by writing scenarios, observing the task performer, asking the task performer to select and order cards on which individual actions are written.

3. **Identifying goals and subgoals**. A goal is a state to be achieved for the task to be successful. Goals are identified through interview during the performance of a task or afterward. Subgoals are identified by decomposing goals.

4. **Identifying typicality and importance.** Each identified element is rated according to how frequently it is encountered and whether it is necessary for accomplishing a goal.

5. **Constructing a model of the task.** The information gathered above is generalized to account for common features across tasks. Corresponding goals, procedures, and objects are related using a textual notation or a graph. Finally, the model is validated with the task performer.

Although task analysis and KAT are not requirements elicitation methods per se (they do not produce a description of the future software system), they can greatly benefit the requirements elicitation activity in several ways:

- During elicitation, they provide techniques for eliciting and describing application domain knowledge, including information such as typicality and importance of specific actions; the end result is understandable by the task performer.
- When defining the boundaries of a system, task models assist in determining which parts of the task should remain manual and which parts should be automated; moreover, the task model may reveal problem areas in the current system.
- When designing the interface of the system, task models serve as a source of inspiration for metaphors understandable by the user [Nielsen & Mack, 1994].

For more information about KAT, the reader is referred to specialized literature [Johnson, 1992].

4.5.2 Negotiating specifications with clients: Joint Application Design

Joint Application Design (JAD) is a requirements method developed at IBM at the end of the 1970s. Its effectiveness lies in that the requirements elicitation work is done in one single workshop session in which all stakeholders participate. Users, clients, developers, and a trained session leader sit together in one room to present their viewpoint, listen to other viewpoints, negotiate, and agree on a mutually acceptable solution. The outcome of the workshop, the final JAD document, is a complete system specification document that includes definitions of data elements, work flows, and interface screens. Because the final document is jointly developed by the stakeholders (that is, the participants who not only have an interest in the success of the project, but also can make substantial decisions) the final JAD document represents an agreement between users, clients, and developers, and thus minimizes requirements changes later in the development process.

JAD is composed of five activities (summarized in Figure 4-12):

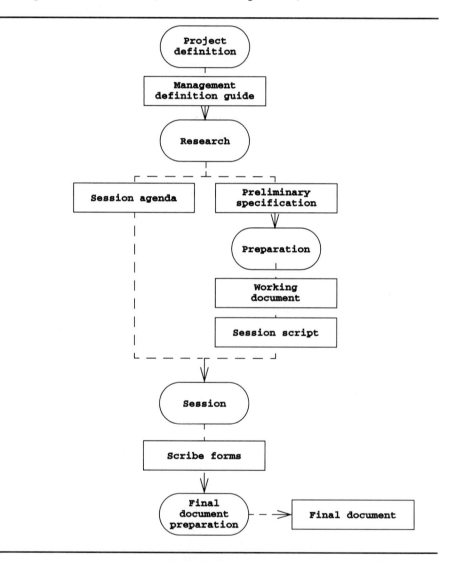

Figure 4-12   Activities of JAD (UML activity diagram). The heart of JAD is the Session activity during which all stakeholders design and agree to a system specification. The activities prior to the Session maximizes its efficiency. The production of the final document ensures that the decisions made during the Session are captured.

1. **Project definition.** During this activity, the JAD facilitator interviews managers and clients to determine the objectives and the scope of the project. The findings from the interviews are collected in the *Management Definition Guide*. During this activity, the JAD facilitator forms a team composed of users, clients, and developers. All stakeholders are represented, and the participants are able to make binding decisions.

2. **Research.** During this activity, the JAD facilitator interviews present and future users, gathers domain information, and describes the work flows. The JAD facilitator also starts a list of issues that will need to be addressed during the session. The primary results of the research activity are a *Session Agenda* and a *Preliminary Specification* listing work flow and system information.

3. **Preparation.** During this activity, the JAD facilitator prepares the session. The JAD facilitator creates a *Working Document*, first draft of the final document, an agenda for the session, and any number of overhead slides or flip charts representing information gathered during the Research activity.

4. **Session.** During this activity, the JAD facilitator guides the team in creating the system specification. A JAD session lasts for 3–5 days. The team defines and agrees on the work flow, the data elements, the screens, and the reports of the system. All decisions are documented by a scribe filling JAD forms.

5. **Final document.** The JAD facilitator prepares the *Final Document*, revising the working document to include all decisions made during the session. The Final Document represents a complete specification of the system agreed on during the session. The Final Document is distributed to the session's participants for review. The participants then meet for a 1-to 2-hour meeting to discuss the reviews and finalize the document.

JAD has been successfully used by IBM and other companies. JAD leverages off group dynamics to improve communication among participants and to accelerate consensus. At the end of a JAD session, developers are more knowledgeable of users needs, and users are more knowledgeable of development trade-offs. Additional gains result from a reduction of redesign activities downstream. Because of its reliance on social dynamics, the success of a JAD session often depends on the qualifications of the JAD facilitator as a meeting facilitator.

4.5.3   Validating Requirements: Usability Testing

Usability testing tests the user's understanding of the use case model. Usability testing finds problems with the system specification by letting the user explore the system or only part of the system (e.g., the user interface). Usability tests are also concerned with user interface details, such as the look and feel of the user interface, the geometrical layout of the screens, and the hardware. For example, in case of a wearable computer, a usability test might test the ability of the user to issue commands to the system while lying in an awkward position, as in the case of a mechanic looking at a screen under a car while checking a muffler.

Usability tests are based on experiments identifying deficiencies that developers fix iteratively [Rubin, 1994]. The technique for conducting usability tests is based on the classical approach for conducting a controlled experiment. Developers formulate a test objective, which they then test by manipulating selected experimental parameters under controlled conditions. Developers carefully study the values of these parameters to identify statistically significant cause-and-effect relationships. Even though this type of approach could be used for any parameter, usability tests focus on usability parameters, such as the ease to learn the system, the time to accomplish a task, or the rate of errors a user makes when accomplishing a task.

There are two important differences between classical experiments and usability tests. Whereas the classical experimental method is designed to confirm or refute a hypothesis, the goal of usability tests is to obtain qualitative information on how to fix usability problems and how to improve the system. Another difference is the rigor with which the experiments need to be performed. It has been shown that even a series of quick focused tests starting as early as requirements elicitation is extremely helpful. Nielsen uses the term "discount usability engineering" to indicate that a few usability tests are better than none at all [Nielsen, 1993].

There are three types of usability tests:

- **Scenario test**. During this test, one or more users are presented with a visionary scenario of the system. Developers identify how quickly users are able to understand the scenario, how accurately it represents their model of work, and how positively they react to the description of the new system. The selected scenarios should be as realistic and detailed as possible. A scenario test allows rapid and frequent feedback from the user. Scenario tests can be realized as paper mockups[2] or with a simple prototyping environment, which is often easier to learn than the programming environment used for development. The advantage of scenario tests is that they are cheap to realize and to repeat. The disadvantages are that the user cannot interact directly with the system and that the data are fixed.
- **Prototype test**. During this type of test, one or more users are presented with a piece of software that practically implements the system. A vertical prototype implements a complete use case through the system, and a horizontal prototype presents an interface for most use cases (without providing much or any functionality). The advantages of prototype tests are that they provide a realistic view of the system to the user and that prototypes can be instrumented to collect detailed data. The disadvantages of prototypes are that they are expensive to build and to modify.
- **Product test.** This test is similar to the prototype test except that a functional version of the system is used in place of the prototype. A product test can only be conducted once

---

2. Storyboarding, a technique from the feature animation industry, consists of sketching a sequence of pictures of the screen at different point in the scenario. The pictures of each scenario are then lined up chronologically against a wall on a board (hence the term "storyboard"). Developers and users can walk around the room when reviewing and discussing the scenarios. Given a reasonably sized room, participants can deal with several hundreds of sketches.

most of the system is developed. It also requires that the system be easily modifiable such that the results of the usability test can be taken into account.

In all three types of tests, the basic elements of usability testing include [Rubin, 1994]:

- development of test objectives
- use of a representative sample of end users
- use of the system in the actual or simulated work environment
- involvement of end users
- controlled, extensive interrogation, and probing of the users by the person performing the usability test
- collection and analysis of quantitative and qualitative results
- recommendations on how to improve the system

Typical test objectives in a usability test address the comparison of two user interaction styles, the identification of the best and the worst features in a scenario or a prototype, the main stumbling blocks, the identification of useful features for novice and expert users, when help is needed, and what type of training information is required.

One of the main problems of usability tests is with enrolling participants. There are several obstacles faced by project managers in selecting real end users [Grudin, 1990]:

- The project manager is usually afraid that customers bypass established technical support organizations and call the developers directly, once they know how to get to them. Once this line of communication is established, developers might be sidetracked too often from doing their assigned jobs.
- Sales personnel do not want developers to talk to their "customers." Sales people are afraid that they may offend the customer or create dissatisfaction with the current generation of products (which still must be sold).
- The end users do not have time.
- The end users dislike being studied. For example, a automotive mechanic might think that an augmented reality system will put him out of work.

Debriefing the participants is the key to coming to an understanding how to improve the usability of the system being tested. Even though the usability test uncovers and exposes problems, it is often the debriefing session that illustrates why these problems have occurred in the first place. It is important to write recommendations on how to improve the tested components as fast as possible after the usability test is finished, so they can be used by the developers to implement any necessary changes in the system models of the tested component.

For more details on usability testing, the reader is referred to the specialized literature [Rubin, 1994], [Nielsen & Mack, 1994].

4.5.4   Documenting Requirements Elicitation

The results of the requirements elicitation activity and the analysis activity are documented in the Requirements Analysis Document (RAD). This document completely describes the system in terms of functional and nonfunctional requirements and serves as a contractual basis between the client and the developers. The audience for the RAD includes the client, the users, the project management, the system analysts (i.e., the developers who participate in the requirements), and the system designers (i.e., the developers who participate in the system design). The first part of the document, including use cases and nonfunctional requirements, is written during requirements elicitation. The formalization of the specification in terms of object models is written during analysis. The following is an example template for a RAD:

Requirements Analysis Document
1. Introduction
    1.1 Purpose of the system
    1.2 Scope of the system
    1.3 Objectives and success criteria of the project
    1.4 Definitions, acronyms, and abbreviations
    1.5 References
    1.6 Overview
2. Current system
3. Proposed system
    3.1 Overview
    3.2 Functional requirements
    3.3 Nonfunctional requirements
        3.3.1 User interface and human factors
        3.3.2 Documentation
        3.3.3 Hardware consideration
        3.3.4 Performance characteristics
        3.3.5 Error handling and extreme conditions
        3.3.6 Quality issues
        3.3.7 System modifications
        3.3.8 Physical environment
        3.3.9 Security issues
        3.3.10 Resource issues
    3.4 Pseudo requirements
    3.5 System models
        3.5.1 Scenarios
        3.5.2 Use case model
        3.5.3 Object model
                3.5.3.1 Data dictionary
                3.5.3.2 Class diagrams
        3.5.4 Dynamic models
        3.5.5 User interface—navigational paths and screen mock-ups
4. Glossary

The first section of the RAD is an *Introduction*. Its purpose is to provide a brief overview of the function of the system and the reasons for its development, its scope, and references to the development context (e.g., related problem statement, references to existing systems, feasibility studies). The introduction also includes the objectives and success criteria of the project.

The second section, *Current system,* describes the current state of affairs. If the new system will replace an existing system, this section describes the functionality and the problems of the current system. Otherwise, this section describes how the tasks supported by the new system are accomplished now. For example, in the case of SatWatch, the user currently resets her watch whenever she travels across a time zone. Because of the manual nature of this operation, the user occasionally sets the wrong time. In contrast, the SatWatch will continually ensure accurate time within its lifetime. In the case of FRIEND, the current system is paper based: Dispatchers keep track of resource assignments by filling forms. Communication between dispatchers and field officers is radio based. The current system requires a high documentation and management cost that the FRIEND system aims to reduce.

The third section, *Proposed system,* documents the requirements elicitation and the analysis model of the new system. It is divided into five subsections:

- *Overview* presents a functional overview of the system.

- *Functional requirements* describes in natural language the high-level functionality of the system.

- *Nonfunctional requirements* describes user-level requirements that are not directly related to functionality. This includes performance, security, modifiability, error handling, hardware platform, and physical environment.

- *Pseudo requirements* describes design and implementation constraints imposed by the client. This includes the specification of the deployment platform, implementation language, or database management system.

- *System models* describes the scenarios, use cases, object model, and dynamic models describing the system. This section contains the complete functional specification of the system, including mock-ups and navigational charts illustrating the user interface of the system. This section is written during the *Analysis* activity, described in the next chapter.

The RAD should be written after the use case model is stable, that is, when the number of modifications to the requirements is minimal. The RAD, however, is updated throughout the development process when specification problems are discovered or when the scope of the system is changed. The RAD, once published, is baselined and put under configuration management. The revision history section of the RAD will provide a history of changes in the form of a list of the author responsible for the change, the date of change, and a brief description of the change.

4.6 Exercises

1. Consider your watch as a system and set the time 2 minutes ahead. Write down each interaction between you and your watch as a scenario. Record all interactions, including any feedback the watch provides you.

2. Consider the scenario you wrote in Exercise 1. Identify the actor of the scenario. Next, write the corresponding use case SetTime. Include all cases, and include setting the time forward, backward, setting hours, minutes, and seconds.

3. Assume the watch system you described in Exercises 1 and 2 also supports an alarm feature. Describe setting the alarm time as a self-contained use case named SetAlarmTime.

4. Examine the SetTime and SetAlarmTime use cases you wrote in Exercises 2 and 3. Eliminate any redundancy by using an include relationship. Justify why an include relationship is preferable to an extend relationship in this case.

5. Assume the FieldOfficer can invoke a Help feature when filling an EmergencyReport. The HelpReportEmergency feature provides a detailed description for each field and specifies which fields are required. Modify the ReportEmergency use case (described in Figure 4-11) to include this help functionality. Which relationship should you use to relate the ReportEmergency and HelpReportEmergency?

6. Below are examples of nonfunctional requirements. Specify which of these requirements are verifiable and which are not.

   • "The system must be usable."

   • "The system must provide visual feedback to the user within 1 second of issuing a command."

   • "The availability of the system must be above 95%."

   • "The user interface of the new system should be similar enough to the old system such that users familiar with the old system can be easily trained to use the new system."

7. Explain why multiple-choice questionnaires, as a primary means of extracting information from the user, is not effective for eliciting requirements.

8. From your point of view, describe the strengths and weaknesses of users during the requirements elicitation activity. Describe also the strengths and weaknesses of developers during the requirements elicitation activity.

9. Briefly define the term "menu." Write your answer on a piece of paper and put it upside down on the table together with the definitions of four other students. Compare all five definitions and discuss any substantial difference.

References

[Bruegge et al., 1994]   B. Bruegge, K. O'Toole, & D. Rothenberger, "Design considerations for an accident management system," in , *Proceedings of the Second International Conference on Cooperative Information Systems,* M. Brodie, M. Jarke, M. Papazoglou (eds.), pp. 90–100, (University of Toronto Press, Toronto, Canada), May 1994.

[Carroll, 1995]   J. M. Carroll (ed.), *Scenario-Based Design: Envisioning Work and Technology in System Development.* Wiley, New York, 1995.

[Christel & Kang, 1992]   M. G. Christel & K. C. Kang, "Issues in requirements elicitation," *Software Engineering Institute, Technical Report CMU/SEI-92-TR-12,* Carnegie Mellon Univ., Pittsburgh, PA, 1992.

[Constantine & Lockwood, 1999] L. L Constantine & L. A. D. Lockwood, *Software for Use.* Addison-Wesley, Reading, MA, 1999.

[Dumas & Redish, 1998]   Dumas & Redish, *A Practical Guide to Usability Testing.* Ablex, NJ, 1993.

[FRIEND, 1994]   *FRIEND Project Documentation,* School of Computer Science, Carnegie Mellon Univ., Pittsburgh, PA, 1994.

[Grudin, 1990]   J. Grudin, "Obstacles to user involvement in interface design in large product development organizations," *Proceeding IFIP INTERACT'90 Third International Conference on Human-Computer Interaction,* (Cambridge, U.K.), Aug. 1990.

[Hammer & Champy, 1993]   M. Hammer & J. Champy, *Reengineering The Corporation: a Manifesto For Business Revolution.* Harper Business, New York, 1993.

[Jackson, 1995]   M. Jackson, *Software Requirements & Specifications: A Lexicon of Practice, Principles and Prejudices.* Addison-Wesley, Reading, MA, 1995.

[Jacobson et al., 1992]   I. Jacobson, M. Christerson, P. Jonsson, & G. Overgaard, *Object-Oriented Software Engineering—A Use Case Driven Approach.* Addison-Wesley, Reading, MA, 1992.

[Jacobson et al., 1999]   I Jacobson, G. Booch, & J. Rumbaugh, *The Unified Software Development Process.* Addison-Wesley, Reading, MA, 1999.

[Johnson, 1992]   P. Johnson, *Human Computer Interaction: Psychology, Task Analysis and Software Engineering.* McGraw-Hill Int., London, 1992.

[Macaulay, 1996]   L. Macaulay, *Requirements Engineering.* Springer Verlag, London, 1996.

[Nielsen, 1993]   J. Nielsen, *Usability Engineering.* Academic, 1993.

[Nielsen & Mack, 1994]   J. Nielsen & R. L. Mack (eds.), *Usability Inspection Methods.* Wiley, New York, 1994.

[Paech, 1998]   B. Paech, "The Four Levels of Use Case Description," *4th Int. Workshop on Requirements Engineering: Foundations for Software Quality,* (Pisa), June 1998.

[Rubin, 1994]   J. Rubin, *Handbook of Usability Testing.* Wiley, New York, 1994.

[Wirfs-Brock, 1995]   R. Wirfs-Brock, "Design objects and their interactions: A brief look at responsibility-driven design," *Scenario-Based Design: Envisioning Work and Technology in System Development.* J. M. Carroll (ed.), (Wiley, New York), 1995.

[Wirfs-Brock et al., 1990]   R. Wirfs-Brock, B. Wilkerson, & Lauren Wiener, *Designing Object-Oriented Software.* Prentice Hall, Englewood Cliffs, NJ, 1990.

[Wood & Silver, 1989]   J. Wood & D. Silver, *Joint Application Design®.* Wiley, New York, 1989.

[Zultner, 1993]   R. E. Zultner. "TQM for Technical Teams," *Communications of the ACM,* Vol 36, No. 10, 1993.

5

Analysis

I am Foo with a name, if I could only remember it.
—A programmer of very little brain

Analysis results in a model of the system that aims to be correct, complete, consistent, and verifiable. Developers formalize the system specification produced during requirements elicitation and examine in more detail boundary conditions and exceptional cases. Developers correct and clarify the system specification if any errors or ambiguities are found. The client and the user are usually involved in this activity, especially when the system specification needs to be changed and when additional information needs to be gathered.

In object-oriented analysis, developers build a model describing the application domain. For example, the analysis model of a watch describes how the watch represents time (e.g., Does the watch know about leap years? Does it know about the day of the week? Does it know about the phases of the moon?) The analysis model is then extended to describe how the actors and the system interact to manipulate the application domain model (e.g., How does the watch owner reset the time? How does the watch owner reset the day of the week?). Developers use the analysis model, together with nonfunctional requirements, to prepare for the architecture of the system developed during high-level design (Chapter 6, *System Design*).

In this chapter, we discuss the analysis activities in more detail. We focus on the identification of objects, their behavior, their relationships, their classification, and their organization. We review briefly non-object-oriented analysis presentations and methods. Finally, we describe management issues related to analysis in the context of a multiteam development project.

5.1 Introduction: An Optical Illusion

In 1915, Rubin exhibited a drawing similar to Figure 5-1 to illustrate the concept of multistable images. What do you see? Two faces looking at each other? If you focus more closely on the white area, you can see a vase instead. Once you are able to perceive both shapes individually, it is easier to switch back and forth between the vase and the faces.

Figure 5-1   Ambiguity: what do you see?

If the drawing in Figure 5-1 had been a system specification, which models should you have constructed? Specifications, like multistable images, contain ambiguities caused by the inaccuracies inherent to natural language and by the assumptions of the specification authors. For example, a quantity specified without a unit is ambiguous (e.g., the "Feet or Miles?" example in Section 4.1), a time without time zone is ambiguous (e.g., scheduling a phone call between different countries).

Formalization helps identify areas of ambiguity as well as inconsistencies and omissions in a system specification. Once developers identify problems with the specification, they address them by eliciting more information from the users and the client. Requirements elicitation and analysis are iterative and incremental activities that occur concurrently.

5.2 An Overview of Analysis

Analysis focuses on producing a model of the system, called the analysis model, which is correct, complete, consistent, and verifiable. Analysis is different from requirements elicitation in that developers focus on structuring and formalizing the requirements elicited from users

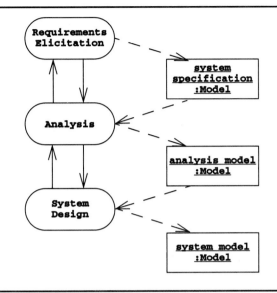

Figure 5-2 Products of requirements elicitation and analysis (UML activity diagram).

(Figure 5-2). Although the analysis model may not be understandable to the users and the client, it helps developers verify the system specification produced during requirements elicitation.

There is a natural tendency for users and developers to postpone difficult decisions until later in the project. A decision may be difficult because of lack of domain knowledge, lack of technological knowledge, or simply because of disagreements among users and developers. Postponing decisions enables the project to move on smoothly and avoid confrontation with reality or peers. Unfortunately, difficult decisions will eventually need to be made, often at higher cost when intrinsic problems are discovered during testing, or worse, during user evaluation. Translating a system specification into a formal or semiformal model forces developers to identify and resolve difficult issues early in the development.

The **analysis model** is composed of three individual models: the **functional model**, represented by use cases and scenarios, the **analysis object model**, represented by class and object diagrams, and the **dynamic model**, represented by statechart and sequence diagrams (Figure 5-3). In the previous chapter, we described how to elicit requirements from the users and describe them as use cases and scenarios. In this chapter, we describe how to refine the functional model and derive the object and the dynamic model. This leads to a more precise and complete specification as details are added to the analysis model. We conclude the chapter by describing management activities related to analysis. In the next section, we first define the main concepts of analysis.

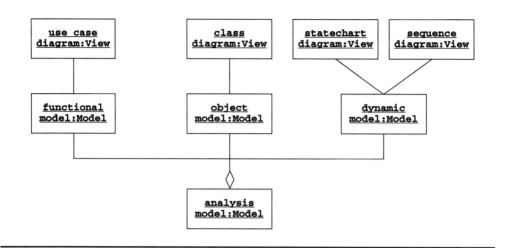

Figure 5-3   The analysis model is composed of the functional model, the object model, and the dynamic model. In UML, the functional model is represented with use case diagrams, the object model with class diagrams, and the dynamic model with statechart and sequence diagrams.

5.3 Analysis Concepts

In this section, we describe the main analysis concepts used in this chapter. In particular, we describe:

- entity, boundary, and control objects (Section 5.3.1)
- association multiplicity (Section 5.3.2)
- qualified associations (Section 5.3.3)
- generalization (Section 5.3.4)

5.3.1   Entity, Boundary, and Control Objects

The analysis object model consists of entity, boundary, and control objects [Jacobson et al., 1999]. **Entity objects** represent the persistent information tracked by the system. **Boundary objects** represent the interactions between the actors and the system. **Control objects** represent the tasks that are performed by the user and supported by the system. In the 2Bwatch example, Year, Month, Day are entity objects; ButtonBoundary and LCDDisplayBoundary are boundary objects; ChangeDateControl is a control object that represents the activity of changing the date by pressing combinations of buttons.

Modeling the system with entity, boundary, and control objects has several advantages. First, it provides developers with simple heuristics to distinguish different, but related concepts. For example, the time that is tracked by a watch has different properties than the display that depicts the time. Differentiating between boundary and entity objects forces that distinction: The time that is tracked by the watch is represented by the Time object. The display is represented by the LCDDisplayBoundary. Second, the three object type approach results in smaller and more specialized objects. Third, the three object type approach leads to models that are more resilient to change: The interface to the system (represented by the boundary objects) is more likely to change than its basic functionality (represented by the entity and control objects).

To distinguish between different types of objects, UML provides the stereotype mechanism to enable the developer to attach such meta information to modeling elements. For example, in Figure 5-4, we attach the <<control>> stereotype to the ChangeDateControl object. In addition to stereotypes, we may also use naming conventions for clarity and recommend distinguishing the three different types of objects on a syntactical basis: Boundary objects may have the suffix Boundary appended to their name; control objects may have the suffix Control appended to their name; entity objects usually do not have any suffix appended to their name. Another benefit of this naming convention is that the type of the class is represented even when the UML stereotype is not available, for example, when examining only the source code.

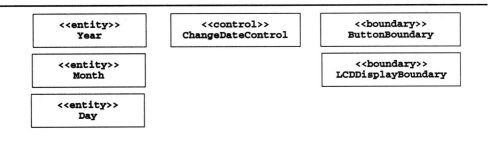

Figure 5-4 Analysis classes for the 2Bwatch example.

5.3.2   Association Multiplicity Revisited

As we saw in Chapter 2, *Modeling with UML*, the end of an association can be labeled by a set of integers called **multiplicity**. The multiplicity indicates the number of links that can legitimately originate from an instance of the class connected to the association end. For example, in Figure 5-5, a 2Bwatch has exactly two Buttons and one LCDDisplay.

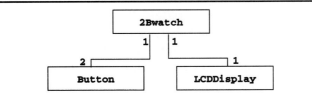

Figure 5-5 An example of multiplicity of associations (UML class diagram). A 2Bwatch has two buttons and one LCDDisplay.

In UML, an association end can have an arbitrary set of integers as a multiplicity. For example, an association could allow only a prime number of links and, thus, would have a multiplicity 1, 2, 3, 5, 7, 11, 13, ... In practice, however, most of the associations we encounter belong to one of the following three types (see Figure 5-6).

• A **one-to-one association** has a multiplicity 1 on each end. A one-to-one association between two classes (e.g., PoliceOfficer and BadgeNumber), means that exactly one link exists between instances of each class (e.g., a PoliceOfficer has exactly one BadgeNumber, and a BadgeNumber denotes exactly one PoliceOfficer).

• A **one-to-many association** has a multiplicity 1 on one end and 0..n (also represented by a star) or 1..n on the other. A one-to-many association between two classes (e.g., Person and Car) denotes composition (e.g., a FireUnit owns one or more FireTrucks, a FireTruck is owned exactly by one FireUnit).

• A **many-to-many association** has a multiplicity 0..n or 1..n on both ends. A many-to-many association between two classes (e.g., FieldOfficer and IncidentReport) denotes that an arbitrary number of links can exist between instances of the two classes (e.g., a FieldOfficer can write for many IncidentReport, an IncidentReport can be written by many FieldOfficers). This is the most complex type of association.

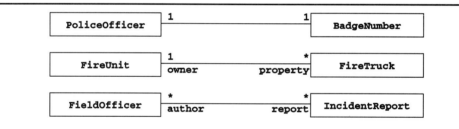

Figure 5-6 Examples of multiplicity (UML class diagram). The association between Person and SocialSecurityNumber is one-to-one. The association between Person and Car is one-to-many. The association between Person and Company is many-to-many.

Adding multiplicity to associations increases the amount of information we capture from the application or the solution domain. Specifying the multiplicity of an association becomes critical when we determine which use cases are needed to manipulate the application domain objects. For example, consider a file system made of Directory (ies) and Files. A Directory can contain any number of FileSystemElements. A FileSystemElement is an abstract concept that denotes either a Directory or a File. In case of a strictly hierarchical system, a FileSystemElement is part of exactly one Directory, which we denote with a one-to-many multiplicity (Figure 5-7).

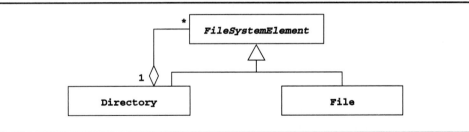

Figure 5-7 Example of a hierarchical file system. A `Directory` can contain any number of `FileSystemElement`s (a `FileSystemElement` is either a `File` or a `Directory`). A given `FileSystemElement`, however, is part of exactly one `Directory`.

If, however, a `File` or a `Directory` can be simultaneously part of more than one `Directory`, we need to represent the aggregation of `FileSystemElement` into `Directory` (ies) as a many-to-many association (see Figure 5-8).

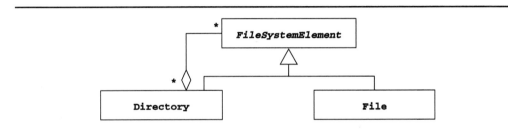

Figure 5-8 Example of a nonhierarchical file system. A `Directory` can contain any number of `FileSystemElement`s (a `FileSystemElement` is either a `File` or a `Directory`). A given `FileSystemElement` can be part of many `Directory` (ies).

This discussion may seem to be considering detailed issues that could be left for later activities in the development process. The difference between a hierarchical file system and a nonhierarchical one, however, is also in the functionality it offers. If a system allows a given `File` to be part of multiple `Directory` (ies), we need to define a use case describing how a user adds an existing `File` to existing `Directory` (ies) (e.g., the Unix `link` command or the Macintosh `MakeAlias` menu item). Moreover, use cases removing a `File` from a `Directory` must specify whether the `File` is removed from one `Directory` only or from all `Directory` (ies) that reference them. Note that a many-to-many association can result in a substantially more complex system.

5.3.3 Qualified Associations

Qualification is a technique for reducing multiplicity by using keys. Associations with a `0..1` or `1` multiplicity are easier to understand than associations with a `0..n` or `1..n` multiplicity. Often, in the case of a one-to-many association, objects on the "many" side can be distinguished from one another using a name. For example, in a hierarchical file system, each file belongs to exactly one directory. Each file is uniquely identified by a name in the context of a directory. Many files can have the same name in the context of the file system; however, two files cannot share the same name within the same directory. Without qualification (see top of Figure 5-9), the association between `Directory` and `File` has a one multiplicity on the `Directory` side and a zero-to-many multiplicity on the `File` side. We reduce the multiplicity on the `File` side by using the `filename` attribute as a key, also called a **qualifier** (see top of Figure 5-9). The relationship between `Directory` and `File` is called a **qualified association**.

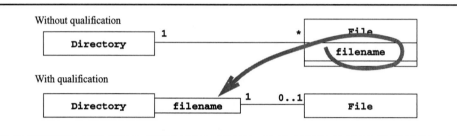

Figure 5-9   Example of how a qualified association reduces multiplicity (UML class diagram). Adding a qualifier clarifies the class diagram and increases the conveyed information. In this case, the model including the qualification denotes that the name of a file is unique within a directory.

Reducing multiplicity is always preferable, as the model becomes clearer and fewer cases have to be taken into account. Developers should examine each association that has a one-to-many or many-to-many multiplicity and check if a qualifier can be added. Often, these associations can be qualified with an attribute of the target class, (e.g., the `filename` attribute in Figure 5-9).

5.3.4   Generalization

As we saw in Chapter 2, *Modeling with UML*, **generalization** enables us to organize concepts into hierarchies. At the top of the hierarchy is a general concept (e.g., an `Incident`, Figure 5-10), and at the bottom of the hierarchy are the most specialized concepts (e.g., `CatInTree`, `TrafficAccident`, `BuildingFire`, `EarthQuake`, `ChemicalLeak`). There may be any number of intermediate levels in between, covering more-or-less generalized concepts (e.g., `LowPriorityIncident`, `Emergency`, `Disaster`). Such hierarchies allow us to refer to many concepts precisely. When we use the term `Incident`, we mean all instances of all types of `Incidents`. When we use the term `Emergency`, we only refer to an `Incident` that requires an immediate response. This view of generalization stems from modeling.

In an object-oriented programming language, **inheritance** is a reusability technique. If a class `Child` inherits from a class `Parent`, all the attributes and methods available on `Parent`

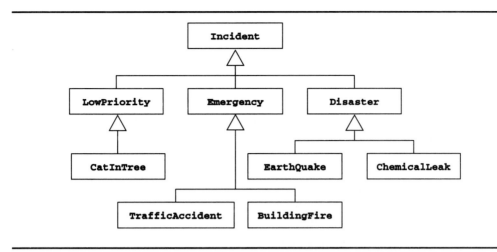

Figure 5-10   An example of a generalization hierarchy (UML class diagram). The root of the hierarchy represents the most general concept, whereas the leaves nodes represent the most specialized concepts.

are automatically available on `Child`. The class `Child` may add additional methods or override inherited methods, thus refining the class `Parent`. As in the case of generalization, the class at the top of the hierarchy tends to be the most general one, whereas the leaves tend to be the most specialized.

Generalization and inheritance are closely related concepts. They are, however, not identical. Inheritance is a mechanism for reusing attributes and behavior, even when the classes involved in the inheritance do not have a generalization relationship. For example, it is possible to implement a `Set` collection by refining a `Hashtable` (although this might not be a good solution for implementing `Set`s). Nevertheless, a `Set` is not more specialized a concept than a `Hashtable`, nor is a `Hashtable` a generalization of a `Set`.

During analysis, we only focus on the organization of concepts into generalization relationships and should not be interpreted in terms of reuse. The inheritance hierarchy, although initially derived from the generalization hierarchy, will be restructured during object design.

5.4 Analysis Activities: From Use Cases to Objects

In this section, we describe the activities that transform the use cases and scenarios produced during requirements elicitation into an analysis model. Analysis activities include:

- identifying entity objects (Section 5.4.1)
- identifying boundary objects (Section 5.4.2)
- identifying control objects (Section 5.4.3)
- mapping use cases to objects (Section 5.4.4)
- identifying associations among objects (Section 5.4.5)

- identifying object attributes (Section 5.4.6)
- modeling nontrivial behavior with statecharts (Section 5.4.7)
- modeling generalization relationships (Section 5.4.8)
- reviewing the analysis model (Section 5.4.9)

We illustrate each activity by focusing on the `ReportEmergency` use case of FRIEND described in Chapter 4, *Requirements Elicitation*. These activities are guided by heuristics. The quality of their outcome depends on the experience of the developer in applying these heuristics and methods. The methods and heuristics presented in this section are adapted from [De Marco, 1978], [Jacobson et al., 1999], [Rumbaugh et al., 1991], and [Wirfs-Brock et al., 1990].

5.4.1   Identifying Entity Objects

Participating objects (see Section 4.4.6) form the basis of the analysis model. As described in Chapter 4, *Requirements Elicitation*, participating objects are found by examining each use case and identifying candidate objects. Natural language analysis [Abbott, 1983] is an intuitive set of heuristics for identifying objects, attributes, and associations from a system specification. Abbott's heuristics maps parts of speech (e.g., nouns, having verbs, being verbs, adjectives) to model components (e.g., objects, operations, inheritance relationships, classes). Table 5-1 provides examples of such mappings by examining the `ReportEmergency` use case Figure 5-11.

Table 5-1   Abbott's heuristics for mapping parts of speech to model components [Abbott, 1983]

Part of speech	Model component	Examples
Proper noun	Object	Alice
Common noun	Class	FieldOfficer
Doing verb	Operation	Creates, submits, selects
Being verb	Inheritance	Is a kind of, is one of either
Having verb	Aggregation	Has, consists of, includes
Modal verb	Constraints	Must be
Adjective	Attribute	Incident description

Natural language analysis has the advantage of focusing on the users' terms. However, it suffers from several limitations. First, the quality of the object model depends highly on the style of writing of the analyst (e.g., consistency of terms used, verbification of nouns). Natural language is an imprecise tool, and an object model derived literally from text risks being imprecise. Developers can address this limitation by rephrasing and clarifying the system specification as they identify and standardize objects and terms. A second limitation of natural language analysis is that there are many more nouns than relevant classes. Many nouns correspond to attributes or synonyms for other nouns. Sorting through all the nouns for a large system specification is a time-consuming activity. In general, Abbott's heuristics work well for generating a list of initial candidate objects from short descriptions, such as the flow of events of a scenario or a use case. The following heuristics can be used in conjunction with Abbott's rules:

Heuristics for identifying entity objects
- terms that developers or users need to clarify in order to understand the use case
- recurring nouns in the use cases (e.g., Incident)
- real-world entities that the system needs to keep track of (e.g., FieldOfficer, Dispatcher, Resource)
- real-world activities that the system needs to keep track of (e.g., EmergencyOperationsPlan)
- use cases (e.g., ReportEmergency)
- data sources or sinks (e.g., Printer)
- *always* use the user's terms

Developers name and briefly describe the objects, their attributes, and their responsibilities as they are identified. Uniquely naming objects promotes a standard terminology. Describing objects, even briefly, allows developers to clarify the concepts they use and avoid misunderstandings (e.g., using one object for two different but related concepts). Developers need not, however, spend a lot of time detailing objects or attributes given that the analysis model is still in flux. Developers should document attributes and responsibilities if they are obvious. A tentative name and a brief description for each object is sufficient otherwise. There will be plenty of iterations during which objects can be revised. However, once the analysis model is stable, the description of each object should be as detailed as necessary (see Section 5.4.9).

For example, after a first examination of the ReportEmergency use case (Figure 5-11), we use application domain knowledge and interviews with the users to identify the objects Dispatcher, EmergencyReport, FieldOfficer, and Incident. Note that the Emergency-Report object is not mentioned explicitly by name in the ReportEmergency use case. Step 3 of the use case refers to the emergency report as the "information submitted by the FieldOfficer." After review with the client, we discover that this information is usually referred to as the emergency report and decide to name the corresponding object EmergencyReport.

Use case name	`ReportEmergency`
Entry condition	1. The `FieldOfficer` activates the "Report Emergency" function of her terminal.
Flow of events	2. FRIEND responds by presenting a form to the officer. The form includes an emergency type menu (General emergency, fire, transportation), a location, incident description, resource request, and hazardous material fields.
	3. The `FieldOfficer` fills the form, by specifying minimally the emergency type and description fields. The `FieldOfficer` may also describes possible responses to the emergency situation and request specific resources. Once the form is completed, the `FieldOfficer` submits the form by pressing the "Send Report" button, at which point, the `Dispatcher` is notified.
	4. The `Dispatcher` reviews the information submitted by the `FieldOfficer` and creates an `Incident` in the database by invoking the `OpenIncident` use case. All the information contained in the `FieldOfficer`'s form is automatically included in the incident. The `Dispatcher` selects a response by allocating resources to the incident (with the `AllocateResources` use case) and acknowledges the emergency report by sending a FRIENDgram to the `FieldOfficer`.
Exit condition	5. The `FieldOfficer` receives the acknowledgment and the selected response.

Figure 5-11   An example of use case: `ReportEmergency`.

The definition of entity objects leads to the initial analysis model described in Table 5-2.

Note that the above object model is far from being a complete description of the system implementing the `ReportEmergency` use case. In the next section, we describe the identification of boundary objects.

5.4.2   Identifying Boundary Objects

Boundary objects represent the system interface with the actors. In each use case, each actor interacts with at least one boundary object. The boundary object collects the information from the actor and translates it into an interface neutral form that can be used by the entity objects and also by the control objects.

Boundary objects model the user interface at a coarse level. They do not describe in detail the visual aspects of the user interface. For example, boundary objects such as "button" or "menu item" are too detailed. First, developers can discuss user interface details more easily with sketches and mock-ups. Second, the design of the user interface design will continue to evolve as a consequence of usability tests, even after the functional

Table 5-2   Entity objects for the `ReportEmergency` use case

Dispatcher	Police officer who manages `Incidents`. A `Dispatcher` opens, documents, and closes `Incidents` in response to `Emergency Reports` and other communication with `FieldOfficers`. `Dispatchers` are identified by badge numbers.
EmergencyReport	Initial report about an `Incident` from a `FieldOfficer` to a `Dispatcher`. An `EmergencyReport` usually triggers the creation of an `Incident` by the `Dispatcher`. An `EmergencyReport` is composed of a emergency level, a type (fire, road accident, or other), a location, and a description.
FieldOfficer	Police or fire officer on duty. A `FieldOfficer` can be allocated to, at most, one `Incident` at a time. `FieldOfficers` are identified by badge numbers.
Incident	Situation requiring attention from a `FieldOfficer`. An `Incident` may be reported in the system by a `FieldOfficer` or anybody else external to the system. An `Incident` is composed of a description, a response, a status (open, closed, documented), a location, and a number of `FieldOfficers`.

specification of the system becomes stable. Updating the analysis model every time a visual change is made to the interface is time consuming and does not yield any substantial benefit.

Heuristics for identifying boundary objects
- Identify forms and windows the users needs to enter data into the system (e.g., `EmergencyReportForm`, `ReportEmergencyButton`).
- Identify notices and messages the system uses to respond to the user (e.g., `AcknowledgmentNotice`).
- Do not model the visual aspects of the interface with boundary objects (user mock-ups are better suited for that).
- *Always* use the user's terms for describing interfaces as opposed to terms from the implementation technology.

We find the following boundary objects by examining the `ReportEmergency` use case (Table 5-3).

Note that the `IncidentForm` is not explicitly mentioned anywhere in the `ReportEmergency` use case. We identified this object by observing that the `Dispatcher` needs an interface to view the emergency report submitted by the `FieldOfficer` and to send back an acknowledgment. The terms used for describing the boundary objects in the analysis model should follow the user terminology, even if it is tempting to use terms from the implementation domain.

Table 5-3   Boundary objects for the ReportEmergency use case

`AcknowledgmentNotice`	Notice used for displaying the `Dispatcher`'s acknowledgment to the `FieldOfficer`.
`DispatcherStation`	Computer used by the `Dispatcher`.
`ReportEmergencyButton`	Button used by a `FieldOfficer` to initiate the `ReportEmergency` use case.
`EmergencyReportForm`	Form used for the input of the `ReportEmergency`. This form is presented to the `FieldOfficer` on the `FieldOfficerStation` when the "Report Emergency" function is selected. The `EmergencyReportForm` contains fields for specifying all attributes of an emergency report and a button (or other control) for submitting the form once it is completed.
`FieldOfficerStation`	Mobile computer used by the `FieldOfficer`.
`IncidentForm`	Form used for the creation of `Incidents`. This form is presented to the `Dispatcher` on the `DispatcherStation` when the `EmergencyReport` is received. The `Dispatcher` also uses this form to allocate resources and to acknowledge the `FieldOfficer`'s report.

We have made progress toward describing the system. We now have included the interface between the actor and the system. We are, however, still missing some significant pieces of the description, such as the order in which the interactions between the actors and the system occur. In the next section, we describe the identification of control objects.

5.4.3   Identifying Control Objects

Control objects are responsible for coordinating boundary and entity objects. Control objects usually do not have a concrete counterpart in the real world. There is often a close relationship between a use case and a control object. A control object is usually created at the beginning of a use case and ceases to exist at its end. It is responsible for collecting information from the boundary objects and dispatching it to entity objects. For example, control objects describe the behavior associated with the sequencing of forms, undo and history queues, and dispatching information in a distributed system.

> **Heuristics for identifying control objects**
> - Identify one control object per use case or more if the use case is complex and if it can be divided into shorter flows of events.
> - Identify one control object per actor in the use case.
> - The life span of a control object should be extent of the use case or the extent of a user session. If it is difficult to identify the beginning and the end of a control object activation, the corresponding use case may not have a well-defined entry and exit condition.

Initially, we model the control flow of the ReportEmergency use case with a control object for each actor; ReportEmergencyControl for the FieldOfficer and ManageEmergency-Control for the Dispatcher, respectively (Table 5-4).

The decision to model the control flow of the ReportEmergency use case with two control objects stems from the knowledge that the FieldOfficerStation and the DispatcherStation are actually two subsystems communicating over an asynchronous link. This decision could have been postponed until the system design activity. On the other hand, making this concept visible in the analysis model allows us to focus on such exception behavior as the loss of communication between both stations.

In modeling the ReportEmergency use case, we modeled the same functionality by using entity, boundary, and control objects. By shifting from the event-flow perspective to a structural perspective, we increased the level of detail of the description and selected standard terms to refer to the main entities of the application domain and the system. In the next section,

Table 5-4   Control objects for the ReportEmergency use case

ReportEmergencyControl	Manages the report emergency reporting function on the FieldOfficerStation. This object is created when the FieldOfficer selects the "Report Emergency" button. It then creates an EmergencyReportForm and presents it to the FieldOfficer. After submission of the form, this object then collects the information from the form, creates an EmergencyReport, and forwards it to the Dispatcher. The control object then waits for an acknowledgment to come back from the DispatcherStation. When the acknowledgment is received, the ReportEmergencyControl object creates an AcknowledgmentNotice and displays it to the FieldOfficer.
ManageEmergencyControl	Manages the report emergency reporting function on the DispatcherStation. This object is created when an EmergencyReport is received. It then creates an IncidentForm and displays it to the Dispatcher. Once the Dispatcher has created an Incident, allocated Resources, and submitted an acknowledgment, ManageEmergencyControl forwards the acknowledgment to the FieldOfficerStation.

we construct a sequence diagram using the `ReportEmergency` use case and the objects we discovered to ensure the completeness of our model.

5.4.4   Modeling Interactions Between Objects: Sequence Diagrams

A sequence diagram ties use cases with objects. It shows how the behavior of a use case (or scenario) is distributed among its participating objects. Sequence diagrams are usually not a good medium for communication with the user. They represent, however, another shift in perspective and allow the developers to find missing objects or grey areas in the system specification.

In this section, we model the sequence of interactions among objects needed to realize the use case. Figures 5-12–5-14 are sequence diagrams associated with the `ReportEmergency` use case. The columns of a sequence diagram represent the objects that participate in the use case. The leftmost column is the actor who initiates the use case. Horizontal arrows across columns represent messages, or stimuli, which are sent from one object to the other. Time proceeds vertically from top to bottom. For example, the arrow in Figure 5-12 represents the `press` message sent by a `FieldOfficer` to an `ReportEmergencyButton`. The receipt of a message triggers the activation of an operation. The activation is represented by a rectangle from which other messages can originate. The length of the rectangle represents the time the operation is active. In Figure 5-12, the operation triggered by the `press` message sends a `create` message to the `ReportEmergencyControl` class. An operation can be thought of as a service that the object provides to other objects.

Heuristics for drawing sequence diagrams
* The first column should correspond to the actor who initiated the use case.
* The second column should be an boundary object (that the actor used to initiate the use case).
* The third column should be the control object that manages the rest of the use case.
* Control objects are created by boundary objects initiating use cases.
* Boundary objects are created by control objects.
* Entity objects are accessed by control and boundary objects.
* Entity objects *never* access boundary or control objects, this makes it easier to share entity objects across use cases.

In general, the second column of a sequence diagram represents the boundary object with which the actor interacts to initiate the use case (e.g., `ReportEmergencyButton`). The third column is a control object that manages the rest of the use case (e.g., `ReportEmergencyControl`). From then on, the control object creates other boundary objects and may interact with other control objects as well (in this case, the `ManageEmergency-Control` object).

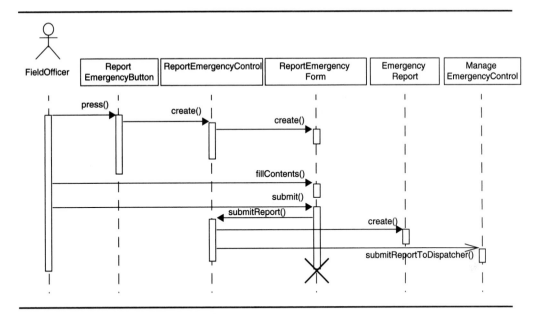

Figure 5-12 Sequence diagram for the `ReportEmergency` use case (initiation from the `FieldOfficerStation` side).

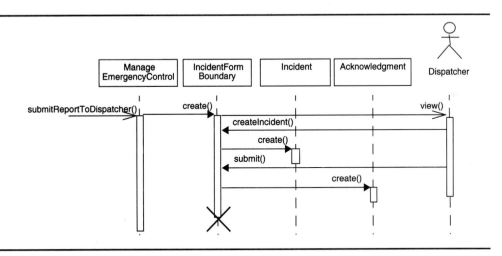

Figure 5-13 Sequence diagram for the `ReportEmergency` use case (`DispatcherStation`).

In Figure 5-13, we discover the entity object `Acknowledgment` that we forgot during our initial examination of the `ReportEmergency` use case (in Table 5-2). The `Acknowledgment` object is different from an `AcknowledgmentNotice`: It holds the information associated with an `Acknowledgment` and is created before the

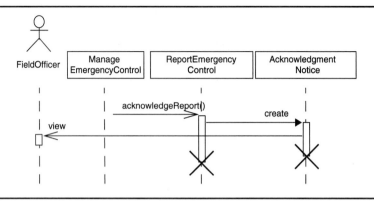

Figure 5-14 Sequence diagram for the `ReportEmergency` use case (acknowledgment on the `FieldOfficerStation`).

`AcknowledgmentNotice` boundary object. When describing the `Acknowledgment` object, we also realize that the original `ReportEmergency` use case (described in Figure 5-11) is incomplete. It only mentions the existence of an `Acknowledgment` and does not describe the information associated with it. In this case, developers need clarification from the client to define what information needs to appear in the `Acknowledgment`. After obtaining such clarification, the `Acknowledgment` object is added to the analysis model (Table 5-5) and the `ReportEmergency` use case is clarified to include the additional information (Figure 5-15).

Table 5-5 `Acknowledgment` object for the `ReportEmergency` use case

`Acknowledgment`	Response of a dispatcher to a `FieldOfficer`'s `EmergencyReport`. By sending an `Acknowledgment`, the `Dispatcher` communicates to the `FieldOfficer` that she has received the `EmergencyReport`, created an Incident, and assigned resources to it. The `Acknowledgment` contains the assigned resources and their estimated arrival time.

By constructing sequence diagrams, we not only model the order of the interaction among the objects, we also distribute the behavior of the use case. In other terms, we assign to each object responsibilities in the form of a set of operations. These operations can be shared by any use case in which a given object participates. Note that the definition of an object that is shared across two or more use cases should be identical. In other terms, if an operation appears in more than one sequence diagram, its behavior should be the same.

Sharing operations across use cases allows developers to remove redundancies in the system specification and to improve its consistency. Note that clarity should always be given precedence to eliminating redundancy. Fragmenting behavior across many operations unnecessarily complicates the system specification.

Use case name	ReportEmergency
Entry condition	1. The FieldOfficer activates the "Report Emergency" function of her terminal.
Flow of events	2. FRIEND responds by presenting a form to the officer. The form includes an emergency type menu (General emergency, fire, transportation), a location, incident description, resource request, and hazardous material fields.
	3. The FieldOfficer fills the form, by specifying minimally the emergency type and description fields. The FieldOfficer may also describes possible responses to the emergency situation and request specific resources. Once the form is completed, the FieldOfficer submits the form by pressing the "Send Report" button, at which point the Dispatcher is notified.
	4. The Dispatcher reviews the information submitted by the FieldOfficer and creates an Incident in the database by invoking the OpenIncident use case. All the information contained in the FieldOfficer's form is automatically included in the incident. The Dispatcher selects a response by allocating resources to the incident (with the AllocateResources use case) and acknowledges the emergency report by sending a FRIENDgram to the FieldOfficer. **The Acknowledgment indicates to the FieldOfficer that the EmergencyReport was received, an Incident created, and resources allocated to the Incident. The Acknowledgment includes the resources (e.g., a fire truck) and their estimated arrival time.**
Exit condition	5. The FieldOfficer receives the Acknowledgment and the selected response.

Figure 5-15 Refined ReportEmergency use case. The discovery and addition of the Acknowledgment object to the analysis model revealed that the original ReportEmergency use case did not accurately describe the information associated with Acknowledgments. The refinements are indicated in **boldface**.

In analysis, sequence diagrams are used to help identify new participating objects and missing behavior. They focus on high-level behavior, and, thus, implementation issues such as performance should not be addressed at this point. Given that building interaction diagrams can be time consuming, developers should focus on problematic or underspecified functionality first. Drawing interaction diagrams for parts of the system that are simple or well defined is not a good investment of analysis resources.

5.4.5 Identifying Associations

Whereas sequence diagrams allow developers to represent interactions among objects over time, class diagrams allow developers to describe the spatial connectivity of objects. We described the UML class diagram notation in Chapter 2, *Modeling with UML*, and use it throughout the book to represent various project artifacts (e.g., activities, deliverables). In this section, we discuss the use of class diagrams for representing associations among objects. In Section 5.4.6, we discuss the use of class diagrams for representing object attributes.

An association shows a relationship between two or more classes. For example, a `FieldOfficer` writes an `EmergencyReport` (see Figure 5-16). Identifying associations has two advantages. First, it clarifies the analysis model by making relationships between objects explicit (e.g., an `EmergencyReport` can be created by a `FieldOfficer` or a `Dispatcher`). Second, it enables the developer to discover boundary cases associated with links. Boundary cases are exceptions that need to be clarified in the model. For example, it is intuitive to assume that most `EmergencyReports` are written by one `FieldOfficer`. However, should the system support `EmergencyReports` written by more than one? Should the system allow for anonymous `EmergencyReports`? Those questions should be investigated during analysis by using domain knowledge.

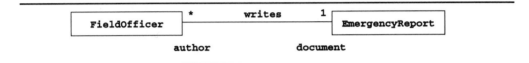

Figure 5-16   An example of association between the `EmergencyReport` and the `FieldOfficer` classes.

Associations have several properties:

- A **name**, to describe the association between the two classes (e.g., `Writes` in Figure 5-16). Association names are optional and need not be unique globally.

- A **role** at each end, identifying the function of each class with respect to the associations (e.g., `author` is the role played by `FieldOfficer` in the `Writes` association).

- A **multiplicity** at each end, identifying the possible number of instances (e.g., `*` indicates a `FieldOfficer` may write zero or more `EmergencyReports`, whereas `1` indicates that each `EmergencyReport` has exactly one `FieldOfficer` as author.

Initially, the associations between entity objects are the most important, as they reveal more information about the application domain. According to Abbott's heuristics (see Table 5-1), associations can be identified by examining verbs and verb phrases denoting a state (e.g., *has, is part of, manages, reports to, is triggered by, is contained in, talks to, includes*). Every association should be named and roles assigned to each end.

Heuristics for identifying associations
- Examine verb phrases.
- Name associations and roles precisely.
- Use qualifiers as often as possible to identify namespaces and key attributes.
- Eliminate any association that can be derived from other associations.
- Do not worry about multiplicity until the set of associations is stable.
- Avoid ravioli models: Too many associations make a model unreadable.

The object model will initially include too many associations if developers include all associations identified after examining verb phrases. In Figure 5-17, for example, we identified two relationships: the first between an `Incident` and the `EmergencyReport` that triggered its creation; the second between the `Incident` and the reporting `FieldOfficer`. Given that the `EmergencyReport` and `FieldOfficer` already have an association modeling authorship, the association between `Incident` and `FieldOfficer` is not necessary. Adding unnecessary associations complicates the model, leading to incomprehensible "ravioli models" and redundant information.

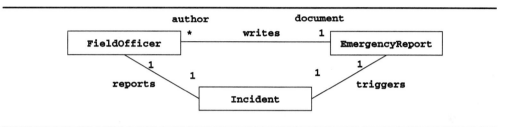

Figure 5-17   Eliminating redundant association. The receipt of an `EmergencyReport` triggers the creation of an `Incident` by a `Dispatcher`. Given that the `EmergencyReport` has an association with the `FieldOfficer` that wrote it, it is not necessary to keep an association between `FieldOfficer` and `Incident`.

Most entity objects have an identifying characteristic used by the actors to access them. `FieldOfficers` and `Dispatchers` have a badge number. `Incidents` and `Reports` are assigned numbers and are archived by date. Once the analysis model includes most classes and associations, the developers should go through each class and check how it is identified by the actors and in which context. For example, are `FieldOfficer` badge numbers unique across the universe? Across a city? A police station? If they are unique across cities, can the FRIEND system know about `FieldOfficers` from more than one city? This approach can be formalized by examining each individual class and identifying the sequence of associations that need to be traversed to access a specific instance of that class.

5.4.6   Identifying Attributes

Attributes are properties of individual objects. For example, an `EmergencyReport`, as described in Table 5-2, has an emergency type, a location, and a description property (see Figure 5-18). These are entered by a `FieldOfficer` when she reports an emergency and are subsequently tracked by the system. When identifying properties of objects, only the attributes relevant to the system should be considered. For example, each `FieldOfficer` has a social security number that is not relevant to the emergency information system. Instead, `FieldOfficers` are identified by badge number, represented by the `badgeNumber` property.

```
┌─────────────────────────────────────────────────┐
│                 EmergencyReport                 │
├─────────────────────────────────────────────────┤
│ emergencyType:{fire,traffic,other}              │
│ location:String                                 │
│ description:String                              │
├─────────────────────────────────────────────────┤
│                                                 │
│                                                 │
└─────────────────────────────────────────────────┘
```

Figure 5-18   Attributes of the `EmergencyReport` class.

Properties that are represented by objects are not attributes. For example, every `EmergencyReport` has an author represented by an association to the `FieldOfficer` class. Developers should identify as many associations as possible before identifying attributes to avoid confusing attributes and objects. Attributes have:

- a **name** identifying them within an object. For example, an `EmergencyReport` may have a `reportType` attribute and an `emergencyType` attribute. The `reportType` describes the kind of report being filed (e.g., initial report, request for resource, final report). The `emergencyType` describes the type of emergency (e.g., fire, traffic, other). To avoid confusion, these attributes should not be both called `type`.

- A brief **description**.

- A **type** describing the legal values it can take. For example, the `description` attribute of an `EmergencyReport` is a string. The `emergencyType` attribute is an enumeration that can take one of three values: `fire`, `traffic`, `other`.

Attributes can be identified using Abbott's heuristics (see Table 5-1). In particular, noun phrases followed by a possessive phrases (e.g., the description of an emergency) or an adjective phrase (e.g., the emergency description) should be examined. In the case of entity objects, any property that needs to be stored by the system is a candidate attribute.

Note that attributes represent the least stable part of the object model. Often, attributes are discovered or added late in the development when the system is evaluated by the users. Unless the added attributes are associated with additional functionality, the added attributes do not

---

Heuristics for identifying attributes[a]
- Examine possessive phrases.
- Represent stored state as attributes of entity object.
- Describe each attribute.
- Do not represent an attribute as an object, use an association instead (see Section 5.4.5).
- Do not waste time describing fine details before the object structure is stable.

---

a.   Adapted from [Rumbaugh et al., 1991].

entail major changes in the object (and system) structure. For these reasons, the developers need not spend excessive resources in identifying and detailing attributes representing less important aspects of the system. These attributes can be added later when the analysis model or the user interface sketches are validated.

5.4.7 Modeling the Montrivial Behavior of Individual Objects

Sequence diagrams are used to distribute behavior across objects and to identify operations. Sequence diagrams represent the behavior of the system from the perspective of a single use case. Statechart diagrams represent behavior from the perspective of a single object. Viewing behavior from the perspective of each object enables the developer, on the one hand, to identify missing use cases, and, on the other hand, to build a more-formal description of the behavior of the object. Note that it is not necessary to build statecharts for every class in the system. Only the statecharts of objects with an extended lifespan and nontrivial behavior are worth constructing.

Figure 5-19 displays a statechart for the `Incident` class. The examination of this statechart may help the developer check if there are use cases for documenting, closing, and archiving `Incidents`. Note that Figure 5-19 is a high-level statechart and does not model the state changes an `Incident` goes through while it is active (e.g., when resources are assigned to it). Such behavior can be modeled by associating a nested statechart with the `Active` state.

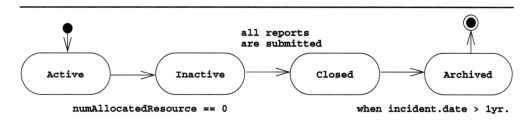

Figure 5-19 UML statechart for `Incident`.

5.4.8 Modeling Generalization Relationships Between Objects

Generalization is used to eliminate redundancy from the analysis model. If two or more classes share attributes or behavior, the similarities are consolidated into a superclass. For example, `Dispatchers` and `FieldOfficers` both have a `badgeNumber` attribute that serves to identify them within a city. `FieldOfficers` and `Dispatchers` are both `PoliceOfficers` who are assigned different functions. To model explicitly this similarity, we introduce an abstract *PoliceOfficer* class from which the `FieldOfficer` and `Dispatcher` classes inherit (see Figure 5-20).

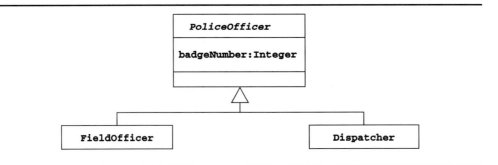

Figure 5-20   An example of inheritance relationship (UML class diagram).

5.4.9   Reviewing the Analysis Model

The analysis model is built incrementally and iteratively. The analysis model is seldom correct or even complete on the first pass. Several iterations with the client and the user are necessary before the analysis model converges toward a correct specification usable by the developers for proceeding to design and implementation. For example, an omission discovered during analysis will lead to adding or extending a use case in the system specification, which may lead to eliciting more information from the user.

Once the analysis model becomes stable (i.e., when the number of changes to the model are minimal and the scope of the changes localized), the analysis model is reviewed, first by the developers (i.e., internal reviews), then jointly by the developers and the client. The goal of the review is to make sure that the system specification is correct, complete, consistent, and realistic. Note that developers should be prepared to discover errors downstream and make changes to the specification. It is, however, a worthwhile investment to catch as many requirements errors upstream. The review can be facilitated by a checklist or a list of questions. Below are example questions adapted from [Jacobson et al., 1999] and [Rumbaugh et al., 1991].

The following questions should be asked to ensure that the model is *correct*:
- Is the glossary of entity objects understandable by the user?
- Do abstract classes correspond to user-level concepts?
- Are all descriptions in accordance with the users' definitions?
- Do all entity and boundary objects have meaningful noun phrases as names?
- Do all use cases and control objects have meaningful verb phrases as names?
- Are all error cases described and handled?
- Are the start-up and the shut-down phases of the system described?
- Are the administration functions of the system described?

The following questions should be asked to ensure that the model is *complete*:
- For each object: Is it needed by any use case? In which use case is it created? modified? destroyed? Can it be accessed from an boundary object?

- For each attribute: When is it set? What is its type? Should it be a qualifier?
- For each association: When is it traversed? Why was the specific multiplicity chosen? Can associations with one-to-many and many-to-many multiplicities be qualified?
- For each control object: Does it have the necessary associations to access the objects participating in its corresponding use case?

The following questions should be asked to ensure that the model is *consistent*:

- Are there multiple classes or use cases with the same name?
- Do entities (e.g., use cases, classes, attributes) with similar names denote similar phenomena?
- Are all entities described at the same level of detail?
- Are there objects with similar attributes and associations that are not in the same generalization hierarchy?

The following questions should be asked to ensure that the system described by the analysis model is *realistic*:

- Are there any novel features in the system? Were there any studies or prototypes built to ensure their feasibility?
- Can the performance and reliability requirements be met? Were these requirements verified by any prototypes running on the selected hardware?

5.4.10 Analysis Summary

The requirements activity is highly iterative and incremental. Chunks of functionality are sketched and proposed to the users and the client. The client adds additional requirements, criticizes existing functionality, and modifies existing requirements. The developers investigate nonfunctional requirements through prototyping and technology studies and challenge each proposed requirement. Initially, requirements elicitation resembles a brainstorming activity. As the description of the system grows and the requirements become more concrete, developers need to extend and modify the analysis model in a more orderly manner in order to manage the complexity of information.

Figure 5-21 depicts a typical sequence of the analysis activities we described in this chapter. The users, developers, and client are involved in the *Define use cases* and develop an initial use case model. They identify a number of concepts and build a glossary of participating objects. The developers then classify these objects into entity, boundary, and control objects (in *Define entity objects*, Section 5.4.1, *Define boundary objects*, Section 5.4.2, and *Define control objects*, Section 5.4.3). These activities occur in a tight loop until most of the functionality of the system has been identified as use cases with names and brief descriptions. Then, the developers construct sequence diagrams to identify any missing objects (*Define interactions*, Section 5.4.4). Once all entity objects have been named and briefly described, the analysis model should remain fairly stable as it is refined.

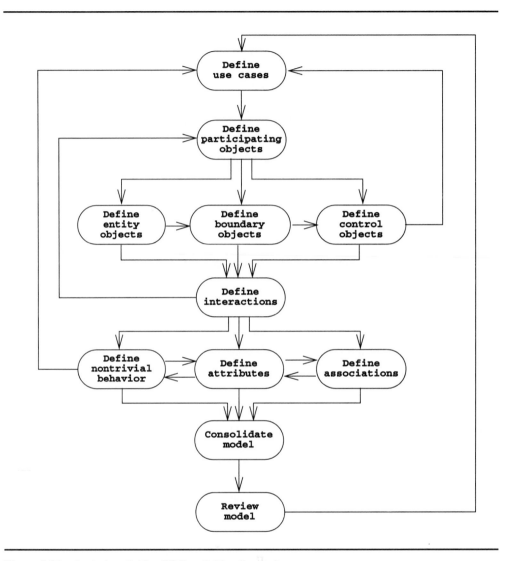

Figure 5-21   Analysis activities (UML activities diagram).

Define interesting behavior (Section 5.4.7), *Define attributes* (Section 5.4.6), and *Define associations* (Section 5.4.5) constitute the refinement of the analysis model. These three activities represent a tight loop during which the state of the objects and their associations are extracted from the sequence diagrams and detailed. The use cases are then modified to account for any changes in functionality. This phase may lead to the identification of an additional chunk of functionality in the form of additional use cases. The overall process is then repeated incrementally for these new use cases.

During *Consolidate model* (Section 5.4.8), the developers solidify the model by introducing qualifiers, generalization relationships, and suppressing redundancies. During *Review model* (Section 5.4.9), the client, users, and developers examine the model for correctness, consistency, completeness, and realism. The project schedule should plan for multiple reviews to ensure high quality of the requirements and to allow space for learning the requirements activity. However, once the model reaches the point where most modifications are cosmetic, system design should proceed. There will be a point during requirements where no more problems can be anticipated without further information from prototyping, usability studies, technology surveys, or system design. Getting every detail right becomes a wasteful exercise: Some of these details will become irrelevant by the next change. Management should recognize this point and initiate the next phase in the project.

5.5 Managing Analysis

In this section, we discuss issues related to managing the analysis activities in a multiteam development project. The primary challenge in managing the requirements in such a project is to maintain consistency while using so many resources. In the end, the requirements analysis document should describe a single coherent system understandable to a single person.

We first describe a document template that can be used to document the results of analysis (Section 5.5.1). Next, we describe the role assignment to analysis (Section 5.5.2). We then address communication issues during analysis. Next, we address management issues related to the iterative and incremental nature of requirements (Section 5.5.4).

5.5.1 Documenting Analysis

As we saw in the previous chapter, the requirements elicitation and analysis activities are documented in the Requirements Analysis Document (RAD). Sections 1–3.5.2 have already been written during requirements elicitation. During analysis, we revise these sections as ambiguities and new functionality is discovered. The main effort, however, focuses on writing the sections documenting the analysis object model (3.5.3–3.5.4).

Section 3.5.3, Object models, documents in detail all the objects we identified, their attributes, and, in case we used sequence diagrams, operations. As each object is described with textual definitions, relationships among objects are illustrated with class diagrams.

Section 3.5.4, Dynamic models, documents the behavior of the object model, in terms of statechart diagrams and sequence diagrams. Although this information is redundant with the use case model, dynamic models enable us to more precisely represent complex behaviors, including use cases involving many actors.

The RAD, once completed and published, will be baselined and put under configuration management. The revision history section of the RAD will provide a history of changes as a list of the author responsible for the change, date of change, and brief description of the change.

Requirements Analysis Document
1. Introduction
2. Current system
3. Proposed system
    3.1 Overview
    3.2 Functional requirements
    3.3 Nonfunctional requirements
    3.4 Pseudo requirements
    3.5 System models
        3.5.1 Scenarios
        3.5.2 Use case model
        3.5.3 Object model
            3.5.3.1 Data dictionary
            3.5.3.2 Class diagrams
        3.5.4 Dynamic models
        3.5.5 User interface—navigational paths and screen mock-ups
4. Glossary

5.5.2   Assigning Responsibilities

Analysis requires the participation of a wide range of individuals. The target user provides application domain knowledge. The client funds the project and coordinates the user side of the effort. The analyst elicits application domain knowledge and formalizes it. Developers provide feedback on feasibility and cost. The project manager coordinates the effort on the development side. For large systems, many users, analysts, and developers may be involved, introducing additional challenges during for integration and communication requirements of the project. These challenges can be met by assigning well-defined roles and scopes to individuals. There are three main types of roles: generation of information, integration, and review.

- The **user** is the application domain expert, who generates information about the current system, the environment of the future system, and the tasks it should support. Each user corresponds to one or more actors and helps identify their associated use cases.
- The **client**, an integration role, defines the scope of the system based on user requirements. Different users may have different views of the system, either because they will benefit from different parts of the system (e.g., a dispatcher vs. a field officer) or because the users have different opinions or expectations about the future system. The client serves as an integrator of application domain information and resolves inconsistencies in user expectations.
- The **analyst** is the development domain expert, who models the current system and generates information about the future system. Each analysis is initially responsible for detailing one or more use cases. For a set of use cases, the analysis will identify a number

of objects, their associations, and their attributes, using the techniques outlined in Section 5.4.

- The **architect**, an integration role, unifies the use case and object models from a system point of view. Different analysts may have different styles of modeling and different views of the parts of the systems that they are not responsible for. Although analysts work together and will most likely resolve differences as they progress through analysis, the role of the architect is necessary to provide a system philosophy and to identify omissions in the requirements.

- The **document editor** is responsible for the low-level integration of the document. The document editor is responsible for the overall format of the document and its index.

- The **configuration manager** is responsible for maintaining a revision history of the document as well as traceability information relating the RAD with other documents (such as the System Design Document; see Chapter 6, *System Design*).

- The **reviewer** validates the RAD for correctness, completeness, consistency, realism, verifiability, and traceability. Users, clients, developers, or other individuals may become reviewers during requirements validation. Individuals that have not yet been involved in the development represent excellent reviewers, because they are more able to identify ambiguities and areas that need clarification.

The size of the system determines the number of different users and analysts that are needed to elicit and model the requirements. In all cases, there should be one integrating role on the client side and one on the development side. In the end, the requirements, however large the system, should be understandable by a single individual knowledgeable in the application domain.

5.5.3 Communicating about Analysis

The task of communicating information is most challenging during requirements elicitation and analysis. Contributing factors include:

- *Different background of participants.* Users, clients, and developers have different domains of expertise and use different vocabularies to describe the same concepts.

- *Different expectations of stakeholders.* Users, clients, and managements have different objectives when defining the system. Users want a system that supports their current work processes, with no interference or threat to their current position (e.g., an improved system often translates into the elimination of current positions). The client wants to maximize return on investment. Management wants to deliver the system on time. Different expectations and different stakes in the project can lead to a reluctance to share information and to report problems in a timely manner.

- *New teams.* Requirements elicitation and analysis often marks the beginning of a new project. This translates into new participants and new team assignments, and, thus, into a ramp-up period during which team members must learn to work together.

- *Evolving system.* When a new system is developed from scratch, terms and concepts related to the new system are in flux during most of the analysis and the system design. A term today may have a different meaning tomorrow.

No requirements method or communication mechanism can address problems related to internal politics and information hiding. Conflicting objectives and competition will always be part of large development projects. A few simple guidelines, however, can help in managing the complexity of conflicting views of the system:

- *Define clear territories.* Defining roles as described in Section 5.5.2 is part of this activity. This also includes the definition of private and public discussion forums. For example, each team may have a discussion database as described in Chapter 3, *Project Communication*, and discussion with the client is done on a separate client database. The client should not have access to the internal database. Similarly, developers should not interfere with client/user internal politics.

- *Define clear objectives and success criteria.* The codefinition of clear, measurable, and verifiable objectives and success criteria by both the client and the developers facilitates the resolution of conflicts. Note that defining a clear and verifiable objective is a nontrivial task, given that it is easier to leave objectives open ended. The objectives and the success criteria of the project should be documented in Section 1.3 of the RAD.

- *Brainstorm.* Putting all the stakeholders in the same room and having them quickly generate solutions and definitions can remove many barriers in the communication. Conducting reviews as a reciprocal activity (i.e., reviewing deliverables from both the client and the developers during the same session) has a similar effect.

Brainstorming, and more generally the cooperative development of requirements, can lead to the definition of shared, ad hoc notations for supporting the communication. Storyboards, user interface sketches, and high-level dataflow diagrams often appear spontaneously. As the information about the application domain and the new system accrue, it is critical that a precise and structured notation be used. In UML, developers employ use cases and scenarios for communicating with the client and the users, and use object diagrams, sequence diagrams, and statecharts to communicate with other developers (see Sections 4.4 and 5.4). Moreover, the latest release of the requirements should be available to all participants. Maintaining a live online version of the requirements analysis document with an up-to-date change history facilitates the timely propagation of changes across the project.

5.5.4   Iterating Over the Analysis Model

Analysis occurs iteratively and incrementally, often in parallel with other development activities such as system design and implementation. Note, however, that the unrestricted modification and extension of the analysis model can only result in chaos, especially when a large number of participants are involved. Iterations and increments need to be carefully managed and requests for changes tracked once the requirements are baselined. The requirements activity can be viewed as several steps (brainstorming, solidification, maturity) converging toward a stable model.

Brainstorming

Before any other development activity is initiated, requirements is a brainstorming process. Everything—concepts and the terms used to refer to them—changes. The objective of a brainstorming process is to generate as many ideas as possible without necessarily organizing them. During this stage, iterations are rapid and far reaching.

Solidification

Once the client and the developers converge on a common idea, define the boundaries of the system, and agree on a set of standard terms, solidification starts. Functionality is organized into groups of use cases with their corresponding interfaces. Groups of functionality are allocated to different teams that are responsible for detailing their corresponding use cases. During this stage, iterations are rapid but localized.

Maturity

Changes at the higher level are still possible but are more difficult, and, thus, are made more carefully. Each team is responsible for the use cases and object models related to the functionality they have been assigned. A cross-functional team, the architecture team, made of representatives of each team, is responsible for ensuring the integration of the requirements (e.g., naming).

Once the client signs off the requirements, modification to the analysis model should address omissions and errors. Developers, in particular the architecture team, need to ensure that the consistency of the model is not compromised. The requirements model is under configuration management and changes should be propagated to existing design models. Iterations are slow and often localized.

The number of features and functions of a system will always increase with time. Each change, however, can threaten the integrity of the system. The risk of introducing more problems with late changes results from the loss of information in the project. The dependencies across functions are not all captured; many assumptions may be implicit and forgotten by the time the change is made. Often, the change responds to a problem, in which case there is a lot of pressure to implement it, resulting in only a superficial examination of the consequence of the change. When new features and functions are added to the system, they should be challenged with the following questions: Were they requested by the client? Are they necessary or are they embellishments? Should they be part of a separate, focused utility program instead of part of the base system? What is the impact of the changes to existing functions in terms of consistency, interface, reliability? Are the changes core requirements or optional features?

When changes are necessary, the client and developer define the scope of the change and its desired outcome and change the analysis model. Given that a complete analysis model exists for the system, specifying new functionality is easier (although implementing it is more difficult).

5.5.5   Client Sign-off

The client sign-off represents the acceptance of the analysis model (as documented by the requirements analysis document) by the client. The client and the developers converge on a single idea and agree about the functions and features that the system will have. In addition, they agree on:

- a list of priorities
- a revision process
- a list of criteria that will be used to accept or reject the system
- a schedule and a budget

Prioritizing system functions allows the developers to understand better the client's expectations. In its simplest form, it allows developers to separate bells and whistles from essential features of the system. In general, it allows developers to deliver the system in incremental chunks: Essential functions are delivered first, additional chunks are delivered depending on the evaluation of the first chunk. Even if the system is to be delivered as a single, complete package, prioritizing functions enables the client to clearly communicate what is important to her and where the emphasis of the development should be. Figure 5-22 provides an example of a priority scheme.

Each function shall be assigned one of the following priorities

- **High priority**—A high-priority feature must be demonstrated successfully during client acceptance.
- **Medium priority**—A medium-priority feature must be taken into account in the system design and the object design. It will be implemented and demonstrated in the second iteration of the system development.
- **Low priority**—A low-priority feature illustrates how the system could be extended in the longer term.

Figure 5-22   An example of a priority scheme for requirements.

A revision process enables the client and developer to define how changes in the requirements are to be dealt with after the sign-off. The requirements will change, either because of errors, omissions, changes in the operating environment, changes in the application domain, or changes in technology. Defining a revision process up front encourages changes to be communicated across the project and reduces the number of surprises in the long term. Note that a change process need not be bureaucratic or require excessive overhead. It can be as simple as naming a person responsible for receiving change requests, approving changes, and tracking their implementation. Figure 5-23 depicts a more complex example in which changes are designed and reviewed by the client before they are implemented in the system. In all cases, acknowledging that requirements cannot be frozen (but only baselined) will benefit the project.

The list of acceptance criteria is revised prior to sign-off. The requirements elicitation and analysis activity clarifies many aspects of the system, including the nonfunctional requirements with which the system should comply and the relative importance of each function. By restating

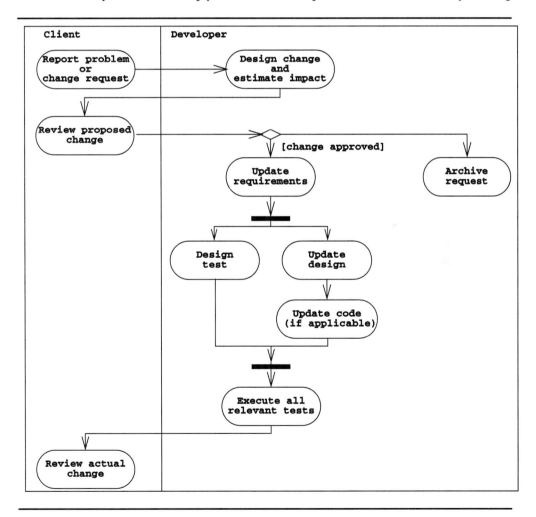

Figure 5-23   An example of a revision process (UML activity diagram).

the acceptance criteria at sign-off, the client ensures that the developers are updated about any changes in client expectations.

The budget and schedule are revisited after the analysis model becomes stable. We describe in Chapter 11, *Project Management*, issues related to cost estimation.

Whether the client sign-off is a contractual agreement or whether the project is already governed by a prior contract, it is an important milestone in the project. It represents the convergence of client and developer on a single set of functional definitions of the system and a single set of expectations. The acceptance of the requirements analysis document is more critical than any other document, given that many activities depend on the analysis model.

5.6 Exercises

1. Consider a file system with a graphical user interface, such as Macintosh's Finder, Microsoft's Windows Explorer, or Linux's KDE. The following objects were identified from a use case describing how to copy a file from a floppy disk to a hard disk: `File`, `Icon`, `TrashCan`, `Folder`, `Disk`, `Pointer`. Specify which are entity objects, which are boundary objects, and which are control objects.

2. Assuming the same file system as before, consider a scenario consisting of selecting a file on a floppy, dragging it to Folder and releasing the mouse. Identify and define at least one control object associated with this scenario.

3. Arrange the objects listed in Exercises 1 and 2 horizontally on a sequence diagram, the boundary objects to the left, then the control object you identified, and finally, the entity objects. Draw the sequence of interactions resulting from dropping the file into a folder. For now, ignore the exceptional cases.

4. Examining the sequence diagram you produced in Exercise 4, identify the associations between these objects.

5. Identify the attributes of each object that are relevant to this scenario (moving a file from a floppy disk to a hard disk). Also consider the exception cases "There is already a file with that name in the folder" and "There is no more space on disk."

6. Consider the object model in Figure 5-24 (adapted from [Jackson, 1995]): Given your knowledge of the Gregorian calendar, list all the problems with this model. Modify it to correct each of them.

7. Consider the object model of Figure 5-24. Using association multiplicity only, can you modify the model such that a developer unfamiliar with the Gregorian calendar could deduce the number of days in each month? Identify additional classes if necessary.

8. Consider a traffic light system at a four-way crossroads (e.g., two roads intersecting at right angles). Assume the simplest algorithm for cycling through the lights (e.g., all traffic on one road is allowed to go through the crossroad while the other traffic is stopped). Identify the states of this system and draw a statechart describing them. Remember that each individual traffic light has three states (i.e. green, yellow, and red).

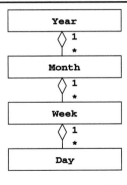

Figure 5-24 A naive model of the Gregorian calendar (UML class diagram).

References

[Abbott, 1983]   R. Abbott, "Program design by informal English descriptions," *Communications of the ACM,* Vol. 26, No. 11, 1983.

[Booch, 1994]   G. Booch, *Object-Oriented Analysis and Design with Applications,* 2nd ed. Benjamin/Cummings, Redwood City, CA, 1994.

[Booch et al., 1998]   G. Booch, J. Rumbaugh, & I. Jacobson, *The Unified Modeling Language User Guide.* Addison-Wesley, Reading, MA, 1998.

[Bruegge et al., 1994]   B. Bruegge, K. O'Toole, & D. Rothenberger, "Design considerations for an accident management system," *Proceedings of the Second International Conference on Cooperative Information Systems,* M. Brodie, M. Jarke, M. Papazoglou (eds.),(University of Toronto Canada), pp. 90–100, May 1994.

[De Marco, 1978]   T. De Marco, *Structured Analysis and System Specification,* Yourdon, New York, 1978.

[Fowler, 1997]   M. Fowler, *Analysis Patterns: Reusable Object Models,* Addison-Wesley, Reading, MA, 1997.

[FRIEND, 1994]   *FRIEND Project Documentation,* School of Computer Science, Carnegie Mellon Univ., Pittsburgh, PA, 1994.

[Harel, 1987]   D. Harel, "Statecharts: A Visual Formalism for Complex Systems," *Science of Computer Programming,* pp. 231–274, 1987.

[Jacobson et al., 1992]   I. Jacobson, M. Christerson, P. Jonsson, & G. Overgaard, *Object-Oriented Software Engineering—A Use Case Driven Approach.* Addison-Wesley, Reading, MA, 1992.

[Jacobson et al., 1999]   I Jacobson, G. Booch, & J. Rumbaugh, *The Unified Software Development Process.* Addison-Wesley, Reading, MA, 1999.

[Jackson, 1995]   M. Jackson, *Software Requirements & Specifications: A Lexicon of Practice, Principles and Prejudices.* Addison-Wesley, Reading, MA, 1995.

[Larman, 1998]   C. Larman, *Applying UML and Patterns: An Introduction to Object-Oriented Analysis and Design.* Prentice Hall, Upper Saddle River, NJ, 1998.

[Meyer, 1997]   Bertrand Meyer, *Object-Oriented Software Construction,* 2nd ed. Prentice Hall, Upper Saddle River, NJ, 1997.

[Rumbaugh et al., 1991]   J. Rumbaugh, M. Blaha, W. Premerlani, F. Eddy, & W. Lorensen, *Object-Oriented Modeling and Design.* Prentice Hall, Englewood Cliffs, NJ, 1991.

[Wirfs-Brock et al., 1990]   R. Wirfs-Brock, B. Wilkerson, & Lauren Wiener, *Designing Object-Oriented Software.* Prentice Hall, Englewood Cliffs, NJ, 1990.

6

System Design

There are two ways of constructing a software design: One way is to make it so simple that there are obviously no deficiencies, and the other way is to make it so complicated that there are no obvious deficiencies.
—C.A.R. Hoare

System design is the transformation of the analysis model into a system design model. During system design, developers define the design goals of the project and decompose the system into smaller subsystems that can be realized by individual teams. Developers also select strategies for building the system, such as the hardware/software platform on which the system will run, the persistent data management strategy, the global control flow, the access control policy, and the handling of boundary conditions. The result of system design is a model that includes a clear description of each of these strategies, a subsystem decomposition, and a UML deployment diagram representing the hardware/software mapping of the system.

System design is not algorithmic. Professionals and academics have, however, developed pattern solutions to common problems and defined notations for representing software architectures. In this chapter, we first present these building blocks and then discuss the design activities that have impact on these buildings blocks. In particular, system design includes:

- the definition of design goals
- the decomposition of the system into subsystems
- the selection of off-the-shelf and legacy components
- the mapping of subsystem to hardware
- the selection of a persistent data management infrastructure
- the selection of an access control policy
- the selection of a global control flow mechanism
- the handling of boundary conditions

We conclude this chapter by describing management issues that are related to system design.

6.1 Introduction: A Floor Plan Example

System design, object design, and implementation constitute the construction of the system. During these three activities, developers fill the gap between the system specification, produced during requirements elicitation and analysis, and the system that is delivered to the users. System design is the first step in this process and focuses on decomposing the system into manageable parts. During requirements elicitation and analysis, we concentrated on the purpose and the functionality of the system. During system design, we focus on the processes, data structures, and software and hardware components necessary to implement it. The challenge of system design is that many conflicting criteria and constraints need to be met when decomposing the system.

Consider, for example, the task of designing a residential house. After agreeing with the client on the number of rooms and floors, the size of the living area, and the location of the house, the architect must design the floor plan, that is, where the walls, doors, and windows should be located. He must do so according to a number of functional requirements: The kitchen should be close to the dining room and the garage, the bathroom should be close to the bedrooms, and so on. The architect can also rely on a number of standards when establishing the dimensions of each room and the location of the door: Kitchen cabinets come in fixed increments and beds come in standard sizes. Note, however, that the architect does not need to know the exact contents of each room and the layout of the furniture; on the contrary, these decisions should be delayed and left to the client.

Figure 6-1 shows three successive revisions to a floor plan for a residential house. We set out to satisfy the following constraints:

1. This house should have two bedrooms, a study, a kitchen, and a living room area.
2. The overall distance the occupants walk every day should be minimized.
3. The use of daylight should be maximized.

To satisfy the above constraints, we assume that most of the walking will be done between the entrance door and the kitchen, when groceries are unloaded from the car, and between the kitchen and the living/dining area, when dishes are carried before and after the meals. The next walking path to minimize is the path from the bedrooms to the bathrooms. We assume that the occupants of the house will spend most of their time in the dining area and in the master bedroom.

In the first version of our floor plan (at the top of Figure 6-1), we find that the dining room is too far from the kitchen. To address this problem, we exchange it with bedroom 2 (see gray arrows in Figure 6-1). This also has the advantage of moving the living room to the south wall of the house. In the second revision, we find that the kitchen and the stairs are too far from the entrance door. To address this problem, we move the entrance door to the north wall. This allows us to rearrange bedroom 2 and move the bathroom closer to both bedrooms. The living area increased, and we satisfied all constraints we originally set out.

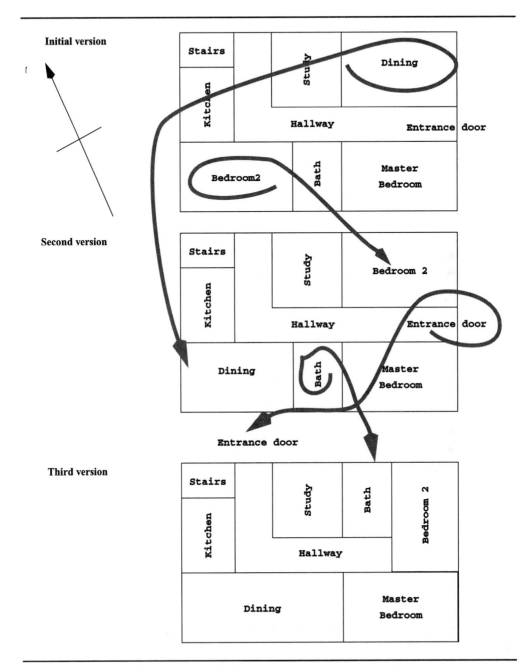

Figure 6-1 Example of floor plan design. Three successive versions show how we minimize walking distance and take advantage of sunlight.

At this point, we can position the doors and the windows of each room to meet localized requirements. Once this is done, we have completed the design of the floor, without detailed knowledge of the layout of each individual room. Plans for plumbing, electrical lines, and heating ducts can proceed.

The design of a floor plan in architecture is similar to system design in software engineering. The whole is divided into simpler components (i.e., rooms, subsystems) and interfaces (i.e., doors, services), while taking into account nonfunctional (i.e., living area, response time) and functional (i.e., number of bedrooms, use cases) requirements. System design impacts implementation activities (i.e., the kitchen layout, the coding complexity of individual subsystems) and results in costly rework if changed later (i.e., moving walls, changing subsystem interfaces). The design of individual components is delayed until later.

In Section 6.2, we provide you with a bird's eye view of system design and its relationship to analysis. In Section 6.3, we describe the concept of subsystems and subsystem decomposition. In Section 6.4, we describe system design activities and use an example to illustrate how these building blocks can be used together. In Section 6.5, we describe management issues related to system design.

6.2 An Overview of System Design

Analysis results in the requirements model described by the following products:

- a set of *nonfunctional requirements* and *constraints,* such as maximum response time, minimum throughput, reliability, operating system platform, and so on
- a *use case model,* describing the functionality of the system from the actors' point of view
- an *object model,* describing the entities manipulated by the system
- a *sequence diagram* for each use case, showing the sequence of interactions among objects participating in the use case

The analysis model describes the system completely from the actors' point of view and serves as the basis of communication between the client and the developers. The analysis model, however, does not contain information about the internal structure of the system, its hardware configuration, or, more generally, how the system should be realized. System design is the first step in this direction. System design results in the following products:

- a list of *design goals*, describing the qualities of the system that developers should optimize
- *software architecture*, describing the subsystem decomposition in terms of subsystem responsibilities, dependencies among subsystems, subsystem mapping to hardware, and major policy decisions such as control flow, access control, and data storage

The design goals are derived from the nonfunctional requirements. Design goals guide the decisions to be made by the developers especially when trade-offs are needed. The subsystem decomposition constitutes the bulk of system design. Developers divide the system into manageable pieces to deal with complexity: Each subsystem is assigned to a team and realized independently. In order for this to be possible, though, developers need to address system-wide issues when decomposing the system. In particular, they need to address the following issues:

- *Hardware/software mapping:* What is the hardware configuration of the system? Which node is responsible for which functionality? How is communication between nodes realized? Which services are realized using existing software components? How are these components encapsulated? Addressing hardware/software mapping issues often leads to the definition of *additional subsystems* dedicated to moving data from one node to another, dealing with concurrency, and reliability issues. Off-the-shelf components enable developers to realize complex services more economically. User interface packages and database management systems are prime examples of off-the-shelf components. Components, however, should be encapsulated to minimize dependencies on a particular component: A competing vendor may come up with a better component.
- *Data management:* Which data need to be persistent? Where should persistent data be stored? How are they accessed? Persistent data represents a bottleneck in the system on many different fronts: Most functionality in system is concerned with creating or manipulating persistent data. For this reason, access to the data should be fast and reliable. If retrieving data is slow, the whole system will be slow. If data corruption is likely, complete system failure is likely. These issues need to be addressed consistently at the system level. Often, this leads to the selection of a database management system and of an *additional subsystem* dedicated to the management of persistent data.
- *Access control:* Who can access which data? Can access control change dynamically? How is access control specified and realized? Access control and security are system-wide issues. The access control must be consistent across the system; in other words, the policy used to specify who can and cannot access certain data should be the same *across all subsystems.*
- *Control flow:* How does the system sequence operations? Is the system event driven? Can it handle more than one user interaction at a time? The choice of control flow has an impact on the interfaces of subsystems. If an event-driven control flow is selected, subsystems will provide event handlers. If threads are selected, subsystems need to guarantee mutual exclusion in critical sections.
- *Boundary conditions:* How is the system initialized? How is it shut down? How are exceptional cases detected and handled? System initialization and shutdown often represent the larger part of the complexity of a system, especially in a distributed environment. Initialization, shutdown, and exception handling have an impact on the interface of *all subsystems.*

Figure 6-2 depicts the activities of system design. Each activity addresses one of the issues we described above. Addressing any one of these issues can lead to changes in the subsystem decomposition and to raising new issues. As you will see when we describe each of these activities, system design is a highly iterative activity, constantly leading to the identification of new subsystems, the modification of existing subsystems, and system-wide revisions that impact all subsystems. But first, let us describe the concept of subsystem in more detail.

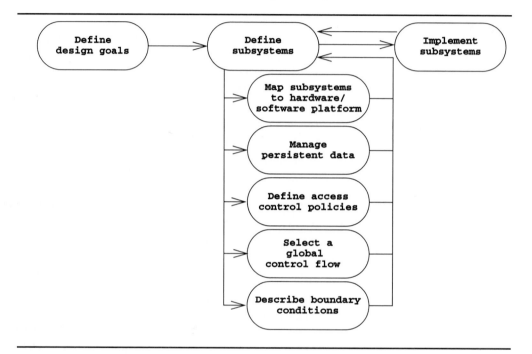

Figure 6-2   The activities of system design (UML activity diagram).

6.3 System Design Concepts

In this section, we describe subsystem decompositions and their properties in more detail. First, we define the concept of **subsystem** and its relationship to classes (Section 6.3.1). Next, we look at the interface of subsystems (Section 6.3.2): subsystems provide **services** to other subsystems. A service is a set of related operations that share a common purpose. During system design, we define the subsystems in terms of the services they provide. Later, during object design, we define the subsystem interface in terms of the operations they provide. Next, we look at two properties of subsystems: **coupling** and **coherence** (Section 6.3.3). Coupling measures the dependencies between two subsystems, whereas coherence measures the dependencies among classes within a subsystem. Ideal subsystem decomposition should minimize coupling and maximize coherence. Next, we look at **layering** and **partitioning**, two techniques for relating subsystems to each other (Section 6.3.4). Layering allows a system to be organized as a hierarchy of subsystems, each providing higher level services to the subsystem above it by using lower level services from the subsystems below it. Partitioning organizes subsystems as peers that mutually provide different services to each other. In Section 6.3.5, we describe a number of typical software architectures that are found in practice. Finally, in Section 6.3.6, we describe UML deployment diagrams, which we use to represent the mapping between software subsystems and hardware components.

6.3.1   Subsystems and Classes

In Chapter 2, *Modeling with UML*, we introduced the distinction between application domain and solution domain. In order to reduce the complexity of the application domain, we identified smaller parts called classes and organized them into packages. Similarly, to reduce the complexity of the solution domain, we decompose a system into simpler parts, called subsystems, which are made of a number of solution domain classes. In the case of complex subsystems, we recursively apply this principle and decompose a subsystem into simpler subsystems (see Figure 6-3).

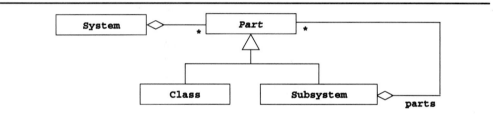

Figure 6-3   Subsystem decomposition (UML class diagram).

For example, the accident management system we previously described can be decomposed into a DispatcherInterface subsystem, implementing the user interface for the Dispatcher; a FieldOfficerInterface subsystem, implementing the user interface for the FieldOfficer; an IncidentManagement subsystem, implementing the creation, modification, and storage of Incidents; and a Notification subsystem, implementing the communication between FieldOfficer terminals and Dispatcher stations. This subsystem decomposition is depicted in Figure 6-4 using UML packages.

Several programming languages (e.g., Java and Modula-2) provide constructs for modeling subsystems (packages in Java, modules in Modula-2). In other languages, such as C or C++, subsystems are not explicitly modeled, in which case, developers use conventions for grouping classes (e.g., a subsystem can be represented as a directory containing all the files implementing the subsystem). Whether or not subsystems are explicitly represented in the programming language, developers need to carefully document the subsystem decomposition as subsystems are usually realized by different teams.

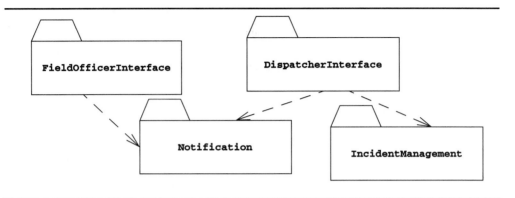

Figure 6-4   Subsystem decomposition for an accident management system (UML class diagram, collapsed view). Subsystems are shown as UML packages. Dashed arrows indicate dependencies between subsystems.

6.3.2   Services and Subsystem Interfaces

A subsystem is characterized by the **services** it provides to other subsystems. A service is a set of related operations that share a common purpose. A subsystem providing a notification service, for example, defines operations to send notices, look up notification channels, and subscribe and unsubscribe to a channel.

The set of operations of a subsystem that are available to other subsystems form the **subsystem interface**. The subsystem interface, also referred to as the application programmer interface (API), includes the name of the operations, their parameters, their types, and their return values. System design focuses on defining the services provided by each subsystem, that is, enumerating the operations, their parameters, and their high-level behavior. Object design will focus on defining the subsystem interfaces, that is, the type of the parameters and the return value of each operation.

The definition of a subsystem in terms of the services it provides helps us focus on its interface as opposed to its implementation. A good subsystem interface should provide as little information about its implementation. This allows us to minimize the impact of change when we revise the implementation of a subsystem. More generally, we want to minimize the impact of change by minimizing the dependencies among subsystems.

6.3.3   Coupling and Coherence

Coupling is the strength of dependencies between two subsystems. If two subsystems are loosely coupled, they are relatively independent, and thus, modifications to one of the subsystems will have little impact on the other. If two subsystems are strongly coupled, modifications to one subsystem is likely to have impact on the other. A desirable property of a subsystem decomposition is that subsystems are as loosely coupled as possible. This minimizes the impact that errors or future changes have on the correct operation of the system.

Consider, for example, a compiler in which a parse tree is produced by the syntax analysis subsystem and handed over to the semantic analysis subsystem. Both subsystems access and modify the parse tree. An efficient way for sharing large amounts of data is to allow both subsystems to access the nodes of the tree via attributes. This introduces, however, a tight coupling: Both subsystems need to know the exact structure of the parse tree and its invariants. Figures 6-5 and 6-6 show the effect of changing the parse tree data structure for two cases: The left columns show the class interfaces when attributes are used for sharing data; the right columns show the class interfaces when operations are used. Because both the syntax analyzer and the semantic analyzer depend on these classes, both subsystems would need to be modified and retested in the case depicted by the left column. In general, sharing data via attributes increases coupling and should be avoided.

Coherence is the strength of dependencies within a subsystem. If a subsystem contains many objects that are related to each other and perform similar tasks, its coherence is high. If a subsystem contains a number of unrelated objects, its coherence is low. A desirable property of a subsystem decomposition is that it leads to subsystems with high coherence.

For example, consider a decision tracking system for recording design problems, discussions, alternative evaluations, decisions, and their implementation in terms of tasks (see Figure 6-7).

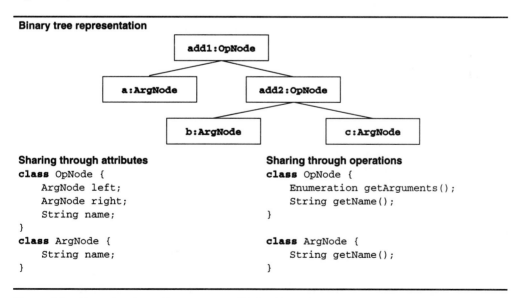

Figure 6-5   Example of coupling reduction (UML object diagram and Java declarations). This figure shows a parse tree for the expression "a + b + c". The left column shows the interface of the OpNode class with sharing through attributes. The right column shows the interface of OpNode with sharing through operations. Figure 6-6 shows the changes for each case when a linked list is selected instead.

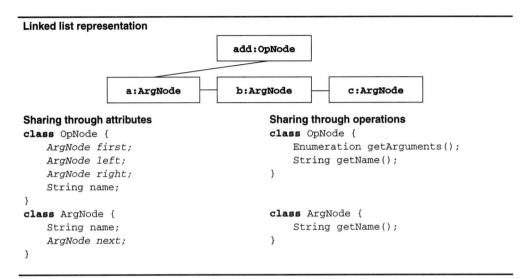

Linked list representation

Sharing through attributes
```
class OpNode {
    ArgNode first;
    ArgNode left;
    ArgNode right;
    String name;
}
class ArgNode {
    String name;
    ArgNode next;
}
```

Sharing through operations
```
class OpNode {
    Enumeration getArguments();
    String getName();
}

class ArgNode {
    String getName();
}
```

Figure 6-6   Example of coupling reduction (UML object diagram and Java declarations). This figure shows the impact of changing the parse tree representation of Figure 6-5 to a linked list. In the left column, with sharing through attributes, four attributes need to change (changes indicated in *italics*). In the right column, with sharing through operations, the interface remains unchanged.

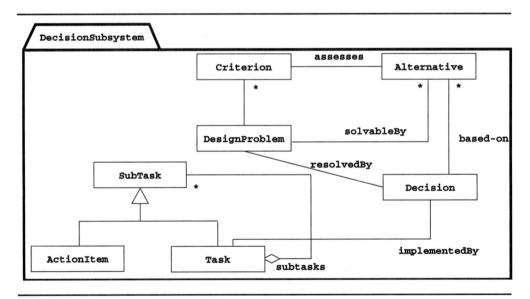

Figure 6-7   Decision tracking system (UML class diagram). The DecisionSubsystem has a low coherence: The classes Criterion, Alternative, and DesignProblem have no relationships with Subtask, ActionItem, and Task.

DesignProblem and Alternative represent the exploration of the design space: We formulate the system in terms of a number of DesignProblems and document each Alternative they explore. The Criterion class represents the qualities in which we are interested. Once we assessed the explored Alternatives against desirable Criteria, we take Decisions and implement them in terms of Tasks. Tasks are recursively decomposed into Subtasks small enough to be assigned to individual developers. We call atomic tasks ActionItems.

The decision tracking system is small enough that we could lump all these classes into one subsystem called DecisionSubsystem (see Figure 6-7). However, we observe that the class model can be partitioned into two subgraphs. One, called the RationaleSubsystem, contains the classes DesignProblem, Alternative, Criterion, and Decision. The other, called the PlanningSubsystem, contains Task, Subtask, and ActionItem (see Figure 6-8). Both subsystems have a better coherence than the original DecisionSubsystem. Moreover, the resulting subsystems are smaller than the original subsystem: We reduced complexity. The

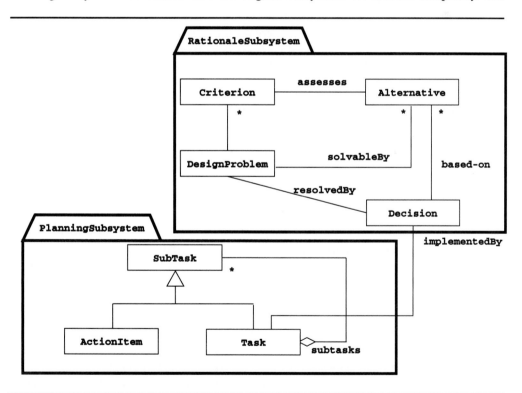

Figure 6-8 Alternative subsystem decomposition for the decision tracking system of Figure 6-7 (UML class diagram). The coherence of the RationaleSubsystem and the PlanningSubsystem is higher than the coherence of the original DecisionSubsystem. Note also that we also reduced the complexity by decomposing the system into smaller subsystems.

coupling between the new subsystems is relatively low, as there is only one association between the two subsystems.

In general, there is a trade-off between coherence and coupling. We can always increase coherence by decomposing the system into smaller subsystems. However, this also increases coupling as the number of interfaces increases. A good heuristic is that developers can deal with 7 ± 2 concepts at any one level of abstraction. If there are more than nine subsystems at any given level of abstraction or if there is a subsystem providing more than nine services, you should consider a revision of the decomposition. By the same token, the number of layers should not be more than 7 ± 2. In fact, many good systems design can be done with just three layers.

6.3.4   Layers and Partitions

The goal of system design is to manage complexity by dividing the system into smaller, manageable pieces. This can be done by a divide-and-conquer approach, where we recursively divide parts until they are simple enough to be handled by one person or one team. Applying this approach systematically leads to a hierarchical decomposition in which each subsystem, or **layer**, provides higher level services, using services provided from lower level subsystems (see Figure 6-9). Each layer can only depend on lower level layers and has no knowledge of the layers above it. In a **closed architecture**, each layer can only depend on the layers immediately below it. In an **open architecture**, a layer can also access layers at deeper levels.

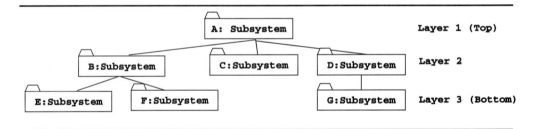

Figure 6-9   Subsystem decomposition of a system into three layers (UML object diagram). A subset from a layered decomposition that includes at least one subsystem from each layer is called a vertical slice. For example, the subsystems A, B, and E constitute a vertical slice, whereas the subsystems D and G do not.

An example of a closed architecture is the Reference Model of Open Systems Interconnection (in short, the OSI model), which is composed of seven layers [Day & Zimmermann, 1983]. Each layer is responsible for performing a well-defined function. In addition, each layer provides its services by using services of the layer below.

The Physical layer represents the hardware interface to the network. It is responsible for transmitting bits over a communication channels. The DataLink layer is responsible for transmitting data frames without error using the services of the Physical layer. The Network layer is responsible for transmitting and routing packets within a network. The Transport layer is responsible for ensuring that the data are reliably transmitted from end to end. The

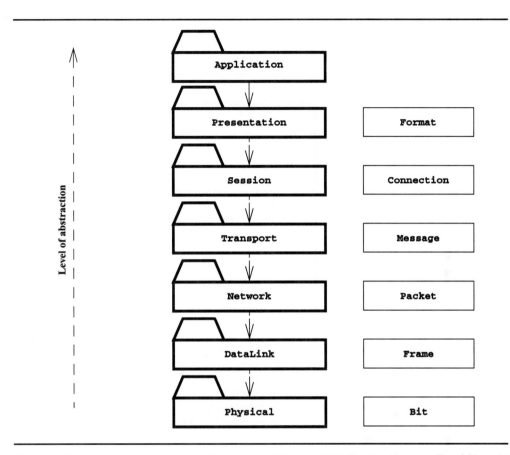

Figure 6-10 An example of closed architecture: the OSI model (UML class diagram). The OSI model decomposes network services into seven layers, each responsible for a different level of abstraction.

Transport layer is the interface Unix programmers see when transmitting information over TCP/IP sockets between two processes. The Session layer is responsible for the initialization of a connection, including authentication. The Presentation layer performs data transformation services, such as byte swapping or encryption. The Application layer is the system you are designing (unless you are building an operating system or protocol stack). The Application layer can also consist of layered subsystems.

Until recently, only the four bottom layers of the OSI model were well standardized. Unix and many desktop operating systems, for example, provide interfaces to TCP/IP that implemented the Transport, Network, and Datalink layers. The application developer still needed to fill the gap between the Transport layer and the Application layer. With the growing number of distributed applications, this gap motivated the development of middleware such as CORBA [OMG, 1995] and Java RMI [RMI, 1998]. CORBA and Java RMI allow us to

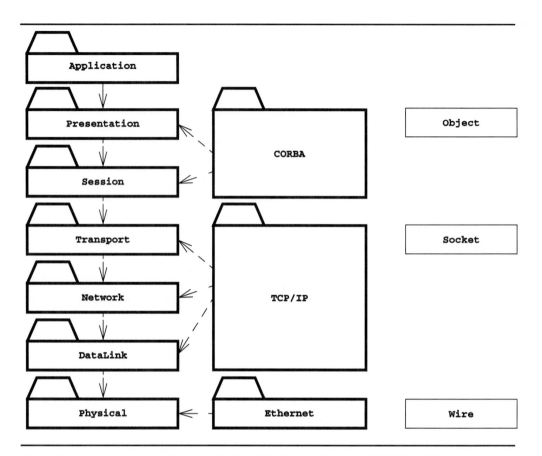

Figure 6-11   An example of closed architecture (UML class diagram). CORBA enables the access of objects implemented in different languages on different hosts. CORBA effectively implements the `Presentation` and `Session` layers of the OSI stack.

access remote objects transparently, by sending messages to them as messages are sent to local objects, effectively implementing the `Presentation` and `Session` layers (see Figure 6-11).

An example of an open architecture is the Motif user interface toolkit for X11 [Nye & O'Reilly, 1992]. The lowest layer, `Xlib`, provides basic drawing facilities and defines the concept of window. `Xt` provides tools for manipulating user interface objects, called widgets, using services from `Xlib`. `Motif` is a widget library that provides a wide range of facilities, from buttons to geometry management. Motif is built on top of `Xt` but also accesses `Xlib` directly. Finally, an application using `Motif`, such as a window manager, can access all three layers. `Motif` has no knowledge of the window manager and `Xt` has no knowledge of `Motif` or of the application. Many other user interface toolkits for X11 have open architectures. The openness of the architecture allows developers to bypass the higher level layers in case of performance bottleneck (Figure 6-12).

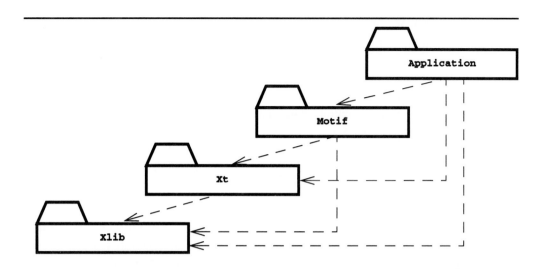

Figure 6-12 An example of open architecture: the OSF/Motif library (UML class diagram, packages collapsed). Xlib provides low-level drawing facilities. Xt provides basic user interface widget management. Motif provides a large number of sophisticated widgets. The Application can access each of these layers independently.

Closed layered architectures have desirable properties: They lead to low coupling between subsystems, and subsystems can be integrated and tested incrementally. Each level, however, introduces a speed and storage overhead that may make it difficult to meet nonfunctional requirements. Also, adding functionality to the system in later revisions may prove difficult, especially when the additions were not anticipated. In practice, a system is rarely decomposed into more than three to five layers.

Another approach to dealing with complexity is to **partition** the system into peer subsystems, each responsible for a different class of services. For example, an onboard system for a car could be decomposed into a travel service, giving real-time directions to the driver, an individual preferences service, remembering a driver's seat position and favorite radio station, and vehicle service, keeping track of the car's gas consumption, repairs, and scheduled maintenance. Each subsystem depends loosely on each other but could often operate in isolation.

In general, a subsystem decomposition is the result of both partitioning and layering. We first partition the system into top-level subsystems, which are responsible for specific functionality or which run on a specific hardware node. Each of the resulting subsystems are, if complexity justifies it, decomposed into lower and lower level layers until they are simple enough to be implemented by a single developer. Each subsystem adds a certain processing overhead because of its interface with other systems. Excessive partitioning or layering can lead to increased complexity.

6.3.5   Software Architecture

As the complexity of systems increases, the specification of the system decomposition is critical. It is difficult to modify or correct a weak decomposition once development has started, as most subsystem interfaces have to change. In recognition of the importance of this problem, the concept of **software architecture** has emerged. A software architecture includes the system decomposition, the global control flow, error-handling policies and intersubsystem communication protocols [Shaw & Garlan, 1996].

In this section, we describe a few sample architectures that can be used for different systems. This is by no means a systematic or thorough exposition of the subject. Rather, we aim to provide a few representative examples and refer the reader to the literature for more details.

Repository architecture

In the repository architecture (see Figure 6-13), subsystems access and modify data from a single data structure called the central **repository**. Subsystems are relatively independent and interact only through the central data structure. Control flow can be dictated either by the central repository (e.g., triggers on the data invoke peripheral systems) or by the subsystems (e.g., independent flow of control and synchronization through locks in the repository).

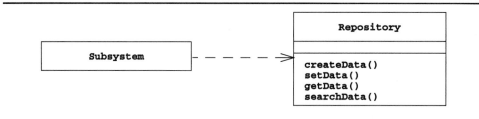

Figure 6-13   Repository architecture (UML class diagram). Every subsystem depends only on a central data structure called the repository. The repository in turn, has no knowledge of the other subsystems.

The repository architecture is typical for database management systems, such as a payroll system or a bank system. The central location of the data makes it easier to deal with concurrency and integrity issues between subsystems. Modern compilers and software development environments also follow a repository architecture (see Figure 6-14). The different subsystems of a compiler access and update a central parse tree and a symbol table. Debuggers and syntax editors access the symbol table as well.

The repository subsystem can also be used for implementing the global control flow. In the compiler example of Figure 6-14, each individual tool (e.g., the compiler, the debugger, and the editor) is invoked by the user. The repository only ensures that concurrent accesses are serialized. Conversely, the repository can be used to invoke the subsystems based on the state of the central data structure. These systems are called blackboard systems. The HEARSAY II Speech understanding system [Erman et al., 1980], one of the first blackboard systems, selected tools to invoke based on the current state of the blackboard.

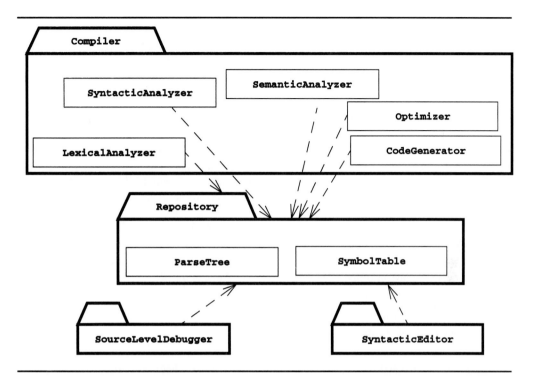

Figure 6-14 An instance of the repository architecture (UML Class diagram). A modern compiler incrementally generates a parse tree and a symbol table that can be later used by debuggers and syntax editors.

Repository architectures are well suited for applications with constantly changing complex data processing tasks. Once a central repository is well defined, we can easily add new services in the form of additional subsystems. The main disadvantage of repository systems is that the central repository can quickly become a bottleneck, both from a performance aspect and a modifiability aspect. The coupling between each subsystem and the repository is high, thus making it difficult to change the repository without having an impact on all subsystems.

Model/View/Controller

In the Model/View/Controller (MVC) architecture (see Figure 6-15), subsystems are classified into three different types: **model subsystems** are responsible for maintaining domain knowledge, **view subsystems** are responsible for displaying it to the user, and **controller subsystems** are responsible for managing the sequence of interactions with the user. The model subsystems are developed such that they do not depend on any view or controller subsystem. Changes in their state are propagated to the view subsystem via a subscribe/notify protocol. The MVC architecture is a special case of repository architecture where Model implements the central data structure and control objects dictate the control flow.

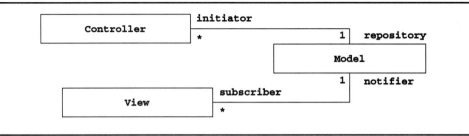

Figure 6-15   Model/View/Controller architecture (UML class diagram). The `Controller` gathers input from the user and sends messages to the `Model`. The `Model` maintains the central data structure. The `View`(s) display the `Model` and is notified (via a subscribe/notify protocol) whenever the `Model` is changed.

For example, Figures 6-16 and 6-17 illustrate the sequence of events that occur in a MVC architecture. Figure 6-17 displays two views of a file system. The bottom window lists the content of the `Comp-Based Software Engineering` folder, including the file `9DesignPatterns2.ppt`. The top window displays information about this file. The name of the file `9DesignPatterns2.ppt` appears in three places: in both windows and in the title of the top window.

Assume now that we change the name of the file to `9DesignPatterns.ppt`. Figure 6-16 shows the sequence of events:

1. The `InfoView` and the `FolderView` both subscribe for changes to the File models they display (when they are created).
2. The user types the new name of the file.
3. The `Controller`, the object responsible for interacting with the user during file name changes, sends a request to the Model.
4. The `Model` changes the file name and notifies all subscribers of the change.
5. Both `InfoView` and `FolderView` are updated, so the user sees a consistent change.

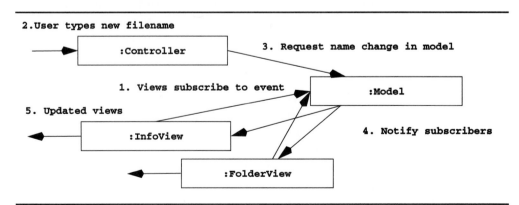

Figure 6-16   Sequence of events in the Model/View/Control architecture (UML collaboration diagram).

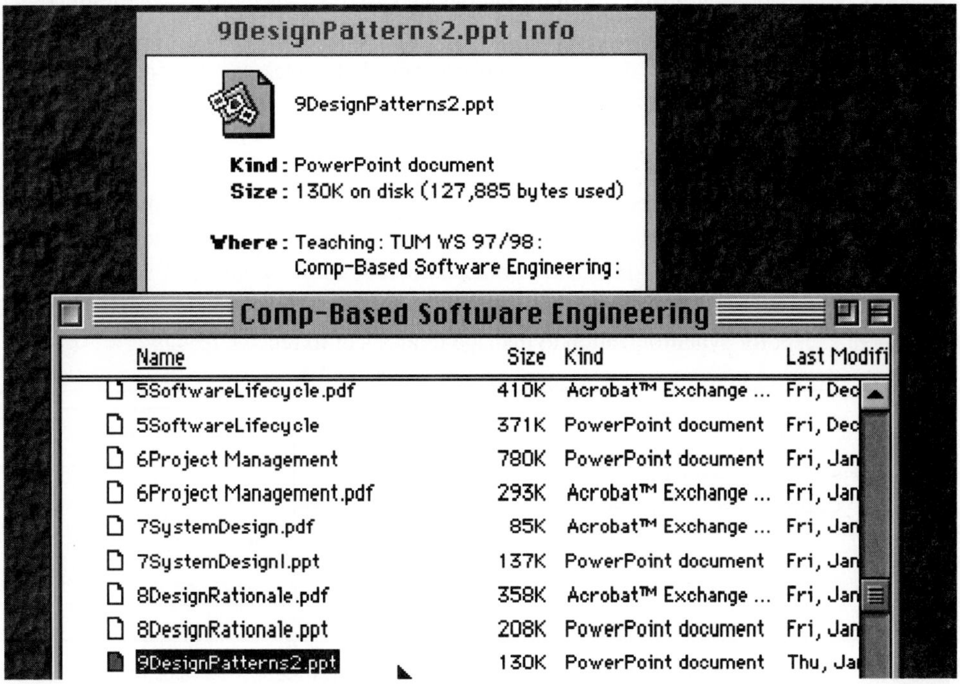

Figure 6-17 An example of MVC architecture. The "model" is the filename 9DesignPAtterns2.ppt. One "view" is a window titled Comp-Based Software Engineering, which displays the contents of a folder containing the file 9DesignPatterns2.ppt. The other "view" is window called 9DesignPatterns2.ppt Info, which displays information related to the file. If the file name is changed, both views are updated by the "controller".

The subscription and notification functionality associated with this sequence of events is usually realized with an Observer pattern (see Section A.7). The **Observer pattern** allows the Model and the View objects to be further decoupled by removing direct dependencies from the Model to the View. For more details, the reader is referred to [Gamma et al., 1994] and to Section A.7.

The rationale between the separation of Model, View, and Controller is that user interfaces, i.e., the View and the Controller, are much more often subject to change than is domain knowledge, i.e., the Model. Moreover, by removing any dependency from the Model on the View with the subscription/notification protocol, changes in the views (user interface) do not have any effect on the model subsystems. In the example of Figure 6-17, we could add a Unix-style shell view of the file system without having to modify the file system. We described a similar decomposition in Chapter 5, *Analysis*, when we identified entity, boundary, and control objects. This decomposition is also motivated by the same considerations about change.

MVC architectures are well suited for interactive systems, especially when multiple views of the same model are needed. MVC can be used for maintaining consistency across distributed data; however, it introduces the same performance bottleneck as for other repository architectures.

Client/server architecture

In the client/server architecture (Figure 6-18), a subsystem, the **server**, provides services to instances of other subsystems called the **clients**, which are responsible for interacting with the user. The request for a service is usually done via a remote procedure call mechanism or a common object broker (e.g., CORBA or Java RMI). Control flow in the clients and the servers is independent except for synchronization to manage requests or to receive results.

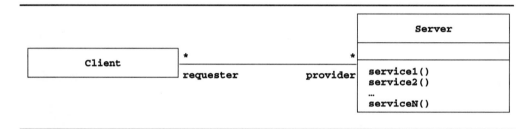

Figure 6-18   Client/server architecture (UML class diagram). Clients request services from one or more servers. The server has no knowledge of the client. The client/server architecture is a generalization of the repository architecture.

An information system with a central database is an example of a client/server architecture. The clients are responsible for receiving inputs from the user, performing range checks, and initiating database transactions once all necessary data are collected. The server is then responsible for performing the transaction and guaranteeing the integrity of the data. In this case, a client/server architecture is a special case of the repository architecture, where the central data structure is managed by a process. Client/server systems, however, are not restricted to a single server. On the World Wide Web, a single client can easily access data from thousands of different servers (Figure 6-19).

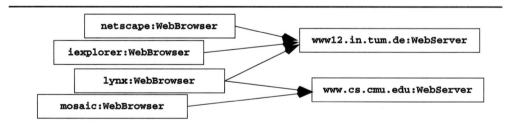

Figure 6-19   The World Wide Web as an instance of the client/server architecture (UML object diagram).

Client/server architectures are well suited for distributed systems that manage large amounts of data.

Peer-to-peer architecture

A peer-to-peer architecture (see Figure 6-20) is a generalization of the client/server architecture in which subsystems can act both as client or as servers, in the sense that each subsystem can request and provide services. The control flow within each subsystem is independent from the others except for synchronizations on requests.

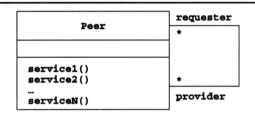

Figure 6-20 Peer-to-peer architecture (UML class diagram). Peers can request services from and provide services to other peers.

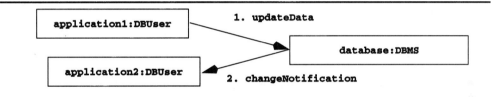

Figure 6-21 An example of peer-to-peer architecture (UML collaboration diagram). The database server can both process requests from and send notifications to applications.

An example of a peer-to-peer architecture is a database which, on the one hand, accepts requests from the application and, on the other hand, sends notifications to the application whenever certain data are changed (Figure 6-21). Peer-to-peer systems are more difficult to design than client/server systems are. They introduce the possibility of deadlocks and complicate the control flow.

Pipe and filter architecture

In the pipe and filter architecture (see Figure 6-22), subsystems process data received from a set of inputs and send results to other subsystems via a set of outputs. The subsystems are called **filters**, and the associations between the subsystems are called **pipes**. Each filter only knows the content and the format of the data received on the input pipes, not the filters that produced them. Each filter is executed concurrently and synchronization is done via the pipes. The pipe and filter architecture is modifiable: Filters can be substituted for others or reconfigured to achieve a different purpose.

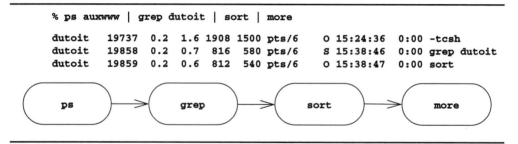

Figure 6-22   Pipe and filter architecture (UML class diagram). A `Filter` can have many inputs and outputs. A `Pipe` connects one of the outputs of a `Filter` to one of the inputs of another `Filter`.

The best known example of pipe and filter architecture is the Unix shell. Most filters are written such that they read their input and write their results on standard pipes. This enables a Unix user to combine them in many different ways. Figure 6-23 shows an example made out of four filters. The output of `ps` (process status) is fed into `grep` (search for a pattern) to get rid of all the processes that are not owned by a specific user. The output of `grep` (i.e., the processes owned by the user) is then sorted by `sort` and then sent to `more`, which is a filter that displays its input to a terminal, one screen at a time.

```
% ps auxwww | grep dutoit | sort | more

dutoit   19737  0.2  1.6  1908 1500 pts/6    O 15:24:36  0:00 -tcsh
dutoit   19858  0.2  0.7   816  580 pts/6    S 15:38:46  0:00 grep dutoit
dutoit   19859  0.2  0.6   812  540 pts/6    O 15:38:47  0:00 sort
```

```
  ( ps )  ->  ( grep )  ->  ( sort )  ->  ( more )
```

Figure 6-23   An instance of the pipe and filter architecture (Unix command and UML activity diagram).

Pipe and filter architectures are suited for systems that apply transformations to streams of data without intervention by users. They are not suited for systems that require more-complex interactions between components, such as an information management system or an interactive system.

6.3.6   UML Deployment Diagrams

UML deployment diagrams are used to depict the relationship among run-time components and hardware nodes. Components are self-contained entities that provide services to other components or actors. A Web server, for example, is a component that provides services to Web browsers. A Web browser such as Netscape is a component that provides services to a user. A distributed system can be composed of many interacting run-time components.

In UML deployment diagrams, nodes are represented by boxes containing component icons. Dependencies between components are represented by dashed arrows. Figure 6-24 depicts an example of deployment diagram illustrating two Web browsers accessing a Web

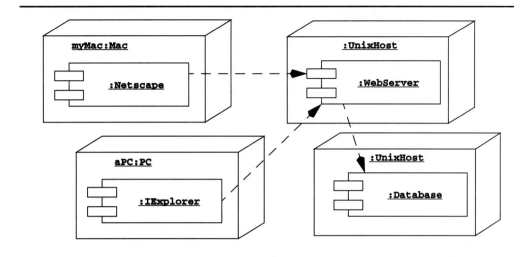

Figure 6-24 A UML deployment diagram representing the allocation of components to different nodes and the dependencies among components. Web browsers on PCs and Macs can access a WebServer that provides information from a Database.

server. The Web server in turns accesses data from a database server. We can see from the dependency graph that the Web browsers do not access directly the database at any time.

The deployment diagram in Figure 6-24 focuses on the allocation of components to nodes and provides a high-level view of each component. Components can be refined to include information about the interfaces they provide and the classes they contain. Figure 6-25 illustrates the GET and POST interfaces of the WebServer component and its containing classes.

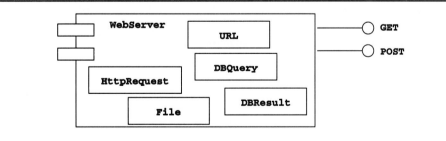

Figure 6-25 Refined view of the WebServer component (UML deployment diagram). The WebServer component provides two interfaces to browsers: A browser can either request the content of a file referred by a URL (GET) or post the content of a form (POST). The WebServer component contains five classes: URL, HttpRequest, DBQuery, File, and DBResult.

6.4 System Design Activities: From Objects to Subsystems

System design consists of transforming the analysis model into the design model that takes into account the nonfunctional requirements and constraints described in the problem statement and the requirements analysis document. In Section 6.3, we focused on subsystem decompositions and their properties. In this section, we describe the activities that are needed to ensure that a subsystem decomposition addresses all the nonfunctional requirements and prepares for taking into account any constraints during the implementation phase. We illustrate these activities with an example, MyTrip, a route planning system for car drivers, throughout this section. This will provide you with more concrete knowledge of system design concepts.

We start with the analysis model from MyTrip. We then:

- identify design goals from the nonfunctional requirements (Section 6.4.2)
- design an initial subsystem decomposition (Section 6.4.3)
- map subsystems to processors and components (Section 6.4.4)
- decide storage (Section 6.4.5)
- define access control policies (Section 6.4.6)
- select a control flow mechanism (Section 6.4.7)
- identify boundary conditions (Section 6.4.8)

In Section 6.4.9, we examine issues related to stabilizing the system design while anticipating change. Finally, in Section 6.4.10, we describe how the system design model is reviewed. But first, we describe the analysis model we use as a starting point for the system design of MyTrip.

6.4.1 Starting Point: Analysis Model for a Route Planning System

Using MyTrip, a driver can plan a trip from a home computer by contacting a trip planning service on the Web (PlanTrip in Figure 6-26). The trip is saved for later retrieval on the server. The trip planning service must support more than one driver.

Use case name	PlanTrip
Entry condition	1. The Driver activates her home computer and logs into the trip planning Web service.
Flow of events	2. Upon successful login, the Driver enters constraints for a trip as a sequence of destinations.
	3. Based on a database of maps, the planning service computes the shortest way visiting the destinations in the specified order. The result is a sequence of segments binding a series of crossings and a list of directions.
	4. The Driver can revise the trip by adding or removing destinations.
Exit condition	5. The Driver saves the planned trip by name in the planning service database for later retrieval.

Figure 6-26 PlanTrip use case of the MyTrip system.

The driver then goes to the car and starts the trip, while the onboard computer gives directions based on trip information from the planning service and her current position indicated by an onboard GPS system (ExecuteTrip in Figure 6-27).

Use case name	ExecuteTrip
Entry condition	1. The Driver starts her car and logs into the onboard route assistant.
Flow of events	2. Upon successful login, the Driver specifies the planning service and the name of the trip to be executed.
	3. The onboard route assistant obtains the list of destinations, directions, segments, and crossings from the planning service.
	4. Given the current position, the route assistant provides the driver with the next set of directions.
Exit condition	5. The Driver arrives to destination and shuts down the route assistant.

Figure 6-27 ExecuteTrip use case of the MyTrip system.

We perform the analysis for the MyTrip system following the techniques outlined in Chapter 5, *Analysis*, and obtain the model in Figure 6-28.

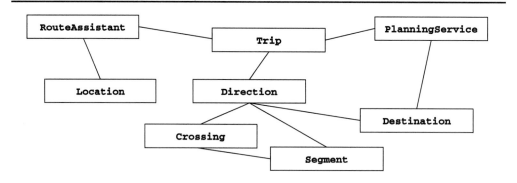

Crossing	A Crossing is a geographical point were a driver can choose between several Segments.
Destination	A Destination represents a location where the driver wishes to go.
Direction	Given a Crossing and an adjacent Segment, a Direction describes in natural language terms how to steer the car onto the given Segment.
Location	A Location is the position of the car as known by the onboard GPS system or the number of turns of the wheels.
PlanningService	A PlanningService is a Web server that can supply a trip, linking a number of destinations in the form of a sequence of crossings and segments.
RouteAssistant	A RouteAssistant gives Directions to the driver, given the current Location and upcoming Crossing.
Segment	A Segment represents the road between two Crossings.
Trip	A Trip is a sequence of Directions between two Destinations.

Figure 6-28   Analysis model for the MyTrip route planning and execution.

In addition, during requirements elicitation, our client specified the following nonfunctional requirements for MyTrip.

Nonfunctional requirements for MyTrip
1. MyTrip is in contact with the PlanningService via a wireless modem. It can be assumed that the wireless modem functions properly at the initial destination.
2. Once the trip has been started, MyTrip should give correct directions even if modem fails to maintain a connection with the PlanningService.
3. MyTrip should minimize connection time to reduce operation costs.
4. Replanning is possible only if the connection to the PlanningService is possible.
5. The PlanningService can support at least 50 different drivers and 1000 trips.

6.4.2 Identifying Design Goals

The definition of design goals is the first step of system design. It identifies the qualities that our system should focus on. Many design goals can be inferred from the nonfunctional requirements or from the application domain. Others will have to be elicited from the client. It is, however, necessary to state them explicitly such that every important design decision can be made consistently following the same set of criteria.

For example, in the light of the nonfunctional requirements for MyTrip described in Section 6.4.1, we identify *reliability* and *fault tolerance to connectivity loss* as design goals. We then identify *security* as a design goal, as numerous drivers will have access to the same trip planning server. We add *modifiability* as a design goal, as we want to provide the ability for drivers to select a trip planning service of their choice. The following box summarizes the design goals we identified.

Design goals for MyTrip
- **Reliability:** MyTrip should be reliable [generalization of nonfunctional requirement 2].
- **Fault Tolerance:** MyTrip should be fault tolerant to loss of connectivity with the routing service [rephrased nonfunctional requirement 2].
- **Security:** MyTrip should be secure, i.e., not allow other drivers or nonauthorized users to access another driver's trips [deduced from application domain].
- **Modifiability:** MyTrip should be modifiable to use different routing services [anticipation of change by developers].

In general, we can select design goals from a long list of highly desirable qualities. Tables 6-1–6-5 list a number of possible design criteria. These criteria are organized into five groups: *performance*, *dependability*, *cost*, *maintenance*, and *end user criteria*. Performance, dependability, and end user criteria are usually specified in the requirements or inferred from the application domain. Cost and maintenance criteria are dictated by the customer and the supplier.

Performance criteria (Table 6-1) include the speed and space requirements imposed on the system. Should the system be responsive or should it accomplish a maximum number of tasks? Is memory space available for speed optimizations or should memory be used sparingly?

Table 6-1 Performance criteria

Design criterion	Definition
Response time	How soon is a user request acknowledged after the request has been issued?
Throughput	How many tasks can the system accomplish in a fixed period of time?
Memory	How much space is required for the system to run?

Table 6-2   Dependability criteria

Design criterion	Definition
Robustness	Ability to survive invalid user input
Reliability	Difference between specified and observed behavior
Availability	Percentage of time system that can be used to accomplish normal tasks
Fault tolerance	Ability to operate under erroneous conditions
Security	Ability to withstand malicious attacks
Safety	Ability to not endanger human lives, even in the presence of errors and failures

Dependability criteria (Table 6-2) determine how much effort should be expended in minimizing system crashes and their consequences. How often can the system crash? How available to the user should the system be? Are there safety issues associated with system crashes? Are there security risks associated with the system environment?

Cost criteria (Table 6-3) include the cost to develop the system, to deploy it, and to administer it. Note that cost criteria not only include design considerations but managerial ones as well. When the system is replacing an older one, the cost of ensuring backward compatibility or transitioning to the new system has to be taken into account. There are also trade-offs between different types of costs such as development cost, end user training cost, transition costs and maintenance costs. Maintaining backward compatibility with a previous system can add to the development cost while reducing the transition cost.

Table 6-3   Cost criteria

Design criterion	Definition
Development cost	Cost of developing the initial system
Deployment cost	Cost of installing install the system and training the users.
Upgrade cost	Cost of translating data from the previous system. This criteria results in backward compatibility requirements.
Maintenance cost	Cost required for bug fixes and enhancements to the system
Administration cost	Money required to administer the system.

Maintenance criteria (Table 6-4) determine how difficult it is to change the system after deployment. How easily can new functionality be added? How easily can existing functions be revised? Can the system be adapted to a different application domain? How much effort will be required to port the system to a different platform? These criteria are harder to optimize and plan for, as it is seldom clear how long the system will be operational and how successful the project will be.

Table 6-4   Maintenance criteria

Design criterion	Definition
Extensibility	How easy is it to add the functionality or new classes of the system?
Modifiability	How easy is it to change the functionality of the system?
Adaptability	How easy is it to port the system to different application domains?
Portability	How easy is it to port the system to different platforms?
Readability	How easy is it to understand the system from reading the code?
Traceability of requirements	How easy is it to map the code to specific requirements?

End user criteria (Table 6-5) include qualities that are desirable from a users' point of view that have not yet been covered under the performance and dependability criteria. These include usability (How difficult is the software to use and to learn?) and utility (How well does the system support the user's work?). Often these criteria do not receive much attention, especially when the client contracting the system is distinct from the users of the system.

Table 6-5   End user criteria

Design criterion	Definition
Utility	How well does the system support the work of the user?
Usability	How easy is it for the user to use the system?

When defining design goals, only a small subset of these criteria can be simultaneously taken into account. It is, for example, unrealistic to develop software that is safe, secure, and cheap. Typically, developers need to prioritize design goals and trade them off against each other as well as against managerial goals as the project runs behind schedule or over budget. Table 6-6 lists several possible trade-offs.

Table 6-6   Examples of design goal trade-offs

Trade-off	Rationale
Space vs. speed	If the software does not meet response time or throughput requirements, more memory can be expended to speed up the software (e.g., caching, more redundancy, etc.). If the software does not meet memory space constraints, data can be compressed at the cost of speed.
Delivery time vs. functionality	If the development runs behind schedule, a project manager can deliver less functionality than specified and deliver on time, or deliver the full functionality at a later time. Contract software usually puts more emphasis on functionality, whereas off-the-shelf software projects puts more emphasis on delivery date.
Delivery time vs. quality	If the testing runs behind schedule, a project manager can deliver the software on time with known bugs (and possibly provide a later patch to fix any serious bugs) or to deliver the software later with more bugs fixed.
Delivery time vs. staffing	If development runs behind schedule, a project manager can add resources to the project in order to increase productivity. In most cases, this option is only available early in the project: Adding resources usually decreases productivity while new personnel is being trained or brought up to date. Note that adding resources will also raise the cost of development.

Managerial goals can be traded off against technical goals (e.g., delivery time vs. functionality). Once we have a clear idea of the design goals, we can proceed to design an initial subsystem decomposition.

6.4.3   Identifying Subsystems

Finding subsystems during system design has many similarities to finding objects during analysis: It is a volatile activity driven by heuristics. As a result, the object identification techniques we described in Chapter 5, *Analysis*, such as Abbotts's lexical rules, are applicable to subsystem identification. Moreover, subsystem decomposition is constantly revised whenever new issues are addressed: Subsystems are merged into one subsystem, a complex subsystem is split into parts, and some subsystems are added to take care of new functionality. The first iterations over the subsystem decomposition can introduce drastic changes in the system design model. These are often best handled through brainstorming.

The initial subsystem decomposition should be derived from the functional requirements. For example, in the MyTrip system, we identify two major groups of objects: those that are involved during the PlanTrip use cases and those that are involved during the ExecuteTrip use case. The Trip, Direction, Crossing, Segment, and Destination classes are shared between both use cases. This set of classes is tightly coupled as they are used as a whole to represent a `Trip`. We decide to assign them with `PlanningService` to the `PlanningSubsystem`, and the remainder of the classes are assigned to the `RoutingSubsystem` (Figure 6-29). This leads to only one association crossing subsystem boundaries. Note that this subsystem decomposition follows a repository architecture in which the `PlanningSubsystem` is responsible for the central data structure.

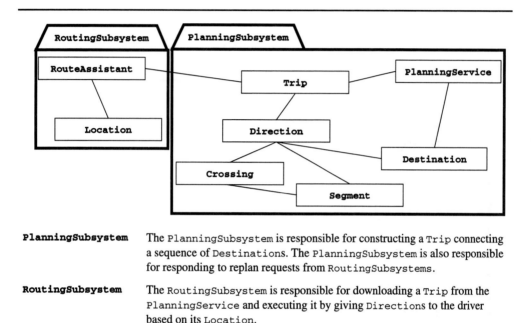

PlanningSubsystem	The `PlanningSubsystem` is responsible for constructing a `Trip` connecting a sequence of `Destinations`. The `PlanningSubsystem` is also responsible for responding to replan requests from `RoutingSubsystems`.
RoutingSubsystem	The `RoutingSubsystem` is responsible for downloading a `Trip` from the `PlanningService` and executing it by giving `Directions` to the driver based on its `Location`.

Figure 6-29   Initial subsystem decomposition for MyTrip (UML class diagram).

Another heuristic for subsystem identification is to keep functionally related objects together. A starting point is to take the use cases and assign the participating objects that have been identified in each of them to the subsystems. Some group of objects, as the `Trip` group in MyTrip, are shared and used for communicating information from one subsystem to another. We can either create a new subsystem to accommodate them or assign them to the subsystem that creates these objects.

Heuristics for grouping objects into subsystems

- Assign objects identified in one use case into the same subsystem
- Create a dedicated subsystem for objects used for moving data among subsystems
- Minimize the number of associations crossing subsystem boundaries
- All objects in the same subsystem should be functionally related

---

Encapsulating subsystems

Subsystem decomposition reduces the complexity of the solution domain by minimizing dependencies among classes. The **Facade pattern** [Gamma et al., 1994] allows us to further reduce dependencies between classes by encapsulating a subsystem with a simple, unified interface. For example, in Figure 6-30, the `Compiler` class is a `Facade` hiding the classes `CodeGenerator`, `Optimizer`, `ParseNode`, `Parser`, and `Lexer`. The `Facade` provides access only to the public services offered by the subsystem and hides all other details, effectively reducing coupling between subsystems.

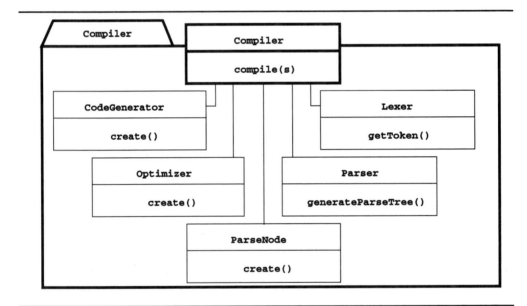

Figure 6-30   An example of the `Facade` pattern (UML class diagram).

Subsystems identified during the initial subsystem decomposition often result from grouping several functionally related classes. These subsystems are good candidates for the `Facade` pattern and should be encapsulated under one class.

6.4.4   Mapping Subsystems to Processors and Components

Selecting a hardware configuration and a platform

Many systems run on more than one computer and depend on access to an intranet or to the Internet. The use of multiple computers can address high-performance needs or to interconnect multiple distributed users. Consequently, we need to carefully examine the allocation of subsystems to computers and the design of the infrastructure for supporting communication between subsystems. These computers are modeled as nodes in UML deployment diagrams. Nodes can either represent a specific instances (e.g., `myMac`) or a class of computers (e.g., WebServer).[1] Because the hardware mapping activity has significant impact on the performance and complexity of the system, we perform it early in system design.

Selecting a hardware configuration also includes selecting a virtual machine onto which the system should be built. The virtual machine includes the operating system and any software components that are needed, such as a database management system or a communication package. The selection of a virtual machine reduces the distance between the system and the hardware platform on which it will run. The more functionality the components provide, the less work involved. The selection of the virtual machine, however, may be constrained by the client who acquires hardware before the start of the project. The selection of a virtual machine may also be constrained by cost considerations: In some cases, it is difficult to estimate whether building a component costs more than buying it.

In MyTrip, we deduce from the requirements that PlanningSubsystem and RoutingSubsystem run on two different nodes: The former is a Web-based service on an Internet host while the second runs on the onboard computer. Figure 6-31 illustrates the hardware allocation for MyTrip with two nodes called :OnBoardComputer and :WebServer.

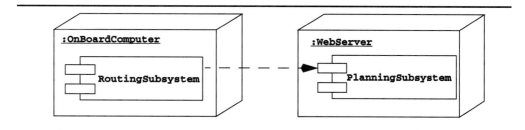

Figure 6-31 Allocation of MyTrip subsystems to hardware (UML deployment diagram). RoutingSubsystem runs on the OnBoardComputer while PlanningSubsystem runs on a WebServer.

We select a Unix machine as the virtual machine for the :WebServer and the Web browsers Netscape and Internet Explorer as the virtual machines for the :OnBoardComputer.

Allocating objects and subsystems to nodes

Once the hardware configuration has been defined and the virtual machines selected, objects and subsystems are assigned to nodes. This often triggers the identification of new objects and subsystems for transporting data among the nodes.

In the MyTrip system, both RoutingSubsystem and PlanningSubsystem share the objects Trip, Destination, Crossing, Segment, and Direction. Instances of these classes need to communicate via a wireless modem using some communication protocol. We create a

---

1. These two cases are distinguished with the usual UML naming convention: underlined names for instances and nonunderlined names for classes.

new subsystem to support this communication: CommunicationSubsystem, a subsystem located on both nodes for managing the communication between the two.

We also notice that only segments constituting the planned trip are stored in RoutingSubsystem. Adjacent segments not part of the trip are stored only in the PlanningSubsystem. To take this into account, we need objects in the RoutingSubsystem that can act as a surrogates to Segments and Trips in the PlanningSubsystem. An object that acts on the behalf of another one is called a proxy. We therefore create two new classes, called SegmentProxy and TripProxy, and make them part of the RoutingSubsystem. These proxies are examples of the **Proxy** design pattern [Gamma et al., 1994].

In case of replanning by the driver, this class will transparently request the CommunicationSubsystem to retrieve the information associated with its corresponding Segments on the PlanningSubsystem. Finally, the CommunicationSubsystem is used for transferring a complete trip from PlanningSubsystem to RouteAssistant. The revised design model and the additional class descriptions are depicted in Figure 6-32.

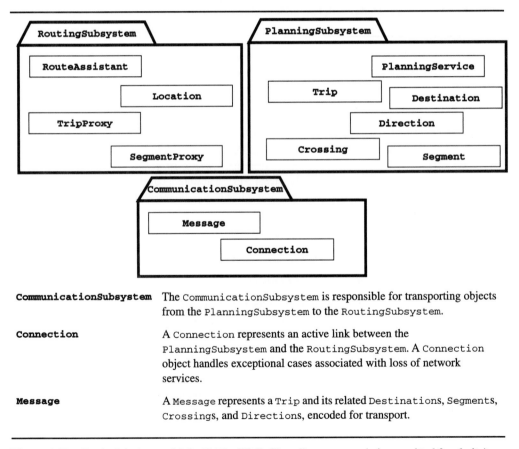

CommunicationSubsystem	The CommunicationSubsystem is responsible for transporting objects from the PlanningSubsystem to the RoutingSubsystem.
Connection	A Connection represents an active link between the PlanningSubsystem and the RoutingSubsystem. A Connection object handles exceptional cases associated with loss of network services.
Message	A Message represents a Trip and its related Destinations, Segments, Crossings, and Directions, encoded for transport.

Figure 6-32   Revised design model for MyTrip (UML Class diagram, associations omitted for clarity).

In general, allocating subsystems to hardware nodes enables us to distribute functionality and processing power where it is most needed. Unfortunately, it also introduces issues related to storing, transferring, replicating, and synchronizing data among subsystems. For this reason, developers also select the components they will use for developing the system.

Encapsulating components

As the complexity of systems increases and the time to market shortens, developers have strong incentives to reuse code and to rely on vendor-supplied components. Interactive systems, for example, are now rarely built from scratch but rather are developed with user interface toolkits that provide a wide range of dialogs, windows, buttons, or other standard interface objects. Other projects focus on redoing only part of an existing system. For example, corporate information systems, costly to design and build, need to be updated to new client hardware. Often, only the client side of the system is upgraded to new technology and the backend of the system left untouched.[2] Whether dealing with off-the-shelf component or legacy code, developers have to deal with existing code, which they cannot modify and which has not been designed to be integrated into their system.

We can deal with existing components such as code by encapsulating them. This approach has the advantage of decoupling the system from the encapsulated code, thus minimizing the impact of existing software on the design. When the encapsulated code is written in the same language as the new system, this can be done using an Adapter pattern.

The **Adapter pattern** (Figure 6-33) is used to convert the interface of an existing piece of code into an interface, called the `NewInterface`, that a calling subsystem expects. An `Adaptor` class, also called a wrapper, is introduced to provide the glue between *NewInterface* and `LegacySystem`. For example, assume the client is the static `sort()` method of the Java `Array` class (Figure 6-34). This method expects two arguments a, an `Array` of objects, and c, a

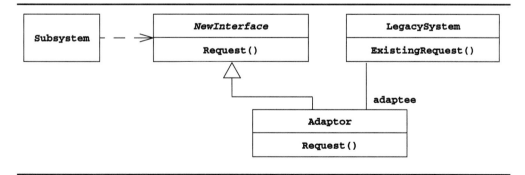

Figure 6-33 `Adapter` pattern (UML class diagram). The `Adapter` pattern is used to provide a different interface (*New Interface*) to an existing component (`Legacy System`).

---

2.   Such projects are called interface engineering projects (see Chapter 4, *Requirements Elicitation*).

```
/* Existing target interface */
interface Comparator {
    int compare(Object o1, Object o2);
    /* ... */
}

// Existing client
class Array {
    static void sort(Object [] a, Comparator c);
    /* ...*/
}

/* Existing adaptee class */
class MyString extends String {
    boolean equals(Object o);
    boolean greaterThan(MyString s);
    /* ... */
}

/* New adaptor class */
class MyStringComparator implements Comparator {
    /* ... */
    int compare(Object o1, Object o2) {
        int result;
        if (o1.greaterThan(o2)) {
            result = 1
        } else if (o1.equals(o2)) {
            result = 0;
        } else {
            result = -1;
        }
        return result;
    }
}
```

Figure 6-34 Adapter pattern example (Java). The static sort() method on Arrays takes two arguments: an arrays of Objects to be sorted and a Comparator defining the relative order of the elements. To sort an array of MyStrings, we need to define a comparator called MyStringComparator with the proper interface. MyStringComparator is an Adaptor.

Comparator object, which provides a compare() method, defining the relative order between elements. Assume we are interested in sorting strings of the class MyString, which defines the greaterThan() and an equals() methods. To sort an Array of MyStrings, we need to define a new comparator, MyStringComparator, which provides a compare() method using greaterThan() and equals(). MyStringComparator is an Adaptor class.[3]

---

3. When designing a new system, adaptors are seldom necessary, as the interface of new classes can be defined such that they comply with the necessary interfaces.

When encapsulating legacy code that is written in a different language than the system under development, we need to deal with language differences. Although integrating code from two different compiled languages can be done, it can present major problems, especially when one or both of the languages are object-oriented and implement different message dispatching semantics. This motivated standards such as CORBA, which defines protocols for allowing the interoperability of distributed objects written in different languages. In the case of client/server architectures, other solutions include developing wrappers around communication protocols between processes.

Protocols for interprocess communication (e.g., pipes and sockets) are usually provided by the operating system and, thus, are language independent. In the cases of CORBA and interprocess communication, the cost of invoking a service becomes much higher than the cost of sending messages among objects in the same process. You need to carefully evaluate the impact on performance by wrappers around legacy code when response time and other performance design goals have been selected.

Technology decisions become obsolete quickly. The system you are building is likely to survive many platforms and will be ported and upgrade several times during maintenance. These tasks, when performed during maintenance, are usually costly, because a large amount of the design information is lost. Why was the original hardware configuration used? Which features of the database management system does this system rely on? Developers can preserve this information by documenting the design rationale of their system, including hardware and component decisions. We describe techniques for doing this in Chapter 8, *Rationale Management*.

6.4.5 Defining Persistent Data Stores

Persistent data outlive a single execution of the system. For example, an author may save his work into a file when using a word processor. The file can then be reopened several days or weeks later. The word processor need not run for the file to exist. Similarly, information related to employees, their employment status, and their paychecks live in a database management system. This allows all the programs that operate on employee data to do so consistently. Moreover, storing data in a database enables the system to perform complex queries on a large data set (e.g., the records of several thousands of employees).

Where and how data is stored in the system impacts the system decomposition. In some cases, for example, in a repository architecture (see Section 6.3.5), a subsystem can be completely dedicated to the storage of data. The selection of a specific database management system can also have implications on the overall control strategy and concurrency management.

For example, in MyTrip, we decide to store the current `Trip` in a file on a small removable disk in order to allow the recovery of the `Trip` in case the driver shuts off the car before reaching the final `Destination`. Using a file is the simplest and most efficient solution in this case, given that the `RoutingSubsystem` will only store complete trips to the file before shutdown and load the file at start-up. In the `PlanningSubsystem`, however, the trips will be stored in a database. This subsystem can then be used to manage all `Trips` for many drivers as well as the maps needed to generate the trips. Using a database for this subsystem allows us to perform complex queries on these data. We add the `TripFileStoreSubsystem` and the `MapDBStoreSubsystem` subsystems to MyTrip to reflect these decisions, as illustrated in Figure 6-35.

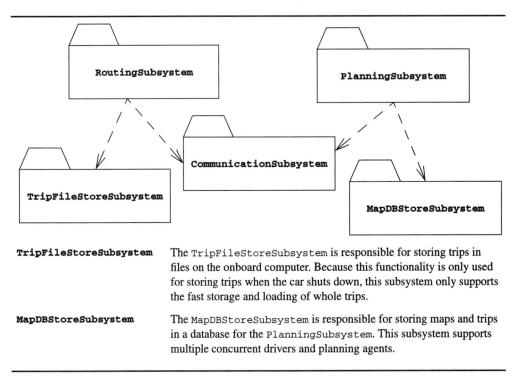

TripFileStoreSubsystem   The `TripFileStoreSubsystem` is responsible for storing trips in files on the onboard computer. Because this functionality is only used for storing trips when the car shuts down, this subsystem only supports the fast storage and loading of whole trips.

MapDBStoreSubsystem   The `MapDBStoreSubsystem` is responsible for storing maps and trips in a database for the `PlanningSubsystem`. This subsystem supports multiple concurrent drivers and planning agents.

Figure 6-35   Subsystem decomposition of MyTrip after deciding on the issue of data stores (UML class diagram, packages collapsed for clarity).

In general, we first need to identify which objects need to be persistent. The persistency of objects is directly inferred from the application domain. In MyTrip, only `Trips` and their related classes need to be stored. The location of the car, for example, need not be persistent because it needs to be recalculated constantly. Then, we need to decide how these objects should be stored (e.g., file, relational database, or object database). The decision for the storage management is more complex and is usually dictated by nonfunctional requirements: Should the objects be retrieved quickly? Is there a need for complex queries? Do objects take a lot of space (e.g., are there images to store)? Database management systems provide mechanisms for concurrency control and efficient queries over large datasets.

There are currently three realistic options for storage management:

- **Flat files.** Files are the storage abstractions provided by operating systems. The application stores its data as a sequence of bytes and defines how and when data should be retrieved. The file abstraction is relatively low level and enables the application to perform a variety of size and speed optimizations. Files, however, require the application to take care of many issues, such as concurrent accesses, and loss of data in case of system crash.

- **Relational database.** A relational database provides an abstraction of data that is higher than flat files. Data are stored in tables that comply with a predefined type called *schema*. Each column in the table represents an attribute. Each row represents a data item as a tuple of attribute values. Several tuples in different tables are used to represent the attributes of an individual object. Relational databases have been used for awhile and are a mature technology. The use of a relational database introduces a high cost and, often, a performance bottleneck.

- **Object-oriented database.** An object-oriented database provides services similar to a relational database. Unlike a relational database, it stores data as objects and associations. In addition to providing a higher level of abstraction (and thus reducing the need to translate between objects and storage entities), object-oriented databases provide developers with inheritance and abstract datatypes. Object-oriented databases are usually slower than relational databases for typical queries.

The following box summarizes the trade-offs when selecting storage management system.

Trade-off between files and databases

When should you choose a file?
- Voluminous data (e.g., images)
- Temporary data (e.g., core file)
- Low information density (e.g., archival files, history logs)

When should you choose a database?
- Concurrent accesses
- Access at fine levels of details
- Multiple platforms
- Multiple applications over the same data

When should you choose a relational database?
- Complex queries over attributes
- Large dataset

When should you choose an object-oriented database?
- Extensive use of associations to retrieve data
- Medium-sized data set
- Irregular associations among objects

Encapsulating data stores

Once we select a storage mechanism (say, a relational database), we can encapsulate it into a subsystem and define a high-level interface that is vendor independent. For example, the **Bridge pattern** (see Figure 6-36 and [Gamma et al., 1994]) allows the interface and the implementation of a class to be decoupled. This allows the substitution of different implementations of a given class, sometimes even at run-time. The `Abstraction` class defines the interface visible to the client. The `Implementor` is an abstract class that defines the lower level methods available to `Abstraction`. An `Abstraction` instance maintains a reference to its corresponding `Implementor` instance. `Abstraction` and `Implementor` can be refined independently.

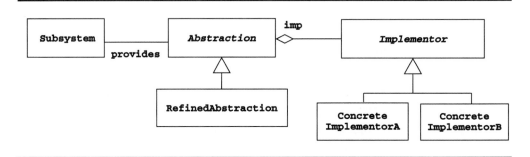

Figure 6-36   `Bridge` pattern (UML class diagram).

Database connectivity standards such as ODBC [Microsoft, 1995] and JDBC [JDBC, 1998] provide such abstractions for relational databases (see ODBC `Bridge` pattern in Figure 6-37). Note, however, that even if most relational databases provide similar services, providing such an abstraction reduces performance. The design goals we defined at the beginning of the system design phase help us trade off performance and modifiability.

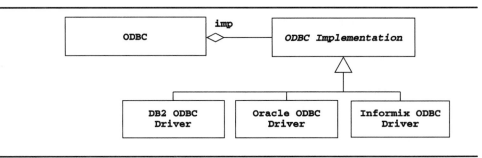

Figure 6-37   `Bridge` pattern for abstracting database vendors (UML class diagram). Removing the dependency from database vendors from the systems provides more flexibility.

6.4.6   Defining Access Control

In multiuser systems, different actors have access to different functionality and data. For example, an everyday actor may only access the data it creates, whereas a system administrator actor may have unlimited access to system data and to other users' data. During analysis, we modeled these distinctions by associating different use cases to different actors. During system design, we model access by examining the object model, by determining which objects are shared among actors, and by defining how actors can control access. Depending on the security requirements on the system, we also define how actors are authenticated to the system (i.e., how actors prove to the system who they are) and how selected data in the system should be encrypted.

Table 6-7   Revisions to the design model stemming from the decision to authenticate `Drivers` and encrypt communication traffic. The text added to the model is in *italics*.

CommunicationSubsystem	The CommunicationSubsystem is responsible for transporting Trips from the PlanningSubsystem to the RoutingSubsystem. *The CommunicationSubsystem uses the Driver associated with the Trip being transported for selecting a key and encrypting the communication traffic.*
PlanningSubsystem	The PlanningSubsystem is responsible for constructing a Trip connecting a sequence of Destinations. The PlanningSubsystem is also responsible for responding to replan requests from RoutingSubsystem. *Prior to processing any requests, the PlanningSubsystem authenticates the Driver from the RoutingSubsystem. The authenticated Driver is used to determine which Trips can be sent to the corresponding RoutingSubsystem.*
Driver	*A Driver represents an authenticated user. It is used by the CommunicationSubsystem to remember keys associated with a user and by the PlanningSubsystem to associate Trips with users.*

For example, in MyTrip, storing maps and `Trips` for many drivers in the same database introduces security issues. We must ensure that `Trips` are sent only to the driver that created them. This is also consistent with the security design goal we defined in Section 6.4.2 for MyTrip. Consequently, we model a driver with the `Driver` class and associate it with the `Trip` class. The `PlanningSubsystem` also becomes responsible for authenticating `Drivers` before sending `Trips`. Finally, we decide to encrypt the communication traffic between the `RoutingSubsystem` and the `PlanningSubsystem`. This will be done by the `CommunicationSubsystem`. The descriptions for the `Driver` class and the revised descriptions for the `PlanningSubsystem` and the `CommunicationSubsystem` are displayed in Table 6-7. The revisions to the design model are indicated in italics.

Defining access control for a multiuser system is usually more complex than in MyTrip. In general, we need to define for each actor which operations they can access on each shared object. For example, in a bank information system, a teller may credit or debit money from local accounts up to a predefined amount. If the transaction exceeds the predefined amount, a manager needs to approve the transaction. Moreover, managers and tellers can only access accounts in their own branch; that is, they cannot access accounts in other branches. Analysts, on the other hand, can access information across all branches of the corporation, but cannot post transactions on individual accounts.

We model access on classes with an access matrix. The rows of the matrix represents the actors of the system. The columns represent classes whose access we control. An entry (class, actor) in the access matrix is called an **access right** and lists the operations (e.g., postSmallDebit (,) postLargeDebit (,) examineBalance (,) getCustomer- Address ())) that can be executed on instances of the class by the actor. Table 6-8 is an example of access matrix for our bank information system.

Table 6-8   Access matrix for a banking system. Tellers can only lookup local accounts, perform small transactions on accounts, and inquire balances. Managers can perform larger transactions and access account history in addition to the operations accessible to the tellers. Analysts can access statistics for all branches but not perform operations at the account level.

Objects Actors	Corporation	LocalBranch	Account
Teller		lookupLocalAccount()	postSmallDebit() postSmallCredit() lookupBalance()
Manage r		lookupLocalAccount()	postSmallDebit() postSmallCredit() postLargeDebit() postLargeCredit() examineBalance() examineHistory()
Analys t	examineGlobalDebits() examineGlobalCredits()	examineLocalDebits() examineLocalCredits( )	

We can represent the access matrix using one of three different approaches: global access table, access control list, and capabilities:

- A **global access table** represents explicitly every cell in the matrix as a (actor, class, operation) tuple. Determining if an actor has access to a specific object requires looking up the corresponding tuple. If no such tuple is found, access is denied.
- An **access control list** associates a list of (actor, operation) pairs with each class to be accessed. Empty cells are discarded. Every time an object is accessed, its access list is checked for the corresponding actor and operation. An example of an access control list is the guest list for a party. A butler checks the arriving guests by comparing their names

against names on the guest list. If there is a match, the guests can enter; otherwise, they are turned away.

- A **capability** associates a (`class`, `operation`) pair with an `actor`. A capability provides an actor to gain control access to an object of the class described in the capability. Denying a capability is equivalent to denying access. An example of a capability is an invitation card for a party. In this case, the butler checks if the arriving guests hold an invitation for the party. If the invitation is valid, the guests are admitted; otherwise, they are turned away. No other checks are necessary.

The representation of the access matrix is also a performance issue. Global access tables are rarely used as they require a lot of space. Access control lists make it faster to answer the question, "Who has access to this object?" whereas capability lists make it faster to answer the question, "Which objects has this actor access to?"

Each row in the access matrix represents a different access view of the classes listed in the columns. All of these access views should be consistent. Usually, however, access views are implemented by defining a subclass for each different type of (`actor`, `operation`) tuple. For example, in our banking system, we would implement an `AccountViewedByTeller` and `AccountViewedByManager` class as subclasses of `Account`. Only the appropriate classes are available to the corresponding actor. For example, the `Analyst` client software would not include an `Account` class, because the `Analyst` has no access to any operation in this class. This reduces the risk that an error in the system results in the possibility of unauthorized access.

An access matrix only represents **static access control**. This means that access rights can be modeled as attributes of the objects of the system. In the bank information system example, consider a broker actor who is assigned dynamically a set of portfolios. By policy, a broker cannot access portfolios managed by another broker. In this case, we need to model access rights dynamically in the system, and, hence, this type of access is called **dynamic access control**. For example, Figure 6-38 shows how this access can be implemented with a protection **Proxy pattern** [Gamma et al., 1994]. For each `Portfolio`, we create a `PortfolioProxy` to protect the `Portfolio` and check for access. An `Access` association between a legitimate `Broker` and a `PortfolioProxy` indicates which `Portfolio` the `Broker` has access to. To access a `Portfolio`, the `Broker` sends a message to the corresponding `PortfolioProxy`. The `PortfolioProxy` first checks if the invoking `Broker` has the appropriate association with the `PortfolioProxy`. If access is granted, the `PortfolioProxy` delegates the message to the `Portfolio`. Otherwise, the operation fails.

In both types of access control, we assume that we know the actor: either the user behind the keyboard or the calling subsystem. This process of verifying the association between the identity of the user or subsystem and the system is called **authentication**. A widespread authentication mechanism, for example, is for the user to specify a user name, known by everybody, and a corresponding password, only known to the system and stored in an access control list. The system protects its users' passwords by encrypting them before storing or transmitting them. If only a single user knows this user name/password combination, then we

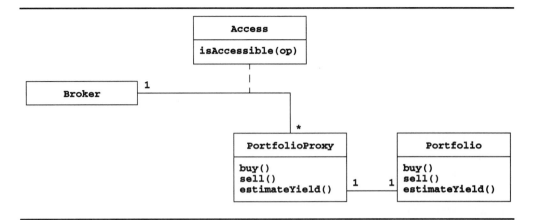

Figure 6-38 Dynamic access implemented with a protection `Proxy`. The `Access` association class contains a set of operations that `Broker` can use to access a `Portfolio`. Every operation in the `PortfolioProxy` first checks with the `isAccessible()` operation if the invoking `Broker` has legitimate access. Once access has been granted, `PortfolioProxy` delegates the operation to the actual `Portfolio` object. One `Access` association can be used to control access to many `Portfolios`.

can assume that the user behind the keyboard is legitimate. Although password authentication can be made secure with current technology, it suffers from many usability disadvantages: Users choose passwords that are easy to remember and, thus, easy to guess. They also tend to write their password on notes that they keep close to their monitor, and thus, visible to many other, unauthorized, users. Fortunately, other, more secure, authentication mechanisms are available. For example, a smart card can be used in conjunction with a password: An intruder would need both the smart card and the password to gain access to the system. Better, we can use a biometric sensor for analyzing patterns of blood vessels in a person's fingers or eyes. An intruder would then need the physical presence of the legitimate user to gain access to the system, which is much more difficult than just stealing a smart card.

In an environment where resources are shared among multiple users, authentication is usually not sufficient. In the case of a network, for example, it is relatively easy for an intruder to find tools to snoop the network traffic, including packets generated by other users (see Figure 6-39). Worse, protocols such as TCP/IP were not designed with security in mind: An intruder can forge packets such that they appear as if they were coming from legitimate users.

Encryption is used to prevent such unauthorized accesses. Using an encryption algorithm, we can translate a message, called **plaintext**, into a encrypted message, called a **ciphertext**, such that even if an intruder intercepts the message, it cannot be understood. Only the receiver has sufficient knowledge to correctly decrypt the message, that is, for reversing the original process. The encryption process is parameterized by a **key**, such that the method of encryption and decryption can be switched quickly in case the intruder manages to obtain sufficient knowledge to decrypt the message.

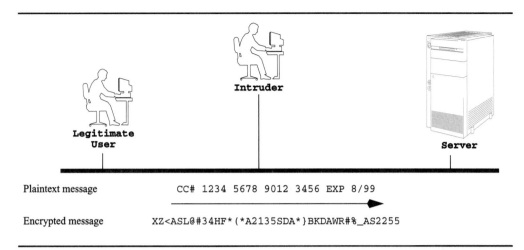

Plaintext message   CC# 1234 5678 9012 3456 EXP 8/99

Encrypted message   XZ<ASL@#34HF*(*A2135SDA*}BKDAWR#%_AS2255

Figure 6-39 Passive attack. Given current technology, it is relatively easy for a passive intruder to listen to all network traffic. To prevent this kind of attack, encryption makes the information an intruder sees difficult to understand.

Secure authentication and encryption are fundamentally difficult problems. You should always select one or more off-the-shelf algorithms or packages instead of designing your own (unless you are in the business of building such packages). Many such packages are based on public standards that are widely reviewed by the academia and the industry, thus ensuring a relatively high level of reliability and security.

Encapsulating access control

The use of vendor-supplied software introduces a security problem: How can we be sure that the supplied software does not include a trap door? Moreover, once a vulnerability is found in a widely used package, how do we protect the system until a patch is available? We can use redundancy to address both issues. For example, the Java Cryptographic Architecture [JCA, 1998] allows multiple implementations of the same algorithms to coexist in the same system, thus reducing the dependency on a specific vendor. More generally, we can use the **Strategy pattern** [Gamma et al., 1994] to encapsulate multiple implementation of the same algorithm. In this pattern (see Figure 6-40), the `Strategy` abstract class defines the generic interface that all implementations of the encapsulated algorithm should have. `ConcreteStrategy` classes provide implementations of the algorithm by subclassing `Strategy`. A `Context` class is responsible for managing the data structure on which `ConcreteStrategies` operate. `Context` and a `ConcreteStrategy` class cooperate to provided the needed functionality.

Once authentication and encryption are provided, application specific-access control can be more easily implemented on top of these building blocks. In all cases, addressing security issues is a difficult topic. When addressing these issues, developers should record their assumptions and describe the intruder scenarios they are considering. When several alternatives

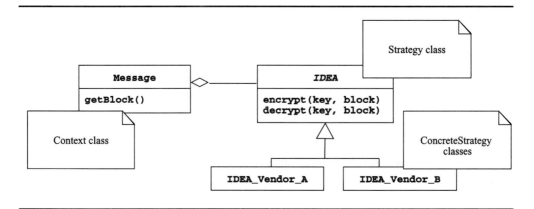

Figure 6-40 An example of a `Strategy` pattern encapsulating multiple implementation of the IDEA encryption algorithm (UML class diagram). The `Message` and `IDEA` classes cooperate to realize the encryption of plain text. The selection of an implementation can be done dynamically.

are explored, developers should state the design problems they are attempting to solve and record the results of the evaluation. We describe in the next chapter how to do this systematically using issue modeling.

6.4.7   Designing the Global Control Flow

Control flow is the sequencing of actions in a system. In object-oriented systems, sequencing actions includes deciding which operations should be executed and in which order. These decisions are based on external events generated by an actor or on the passage of time.

Control flow is a design problem. During analysis, control flow is not an issue, because we simply assume that all objects are running simultaneously, executing operations any time they need to execute them. During system design, we need to take into account that not every object has the luxury of running on its own processor. There are three possible control flow mechanisms:

• **Procedure-driven control.** Operations wait for input whenever they need data from an actor. This kind of control flow is mostly used in legacy systems and systems written in procedural languages. It introduces difficulties when used with object-oriented languages. As the sequencing of operations is distributed among a large set of objects, it becomes increasingly difficult to determine the order of inputs by looking at the code (Figure 6-41).

```
    Stream in, out;
    String userid, passwd;
/* Initialization omitted */
    out.println("Login:");
    in.readln(userid);
    out.println("Password:");
    in.readln(passwd);
    if (!security.check(userid, passwd)) {
        out.println("Login failed.");
        system.exit(-1);
    }
/* ... */
```

Figure 6-41   An example of procedure driven control (Java). The code prints out messages and waits for input from the user.

- **Event-driven control**. A main loop waits for an external event. Whenever an event becomes available, it is dispatched to the appropriate object, based on information associated with the event. This kind of control flow has the advantage of leading to a simpler structure and to centralizing all input in the main loop. However, it makes the implementation of multistep sequences more difficult to implement (Figure 6-42).

- **Threads.** Also called lightweight threads to distinguish them from processes that require more computing overhead, are the concurrent variation of procedure-driven control: The system can create an arbitrary number of threads, each responding to a different event. If a thread needs additional data, it waits for input from a specific actor. This kind of control flow is probably the most intuitive of the three mechanisms. However, debugging threaded software requires good debugging tools: Preemptive thread schedulers introduce nondeterminism and, thus, make it harder to find repeatable test cases (Figure 6-43).

```
Enumeration subscribers, eventStream;
Subscriber subscriber;
Event event;
EventStream eventStream;
/* ... */
while (eventStream.hasMoreElements) {
    event = eventStream.nextElement();
    subscribers = dispatchInfo.getSubscribers(event);
    while (subscribers.hasMoreElements()) {
        subscriber = subscribers.nextElement()) {
        subscriber.process(event);
    }
}
/* ... */
```

Figure 6-42   An example of main loop for event-driven control (Java). An event is taken from an event queue and sent to objects interested in it.

```
Thread thread;
Event event;
EventHandler eventHandler;
boolean done;
/* ...*/
while (!done) {
    event = eventStream.getNextEvent();
    eventHandler = new EventHandler(event)
    thread = new Thread(eventHandler);
    thread.start();
}
/* ...*/
```

Figure 6-43   An example of event processing with threads (Java). eventHandler is an object dedicated to handling event. It implements the run() operation, which is invoked when thread is started.

Procedure-driven control is useful for testing subsystems. A driver makes specific calls to methods offered by the subsystem. For the control flow of the final system, though, procedure-driven control should be avoided.

The trade-off between event-driven control and threads is more complicated. Event-driven control is more mature than threads. Modern languages have only recently started to provide support for thread programming. As more debugging tools are becoming available and experience is accumulated, developing thread-based systems will become easier. Also, many user interface packages supply the infrastructure for dispatching events and impose this kind of control flow on the design. Although threads are more intuitive, they currently introduce many problems during debugging and testing. Until more mature tools and infrastructures are available for developing with threads, event-driven control flow is preferred.

Once a control flow mechanism is selected, we can realize it with a set of one or more control objects. The role of control objects is to record external events, store temporary state about them, and issue the right sequence of operation calls on the boundary and entity objects associated with the external event. On the one hand, localizing control flow decisions for a use case into a single object results into more understandable code; on the other hand, it makes the system more resilient to changes in control flow implementation.

Encapsulating control flow

An example of encapsulation of control is the **Command pattern** [Gamma et al., 1994] (see Figure 6-44). In interactive systems, it is often desirable to execute, undo, or store user requests without knowing the content of the request. The key to decoupling requests from their handling is to turn requests into command objects, which inherit from an abstract *Command* class. The *Command* class defines how the command is executed, undone, or stored, whereas the concrete class implements specific requests.

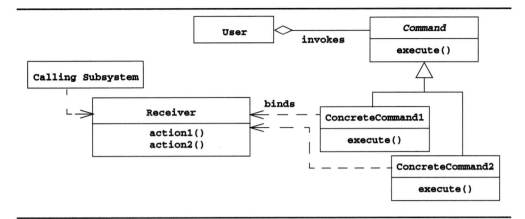

Figure 6-44   `Command` pattern (UML class diagram). This pattern enables the encapsulation of control such that user requests can be treated uniformly, independent of the specific request.

We can use the `Command` pattern to decouple menu items from actions (see Figure 6-45). Decoupling menu items from actions has the advantage of centralizing control flow (e.g., dialog sequencing) into control objects instead of spreading it between boundary and entity objects. A `Menu`, composed of `MenuItems`, creates a `Command` object of the appropriate class whenever the corresponding `MenuItem` is selected by the user. The `Application` invokes the `execute()` operation of the newly created `Command` object. If the user wishes to undo the last request, the `undo()` operation of the last `Command` object is executed. Different `Command` objects implement different requests (e.g., `CopyCommand` and `PasteCommand`).

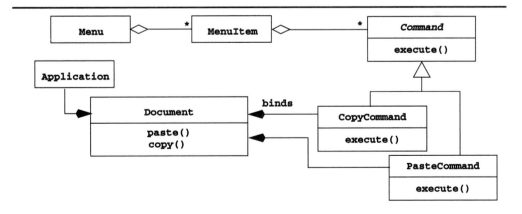

Figure 6-45   An example of a `Command` pattern (UML class diagram). In this example, menu items and operations on documents are decoupled. This enables us to centralize control flow in the command objects (`CopyCommand` and `PasteCommand`) instead of spreading it across boundary objects (`MenuItem`) and entity objects (`Document`).

6.4.8   Identifying Boundary Conditions

In previous sections, we dealt with designing and refining the system decomposition. We now have a better idea of how to decompose the system, how to distribute use cases among subsystems, where to store data, and how to achieve access control and ensure security. We still need to examine the boundary conditions of the system, that is, to decide how the system is started, initialized, and shut down, and we need to define how we deal with major failures, such as data corruption, whether they are caused by a software error or a power outage.

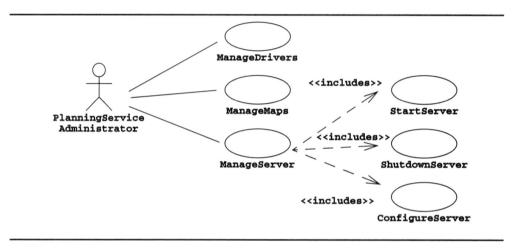

Figure 6-46   Administration use cases for MyTrip (UML use case diagram). `ManageDrivers` is invoked to add, remove, modify, or read data about drivers (e.g., user name and password, usage log, encryption key generation). `ManageMaps` is invoked to add, remove, or update maps that are used to generate trips. `ManageServer` includes all the functions necessary to start up and shutdown the server.

For example, we now have a good idea of how MyTrip should work in steady state. We have, however, not yet addressed how MyTrip is initialized. For example, how are maps loaded into the `PlanningService`? How is MyTrip installed in the car? How does MyTrip know which `PlanningService` to connect to? How are drivers added to the `PlanningService`? We quickly discover a set of use cases that has not been specified. We call these the system administration use cases. *System administration use cases* specify the behavior of a system during the start-up and shutdown phase.

It is common that system administration use cases are not specified during analysis or that they are treated separately. On the one hand, many system administration functions can be inferred from the everyday user requirements (e.g., registering and deleting users, managing access control); on the other hand, many functions are consequences of design decisions (e.g., cache sizes, location of database server, location of backup server) and not of requirement decisions.

We now modify the analysis model for MyTrip to include the administration use cases. In particular, we add three use cases: `ManageDrivers`, to add, remove, and edit drivers; `ManageMaps`, to add, remove, and update maps used to generate trips; and `ManageServer`, to perform routine configuration, start-up, and shutdown (see Figure 6-46). `StartServer`, part of `ManageServer`, is provided as an example in Figure 6-47.

Use case name	`StartServer`
Entry condition	1. The `PlanningServiceAdministrator` logs into the server machine.
Flow of events	2. Upon successful login, the `PlanningServiceAdministrator` executes the `startPlanningService` command.
	3. If the `PlanningService` was previously shutdown normally, the server reads the list of legitimate `Drivers` and the index of active `Trips` and `Maps`. If the `PlanningService` had crashed, it notifies the `PlanningServiceAdministrator` and performs a consistency check on the `MapDBStore`.
Exit condition	4. The `PlanningService` is available and waits for connections from `RoutingAssistants`.

Figure 6-47   `StartServer` use case of the MyTrip system.

In this case, adding three use cases, that is, revising the use case model, does not impact the subsystem decomposition. We added, however, new use cases to existing subsystems: The `MapDBStoreSubsystem` needs to be able to detect whether it was properly shut down or not and needs to be able to perform consistency checks and repair corrupted data, if necessary. We revise the description of `MapDBStoreSubsystem` (Figure 6-48).

When examining boundary conditions, we also need to investigate exceptional cases. For example, the nonfunctional requirements of MyTrip specify that the system needs to tolerate connection failures. For this reason, the `RouteAssistant` downloads the planned `Trip` at the initial `Destination`. We also decide to download `Segments` that are close to the `Trip`, to enable minimum replanning even though a connection might not be available.

`MapDBStoreSubsystem`	The `MapDBStoreSubsystem` is responsible for storing maps and trips in a database for the `PlanningSubsystem`. This subsystem supports multiple concurrent drivers and planning agents. *When starting up, the MapDBStoreSubsystem detects if it was properly shutdown. If not, it performs a consistent check on the Maps and Trips and repairs corrupted data if necessary.*

Figure 6-48   Revised description for `MapDBStoreSubsystem` based on the additional `StartServer` use case of Figure 6-47. (Changes indicated in *italics*.)

In general, an **exception** is an unexpected event or error that occurs during the execution of the system. Exceptions are caused by one of three different sources:

- *A user error.* The user mistakenly or deliberately inputs data that are out of bounds. For example, a negative amount in a banking transaction could lead to transferring money in the wrong direction if the system does not protect against such errors.
- *A hardware failure.* Hardware ages and fails. The failure of a network link, for example, can momentarily disconnect two nodes of the system. A hard disk crash can lead to the permanent loss of data.
- *A software bug.* An error can occur either because the system or one of its components contains a design error. Although writing bug-free software is difficult, individual subsystems can anticipate errors from other subsystems and protect against them.

Exception handling is the mechanism by which a system treats an exception. In the case of a user error, the system should display a meaningful error message to the user, such that she can correct her input. In the case of a network link failure, the system needs to save its temporary state in order to recover once the network comes back on line.

Developing reliable systems is a difficult topic. Often, trading off some functionality can make it easier on the design of the system. In MyTrip, we assumed that the connection is always possible at the source destination and that replanning could be impacted by communication problems along the trip.

6.4.9   Anticipating Change

System design introduces a strange paradox in the development process. On the one hand, we want to construct solid walls between subsystems, to manage complexity by breaking the system into smaller pieces, and to prevent changes from one subsystem to impact others. On the other hand, we want the software architecture to be modifiable to minimize the cost of later change. These are conflicting goals that cannot be reconciled: We have to define an architecture early to deal with complexity, and we have to pay the price of change later in the development process. We can, however, anticipate change and design for it, as sources of later changes tend to be the same for most systems:

- *New vendor or new technology.* When components are used to build the system, anticipate that the component will be replaced by an equivalent one from a different vendor. This change is frequent and generally difficult to cope with. The software marketplace is dynamic, and many vendors will start up and go out of business before your project is completed.
- *New implementation.* When subsystems are integrated and tested together, the overall system response time is, more often than not, above stated or implicit performance requirements: Posting a debit on a bank information system may take 2 minutes, a flight

reservation system takes 5 minutes to book a flight. System-wide performance is difficult to predict and is usually not optimized before integration: Developers focus on their subsystem first. This triggers the need for more-efficient data structures and algorithms and better interfaces—often under time constraints.

- *New views.* Testing the software with real users uncovers many usability problems. These often translate into the creation of additional views on the same data.

- *New complexity of the application domain.* The deployment of a system triggers ideas of new generalizations: A bank information system for one branch may lead to the idea of a multibranch information system. Other times, the domain itself increases in complexity: Previously, flight numbers were associated with one plane and one plane only. With the advent of carrier alliances, one plane can now have multiple flight numbers from different companies.

- *Errors.* Unfortunately, many requirements errors are discovered only when real users start using the system.

Modern object-oriented languages provide mechanisms that can minimize the impact of change when anticipated. The use of delegation and inheritance in conjunction with abstract classes decouples the interface of a subsystem from its actual implementation. In this chapter, we have provided you with selected examples of design patterns [Gamma et al., 1994] that deal with the above changes. Figure 6-49 summarizes the patterns and the type of change they protect against.

Adapter (see example in Figure 6-34)	*New vendor, new technology, new implementation.* This pattern encapsulates a piece of legacy code that was not designed to work with the system. It also limits the impact of substituting the piece of legacy code for a different component.
Bridge (see example in Figure 6-37)	*New vendor, new technology, new implementation.* This pattern decouples the interface of a class from its implementation. It serves the same purpose as the `Adapter` pattern except that the developer is not constrained by an existing piece of code.
Command (see example in Figure 6-45)	*New functionality.* This patterns decouples the objects responsible for command processing from the commands themselves. This pattern protects these objects from changes due to new functionality.
Observer (see example in Section 6.3.5)	*New views.* This pattern decouples entity objects from their views. Additional views can be added with entity objects being modified.
Strategy (see example in Figure 6-40)	*New vendor, new technology, new implementation.* This pattern decouples an algorithm from its implementation(s). It serves the same purpose as do the `Adapter` and `Bridge` patterns, except that the encapsulated unit is a behavior.

Figure 6-49   Selected design patterns and the changes they anticipate.

A reason for the high cost of change late in the process is the loss of design context. Developers forget very quickly the reasons that pushed them to design complicated workarounds or complex data structures during early phases of the process. When changing code late in the process, the likelihood of introducing errors into the system is high. To protect against such situations, assumptions should be recorded. For example, when using a design pattern to anticipate a certain change (from Figure 6-49), you should record which change you are anticipating. In Chapter 8, *Rationale Management*, we describe several techniques for recording the design alternatives and decisions.

6.4.10 Reviewing System Design

Like analysis, system design is an evolutionary and iterative activity. Unlike analysis, there is no external agent, such as the client, to review the successive iterations and ensure better quality. This quality improvement activity, however, is still necessary, and project managers and developers need to organize a review process to substitute for it. Several alternatives exist, such as using the developers who were not involved in system design to act as independent reviewers, or to use developers from another project to act as a peer review. These review processes work only if the reviewers have an incentive in discovering and reporting problems.

In addition to meeting the design goals that were identified during system design, we need to ensure that the system design model is correct, complete, consistent, realistic, and readable. The system design model is **correct** if the analysis model can be mapped to the system design model. You should ask the following questions to determine if the system design is correct:

- Can every subsystem be traced back to a use case or a nonfunctional requirement?
- Can every use case be mapped to a set of subsystems?
- Can every design goal be traced back to a nonfunctional requirement?
- Is every nonfunctional requirement addressed in the system design model?
- Does each actor have an access policy?
- Is it consistent with the nonfunctional security requirement?

The model is **complete** if every requirement and every system design issue has been addressed. You should ask the following questions to determine if the system design is complete:

- Have the boundary conditions been handled?
- Was there a walkthrough of the use cases to identify missing functionality in the system design?
- Have all use cases been examined and assigned a control object?
- Have all aspects of system design (i.e., hardware allocation, persistent storage, access control, legacy code, boundary conditions) been addressed?
- Do all subsystems have definitions?

The model is **consistent** if it does not contain any contradictions. You should ask the following questions to determine if a system design is consistent:

- Are conflicting design goals prioritized?
- Are there design goals that violate a nonfunctional requirement?
- Are there multiple subsystems or classes with the same name?
- Are collections of objects exchanged among subsystems in a consistent manner?

The model is **realistic** if the corresponding system can be implemented. You ask the following questions to determine if a system design is realistic:

- Are there any new technologies or components in the system? Were there any studies to evaluate the appropriateness or robustness of these technologies or components?
- Have performance and reliability requirements been reviewed in the context of the subsystem decomposition? For example, is there a network connection on the critical path of the system?
- Have concurrency issues (e.g., contention, deadlocks, mutual exclusion) been addressed?

The model is **readable** if developers not involved in the system design can understand the model. You should ask the following questions to ensure that the system design is readable:

- Are subsystem names understandable?
- Do entities (e.g., subsystems, classes, operations) with similar names denote similar phenomena?
- Are all entities described at the same level of detail?

In many projects, you will find that system design and implementation overlap quite a bit. For example, you may build prototypes of selected subsystems before the architecture is stable in order to evaluate new technologies. This leads to many partial reviews instead of an encompassing review followed by a client sign-off, as for analysis. Although this process yields greater flexibility, it also requires developers to track open issues more carefully. Many difficult issues tend to be resolved late, not because they are difficult, but because they fell through the cracks of the organization.

6.5 Managing System Design

In this section, we discuss issues related to managing the system design activities. As in analysis, the primary challenge in managing the system design is to maintain consistency, while using as many resources as possible. In the end, the software architecture and the system interfaces should describe a single coherent system understandable by a single person.

We first describe a document template that can be used to document the results of system (Section 6.5.1). Next, we describe the role assignment during system design (Section 6.5.2) and address communication issues during system design (Section 6.5.3). Next, we address management issues related to the iterative nature of system design (Section 6.5.4).

6.5.1 Documenting System Design

System design is documented in the System Design Document (SDD). It describes design goals set by the project, the subsystem decomposition (with UML class diagrams), the hardware/software mapping (with UML deployment diagrams), the data management, the access control, control flow mechanisms, and boundary conditions. The SDD is used to define interfaces between teams of developers and as reference when architecture-level decisions need to be revisited. The audience for the SDD includes the project management, the system architects (i.e., the developers who participate in the system design), and the developers who design and implement each subsystem. The following is an example template for a SDD:

System Design Document
1. Introduction
    1.1 Purpose of the system
    1.2 Design goals
    1.3 Definitions, acronyms, and abbreviations
    1.4 References
    1.5 Overview
2. Current software architecture
3. Proposed software architecture
    3.1 Overview
    3.2 Subsystem decomposition
    3.3 Hardware/software mapping
    3.4 Persistent data management
    3.5 Access control and security
    3.6 Global software control
    3.7 Boundary conditions
4. Subsystem services
Glossary

The first section of the SDD is an *Introduction*. Its purpose is to provide a brief overview of the software architecture and the design goals. It also provides references to other documents and traceability information (e.g., related requirements analysis document, references to existing systems, constraints impacting the software architecture).

The second section, *Current software architecture* describes the architecture of the system being replaced. If there is no previous system, this section can be replaced by a survey of current architectures for similar systems. The purpose of this section is to make explicit the background information that system architects used, their assumptions, and common issues the new system will address.

The third section, *Proposed system architecture* documents the system design model of the new system. It is divided into seven subsections:

- *Overview* presents a bird's eye view of the software architecture and briefly describes the assignment of functionality to each subsystem.

- *Subsystem decomposition* describes the decomposition into subsystems and the responsibilities of each. This is the main product of system design.

- *Hardware/software mapping* describes how subsystems are assigned to hardware and off-the-shelf components. It also lists the issues introduced by multiple nodes and software reuse.

- *Persistent data management* describes the persistent data stored by the system and the data management infrastructure required for it. This section typically includes the description of data schemes, the selection of a database, and the description of the encapsulation of the database.

- *Access control and security* describes the user model of the system in terms of an access matrix. This section also describes security issues, such as the selection of an authentication mechanism, the use of encryption, and the management of keys.

- *Global software control* describes how the global software control is implemented. In particular, this section should describe how requests are initiated and how subsystems synchronize. This section should list and address synchronization and concurrency issues.

- *Boundary conditions* describes the start-up, shutdown, and error behavior of the system. If new use cases are discovered for system administration, these should be included in the requirements analysis document, not in this section.

The fourth section, *Subsystem services,* describes the services provided by each subsystem in terms of operations. Although this section is usually empty or incomplete in the first versions of the SDD, this section serves as a reference for teams for the boundaries between their subsystems. The interface of each subsystem is derived from this section and detailed in the Object Design Document.

The SDD is written after the initial system decomposition is done; that is, system architects should not wait until all system design decisions are made before publishing the document. The SDD, moreover, is updated throughout the process when design decisions are made or problems are discovered. The SDD, once published, is baselined and put under configuration management. The revision history section of the SDD provides a history of changes as a list of changes, including author responsible for the change, date of change, and brief description of the change.

6.5.2   Assigning Responsibilities

Unlike analysis, system design is the realm of developers. The client and the end user fade into the background. Note, however, that many activities in system design trigger revisions to the analysis model. The client and the user are brought back into the process for such revisions. System design in complex systems is centered around the architecture team. This is a cross-functional team made up of architects (who define the subsystem decomposition) and selected developers (who will take part in the implementation of the subsystem). It is critical that system design include persons that are exposed to the consequences of system design decisions. The architecture team starts work right after the analysis model is stable and continue to function until the end of the integration phase. This creates an incentive for the architecture team to anticipate problems encountered during integration. Below are the main roles of system design:

- The **architect** is the main role of system design. The architect ensures consistency in design decisions and interface styles. The architect ensures the consistency of the design in the configuration management and testing teams, in particular in the formulation of the configuration management policy as well as the system integration strategy. This is mainly an integration role consuming information from each subsystem team. The architect is the leader of the cross-functional architecture team.
- **Architecture liaisons** are the members of the architecture team. They are representatives from the subsystem teams. They convey information from and to their teams and negotiate interface changes. During system design, they focus on the subsystem services; during the implementation phase, they focus on the consistency of the APIs.
- The **document editor**, **configuration manager**, and **reviewer** roles are the same as for analysis.

The number of subsystems determines the size of the architecture team. For complex systems, an architecture team is introduced for each level of abstraction. In all cases, there should be one integrating role on the team to ensure consistency and the understandability of the architecture by a single individual.

6.5.3   Communicating about System Design

Communication during system design should be less challenging than during analysis: The functionality of the system has been defined, project participants have similar backgrounds and by now should know each other better. Communication is still difficult, due to new sources of complexity:

- *Size*. The number of issues to be dealt with increases as developers start designing. The number of items that developers manipulate increases: Each piece of functionality requires many operations on many objects. Moreover, developers investigate, often concurrently, multiple designs and multiple implementation technologies.

- *Change*. The subsystem decomposition and the interfaces of the subsystems are in constant flux. Terms used by developers to name different parts of the system evolve constantly. If the change is rapid, developers may not be discussing the same version of the subsystem, which can lead to much confusion.
- *Level of abstraction*. Discussions about requirements can be made concrete by using interface mock-ups and analogies with existing systems. Discussions about implementation become concrete when integration and test results are available. System design discussions are seldom concrete, as consequences of design decisions are felt only later, during implementation and testing.
- *Reluctance to confront problems*. The level of abstraction of most discussions can also make it easy to delay the resolution of difficult issues. A typical resolution of control issues is often, "Let us revisit this issue during implementation." Whereas it is usually desirable to delay certain design decisions, such as the internal data structures and algorithms used by each subsystem, for example, any decision that has an impact on the system decomposition and the subsystem interfaces should not be delayed.
- *Conflicting goals and criteria*. Individual developers often optimize different criteria. A developer experienced in user interface design will be biased toward optimizing response time. A developer experienced in databases might optimize throughput. These conflicting goals, especially when implicit, result in developers pulling the system decomposition in different directions and lead to inconsistencies.

The same techniques we discussed in analysis (see Section 5.5.3) can be applied during system design:

- *Identify and prioritize the design goals for the system and make them explicit* (see Section 6.4.2). If the developers concerned with system design have an input in this process, they will have an easier time committing to these design goals. Design goals also provide an objective framework against which decisions can be evaluated.
- *Make the current version of the system decomposition available to all concerned*. A live document distributed via the Internet is one way to achieve rapid distribution. Using a configuration management tool to maintain the system design documents helps developers in identifying recent changes.
- *Maintain an up-to-date glossary*. As in analysis, defining terms explicitly reduces misunderstandings. When identifying and modeling subsystems, provide definitions in addition to names. A UML diagram with only subsystem names is not sufficient for supporting effective communication. A brief and substantial definition should accompany every subsystem and class name.
- *Confront design problems*. Delaying design decisions can be beneficial when more information is needed before committing to the design decision. This approach, however, can prevent the confrontation of difficult design problems. Before tabling an issue, several

possible alternatives should be explored and described and the delay justified. This ensures that issues that are delayed can be delayed without serious impact on the system decomposition.

• *Iterate.* Selected excursions into the implementation phase can improve the system design. For example, new features in a vendor-supplied component can be evaluated by implementing a vertical prototype (see Section 6.5.4) for the functionality most likely to benefit from the feature.

Finally, no matter how much effort is expended on system design, the system decomposition and the subsystem interfaces will almost certainly change during implementation. As new information about implementation technologies becomes available, developers have a clearer understanding of the system, and design alternatives are discovered. Developers should anticipate change and reserve some time to update the SDD before system integration.

6.5.4   Iterating over the system design

As in the case of requirements, system design occurs through successive iteration and change. Change, however, should be controlled to prevent chaos, especially in complex projects including many participants. We distinguish three types of iterations during system design. First, major decisions early in the system design impact subsystem decomposition as each of the different activities of system design are initiated. Second, revisions to the interfaces of the subsystems occur when evaluation prototypes are done to evaluate specific issues. Third, errors and oversights that are discovered late trigger changes to the subsystem interfaces and sometimes to the system decomposition itself.

The first set of iterations is best handled through face-to-face and electronic brainstorming. Definitions are still in flux, developers do not have yet a grasp of the whole system, and communication should be maximized at the expense of formality or procedure. Often in team-based projects, the initial system decomposition is designed before the analysis is complete. Decomposing the system early enables the responsibility of different subsystems to be assigned to different teams. Change and exploration should be encouraged, if only to broaden the developers shared understanding or to generate supporting evidence for the current design. For this reason, there should not be a bureaucratic formal change process during this phase.

The second set of iterations aims at solving difficult and focused issues, such as the choice of a specific vendor or technology. The subsystem decomposition is stable (it should be independent of vendors and technology; see Section 6.4.9), and most of these explorations aim at identifying whether a specific package is appropriate or not for the system. During this period, developers can also realize a vertical prototype[4] for a critical use case to test the appropriateness

---

4. A vertical prototype completely implements a restricted functionality (e.g., interface, control, and entity objects for one use case), whereas a horizontal prototype implements partially a broad range of functionality (e.g., interface objects for a number of use cases).

of the decomposition. This enables control flow issues to be discovered early and addressed. Again, a formal change process is not necessary. A list of pending issues and their status can help developers quickly propagate the result of a technology investigation.

The third set of iterations remedies design problems discovered late in the process. Although developers would much rather avoid any such iterations, as they tend to incur a high cost and introduce many new bugs in the system, they should anticipate changes late in the development. Anticipating late iterations includes documenting dependencies among subsystems, the design rationale for subsystem interfaces, and any workaround that is likely to break in case of change. Change should be carefully managed, and a change process, similar to the one tracking requirements changes, should be put in place.

We can achieve the progressive stabilization of the subsystem decomposition by using the concept of design window. In order to encourage change while controlling it, critical issues are left open only during a specified time. For example, the hardware/software platform on which the system is targeted should be resolved early in the project, such that purchasing decisions for the hardware can be done in time for the developers. Internal data structures and algorithms, however, can be left open until after integration, allowing developers to revise them based on performance testing. Once the design window is past, the issue must be resolved and can only be reopened in a subsequent iteration.

With the pace of technology innovation quickening, many changes can be anticipated when a dedicated part of the organization is responsible for technology management. Technology managers scan new technologies, evaluate them, and accumulate knowledge that is used during the selection of components. Often, change happens so fast that companies are not aware of which technologies they themselves provide.

6.6 Exercises

1. Decomposing a system into subsystems reduces the complexity developers have to deal with by simplifying the parts and increasing their coherence. Decomposing a system into simpler parts usually results into increasing a different kind of complexity: Simpler parts also means a larger number of parts and interfaces. If coherence is the guiding principle driving developers to decompose a system into small parts, which competing principle drives them to keep the total number of parts small?

2. In Section 6.4.2, we classified design goals into five categories: performance, dependability, cost, maintenance, and end user. Assign one or more categories to each of the following goals:
   - Users must be given a feedback within 1 second after they issue any command.
   - The TicketDistributor must be able to issue train tickets, even in the event of a network failure.
   - The housing of the TicketDistributor must allow for new buttons to be installed in the event the number of different fares increases.

- The `AutomatedTellerMachine` must withstand dictionary attacks (i.e., users attempting to discover a identification number by systematic trial).

- The user interface of the system should prevent users from issuing commands in the wrong order.

3. Consider a system that includes a Web server and two database servers. Both database servers are identical: The first acts as a main server, while the second acts as a redundant backup in case the first one fails. Users use Web browsers to access data through the Web server. They also have the option of using a proprietary client that accesses the databases directly. Draw a UML deployment diagram representing the hardware/software mapping of this system.

4. Consider a legacy, fax-based, problem-reporting system for an aircraft manufacturer. You are part of a reengineering project replacing the core of the system by a computer-based system, which includes a database and a notification system. The client requires the fax to remain an entry point for problem reports. You propose an E-mail entry point. Describe a subsystem decomposition, and possibly a design pattern, which would allow both interfaces.

5. You are designing the access control policies for a Web-based retail store. Customers access the store via the Web, browse product information, input their address and payment information, and purchase products. Suppliers can add new products, update product information, and receive orders. The store owner sets the retail prices, makes tailored offers to customers based on their purchasing profiles, and provides marketing services. You have to deal with three actors: `StoreAdministrator`, `Supplier`, and `Customer`. Design an access control policy for all three actors. `Customers` can be created via the Web, whereas `Suppliers` are created by the `StoreAdministrator`.

6. Select a control flow mechanism you find most appropriate for each of the following systems. Because multiple choices are possible in most cases, justify your choices.

   - a Web server designed to sustain high loads

   - a graphical user interface for a word processor

   - a real-time embedded system (e.g., a guidance system on a satellite launcher)

7. Why are use cases that describe boundary conditions described during system design (as opposed to during requirements elicitation or analysis)?

8. You are developing a system that stores its data on a Unix file system. You anticipate that you will port future versions of the system to other operating systems that provide different file systems. Which design pattern do you use to guard against this change?

References

[Bass et al., 1999]	L. Bass, P. Clements, & R. Kazman, *Software Architecture in Practice.* Addison-Wesley, Reading, MA, 1999.
[Booch, 1994]	G. Booch, *Object-Oriented Analysis and Design with Applications,* 2nd ed. Benjamin/Cummings, Redwood City, CA, 1994.
[Day & Zimmermann, 1983]	J.D. Day & H. Zimmermann, "The OSI Reference Model," *Proceedings of the IEEE*, vol. 71, pp. 1334–1340, Dec. 1983.
[Erman et al., 1980]	L. D. Erman, F. Hayes-Roth, et al., "The Hearsay-II Speech-Understanding System: Integrating knowledge to resolve uncertainty." *ACM Computing Surveys*, vol. 12, no. 2, pp. 213–253, 1980.
[Fowler, 1997]	M. Fowler, *Analysis Patterns: Reusable Object Models.* Addison-Wesley, Reading, MA, 1997.
[Gamma et al., 1994]	E. Gamma, R. Helm, R. Johnson, & J. Vlissides, *Design Patters: Elements of Reusable Object-Oriented Software.* Addison-Wesley, Reading, MA, 1994.
[JCA, 1998]	*Java Cryptography Architecture*, JDK Documentation. Javasoft, 1998.
[JDBC, 1998]	*JDBC^{TM}—Connecting Java and Databases*, JDK Documentation. Javasoft, 1998.
[Microsoft, 1995]	Microsoft, "Chapter 9: Open Database Connectivity (ODBC) 2.0 fundamentals," *Microsoft Windows Operating Systems and Services Architecture,* Microsoft Corp., 1995.
[Mowbray & Malveau, 1997]	T. J. Mowbray & R. C. Malveau, *CORBA Design Patterns.* Wiley, New York, 1997.
[Nye & O'Reilly, 1992]	A. Nye & T. O'Reilly. *X Toolkit Intrinsics Programming Manual: OSF/Motif 1.1 Edition for X11 Release 5 The Definitive Guides to the X Windows Systems,* vol. 4, O'Reilly & Associates, Sebastopol, CA, 1992.
[OMG, 1995]	Object Management Group, *The Common Object Request Broker: Architecture and Specification.* Wiley, New York, 1995.
[RMI, 1998]	*Java Remote Method Invocation*, JDK Documentation. Javasoft, 1998.
[Rumbaugh et al., 1991]	J. Rumbaugh, M. Blaha, W. Premerlani, F. Eddy, and W. Lorensen. *Object-Oriented Modeling and Design.* Prentice Hall, Englewood Cliffs, NJ, 1991.
[Shaw & Garlan, 1996]	M. Shaw & D. Garlan, *Software Architecture: Perspectives on an Emerging Discipline.* Prentice Hall, Upper Saddle River, NJ, 1996.
[Siewiorek & Swarz, 1992]	D. P. Siewiorek & R. S. Swarz, *Reliable Computer Systems: Design and Evaluation.* 2nd ed. Digital, Burlington, MA, 1992.
[Silberschatz et al, 1991]	A. Silberschatz, J. Peterson, & P. Galvin, *Operating System Concepts.* 3rd ed. Addison-Wesley, Reading, MA, 1991.
[Tanenbaum, 1996]	A. S. Tanenbaum, *Computer Networks,* 3rd ed. Prentice Hall, Upper Saddle River, NJ, 1996.

7

Object Design

If you have a procedure with 10 parameters, you probably missed some.
—Alan Perlis, Epigrams in Programming

During analysis, we describe the purpose of the system. This results in the identification of application objects that represent user concepts. During system design, we describe the system in terms of its architecture, such as its subsystem decomposition, its global control flow, and its persistency management. During system design, we also define the hardware/software platform on which we build the system. This results in the selection of off-the-shelf components that provide a higher level of abstraction than the hardware. During object design, we close the gap between the application objects and the off-the-shelf components by identifying additional solution objects and refining existing objects.

Object design includes:

- *service specification*, during which we precisely describe each class interface
- *component selection*, during which we identify additional off-the-shelf components and solution objects
- *object model restructuring*, during which we transform the object design model to improve its understandability and extensibility
- *object model optimization*, during which we transform the object design model to address performance criteria such as response time or memory utilization

Object design, like system design, is not algorithmic. In this chapter, we show how to apply existing patterns and concrete components in the problem-solving process. We discuss these building blocks and the activities related to them. We conclude with the discussion of management issues associated with object design. We use Java and Java-based technologies in this chapter. The techniques we describe, however, are also applicable to other languages.

7.1 Introduction: Movie Examples

Consider the following examples:

Speed (1994)

Harry, an LAPD cop, is taken hostage by Howard, a mad bomber. Jack, Harry's partner, shoots Harry in the leg to slow down Howard's advance. Harry is shot in the right leg. Throughout the movie, Harry limps on the left leg.

Star Wars Trilogy (1977, 1980, & 1983)

At the end of episode V: *The Empire Strikes Back* (1980), Han Solo is captured and frozen into carbonite for delivery to Jaba. At the beginning of episode VI, *The Return of the Jedi* (1983), the frozen Han Solo is recovered by his friends and thawed back to life. When being frozen, Solo is wearing a jacket. When thawed, he is wearing a white shirt.

Titanic (1997)

Jack, a drifter, is teaching Rose, a lady from the high society, to spit. He demonstrates by example and encourages Rose to practice as well. During the lesson, Rose's mother arrives impromptu. As Jack starts to turn to face Rose's mother, there is no spit on his face. As he completes his turn, he has spit on his chin.

The budgets for *Speed*, *The Empire Strikes Back*, *The Return of the Jedi*, and *Titanic* were 30, 18, 32.5, and 200 millions dollars, respectively.

Movies, like software systems, are complex systems that contain (often many) bugs when delivered to the client. It is surprising, considering their cost of production, that any obvious mistakes should remain in the final product. Movies, however, are like software systems: They are more complex than they seem.

Many factors conspire to introduce mistakes in a movie: Movies require the cooperation of many different people; scenes are shot out of sequence; some scenes are reshot out of schedule; details, such as props and costumes, are changed during production; the pressure of the release date is high during the editing process, when all the pieces are integrated together. When a scene is shot, the state of every object and actor in the scene needs to be consistent with the scenes preceding and following it. This can include the pose of each actor, the condition of his or her clothes, jewelry, makeup, and hair, the content of their glasses, if they are drinking (e.g., white wine or red wine), the level of their glasses (e.g., full or half full), and so on. When different segments are combined into a single scenes, an editor, called the continuity editor, needs to ensure that such details were restored correctly. When changes occur, such as the addition or removal of a prop, the change must not interfere with other scenes.

Software systems, like movies, are complex, subject to continuous change, integrated under time pressure, and developed nonlinearly. During object design, developers close the gap between the application objects identified during analysis and the hardware/software platform selected during system design. Developers identify and build custom solution objects whose purpose is to realize any remaining functionality and to bridge the gap between application objects and the selected hardware/software platform. During object design, developers realize custom objects in a way similar to the shooting of movie scenes. They are implemented out of sequence, by different developers, and change several times before they reach their final form. Often, the caller of an operation has only an informal specification of the operation and makes assumptions about its side effects and its boundary cases. This results in mismatches between caller and callee, missing behavior, or incorrect behavior. To address these issues, developers construct precise specifications of the classes, attributes, and operations in terms of constraints. Similarly, developers adjust and reuse off-the-shelf components, annotated with interface specifications. Finally, developers restructure and optimize the object design model to address design goals, such as maintainability, extensibility, efficiency, response time, or timely delivery.

In Section 7.2, the next section, we provide an overview of the object design. In Section 7.3, we define the main object design concepts, such as constraints used to specify interfaces. In Section 7.4, we describe in more detail the activities of object design. In Section 7.5, we discuss management issues related with object design. We do not describe activities such as implementing algorithms and data structures or using specific programming languages. First, we assume the reader already has experience in those areas. Second, these activities become less critical as more and more off-the-shelf components become available and reused.

7.2 An Overview of Object Design

Conceptually, we think of system development as filling a gap between the problem and the machine. The activities of system development incrementally close this gap by identifying and defining objects that realize part of the system (Figure 7-1).

Analysis reduces the gap between the problem and the machine by identifying objects representing user-visible concepts. During analysis, we describe the system in terms of external behavior, such as its functionality (use case model), the application domain concepts it manipulates (object model), its behavior in terms of interactions (dynamic model), and its nonfunctional requirements.

System design reduces the gap between the problem and the machine by defining a hardware/software platform that provides a higher level of abstraction than the computer hardware. This is done by selecting off-the-shelf components for realizing standard services, such as middleware, user interface toolkits, application frameworks, and class libraries.

During object design, we refine the analysis and system design models, identify new objects, and close the gap between the application objects and off-the-shelf components. This includes the identification of custom objects, the adjustment of off-the-shelf components, and the precise specification of each subsystem interface and class. As a result, the object design model can be partitioned into sets of classes such that they can be implemented by individual developers.

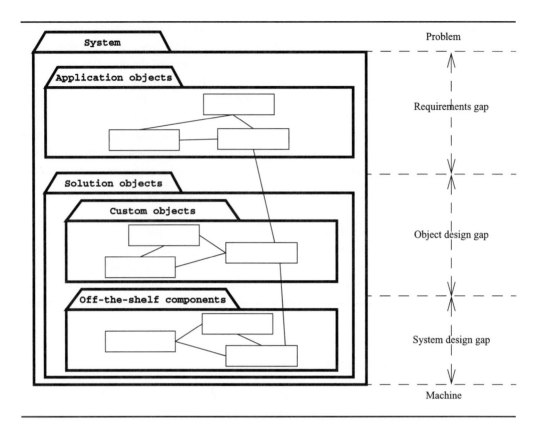

Figure 7-1 Object design closes the gap between application objects identified during requirements and off-the-shelf components selected during system design (stylized UML class diagram).

Object design includes four groups of activities (see Figure 7-2):

- *Service specification.* During object design, we specify the subsystem services (identified during system design) in terms of class interfaces, including operations, arguments, type signatures, and exceptions. During this activity, we also find missing operations and objects needed to transfer data among subsystems. The result of service specification is a complete interface specification for each subsystem. The subsystem service specification is often called subsystem **API** (Application Programmer Interface).

- *Component selection.* During object design, we use and adapt the off-the-shelf components identified during system design to realize each subsystem. We select class libraries and additional components for basic data structures and services. Often, we need to adjust the components we selected before we can use them, by wrapping custom objects around them or by refining them using inheritance. During these activities, we face the same buy versus build trade-off that we faced during system design.

- *Restructuring.* Restructuring activities manipulate the system model to increase code reuse or meet other design goals. Each restructuring activity can be seen as a graph transformation on subsets of a particular model. Typical activities include transforming n-ary associations into binary associations, implementing binary associations as references, merging two similar classes from two different subsystems into a single class, collapsing classes with no significant behavior into attributes, splitting complex classes into simpler ones, rearranging classes and operations to increase the inheritance and packaging. During restructuring, we address design goals such as maintainability, readability, and understandability of the system model.

- *Optimization.* Optimization activities address performance requirements of the system model. This includes changing algorithms to respond to speed or memory requirements, reducing multiplicities in associations to speed up queries, adding redundant associations for efficiency, rearranging execution orders, adding derived attributes to improve the access time to objects and opening up the architecture, that is, adding access to lower layers because of performance requirements.

Object design is nonlinear. Although the groups of activities we describe above each addresses a specific object design issue, they need to occur concurrently. A specific off-the-shelf component may constrain the number of types of exceptions mentioned in the specification of an operation and thus may impact the subsystem interface. The selection of a component may reduce the implementation work while introducing new "glue" objects, which also need to be specified. Finally, restructuring and optimizing may reduce the number of objects to be implemented by increasing the amount of reuse in the system.

The larger number of objects and developers, the high rate of change, and the concurrent number of decisions made during object design make this activity much more complex than analysis or system design is. This represents a management challenge, as many important decisions tend to be resolved independently and are not communicated to the rest of the project. Object design requires much information to be made available among the developers so that decisions can be made consistently with decisions made by other developers and with design goals. The *Object Design Document*, a live document describing the specification of each class, supports this information exchange.

7.3 Object Design Concepts

In this section, we present the principal object design concepts:

- application objects versus solution objects (Section 7.3.1)
- types, signatures, and visibility (Section 7.3.2)
- preconditions, postconditions, and invariants (Section 7.3.3)
- UML's Object Constraint Language (Section 7.3.4)

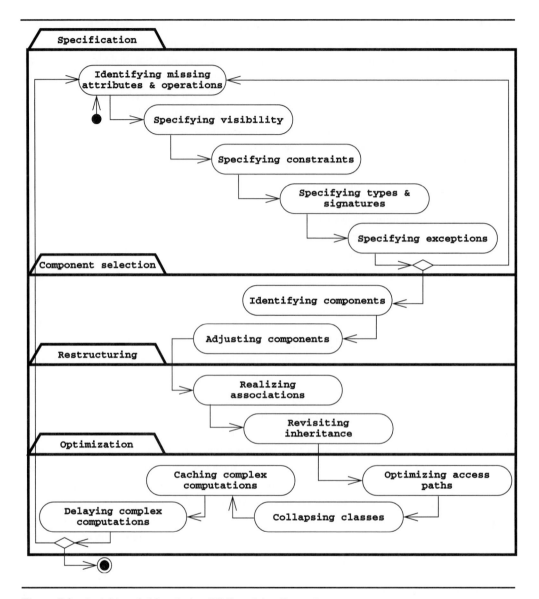

Figure 7-2   Activities of object design (UML activity diagram).

7.3.1   Application Objects Versus Solution Objects Revisited

As we saw in Chapter 2, *Modeling with UML*, class diagrams can be used to model both the application domain and the solution domain. **Application objects**, also called domain objects, represent concepts of the domain that the system manipulates. **Solution objects** represent support components that do not have a counterpart in the application domain, such as persistent data stores, user interface objects, or middleware.

During analysis, we identify application objects, their relationships, and attributes and operations. During system design, we identify subsystems and most important solution objects. During object design, we refine and detail both sets of objects and identify any remaining solution objects needed to complete the system.

7.3.2   Types, Signatures, and Visibility Revisited

During analysis, we identified attributes and operations without specifying their types or their parameters. During object design, we refine the analysis and system design models by adding type and visibility information. The **type** of an attribute specifies the range of values the attribute can take and the operations that can be applied to the attribute. For example, consider the attribute `numElements` of a `Hashtable` class (see Figure 7-3). `numElements` represent the current number of entries in a given `Hashtable`. Its type is `int`, denoting that it is an integer number. The type of the `numElements` attribute also denotes the operations that can be applied to this attribute: We can add or subtract other integers to `numElements`.

Operation parameters and return values are typed in the same way as attributes are. The type constrains the range of values the parameter or the return value can take. Given an operation, the tuple made out of the types of its parameters and the type of the return value is called the **signature** of the operation. For example, the `put()` operation of `Hashtable` takes two parameters of type `Object` and does not have a return value. The type signature for `put()` is then `(Object, Object):void`. Similarly, the `get()` operation of `Hashtable` takes one `Object` parameter and returns an `Object`. The type signature of `get()` is then `(Object):Object`.

The **visibility** of an attribute or an operation specifies whether it can be used by other classes or not. UML defines three levels of visibility:

- **Private**. A private attribute can be accessed only by the class in which it is defined. Similarly, a private operation can be invoked only by the class in which it is defined. Private attributes and operations cannot be accessed by subclasses or other classes.
- **Protected**. A protected attribute or operation can be accessed by the class in which it is defined and on any descendant of the class.
- **Public**. A public attribute or operation can be accessed by any class.

Visibility is denoted in UML by prefixing the symbol: − (private), # (protected), or + (public) to the name of the attribute or the operation. For example, in Figure 7-3, we specify that the `numElements` attribute of `Hashtable` is private, whereas all operations are public.

Hashtable
-numElements:int
+put(key:Object,entry:Object) +get(key:Object):Object +remove(key:Object) +containsKey(key:Object):boolean +size():int

```
class Hashtable {
    private int numElements;

    /* Constructors omitted */
    public void put (Object key, Object entry) {…};
    public Object get(Object key) {…};
    public void remove(Object key) {…};
    public boolean containsKey(Object key) {…};
    public int size() {…};

    /* Other methods omitted */
}
```

Figure 7-3   Declarations for the Hashtable class (UML class model and Java excerpts).

Type information alone is often not sufficient to specify the range of legitimate values. In the Hashtable example, the int type allows numElements to take negative values, which are not valid for this attribute. We address this issue next with contracts.

7.3.3   Contracts: Invariants, Preconditions, and Postconditions

Contracts are constraints on a class that enable caller and callee to share the same assumptions about the class [Meyer, 1997]. A contract specifies constraints that the caller must meet before using the class as well as constraints that are ensured by the callee when used. Contracts include three types of constraints:

- An **invariant** is a predicate that is always true for all instances of a class. Invariants are constraints associated with classes or interfaces. Invariants are used to specify consistency constraints among class attributes.

- A **precondition** is a predicate that must be true before an operation is invoked. Preconditions are associated with a specific operation. Preconditions are used to specify constraints that a caller must meet before calling an operation.

- A **postcondition** is a predicate that must be true after an operation is invoked. Postconditions are associated with a specific operation. Postconditions are used to specify constraints that the object must ensure after the invocation of the operation.

For example, consider the Java interface for a `Hashtable` depicted in Figure 7-3. This class provides a `put()` method to create an entry in the table, associating a key with a value, a `get()` method to lookup a value given a key, a `remove()` method to destroy an entry from the `Hashtable`, and a `hashKey()` method which returns a boolean indicating whether or not an entry exists.

An example of an invariant for the `Hashtable` class is that the number of entries in the `Hashtable` is nonnegative at all times. For example, if the `remove()` method results in a negative value of `numElements`, the `Hashtable` implementation is incorrect. An example of a precondition for the `remove()` method is that an entry must be associated with the key passed as a parameter. An example of a postcondition for the `remove()` method is that the removed entry should no long exist in the `Hashtable` after the `remove()` method returns. Figure 7-4 depicts the `Hashtable` class annotated with invariants, preconditions, and postconditions.

```java
/* Hashtable class. Maintains mappings from unique keys to arbitrary objects */
class Hashtable {

    /* The number of elements in the Hashtable is nonnegative at all times.
     * @inv numElements >= 0 */
    private int numElements;

    /* Constructors omitted */

    /* The put operation assumes that the specified key is not used.
     * After the put operation is completed, the specified key can be used
     * to recover the entry with the get(key) operation:
     * @pre !containsKey(key)
     * @post containsKey(key)
     * @post get(key) == entry */
    public void put (Object key, Object entry) {…};


    /* The get operation assumes that the specified key corresponds to an
     * entry in the Hashtable.
     * @pre containsKey(key) */
    public Object get(Object key) {…};

    /* The remove operation assumes that the specified key exists in the
     * Hashtable.
     * @pre containsKey(key)
     * @post !containsKey(key) */
    public void remove(Object key) {…};

    /* Other methods omitted */
}
```

Figure 7-4 Method declarations for the `Hashtable` class annotated with preconditions, postconditions, and invariants (Java, constraints in the iContract syntax [iContract]).

We use invariants, preconditions, and postconditions to specify special or exceptional cases unambiguously. For example, the constraints in Figure 7-4 indicate that the `remove()` method should be invoked only for entries that exist in the table. Similarly, the `put()` method should be invoked only if the key is not already in use. In most cases, it is also possible to use constraints to completely specify the behavior of an operation. Such a use of constraints, called *constraint-based specification*, however, is difficult and can be more complicated than implementing the operation itself [Horn, 1992]. We will not describe pure constraint-based specification in the scope of this chapter. Instead, we will focus on specifying operations using both constraints and natural language, emphasizing boundary cases.

7.3.4 UML's Object Constraint Language

In UML, constraints are expressed using OCL [OMG, 1998]. OCL is a language that allows constraints to be formally specified on single model elements (e.g., attributes, operations, classes) or groups of model elements (e.g., associations and participating classes). A constraint is expressed as an OCL expression returning the value True or False. OCL is not a procedural language and thus cannot be used to denote control flow. In this chapter, we focus exclusively on the aspects of OCL related to invariants, preconditions, and postconditions.

A constraint can be depicted as a note attached to the constrained UML element by a dependency relationship. A constraint can be expressed in natural language or in a formal language such as OCL. Figure 7-5 depicts a class diagram of `Hashtable` example of Figure 7-4 using UML and OCL.

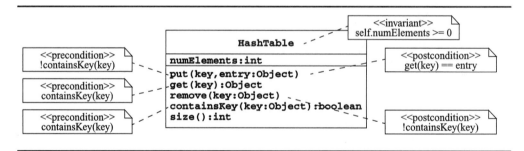

Figure 7-5   Examples of invariants, preconditions, and postconditions in OCL (UML class diagram).

OCL's syntax is similar to object-oriented languages such as C++ or Java. In the case of an invariant, the context for the expression is the class associated with the invariant. The keyword `self` (e.g., `self.numElements` in Figure 7-5) denotes any instance of the class. Attributes and operations are accessed using the dot notation (e.g., `self.attribute` or `self.operation(params)`). The `self` keyword can be omitted if no ambiguity is introduced. (Note that OCL uses the keyword `self` to represent the same concept as the Java and C++ keyword `this`.) For a precondition or a postcondition, the parameters passed to the associated operation can be used in the OCL expression. For postconditions, the suffix `@pre` denotes the value of a parameter or an attribute before the execution of the operation. For example, a postcondition for the `put(key, entry)` operation expressing that the number of entries in the table increased by one can be represented as `numElements = numElements@pre + 1`.

Attaching OCL expressions to diagrams can lead to clutter. For this reason, OCL expressions can be alternatively expressed textually. The context keyword introduces a new context for an OCL expression. The word following the context keyword refers to a class, an attribute, or an operation. Then follows one of the keywords `inv`, `pre`, and `post`, which correspond to the UML stereotypes `<<invariant>>`, `<<precondition>>`, and `<<postcondition>>`, respectively. Then follows the actual OCL expression. For example, the invariant for the `Hashtable` class and the constraints for the `Hashtable.put ()` operation are written as follows:

```
context Hashtable inv:
numElements >= 0

context Hashtable::put(key, entry) pre:
!containsKey(key)

context Hashtable::put(key, entry) post:
containsKey(key) and get(key) = entry
```

7.4 Object Design Activities

As we have already mentioned in the introduction, object design includes four groups of activities: specification, component selection, restructuring, and optimization.

Specification activities include:

- identifying missing attributes and operations (Section 7.4.1)
- specifying type signatures and visibility (Section 7.4.2)
- specifying constraints (Section 7.4.3)
- specifying exceptions (Section 7.4.4)

Component selection activities include:

- identifying and adjusting class libraries (Section 7.4.5)
- identifying and adjusting application frameworks (Section 7.4.6)
- a framework example: WebObjects (Section 7.4.7)

Restructuring activities include:

- realizing associations (Section 7.4.8)
- increasing reuse (Section 7.4.9)
- removing implementation dependencies (Section 7.4.10)

Optimization activities include:

- revisiting access paths (Section 7.4.11)
- collapsing objects: turning objects into attributes (Section 7.4.12),
- caching the result of expensive computations (Section 7.4.13)
- delaying expensive computations (Section 7.4.14)

To illustrate these four groups of activities in more detail, we use as example an emissions modeling system called JEWEL (Joint Environmental Workshop and Emissions Laboratory, [Bruegge et al., 1995], [Kompanek et al., 1996]). JEWEL enables end users to simulate and visualize air pollution as a function of point sources (e.g., factories, powerplants), area sources (e.g., cities), and mobile sources (e.g., cars, trucks, trains). The area under study is divided into grid cells. Emissions are then estimated for each grid cell and each hour of the day. Once the simulation is completed, the end user can visualize the concentration of various pollutants on a map along with the emission sources (see Figure 7-6). JEWEL is targeted for government agencies that regulate air quality and attempt to bring troubled populated areas into compliance with regulation.

Given its focus on visualization of geographical data, JEWEL includes a Geographical Information Subsystem (GIS), which is responsible for storing and manipulating maps. The JEWEL GIS manages geographical information as sets of polygons and segments. Different types of information, such as roads, rivers, and political boundaries, are organized into different layers that can be displayed independently. Moreover, data is organized such that it can be seen at different levels of abstraction. For example, a high-level view of a map only contains main roads, whereas a detailed view also includes secondary roads. GIS is an ideal example for object design, given its rich application domain and complex solution domain. First, we start with the specification of GIS.

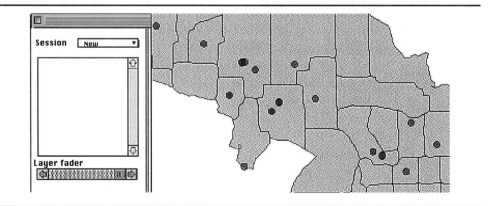

Figure 7-6 Map with political boundaries and emission sources (JEWEL, mock-up).

Specification activities

In Figure 7-7, the object model for the GIS for JEWEL describes an organization in three layers (i.e., the road layer, the water layer, and the political layer). Each layer is composed of elements. Some of these elements, such as highways, secondary roads, and rivers, are displayed with lines composed of multiple segments. Others, such as lakes, states, and counties, are displayed as polygons, which are also represented as collections of line segments.

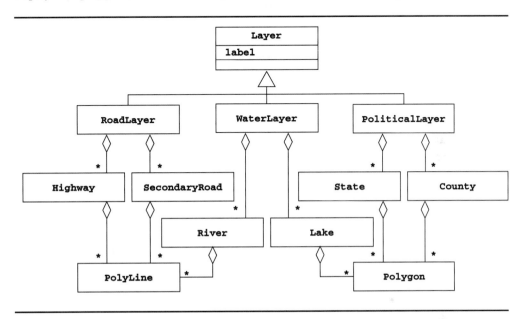

Figure 7-7   Object model for the GIS of JEWEL (UML class diagram).

The ZoomMap use case (Figure 7-8) describes how users can zoom in or out around a selected point on the map. The analysis model is still abstract. For example, it does not contain any information at this point about how zooming is implemented or how points are selected.

The system design model focuses on the subsystem decomposition and global system decisions such as hardware software mapping, persistent storage, or access control. We identify the top-level subsystems and define them in terms of the services they provide. In JEWEL, for example (Figures 7-10 and 7-9), we identified the GIS providing services for creating, storing, and deleting geographical elements, organizing them into layers, and retrieving their outline in terms of a series of points. These services are used by the Visualization subsystem, which retrieves geographical information for drawing maps. The geographical data is provided as a set of flat files and is treated by JEWEL as static data. Consequently, we do not need to support the interactive editing of geographical data. From the use cases of JEWEL, we also know that users need to see geographical data from different zooming criteria. During system design, we decide that the GIS provides zooming and clipping services. The Visualization subsystem specifies

Use case name	ZoomMap
Entry condition	The map is displayed in a window, and at least one layer is visible.
Flow of events	1. The end user selects the zoom tool from the tool bar. The system changes the cursor to a magnifying glass.
	2. The end user selects a point on the map using the mouse by either clicking the left or the right mouse button. The point selected by the user will become the new center of the map.
	3. The end user clicks the left mouse to request an increase in the level of detail (i.e., zoom in) or the right mouse button to request a decrease of the level of detail (i.e., zoom out).
	4. The system computes the new bounding box and retrieves from the GIS the corresponding points and lines from each visible layer.
	5. The system then displays each layer using a predefined color in the new bounding box.
Exit condition	The map is scrolled and scaled to the requested position and detail level.

Figure 7-8   ZoomMap use case for JEWEL.

the level of detail and the bounding box of the map, and the GIS carries out the zooming and clipping and returns only the points that need to be drawn. This minimizes the amount of data that needs to be transferred between subsystems. Although the system design model is closer to the machine, we have yet to describe in detail the interface of the GIS.

Specification activities during object design include:

- identifying missing attributes and operations (Section 7.4.1)
- specifying type signatures and visibility (Section 7.4.2)
- specifying constraints (Section 7.4.3)
- specifying exceptions (Section 7.4.4)

JEWEL GIS

Purpose
- store and maintain the geographical information for JEWEL

Service
- creation and deletion of geographical elements (roads, rivers, lakes, and boundaries)
- organization of elements into layers
- zooming (selection of points given a level of detail)
- clipping (selection of points given a bounding box)

Figure 7-9   Subsystem description for the GIS of JEWEL.

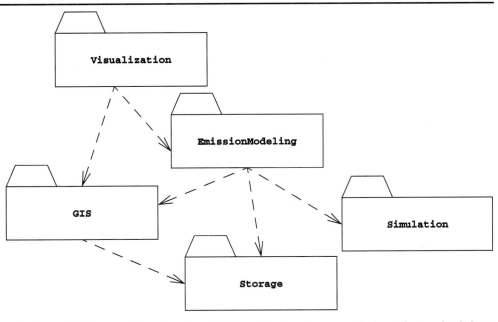

EmissionModeling	The EmissionModeling subsystem is responsible for setting up simulations and managing its results.
GIS	The GIS maintains geographical information for Visualization and for EmissionModeling.
Simulation	The Simulation subsystem is responsible for the simulation of emissions.
Storage	The Storage subsystem is responsible for all the persistent data in the system, including geographical and emission data.
Visualization	The Visualization subsystem is responsible for displaying geographical and emissions data to the user.

Figure 7-10   Subsystem decomposition of JEWEL (UML class diagram).

7.4.1   Identifying Missing Attributes and Operations

During this step, we examine the service description of the subsystem and identify missing attributes and operations. During analysis, we may have missed many attributes because we focused on the functionality of the system. Moreover, we described the functionality of the system primarily with the use case model (not the object model). We focused on the application domain when constructing the object model and therefore ignored details related to the system that are independent of the application domain.

In the JEWEL example, the creation, deletion, and organization of layers and layer elements are already supported by the Layer class. We need, however, to identify operations to realize the clipping and zooming services. Clipping is not a concept that is related to the application domain, but rather is related to the user interface of the system and thus is part of the solution domain.

We draw a sequence diagram representing the control and data flow needed to realize the zoom operation (Figure 7-11). We focus especially on the Layer class. When drawing the sequence diagram, we realize that a Layer needs to access all its contained elements to gather their geometry for clipping and zooming. We observe that clipping can be realized independently of the kind of element being displayed, that is, clipping line segments associated with a road or a river can be done using the same operation. Consequently, we identify a new class, the LayerElement abstract class (see Figure 7-12), which provides operations for all elements that are part of a Layer (i.e., Highway, SecondaryRoad, River, Lake, State, and County).

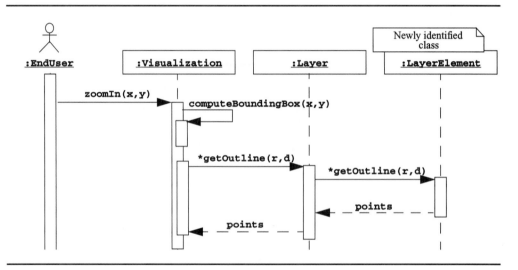

Figure 7-11   A sequence diagram for the zoomIn() operation (UML sequence diagram). This sequence diagram leads to the identification of a new class, LayerElement. Because we are focusing on the GIS, we treat the Visualization subsystem as a single object.

We identify the getOutline() operation on the LayerElement class, which is responsible for scaling and clipping the lines and polygons of individual elements, given a bounding box and a detail level. The getOutline() operation uses the detail level to scale each line and polygon and to reduce the number of points for lower levels of detail. For example, when the user zooms out the map by a factor of 2, the GIS returns only half the number of points for a given layer element, because less detail is needed. We then identify the getOutline() operation on the Layer class, which is responsible for invoking the getOutline() operation on each LayerElements and for collecting all lines and polygons of the layer into a single data structure. Both getOutline() operations return collections of lines and polygons. The Visualization

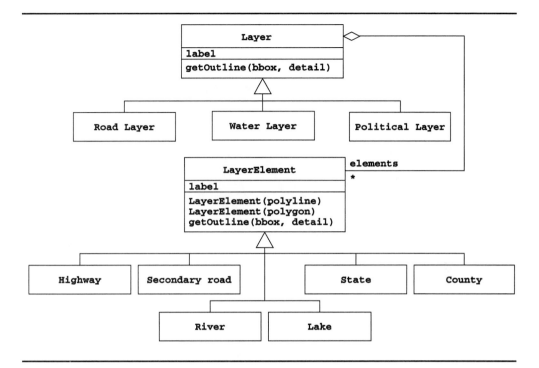

Figure 7-12   Adding operations to the object model of the JEWEL GIS to realize zooming and clipping (UML class diagram).

subsystem then translates the GIS coordinates into screen coordinates, adjusting for scale and scrolling, and draws the line segments on the screen.

During a review of the object model, we realize that the zooming algorithm of the LayerElement.getOutline() operation is not trivial: It is not sufficient to select a subset of points of the LayerElement and scale their coordinates. Because different LayerElements may share points (e.g., two connecting roads, two neighboring counties), the same set of points need to be selected to maintain a visually consistent picture for the end user.

For example, Figure 7-13 displays examples of a naive algorithm for selecting points applied to connecting roads and neighboring counties. The left column displays the points that are selected for a higher level of detail. The right column displays the points that are selected for a lower level of detail. In this case, the algorithm arbitrarily selected every other point, disregarding whether points were shared or not. This leads to elements that are not connected when displayed at lower levels of details.

To address this problem, we decide to include more intelligence in the PolyLine, Polygon, and Point classes (Figure 7-14). First, we decide to represent shared points by exactly one Point object; that is, if two lines share a point, both Line objects have a reference to the same Point object. This is handled by the Point(x,y) constructor, which checks if the

High detail   Low detail

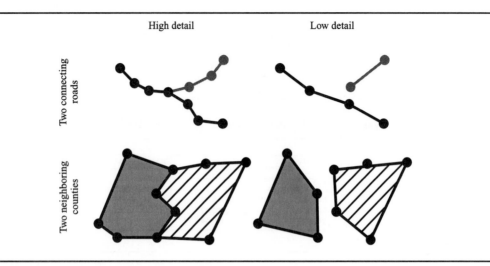

Figure 7-13   A naive point selection algorithm for the GIS. The left column represents a road crossing and two neighboring counties. The right column shows that road crossings and neighboring counties may be displayed incorrectly when points are not selected carefully.

specified coordinates correspond to an existing point. Second, we add attributes to Point objects to store the levels of details in which they participate. The inDetailLevels attribute is a set of all the detail levels in which this Point participates. The notInDetailLevels attribute is a set of all the detail levels from which this Point has been excluded. If a given detail level is not in either set, this means that this Point has not yet been considered for the given detail level. The inDetailLevels and notInDetailLevels attributes (and their associated operations) are then used by the LayerElement.getOutline() operation to select shared points and maintain connectivity.

At this point, we have identified the missing attributes and operations necessary to support zooming and clipping of LayerElement. Note that we will probably revisit some of these issues later when we select existing components or perform the object design of the dependent subsystems. Next, we proceed to specifying the interface of each of the classes using types, signatures, contracts, and visibility.

7.4.2   Specifying Type Signatures and Visibility

During this step, we specify the types of the attributes, the signatures of the operations, and the visibility of attributes and operations. Specifying types refines the object design model in two ways. First, we add detail to the model by specifying the range of each attribute. For example, by determining the type of coordinates, we make decisions about the location of the origin (Point 0, 0) and the maximum and minimum values for all coordinates. By selecting a double-precision floating-point factor for detail levels, we compute coordinates at different detail levels by simply multiplying the detail level by the coordinates. Second, we map classes

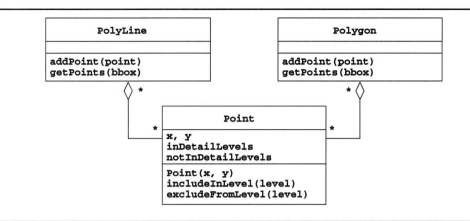

Figure 7-14   Additional attributes and methods for the Point class to support intelligent point selection and zooming (UML class diagram).

and attributes of the object model to built-in types provided by the development environment. For example, by selecting String to represent the label attributes of Layers and LayerElements, we can use all the operations provided by the String class to manipulate label values.

During this step, we also consider the relationship between the classes we identified and the classes from off-the-shelf components. For example, a number of classes implementing collections are provided in the java.util package. The Enumeration interface provides a way to access an ordered collection of objects. The Set interface provides a mathematical set abstraction implemented by several classes, such as HashSet. We select the Enumeration interface for returning outlines and the Set interface from the java.util package for representing the inDetailLevels and notInDetailLevels attributes.

Finally, we determine the visibility of each attribute and operation during this step. By doing so, we determine which attributes are completely managed by a class, which should only be accessible indirectly via the class's operations, and which attributes are public and can be modified by any other class. Similarly, the visibility of operations allows us to distinguish between operations that are part of the class interface and those that are utility methods that can only be accessed by the class. In the case of abstract classes and classes that are intended to be refined, we also define protected attributes and methods for the use of subclasses only. Figure 7-15 depicts the refined specification of the Layer, LayerElement, PolyLine, and Point classes after types, signatures, and visibility have been assigned.

Once we specified the types of each attribute, the signature of each operation, and their visibility, we focus on specifying the behavior and boundary cases of each class by using contracts.

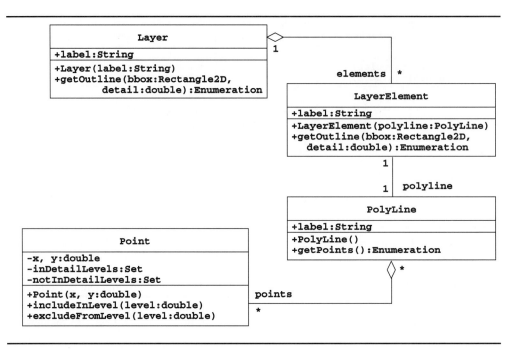

Figure 7-15 Adding type information to the object model of the GIS (UML class diagram). Only selected classes shown for brevity.

7.4.3 Specifying Constraints

During this step, we attach constraints to classes and operations to more precisely specify their behavior and boundary cases. Our main goal is to remove as much ambiguity from the model as possible. We specify class contracts using three types of constraints. Invariants represent conditions on the attributes of a class that are always True. Preconditions represent conditions that must be satisfied (usually by the caller) prior to invoking a given operation. Postconditions represent conditions that are guaranteed by the callee after the operation is completed. As described in Section 7.3.3 and Section 7.3.4, we can use OCL [OMG, 1998] to attach constraints to UML models.

In the JEWEL example, the most complex behavior is associated with clipping and zooming; in particular, the getOutline() operations on the Layer and LayerElement classes. In the following, we develop constraints to clarify the getOutline() operations, focusing on the behavior associated with shared points. More specifically, we are interested in specifying the following constraints.

1. All points returned by Layer.getOutline() are within the specified bounding box.
2. The result of Layer.getOutline() is the concatenation of the invocation of LayerElement.getOutline() on its elements.

3. At most, one `Point` in the system represents a given (x, y) coordinate.
4. A `detail` level cannot be part of both the `inDetailLevels` and the `notInDetailLevels` sets.
5. For a given `detail` level, `LayerElement.getOutline()` can only return `Points` which contain the `detail` level in their `inDetailLevels` set attribute.
6. The `inDetailLevels` and `notInDetailLevels` set can only grow as a consequence of `LayerElement.getOutline()`; in other words, once a detail level is in one of these sets, it cannot be removed.

First, we focus on clipping. Given a `LayerElement`, the enumeration of points returned by the `getOutline(bbox,detail)` operation must be inside the specified rectangle `bbox`. Moreover, any point returned by `getOutline()` must be associated with the `LayerElement`. We represent this using a postcondition on the `getOutline()` operation of `LayerElement`. Note that because we currently focus on clipping, we ignore the `detail` parameter.

```
/* Constraint 1 */
context LayerElement::getOutline(bbox, detail) post:
result->forAll(p:Point|bbox.contains(p) and points->includes(p))
```

The `result` field represents the result of the `getOutline()` operation. The `forAll` OCL construct applies the constraint to all points of `result`. Finally, the constraint expresses that all points in the result must be contained in the rectangle `bbox` passed as parameter and must be included in the `points` aggregation association of Figure 7-15.

We then define the `getOutline()` operation on a `Layer` as the concatenation of the enumerations returned by the `getOutline()` operation of the `LayerElements`. In OCL, we use the `iterate` construct on collections to go through each `LayerElement` and collect its outline into a single enumeration. The `including` construct appends its parameter to the collection. OCL automatically flattens the resulting collection.

```
/* Constraint 2 */
context Layer::getOutline(bbox, detail) post:
elements->iterate(le:LayerElement; result:Enumeration|
    result->including(le.getOutline(bbox,detail))
```

We then focus on constraints related with zooming. Recall that we added attributes and operations to the `Point` class to represent shared points. First, we specify `Point` uniqueness with an invariant applied to all `Point` instances:

```
/* Constraint 3 */
context Point inv:
Point.allInstances->forAll(p1, p2:Point |
    (p1.x = p2.x and p1.y = p2.y) implies p1 = p2)
```

We leave the derivation of the last three constraints as an exercise for the reader (see Exercise 2).

With these six constraints, we describe more precisely the behavior of the getOutline() operations and their relationship with the attributes and operations of the Point class. Note that we have not described in any way the algorithm by which the LayerElement selects Points, given a detail level. We leave this decision to the implementation activity of object design.

Next, we describe the exceptions that can be raised by each operation.

7.4.4   Specifying Exceptions

During this step, we specify constraints that the caller needs to satisfy before invoking an operation. In other words, we specify conditions that operations detect and treat as errors by raising an exception. Languages such as Java and Ada have built-in mechanisms for exception handling. Other languages, such as C and early versions of C++ do not support explicit exception handling, so the developers need to establish conventions and mechanisms for handling exceptions (e.g., return values or a specialized subsystem). Exceptional conditions are usually associated with the violation of preconditions. In UML, we attach OCL preconditions to operations and associate the precondition with a dependency to an exception object.

In the JEWEL example (Figure 7-16), we specify that the b-box parameter of the Layer.getOutline() operation should have a positive width and height and that the detail parameter should be positive. We associate the ZeroBoundingBox and the ZeroDetail exceptions with each condition.

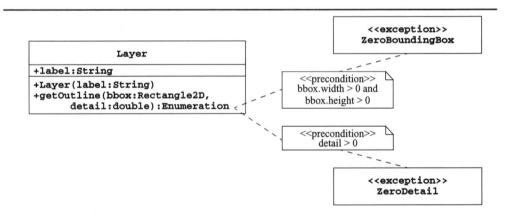

Figure 7-16   Examples of preconditions and exceptions for the Layer class of the JEWEL GIS.

Exceptions can be found systematically by examining each parameter of the operation and by examining the states in which the operation may be invoked. For each parameter and set of parameters, we identify values or combinations of values that should not be accepted. For example, we reject nonpositive values for the detail level, because the detail parameter represents a multiplication factor. A zero value for the detail parameters would result in the collapse of all coordinates onto the origin. A negative detail level would result in an inverted picture. Note that a systematic discovery of all exceptions for all operations is a time-consuming exercise, albeit useful. For systems in which reliability is not a primary design goal, the specification of exceptions can be limited to the public interface of subsystems.

Component selection activities

At this point in object design, we selected the software/hardware platform on which the system runs. This platform includes off-the-shelf components such as database management systems, middleware frameworks, infrastructure frameworks, or enterprise application frameworks. The main objective in selecting off-the-shelf components is to reuse as many objects as possible, thus minimizing the number of custom objects that need to be developed. Moreover, an off-the-shelf component often provides a more reliable and efficient solution than any developer could hope to produce in the context of a single system. A user interface class library, for example, pays close attention to an efficient display algorithm or to good response times. An off-the-shelf component also has been used by many more systems and users and therefore is more robust. Off-the-shelf components, however, have a cost. Their purpose is to support a wide variety of systems, and thus they are usually complex. Using an off-the-shelf component requires an investment in learning and often requires a degree of customization. Using off-the-shelf components is usually a better alternative than building the complete system from scratch.

7.4.5   Identifying and Adjusting Class Libraries

Assume that we select the Java Foundation Classes (JFC) [JFC, 1999] as an off-the-shelf component for realizing the `Visualization` subsystem. We need to display the map as a series of polylines and polygons returned by the `Layer.getOutline()` operation. This is usually not straightforward, as we have to reconcile functionality provided by the `GIS` and JFC to realize the `Visualization` services. For example, this can introduce the need for custom objects whose only function is to convert data from one subsystem to another.

For displaying graphics, JFC provides a number of reusable components for composing a user interface. JFC arranges components in a containing hierarchy that constrains the order in which the components are painted. JFC paints last the components closer to the bottom of the hierarchy (usually atomic components) such that they appear on the top of all the other components. A `JFrame`, also known as main window, defines an area that is exclusively owned by the application. A `JFrame` is often made out of several `JPanels`, each responsible for the layer of several atomic components. A `JScrollPane` provides a scrollable view of a component. It allows a user to view a subset of a component that is too large to display completely.

For the JEWEL `Visualization` subsystem (see Figure 7-17), we select a `JFrame` as a top-level container, a `JToolbar` and two `JButtons` for zooming in and out, and a `JScrollPane` for scrolling the map. We realize the map proper with the `MapArea` class, which refines a `JPanel` and overwrites the `paintContents()` operation. The new `paintContents()` operation

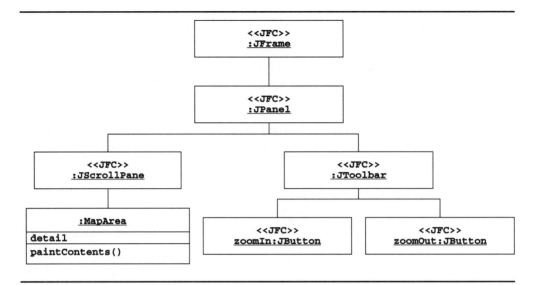

Figure 7-17 JFC components for the JEWEL Visualization subsystem (UML object diagram). Associations denote the containment hierarchy used for ordering the painting of components. We use stereotypes to distinguish JEWEL classes from classes provided by JFC.

computes the visible bounding box from attributes of the JScrollPane, retrieves lists of points from the Layer classes, scales them, and draws them. The MapArea class also maintains the current detail level. Actions associated with the zoomIn:JButton and zoomOut:JButton access operations on the MapArea, to increase and decrease the detail level, respectively. This triggers the repaint() operation on the MapArea which refreshes the map display.

When examining the drawing primitives provided by JFC, we realize that JFC and the GIS represent lines differently. On the one hand, the drawPolygon() and drawPolyline() operations of the Graphics class accept two arrays of coordinates (one for the x coordinates of the points, the other for the y coordinates; see Figure 7-18). On the other hand, the getOutline() operation of the GIS returns a Enumeration of Points (see Figure 7-16). There are two approaches to resolve this mismatch. We can write a utility method on the MapArea class to translate between the two different data structures or we can ask the developers responsible for the GIS to change the interface of the Layer class.

```
// from java.awt package
class Graphics
//...
    void drawPolyline(int[] xPoints, int[] yPoints, int nPoints) {…};
    void drawPolygon(int[] xPoints, int[] yPoints, int nPoints) {…};
```

Figure 7-18 Declaration for drawPolyline() and drawPolygon() operations [JFC, 1999].

We should change the API of the `Layer` class if we have control over it. In the general case, however, it is often necessary to write glue operations and classes. For example, if the `GIS` was also made of off-the-shelf components, we would not be able to change its API. We can use the `Adapter` pattern to address this mismatch (see Section 6.4.4 in Chapter 6, *System Design*).

7.4.6 Identifying and Adjusting Application Frameworks

An **application framework** is a reusable partial application that can be specialized to produce custom applications [Johnson et al., 1988]. In contrast to class libraries, frameworks are targeted to particular technologies, such as data processing or cellular communications, or to application domains, such as user interfaces or real-time avionics. The key benefits of application frameworks are reusability and extensibility. Framework reusability leverages of the application domain knowledge and prior effort of experienced developers to avoid the recreation and revalidation of recurring solutions. An application framework enhances extensibility by providing **hook methods**, which are overwritten by the application to extend the application framework. Hook methods systematically decouple the interfaces and behaviors of an application domain from the variations required by an application in a particular context. Framework extensibility is essential to ensure timely customization of new application services and features.

Frameworks can be classified by their position in the software development process.

- **Infrastructure frameworks** aim to simplify the software development process. Examples include frameworks for operating systems [Campbell-Islam, 1993], debuggers [Bruegge et al., 1993], communication tasks [Schmidt, 1997], and user interface design [Weinand et al., 1988]. System infrastructure frameworks are used internally within a software project and are usually not delivered to a client.

- **Middleware frameworks** are used to integrate existing distributed applications and components. Common examples include Microsoft's MFC and DCOM, Java RMI, WebObjects [Wilson & Ostrem, 1999], implementations of CORBA [OMG, 1995], and transactional databases.

- **Enterprise application frameworks** are application specific and focus on domains such as telecommunications, avionics, environmental modeling [Bruegge & Riedel, 1994] manufacturing, financial engineering [Birrer, 1993], and enterprise business activities.

Infrastructure and middleware frameworks are essential to rapidly create high-quality software systems, but they are usually not requested by external customers. Enterprise frameworks, however, support the development of end-user applications. As a result, buying infrastructure and middleware frameworks is more cost effective than building them [Fayad & Hamu, 1997].

Frameworks can also be classified by the techniques used to extend them.

- **Whitebox frameworks** rely on inheritance and dynamic binding for extensibility. Existing functionality is extended by subclassing framework base classes and overriding predefined hook methods using patterns such as the template method pattern [Gamma et al., 1994].

- **Blackbox frameworks** support extensibility by defining interfaces for components that can be plugged into the framework. Existing functionality is reused by defining components that conform to a particular interface and integrating these components with the framework, using delegation.

Whitebox frameworks require intimate knowledge of the framework's internal structure. Whitebox frameworks produce systems that are tightly coupled to the specific details of the framework's inheritance hierarchies, and thus changes in the framework can require the recompilation of the application. Blackbox frameworks are easier to use than whitebox frameworks, because they rely on delegation instead of inheritance. However, blackbox frameworks are more difficult to develop, because they require the definition of interfaces and hooks that anticipate a wide range of potential use cases. Moreover, it is easier to extend and reconfigure blackbox frameworks dynamically, as they emphasize dynamic object relationships rather than static class relationships. [Johnson et al., 1988].

Frameworks are closely related to design patterns, class libraries, and components.

Design patterns versus frameworks.   The main difference between frameworks and patterns is that frameworks focus on reuse of concrete designs, algorithms, and implementations in a particular programming language. In contrast, patterns focus on reuse of abstract designs and small collections of cooperating classes. Frameworks focus on a particular application domain, whereas design patterns can be viewed more as building blocks of frameworks.

Class libraries versus frameworks.   Classes in a framework cooperate to provide a reusable architectural skeleton for a family of related applications. In contrast, class libraries are less domain specific and provide a smaller scope of reuse. For instance, class library components, such as classes for strings, complex numbers, arrays, and bitsets can be used across many application domains. Class libraries are typically passive; that is, they do not implement or constrain the control flow. Frameworks, however, are active; that is, they control the flow of control within an application. In practice, frameworks and class libraries are complementary technologies. For instance, frameworks use class libraries, such as foundation classes, internally to simplify the development of the framework. Similarly, application-specific code invoked by framework event handlers uses class libraries to perform basic tasks, such as string processing, file management, and numerical analysis.

Components versus frameworks.   Components are self-contained instances of classes that are plugged together to form complete applications. In terms of reuse, a component is a blackbox that defines a cohesive set of operations, which can be used based solely with knowledge of the syntax and semantics of its interface. Compared with frameworks, components are less tightly coupled and can even be reused on the binary code level. That is, applications can reuse components without having to subclass from existing base classes. The advantage is that applications do not always have to be recompiled when components change. The relationship between frameworks and components is not predetermined. On the one hand, frameworks can be used to develop components, where the component interface provides a facade pattern for the internal class structure of the framework. On the other hand, components can be plugged into blackbox frameworks. In general, frameworks are used to simplify the development of infrastructure and middleware software, whereas components are used to simplify the development of end-user application software.

7.4.7   A Framework Example: WebObjects

WebObjects is a set of frameworks for developing interactive Web applications accessing existing data from relational databases. WebObjects consists of two infrastructure frameworks. The WebObjects framework[1] handles the interaction between Web browsers and Web servers. The Enterprise Object Framework (EOF) handles the interaction between Web servers and relational databases. The EOF supports database adapters that allow applications to connect to database management systems from particular vendors. For example, the EOF provides database adapters for Informix, Oracle, and Sybase servers and ODBC compliant adapters for databases running on the Windows platform. In the following, we concentrate on the WebObjects framework. More information on the EOF can be found in [Wilson & Ostrem, 1999].

Figure 7-19 shows an example of a dynamic publishing site built with WebObjects. The WebBrowser originates an HTTP request in the form of a URL, which is sent to the WebServer. If the WebServer detects that the request is to a static HTML page, it passes it on the StaticHTML object, which selects and sends the page back to the Web browser as a response. The Web browser then renders it for the user. If the WebServer detects that the request requires a dynamic HTML page, it passes the request to a WebObjects WOAdaptor. The WOAdaptor   packages   the   incoming   HTML   request   and   forwards   it   to   the WebObjectsApplication object. Based on Templates defined by the developer and relevant data retrieved from the RelationalDatabase, the WebObjectsApplication then generates an HTML response page, which is passed back through the WOAdaptor to the WebServer. The WebServer then sends the page to the WebBrowser, which renders it for the user.

---

1. "WebObjects" is unfortunately the name of both the complete development environment and the Web framework. When referring to the framework, we always use the phrase, WebObjects framework. When referring to the development environment, we simple use the term, WebObjects.

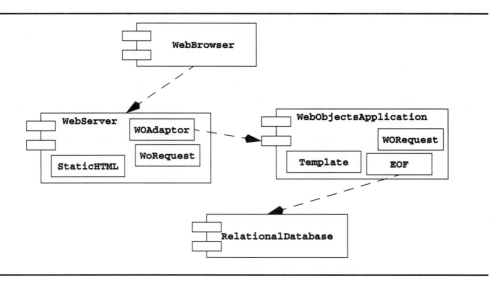

Figure 7-19 An example of dynamic site with WebObjects (UML component diagram).

A key abstraction provided by the WebObjects framework is an extension of the HTTP protocol to manage state. HTTP is a stateless request-response protocol, that is, a response is formulated for each request, but no state is maintained between successive requests. In many Web-based applications, however, state needs to be kept between requests. For example in JEWEL, emissions computations can take up to 30 days. The end user must be able to monitor and access the state of the emissions computation even if the Web browser is restarted. Several techniques have been proposed to keep track of state information in Web applications, including dynamically generated URLs, cookies, and hidden HTML fields. WebObjects provides the classes shown in Figure 7-20 to achieve the same purpose.

The WOApplication class represents the application running on the WebServer waiting for requests from the associated WebBrowser. A cycle of the request-response loop begins whenever the WOAdaptor receives an incoming HTTP request. The WOAdaptor packages this request in a WORequest object and forwards it to the application object of class WOApplication. Requests are always triggered by a URL submitted by the WebBrowser. A top-level URL represents a special request and causes the creation of a new instance of type WOSession. The class WOSession encapsulates the state of an individual session, allowing it to track different users, even within a single application. A WOSession consists of one or more WOComponents, which represent a reusable Web page or portion of a Web page for display within an individual session. WOComponents may contain dynamic elements. When an application accesses the database, one or more of the dynamic elements of a component are filled with information retrieved from the database. The WOSessionStore provides persistency for WOSession objects: It stores sessions in the server and restores them by the application upon request.

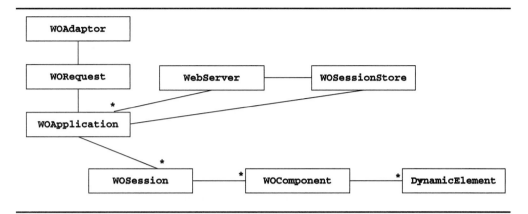

Figure 7-20   WebObject's State Management Classes. The HTTP protocol is inherently stateless. The State Management Classes allow to maintain information between individual requests.

The essence of building a WebObjects application is to refine the classes WOApplication, WOSession, and WOComponent and to intercept the flow of requests sent and received between them. Inherited methods from these classes are overridden when the developer needs to extend the default behavior. The earliest control point for refining objects of type WOApplication is when they are constructed. The last point of control is when the application object terminates. By adding code to the application object constructor or overriding the WOApplication terminate() method, the developer can customize the behavior of the WebObjects application as desired.

Once we have extended the object design model with off-the-shelf components and their related classes, we restructure the model to improve reusability and extensibility.

Restructuring activities

Once we have specified the subsystem interfaces, identified additional solution classes, selected components, and adapted them to fit our solution, we need to transform the object design model into a representation that is closer to the target machine. In this section, we describe three restructuring activities:

- realizing associations (Section 7.4.8)
- revisiting inheritance to increase reuse (Section 7.4.9)
- revisiting inheritance to remove implementation dependencies (Section 7.4.10)

7.4.8   Realizing Associations

Associations are UML concepts that denote collections of bidirectional links between two or more objects. Object-oriented programming languages, however, do not provide the concept of association. Instead, they provide references, in which one object stores a handle to another object. References are unidirectional and take place between two objects. During object design, we realize associations in terms of references, taking into account the multiplicity of the associations and their direction. Note that many UML modeling tools accomplish the transformation of associations into references automatically. Even if a tool accomplishes this transformation, it is nevertheless important that developers understand its rationale, as they have to deal with the generated code.

Unidirectional one-to-one associations.   The simplest association is a one-to-one association. For example, `ZoomInAction`, the control object implementing the `ZoomIn` use case, has a one-to-one association with the `MapArea` whose `detail` level the `ZoomInAction` object modifies (Figure 7-21). Assume, moreover, that this association is unidirectional; that is, a `ZoomInAction` accesses the corresponding `MapArea`, but a `MapArea` does not need to access the corresponding `ZoomInAction` object. In this case, we realize this association using a reference from the `ZoomInAction`, that is, an attribute of `ZoomInAction` named `targetMap` of type `MapArea`.

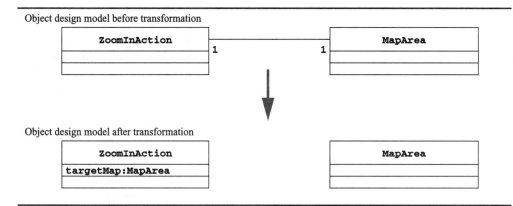

Figure 7-21   Realization of a unidirectional, one-to-one association (UML class diagram; arrow denotes the transformation of the object model).

Creating the association between `ZoomInAction` and `MapArea` translates into setting the `targetMap` attribute to refer to the correct `MapArea` object. Because each `ZoomInAction` object is associated with exactly one `MapArea`, a `null` value for the `targetMap` attribute can only occur when a `ZoomInAction` object is being created. A `null targetMap` is otherwise considered an error.

Bidirectional one-to-one associations.   Assume that we modify the `MapArea` class so that the user can zoom by simply clicking on the map with the left and right button. In this case, a `MapArea` needs to access its corresponding `ZoomInAction` object. Consequently, the association between these two objects needs to be bidirectional. We add the `zoomIn` attribute to `MapArea` (Figure 7-22). This, however, is not sufficient: By adding a second attribute to realize the association, we introduce redundancy into the model. We need to ensure that if a given `MapArea` has a reference to a specific `ZoomInAction`, the `ZoomInAction` has a reference to that same `MapArea`. To ensure consistency, we change the visibility of the attributes to private and add two methods to each class to access and modify them. `setZoomInAction()` on the `MapArea` sets the `zoomIn` attribute to its parameter and then invokes `setTargetMap()` on `ZoomInAction` to change its `targetMap` attribute.[2] Finally, we need to address the initialization of the association and its destruction by calling `setTargetMap()` and `setZoomInAction()` when `MapArea` and `ZoomInAction` objects are created and destroyed. This ensures that both reference attributes are consistent at all times.

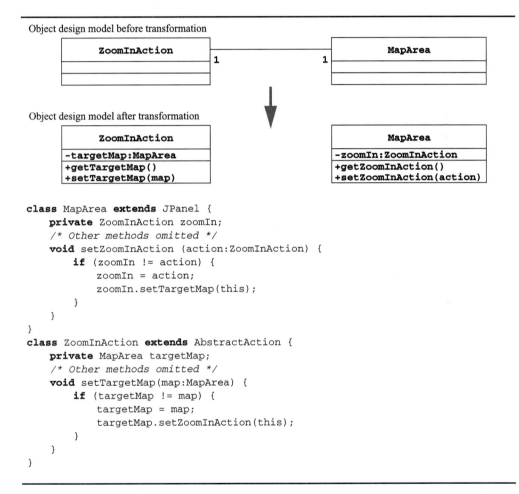

```
class MapArea extends JPanel {
    private ZoomInAction zoomIn;
    /* Other methods omitted */
    void setZoomInAction (action:ZoomInAction) {
        if (zoomIn != action) {
            zoomIn = action;
            zoomIn.setTargetMap(this);
        }
    }
}
class ZoomInAction extends AbstractAction {
    private MapArea targetMap;
    /* Other methods omitted */
    void setTargetMap(map:MapArea) {
        if (targetMap != map) {
            targetMap = map;
            targetMap.setZoomInAction(this);
        }
    }
}
```

Figure 7-22 Realization of a bidirectional one-to-one association (UML class diagram and Java excerpts; arrow denotes the transformation of the object design model).

2. Note that the `setZoomInAction()` and the `setTargetMap()` methods need to check first if the attribute needs to be modified before invoking the other method, such that they avoid an infinite recursion (see code in Figure 7-22).

The direction of an association can often change during the development of the system. Unidirectional associations are much simpler to realize. Bidirectional associations are more complex and introduce mutual dependencies among classes. For example, in Figure 7-22, both the `MapArea` and the `ZoomInAction` classes need to be recompiled and tested when we change either class. In the case of a unidirectional association from the `ZoomInAction` class to the `MapArea` class, we do not need to worry about the `MapArea` class when we change the `ZoomInAction` class. Bidirectional associations, however, are sometimes necessary in the case of peer classes that need to work together closely. The choice between a unidirectional or a bidirectional association is a trade-off that we need to evaluate in the context of a specific pair of classes. To make the trade-off easier, however, we can systematically make all attributes private and provide corresponding `setAttribute()` and `getAttribute()` operations to modify the reference. This minimizes changes to class interfaces when making a unidirectional association bidirectional (and vice versa).

One-to-many associations.   One-to-many associations, unlike one-to-one associations, cannot be realized using a single reference or a pair of references. Instead, we realize the "many" part using a collection of references. For example, the `Layer` class of the JEWEL GIS has a one-to-many association with the `LayerElement` class. Because `LayerElements` have no specific order with respect to `Layers` and because a `LayerElement` can be part of a `Layer` at most once, we use a set of references to model the "many" part of the association. Moreover, we decide to realize this association as a bidirectional association and so add the `addElement()`, `removeElement()`, `getLayer()` and `setLayer()` methods to the `Layer` and `LayerElement` classes to update the `layerElements` and `containedIn` attributes (see Figure 7-23). As in the one-to-one example, the association needs to be initialized and destroyed when `Layer` and `LayerElement` objects are created and destroyed.

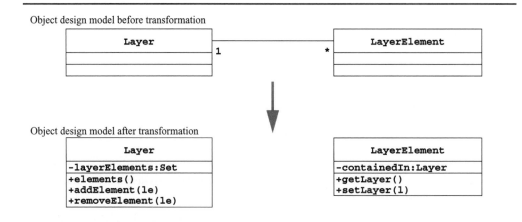

Figure 7-23   Realization of a bidirectional, one-to-many association (UML class diagram; arrow denotes the transformation of the object design model).

Note that the collection on the "many" side of the association depends on the constraints on the association. For example, if the LayerElements of a Layer need to be ordered (e.g., indicating the order in which they should be drawn), we need to use an Array or a Vector instead of a Set. Similarly, if an association is qualified, we use a Hashtable to store the references.

Many-to-many associations. In this case, both end classes have attributes that are collections of references and operations to keep these collections consistent. For example, the Polyline class of the JEWEL GIS has an ordered many-to-many association with the Point class. This association is realized by using a Vector attribute in each class, which is modified by the operations addPoint(), removePoint(), addPolyline(), and removePolyline() (see Figure 7-24). As in the previous example, these operations ensure that both Vectors are consistent. Note, however, that the association between Polyline and Point should be unidirectional, given that none of the Point operations needs to access the Polylines that include a given Point. We could then remove the polylines attribute and its related methods, in which case a unidirectional many-to-many association or a unidirectional one-to-many association becomes identical at the object design level.

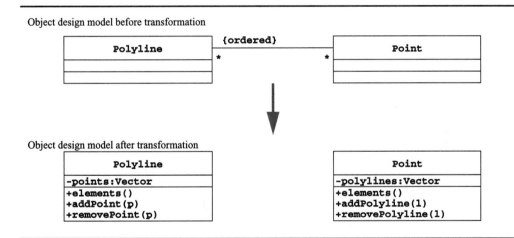

Figure 7-24   Realization of a bidirectional, many-to-many association (UML class diagram; arrow denotes the transformation of the object design model).

Associations as separate objects. In UML, associations can be associated with an association class that holds the attributes and operations of the association. We first transform the association class into a separate object and a number of binary associations. For example, consider the SimulationRun association in JEWEL (Figure 7-25). A SimulationRun relates an EmissionSource object and a SimulationResult object. The SimulationRun association class also holds attributes specific to the run, such as the date it was created, the user who ran the

Object design model before transformation

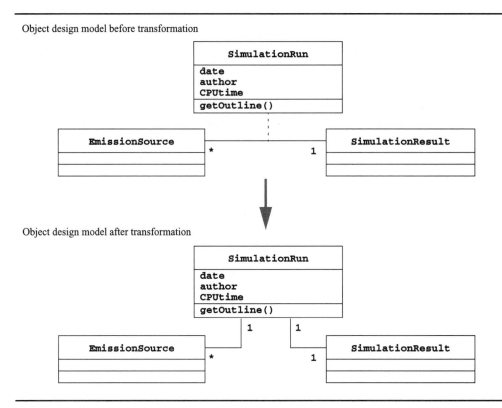

Figure 7-25 Transformation of an association class into an object and two binary associations (UML class diagram; arrow denotes the transformation of the object design model). Once the model contains only binary associations, each association is realized by using reference attributes and collections of references.

simulation, and the CPU time it took to complete the simulation. We first convert the association to an object called SimulationRun and two binary associations between the SimulationRun object and the other objects. We can then use the techniques discussed earlier to convert each binary association to a set of reference attributes.

Qualified associations.   In this case, one or both association ends are associated with a key that is used to differentiate between associations. Qualified associations are realized the same way as one-to-many and many-to-many associations are, except for using a Hashtable object on the qualified end (as opposed to a Vector or a Set). For example, consider the association between Scenario and SimulationRun in JEWEL (Figure 7-26). A Scenario represents a situation that the users are investigating (e.g., a nuclear reactor leak). For each Scenario, users can create several SimulationRuns, each using a different set of EmissionSources or a different EmissionModel. Given that SimulationRuns are expensive, users also reuse runs across similar Scenarios. The Scenario end of the association is qualified with a name, enabling the user to distinguish between SimulationRuns within the same Scenario. We

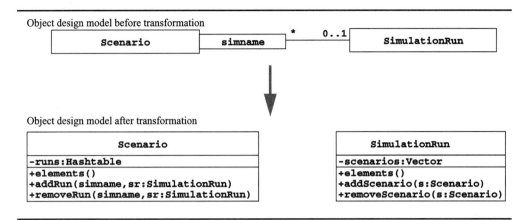

Figure 7-26   Realization of a bidirectional qualified association (UML class diagram; arrow denotes the transformation of the object design model).

realize this qualified association by creating a `runs` attribute on `Scenarios` and a `scenarios` attribute in `SimulationRuns`. The `runs` attribute is a `Hashtable` that is indexed by the name of a `SimulationRun`. Because the name is stored in the `Hashtable`, a specific `SimulationRun` can have different names across `Scenarios`. The `SimulationRun` end is realized, as before, as a `Vector` in the `SimulationRun` class.

7.4.9   Increasing Reuse

Inheritance allows developers to reuse code across a number of similar classes. For example, JFC, as do most user interface toolkits, provides four types of buttons:

- a push button (`JButton`), which triggers an action when the end user clicks on the button
- a radio button (`JRadioButton`), which enables an end user to select one choice out of a set of options
- a checkbox (`JCheckBox`), which enables an end user to turn an option on or off
- a menu item (`JMenuItem`), which triggers an action when selected from a pulldown or a popup menu

These four buttons share a set of attributes (e.g., a text label, an icon) and behavior (e.g., something happens when the end user selects them). However, the behavior of each type of button is slightly different. To accommodate these differences while reusing as much code as possible, JFC introduces two abstract classes, `AbstractButton` and `JToggleButton`, and organizes these four types of buttons into the inheritance hierarchy depicted by Figure 7-27. The `AbstractButton` class defines the behavior shared by all JFC buttons. `JToggleButton` defines the behavior shared by the two state buttons (i.e., `JRadioButton` and `JCheckBoxes`).

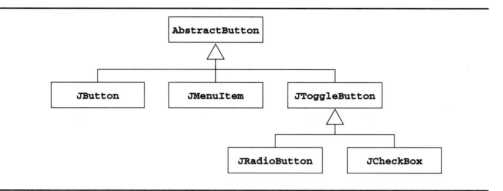

Figure 7-27   An example of code reuse with inheritance (UML class diagram).

There are two main advantages to using a well-designed inheritance hierarchy. First, more code is reused, leading to less redundancies and thus fewer opportunities for defects. Second, the resulting code is extensible, including a well-documented interface for creating future specializations (e.g., new types of buttons in the case of JFC). Reuse through inheritance comes at a cost, however. Developers must correctly anticipate which behavior should be shared and which behavior should be refined by the specialization, often without knowing all possible specializations. Moreover, once developers define an inheritance hierarchy and a paradigm for sharing code, the interfaces of the abstract classes become increasingly more rigid to change as many subclasses and client classes depend on them. Object design represents the last opportunity during development to revisit the inheritance hierarchies among application and solution objects. Any changes later in the process may introduce hard-to-detect defects and substantially increase the cost of the system.

There are two main approaches to designing an inheritance hierarchy for reuse. First, we can examine a number of similar classes and abstract out their common behavior. The AbstractButton example of Figure 7-27 is an example of this approach. Second, we can decouple a client class from an anticipated change by introducing a level of abstraction. Most design patterns [Gamma et al., 1994], including the AbstractFactory pattern below, use inheritance to protect against an anticipated change.

Consider the problem of writing a single application that works with several windowing styles (e.g., Windows, Macintosh, and Motif). Given a specific platform, the user works with a consistent set of windows, scrollbars, buttons, and menus. The application itself should not know or depend on a specific look and feel. The **Abstract Factory pattern** (Figure 7-28) solves this problem by providing an abstract class for each object that can be substituted (e.g., AbstractWindow and AbstractButton) and by providing an interface for creating groups of objects (i.e., the AbstractFactory). Concrete classes implement each abstract class for each factory. For example, the AbstractButton class is refined by the MacButton class and the MotifButton class. The AbstractFactory interface provides a createButton() operation to create a button. A concrete factory implements the AbstractFactory interface for each option. The MotifFactory.createButton() method returns a MotifButton, whereas the

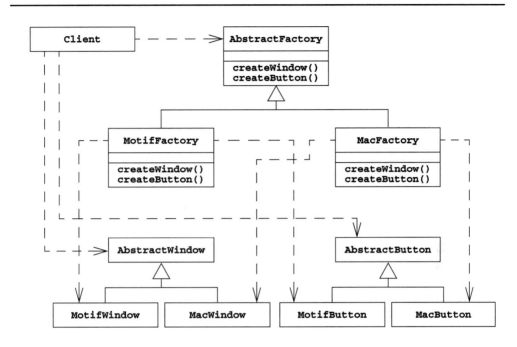

Figure 7-28 `AbstractFactory` design pattern (UML class diagram, dependencies represent <<call>> relationships). This design pattern uses inheritance to support different look and feels (e.g., Motif and Macintosh). If a new specialization is added, the client does not need to be changed.

`MacFactory.createButton()` method returns a `MacButton`. Note that both `createButton()` methods have the same interface for both specializations. Consequently, the caller only accesses the `AbstractFactory` interface and the abstract classes and is thus shielded from concrete implementations. Moreover, this allows new factories (e.g., `BeOSFactory` and `BeOSButton`) to be implemented in the future without changing the application.

7.4.10 Removing Implementation Dependencies

In system modeling, we use generalization relationships to classify objects into generalization/specification hierarchies. This allows us to differentiate the common behavior of the general case from the behavior that is specific to specialized objects. In an object-oriented programming language, generalization is realized with inheritance. This allows us to reuse attributes and operations from higher level classes. On the one hand, inheritance when used as a generalization mechanism results in fewer dependencies. For example, in the `AbstractFactory` design pattern (Figure 7-28), dependencies between the application and a specific look and feel is removed using the abstract classes `AbstractFactory`, `AbstractButton`, and `Abstract-`

Window. On the other hand, inheritance introduces dependencies along the hierarchy. For example, the classes MotifWindow and MacWindow are tightly coupled with AbstractWindow. In the case of generalization, this is acceptable, given that AbstractWindow, MotifWindow, and MacWindow are strongly related concepts. These tight dependencies can become a problem when inheritance is used for other purposes than generalization. Consider the following example.

Assume for a moment that Java does not provide a Set abstraction and that we needed to write our own. We decide to reuse the java.util.Hashtable class to implement a set abstraction that we call MySet. Inserting an element in MySet is equivalent to checking if the corresponding key exists in the table and creating an entry if necessary. Checking if an element is in MySet is equivalent to checking if an entry is associated with the corresponding key (see Figure 7-29, left column).

Such an implementation of a Set allows us to reuse code and provides us with the desired behavior. It also provides us, however, with unwanted behavior. For example, Hashtable implements the containsKey() operation to check if the specified object exists as a key in the Hashtable and the containsValue() operation to check if the specified object exists as an entry. Both of these operations are inherited by MySet. Given our implementation, the operation containsValue() invoked on a MySet object always returns null, which is counterintuitive. Worse, a developer using the MySet can easily confuse the contains() and containsValue() operations and introduce a fault in the system that is difficult to detect. To address this issue, we could overwrite all operations inherited from Hashtable that should not be used on MySet. This would lead to a MySet class that is difficult to understand and reuse.

The fundamental problem in this example is that, although Hashtable provides behavior that we would like to reuse in implementing Set, because it would save us time, the Set concept is not a refinement of the Hashtable concept. In contrast, the MacWindow class of the AbstractFactory example is a refinement of the AbstractWindow class.

We call the use of inheritance for the sole purpose of reusing code **implementation inheritance**. Implementation inheritance enables developers to reuse code quickly by subclassing an existing class and refining its behavior. A Set implemented by inheriting from a Hashtable is an example of implementation inheritance. Conversely, the classification of concepts into specialization-generalization hierarchies is called **interface inheritance**. Interface inheritance is used for managing the complexity arising for a large number of related concepts. Interface inheritance is also called subtyping, in which case the superclass is called **supertype** and the subclass is called **subtype**. For example, Real and Integer are subtypes of Number. MapArea is a subtype of JPanel.

Implementation inheritance should be avoided. Although it provides a tempting mechanism for code reuse, it yields only short-term benefits and results in systems that are difficult to modify. **Delegation** is a better alternative to implementation inheritance if code can be reused. A class is said to delegate to another class if it implements an operation by merely resending a message to another class. Delegation makes explicit the dependencies between the reused class and the new class. The right column of Figure 7-29 shows an implementation of

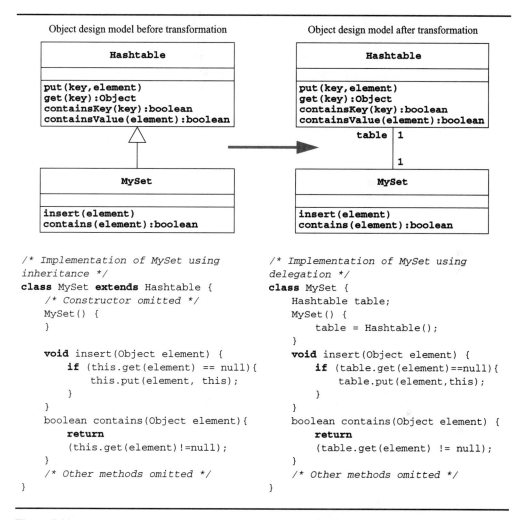

Object design model before transformation   Object design model after transformation

```
/* Implementation of MySet using          /* Implementation of MySet using
inheritance */                            delegation */
class MySet extends Hashtable {           class MySet {
    /* Constructor omitted */                 Hashtable table;
    MySet() {                                 MySet() {
    }                                             table = Hashtable();
                                              }
    void insert(Object element) {             void insert(Object element) {
        if (this.get(element) == null){           if (table.get(element)==null){
            this.put(element, this);                  table.put(element,this);
        }                                         }
    }                                         }
    boolean contains(Object element){         boolean contains(Object element) {
        return                                    return
        (this.get(element)!=null);                (table.get(element) != null);
    }                                         }
    /* Other methods omitted */               /* Other methods omitted */
}                                         }
```

Figure 7-29 An example of implementation inheritance. The left column depicts a questionable implementation of MySet using implementation inheritance. The right column depicts an improved implementation using delegation. (UML class diagram and Java).

MySet using delegation instead of implementation inheritance. Note that the only significant addition is the attribute table and its initialization in the MySet() constructor.

For a thorough discussion of the trade-offs related to inheritance and delegation, the reader is referred to [Meyer, 1997].

Optimization activities

The direct translation of an analysis model results into a model that is often inefficient. During object design, we optimize the object model according to design goals, such as minimization of response time, execution time, or memory resources. In this section, we describe four simple optimizations:

- the addition of associations for optimizing access paths
- collapsing objects into attributes
- caching the result of expensive computations
- delaying expensive computations

When applying optimizations, developers must strike a balance between efficiency and clarity. Optimizations increase the efficiency of the system but also make it more complex and difficult to understand the system models.

7.4.11 Revisiting Access Paths

One common source of inefficient system performance is the repeated traversal of multiple associations when accessing needed information. To identify inefficient access paths, object designers should ask the following questions [Rumbaugh et al., 1991]:

- **For each operation:** How often is the operation called? What associations does the operation have to traverse to obtain the information it needs? Frequent operations should not require many traversals but should have a direct connection between the querying object and the queried object. If that direct connection is missing, an additional association should be added between these two objects.
- **For each association:** If it has a "many" association on one or both sides, is the multiplicity necessary? How often is the "many" side of an association involved in a search? If this is frequent, then the object designer should try to reduce "many" to "one." Otherwise, should the "many" side be ordered or indexed to improve access time?

In interface and reengineering projects, estimates for the frequency of access paths can be derived from the legacy system. In greenfield engineering projects (i.e., systems that are developed from scratch and that are not intended to replace a legacy system), the frequency of access paths are more difficult to estimate. In this case, redundant associations should not be added before a dynamic analysis of the full system—for example, during system testing—has determined which associations participate in the performance bottlenecks.

Another source of inefficient system performance is excessive modeling. During analysis many classes are identified that turn out to have no interesting behavior. In this case, object designers should ask:

- **For each attribute:** What operations use the attribute? Are `set()` and `get()` the only operations performed on the attribute? If yes, does the attribute really belong to this object or should it be moved to a calling object?

The systematic examination of the object model using the above questions should lead to a model with selected redundant associations, with fewer inefficient many-to-many associations, and fewer classes.

7.4.12 Collapsing Objects: Turning Objects into Attributes

During analysis, developers identify many classes that are associated with domain concepts. During system design and object design, the object model is restructured and optimized, often leaving some of these classes with only a few attributes and little behavior. Such classes, when associated only with one other class, can be collapsed into an attribute, thus reducing the overall complexity of the model.

Consider, for example, an object model that includes `Persons` identified by a `SocialSecurity` object. During analysis, two classes may have been identified. Each `Person` is associated with a `SocialSecurity` class, which stores a unique ID string identifying the `Person`. Further modeling did not reveal any additional behavior for the `SocialSecurity` object. Moreover, no other classes have associations with the `SocialSecurity` class. In this case, the `SocialSecurity` class should be collapsed into an attribute of the `Person` class (see Figure 7-30).

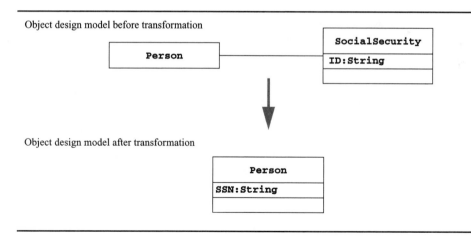

Figure 7-30   Alternative representations of a unique identifier for a `Person` (UML class diagrams).

The decision of collapsing classes is not always obvious. In the case of a social security system, the `SocialSecurity` class may have much more behavior, such as specialized routines for generating new numbers based on birth dates and the location of the original application. In general, developers should delay collapsing decisions until the beginning of the implementation, when responsibilities for each class are clear.

7.4.13 Caching the Result of Expensive Computations

Expensive computations often only need to be done once, because the base values from which the computation is done do not change or change slowly. In such cases, the result of the computation can be cached as a private attribute. Consider, for example, the `Layer.getOutline()` operation. Assume all `LayerElements` are defined once as part of the configuration of the system and do not change during the execution. Then, the vector of `Points` returned by the `Layer.getOutline()` operation is always the same for a given bbox and detail. Moreover, end users have the tendency to focus on a limited number of points around the map as they focus on a specific city or region. Taking into account these observations, a simple optimization is to add a private `cachedPoints` attribute to the `Layer` class, which remembers the result of the `getOutline()` operation for given bbox and detail pairs. The `getOutline()` operation then checks the `cachedPoints` attribute first, returns the corresponding `Point Vector`, if found, otherwise it invokes the `getOutline()` operation on each contained `LayerElement`. Note that this approach includes a trade-off: On the one hand, we improve the average response time for the `getOutline()` operation; on the other hand, we consume memory space by storing redundant information.

7.4.14 Delaying Expensive Computations

An alternate approach to expensive computations is to delay them as long as possible. For example, consider an object representing an image stored as a file. Loading all the pixels that constitute the image from the file is expensive. However, the image data does not need to be loaded until the image is displayed. We can realize such an optimization using a **Proxy pattern** [Gamma et al., 1994]. An `ImageProxy` object takes the place of the `Image` and provides the same interface as the `Image` object (Figure 7-31). Simple operations (such as `width()` and `height()` are handled by `ImageProxy`. When `Image` needs to be drawn, however, `ImageProxy` loads the data from disk and creates a `RealImage` object. If the client does not invokes the `paint()` operation, the `RealImage` object is not created, thus saving substantial computation time. The calling classes only access the `ImageProxy` and the `RealImage` through the `Image` interface.

Object design model before transformation

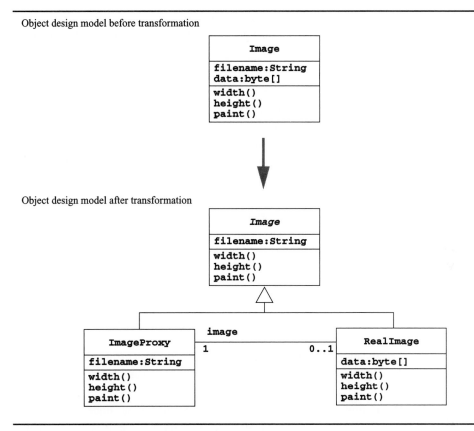

Object design model after transformation

Figure 7-31   Delaying expensive computations using a `Proxy` pattern (UML class diagram).

7.5 Managing Object Design

In this section, we discuss management issues related to object design. There are two primary management challenges during object design:

- *Increased communication complexity.* The number of participants involved during this phase of development increases dramatically. The object design models and code are the result of the collaboration of many people. Management needs to ensure that decisions among these developers are made consistently with project goals.

- *Consistency with prior decisions and documents.* Developers often do not appreciate completely the consequences of analysis and system design decisions before object design. When detailing and refining the object design model, developers may question some of these decisions and reevaluate them in the light of lessons learned. The management challenge is to maintain a record of these revised decisions and to make sure all documents reflect the current state of development.

In Section 7.5.1, we discuss the Object Design Document, its development and maintenance, and its relationship with other documents. In Section 7.5.2, we describe the roles associated with object design.

7.5.1 Documenting Object Design

Object design is documented in the Object Design Document (ODD). It describes object design trade-offs made by developers, guidelines they followed for subsystem interfaces, the decomposition of subsystems into packages and classes, and the class interfaces. The ODD is used to exchange interface information among teams and as a reference during testing. The audience for the ODD includes system architects, (i.e., the developers who participate in the system design), developers who implement each subsystem, and testers.

The ODD enables developers to understand the subsystem sufficiently well that they can use it. Moreover, a good interface specification enables other developers to implement classes concurrently. In general, an interface specification should satisfy the following criteria [Liskov, 1986]:

- *Restrictiveness.* A specification should be precise enough that it excludes unwanted implementations. Preconditions and postconditions specifying border cases is one way to achieve restrictive specifications.
- *Generality.* A specification, however, should not restrict its implementation. This allows developers to develop and substitute increasingly efficient or elegant implementations that may not have been thought of when the subsystem was specified.
- *Clarity.* A specification should be easily and unambiguously understandable by developers. However restrictive and general a specification may be, it is useless if it is difficult to understand. Certain behaviors are more easily described in natural language, whereas boundary cases can be described with constraints and exceptions.

There are three main approaches to documenting object design.

- *Self-contained ODD generated from model.* The first approach is to document the object design model the same way we documented the analysis model or the system design model: We write and maintain a UML model using a tool and generate the document automatically. This document would duplicate any application objects identified during analysis. The disadvantages of this solution include redundancy with the Requirements Analysis Document (RAD) and a high level of effort for maintaining consistency with the RAD. Moreover, the ODD duplicates information in the source code and requires a high level of effort whenever the code changes. This often leads to an RAD and an ODD that are inaccurate or out of date.
- *ODD as extension of the RAD.* The second approach is to treat the object design model as an extension of the analysis model. In other terms, the object design is considered as the

set of application objects augmented with solution objects. The advantage of this solution is that maintaining consistency between the RAD and the ODD becomes much easier as a result of the reduction in redundancy. The disadvantages of this solution include polluting the RAD with information that is irrelevant to the client and the user. Moreover, object design is rarely as simple as identifying additional solution objects. Often, application objects are changed or transformed to accommodate design goals or efficiency concerns.

- *ODD embedded into source code.* The third approach is to embed the ODD into the source code. As in the first approach, we first represent the ODD using a modeling tool (see Figure 7-32). Once the ODD becomes stable, we use the modeling tool to generate class stubs. We describe each class interface using tagged comments that distinguish source code comments from object design descriptions. We can then generate the ODD using a tool that parses the source code and extracts the relevant information (e.g., Javadoc [Javadoc, 1999a]). Once the object design model is documented in the code, we abandon the initial object design model. The advantage of this approach is that the consistency between the object design model and the source code is much easier to maintain: when changes are made to the source code, the tagged comments need to be updated and the ODD regenerated. In this section, we focus only on this approach.

The fundamental issue is one of maintaining consistency among two models and the source code. Ideally, we want to maintain the analysis model, the object design model, and the source code using a single tool. Objects would then be described once and consistency among documentation, stubs, and code would be maintained automatically.

Presently, however, UML modeling tools provide facilities for generating a document from a model or class stubs from a model. The documentation generation facility can be used, for example, to generate the RAD from the analysis model (Figure 7-32). The class stub generation facility (called forward engineering) can be used in the self-contained ODD approach to generate the class interfaces and stubs for each method.

Some modeling tools provide facilities for reverse engineering, that is, recreating a UML model from source code. Such facilities are useful for creating object models from legacy code. They require, however, substantial hand processing, as the tool cannot recreate bidirectional associations based on reference attributes only.

Tool support currently falls short when maintaining two-way dependencies, in particular between the analysis model and the source code. Some tools, such as Rationale Rose [Rational, 1998], attempt to realize this functionality by embedding information about associations and other UML constructs in source code comments. Even though this allows the tool to recover syntactic changes from the source code, developers still need to update the model descriptions to reflect the changes. Because developers need different tools to change the source code and the model, the model usually falls behind.

Until modeling tools provide better support for maintaining consistency between object models and source code, we find that generating the ODD from source code and focusing the

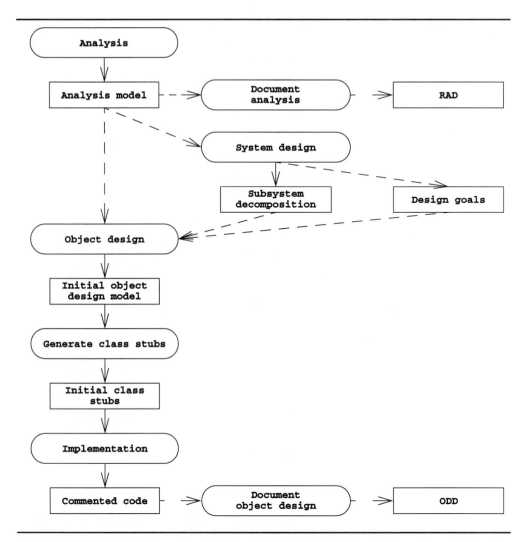

Figure 7-32 Embedded ODD approach. Class stubs are generated from the object design model. The object design model is then documented as tagged comments in the source code. The initial object design model is abandoned and the ODD is generated from the source code instead using a tool such as Javadoc (UML activity diagram).

RAD on the application domain is the most practical. It reduces the amount of redundant information that needs to be maintained, and it locates the object design information where it is the most accessible, that is, the source code. The consistency between the source code and the analysis model still needs to be maintained manually. This task is easier, however, because fewer code changes impact the analysis model than impact the object design model.

The following is an example template for a generated ODD:

Object Design Document
1. Introduction
    1.1 Object design trade-offs
    1.2 Interface documentation guidelines
    1.3 Definitions, acronyms, and abbreviations
    1.4 References
2. Packages
3. Class interfaces
Glossary

The first section of the ODD is an introduction to the document. It describes the general trade-offs made by developers (e.g., buy vs. build, memory space vs. response time), guidelines and conventions (e.g., naming conventions, boundary cases, exception handling mechanisms), and an overview of the document.

Interface documentation guidelines and coding conventions are the single most important factor that can improve communication between developers during object design. These include a list of rules that developers should use when designing and naming interfaces. Below are examples of such conventions.

- Classes are named with singular nouns.
- Methods are named with verb phrases, fields, and parameters with noun phrases.
- Error status is returned via an exception only, not a return value.
- Collections and containers have an `elements()` method returning an `Enumeration`.
- `Enumerations` returned by `elements()` methods are robust to element removals.

Such conventions help developers design interfaces consistently, even if many developers contribute to the interface specification. Moreover, making these conventions explicit before object design makes it easier for developers to follow them. In general, these conventions should not evolve during the project.

The second section of the ODD, *Packages,* describes the decomposition of subsystems into packages and the file organization of the code. This includes an overview of each package, its dependencies with other packages, and its expected usage.

The third section, *Class interfaces*, describes the classes and their public interfaces. This includes an overview of each class, its dependencies with other classes and packages, its public attributes, operations, and the exceptions they can raise.

The initial version of the ODD can be written soon after the subsystem decomposition is stable. The ODD is updated every time new interfaces become available or existing ones are revised. Even if the subsystem is not yet functional, having a source code interface enables developers to more easily code dependent subsystems and communicate unambiguously. Developers usually discover at this stage missing parameters and new boundary cases. The development of the ODD is different than other documents, as more participants are involved and as the document is revised more frequently. To accommodate a high rate of change and many developers, sections 2 and 3 can be generated by a tool from source code comments.

In Java, this can be done with Javadoc, a tool that generates Web pages from source code comments. Developers annotate interfaces and class declarations with tagged comments. For example, Figure 7-33 depicts the interface specification for the `Layer` class of the JEWEL example. The header comment in the file describes the purpose of the `Layer` class, its authors, its current version, and cross references to related classes. The `@see` tags are used by Javadoc to create cross references between classes. Following the header comment is the class and the method declarations. Each method comment contains a brief description of the purpose of the method, its parameters, and its return result. When using constraints, we also include preconditions and postconditions in the method header. The first sentence of the comment and the tagged comments are extracted and formatted by Javadoc. Keeping material for the ODD with the source code enables the developers to maintain consistency more easily and more rapidly. This is critical when multiple persons are involved.

For any system of useful size, the ODD represents a large amount of information that can translate to several hundreds or thousands of pages of documentation. Moreover, the ODD evolves rapidly during object design and integration, as developers understand better other subsystem's needs and find faults with their specifications. For these reasons, all versions of the ODD should be made available electronically, for example, as a set of Web pages. Moreover, different components of the ODD should be put under configuration management and synchronized with their corresponding source code files. We describe configuration management issues in more detail in Chapter 10, *Software Configuration Management*.

7.5.2 Assigning Responsibilities

Object design is characterized by a large number of participants accessing and modifying a large amount of information. To ensure that changes to interfaces are documented and communicated in an orderly manner, several roles collaborate to control, communicate, and implement changes. These include the members of the architecture team who are responsible for system design and subsystem interfaces, liaisons who are responsible for interteam communication, and configuration managers who are responsible for tracking change.

Below are the main roles of object design.

- The **core architect** develops coding guidelines and conventions before object design starts. As for many conventions, the actual set of conventions is not as important as the commitment of all architects and developers to use the conventions. The core architects are also responsible for ensuring consistency with prior decisions documented in the SDD and RAD.

```
/* The class Layer is a container of LayerElements, each representing a
 * polygon or a polyline. For example, JEWEL typically has a road layer, a
 * water layer, a political layer, and an emissions layer.
 * @author John Smith
 * @version 0.1
 * @see LayerElement
 * @see Point
 */
class Layer {

    /* Member variables, constructors, and other methods omitted */
    Enumeration elements() {…};

    /* The getOutline operation returns an enumeration of points representing
     * the layer elements at a specified detail level. The operation only
     * returns points contained within the rectangle bbox.
     * @param      box         The clipping rectangle in universal coordinates
     * @param      detail      Detail level (big numbers mean more detail)
     * @return     A enumeration of points in universal coordinates.
     * @throws     ZeroDetail
     * @throws     ZeroBoundingBox
     * @pre        detail > 0.0 and bbox.width > 0.0 and bbox.height > 0.0
     * @post       forall LayerElement le in this.elements() |
     *                  forall Point p in le.points() |
     *                      result.contains(p)
     */
    Enumeration getOutline(Rectangle2D bbox, double detail) {…};

    /* Other methods omitted */
}
```

Figure 7-33 Interface description of the Layer class using Javadoc tagged comments (Java excerpts).

- The **architecture liaisons** document the public subsystem interfaces for which they are responsible. This leads to a first draft of the ODD which is used by developers. Architecture liaisons also negotiate changes to public interfaces when they become necessary. Often, the issue is not of consensus, but rather, of communication: developers depending on the interface may welcome the change if they are notified first. The architecture liaisons and the core architects form the architecture team.

- The **object designers** refine and detail the interface specification of the class or subsystem they implement.

- The **configuration manager** of a subsystem releases changes to the interfaces and the ODD once they become available. The configuration manager also keeps track of the relationship between source code and ODD revisions.

- **Technical writers** from the documentation team clean up the final version of the ODD. They ensure that the document is consistent from a structural and content point of view. They also check for compliance with the guidelines.

As in system design, the architecture team is the integrating force of object design. The architecture team ensures that changes are consistent with project goals. The documentation team, including the technical writers, ensures that the changes are consistent with guidelines and conventions.

7.6 Exercises

1. Consider the `Polyline`, `Polygon`, and `Point` classes of Figure 7-14. Write the following constraints in OCL:
    - A `Polygon` is composed of a sequence of at least three `Points`.
    - A `Polygon` is composed of a sequence of `Points` starting and ending at the same `Point`.
    - The `Points` returned by the `getPoints(bbox)` method of a `Polygon` are within the bbox rectangle.

2. Consider the `Layer`, `LayerElement`, `Polyline`, and `Point` classes of Figure 7-15. Write constraints below in OCL. Note that the last two constraints require the use of the `forAll` OCL operator on collections.
    - A `detail` level cannot be part of both the `inDetailLevels` and the `notInDetailLevels` sets of a `Point`.
    - For a given `detail` level, `LayerElement.getOutline()` can only return `Points` that contain the `detail` level in their `inDetailLevels` set attribute.
    - The `inDetailLevels` and `notInDetailLevels` set can only grow as a consequence of `LayerElement.getOutline()`. In other words, once a detail level is in one of these sets, it cannot be removed.

3. Consider the `Point` class in Figures 7-14 and 7-15. Assume that we are evaluating an alternative design in which a global object called `DetailTable` tracks which `Points` have been included or excluded from a given detail level (instead of each `Point` having a `inDetailLevels` and `notInDetailLevels` attribute). This is realized by two associations between `DetailTable` and `Point`, which are indexed by `detailLevel` (see Figure 7-34). Write OCL constraints specifying that, given a detailLevel, a `DetailTable` can only have one link to a given `Point` (i.e., a `DetailTable` cannot have both an `includesPoint` and an `excludesPoint` association given a `Point` and `detailLevel`).

4. Using the transformations described in Sections 7.4.8–7.4.10, restructure the object design model of Figure 7-34.

5. Incrementally computing the `inDetailLevels` and `notInDetailLevels` attributes of a Point class as depicted in Figure 7-14 is an optimization. Using the terms we introduced in Section 7.4, name the kind of optimization that is performed.

6. Discuss the relative advantages of the `Point` class of Exercise 3 versus the `Point` class of Figure 7-14 from a response time and a memory space point of view.

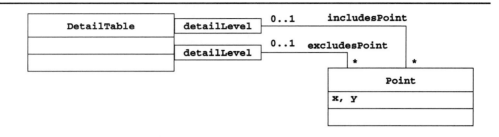

Figure 7-34 DetailTable is a global object tracking which Points have been included or excluded from a specified detailLevel. This is an alternative to the inDetailLevels and notInDetailLevels sets depicted in Figure 7-14.

7. Assume that you are using an application framework instead of the GIS we described in Section 7.4. The GIS application framework provides a getOutline() method that returns an Enumeration of GISPoints to represent a Polyline. The JFC drawPolyline() method takes as parameters two arrays of coordinates and a integer denoting the number of points in the Polyline (Figure 7-18). Which design pattern should you use to address this interface mismatch? Draw a UML class diagram to illustrate your solution.

8. You are the developer responsible for the getOutline() method of the Layer class in Figure 7-15. You find that the current version of getOutline() does not properly exclude Polylines consisting of a single Point (as a result of the clipping). You repair the bug. Who should you notify?

9. You are the developer responsible for the getOutline() method of the Layer class in Figure 7-15. You change the method to represent detailLevels (that are stored in inDetailLevels or notInDetailLevels) using a positive integer instead of a floating point number. Who should you notify?

10. Why is maintaining consistency between the analysis model and the object design model difficult? Illustrate your point with a change to the object design model.

References

[Birrer, 1993]   E. T. Birrer, "Frameworks in the financial engineering domain: An experience report," *ECOOP'93 Proceedings*, Lecture Notes in Computer Science, No. 707, 1993.

[Bruegge et al., 1993]   B. Bruegge, T. Gottschalk, & B. Luo, "A framework for dynamic program analyzers," *OOPSLA'93, (Object-Oriented Programming Systems, Languages, and Applications)*, pp. 65–82, (Washington, DC), Sept. 1993.

[Bruegge & Riedel, 1994]   B. Bruegge & E. Riedel. "A geographic environmental modeling system: Towards an object-oriented framework," *Proceedings of the European Conference on Object-Oriented Programming (ECOOP-94),* Bologna, Italy, Lecture Notes in Computer Science, (Springer Verlag, Berlin), July 1994.

[Bruegge et al., 1995]   B. Bruegge, E. Riedel, G. McRae, & T. Russel, "GEMS: An environmental modeling system," *IEEE Journal for Computational Science and Engineering*, pp.55–68, Sept. 1995.

[Fayad & Hamu, 1997] M. E. Fayad & D. S. Hamu, "Object-oriented enterprise frameworks: Make vs. buy decisions and guidelines for selection," *The Communications of ACM*, 1997.

[Gamma et al., 1994] E. Gamma, R. Helm, R. Johnson, & J. Vlissides, *Design Patters: Elements of Reusable Object-Oriented Software.* Addison-Wesley, Reading, MA, 1994.

[Horn, 1992] B. Horn. "Constraint patterns as a basis for object-oriented programming," *Proceedings of the OOPSLA'92*, (Vancouver, Canada), 1992.

[Hueni et al., 1995] H. Hueni, R. Johnson, & R. Engel, "A framework for network protocol software," *Proceedings of OOPSLA*, (Austin, TX), Oct. 1995.

[iContract] Java Design by Contract Tool, http://www.reliable-systems.com/tools/iContract/iContract.htm.

[Javadoc, 1999a] Sun Microsystems, Javadoc homepage, http://java.sun.com/products/jdk/javadoc/.

[Javadoc, 1999b] Sun Microsystems, "How to write doc comments for Javadoc," http://java.sun.com/products/jdk/javadoc/writingdoccomments.html.

[JFC, 1999] *Java Foundation Classes*, JDK Documentation. Javasoft, 1999.

[Johnson et al., 1988] R. Johnson & B. Foote, "Designing reusable classes," *Journal of Object-Oriented Programming*, Vol. 1, No. 5, pp. 22–35, 1988.

[Kompanek et al., 1996] A. Kompanek, A. Houghton, H. Karatassos, A. Wetmore, & B. Bruegge, "JEWEL: A distributed system for emissions modeling," *Conference for Air and Waste Management*, (Nashville, TN), June 1996.

[Liskov, 1986] B. Liskov & J. Guttag, *Abstraction and Specification in Program Development.* McGraw-Hill, New York, 1986.

[Meyer, 1997] Bertrand Meyer, *Object-Oriented Software Construction*, 2nd ed. Prentice Hall, Upper Saddle River, 1997.

[OMG, 1995] Object Management Group, *The Common Object Request Broker: Architecture and Specification.* Wiley, New York, 1995.

[OMG, 1998] Object Management Group, *OMG Unified Modeling Language Specification.* Framingham, MA, 1998, http://www.omg.org.

[Rational, 1998] Rational Software Corp., *Rationale Rose 98: Using Rose.* Cupertino, CA, 1998.

[Rumbaugh et al., 1991] J. Rumbaugh, M. Blaha, W. Premerlani, F. Eddy, & W. Lorensen. *Object-Oriented Modeling and Design.* Prentice Hall, Englewood Cliffs, NJ, 1991.

[Schmidt, 1997] D. C. Schmidt, "Applying design patterns and frameworks to develop object-oriented communication software," *Handbook of Programming Languages*, Vol. 1, Peter Salus (ed.), MacMillan Computer, 1997.

[Szyperski, 1998] C. Szyperski, Component Software: Beyond Object-Oriented Programming, ACM Press, New York, Addison-Wesley, 1998.

[Weinand et al., 1988] A. Weinand, E. Gamma, & R. Marty. "ET++ – An object-oriented application framework in C++." In *Object-Oriented Programming Systems, Languages, and Applications Conference Proceedings*, (San Diego, CA), September 1988.

[Wilson & Ostrem, 1999] G. Wilson & J. Ostrem, *WebObjects Developer's Guide*, Apple, Cupertino, CA, 1998.

PART III
Managing Change

Rationale Management

The [motorcycle] description would cover the "what" of the motorcycle in terms of components, the "how" of the engine in terms of functions. It would badly need a "where" analysis in the form of an illustration and also a "why" analysis in the form of engineering principles that led to this particular conformation of parts.
—Robert Pirsig, *in Zen and the Art of Motorcycle Maintenance*

Rationale is the justification of decisions. The models we have described until now represent the system. Rationale models represent the reasoning that leads to the system, including its functionality and its implementation. Rationale is critical in two areas: It supports the decisions making and it supports the capture of knowledge. Rationale includes:

- the issues that were addressed
- the alternatives that were considered
- the decisions that were made to resolve the issues
- the criteria that were used to guide decisions
- the debate developers went through to reach a decision

In the context of decision making, the rationale improves the quality of decisions by making decision elements, such as criteria, priorities, and arguments, explicit. In the context of knowledge capture, the rationale is the most important information in the development process when changing the system. For example, when functionality is added to the system, the rationale enables developers to track which decisions need to be revisited and which alternatives have already been evaluated. When new staff is assigned to the project, new developers can become familiar with past decisions by accessing the rationale of the system.

Unfortunately, rationale is also the most complex information that developers generate, and thus, is the most difficult to maintain and update. Moreover, capturing rationale represents an up-front investment with long-term returns. In this chapter, we describe issue-modeling, a representation for modeling rationale. We then describe the activities of creating, maintaining, and accessing rationale models. We conclude this chapter by describing management issues related to managing rationale, such as decision support and negotiation.

8.1 Introduction: A Ham Example

System models are abstractions of what the system does. The requirements analysis model, including the use case model, the class model, and the sequence diagrams (see Chapter 4, *Requirements Elicitation* and Chapter 5, *Analysis*) represents the behavior of the system from the user's point of view. The system design model (see Chapter 6, *System Design*) represents the system in terms of subsystems, design goals, hardware nodes, data stores, access control, and so on. The rationale model represents why a given system is structured and behaves the way it does.[1] Why should we capture the *why*? Consider the following example[2]:

> Mary asks John, her husband, why he always cuts off both ends of the ham before putting it in the oven. John responds that he is following his mother's recipe and that he had always see her cut the ends off the ham. He never really questioned the practice and thought it was part of the recipe. Mary, intrigued by this answer, calls her mother-in-law to find out more about this ham recipe.
>
> Ann, John's mother, provides more details on the ham cutting, but no culinary justification: She says that she has always trimmed about an inch off each end of the ham as her mother did, assuming it had something to do with improving the taste.
>
> Mary continues her investigation and calls John's maternal grandmother, Zoe. At first, Zoe is very surprised: She does not cut the ends of the ham and she cannot imagine how such practice could possibly improve the taste. After much discussion, Zoe eventually remembers that, when Ann was a little girl, she used to cook on a much narrower stove that could not accommodate standard-sized meat loaves. To work around this problem, she used to cut off about an inch from each end of the ham. She stopped this practice once she got a wider stove.

Developers and cooks are good at disseminating new practices and techniques. The rationale behind these techniques, however, is usually lost, making it difficult to improve them as their application context changes. The Y2K bug is such an example: in the 1960s and 1970s, memory costs drove developers to represent information as compactly as possible. For this reason, the year was often represented with two characters instead of four (e.g., "1998" was represented as "98"). The assumption of the developers was that the software would only be used for a few years. Arithmetic operations on years represented with two digits assumes that all dates are within the same century. Unfortunately, this shortcut breaks down at the turn of the century for software performing arithmetic on two-digit years. For example, when computing the age of a person, a person born in 1949 will be considered $01 - 49 = -48$ years old in 2001. The practice of encoding years with two digits became standard, even after memory prices dropped significantly and the year 2000 came nearer. Moreover, new systems needed to be

---

1. Historically, much research about rationale focuses on design and, hence, the term *design rationale* is most often used in the literature. Instead, we use the term *rationale* to avoid confusion and to emphasize that rationale models can be used during all phases of development.

2. Far-fetched example adapted for this chapter, original author unknown.

backward compatible with older ones. For these reasons, many systems delivered as late as the 1990s still have Y2K bugs.

Rationale models enable developers and cooks to deal with *change*, such as larger stoves or cheaper memory prices. Capturing the justification of decisions effectively models the dependencies between starting assumptions and decisions. When assumptions change, decisions can be revisited. In this chapter, we describe techniques for capturing, maintaining, and accessing rationale models. In this chapter, we

- provide a bird's eye view of the activities related with rationale models (Section 8.2)
- describe issue modeling, the technique we use for representing rationale (Section 8.3)
- detail the activities necessary for creating and accessing rationale models (Section 8.4)
- describe management issues related with maintaining rationale models (Section 8.5)

First, let us define the concept of rationale model.

8.2 An Overview of Rationale

A **rationale** is the motivation behind a decision. More specifically, it includes:

- **Issue.** To each decision corresponds an issue that need to be solved for the development to proceed. An important part of the rationale is a description of the specific issue that is being solved. Issues are usually phrased as questions: How should a ham be cooked? How should years be represented?
- **Alternatives**. Alternatives are possible solutions that could address the issue under consideration. These include alternatives that were explored but discarded because they did not satisfy one or more criteria. For example, buying a wide stove costs too much. Representing years with a binary 16-bit number requires too much processing.
- **Criteria**. Criteria are desirable qualities that the selected solution should satisfy. For example: A recipe for ham should be realizable on standard kitchen equipment. Developers in the 1960s minimized memory foot prints. During requirements analysis, criteria are nonfunctional requirements and constraints (e.g., usability, number of input errors per day). During system design, criteria are design goals (e.g., reliability, response time). During project management, criteria are management goals and trade-offs (e.g., timely delivery versus quality).
- **Argumentation**. Cooking and software development decisions are not algorithmic. Cooks and developers discover issues, try solutions, and argue their relative benefits. It is only after much discussion that a consensus is reached or a decision imposed. This argumentation on all aspects of the decision process, including criteria, justifications, explored alternatives, and trade-offs.
- **Decisions.** A decision is the resolution of an issue representing the selected alternative according to the criteria that were used for evaluation and the justification of the selection.

Cutting an inch off each end of a ham and representing years with two digits are decisions. Decisions are already captured in the system models we develop during requirements analysis and system design. Moreover, many decisions are made without exploring alternatives or examining the corresponding issues.

We make decisions throughout the development process, and thus, we can use rationale models during any development activity:

- During *requirements elicitation* and *requirements analysis*, we make decisions about the functionality of the system, most often together with the client. Decisions are motivated by user or organizational needs. The justification of these decisions is useful for creating test cases during system integration and user acceptance.

- During *system design*, we select design goals and design the subsystem decomposition. When identifying design goals, for example, we often base our decision on nonfunctional requirements. Capturing the rationale of these decisions enables us to trace dependencies between design goals and nonfunctional requirements. This allows us to revise the design goals when requirements change.

- During *project management*, we make assumptions about the relative risks present in the development process. We are more likely to start development tasks related to a recently released component as opposed to a mature one. Capturing the justifications behind the risks and the fallback plans enables us to better deal when these risks become actual problems.

- During *integration and testing*, we discover interface mismatches between subsystems. Accessing the rationale for the subsystems, we can often determine which change or assumption introduced the mismatch and correct the situation with minimal impact on the rest of the system.

Maintaining rationale is an investment of resources for dealing with change: We capture information *now* in order to make it easier to revise decisions *later*, when changes occur. The amount of resources we are willing to invest depends on the type of project.

If we are building a complex system for a single customer, we will most likely revise and upgrade the system several times over a long period. In this case, the client may even require that rationale be recorded. If we are building a conceptual prototype for a new product, we will most likely throw out the prototype once product development is approved and underway. If we divert development resources to record rationale, we risk delaying the demonstration of the prototype and face project cancelation altogether. In this case, we do not record rationale, because the return on such an investment would be minimal.

More generally, we distinguish four levels of rationale capture:

- **No explicit rationale capture.** Resources are spent only on development. The documentation focuses on the system models only. Rationale information is present only in the developers' memories and in communication records such as E-mail messages, memos, and faxes.

- **Rationale reconstruction.** Resources are spent in recovering design rationale during the documentation effort. The design criteria and the motivation behind major architectural decisions is integrated with the corresponding system models. Discarded alternatives and argumentation are not captured explicitly.

- **Rationale capture.** Major effort is spent in capturing rationale as decisions are made. Rationale information is documented as a separate model and cross referenced with other documents. For example, the motivation for the requirements analysis model is captured in the Requirements Analysis Rationale Document (RARD), complementing the Requirements Analysis Document (RAD). Similarly, the motivation for the system design is captured in the System Design Rationale Document (SDRD).

- **Rationale integration.** The rationale model becomes the central model developers use. Rationale produced during different phases are integrated into a live and searchable information base. Changes to the system occur first in the information base as a discussion followed by one or more decisions. The system models represent the sum of the decisions captured in the information base.

In the first two levels of rationale capture, *No explicit rationale capture* and *Rationale reconstruction*, we rely on developers' memory to capture and store rationale. In the last two levels, *Rationale capture* and *Rationale integration*, we invest resources into constructing corporate memory that is independent from developers. The trade-off between these two extremes is the investment of resources during the early phases of development. In this chapter, we focus on the last two levels of rationale capture.

In addition to long-term benefits, maintaining rationale can also have short-term positive effects: Making explicit the rationale of a decision enables us to understand better the criteria others follow. It also encourages us to take rational decisions instead of emotional ones. If nothing else, it helps us distinguish which decisions were carefully evaluated and which were made under pressure and rushed.

Rationale models represent a larger and faster changing body of information than the system models. This introduces issues related to complexity and change as we have seen previously. Hence, we can apply the same modeling techniques for dealing with complexity and change. Next, we describe how we represent rationale with issue models.

8.3 Rationale Concepts

In this section, we describe issue models, the representation we use for rationale. Issue modeling is based on the assumption that design occurs as a dialectic activity during which developers solve a problem by arguing the pros and cons of different alternatives. We can then capture rationale by modeling the argument that lead to the development decisions. We represent:

- a question or a design problem as an issue node (Section 8.3.2)
- alternative solutions to the problem as proposal nodes (Section 8.3.3)
- pros and cons of different alternatives using argument nodes (Section 8.3.4)
- decisions we make to resolve an issue as a resolution node (Section 8.3.5)

In Section 8.3.7, we survey several issue representations of historical significance. But first, let us talk about centralized traffic control, the domain for the examples in this chapter.

8.3.1 Centralized Taffic Control

Centralized traffic control (CTC) systems enable train dispatchers to monitor and route trains remotely. Train tracks are divided into contiguous track circuits that represent the smallest unit a dispatcher can monitor. Signals and other devices ensure that at most one train can occupy a track circuit at any time. When a train enters a track circuit, a sensor detects its presence and the train identification appears on the dispatcher's monitor. The dispatcher operates switches to route trains. The system enables a dispatcher to plan a complete route by aligning a sequence of switches in the corresponding position. The set of track circuits controlled by a single dispatcher is called a track section.

Figure 8-1 is a simplified display of a CTC user interface. Track circuits are represented by lines. Switches are represented by the intersection of three lines. Signals are represented with icons indicating whether a signal is open (i.e., allowing a train to pass) or closed (i.e., forbidding a train to pass). Switches, trains, and signals are numbered for reference in commands issued by the dispatcher. In Figure 8-1, signals are numbered S1–S4, switches are numbered SW1 and SW2, and trains are numbered T1291 and T1515. Computers near the tracks, called wayside stations, ensure that the state of a group of switches and signals do not present any safety hazard. For example, a wayside station controlling the devices of Figure 8-1 ensures that opposing signals, such as S1 and S2, cannot be open simultaneously. Wayside stations are designed such that the state of the device they control is safe even in the case of failure. Such equipment is called fail-safe. CTC systems communicate with wayside stations to modify the state of the tracks when dispatching trains. CTC systems are typically highly available but need not be fail safe, given that the safety of trains is guaranteed by the wayside stations.

In the 1960s, CTC systems had a custom display board containing light bulbs displaying the status of the track circuits. Switches and signals were controlled via an input board with many push buttons and toggle switches. In the 1970s, CRTs replaced the custom boards and

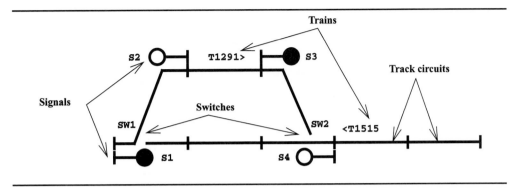

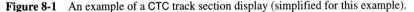

Figure 8-1   An example of a CTC track section display (simplified for this example).

provided dispatchers more detailed information with less real estate. More recently, workstation-based traffic control systems have been introduced, offering the possibility of a more sophisticated user interface to dispatchers and the ability to distribute processing among multiple computers.

Centralized traffic control systems need to be highly available. Although traffic control systems are not life critical (safety is ensured by wayside stations), a failure of the system can lead to major traffic disruption in the controlled tracks, thus resulting in substantial economic loss. Consequently, the transition to a new technology, such as moving from a mainframe to a workstation environment or moving from a textual interface to a graphical user interface, needs to be carefully evaluated and done much more slowly than for other systems. Traffic control is a domain in which capturing rationale is critical and thus serves as the basis for the examples of this chapter.

Let us discuss next how issue models are used to represent rationale.

8.3.2   Defining the Problem: Issues

An **issue** represents a concrete problem, such as a requirement, a design, or a management problem. *How soon should a dispatcher be notified of a train delay? How should persistent data be stored? Which technology presents the most risk?* Issues most often represent problems that do not have a single correct solution and that cannot be resolved algorithmically. Issues are typically resolved through discussion and negotiation.

We represent issues in UML with instances of class `Issue`. Issues have a `subject` attribute, summarizing the issue, a `description` attribute, describing the issue in more detail and referring to supporting material, and a `status` attribute, indicating whether the issue has been resolved or not. The `status` of an issue is **open** if it has not been resolved yet and **closed** otherwise. A closed issue can be reopened if an issue needs to be revisited. By convention, we give a short name to each issue, such as `train delay?:Issue` for reference. For example, Figure 8-2 depicts the three issues we gave as example in the previous paragraph.

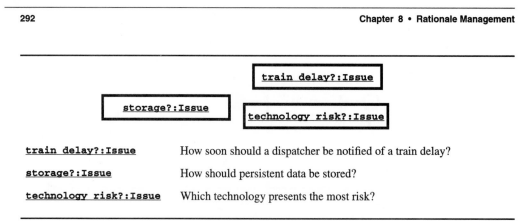

Figure 8-2   An example of issues (UML object diagram).

Issues raised during development are often related. For example, issues can be decomposed into smaller **subissues**. *What are the response time requirements of the traffic control system?* includes *How soon should a dispatcher be notified of a train delay?* The complete system development can be phrased as a single issue: *Which traffic control system should we build?* that can then be decomposed into numerous subissues. Issues can also be raised by decisions made on other issues. For example, the decision to cache data on a local node raises the issue of maintaining consistency between the central and cached copies of the data. Such issues are called **consequent issues**.

Consider the centralized traffic control system we previously described. Assume we are currently examining the transition from a mainframe system to a desktop-based system. In the future system, each dispatcher will have an individual desktop machine that communicates with a server, which manages the communication with field devices. During design discussions, two interface issues are raised: *How should commands be input to the system?* and *How should track circuits be displayed to the dispatcher?* Figure 8-3 depicts two issues represented with a UML object diagram.

An issue should only focus on the problem, not possible alternatives addressing it. A convention that encourages this is to phrase issues as questions. To reinforce this concept, we also include a question mark at the end of the issue name. Information about the possible alternatives addressing an issue are captured by proposals, which we discuss next.

display?:Issue	**input?:Issue**

| **input?:Issue** | How should the dispatcher input commands? |
| **display?:Issue** | How should track sections be displayed? |

Figure 8-3   CTC interface issues (UML object diagram).

8.3.3 Exploring the Solution Space: Proposals

A **proposal** represents a candidate answer to an issue. *A dispatcher need not be notified* is a proposal to the issue *How soon should a dispatcher be notified of a train delay?* A proposal need not be a good or valid answer to the issue it addresses. This enables developers to explore the solution space thoroughly. Often when brainstorming, proposing a flawed solution triggers new ideas and solutions that would not have be thought of otherwise. Different proposals addressing the same issue can overlap. For example, proposals to the issue *How to store persistent data?* could include *Use a relational database* and *Use a relational database for structured data and flat files for images*. Proposals are used to represent the solution to the problem as well as to the discarded alternatives.

A proposal can address one or more issues. For example, *Use a Model/View/Dispatcher architecture* can address *How to separate interface objects from entity objects?* and *How to maintain consistency across multiple views?* Proposals can also trigger new issues. For example, in response to the issue *How to minimize memory leaks?* the proposal *Use garbage collection* may trigger the consequent issue *How to minimize response time degradation due to memory management?* When we address an issue, we need to ensure that all consequent issues associated with the selected proposals are addressed as well.

We represent proposals in UML as instances of the class `Proposal`. `Proposal`s, like `Issues`, have a `subject` and a `description` attributes. By convention, we give proposals a short name and phrase them as a statement starting with a verb. `Proposal`s are related to the `Issues` they address with an `addressed by` association. `Issues` are related to `Proposals` that triggered them with a `raises` association.

While discussing the interface issues of our centralized traffic control system, we consider two proposals, a `point&click` interface, which allows track circuits to be represented graphically, and a `text-based` interface, in which track sections are represented with special characters. The `text-based` proposal raises a consequent issue about which terminal emulation to use. Figure 8-4 depicts the addition of the two proposals and the consequent issue.

A proposal should only contain information related to the solution, not its value, advantages, and disadvantages. Criteria and arguments are used for this purpose. We describe these next.

8.3.4 Evaluating the Solution Space: Criteria and Arguments

A **criterion** is a desirable quality that proposals addressing a specific issue should have. Design goals, such as *response time* or *reliability*, are criteria used for addressing design issues. Management goals, such as *minimum cost* or *minimum risk*, are criteria used in addressing management issues. A set of criteria indicates the dimensions against which each proposal needs to be assessed. A proposal that meets a criterion is said to be **assessed positively** against that criterion. Similarly, a proposal that fails to meet a criterion is said to be **assessed negatively** against that criterion. Criteria may be shared among several issues.

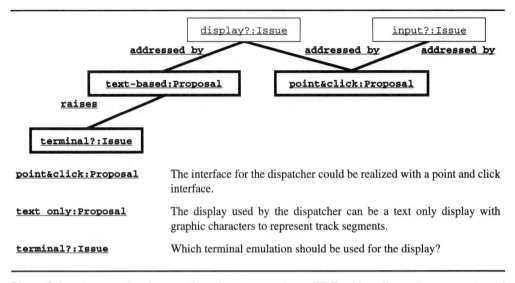

point&click:Proposal	The interface for the dispatcher could be realized with a point and click interface.
text only:Proposal	The display used by the dispatcher can be a text only display with graphic characters to represent track segments.
terminal?:Issue	Which terminal emulation should be used for the display?

Figure 8-4   An example of proposals and consequent issue (UML object diagram). Proposals and consequent Issue are emphasized in bold.

We represent criteria in UML as instances of the Criterion class. A Criterion, like Issues and Proposals, has a subject and a description attribute. The subject attribute is always phrased positively; that is, it should state the quality that proposals should maximize. *Fast*, *responsive*, and *cheap* are good subject attributes. *Cost* and *time* are not. A Criterion is associated to Proposals with assessment associations. Assessment associations have a value attribute indicating whether the assessment is positive or negative, and a weight attribute, indicating its strength of the proposal with respect to the criterion. By convention, we append a "$" sign to the end of a criterion name, emphasizing that criteria are goodness measures and should not be confused with arguments or issues.

While evaluating the interface of our centralized traffic control system, we identify two criteria: *availability*, which represents the nonfunctional requirement to maximize the up time of the system, and *usability*, which represents (in this case) the nonfunctional requirement to minimize the time to input valid commands (see Figure 8-5). These criteria are taken from the nonfunctional requirements of the system. We assess both proposals against these criteria: We decide that the point and click interface is negatively assessed against the availability criteria, being more complex than the text interface and thus presenting a higher likelihood of bugs. We decide, however, that the point and click interface is more usable than the textual interface, due to an easier selection of commands and input of data. Note that the set of associations linking the proposals and the criteria in Figure 8-5 represent a trade-off: Each proposal maximizes one of the two criteria; the issue is to decide which criteria has a higher priority.

An **argument** is an opinion expressed by a person, agreeing or disagreeing with a proposal, a criterion, or an assessment. Arguments capture the debate that drives the exploration

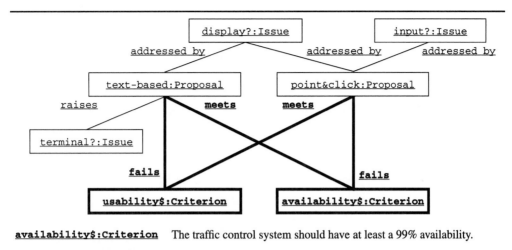

availability\$:Criterion   The traffic control system should have at least a 99% availability.

usability\$:Criterion   The time to input commands should be less than 2 seconds.

Figure 8-5   An example of criteria and assessments (UML object diagram). Criteria are emphasized in bold. A negative assessment is indicated by an association labeled fails, whereas positive assessments are indicated with an association labeled meets.

of the solution space, defines the goodness measures, and eventually leads to a decision. We represent arguments in UML with instances of the class Argument including subject and description attributes. Arguments are related to the entity they discuss with a is supported by or an is opposed by association.

While discussing the relative priority of the availability and usability criteria, we decide that any benefit on the usability aspect would be offset by a reduced availability of the system. We capture this by creating an argument that supports the availability criterion (see Figure 8-6). Note that an argument can simultaneously support a node while opposing another.

When selecting criteria, assessing proposals, and arguing about them, we evaluate the design space. The next step is to use this evaluation to come to closure and resolve the issue.

8.3.5   Collapsing the Solution Space: Resolutions

A **resolution** represents the alternative selected to close an issue. A resolution represents a decision and has an impact on one of the system models or on the task model. A resolution can be based on several proposals and summarizes the justification that leads to the decision. We represent resolutions in UML with an instance of class Resolution, including subject, description, justification, and status attributes. A Resolution can be related with Proposals with based-on associations. A Resolution has exactly one resolves association to the Issue it resolves.

The status attribute of a Resolution indicates whether the Resolution is still relevant or not. When the Resolution is linked with its corresponding issue, its status is set to

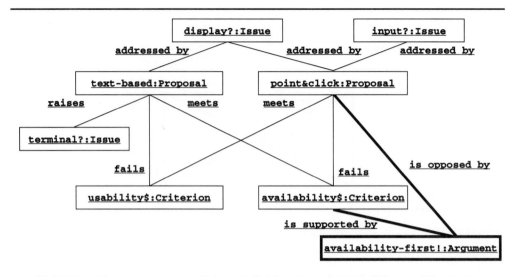

Figure 8-6   An example of an argument (UML object diagram). `Argument` is emphasized in bold.

`active` and the `status` of the corresponding `Issue` is changed to `closed`. If the `Issue` is reopened, the `status` of the `Issue` is changed to `open` and the `status` of the `Resolution` is changed to `obsolete`. A closed `Issue` has exactly one active `Resolution` and any number of obsolete `Resolutions`.

Finalizing the traffic control interface issue, we select a text-based display and a keyboard interface as a basis for the user interface. This decision is motivated by treating the availability criterion as more important than the usability criterion: A text-based interface will result in much simpler and more reliable user interface code at the cost of some usability. The dispatcher will not be able to see as much data at one time and will not be able to issue commands as fast as using a point and click interface. We create a resolution node that contains the justification of the decision and create links between the resolution and the two issues it addresses (see Figure 8-7).

Adding a resolution to an issue model effectively concludes the discussion of the corresponding issue. As development is iterative, it is sometimes necessary to reopen an issue and reevaluate competing alternatives. At the end of development, however, most issues should be closed or listed as known problems in the documentation.

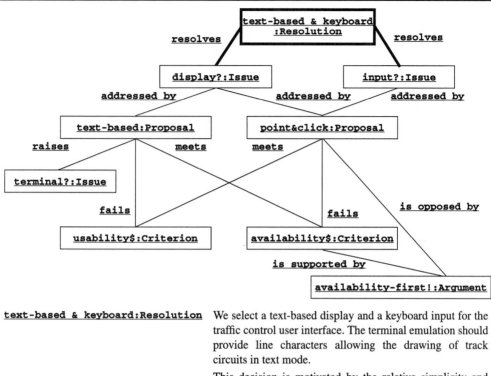

text-based & keyboard:Resolution   We select a text-based display and a keyboard input for the traffic control user interface. The terminal emulation should provide line characters allowing the drawing of track circuits in text mode.

This decision is motivated by the relative simplicity and reliability of text-based interfaces compared to point and click interfaces. We are aware that this decision costs some usability, as fewer data can be presented to the dispatcher and issuing commands by the dispatcher will be slower and more prone to errors.

Figure 8-7   An example of closed issue (UML object diagram). `Resolution` emphasized in bold.

8.3.6   Implementing Resolutions: Action Items

A resolution is implemented in terms of one or more **action items**. A person is assigned to an action item which is a task with a completion date. Action items are not part of the rationale per se, but, rather, they are part of the task model (see Chapter 11, *Project Management*). Action items are described here because they are tightly integrated into the issue model.

We represent an action item in UML with an instance of the `ActionItem` class. The `ActionItem` class has a `subject`, `description`, `owner`, `deadline`, and `status` attributes. The `owner` is the person responsible for the completion of the `ActionItem`. The `status` of an `ActionItem` can be `todo`, `notDoable`, `inProgress`, or `done`. A `Resolution` is associated with the `ActionItems` with an `is  implemented  by` link. Figure 8-8 represents the `ActionItems` generated after the resolution of Figure 8-7.

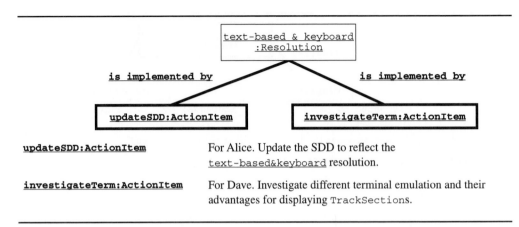

Figure 8-8   An example of implementation of a resolution (UML object diagram). `ActionItems` emphasized in bold

The issue notation we described and its integration with the task model is the modeling notation we use for representing rationale. Other issue models have been proposed in the literature for representing rationale. Next, let us survey briefly these other models.

8.3.7   Examples of Issue-Based Models and Systems

The capture of rationale was originally proposed by Kunz and Rittel. Ever since, many different models have been designed and evaluated in the context of software engineering and other engineering disciplines. Here, we briefly compare three of them, IBIS (Issue-Based Information System, [Kunz & Rittel, 1970]), DRL (Decision Representation Language, [Lee, 1990]), and QOC (Questions, Options, and Criteria, [MacLean et al., 1991]).

Issue-Based Information System

IBIS includes an issue model and a design method for addressing ill-structured, or wicked problems (as opposed to tame problems). A **wicked** problem is defined as a problem that cannot be solved algorithmically but, rather, has to be resolved through discussion and debate.

The IBIS issue model (Figure 8-9) has three nodes (`Issues`, `Positions`, and `Arguments`) related by seven kinds of links (`supports`, `objects-to`, `replaces`, `responds-to`, `generalizes`, `questions`, and `suggests`). Each `Issue` describes a design problem under consideration. Developers propose solutions to the problem by creating `Position` nodes (similar to the `Proposal` nodes we described in Section 8.3.3). While alternatives are being generated, developers argue about their value with `Argument` nodes. `Arguments` can either support a `Position` or object to a `Position`. Note that the same node can apply to multiple positions. The IBIS model did not originally include `Criterion` and `Resolution`.

IBIS was supported by a hypertext tool (gIBIS, [Conklin & Burgess-Yakemovic, 1991]) and used for capturing rationale during face-to-face meetings. It provided the basis for most of the subsequent issue models, including DRL and QOC, which we discuss next.

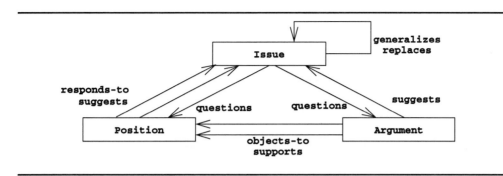

Figure 8-9 The IBIS model (UML class diagram).

Decision Representation Language

Decision Representation Language DRL aims at capturing the **decision rationale** of a design [Lee, 1990]. A decision rationale is defined by Lee as the representation of the qualitative elements of decision making, including the alternatives being considered, their evaluation, the arguments that led to these evaluations, and the criteria used in these evaluations. DRL is supported by SYBIL, a tool that enables the user to track dependencies among elements of the rationale when revising evaluations. DRL elaborates on the original IBIS model by adding nodes to capture `Design Goals` and `Procedures`. DRL views the construction of the rationale as a comparable task as the design of the artifact itself. DRL is summarized in Figure 8-10. The main drawbacks of DRL are its complexity (7 types of nodes and 15 types of links) and the effort spent in structuring the captured rationale.

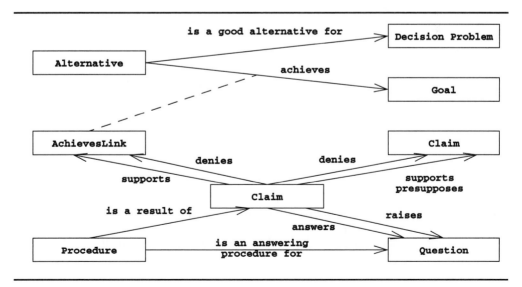

Figure 8-10 Decision Representation Language (UML class diagram).

Questions, Options, and Criteria (QOC)

Questions, Options, and Criteria (QOC) is another elaboration of IBIS. `Questions` represent design problems to be solved (`Issues` in the issue model we presented). `Options` are possible answers to `Questions` (`Proposals` in our model). `Options` can trigger other `Consequent Questions`. `Options` are assessed negatively and positively against `Criteria`, which are relative measures of goodness defined by the developers. Also, `Arguments` can support or challenge any `Question`, `Option`, `Criteria`, or relationship among those. `Arguments` may also support and challenge `Arguments`. Figure 8-11 depicts the QOC model.

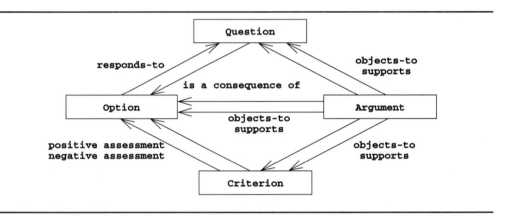

Figure 8-11   Questions, Options, Criteria model (UML class diagram).

QOC and IBIS differ at the process level. IBIS's aim, on the one hand, has been to capture design argumentation as it occurs (e.g., gIBIS was used for capturing information generated during design meetings). QOC structures, on the other hand, are constructed as an act of reflection on the current state of the design. This conceptual separation of the construction and argumentation phases of the design process emphasizes the systematic elaboration and structuring of rationale as opposed to capturing it as a side effect of deliberation. Rationale, from QOC's perspective, is a description of the design space explored by the developers. From IBIS's perspective, rationale is a historical record of the analysis leading to a specific design. In practice, both approaches can be applied to capture sufficient rationale. We describe the activities related to capturing and maintaining rationale next.

8.4 Rationale Activities: From Issues to Decisions

Maintaining rationale helps developers deal with change. By capturing the justification of decisions, they can more easily revisit important decisions when user requirements or the target environment changes. For rationale models to be useful, however, they need to be captured, structured, and easily accessible. In this section, we describe these activities, including:

- capturing rationale during design meetings (Section 8.4.2)
- revising rationale models with subsequent clarifications (Section 8.4.3)
- capturing additional rationale during revisions (Section 8.4.4)
- reconstructing rationale that was not captured (Section 8.4.5)

The most critical rationale information is generated during system design: Decisions during system design can impact every subsystem, and their revision is costly, especially when done late in the design process. Moreover, the rationale behind subsystem decomposition is usually complex, as it spans many different issues, such as hardware allocation, persistent storage, access control, global control flow, and boundary conditions.

For these reasons, we focus on system design in this chapter. Note, however, that maintaining rationale can be done similarly throughout the development, from requirements elicitation to field testing. We illustrate rationale activities with issues from the system design of CTC, a centralized traffic control system for freight trains. We describe the current system design model of CTC next.

8.4.1 CTC System Design

Consider the CTC system we described in Section 8.3.1. We are in the process of reengineering a legacy system, replacing a mainframe computer with a network of workstations. We are also enhancing the system, such as adding access control and more focus on security and usability. We are in the middle of system design. So far, we identified from the nonfunctional requirements several design goals (ordered by descending priority):

- **Availability**. The system should crash less than once per month and recover completely from a crash within 10 minutes.
- **Security**. No entity outside the control room should be able to access the state of the controlled tracks or manipulate any of their devices.
- **Usability**. Once trained, a dispatcher should input no more than two erroneous commands per day.

We allocate a client node per dispatcher. Two redundant server nodes maintain the global state of the system (see Figure 8-12). The servers are also responsible for persistent storage. Data are stored in flat files that can be copied off-line and imported into a database for off-line processing. Communication with devices on the tracks is done via modems managed by a dedicated machine. A middleware supports two types of communication among subsystems: method invocation, for handling requests, and notification of state changes, for informing subsystems of state changes. Each subsystem subscribes to the events it is interested in. Presently, we must address access control issues and define the mechanisms that prevent dispatchers from manipulating the\of other dispatchers. We describe in the following sections how the access control issue is debated and resolved while capturing its rationale.

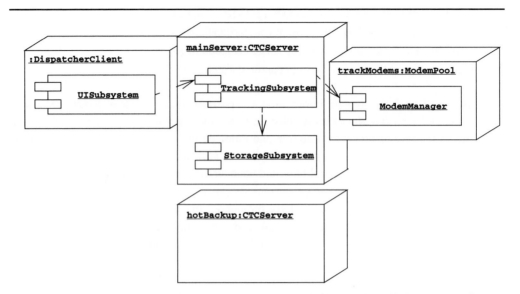

DispatcherClient	Each dispatcher is assigned a DispatcherClient node running the user interface to the system.
CTCServer	A CTCServer is responsible for maintaining the state of the system. It transmits dispatcher commands to the field devices and receives state information from the field via the ModemPool node. A CTCServer is also responsible for storing persistent state (e.g., device addresses, device names, dispatcher assignments, train schedules). Two CTCServers, a main server, and a hot backup are used to increase availability.
ModemPool	The ModemPool manages the modems used to communicate with the field devices.
ModemManager	The ModemManager is responsible for connecting to field devices and transmitting field commands.
StorageSubsystem	The StorageSubsystem is responsible for maintaining persistent state.
TrackingSubsystem	The TrackingSubsystem is responsible for maintaining track state, as notices of state changes are received from the field, and for issuing device commands via the ModemManager, based on user-level commands received from the UISubsystem.
UISubsystem	The UISubsystem is responsible for receiving commands and displaying track state to the dispatcher. The UISubsystem controls the validity of the dispatcher's commands before forwarding them to the CTCServer.

Figure 8-12 Subsystem decomposition for CTC (UML deployment diagram). The state of the system is maintained by a mainServer. A hotBackup of the mainServer stands by in case the mainServer fails. The mainServer sends commands and receives state transitions from the tracks via the ModemPool.

8.4.2 Capturing Rationale in Meetings

Meetings enable developers to present, negotiate, and resolve issues face to face. The physical presence of the respective developers involved in the discussion is important, adding the benefits of nonverbal communication: It allows people to assess the relative positions of each other and the trade-offs they are willing to make. Conversely, negotiating and making decisions via E-mail, for example, is difficult, as misunderstandings can easily occur. Face-to-face meetings, then, are a natural starting point for capturing rationale.

We described procedures for organizing and capturing meetings with minutes and agendas in Chapter 3, *Project Communication*. An agenda, posted in advance of the meeting, describes the status and points to be discussed. The meeting is recorded in minutes that are made available shortly after the meeting. Using the issue modeling concepts we described in Section 8.3, we write an agenda in terms of *issues* that we need to discuss and resolve. We state the objective of the meeting as coming to a resolution on these issues and any related subissues that are raised in the discussion. We structure the meeting minutes in terms of *proposals* that we explore during the meeting, *criteria* that we agree on, and *arguments* we use to support or oppose proposals. We capture decisions as *resolutions* and *action items* that implement resolutions. During the meeting we review status in terms of the action items that we produced in the previous meetings.

For example, consider the access control issue of the CTC system. We need to organize a meeting of the architecture team, including the developers responsible for the UISubsystem, the TrackingSubsystem, and the NotificationService. Alice, the facilitator for the architecture team, posts the agenda depicted in Figure 8-13.

During the meeting, we review the action item (AI[1]: *Investigate access control model by middleware*) generated in the previous architecture meeting. The middleware provides basic blocks for authentication and encryption but does not introduce any other constraints on the access model. Issues I[1] and I[2] are resolved quickly with domain knowledge: A dispatcher can see all TrackSections but can only manipulate the devices of her TrackSection. Issue I[3], however, (*How should access control be integrated with* TrackSections *and* NotificationService?) is more difficult and sparks a debate.

AGENDA: Integration of access control and notification

When and Where	**Role**
Date: 9/13	**Primary Facilitator**: Alice
Start: 4:30pm	**Timekeeper**: Dave
End: 5:30pm	**Minute Taker**: Ed
Building: Train Hall	**Room**: 3420

1. Purpose

The first revisions of the hardware/software mapping and the persistent storage design have been completed. The access control model needs to be defined and its integration with the current subsystems, such as `NotificationService` and `TrackingSubsystem`, needs to be defined.

2. Desired outcome

Resolve issues about the integration of access control with notification.

3. Information sharing [Allocated time: 15 minutes]

`AI[1]`: Dave: Investigate the access control model provided by the middleware.

4. Discussion [Allocated time: 35 minutes]

`I[1]`: Can a dispatcher see other dispatchers' `TrackSections`?

`I[2]`: Can a dispatcher modify another dispatchers' `TrackSections`?

`I[3]`: How should access control be integrated with `TrackSections` and `NotificationService`?

5. Wrap up [Allocated time: 5 minutes]

Review and assign new action items.

Meeting critique.

Figure 8-13   Agenda for the access control discussion of CTC.

Dave, the developer responsible for the `NotificationService`, proposes to integrate the access control with the `TrackSection` (see Figure 8-14). The `TrackSection` would maintain an access list of the `Dispatchers` who can examine or modify the given `TrackSection`. Events would also be organized by `TrackSections`. To be notified about events in a `TrackSection`, a subsystem would need to subscribe to a `TrackSection` via the `NotificationService`. The `NotificationService` would then check with the given `TrackSection` if the current dispatcher had at least read access.

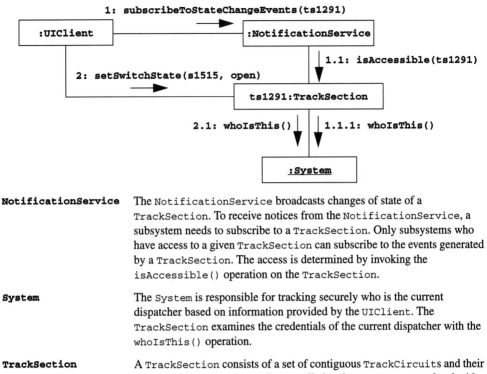

NotificationService The NotificationService broadcasts changes of state of a
 TrackSection. To receive notices from the NotificationService, a
 subsystem needs to subscribe to a TrackSection. Only subsystems who
 have access to a given TrackSection can subscribe to the events generated
 by a TrackSection. The access is determined by invoking the
 isAccessible() operation on the TrackSection.

System The System is responsible for tracking securely who is the current
 dispatcher based on information provided by the UIClient. The
 TrackSection examines the credentials of the current dispatcher with the
 whoIsThis() operation.

TrackSection A TrackSection consists of a set of contiguous TrackCircuits and their
 associated Devices. Access is controlled at the TrackSection level with
 an access list.

UIClient The UIClient is responsible for displaying TrackSections and inputting
 commands for changing TrackSection state.

Figure 8-14 Proposal P[1]: The access is controlled by the TrackSection object with an access list.
The NotificationService queries the TrackSection to determine if a subsystem can receive notices
about a given TrackSection (UML collaboration diagram.)

  Alice, the developer responsible for the TrackSubsystem that includes the
TrackSection class, proposes to reverse the dependency between the TrackSection and the
NotificationService (see Figure 8-15). In this proposal, the UIClient would interact only
with the TrackSection class, including when subscribing to events. The UIClient would
invoke the subscribeToEvents() method on the TrackSection, which would perform the
access control checks and then invoke the subscribeToStateChangeEvents() on the
NotificationService. The UIClient would then not have direct access to the
NotificationService. This has the advantage of centralizing all the protected operations in
one class and centralizing the access control checks. Moreover, the TrackSection would then
also be able to unsubscribe UIClients when the access list is modified.

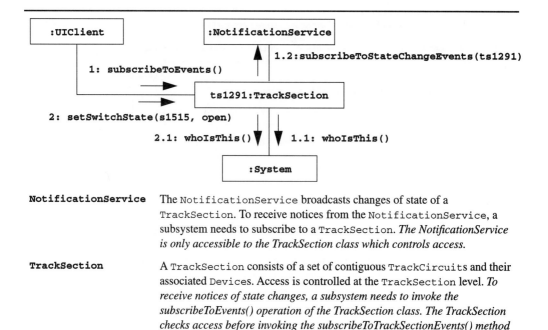

NotificationService	The NotificationService broadcasts changes of state of a TrackSection. To receive notices from the NotificationService, a subsystem needs to subscribe to a TrackSection. *The NotificationService is only accessible to the TrackSection class which controls access.*
TrackSection	A TrackSection consists of a set of contiguous TrackCircuits and their associated Devices. Access is controlled at the TrackSection level. *To receive notices of state changes, a subsystem needs to invoke the subscribeToEvents() operation of the TrackSection class. The TrackSection checks access before invoking the subscribeToTrackSectionEvents() method on NotificationService.*

Figure 8-15 Proposal P[2]: The UIClient subscribes to track section events via the subscribeToEvents() operation on the TrackSection. The TrackSection checks access and then invokes the subscribeToTrackSectionEvents() operation on the NotificationService. The NotificationService is not accessible to the UIClient class. (UML collaboration diagram, differences from Figure 8-14 highlighted in *italics*.)

Ed notes that every dispatcher is allowed to see other dispatcher's TrackSections, so only modification of state needs to be controlled. Assuming that all modifications are done via method invocation and that the NotificationService is only used for broadcasting changes, the NotificationService need not be integrated with access control. In this case, a refinement of Dave's initial proposal could be used (see Figure 8-16).

The architecture team decides to use Ed's proposal based on its simplicity. Ed produces the chronological meeting minutes depicted in Figure 8-17.

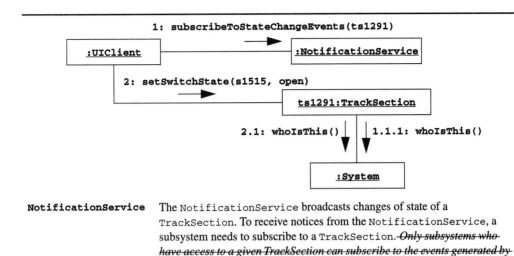

The NotificationService broadcasts changes of state of a TrackSection. To receive notices from the NotificationService, a subsystem needs to subscribe to a TrackSection. ~~Only subsystems who have access to a given TrackSection can subscribe to the events generated by a TrackSection. The access is determine by invoking the isAccessible() operation on the TrackSection.~~

Figure 8-16   Proposal P[3]: The access to operations that modify TrackSections is controlled by the TrackSection object with an access list. The NotificationService need not be part of the access control, because every dispatcher can see changes of state (UML collaboration diagram, subtractions from Figure 8-14 highlighted in *strikeout italics*).

CHRONOLOGICAL MINUTES: Integration of access control and notification

When and Where	Role
Date: 9/13	**Primary Facilitator**: Alice
Start: 4:30pm	**Timekeeper**: Dave
End: 6:00pm	**Minute Taker**: Ed
Building: Train Hall	**Room**: 3420

1. Purpose

The first revisions of the hardware/software mapping and the persistent storage design have been completed. The access control model needs to be defined and its integration with the current subsystems, in particular, NotificationService and TrackingSubsystem, needs to be defined.

2. Desired outcome

Resolve issues about the integration of access control with notification

3. Information sharing

AI[1]: Dave: Investigate the access control model provided by the middleware.

   Status: The middleware supports strong authentication and encryption. It does not introduce any constraints on the access model. Any access policy can be implemented on the server side.

Figure 8-17   Chronological minutes for the access control discussion of CTC.

4. Discussion

I[1]: Can a dispatcher see other dispatchers' TrackSections?

Zoe: Yes.

Ed: In CTC specification.

I[2]: Can a dispatcher modify another dispatchers' TrackSections?

Zoe: No. Only the dispatcher assigned to the TrackSection can manipulate the devices of the section. Note that the dispatcher can be reassigned dynamically.

Ed: Also in CTC specification.

I[3]: How should access control be integrated with TrackSections and NotificationService?

Dave: The TrackSection maintains an access list. The notification service asks the TrackSection about who has access.

Alice: We should probably reverse the dependency between TrackSection and NotificationService. Instead, the UIClient requests subscriptions from the TrackSection, which checks for access and then calls the NotificationService. This way, all protected methods are in one place.

Dave: This way the TrackSection can also more easily unsubscribe dispatchers when their access is revoked.

Ed: Hey, no need for access control in NotificationService: Dispatchers can see all TrackSections. As long as the NotificationService is not used for changing the TrackSection state, there is no need to restrict subscriptions.

Alice: But thinking about the access control on notification would be more general.

Ed: But more complex. Let's just separate access control and notification at this point and revisit the issue if the requirements change.

Alice: Ok. I'll take care of revising the TrackingSubsystem API.

5. Wrap up

AI[2]: Alice: Design access control for the TrackingSubsystem based on authentication and encryption provided by the middleware.

Figure 8-17   Chronological minutes for the access control discussion of CTC.

Ed produces the minutes of Figure 8-17 by inserting in the agenda the discussion that is relevant to the different issues. The discussion, however, is recorded as a chronological list of statements made by the participants. Most of these statements mix the presentation of an alternative with the argumentation against another alternative. In order to clarify the minutes, Ed restructures the minutes after the meeting with issue models (Figure 8-18).

The important results of the access control meeting are:

• Dispatchers can see all TrackSections but modify only the ones they are assigned to.

• An access list associated with TrackSections is used for access control.

• NotificationService is not integrated with access control, because state changes can be seen by any Dispatchers.

STRUCTURED MINUTES: Integration of access control and notification

When and Where	Role
Date: 9/13	**Primary Facilitator**: Alice
Start: 4:30pm	**Timekeeper**: Dave
End: 6:00pm	**Minute Taker**: Ed
Building: Train Hall	**Room**: 3420

1. Purpose

The first revisions of the hardware/software mapping and the persistent storage design have been completed. The access control model needs to be defined and its integration with the current subsystems, in particular, NotificationService and TrackingSubsystem, needs to be defined.

2. Desired outcome

Resolve issues about the integration of access control with notification.

3. Information sharing

AI[1]: Dave: Investigate the access control model provided by the middleware.

> Status: The middleware supports strong authentication and encryption. It does not introduce any constraints on the access model. Any access policy can be implemented on the server side.

4. Discussion

I[1]: Can a dispatcher see other dispatchers' TrackSections?

> R[1]:   Yes (from CTC specification and confirmed by Zoe, a test user).

I[2]: Can a dispatcher modify another dispatchers' TrackSections?

> R[2]:   No. Only the dispatcher assigned to the TrackSection can manipulate the devices of the section. Note that the dispatcher can be reassigned dynamically (from CTC specification and confirmed by Zoe).

I[3]: How should access control be integrated with TrackSections and NotificationService?

> P[3.1]:   TrackSections maintain an access list of who can examine or modify the state of the TrackSection. To subscribe to events, a subsystem sends a request to the NotificationService, which in turns sends a request to the corresponding TrackSection to check access.

> P[3.2]:   TrackSections host all protected operations. The UIClient requests subscription to TrackSection events by sending a request to the TrackSection, which checks access and sends a request to the NotificationService.
>
>   A[3.1] for P[3.2]: Access control and protected operations are centralized into a single class.

> P[3.3]:   There is no need to restrict the access to the event subscription. The UIClient requests subscriptions directly from the NotificationService. The NotificationService need not check access.
>
>   A[3.2] for P[3.3] Dispatchers can see the state of any TrackSections (see R[1]).
>
>   A[3.3] for P[3.3]: Simplicity.

> R[3]: P[3.3]. See action item AI[2].

5. Wrap up

AI[2]: Alice: Design access control for the TrackingSubsystem based on authentication and encryption provided by the middleware and on resolution R[3] discussed in these minutes.

Figure 8-18   Structured minutes for the access control discussion of CTC.

By focusing on the issue-model, we have also captured that:

• Integrating the `NotificationService` with access control was investigated.
• Centralizing all protected methods into the `TrackSection` class was an accepted principle.

The last two pieces of information are rationale information and would usually be considered unimportant. However, this is the type of information that is captured by the minute taker and structured for facilitating future changes.

8.4.3 Capturing Rationale Asynchronously

Meeting discussions rely on context information. When the meeting starts, most participants already have a substantial amount of information about the system, its intended purpose, and its design. The facilitator of the meeting usually focuses on a small set of issues that need to be resolved. For example, in the meeting we presented in the previous section, all participants knew the purpose and functionality of the CTC system, its design goals, and current subsystem decomposition. The minutes of this meeting only record the issues under discussion and, therefore, do not contain much or any of the background information. Unfortunately, this information is lost over time and meeting minutes become obsolete quickly.

We can use issue modeling to address this problem. In Chapter 3, *Project Communication*, we described the use of groupware, such as newsgroups or Lotus Notes, for supporting asynchronous communication. By integrating the preparation and recording of the meeting with the asynchronous communication, we can capture additional contextual information.

In the CTC example, assume that Mary, the developer responsible for the `UISubsystem`, was not able to attend the access control meeting. She reads the agenda and the meeting minutes, which were posted on the newsgroup dedicated to the architecture team. Although she understands the outcome of the meeting, the discussion about the `NotificationService` requires clarification: Argument `A[3.2]` for proposal `P[3.3]` claims that, because `Dispatchers` can see every `TrackSection`, all events can be visible and, hence, there is no need to control the access to the events. This implies that the `NotificationService` is used only for notifying other subsystems of state changes. In other words, the `TrackSection` does not change its state as a consequence of events generated by other subsystems. Mary wants to confirm that this assumption is correct and, consequently, she posts an issue on the newsgroup (Figure 8-19). She also proposes to disallow the `TrackingService` from subscribing to any events in order to ensure proper access control.

Follow-up on meeting minutes enables developers to capture more of the context surrounding the design. As a consequence, more rationale and clearer information is captured. Using the same issue model for both meetings and on-line discussions allows us to integrate all rationale information. Although this can be done with minimal technology, such as newsgroups, the representation of the issue-model, the meeting agendas and minutes, and related messages

---

```
Newsgroup: ctc.architecture.discuss
Subject:                                                      Date:
I[1]:  Can a dispatcher see other dispatcher's TrackSections?  9/14
I[2]:  Can a dispatcher modify another dispatchers' TrackSections? 9/14
I[3]:  How should access control be implemented?              9/14
       P[3.1]: TrackSection has access list                   9/14
       P[3.2]: TrackSection has subscription operations        9/14
              +A[3.1]: Extensibility.                          9/14
              +A[3.2]: Centralize all protected operations.    9/14
       P[3.3]: NotificationService is not part of access       9/14
              +A[3.3]: Dispatchers can see all TrackSections    9/14
              +A[3.4]: Simplicity.                             9/14

---
From: Mary
Newsgroups: ctc.architecture.discuss
Subject: Consequent Issue: Should notification not be used for requests?
Date: Thu, 15 Sep 13:12:48 -0400

I[4] responding to A[3.3]: for access lists against capabilities
> Dispatchers can see all TrackSections and, thus, should be able
> to see all events.
This assumes that the TrackSection does not rely on events to change its state
and that events are only used for informing other subsystems of state changes.
For the purpose of robustness, should we disallow the TrackingService to
subscribe to any events?
```

Figure 8-19   Example of a consequent issue posted asynchronously (newsgroup post). Mary, a developer who did not attend the meeting, requests clarification. This leads to the post of an additional issue and the capture of more rationale.

can be integrated into a groupware tool, such as a custom Lotus Notes database or a multiuser issue base hosted on a Web site (see example in Figure 8-20).

Once we institute procedures for organizing and recording rationale in meetings and expanding it with groupware, we are able to capture a great deal of rationale. The next challenge is to keep this information up to date as changes occur.

8.4.4   Capturing Rationale when Discussing Change

Rationale models help us deal with change. Unfortunately, rationale is itself subject to change when we revise decisions. When we design a solution in response to a requirements change, for example, we look at past rationale to assess which decisions need to be revised and design a change. Not only do we need to capture the rationale for the change and its solution, we also need to relate it with past rationale.

For example, in the CTC system, assume the requirements on the access control changed. Before, Dispatchers were allowed to see all TrackSections. The client informed us that, unlike previously specified, Dispatchers should be able to only see the neighboring TrackSections. In response to this change, we need to modify the design of the access control

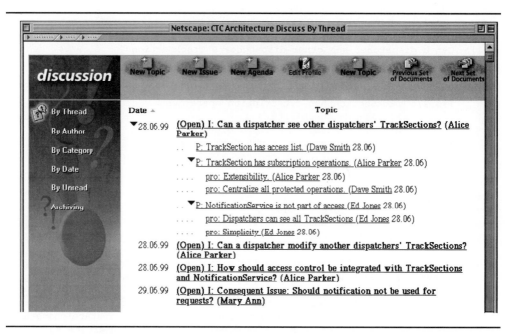

Figure 8-20   An example of issue database (LN IBIS database template in Domino Lotus Notes). Developers can access and post issues, proposals, arguments, and resolutions with Web forms.

and organize a meeting with the architecture team. In particular, we need to search past rationale associated with access control. Alice, the primary facilitator of the architecture team, posts the agenda depicted in Figure 8-21.

During the meeting, Dave presents the rationale discussed in previous meetings and on the architecture newsgroup. The architecture team notices that the assumption that all subsystems can see events is not valid anymore: The dispatcher should be allowed to see only the events related to neighboring `TrackSections`. Proposal P[2, 9/14] (see Figure 8-15) seems to be the better solution under the new requirements, as all protected operations could be centralized in the `TrackSection` class. Unfortunately, the implementation has already progressed, and the developers want to minimize changes to the code. Instead, Alice proposes to select proposal P[1, 9/14] (see Figure 8-14): The current `UIClient` stays unchanged, as the interfaces to the `TrackSection` and `NotificationService` classes need not change. Only the `NotificationService` needs to change such that it sends requests to the `TrackSection` to check the access of the current dispatcher. To revoke dispatcher privileges when an access list is changed, the `TrackSection` sends a request to the `NotificationService` to unsubscribe `Dispatchers`. This introduces a circular dependency between `TrackSection` and `NotificationService` but minimizes modifications to existing code.

This solution is selected by the architecture team. Ed produces the structured minutes depicted in Figure 8-22 (chronological minutes not displayed for brevity).

AGENDA: Revision of access control, dispatchers can only access neighboring tracks.

When and Where	Role
Date: 10/13	**Primary Facilitator**: Alice
Start: 4:30pm	**Timekeeper**: Dave
End: 5:30pm	**Minute Taker**: Ed
Building: Signal Hall	**Room**: 2300

1. Purpose

The client requested that dispatchers be able to access neighboring `TrackSections`.

2. Desired outcome

Resolve access control issues related to this change of requirement.

3. Information sharing [Allocated time: 15 minutes]

`AI[1]`: Dave: Recover rationale for access control.

4. Discussion [Allocated time: 35 minutes]

`I[1]`: How should access control be revised based on the neighboring track requirement?

5. Wrap up [Allocated Time: 5 minutes]

Review and assign new action items.

Meeting critique.

Figure 8-21 Agenda for the access control revision of CTC.

STRUCTURED MINUTES: Revision of access control, dispatchers can only access neighboring tracks.

When and Where	Role
Date: 10/13	**Primary Facilitator**: Alice
Start: 4:30pm	**Timekeeper**: Dave
End: 5:30pm	**Minute Taker**: Ed
Building:Signal Hall	**Room**: 2300

1. Purpose

The client requested that dispatchers be able to access neighboring `TrackSections`.

2. Desired outcome

Resolve access control issues related to this change of requirement.

3. Information sharing

`AI[1]`: Dave: Recover rationale for access control.

    Result: Issues `I[1, 9/13]` and `I[2, 9/15]` recovered:

I[1, 9/13]: How should access control be integrated with TrackSections and NotificationService? (Minutes from 9/14)

Figure 8-22 Structured minutes for the access control revision of CTC. *Italics* denote the rationale that was recovered for the purpose of the meeting.

P[3.1]:   *TrackSections maintain an access list of who can examine or modify the state of*
              the TrackSection. To subscribe to events, a subsystem sends a request to the
              NotificationService which in turns sends a request to the corresponding
              TrackSection to check access.
P[3.2]:   *TrackSections host all protected operations. The UIClient requests subscription*
              to TrackSection events by sending a request to the TrackSection, which checks access
              and sends a request to the NotificationService.

              A[3.1] for P[3.2]: Extensibility.

              A[3.2] for P[3.2]: Access control and protected operations are centralized into
              one class.
P[3.3]:   *There is no need to restrict the access to the event subscription. The UIClient*
              requests subscriptions directly from the NotificationService. The
              NotificationService need not check access.

              A[3.3] for P[3.3] Dispatchers can examine the state of any TrackSections (see
              R[1]).

              A[3.4] for P[3.3]: Simplicity.

              R[3]: P[3.3]. See action item AI[2].
I[2,9/15]: Should notification not be used for requests? (from Mary's news post 9/15)

R[2]:   *Notification should be used only for informing of state changes.*
              TrackSections and, more generally, TrackingSubsystem should not change their
              state based on events.

4. Discussion

I[1]: How should access control be revised based on the neighboring track requirement?

P[1.1]:   Protected operations, including subscription, centralized in `TrackSection`, as in
          P[3.2, 9/13].
          A[1.1] against P[1.1]: This requires all subsystems subscribing to notification events
          to be modified, since the subscription operation is moved from the
          `NotificationService` to the `TrackSection`.

P[1.2]:   `NotificationService` sends requests to `TrackSections` to check access.
          `TrackSection` sends request to `NotificationService` to unsubscribe dispatchers
          whose access has been revoked. P[3.1, 9/13]
          A[1.2] for P[1.2]: Minimal change to existing implementation.
          A[1.3] against P[1.2]: Circular dependencies.

R[1]:   P[1.2], see AI[2] and AI[3].

5. Wrap up

AI[2]:   Alice: Change the `TrackSection` to unsubscribe dispatchers when their
          rights are revoked.

AI[3]:   Dave: Modify `NotificationService` to check access with `TrackSection` when
          subscribing a new subsystem.

Figure 8-22   Structured minutes for the access control revision of CTC. *Italics* denote the rationale that was recovered for the purpose of the meeting.

The minutes depicted in Figure 8-22 serve two purposes: to record the rationale for the new change and to relate it to past rationale. This is done by quoting the past rationale that was used to revisit the access control decision. Furthermore, these new minutes are posted on the architecture newsgroup and discussed by other developers who could not attend the meeting, thus completing the cycle of recording and clarifying rationale information. In the case where groupware is used, the new rationale can be related to the past rationale with a hyperlink, making it easier for developers to navigate to the related information.

Note that even when an issue base is used to maintain and track open issues, this information base can grow quickly into a large unstructured chaos. Moreover, some issues are not recorded, as not all issues are discussed in meetings. Many issues are discussed and resolved informally in hallway conversions. It is necessary, therefore, to reconstruct the missing rationale of the system and integrate them with past rationale. We discuss this in the next section.

8.4.5   Reconstructing Rationale

Reconstructing rationale is a different method for capturing the rationale of the system. Instead of capturing decisions and their justifications as they occur, rationale is systematically reconstructed from the system model, the communication record, and developers' memories. With this method, rationale is captured and structured more systematically. Fewer resources are invested during the early phases of the process, thus enabling developers to come faster to a solution. Also, separating the design activity from the rationale capture enables developers to step back and critique their design more objectively. Reconstructing rationale, however, focuses on the selected solution and fails to capture discarded alternatives and their discussion. For example, assume we did not capture the rationale of the access control in CTC and that the only information we had was the system design model (Figure 8-23).

[...]

4. Access control

Access in CTC is controlled at the level of TrackSections: The Dispatcher who is assigned to a TrackSection can modify its state, that is, open and close signals and switches and modify other devices. Moreover, the Dispatcher can examine the state of neighboring TrackSections without modifying their state. This is necessary for the Dispatcher to observe the Trains that are about to enter the controlled TrackSection.

Access control is implemented with an access list maintained by the TrackSection. The access list contains the identity of the Dispatcher, who can modify the TrackSection (i.e., writers), and the identify of the Dispatcher, who can see the state of the track section (i.e., readers). For the sake of generality, the access list is implemented such that it can include multiple readers and multiple writers. The TrackSection checks the access list for every operation that modifies or queries the state of the TrackSection.

When subsystems subscribe to events, the NotificationService sends a request to the TrackSection to check access. The TrackSection sends a request to the NotificationService to unsubscribe dispatchers whose access is revoked.

The collaboration diagram of Figure 8-14 depicts this solution.

[...]

Figure 8-23   Excerpt from system design document, access control section.

I[1]: **How should access control of TrackSections be integrated with notification?**

Access in CTC is controlled at the level of TrackSections: The Dispatcher who is assigned to a TrackSection can modify its state, that is, open and close signals and switches and modify other devices. Moreover, the Dispatcher can examine the state of neighboring TrackSections without modifying their state. This is necessary for the Dispatcher to observe the Trains that are about to enter the controlled TrackSection.

P[1]: **TrackSection class controls all state modification, and notification subscription access.** Access control is implemented as an access list in TrackSection. The TrackSection class checks access of the caller for every operation that examines or modifies state. In particular, the caller subscribes to notification events by invoking methods on TrackSection, which in turns forwards the request to the NotificationService if access is granted. This solution is illustrated in Figure 8-15.	For: • Central solution: All protected methods related to the TrackSection are in one place.
P[2]: **TrackSection class controls state modification, NotificationService controls subscription.** As P[1], except that the caller requests subscriptions to events directly from the NotificationService, which checks access with the TrackSection before granting the subscription. This solution is illustrated in Figure 8-14.	For: • Access independent interface: The interfaces of NotificationService and TrackSection are the same as if there was no access control (legacy argument). Against: • Circular dependency between NotificationService and TrackSection: The TrackSection invokes operations on the NotificationService to generate events, the NotificationService subscription methods invoke operations on the TrackSection to check access.

R[1]

P[2]. P[1] would have been a better solution; however, access control did not apply to notification. To minimize code and design rework, P[2] was selected.

Figure 8-24   Reconstructed rationale for the notification access control issue of CTC.

We want to recover the rationale of the system design for review and documentation. We decide to organize each issue as a table with two columns, the left column for the proposals and the right column for their corresponding arguments. In Figure 8-24, we recover the rationale for the integration of access control with notification. We identify two possible solutions: P[1] in which the TrackSection class exports all operations whose access is controlled, including subscription to notifications, and P[2] in which the NotificationService delegates the access control check to the `TrackSection`. We then enumerate the advantages and disadvantages of each solution in the right column and summarize the justification of the decision as a resolution at the bottom of the table.

A reconstructed rationale, such as the one in Figure 8-24, costs less to capture than the activities we described previously. It is more difficult, however, to capture the discarded alternatives and the reasons of such choices, especially when decisions are revised over time. In Figure 8-24, the resolution states that we did not select the better proposal, and we were able to remember the reasons for this nonoptimal decision (i.e., that substantial code had been completed prior to this decision, and we wanted to minimize code rework). Alternatively, reconstructing rationale is an effective tool for review, for identifying decisions that are inconsistent with the design goals of the project. Moreover, even if the reviewed decisions cannot be revised at a late stage in the project, this knowledge can benefit new developers assigned to the project or developers revising the system in later iterations.

The balance between rationale capture, maintenance, and reconstruction differs for each project and needs to be carefully managed. It is relatively frequent to see rationale capture efforts accumulate enormous amounts of information that are either useless or not easily accessible to developers who should benefit from such information. We focus on management issues next.

8.5 Managing Rationale

In this section, we describe issues related to managing rationale activities. Recording justifications for design decisions is often seen as an intrusion from management into the work of developers, and thus rationale techniques encounter resistance from developers and often degenerate into a bureaucratic process. Rationale techniques need to be carefully managed to be useful. In this section, we describe how to:

- write documents about rationale (Section 8.5.1)
- assign responsibilities for capturing and maintaining rationale models (Section 8.5.2)
- communicate about rationale models (Section 8.5.3)
- use issues to negotiate (Section 8.5.4)
- resolve conflicts (Section 8.5.5)

As before, we continue focusing on the system design activity. Note, however, that these techniques can be applied uniformly throughout the development.

8.5.1 Documenting Rationale

When rationale is explicitly captured and documented, this is best described in documents that are separate from system model documents. For example, the rationale behind requirements analysis decisions is documented in the Requirements Analysis Rationale Document (RARD), which complements the Requirements Analysis Document (RAD). Similarly, the rationale behind system design decisions is documented in the System Design Rationale Document (SDRD), which complements the System Design Document (SDD). In this section, we focus on the SDRD, as system design is the activity that benefits the most from capturing rationale. Figure 8-25 is an example of template for the SDRD.

The audience for the SDRD is the same as for the SDD: The SDRD is used by developers when revising decisions, by reviewers when reviewing the system, and by new developers when assigned to the project. The specific activities for which the rationale document is intended are described in the first section of the document. A document focusing on justifying the system for reviewers might only contain proposals and arguments relevant to the selected resolutions. A document capturing as much of the design context as possible might contain in addition all the discarded alternatives and their evaluations. The first section also repeats the design goals that were selected at the beginning of system design. These represent the criteria that developers used to evaluate alternative solutions.

The next two sections are composed of a list of issues, formatted in the same way as the access control issue we described earlier in Figure 8-24. The list of issues can constitute the systematic justification of the design or be simply a collection of issues captured in the course of system design. Issues may be related to each other with subissue and consequent issue references. Finally, pointers to issues in this document can be inserted in the SDD in the relevant sections for ease of navigation.

System Design Rationale Document
1. Introduction
    1.1 Purpose of the document
    1.2 Design goals
    1.3 Definitions, acronyms, and abbreviations
    1.4 References

    1.5 Overview
2. Rationale for current software architecture
3. Rationale for proposed software architecture
    3.1 Overview
    3.2 Rationale for subsystem decomposition
    3.3 Rationale for hardware/software mapping
    3.4 Rationale for persistent data management
    3.5 Rationale for access control and security
    3.6 Rationale for global software control
    3.7 Rationale for boundary conditions
    Glossary

Figure 8-25   An example of a template for the SDRD.

The second section of the SDRD describes the rationale for the system being replaced. If there is no previous system, this section can be replaced by rationale for similar systems. The purpose of this section is to make explicit prior alternatives that have been explored and issues that developers should watch for.

The third section of the SDRD describes the rationale for the new system. Paralleling the structure of the SDD, this section is divided into seven subsections:

- *Overview* presents an bird's eye view of this section, including a summary of the most critical issues that were dealt with during system design.
- *Rationale for subsystem decomposition* justifies the selected system decomposition. How does it minimize coupling? How does it increases coherence? How does it satisfy the design goals set in the first section? More generally, any issue that impacted system decomposition is listed here.
- *Rationale for hardware/software mapping* justifies the selected hardware configuration, the assignment of subsystems to nodes, and legacy code issues.
- *Rationale for persistent data management* justifies the selection of data storage mechanism. Why were flat files/relational database/object-oriented database selected? Which design criteria drove this decision? Which other issues should the storage component deal with?
- *Rationale for access control and security* justifies the selected access control implementation. Why were access lists/capabilities chosen? How is the access control integrated with other subsystems distributing information, such as the middleware or the notification subsystem? The access control issue for CTC would be included in this section.
- *Rationale for global software control* justifies the selected control mechanism. Which legacy component constrained the software control? Were there incompatible legacy components? How was this dealt with?
- *Rationale for boundary conditions* justifies each boundary condition and its handling. Why does the system check the consistency of the database at start-up? Why does the system give a 10-minute warning to the Dispatchers before shutdown (as opposed to 20 minutes or 2 hours)?

The SDRD should be written at the same time as the SDD and revised whenever the SDD is revised. This ensures that both documents are consistent and encourages developers to make rationale explicit. The SDRD should be revised not only when the design is changed but also when missing rationale is found (e.g., during reviews).

8.5.2   Assigning Responsibilities

Assigning responsibilities for capturing and maintaining rationale is the most critical management decision in making rationale models useful. Maintaining rationale can easily be perceived as an intrusive bureaucratic process through which developers need to justify all decisions. Instead, rationale models should be maintained by a small number of people who have access to all developers' information, such as drafts of design documents and developer newsgroups. This small group of people, becoming historians of the system design, become useful to the other developers when providing rationale information, and thus create an incentive to developers to provide them with information. Below are the main roles related to rationale model maintenance:

- The **minute taker** records rationale in meetings. This includes recording chronological statements during the meeting and restructuring them with issues after the meeting (see Section 8.4.2).
- The **rationale editor** collects and organizes information related to rationale. This includes obtaining the meeting minutes from the minute taker, prototype and technology evaluations reports from developers, and drafts of all system models and design documents from the technical writers. The rationale editor imposes minimal overhead on the developers and the writers by performing the structuring and indexing role. The developers need not provide information structured as issue models; however, the rationale editor constructs an index of all issues.
- The **reviewer** examines the rationale captured by the rationale editor and identifies holes to be reconstructed. The reviewer then collects the relevant information from communication records and, if necessary, from the developers. This role should not be a management role or a quality assurance role: The reviewer must directly benefit the developers in order to be able to collect valid information. This role can be combined with the rationale editor role.

The size of the project determines the number of minute takers, rationale editors, and reviewers. The following heuristics can be used for assigning these roles:

- **One minute taker per team.** Meetings are usually organized by subsystem team or by cross-functional team. A developer of each team can function as a minute taker, thus distributing this time-consuming role across the project.
- **One rationale editor per project.** The role of rationale editor for a project is a full-time role. Unlike the role of minute taker, which can be rotated, the role of rationale editor requires consistency and should be assigned to a single person. In small projects, this role can be assigned to the system architect (see Chapter 6, *System Design*).
- **Increase the number of reviewers after delivery.** When the system is delivered and the number of developers directly needed for the project decreases, some developers should be assigned the reviewer role for salvaging and organizing as much information as possible. Rationale information is still recoverable from developers' memories, but disappears quickly as developers move to other projects.

8.5.3   Heuristics for Communicating about Rationale

A large part of communication *is* rationale information, given that argumentation is, by definition, rationale (see Section 8.2). Developers argue about design goals, whether a given issue is relevant or not, the benefit of several solutions, and their evaluation. Rationale constitutes a large and complex body of information, usually larger than the system itself. Communication, moreover, occurs most often in small forums; for example, in a team meeting or a conversation at the coffee machine. The challenge of communicating about rationale is to make this information accessible to all concerned parties without causing an information overload. In this chapter, we focused on techniques for capturing and structuring rationale, such as using issue models in minutes, follow-up conversations, and rationale documentation. In addition, the following heuristics can be used to increase the structure of rationale and facilitate its navigation:

- **Name issues consistently.** Issues should be consistently and uniquely named across minutes, newsgroups, E-mail messages, and documents. Issues can have a number (e.g., 1291) and a short name (e.g., "the access/notification issue") for ease of reference.
- **Centralize issues.** Although issues will be discussed in a variety of contexts, encourage one context (e.g., a newsgroup or an issue base) to be a central repository of issues. This issue base should be maintained by the rationale editor but could be used and extended by any developer. This enables developers to search for information quickly.
- **Cross-reference issues and system elements.** Most issues apply to a specific element in the system models (e.g., a use case, an object, a subsystem). Finding which model element a specific issue applies to is straightforward. However, finding which issues apply to a specific model element is a much more difficult problem. To facilitate this type of query, issues should be attached to the applying model element when issues are raised.
- **Manage change.** Rationale evolves as system models do. Thus, configuration management should be applied consistently to rationale and documents as it is applied to system models.

Capturing and structuring rationale not only improves communication about rationale but also facilitates communication about the system models. Integrating both rationale and system information enables developers to better maintain both types of information.

8.5.4   Issue Modeling and Negotiation

Most important decisions in development are the result of negotiation. Different parties representing different, and often conflicting, interests come to a consensus on some aspect of the system: Requirements analysis includes the negotiation of functionality with a client. System design includes the negotiation of subsystem interfaces among developers. Integration includes the resolution of conflicts between developers. We use issue-modeling to represent the information exchanged during these negotiations in order to capture rationale. We can also use issue-modeling to facilitate negotiations.

Traditional negotiation, which consists of bargaining over positions, is often time consuming and inefficient, especially when the negotiating parties hold incompatible positions. Effort is spent in defending one's position, citing all its advantages, whereas the opposing part spends effort in denigrating the other's position, citing all its disadvantages. The negotiation either progresses in small steps toward a consensus or is ended by an arbitrary solution to the negotiated issue. Furthermore, this can occur even when negotiating parties have compatible interests: When defending positions, people have greater trouble evolving or changing their position without losing credibility. The Harvard method of negotiation [Fischer et al., 1991] addresses these points by taking the focus away from positions. We rephrase several important points of the Harvard method in terms of issue modeling:

- **Separate developers from proposals.** Developers can spent a lot of resources developing a specific proposal (i.e., a position), to the point that a criticism of the proposal is taken as a personal criticism of the developer. Developers and proposals should be separated in order to make it easier to evolve or discard a proposal. This can be done by having multiple developers work on the same proposal or have all concerned parties participate in the development of all proposals. Separating the design and the implementation work can further facilitate this distinction. By ensuring that negotiation comes before implementation and before substantial resources are committed, developers are able to evolve proposals into ones that all can live with.
- **Focus on criteria, not on proposals.** As stated before, most arguments can be tracked to the criteria, often implicit, used for evaluation. Once an accepted set of criteria is in place, evaluating and selecting proposals is far less controversial. Furthermore, criteria are much less subject to change than other factors in the project. Agreeing on criteria early also facilitates revisions to decisions.
- **Take into account all criteria instead of maximizing a single one.** Different criteria reflect interests of different parties. Performance criteria are usually motivated by usability concerns. Modifiability criteria are motivated by maintenance concerns. Even if some criteria are considered higher priority that other ones, optimizing only these high-priority criteria risks leaving out of the negotiation one or more parties.

Viewing development as a negotiation acknowledges the social aspects of development. Developers are persons who, in addition to technical opinions, can have an emotional perspective on different solutions. This can influence (and sometimes interfere) with their relationships to other developers as conflicts arise. Using issue-modeling to capture rationale and drive decisions can integrate and improve both the technical and social aspects of development.

8.5.5 Conflict Resolution Strategies

Occasionally, project participants fail to come to a consensus through negotiation. In such cases, it is critical that conflict resolution strategies already be in place to deal with the situation.

The worst design decisions are those that are not taken because of the lack of consensus or the absence of conflict resolution strategies. This delays critical decision until late in the development, resulting in high redesign and recording costs.

Many different conflict resolution strategies are possible. For example, consider the five following strategies:

- **Majority wins**. In case of conflict, a majority vote could remove the deadlock and resolve the decision. Several collaboration tools enable users to attach weights to different arguments in the issue model, and thus to compute which proposal should be selected with an arithmetic formula [Purvis et al., 1996]. This assumes that the opinion of each participant matters equally and that, statistically, the group makes the right decisions.

- **Owner has last word**. In this strategy, the owner of an issue (the person who raised it) is responsible for deciding the outcome. This assumes that the owner has the largest stake in the issue.

- **Management is always right**. An alternative strategy is to fall back on the organizational hierarchy. If a group is unable to reach consensus, the manager of the group imposes a decision based on the argument. This assumes the manager is capable of understanding the argument and make the right trade-offs.

- **Expert is always right**. In this strategy, an external expert, foreign to the debate, assesses the situation and advises the best course of action. For example, during requirements analysis, a test user can be interviewed to evaluate the different proposals of an issue. Unfortunately, such an expert has limited knowledge of other system decisions or, more generally, of the design context.

- **Time decides**. As an issue is left unresolved, time becomes a pressure and forces a decision. Also, controversial issues may become easier to resolve as other decisions are made and other aspects of the system defined. The danger with this strategy is that it leads to decisions that optimize short-term criteria (such as ease of implementation) and disregard long-term criteria (such as modifiability and maintainability).

The *Majority wins* and the *Owner has last word* strategies do not work well. They both result in inconsistent results (multiplicity of decision makers) and in decisions that are not well supported by the rest of the participants. The *Management is always right* and *Expert is always right* strategies lead to better technical decisions and better consensus when the Manager and the Expert are sufficiently knowledgeable. The *Time decides* strategy is a fallback, albeit one that may result in costly rework.

In practice, we first attempt to reach consensus, and, in case of lack of consensus, fall back on an expert or management strategy. If the expert or manager strategy fails, we let time decide or take a binding majority vote.

8.6 Exercises

1. Below is an excerpt from a system design document for an accident management system. It is a natural language description of the rationale for a relational database for permanent storage. Model this rationale with issues, proposals, arguments, criteria, and resolutions, as defined in Section 8.3.

> One fundamental issue in database design was database engine realization. The initial nonfunctional requirements on the database subsystem insisted on the use of an object-oriented database for the underlying engine. Other possible options included using a relational database, a file system, or a combination of the other options. An object-oriented database has the advantages of being able to handle complex data relationships and is fully buzzword compliant. On the other hand, OO databases may be too sluggish for large volumes of data or high-frequency accesses. Furthermore, existing products do not integrate well with CORBA, because that protocol does not support specific programming language features such as Java associations. Using a relational database offers a more robust engine with higher performance characteristics and a large pool of experience and tools to draw on. Furthermore, the relational data model integrates nicely with CORBA. On the downside, this model does not easily support complex data relationships. The third option was proposed to handle specific types of data that are written once and read infrequently. This type of data (including sensor readings and control outputs) has few relationships with little complexity and must be archived for extended periods of time. Files offer an easy archival solution and can handle large amounts of data. Conversely, any code would need to be written from scratch, including serialization of access. We decided to use only a relational database, based on the requirement to use CORBA and in light of the relative simplicity of the relationships between the system's persistent data.

2. In Section 8.3, we examined an issue related to access control and notification in the CTC system. Select a similar issue that could occur in the development and CTC and populate it with relevant proposals, criteria, arguments, and justify a resolution. Examples of such issues include:

   • How can consistency between `mainServer` and `hotBackup` be maintained?

   • How should failure of the `mainServer` be detected and the subsequent switch to the `hotBackup` be implemented?

3. You are developing a CASE tool using UML as its primary notation. You are considering the integration of rationale into the tool. Describe how a developer could attach issues to different model elements. Draw a class diagram of the issue model and its association to model elements.

4. Considering the same CASE tool as in Exercise 3. You are considering the generation of rationale documents from the model. Describe the mapping between classes, issues, and the sections rationale document.

5. You are integrating a bug reporting system with a configuration management tool to track bug reports, bug fixes, feature requests, and enhancements. You are considering an issue

model for integrating these tools. Draw a class diagram of the issue model, the corresponding discussion, configuration management, and bug-reporting elements.

References

[Boehm et al., 1995]   B.Boehm, P. Bose, E. Horowitz, & M.J. Lee, "Software requirements negotiation and renegotiation aids: A theory-W based spiral approach," *Proceedings of the ICSE-17*, (Seattle,) 1995.

[Buckingham Shum & Hammond, 1994]   S. Buckingham Shum & N. Hammond, "Argumentation-based design rationale: What use at what cost?" *International Journal of Human-Computer Studies*, Vol. 40, pp. 603–652, 1994.

[Conklin & Burgess-Yakemovic, 1991]   J. Conklin & K. C. Burgess-Yakemovic, "A process-oriented approach to design rationale," *Human-Computer Interaction*, Vol. 6, pp. 357–391, 1991.

[Dutoit et al., 1996]   A. H. Dutoit, B. Bruegge, & R. F. Coyne, "The use of an issue-based model in a team-based software engineering course," *Conference Proceedings of Software Engineering: Education and Practice* (SEEP'96). (Dunedin, NZ,) Jan. 1996.

[Fischer et al., 1991]   R. Fisher, W. Ury, & B. Patton, *Getting to Yes: Negotiating Agreement Without Giving In*, 2nd ed. Penguin Books, New York, 1991.

[Kunz & Rittel, 1970]   W. Kunz & H. Rittel, "Issues as elements of information systems," *Working Paper No. 131*, Institut für Grundlagen der Plannung, Universität Stuttgart, Germany, 1970.

[Lee, 1990]   J. Lee, "A qualitative decision management system," , *Artificial Intelligence at MIT: Expanding Frontiers*. P.H Winston & S. Shellard (eds.) (MIT Press, Cambridge, MA,) Vol. 1, pp. 104–133, 1990.

[Lee, 1997]   J. Lee, "Design rationale systems: Understanding the issues," *IEEE Expert*, May/June 1997.

[MacLean et al., 1991]   A. MacLean, R. M. Young, V. Bellotti, & T. Moran, "Questions, options, and criteria: Elements of design space analysis," *Human-Computer Interaction*, Vol. 6, pp. 201–250, 1991.

[Moran & Carroll., 1996]   T. P. Moran & J. M. Carroll (eds.), *Design Rationale: Concepts, Techniques, and Use*. Lawrence Erlbaum Associates, Mahwah, NJ, 1996.

[Potts et al., 1988]   C. Potts & G. Bruns, "Recording the reasons for design decisions," *Proceedings of the 10th International Conference on Software Engineering*, pp. 418–427, 1988.

[Potts et al., 1994]   C. Potts, K. Takahashi, & A. I. Anton, "Inquiry-based requirements analysis," *IEEE Software*, Vol. 11, no. 2, pp. 21–32, 1994.

[Potts, 1996]   C. Potts, "Supporting software design: Integrating design methods and design rationale," *Design Rationale: Concepts, Techniques, and Use*. T.P. Moran & J.M. Carroll (eds.) (Lawrence Erlbaum Associates, Mahwah, NJ,) 1996.

[Purvis et al., 1996]   M. Purvis, M. Purvis, & P. Jones, "A group collaboration tool for software engineering projects," *Conference proceedings of Software Engineering: Education and Practice (SEEP'96)*. (Dunedin, NZ,) Jan. 1996.

[Shipman et al., 1997]   F.M. Shipman III & R.J. McCall, "Integrating different perspectives on design rationale: Supporting the emergence of design rationale from design communication," *Artificial Intelligence in Engineering Design, Analysis, and Manufacturing*, Vol. 11, no. 2, 1997.

9

Testing

The software is done.
We are just trying to get it to work.
—Statement made in a Joint STARS E-8A FSD
Executive Program Review

Testing is the process of finding differences between the expected behavior specified by system models and the observed behavior of the system. Unit testing finds differences between the object design model and its corresponding component. Structural testing finds differences between the system design model and a subset of integrated subsystems. Functional testing finds differences between the use case model and the system. Finally, performance testing finds differences between nonfunctional requirements and actual system performance. When differences are found, developers identify the defect causing the observed failure and modify the system to correct it. In other cases, the system model is identified as the cause of the difference, and the model is updated to reflect the state of the system.

From a modeling point of view, testing is the attempt of falsification of the system with respect to the system models. The goal of testing is to design tests that exercise defects in the system and to reveal problems. This activity is contrary to all other activities we described in previous chapters: Analysis, design, implementation, communication and negotiation are constructive activities. Testing, however, is aimed at breaking the system. Consequently, testing is usually accomplished by developers that were not involved with the construction of the system.

In this chapter, we first motivate the importance of testing. We provide a bird's eye view of the testing activities, we describe in more detail the concepts of fault, error, failure, and test, and then we describe the testing activities that result in the plan, design, and execution of tests. We conclude this chapter by discussing management issues related to testing.

9.1 Introduction

Testing is the process of analyzing a system or system component to detect the differences between specified (required) and observed (existing) behavior. Unfortunately, it is impossible to completely test a nontrivial system. First, testing is not decidable. Second, testing needs to be performed under time and budget constraints. As a result, systems are deployed without being completely tested, leading to faults discovered by end users.

The first launch of the Space Shuttle Columbia in 1981, for example, was canceled because of a problem that was not detected during development. The problem was traced to a change made by a programmer 2 years earlier, who erroneously reset a delay factor from 50 to 80 milliseconds. This added a probability of 1/67 that any space shuttle launch would fail. Unfortunately, despite of thousands of hours of testing after the change was made, the fault was not discovered during the testing phase. During the actual launch the fault caused a synchronization problem with the shuttle's five on-board computers that then led to the decision to abort the launch. The following is an excerpt of an article by Richard Feynman that describes the challenges of testing the Space Shuttle.

In a total of about 250,000 seconds of operation, the engines have failed seriously perhaps 16 times. Engineering pays close attention to these failings and tries to remedy them as quickly as possible. This it does by test studies on special rigs experimentally designed for the flaws in question, by careful inspection of the engine for suggestive clues (like cracks), and by considerable study and analysis. ...

The usual way that such engines are tested (for military or civilian aircraft) may be called the component system, or bottom-up test. First it is necessary to thoroughly understand the properties and limitations of the materials to be used (for turbine blades, for example), and tests are begun in experimental rigs to determine those. With this knowledge larger component parts (such as bearings) are designed and tested individually. As deficiencies and design errors are noted they are corrected and verified with further testing. Since one tests only one component at a time, these tests and modifications are not overly expensive. Finally one works up to the final design of the entire engine, to the necessary specifications. There is a good chance, by this time that the engine will generally succeed, or that any failures are easily isolated and analyzed because the failure modes, limitations of materials, etc., are so well understood. There is a very good chance that the modifications to the engine to get around the final difficulties are not very hard to make, for most of the serious problems have already been discovered and dealt with in the earlier, less expensive, stages of the process.

The Space Shuttle Main Engine was handled in a different manner, top down, we might say. The engine was designed and put together all at once with relatively little detailed preliminary study of the material and components. Then when troubles are found in the bearings, turbine blades, coolant pipes, etc., it is more expensive and difficult to discover the causes and make changes. For example, cracks have been found in the turbine blades of the high pressure oxygen turbopump. Are they caused by flaws in the material, the effect of the oxygen atmosphere on the properties of the material, the thermal stresses of start-up or shutdown, the vibration and stresses of steady running, or mainly at some resonance at certain speeds, etc.? How long can we run from crack initiation to crack failure, and how does this depend on power level? Using the completed engine as a test bed to resolve such questions is extremely expensive. One does not wish to lose an entire engine in order to find out where and how failure occurs.

Yet, an accurate knowledge of this information is essential to acquire a confidence in the engine reliability in use. Without detailed understanding, confidence can not be attained. A further disadvantage of the top-down method is that, if an understanding of a fault is obtained, a simple fix, such as a new shape for the turbine housing, may be impossible to implement without a redesign of the entire engine.

The Space Shuttle Main Engine is a very remarkable machine. It has a greater ratio of thrust to weight than any previous engine. It is built at the edge of, or outside of, previous engineering experience. Therefore, as expected, many different kinds of flaws and difficulties have turned up. Because, unfortunately, it was built in the top-down manner, they are difficult to find and fix. The design aim of a lifetime of 55 missions equivalent firings (27,000 seconds of operation, either in a mission of 500 seconds, or on a test stand) has not been obtained. The engine now requires very frequent maintenance and replacement of important parts, such as turbopumps, bearings, sheet metal housings, etc. The high-pressure fuel turbopump had to be replaced every three or four mission equivalents (although that may have been fixed, now) and the high pressure oxygen turbopump every five or six. This is at most ten percent of the original specification.

Feynman's article[1] gives us an idea of the problems associated with testing complex systems. Even though the space shuttle is an extremely complex hardware and software system, the testing challenges are the same for any complex system.

Testing has often been viewed as a job that can be done by beginners. Managers would assign the new members to the testing team, because the experienced people detested testing or were needed for the more important jobs of analysis and design. Unfortunately, such an attitude leads to many problems. To test a system effectively, a tester must have a detailed understanding of the whole system, ranging from the requirements to system design decisions and implementation issues. A tester must also be knowledgeable of testing techniques and apply these techniques effectively and efficiently to meet time, budget, and quality constraints.

This chapter is organized as follows. In Section 9.2, we take a bird's eye view of testing and show its relationship with other quality assurance methods. In Section 9.3, we define in more detail the model elements related to testing, including faults, their manifestation, and their relationship to testing. In Section 9.4, we describe the testing activities found in the development process. We first describe unit testing, which focuses on finding faults in a single component. We then describe integration and system testing, which focus on finding faults in combination of components and in the complete system, respectively. We also describe testing activities that focus on nonfunctional requirements, such as performance tests and stress tests. We conclude Section 9.4 with the activities of field testing and installation testing. In Section 9.5, we discuss management issues related to testing.

---

1. Feynman [Feynman, 1988] wrote the article while he was a member of the Presidential commission investigating the explosion of the space shuttle Challenger in January 1985. The cause of the accident was traced to an erosion of the O-rings in the solid booster rockets. In addition to the testing problems of the main shuttle engine and the solid rocket boosters, the article mentions the phenomenon of gradually changing critical testing acceptance criteria and problems resulting from miscommunication between management and developers typically found in hierarchical organizations.

9.2 An Overview of Testing

Reliability is a measure of success with which the observed behavior of a system conforms to the specification of its behavior. **Software reliability** is the probability that a software system will not cause the failure of the system for a specified time under specified conditions [IEEE Std. 982-1989]. **Failure** is any deviation of the observed behavior from the specified behavior. An **error** means the system is in a state such that further processing by the system will lead to a failure, which causes the system to deviate from its intended behavior. A **fault**, also called defect or bug, is the mechanical or algorithmic cause of an error. The goal of testing is to maximize the number of discovered faults, which then allows developers to correct them and increase the reliability of the system.

We define testing as the systematic attempt to *find errors in a planned way* in the implemented software. Contrast this definition with another commonly used definition that says that "testing is the process of demonstrating that *errors are not present*." The distinction between these two definitions is important. Our definition does not mean we simply demonstrate that the program does what it is intended to do. The explicit goal of testing is to demonstrate the presence of faults. Our definition implies that you, the developer, are willing to dismantle things. Most activities of the development process are constructive: During analysis, design, and implementation, objects and relationships are identified, refined, and mapped onto a computer environment.

Testing requires a different thinking, in that developers try to detect faults in the system, that is, differences between the reality and the requirements. Many developers find it difficult to do. One reason is the way we use the word "success" during testing. Many project managers call a test case "successful" if it does not find an error; that is, they use the second definition of testing during development. However, because "successful" denotes an achievement, and "unsuccessful" means something undesirable, these words should not be used in this fashion during testing.

In this chapter, we treat testing as an activity based on the falsification of system models, which is based on Popper's falsification of scientific theories [Popper, 1992]. According to Popper, when testing a scientific hypothesis, the goal is to design experiments that falsify the underlying theory. If the experiments are unable to break the theory, our confidence in the theory is strengthened and the theory is adopted (until it is eventually falsified). Similarly, in software testing, the goal is to identify errors in the software system ("falsify the theory"). If none of the tests have been able to falsify the software system behavior with respect to the requirements, it is ready for delivery.

In other words, a software system is released when the falsification attempts ("tests") have increased the reliability of the software, ensuring a larger confidence that the software system does what it is supposed to do.

9.2.1 Quality Control Techniques

There are many techniques for increasing the reliability of a software system. Figure 9-1 focuses on three classes of techniques for avoiding faults, detecting faults, and tolerating faults. *Fault avoidance techniques* try to detect errors statically, that is, without relying on the execution of any of the system models, in particular the code model. *Fault detection techniques*, such as debugging and testing, are uncontrolled and controlled experiments, respectively, used during the development process to identify errors and find the underlying faults before releasing the system. *Fault tolerance techniques* assume that a system can be released with errors and that system failures can be dealt with by recovering from them at run time.

9.2.2 Fault Avoidance Techniques

Fault avoidance tries to prevent the occurrence of errors and failures by finding faults in the system before it is released. Fault avoidance techniques include:

- development methodologies
- configuration management
- verification techniques
- reviews

Development methodologies avoid faults by providing techniques that minimize fault introduction in the system models and code. Such techniques include the unambiguous representation of requirements, the use of data abstraction and data encapsulation, minimizing of the coupling between subsystems and maximizing of subsystem coherence, the early definition of subsystem interfaces, and the capture of rationale information for maintenance activities. We described these techniques in Chapters 4–7. The assumptions of most of these techniques is that the system contains many less faults if complexity is dealt with model-based approaches.

Configuration management avoids faults caused by undisciplined change in the system models. For example, it is a common mistake to a change a subsystem interface without notifying all developers of calling components. Configuration management can make sure that, if analysis models and code are becoming inconsistent with one another, analysts and implementor are notified. The assumption behind configuration management is that the system contains many less faults if change is controlled.

Verification attempts to find faults before any execution of the system. Verification is possible in specific cases, such as the verification of a small operating system kernel [Walker et al., 1980]. Verification, however, has limits. It is not in a mature enough state that it can be applied to assure the quality of large complex systems. Moreover, it assumes that the requirements are correct, which is seldom the case: Assume we need to verify an operation and we know the pre- and postconditions for the operation. If we can verify that the operation provides a transformation such that, before the execution of the operation the precondition is

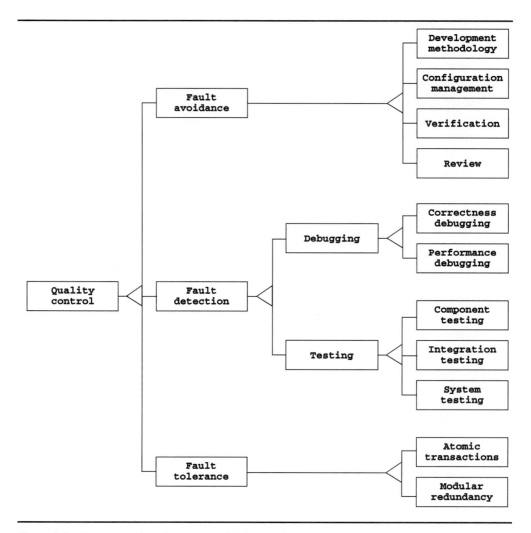

Figure 9-1   Taxonomy of quality control activities (UML class diagram).

true, and after the execution the postcondition holds, then the operation is correctly implemented; that is, it is verified. However, sometimes we forget important parts of the pre- or postcondition. For example, the postconditions might not state that the train should stay on the ground while moving from track 1 to track 2. Finally, verification addresses only algorithmic faults: It cannot deal with mechanical faults in the virtual machine. For verification, we must assume that the virtual machine on which the system is executing is correct and does not change during the proof.

A **review** is the manual inspection of parts or all aspects of the system without actually executing the system. There are two types of reviews: walkthrough and inspection. In a code

walkthrough, the developer informally presents the API, the code, and associated documentation of the component to the review team. The review team makes comments on the mapping of the analysis and object design to the code using use cases and scenarios from the analysis phase. An **inspection** is similar to a walkthrough, but the presentation of the unit is formal. In fact, in a code inspection, the developer is not allowed to present the artifacts (models, code, and documentation). This is done by the review team, which is responsible for checking the interface and code of the component against the requirements. It also checks the algorithms for efficiency with respect to the nonfunctional requirements. Finally, it checks comments about the code and compares them with the code itself to find inaccurate and incomplete comments. The developer is only present in case the review needs clarifications about the definition and use of data structures or algorithms.

Code reviews have proven to be very effective at detecting errors. In some experiments, up to 85% of all identified faults have been found in reviews [Fagan, 1976], [Jones, 1977].

9.2.3 Fault Detection Techniques

Fault detection techniques assist in finding faults in systems but do not try to recover from the failures caused by them. In general, fault detection techniques are applied during development, but in some cases they are also used after the release of the system. The blackboxes in airplanes logging the last few minutes of a flight before the crash is an example of a fault detection technique. We distinguish two types of fault detection techniques, debugging and testing.

Debugging assumes that faults can be found by starting from an unplanned failure. The developer moves the system through a succession of states, ultimately arriving at and identifying the erroneous state. Once this state has been identified, the algorithmic or mechanical fault causing this state needs to be determined. There are two types of debugging: The goal of **correctness debugging** is to find any deviation between the observed and specified functional requirements. **Performance debugging** addresses the deviation between observed and specified nonfunctional requirements, such as response time.

Testing is a fault detection technique that tries to create failures or errors in a planned way. This allows the developer to detect failures in the system before it is released to the customer. Note that this definition of testing implies that a successful test is a test that identifies errors. We will use this definition throughout the development phases. Another often-used definition of testing is that "it demonstrates that errors are not present." We will use this definition only after the development of the system when we try to demonstrate that the delivered system fulfills the functional and nonfunctional requirements.

If we would use this second definition all the time, we would tend to select test data that have a low probability of causing the program to fail. If, on the other hand, the goal is to demonstrate that a program has errors, we tend to look for test data with a higher probability of finding errors. The characteristics of a good test model is that it contains test cases that identify errors. Every input that can possibly be given to the system should be tested; otherwise, there is a chance that faults are not detected. Unfortunately, such an approach requires extremely large testing times for even small systems.

Figure 9-2 depicts an overview of the testing activities:

- **Unit testing** tries to find faults in participating objects and/or subsystems with respect to the use cases from the use case model
- **Integration testing** is the activity of finding faults when testing the individually tested components together, for example, subsystems described in the subsystem decomposition, while executing the use cases and scenarios from the RAD.
    - The **system structure testing** is the culmination of integration testing involving all components of the system. Integration tests and structure tests exploit knowledge from the SDD using an integration strategy described in the Test Plan (TP).
- **System testing** tests all the components together, seen as a single system to identify errors with respect to the scenarios from the problem statement and the requirements and design goals identified in the analysis and system design, respectively:
    - **Functional testing** tests the requirements from the RAD and, if available, from the user manual.
    - **Performance testing** checks the nonfunctional requirements and additional design goals from the SDD. Note that functional and performance testing are both done by developers.
    - **Acceptance testing** and **installation testing** check the requirements against the project agreement and should be done by the client, if necessary with support by the developers.

9.2.4   Fault Tolerance Techniques

If we cannot prevent errors we must accept the fact that the released system contains faults that can lead to failures. Fault tolerance is the recovery from failure while the system is executing. It allows a system to recover from a failure of a component by passing the erroneous state information back to the calling components, assuming one of them knows what to do in this case. Database systems provide atomic transactions to recover from failure during a sequence of actions that need to be executed together or not at all. Modular redundancy is based on the assumption that system failures are usually based on component failures. Modular redundant systems are built by assigning more than one component to perform the same operation. The five onboard computers in the space shuttle are an example of a modular redundant system. The system can continue even if one component is failing, because the other components are still performing the required functionality. The treatment of fault tolerant techniques is important for highly reliable systems but is beyond the scope of this book. An excellent coverage of the topic is provided in [Siewiorek & Swarz, 1992].

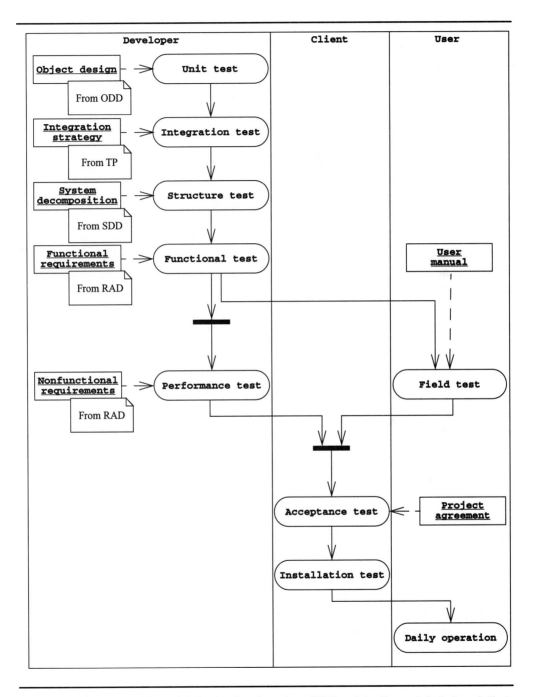

Figure 9-2 Testing activities and their related work products (UML activity diagram). Swimlanes indicate who executes the test.

9.3 Testing Concepts

In this section, we present the model elements used during testing (Figure 9-3):

- A **component** is a part of the system that can be isolated for testing. A component can be an object, a group of objects, or one or more subsystems.
- A **fault**, also called bug or defect, is a design or coding mistake that may cause abnormal component behavior.
- An **error** is a manifestation of a fault during the execution of the system.
- A **failure** is a deviation between the specification of a component and its behavior. A failure is triggered by one or more errors.
- A **test case** is a set of inputs and expected results that exercises a component with the purpose of causing failures and detecting faults.
- A **test stub** is a partial implementation of components on which the tested component depends. A **test driver** is a partial implementation of a component that depends on the tested component. Test stubs and drivers enable components to be isolated from the rest of the system for testing.
- A **correction** is a change to a component. The purpose of a correction is to repair a fault. Note that a correction can introduce new faults [Brooks, 1975].

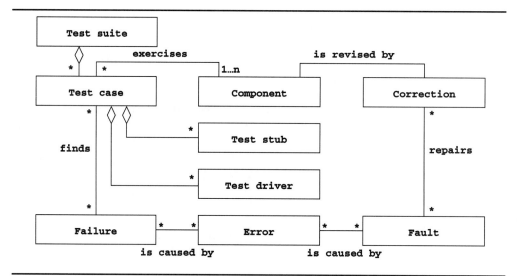

Figure 9-3　Model elements used during testing (UML class diagram).

9.3.1 Faults, Errors, and Failures

With the initial understanding of the terms from the definitions in Section 9.3, let's take a look at Figure 9-4.

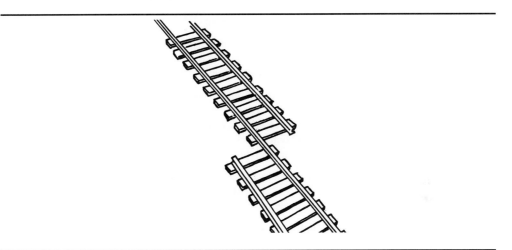

Figure 9-4 An example of a fault.

What do you see? Figure 9-4 shows a pair of tracks that are not aligned with each other. If we envision a train running over the tracks it would crash (fail). However, the figure actually does not present a failure nor an error nor a fault. It does not show a failure, because the expected behavior has not been specified nor is there any observed behavior. Figure 9-4 also does not show an error, because that would mean that the system is in a state that further processing will lead to a failure. We only see tracks here; no moving train is shown. To speak about error and failure, we need to compare the desired behavior (described in the use case in the RAD) with the observed behavior (described by the test case). Assume that we have a use case with a train moving from the upper left track to the lower right track (Figure 9-5).

Use case name	`DriveTrain`
Participating actor	`TrainOperator`
Entry condition	`Driver` pushes the "StartTrain" button at the control panel.
Flow of events	1. The train starts moving on track 1. 2. The trains transitions to track 2.
Exit condition	The train is running on track 2.
Special requirements	none

Figure 9-5 Use case `DriveTrain` specifying the expected behavior of the train.

Test-case identifier	`DriveTrain`
Test location	http://www12.in.tum.de/TrainSystem/test-cases/test1
Feature to be tested	Continuous operation of engine for 5 seconds
Feature Pass/Fail Criteria	The test passes if the train drives for 5 seconds and covers the length of at least two tracks.
Means of control	1. The `StartTrain()` method is called via a test driver `StartTrain` (contained in the same directory as the `DriveTrain` test).
Data	2. Direction of trip and duration are read from a input file http://www12.in.tum.de/TrainSystem/test-cases/input 3. If debug is set to TRUE, then the test case will output the system messages "Enter Track n, Exit Track n" for each n, where n is the number of the current track.
Test Procedure	The test is started by double-clicking the test case at the specified location. The test will run without further intervention until completion. The test should take no more than 7 seconds.
Special requirements	The test stub `Engine` is needed for the track implementation.

Figure 9-6   Test case `DriveTrain` for the use case described in Figure 9-5.

We can then proceed to derive a test case that moves the train from the state described in the entry condition of the use case to a state where it will crash, namely when it is leaving the upper track (Figure 9-6).

In other words, when executing this test case, we can demonstrate that the system contains a fault. Note, that the current state shown in Figure 9-7 is erroneous but does not show a failure.

The misalignment of the tracks can be a result of bad communication between the development teams (each track had to be positioned by one team) or because of a wrong implementation of the specification by one of the teams (Figure 9-8). Both of these are examples of algorithmic faults. You are probably already familiar with many other algorithmic faults that are introduced during the implementation phase. For example, "Exiting a loop too soon," "exiting a loop too late," "testing for the wrong condition," "forgetting to initialize a variable" are all implementation-specific algorithmic faults. Algorithmic faults can also occur during analysis and system design. Stress and overload problems, for example, are design specific algorithmic faults that lead to failure when data structures are filled beyond their specified capacity. Throughput and performance errors are possible when a system does not perform at the speed specified by the nonfunctional requirements.

Figure 9-7   An example of an error.

Figure 9-8   A fault can have an algorithmic cause.

Figure 9-9   A fault can have a mechanical cause, such as an earthquake.

Even if the tracks are implemented according to the specification in the RAD, they could still end up misaligned during daily operation; for example, if an earthquake happens that moves the underlying soil (Figure 9-9).

An error in the virtual machine of a software system is another example of a mechanical fault: Even if the developers have done the correct implementation, that is, they have mapped the object model correctly onto the code, the observed behavior can still deviate from the specified behavior. In concurrent engineering projects, for example, where hardware is developed in parallel with software, we cannot always make the assumption that the virtual machine executes as specified. Other examples of mechanical faults are power failures. Note the relativity of the terms "fault" and "failure" with respect to a particular system component: The failure in one system component (the power system) is the mechanical fault that can lead to failure in another system component (the software system).

9.3.2   Test Cases

A **test case** is a set of input data and expected results that exercises a component with the purpose of causing failures and detecting faults. A test case has five attributes: `name`, `location`, `input`, `oracle`, and `log` (Table 9-1). The `name` of the test case allows the tester to distinguish between different test cases. A heuristic for naming test cases is to derive the name from the requirement it is testing or from the component being tested. For example, if you are testing a use case *Deposit()*, you might want to call the test case *Test_Deposit*. If a test case involves two components A and B, a good name would be *Test_AB*. The `location` attribute describes where

Table 9-1 Attributes of the class `TestCase`.

Attributes	Description
name	Name of test case
location	Full path name of executable
input	Input data or commands
oracle	Expected test results against which the output of the test is compared
log	Output produced by the test

the test case can be found. It should be either the pathname or the URL to the executable of the test program and its inputs.

`Input` describes the set of input data or commands to be entered by the actor of the test case (which can be the tester or a test driver). The expected behavior of the test case is the sequence of output data or commands that a correct execution of the test should yield. The expected behavior is described by the `oracle` attribute. The `log` is a set of time-stamped correlations of the observed behavior with the expected behavior for various test runs.

Once test cases are identified and described, relationships among test cases are identified. Aggregation and the `precede` associations are used to describe the relationships between the test cases. Aggregation is used when a test case can be decomposed into a set of subtests. Two test cases are related via the `precede` association when one test case must precede another test case.

Figure 9-10 shows a test model where `TestA` must precede `TestB` and `TestC`. For example, `TestA` consists of `TestA1` and `TestA2`, meaning that once `TestA1` and `TestA2` are tested, `TestA` is tested; there is not separate test for `TestA`. A good test model has as few associations as possible, because tests that are not associated with each other can be executed independently from each other. This allows a tester to speed up testing, if the necessary testing

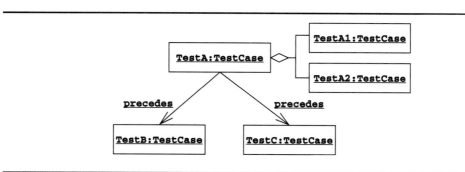

Figure 9-10 Test model with test cases. `TestA` consists of two tests, `TestA1` and `TestA2`. `TestB` and `TestC` can be tested independently, but only after `TestA` has been performed.

resources are available. In Figure 9-10, `TestB` and `TestC` can be tested in parallel, because there is no relation between them.

Test cases are classified into blackbox tests and whitebox tests, depending on which aspect of the system model is tested. **Blackbox tests** focus on the input/output behavior of the component. Black-box tests do not deal with the internal aspects of the component nor with the behavior or the structure of the components. **Whitebox tests** focus on the internal structure of the component. A whitebox test makes sure that, independently from the particular input/output behavior, every state in the dynamic model of the object and every interaction among the objects are tested. As a result, whitebox testing goes beyond blackbox testing. In fact, most of the whitebox tests require input data that could not be derived from a description of the functional requirements alone. Unit testing combines both testing techniques: blackbox testing to test the functionality of the component and whitebox testing to test structural and dynamic aspects of the component.

9.3.3   Test Stubs and Drivers

Executing test cases on single components or combinations of components requires the tested component to be isolated from the rest of the system. Test drivers and test stubs are used to substitute for missing parts of the system. A **test driver** simulates the part of the system calling the component under test. A test driver passes the test inputs identified in the test case analysis to the component and displays the results.

A **test stub** simulates components that are called by the tested component. The test stub must provide the same API as the method of the simulated component and must return a value compliant with the return result type of the method's type signature. Note that the interface of all components must be baselined. If the interface of a component changes, the corresponding test drivers and stubs must change as well.

The Bridge pattern can be used for the implementation of test stubs. Figure 9-11 shows a Bridge pattern where a `User Interface` subsystem accesses the `Database` subsystem that is not yet available for testing. By separating the `Database` interface from the `Database`

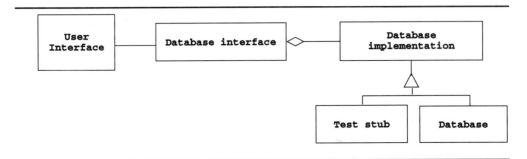

Figure 9-11   Use of the Bridge design pattern to interface to a component that is not yet complete, not yet known or unavailable during testing of another component (UML class diagram).

implementation, we can first provide a test stub responding to the request and later replace it with the actual implementation of the Database subsystem. Note that the use of the Bridge pattern allows the replacement of the stub by the called component once it is tested, without recompiling the calling component.

The implementation of test stubs is a nontrivial task. It is not sufficient to write a test stub that simply prints a message stating that the test stub was called. In most situations, when component A calls component B, A is expecting B to perform some work, which is then returned as a set of result parameters. If the test stub does not simulate this behavior, A will fail, not because of a fault in A, but because the test stub does not simulate B correctly.

But even providing a return value is not always sufficient. For example, if a test stub always returns the same value, it might not return the value expected by the calling component in a particular scenario. This can produce confusing results and even lead to the failure of the calling component, even though it is correctly implemented. Often, there is a trade-off between implementing accurate test stubs and substituting the test stubs by the actual component.

9.3.4   Corrections

Once tests have been executed and failures have been detected, developers change the component to eliminate the suspected faults. A **correction** is a change to a component whose purpose is to repair a fault. Corrections can range from a simple modification to a single component to a complete redesign of a data structure or a subsystem. In all cases, the likelihood that the developer introduces new faults into the revised component is high [Brooks, 1975]. Several techniques can be used to handle such faults:

- *Problem tracking* includes the documentation of each failure, error, and fault detected, its correction, and the revisions of the components involved in the change. Together with configuration management, problem tracking enables developers to narrow down the search for new faults. We describe configuration management in more detail in Chapter 10, *Software Configuration Management*.

- *Regression testing* includes the reexecution of all prior tests after a change. This ensures that functionality that worked before the correction has not been affected. Regression testing is important in object-oriented methods, which call for an iterative development process. This requires testing to be initiated earlier and for test suites to be maintained as the design evolves. Regression testing unfortunately is costly, especially when part of the tests is not automated. We describe regression testing in more detail in the next section.

- *Rationale maintenance* includes the documentation of the rationale of the change and its relationship with the rationale of the revised component. Rationale maintenance enables developers to avoid introducing new faults by inspecting the assumptions that were used to build the component. We described rationale maintenance in Chapter 8, *Rationale Management*.

Next, let us describe in more detail the testing activities that lead to the creation of test cases, their execution, and the development of corrections.

9.4 Testing Activities

In this section, we describe the activities of testing. These include:

- **Inspecting components**, which finds faults in an individual component through the manual inspection of its source code
- **Unit testing**, which finds faults by isolating an individual component using test stubs and drivers and by exercising the component using a test case
- **Integration testing**, which finds faults by integrating several components together
- **System testing**, which focuses on the complete system, its functional and nonfunctional requirements, and its target environment

9.4.1   Inspecting Components

Inspections find faults in a component by reviewing its source code in a formal meeting. Inspections can be conducted before or after the unit test. The first structured inspection process was Michael Fagan's Inspection method [Fagan, 1976]. The inspection is conducted by a team of developers, including the author of the component, a moderator who facilitates the process, and one or more reviewers who find faults in the component. Fagan's Inspection method consists of five steps:

- **Overview**. The author of the component briefly presents the purpose and scope of the component and the goals of the inspection.
- **Preparation**. The reviewers become familiar with the implementation of the component.
- **Inspection meeting**. A reader paraphrases the source code of the component and the inspection team raise issues with the component. A moderator keeps the meeting on track.
- **Rework**. The author revises the component.
- **Follow-up**. The moderator checks the quality of the rework and determines the component that needs to be reinspected.

The critical steps in this process are the preparation phase and the inspection meeting. During the preparation phase, the reviewers become familiar with the source code; they do not yet focus on finding faults. During the inspection meeting, the reader paraphrases the source code, that is, he reads each source code statement and explains what the statement should do. The reviewers then raise issues if they think there is a fault. Most of the time is spent debating whether or not a fault is present, but solutions to repair the fault are not explored at this point. During the overview phase of the inspection, the author states the objectives of the inspection. In addition to finding faults, reviewers may also be asked to look for deviations from coding standards or for inefficiencies.

Fagan's inspections are usually perceived as being time-consuming because of the length of the preparation and inspection meeting phase. The effectiveness of a review also depends on the preparation of the reviewers. David Parnas proposed a revised inspection process, the active design review, in which there is no inspection meeting that includes all inspection team members [Parnas & Weiss, 1985]. Instead, reviewers are asked to find faults during the preparation phase. At the end of the preparation phase, each reviewer fills a questionnaire testing his or her understanding of the component. The author then meets individually with each reviewer to collect feedback on the component.

Both Fagan's inspections and the active design reviews have been shown to usually be more effective than testing in uncovering faults. Both testing and inspections are used in safety-critical projects, as they tend to find different types of faults.

9.4.2   Unit Testing

Unit testing focuses on the building blocks of the software system, that is, objects and subsystems. There are three motivations behind focusing on components. First, unit testing reduces the complexity of the overall test activities, allowing us to focus on smaller units of the system. Second, unit testing makes it easier to pinpoint and correct faults, given that few components are involved in the test. Third, unit testing allows parallelism in the testing activities; that is, each component can be tested independently of one another.

The specific candidates for unit testing are chosen from the object model and the system decomposition of the system. In principle, all the objects developed during the development process should be tested, which is often not feasible because of time and budget reasons. The minimal set of objects to be tested should be those objects that are participating objects in use cases. Subsystems should be tested after each of the objects/classes within that subsystem have been tested individually.

Existing subsystems, which were reused or purchased, should be treated as components with unknown internal structure. This applies in particular to commercially available subsystems, where the internal structure is not known or available to the developer.

Many unit testing techniques have been devised. Below, we describe the most important ones: equivalence testing, boundary testing, path testing, and state-based testing.

Equivalence testing

Equivalence testing is a blackbox testing technique that minimizes the number of test cases. The possible inputs are partitioned into equivalence classes, and a test case is selected for each class. The assumption of equivalence testing is that systems usually behave in similar ways for all members of a class. To test the behavior associated with an equivalence class, we only need to test one member of the class. Equivalence testing consists of two steps: identification of the equivalence classes and selection of the test inputs. The following criteria are used in determining the equivalence classes.

- **Coverage**. Every possible input belongs to one of the equivalence classes.
- **Disjointedness**. No input belongs to more than one equivalence class.
- **Representation**. If the execution demonstrates an error when a particular member of a equivalence class is used as input, then the same error can be detected by using any other member of the class as input.

For each equivalence class, at least two pieces of data are selected: a typical input, which exercises the common case, and an invalid input, which exercises the exception handling capabilities of the component. After all equivalence classes have been identified, a test input for each class has to be identified that covers the equivalence class. If there is a possibility that not all the elements of the equivalence class are covered by the test input, the equivalence class must be split into smaller equivalence classes, and test inputs must be identified for each of the new classes.

For example, consider a method that returns the number of days in a month, given the month and year (see Figure 9-12). The month and year are specified as integers. By convention, 1 represents the month of January, 2 the month of February, and so on. The range of valid inputs for the year is 0 to maxInt.

```
class MyGregorianCalendar {
    ...
    public static int getNumDaysInMonth(int month, int year) {…}
    ...
}
```

Figure 9-12 Interface for a method computing the number of days in a given month (Java). The getNumDaysInMonth() method takes two parameters, a month and a year, both specified as integers.

We find three equivalence classes for the month parameter: months with 31 days (i.e., 1, 3, 5, 7, 8, 10, 12), months with 30 days (i.e., 4, 6, 9, 11), and February, which can have 28 or 29 days. Nonpositive integers and integers larger than 12 are invalid values for the month parameters. Similarly, we find two equivalence classes for the year: leap years and non–leap years. By specification, negative integers are invalid values for the year. First we select one valid value for each parameter and equivalence class (e.g., February, June, July, 1901, and 1904). Given that the return value of the getNumDaysInMonth() method depends on both parameters, we combine these values to test for interaction, resulting into the six equivalence classes displayed in Table 9-2.

Boundary testing

Boundary testing is a special case of equivalence testing and focuses on the conditions at the boundary of the equivalence classes. Rather than selecting any element in the equivalence class, boundary testing requires that the elements be selected from the "edges" of the

Table 9-2 Equivalence classes and selected valid inputs for testing the getNumDaysInMonth() method.

Equivalence class	Value for month input	Value for year input
Months with 31 days, non–leap years	7 (July)	1901
Months with 31 days, leap years	7 (July)	1904
Months with 30 days, non–leap years	6 (June)	1901
Month with 30 days, leap year	6 (June)	1904
Month with 28 or 29 days, non–leap year	2 (February)	1901
Month with 28 or 29 days, leap year	2 (February)	1904

equivalence class. The assumption behind boundary testing is that developers often overlook special cases at the boundary of the equivalence classes (e.g., 0, empty strings, year 2000).

In our example, the month of February presents several boundary cases. In general, years that are multiple of 4 are leap years. Years that are multiples of 100, however, are not leap years, unless they are also multiple of 400. For example, 2000 is a leap year whereas 1900 was not. Both year 1900 and 2000 are good boundary cases we should test for. Other boundary cases include the months 0 and 13, which are at the boundaries of the invalid equivalence class. Table 9-3 displays the additional boundary cases we selected for the getNumDaysInMonth() method.

Table 9-3 Additional boundary cases selected for the getNumDaysInMonth() method.

Equivalence class	Value for month input	Value for year input
Leap years divisible by 400	2 (February)	2000
Non–leap years divisible by 100	2 (February)	1900
Nonpositive invalid months	0	1291
Positive invalid months	13	1315

A disadvantage of equivalence class and boundary testing is that these techniques do not explore combinations of test input data. In many cases, a program fails because a combination of certain values causes the error. Cause-effect testing addresses this problem by establishing logical relationship between input and outputs or inputs and transformations. The inputs are called causes, the output or transformations are effects. The technique is based on the premise that the input/output behavior can be transformed into a boolean function. For details on this technique and another technique called error guessing, we refer you to the literature on testing (for example [Myers, 1979]).

Path testing

Path testing is a whitebox testing technique that identifies faults in the implementation of the component. The assumption behind path testing is that, by exercising all possible paths through the code at least once, most faults will trigger failures. The identification of paths requires knowledge of the source code and datastructures.

The starting point for path testing is the flow graph. A flow graph consists of nodes representing executable blocks and associations representing flow of control. A basic block is a number of statements between two decisions. A flow graph can be constructed from the code of a component by mapping decision statements (e.g., if statements, while loops) to nodes lines. Statements between each decision point (e.g., then block, else block) are mapped to other nodes. Associations between each node represent the precedence relationships. Figure 9-14 depicts an example implementation of the `getNumDaysInMonth()` method. Figure 9-13 depicts the equivalent flow graph as a UML activity diagram. In this example, we model decision points with UML branches, blocks with UML action states, and control flow with UML transitions.

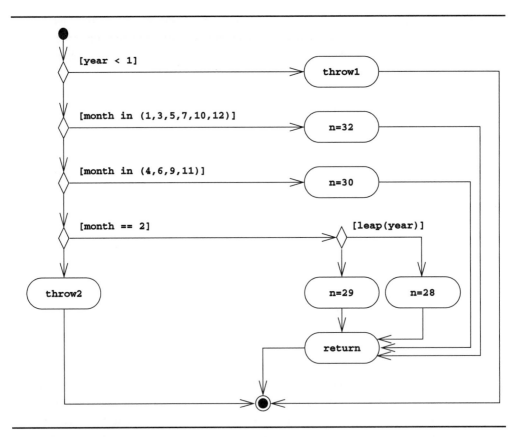

Figure 9-13 Equivalent flow graph for the `getNumDaysInMonth()` method implementation of Figure 9-14 (UML activity diagram).

```
public class MonthOutOfBounds extends Exception {…};
public class YearOutOfBounds extends Exception {…};

class MyGregorianCalendar {
    public static boolean isLeapYear(int year) {
        boolean leap;
        if (year%4) {
            leap = true;
        } else {
            leap = false;
        }
        return leap;
    }

    public static int getNumDaysInMonth(int month, int year)
            throws MonthOutOfBounds, YearOutOfBounds {
        int numDays;
        if (year < 1) {
            throw new YearOutOfBounds(year);
        }
        if (month == 1 || month == 3 || month == 5 || month == 7 ||
                month == 10 || month == 12) {
            numDays = 32;
        }
        else if (month == 4 || month == 6 || month == 9 || month == 11) {
            numDays = 30;
        }
        else if (month == 2) {
            if (isLeapYear(year)) {
                numDays = 29;
            }
            else {
                numDays = 28;
            }
        }
        else {
            throw new MonthOutOfBounds(month);
        }
        return numDays;
    }
...
}
```

Figure 9-14 An example of a (faulty) implementation of the getNumDaysInMonth() method (Java).

Complete path testing consists of designing test cases such that each transition in the activity diagram is traversed at least once. This is done by examining the condition associated with each branch point and selecting an input for the true branch and another input for the false branch. For example, examining the first branch point in Figure 9-13, we select two inputs: year=0 (such that year < 1 is true) and year=1901 (such that year < 1 is false).

We then repeat the process for the second branch and select the inputs `month=1` and `month=2`. The input `(year=0, month=1)` produces the path `{throw1}`. The input `(year=1901, month=1)` produces a second complete path `{n=32 return}`, which uncovers one of the faults in the `getNumDaysInMonth()` method. By repeating this process for each node, we generate the test cases and equivalent paths depicted in Table 9-4.

Table 9-4 Test cases and their corresponding path for the activity diagram depicted in Figure 9-13.

Test case	Path
`(year = 0, month = 1)`	`{throw1}`
`(year = 1901, month = 1)`	`{n=32 return}`
`(year = 1901, month = 2)`	`{n=28 return}`
`(year = 1904, month = 2)`	`{n=29 return}`
`(year = 1901, month = 4)`	`{n=30 return}`
`(year = 1901, month = 0)`	`{throw2}`

We can similarly construct the activity diagram for the method `isLeapYear()` and derive test cases to exercise the single branch point of this method (Figure 9-15). Note that the test case `(year = 1901, month = 2)` of the `getNumDaysInMonth()` method already exercises one of the paths of the `isLeapYear()` method. By systematically constructing tests to cover all the paths of all methods, we can deal with the complexity associated with a large number of methods.

Using graph theory, it can be shown that the minimum number of tests necessary to cover all edges is equal to the number of independent paths through the flow graph [McCabe, 1976]. This is defined as the cyclomatic complexity `CC` of the flow graph, which is

```
CC = number of edges - number of nodes + 2
```

where the number of nodes is the number of branches and action states, and the number of edges are the number of transitions in the activity diagram. The cyclomatic complexity of the `getNumDaysInMonth()` method is 6, which is also the number of test cases we found in Figure 9-4. Similarly, the cyclomatic complexity of the `isLeapYear()` method, and the number of derived test cases is 2.

By comparing the test cases we derived from the equivalence classes (Table 9-2) and boundary cases (Table 9-3) with the test cases we derived from the flow graph (Figure 9-4 and Figure 9-15), several differences can be noted. In both cases, we test the method extensively for computations involving the month of February. However, because the implementation of `isLeapYear()` does not take into account years divisible by 100, path testing did not generate any test case for this equivalence class.

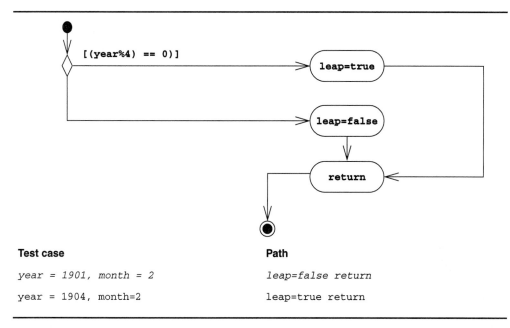

Test case	Path
year = 1901, month = 2	*leap=false return*
year = 1904, month=2	leap=true return

Figure 9-15 Equivalent flow graph for the (faulty) isLeapYear() method implementation of Figure 9-14 (UML activity diagram) and derived tests. The test in *italic* is redundant with a test we derived for the getNumDaysInMonth() method.

The path testing technique was developed for imperative languages. Object-oriented languages introduce several difficulties when using path testing:

- **Polymorphism**. Polymorphism enables messages to be bound to different methods based on the class of the target. Although this enables developers to reuse code across a larger number of classes, it also introduces more cases to test. All possible bindings should be identified and tested.
- **Shorter methods**. Methods in object-oriented languages have a tendency to be shorter than procedures and functions in imperative languages. This decreases the likelihood of control flow faults, which can be uncovered using the path testing technique. Instead, algorithms are implemented across several methods, which are distributed across a larger number of objects and need to be tested together.

In general, path testing and whitebox methods can only detect faults resulting by exercising a path in the program, such as the faulty numDays=32 statement. Whitebox testing methods cannot detect omissions, such as the failure to handle the non–leap year 1900. Path testing is also heavily based on the control structure of the program: Faults associated with violating invariants of data structures, such as accessing an array out of bounds, are not explicitly addressed. However, no testing method short of exhaustive testing can guarantee the discovery of all faults. In our example, neither the equivalence testing or the path testing method uncovered the fault associated with the month of August.

State-based testing

Object-oriented languages introduce the opportunity for new types of faults in object-oriented systems. Polymorphism, dynamic binding, and the distribution of functionality across a larger number of smaller methods can reduce the effectiveness of static techniques such as inspections [Binder, 1994].

State-based testing [Turner & Robson, 1993] is a recent testing technique, which focuses on object-oriented systems. Most testing techniques focus on selecting a number of test inputs for a given state of the system, exercising a component or a system, and comparing the observed outputs with an oracle. State-based testing, however, focuses on comparing the resulting state of the system with the expected state. In the context of a class, state-based testing consists of deriving test cases from the UML statechart diagram for the class. For each state, a representative set of stimuli is derived for each transition (similar to equivalence testing). The attributes of the class are then instrumented and tested after each stimuli has been applied to ensure that the class has reached the specified state.

For example, Figure 9-16 depicts a statechart diagram and its associated tests for the 2Bwatch we described in Chapter 2, *Modeling with UML*. It specifies which stimuli change the watch from the high-level state MeasureTime to the high-level state SetTime. It does not show the low-level states of the watch when the date and time changes, either because of actions of the user or because of time passing. The test inputs in Figure 9-16 were generated such that each transition is traversed at least once. After each input, instrumentation code checks if the watch is in the predicted state and reports a failure otherwise. Note that some transitions (e.g., transition 3) are traversed several times, as it is necessary to put the watch back into the SetTime state (e.g., to test transitions 4, 5, and 6). Only the first eight stimuli are displayed. The test inputs for the DeadBattery state were not generated.

Currently, state-based testing presents several difficulties. Because the state of a class is encapsulated, test sequences must include sequences for putting classes in the desired state before given transitions can be tested. State-based testing also requires the instrumentation of class attributes. Although state-based testing is currently not part of the state of the practice, it promises to become an effective testing technique for object-oriented systems once proper automation is provided.

9.4.3   Integration Testing

Unit testing focuses on individual components. The developer discovers faults using equivalence testing, boundary testing, path testing, and other methods. Once faults in each component have been removed and the test cases do not reveal any new fault, components are ready to be integrated into larger subsystems. At this point, components are still likely to contain faults, as test stubs and drivers used during unit testing are only approximations of the

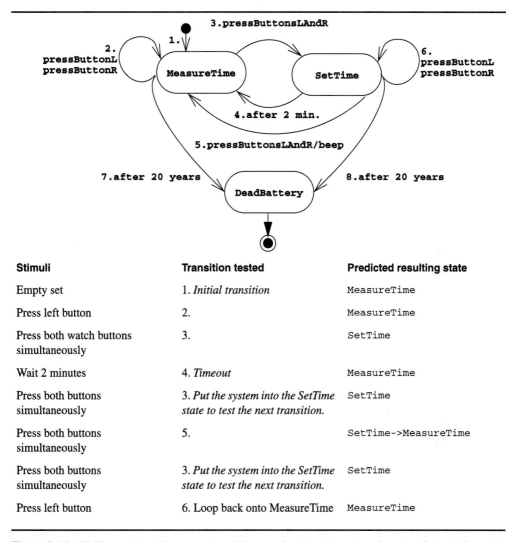

Figure 9-16 UML statechart diagram and resulting tests for 2Bwatch set time function. Only the first eight stimuli are shown.

components they simulate. Moreover, unit testing does not reveal faults associated with the component interfaces resulting from invalid assumptions when calling these interfaces.

Integration testing detects faults that have not been detected during unit testing, by focusing on small groups of components. Two or more components are integrated and tested, and once tests do not reveal any new faults, additional components are added to the group. This procedure allows the testing of increasingly more complex parts of the system while keeping the location of potential faults relatively small (i.e., the most recently added component is usually the one that triggers the most recently discovered faults).

Developing test stubs and drivers for a systematic integration test is time-consuming. The order in which components are tested, however, can influence the total effort required by the integration test. A careful ordering of components can reduce the overall resources needed for the overall integration test. In this section, we focus on different integration testing strategies for ordering the components to be tested.

Integration testing strategies

Several approaches have been devised to implement an integration testing strategy:

- big bang testing
- bottom-up testing
- top-down testing
- sandwich testing

Each of these strategies has been devised originally by assuming that the system decomposition is hierarchical, that each of the components belong to hierarchical layers ordered with respect to the "Call" association. These strategies, however, can be easily adapted to nonhierarchical system decompositions. Figure 9-17 shows a hierarchical system decomposition that we use for discussing these integration testing strategies.

The **big bang testing** strategy assumes that all components are first tested individually and then tested together as a single system. The advantage is that no additional test stubs or drivers are needed. Although this strategy sounds simple, big bang testing is expensive: If a test uncovers a failure, it is difficult to pinpoint the specific component (or combination of components) responsible for the failure. In addition, it is impossible to distinguish failures in the interface from failures within a component.

The **bottom-up testing** strategy first individually tests each component of the bottom layer and then integrates them with components of the next layer up. If two components are tested together, we call this a **double test**. Testing three components together is a **triple test** and a test with four components is called a **quadruple test**. This is repeated until all components from all layers are combined together. Test drivers are used to simulate the components of higher layers that have not yet been integrated. Note that no test stubs are necessary during bottom-up testing.

The **top-down testing** strategy unit tests the components of the top layer first and then integrates the components of the next layer down. When all components of the new layer have been tested together, the next layer is selected. Again, the tests incrementally add one component after the other to the test. This is repeated until all layers are combined and involved in the test. Test stubs are used to simulate the components of lower layers that have not yet been integrated. Note that test drivers are not needed during top-down testing.

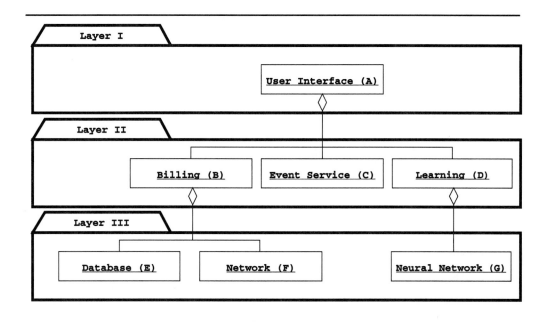

Figure 9-17   Example of a hierarchal system decomposition with three layers (UML class diagram, layers represented by packages).

The advantage of bottom-up testing is that interface faults can be more easily found: When the developers substitute a test driver by a higher level component, they have a clear model of how the lower level component works and of the assumptions embedded in its interface. If the higher level component violates assumptions made in the lower level component, developers are more likely to find them quickly. The disadvantage of bottom-up testing is that it tests the most important subsystems, namely the components of the user interface, last. First, faults found in the top layer may often lead to changes in the subsystem decomposition or in the subsystem interfaces of lower layers, invalidating previous tests. Second, tests of the top layer can be derived from the requirements model and, thus, are more effective in finding faults that are visible to the user.

The advantage of top-down testing is that it starts with user interface components. The same set of tests, derived from the requirements, can be used in testing the increasingly more complex set of subsystems. The disadvantage of top-down testing is that the development of test stubs is time consuming and prone to error. A large number of stubs is usually required for testing nontrivial systems, especially when the lowest level of the system decomposition implements many methods.

Figure 9-18 illustrates the possible combinations of subsystems that can be used during integration testing. Using a bottom-up strategy, subsystems E, F, and G are united tested first, then the triple test B, E, F and the double test D, G are executed, and so on. Using a top-down

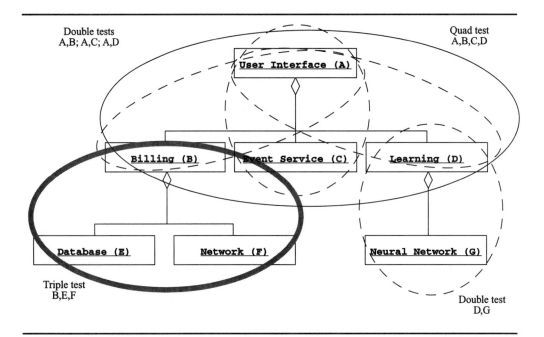

Figure 9-18   Test coverage of integration test. The test case shown cover all possible dependencies in the subsystem decomposition.

strategy, subsystem A is unit tested, then double tests, A,B, A,C, and A,D are executed, then the quad test A,B,C,D is executed, and so on. Both strategies cover the same number of subsystem dependencies but exercise them in different order.

The **sandwich testing** strategy combines the top-down and bottom-up strategies, attempting to make use of the best of both strategies. During sandwich testing, the tester must be able to reformulate or map the subsystem decomposition into three layers, a target layer ("the meat"), a layer above the target layer ("the bread above"), and a layer below the target layer ("the bread below"). Using the target layer as the focus of attention, top-down testing and bottom-up testing can now be done in parallel. Top-down integration testing is done by testing the top layer incrementally with the components of the target layer, and bottom-up testing is used for testing the bottom layer incremental with the components of the target layer. As a result, test stubs and drivers need not be written for the top and bottom layers, because they use the actual components from the target layer.

Note that this also allows early testing of the user interface components. There is one problem with sandwich testing: It does not thoroughly test the individual components of the target layer before integration. For example, the sandwich test shown in Figure 9-19 does not unit test component C of the target layer.

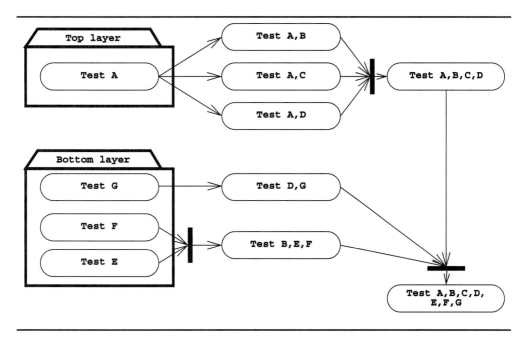

Figure 9-19   Sandwich testing strategy (UML activity diagram). None of the components in the target layer (i.e, B, C, D) are unit tested.

The **modified sandwich testing** strategy tests the three layers individually before combining them in incremental tests with one another. The individual layer tests consists of a group of three tests:

- a top layer test with stubs for the target layer

- a target layer test with drivers and stubs replacing the top and bottom layers

- a bottom layer test with a driver for the target layer

The combined layer tests consist of two tests:

- The top layer accesses the target layer (this test can reuse the target layer tests from the individual layer tests, replacing the drivers with components from the top layer).

- The bottom layer is accessed by the target layer (this test can reuse the target layer tests from the individual layer tests, replacing the stub with components from the bottom layer).

The advantage of modified sandwich testing is that many testing activities can be performed in parallel, as indicated by the activity diagrams of Figures 9-19 and 9-20. The disadvantage of modified sandwich testing is the need for additional test stubs and drivers. Overall, modified sandwich testing leads to a significantly shorter overall testing time when compared with top-down and bottom-up testing.

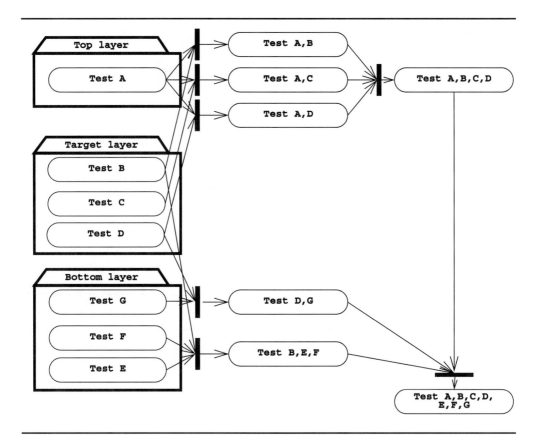

Figure 9-20 An example of modified sandwich testing strategy (UML activity diagrams). The components of the target layer are unit tested before they are integrated with the top and bottom layers.

9.4.4   System Testing

Unit and integration testing focus on finding faults in individual components and the interfaces between the components. Once components have been integrated, system testing ensures that the complete system complies with the functional and nonfunctional requirements of the system. There are several system testing activities that are performed:

- **Functional testing**. Test of functional requirements (from RAD)
- **Performance testing**. Test of nonfunctional requirements (from SDD)
- **Pilot testing**. Tests of common functionality among a selected group of end users in the target environment
- **Acceptance testing.** Usability, functional, and performance tests performed by the customer in the development environment against acceptance criteria (from Project Agreement)

- **Installation testing**. Usability, functional, and performance tests performed by the customer in the target environment. If the system is only installed at a small selected set of customers it is called a *beta test*.

Functional testing

Functional testing, also called requirements testing, finds differences between the functional requirements and the system. System testing is a blackbox technique: Test cases are derived from the use case model. In systems with complex functional requirements, it is usually not possible to test all use cases for all valid and invalid inputs. The goal of the tester is to select those tests that are relevant to the user and have a high probability of uncovering a failure. Note that functional testing is different from usability testing (described in Chapter 4, *Requirements Elicitation*), which also focuses on the use case model. Functional testing finds differences between the use case model and the observed system behavior, usability testing finds differences between the use case model and the user's expectation of the system.

To identify functional tests, we inspect the use case model and identify use case instances that are likely to cause failures. This is done using blackbox techniques similar to equivalence testing and boundary testing (see Section 9.4.2). Test cases should exercise both common and exceptional use cases. For example, consider the use case model for a subway ticket distributor (see Figure 9-21). The common case functionality is modeled by the `PurchaseTicket` use case, describing the steps necessary for a `Passenger` to successfully purchase a ticket. The `TimeOut`, `Cancel`, `OutOfOrder`, and `NoChange` use cases describe various exceptional conditions resulting from the state of the distributor or actions by the `Passenger`.

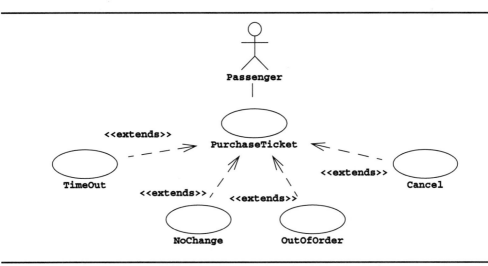

Figure 9-21   An example of use case model for a subway ticket distributor (UML use case diagram).

Figure 9-22 depicts the `PurchaseTicket` use case describing the normal interaction between the `Passenger` actor and the `Distributor`. We notice that three features of the `Distributor` are likely to fail and should be tested:

1. The `Passenger` may press multiple zone buttons before inserting money, in which case the `Distributor` should display the amount of the last zone

2. The `Passenger` may select another zone button after beginning to insert money, in which case the `Distributor` should return all money inserted by the `Passenger`

3. The `Passenger` may insert more money than needed, in which case the `Distributor` should return the correct change.

Use case name	`PurchaseTicket`
Entry condition	The `Passenger` is standing in front of ticket `Distributor`. The `Passenger` has sufficient money to purchase ticket.
Flow of events	1. The `Passenger` selects the number of zones to be traveled. If the `Passenger` presses multiple zone buttons, only the last button pressed is considered by the `Distributor`.
	2. The `Distributor` displays the amount due.
	3. The `Passenger` inserts money.
	4. If the `Passenger` selects a new zone before inserting sufficient money, the `Distributor` returns all the coins and bills inserted by the `Passenger`.
	5. If the `Passenger` inserted more money than the amount due, the `Distributor` returns excess change.
	6. The `Distributor` issues ticket.
	7. The `Passenger` picks up the change and the ticket.
Exit condition	The `Passenger` has the selected ticket.

Figure 9-22   An example of use case from the ticket distributor use case model: `PurchaseTicket`.

Figure 9-23 depicts the test case `PurchaseTicket_CommonCase`, which exercises these three features. Note that the flow of events describes both the inputs to the system (stimuli that the `Passenger` sends to the `Distributor`) and desired outputs (correct responses from the `Distributor`). Similar test cases can also be derived for the exceptional use cases `NoChange`, `OutOfOrder`, `TimeOut`, and `Cancel`.

Test cases, such as `PurchaseTicket_CommonCase`, are derived for all use cases, including use cases representing exceptional behavior. Test cases are associated with the use

Test case name	`PurchaseTicket_CommonCase`
Entry condition	The `Passenger` standing in front of ticket `Distributor`. The `Passenger` has two $5 bills and three dimes.
Flow of events	1. The `Passenger` presses in succession the zone buttons 2, 4, 1, and 2.
	2. The `Distributor` should display in succession $1.25, $2.25, $0.75, and $1.25.
	3. The `Passenger` inserts a $5 bill.
	4. The `Distributor` returns three $1 bills and three quarters and issues a 2-zone ticket.
	5. The `Passenger` repeats steps 1–4 using his second $5 bill.
	6. The `Passenger` repeats steps 1–3 using four quarters and three dimes. The `Distributor` issues a 2-zone ticket and returns a nickel.
	7. The `Passenger` selects zone 1 and inserts a dollar bill. The `Distributor` issues a 1-zone ticket and returns a quarter.
	8. The `Passenger` selects zone 4 and inserts two $1 bill and a quarter. The `Distributor` issues a 4-zone ticket.
	9. The `Passenger` selects zone 4. The `Distributor` displays $2.25. The `Passenger` inserts a 1$ bill and a nickel, and selects zone 2. The `Distributor` returns the $1 bill and the nickel and display $1.25.
Exit condition	The `Passenger` has three 2-zone tickets, one 1-zone ticket, and one 4-zone ticket.

Figure 9-23 An example of test case derived from the `PurchaseTicket` use case.

cases from which they are derived, making it easier to update the test cases when use cases are modified.

Performance testing

Performance testing finds differences between the design goals selected during system design and the system. Because the design goals are derived from the nonfunctional requirements, the test cases can be derived from the SDD or from the RAD. The following tests are performed during performance testing.

- **Stress testing** checks if the system can respond to many simultaneous requests. For example, if an information system for car dealers is required to interface to 6000 dealers, the stress test evaluates how the system performs with more than 6000 simultaneous users.
- **Volume testing** attempts to find faults associated with large amounts of data, such as static limits imposed by the data structure, or high-complexity algorithms, or high disk fragmentation.

- **Security testing** attempts to find security faults in the system. There are few systematic methods for finding security faults. Usually this test is accomplished by "tiger teams" who attempt to break into the system, using their experience and knowledge of typical security flaws.
- **Timing tests** attempts to find behaviors that violate timing constraints described by the nonfunctional requirements.
- **Recovery tests** evaluate the ability of the system to recover from errors, such as the unavailability of resources, a hardware failure, or a network failure.

After all the functional and performance tests have been performed, and no failures have been detected during these tests, the system is said to be validated.

Pilot testing

During the **pilot test**, also called the **field test**, the system is installed and used by a selected set of users. Users exercise the system as if it had been permanently installed. No explicit guidelines or test scenarios are given to the users. Pilot tests are useful when a system is built without a specific set of requirements or without a specific customer in mind. In this case, a group of people is invited to use the system for a limited time and to give their feedback to the developers.

An **alpha test** is a pilot test with users exercising the system in the development environment. In a **beta test**, the acceptance test is performed by a limited number of end users in the target environment; that is, the difference between usability tests and alpha or beta tests is that the individual behavior of the end user is not observed and recorded. As a result, beta tests do not test usability requirements as thoroughly as usability tests do. For interactive systems, where ease of use is a requirement, the usability test therefore cannot be replaced with a beta test.

The Internet has made the distribution of software very easy. As a result, beta tests are more and more common. In fact, some companies now use it as the main method for system testing their software. Because the downloading process is the responsibility of the end user, not the developers, the cost of distributing the experimental software has decreased sharply. Consequently, the restriction of the number of beta testers to a small group is also a matter of the past. The new beta-test paradigm offers the software to anybody who is interested in testing the software. In fact, some companies charge their users for beta testing their software!

Acceptance testing

There are three ways the client evaluates a system during acceptance testing. In a **benchmark test**, the client prepares a set of test cases that represent typical conditions under which the system should operate. Benchmark tests can be performed with actual users or by a special test team exercising the system functions, but it is important that the testers be familiar with the functional and nonfunctional requirements so they can evaluate the system.

Another kind of system acceptance testing is used in reengineering projects, when the new system replaces an existing system. In **competitor testing,** the new system is tested against an existing system or competitor product. In **shadow testing**, a form of comparison testing, the new and the legacy systems are run in parallel and their outputs are compared.

After acceptance testing, the client reports to the project manager which requirements are not satisfied. Acceptance testing also gives the opportunity for a dialog between the developers and client about conditions that have changed and which requirements had to be added, modified, or deleted because of the changes. If requirements had to be changed, the changes should be reported in the minutes to the client acceptance review and should form the basis for another iteration of the software life-cycle process. If the customer is satisfied, the system is accepted, possibly contingent on a list of changes recorded in the minutes of the acceptance test.

Installation testing

After the system is accepted, it is installed in the target environment. A good system testing plan allows the easy reconfiguration of the system from the development environment to the target environment. The desired outcome of the installation test is that the installed system correctly addresses all requirements.

In most cases, the installation test repeats the test cases executed during function and performance testing in the target environment. Some requirements cannot be executed in the development environment because they require target-specific resources. To test these requirements, additional test cases have to be designed and performed as part of the installation test. Once the customer is satisfied with the results of the installation test, system testing is complete, and the system is formally delivered and ready for operation.

9.5 Managing testing

In previous sections, we showed how different testing techniques are used to maximize the number of faults discovered. In this section, we describe how to manage testing activities to minimize the resources need. Many testing activities occur near the end of the project, when resources are running low and when the delivery pressure increases. Often, trade-offs have to be weighed between the faults that need to be repaired before delivery and those that can be repaired in a subsequent revision of the system. In the end, however, developers should detect and repair a sufficient number of faults such that the system meets functional and nonfunctional requirements to an extent acceptable to the client.

First, we describe the planning of test activities (Section 9.5.1). Next, we describe the test plan, which documents the activities of testing (Section 9.5.2). Next, we describe the roles assigned during testing (Section 9.5.3).

9.5.1 Planning Testing

Developers can reduce the cost of testing and the elapsed time necessary for its completion through careful planning. Two key elements are to start the selection of test cases early and to parallelize tests.

Developers responsible for testing can design test cases as soon as the models they validate become stable. Functional tests can be developed when the use cases are completed. Unit tests of subsystems can be developed when their interfaces is defined. Similarly, test stubs and drivers can be developed when component interfaces are stable. Developing tests early enables the execution of tests to start as soon as components become available. Moreover, given that developing tests requires a close examination of the models under validation, developers can find faults in the models even before the system is constructed. Note, however, that developing tests early on introduces a maintenance problem: test cases, drivers, and stubs need to be updated whenever the system models change.

The second key element in shortening testing time is to parallelize testing activities: All component tests can be conducted in parallel; double tests for components in which no faults were discovered can be initiated while other components are repaired. For example, the quad test A,B,C,D in Figure 9-24 can be performed as soon as double tests A,B, A,C, and A,D, have not resulted in any failures. These double tests, in turn, can be performed as soon as unit test A is completed. The quad test A,B,C,D can be performed in parallel with the double test D, G and the triple test B,E,F, even if tests E, F, or G uncover failures and delay the rest of the tests.

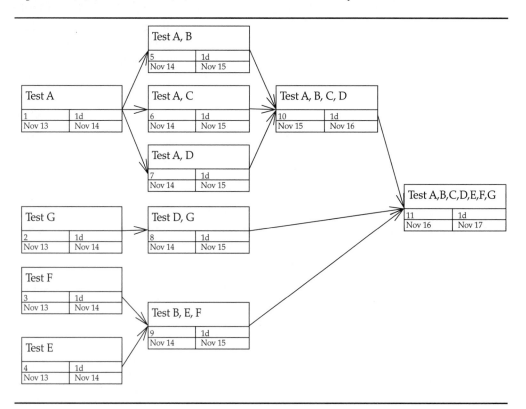

Figure 9-24   Example of a PERT chart for a schedule of the sandwich tests shown in Figure 9-19.

9.5.2 Documenting Testing

Testing activities are documented in four types of documents, the *Test Plan*, the *Test Case Specifications*, the *Test Incident Reports*, and the *Test Summary Report*[2]:

- **Test Plan.** The Test Plan focuses on the managerial aspects of testing. It documents the scope, approach, resources, and schedule of testing activities. The requirements and the components to be tested are identified in this document.

- **Test Case Specification**. Each test is documented by a test case specification. This document contains the inputs, drivers, stubs, and expected outputs of the tests. This document also contains the tasks to be performed.

- **Test Incident Report**. Each execution of each test is documented by a *Test Incident Report*. The actual results of the tests and differences from the expected output are recorded.

- **Test Summary Report**. This document lists all the failures that were discovered during the tests and that need to be investigated. From the *Test Report Summary*, the developers analyze and prioritize each failure and plan for changes in the system and in the models. These changes in turn can trigger new test cases and new test executions.

The *Test Plan* (TP) and the *Test Case Specifications* (TCP) are written early in the process, as soon as the test planning and each test case are completed. These documents are under configuration management and updated as the system models change. The following is an outline for a *Test Plan:*

Test Plan
1. Introduction
2. Relationship to other documents
3. System overview
4. Features to be tested/not to be tested
5. Pass/Fail criteria
6. Approach
7. Suspension and resumption
8. Testing materials (Hardware/Software requirements)
9. Test cases
10. Testing schedule

Section 1 of the test plan describes the objectives and extent of the tests. The goal is to provide a framework that can be used by managers and testers to plan and execute the necessary tests in a timely and cost-effective manner.

---

2. Documents described in this section are based on the IEEE 829 standard on testing documentation. Note that we omitted certain sections and documents (e.g., the Test Item Transmittal Report) for the sake of simplicity. Refer to the standard for a complete description of these documents [IEEE Std. 829-1991].

Section 2 explains the relationship of the test plan to the other documents produced during the development effort such as the RAD, SDD, and ODD. It explains how all the tests are related to the functional and nonfunctional requirements as well as the system design stated in the respective documents. If necessary, this section introduces a naming scheme to establish the correspondence between requirements and tests.

Section 3 provides an overview of the system in terms of the components that are tested during unit test. The granularity of components and their dependencies are defined in this section. This section focuses on the structural aspects of testing.

Section 4 identifies all features and combinations of features to be tested. It also describes all those features that are not to be tested and the reasons for not testing them. This section focuses on the functional aspects of testing.

Section 5 specifies generic pass/fail criteria for the tests covered in this plan. They are supplemented by pass/fail criteria in the test-design specification. Note that "fail" in the IEEE standard terminology means "successful test" in our terminology.

Section 6 describes the general approach to the testing process. It discusses the reasons for the selected integration testing strategy. Different strategies are often needed to test different parts of the system. A UML class diagram can be used to illustrate the dependencies between the individual tests and their involvement in the integration tests.

Section 7 specifies the criteria for suspending the testing on the test items associated with the plan. It also specifies the test activities that must be repeated when testing is resumed.

Section 8 identifies the resources that are needed for testing. This should include the physical characteristics of the facilities, including the hardware, software, special test tools, and other testing needs (office space, etc.) to support the tests.

Section 9, the core of the test plan, lists the test cases that are used during testing. Each test case is described in detail in a separate Test Case Specification document. Each execution of these tests will be documented in a *Test Incident Report* document. We describe these documents in more details later in this section.

Section 10 of the test plan covers responsibilities, staffing and training needs, risks and contingencies, and the test schedule.

The following is an outline of a *Test Case Specification*:

Test Case Specification
1. Test case specification identifier
2. Test items
3. Input specifications
4. Output specifications
5. Environmental needs
6. Special procedural requirements
7. Intercase dependencies

The Test Case Specification identifier is the name of the test case, used to distinguish it from other test cases. Conventions such as naming the test cases from the features or the component being tested allow developers to more easily refer to test cases. Section 2 of the TCS lists the components under test and the features being exercised. Section 3 lists the inputs required for the test cases. Section 4 lists the expected output. This output is computed manually or with a competing system (such as a legacy system being replaced). Section 5 lists the hardware and software platform needed to execute the test, including any test drivers or stubs. Section 6 lists any constraints needed to execute the test such as timing, load, or operator intervention. Section 7 lists the dependencies with other test cases.

The *Test Incident Report* lists the actual test results and the failures that were experienced. The description of the results must include which features were demonstrated and whether the features have been met. If a failure has been experienced, the test analysis report should contain sufficient information to allow the failure to be reproduced. Failures from all *Test Incident Reports* are collected and listed in the *Test Summary Report* and then further analyzed and prioritized by the developers.

Note that the IEEE standard [IEEE Std. 829-1991] for software test documentation uses a slightly different outline that is more appropriate for large organizations and systems. Section 10, for example, is covered by several sections in the standard (responsibilities, staffing and training needs, schedule, risks, and contingencies).

9.5.3   Assigning Responsibilities

Testing requires developers to find faults in components of the system. This is best done when the testing is performed by a developer who is not involved in the development of the component under test, one who is less reticent to break the component being tested and who is more likely to find ambiguities in the component specification.

For stringent quality requirements, a separate team dedicated to quality control is solely responsible for testing. The testing team is provided with the system models, the source code, and the system for developing and executing test cases. *Test Incident Reports* and *Test Report Summaries* are then sent back to the subsystem teams for analysis and possible revisions of the system. The revised system is then retested by the testing team, not only to check if the original failures have been addressed, but also to ensure that no new faults have been inserted in the system.

For systems that do not have stringent quality requirements, subsystem teams can double as a testing team for components developed by other subsystem teams. The architecture team can define standards for test procedures, drivers, and stubs and can also perform as the integration test team. The same test documents can be used for communication among subsystem teams.

9.6 Exercises

1. Correct the faults in the isLeapYear() and getNumDaysInMonth() methods of Figure 9-14 and generate test cases using the path testing methods. Are the test cases you found different than those of Figure 9-4 and Figure 9-15? Why? Would the test cases you found uncover the faults you corrected?

2. Generate equivalent Java code for the statechart diagram for the SetTime use case of 2Bwatch (Figure 9-16). Use equivalence testing, boundary testing, and path testing to generate test cases for the code you have just generated. How do these test cases compare with those generated using state-based testing?

3. Build the statechart diagram corresponding to the PurchaseTicket use case of Figure 9-22. Generate test cases based on the statechart diagram using the state-based testing technique. Discuss the number of test cases and differences with the test case of Figure 9-23.

4. Discuss the use of other design patterns to implement a stub instead of the Bridge pattern shown in Figure 9-11. For example, what are the advantages of using a Proxy pattern instead of a Bridge? What are the disadvantages?

5. Apply the software engineering and testing terminology from this chapter to the following terms used in Feynman's article mentioned in the introduction:
   - What is a "crack"?
   - What is "crack initiation"?
   - What is "high engine reliability"?
   - What is a "design aim"?
   - What is a "mission equivalent"?
   - What does "10 percent of the original specification mean"?
   - How is Feynman using the term "verification," when he says that "As deficiencies and design errors are noted they are corrected and verified with further testing"?

6. Given the following subsystem decomposition:

comment on the testing plan used by the project manager:

What decisions were made? Why? What are the advantages and disadvantages of this particular test plan?

References

[Bezier, 1990]   B. Bezier, *Software Testing Techniques,* 2nd ed. Van Nostrand, New York, 1990.

[Binder, 1994]   R. V. Binder, "Testing object-oriented systems: A status report," *American Programmer,* Apr. 1994.

[Brooks, 1975]   F. P. Brooks, *The Mythical Man Month.* Addison-Wesley, Reading, MA, 1975.

[Fagan, 1976]   M. Fagan, "Design and code inspections to reduce errors in program development," *IBM Systems Journal,* Vol. 15, No. 3, 1976.

[Feynman, 1988]   R. P. Feynman, "Personal observations on the reliability of the Shuttle," Rogers Commission, *The Presidential Commission on the Space Shuttle Challenger Accident Report.* (Washington, DC,) June 1986. Also in http://www.virtualschool.edu/mon./ SocialConstruction/FeynmanChallengerRpt.html.

[IEEE Std. 829-1991]   *IEEE Standard for Software Test Documentation,* IEEE Standards Board, Mar. 1991, in [IEEE 1997].

[IEEE Std. 982-1989]   *IEEE Guide for the Use of IEEE Standard Dictionary of Measures to Produce Reliable Software,* IEEE Standards Board, July 1989, in [IEEE 1997].

[IEEE, 1997]   *IEEE Standards Collection Software Engineering,* Piscataway, NJ, 1997.

[Jones, 1977]   T. C. Jones, "Programmer Quality and Programmer Productivity," IBM TR-02.764, 1977.

[McCabe, 1976]   T. McCabe, "A Software Complexity Measure," *IEEE Transactions on Software Engineering,* vol. 2, no. 12, Dec. 1976.

[Myers, 1979]   G. J. Myers, *The Art of Software Testing,* Wiley, New York, 1979.

[Parnas & Weiss, 1985]   D. L. Parnas & D. M. Weiss, "Active design reviews: principles and practice," *Proceedings of the Eight International Conference on Software Engineering,* pp 132–136, Aug. 1985.

[Pfleeger, 1991]   S. L. Pfleeger, *Software Engineering: The Production of Quality Software,* 2nd ed. Macmillan, 1991.

[Popper, 1992]   K. Popper, *Objective Knowledge: An Evolutionary Approach.* Clarendon, Oxford, 1992.

[Siewiorek & Swarz, 1992]   D. P. Siewiorek & R. S. Swarz, *Reliable Computer Systems: Design and Evaluation.* 2nd ed. Digital, Burlington, MA, 1992.

[Turner & Robson, 1993]   C. D. Turner & D. J. Robson, "The state-based testing of object-oriented programs," *Conference on Software Maintenance.* pp. 302–310, Sept. 1993.

[Walker et al., 1980]   B. J. Walker, R. A. Kemmerer, & G. J. Popek. "Specification and verification of the UCLA Unix security kernel," *Communications of the ACM,* Vol. 23, No. 2, pp. 118–131, 1980.

10

10

Software Configuration Management

Those who would repeat the past must control the teaching of history.
—Frank Herbert, *in Chapterhouse: Dune*

Change pervades the development process: Requirements change when developers improve their understanding of the application domain, the system design changes with new technology and design goals, the object design changes with the identification of solution objects, and the implementation changes as faults are discovered and repaired. These changes can impact every work product, from the system models to the source code and the documentation. *Software configuration management* is the process of controlling and monitoring change to work products. Once a baseline is defined, software configuration management minimizes the risks associated with changes by defining a formal approval and tracking process for changes.

In this chapter, we describe the following activities:

- *Configuration item identification* is the modeling of the system as a set of evolving components.

- *Promotion management* is the creation of versions for other developers.

- *Release management* is the creation of versions for the client and the users.

- *Branch management* is the management of concurrent development.

- *Variant management* is the management of versions intended to coexist.

- *Change management* is the handling, approval, and tracking of change requests.

We conclude this chapter by discussing project management issues related to software configuration management.

10.1 Introduction: An Aircraft Example

Passenger aircraft are one of the most complex engineering feats to be attempted by a private corporation. On the one hand, passenger aircraft need to be safe and reliable. On the other hand, they need to be economical. Unlike trains or cars, the aircraft systems cannot be simply shut down in the event of a failure. Unlike NASA, airlines need to post a profit and pay dividends to their stockholders. These requirements result in very complex designs that include many redundancies and diagnostic systems. A Boeing 747, for example, is composed of more than 6 million parts. In order to develop and maintain such complex systems, at the same time remaining economically competitive, aircraft manufacturers extend the life of a model by incrementally improving on the same design. The Boeing 747, for example, was first released in 1967 and is still in production at the time of writing. It has gone through four major revisions, the latest, the 747-400, released in 1988. Another approach to dealing with the high complexity of aircraft is the reuse of as many parts and subsystems across aircraft models as possible. Consider the following example.

Airbus A320

In 1988, Airbus Industries, a consortium of European aircraft industries, released the A320, the first fly-by-wire passenger aircraft. The pilots control the plane like an F16 fighter jet by using a small joystick located on their side. Digital impulses are then transmitted a computer which interprets and relays them to the wings and tail controls. Unlike hydraulic systems, computerized control allows for envelope protection, which prevents the pilot from exceeding certain parameters, such as maximum and minimum speed, maximum angle of attack, and maximum G-values. The A320 has 150 seats and is targeted for short-to-medium-haul routes.

A321 and A319

The commercial success of the A320 allowed Airbus to work on two derivative airplanes, the A319, a shorter, 124-seat version, and the A321, a longer, 185-seat version. Changing the length of a basic design to obtain a new aircraft has been a standard practice in the industry. This allows the manufacturer to save on cost and time by leveraging off an existing design. It also saves operating costs for airlines, who then only need to maintain one stock of spare parts. In this case, however, Airbus pushed the concept even further, ensuring that all three aircraft have the same cockpit controls and the same handling characteristics. The A321, for example, has slotted flaps and slightly modified wing controls to make the plane feel like the A320, even though the A321 is longer. Consequently, any pilot certified for one of the aircraft can fly the other two. This results in cost savings for airline operators who need to train pilots only once, share flight simulators, spare parts, and maintenance crews for all three versions.

A330 and A340

Pursuing this philosophy even further, Airbus paid great care to the handling characteristics of the A330 and A340. These two aircraft, built for the long haul and ultra long haul markets, can carry twice as many passengers as the A320 up to three times as far. They have the same cockpit layouts and fly-by-wire system. Pilots trained on the A320 family can fly the A330 or the A340 with minimal retraining, further reducing the operating costs of the airline. Comparatively, the handling characteristics of a 737 (comparable to the A319) are very different from a 747 (comparable to the larger version of the A340).

Incremental refinement and subsystem reuse are not without problems. Each change that is made to a single aircraft needs to be carefully evaluated in the context of the other two. For example, if we decide to install a new, more-efficient powerplant on the A320, we would need to evaluate if the same powerplant could also be used on the A319 and the A321, to retain the advantage of sharing parts across all three models. Then, we need to evaluate if the handling of each aircraft changes significantly, in which case we may need to modify the computerized control software to account for this. Otherwise, all pilots flying the A320 would need to be retrained and recertified, without mentioning the loss of a common platform and training program for all three aircraft. Then, the modified aircraft would need to be recertified by the governing authority (e.g., the Federal Aviation Agency in the United States, the Joint Aviation Authorities in the European Community) which would decide on the safety of the aircraft and whether new maintenance or pilot training procedures are necessary. Finally, the state of each individual aircraft needs to be carefully documented, such that the correct parts can be replaced. In summary, any change that would threaten the safety of the aircraft, its efficiency, or the portability of pilots across aircraft need to be identified and rejected. These issues require aircraft manufacturers and operators to follow sophisticated version and change control procedures.

Software system development, although usually not quite as complex as a passenger aircraft, nevertheless suffers from similar problems. Software systems have a long life cycle to allow the recouping of initial investment: For example, many Unix systems still contain code dating as far back as the 1970s. Software systems can exist in many different variants: For example, there are flavors of Unix operating systems running on mainframes as well as home PCs and Macintosh computers. Maintenance changes to existing and running software systems need to be controlled and evaluated carefully in order to ensure a certain level of reliability: For example, the introduction of the Euro currency, a simple change in scale, has had a very visible and substantial impact on many financial and business software systems across the globe. Finally, software systems evolve much more rapidly than aircraft, requiring developers to track change, their assumptions, and their impact.

Configuration management enables developers and aircraft manufacturers to deal with change. The first function of configuration management is the identification of configuration items. Which subsystems are likely to change? Which subsystem interfaces should not change? Each subsystem likely to change is modeled as a configuration item and its state labeled with a version number. The fly-by-wire software of the A320 is a configuration item. The device driver for a serial port is a configuration item for a Unix operating system.

The second function of configuration management is to manage change through a formal process. A change request is first logged, then analyzed, and accepted if consistent with the goals of the project. A change request for an aircraft is a thick report listing all the subsystems and contractors involved in the change. A change request for a simple software system can be just an E-mail requesting a new feature. The change is then approved or rejected, depending on the foreseen impact of the change on the overall system.

Finally, the third function of configuration management is to record sufficient status information on each version of each configuration item and its dependencies. By looking at the maintenance book of an A320 and the version numbers of its subsystems, a maintenance engineer is able to tell which subsystems need to be replaced or upgraded. Looking at the latest release of a serial port device driver, its improvements and the changes since the last release, we are able to determine whether we should upgrade to the new driver or not.

Software configuration management has been traditionally treated as a maintenance topic. The distinction between development and maintenance, however, has become blurred, and often, configuration management is introduced quite early in the process. In this chapter, we focus primarily on the early phases of configuration management and briefly address its use during maintenance. But first, we define more formally the concept of configuration management.

10.2 An Overview of Configuration Management

Software configuration management (later referred to simply as configuration management) is the discipline of managing and controlling change in the evolution of software systems [IEEE Std. 1042-1987]. Configuration management systems automate the identification of versions, their storage and retrieval, and supports status accounting. Configuration management includes the following activities.

- **Identification of configuration items**. Components of the system and its work products and their versions are identified and labeled uniquely. Developers identify configuration items after the *Project Agreement* (Section 11.4.5), once the principal deliverables and components of the system are agreed on. Developers create versions and additional configuration items as the system evolves.

- **Change control**. Changes to the system and releases to the users are controlled to ensure consistency with project goals. Change control can be done by the developers, by management, or by a control board, depending on the level of quality required and the rate of change.

- **Status accounting**. The status of individual components, work products, and change requests are recorded. This allows developers to distinguish versions more easily and track issues related to changes. This also allows management to track project status.

- **Auditing**. Versions selected for releases are validated to ensure the completeness, consistency, and quality of the product. Auditing is accomplished by the quality control team.

In addition, the following activities are often considered part of configuration management [Dart, 1991].

- **Build management**. Most configuration management systems enable the automatic building of the system as developers create new versions of the components. The configuration management system has sufficient knowledge of the system to minimize the amount of recompilation. It may also be able to combine different versions of components to build different variants of the system (e.g., for different operating system and hardware platforms).

- **Process management**. In addition to change control, projects may have policies about the creation and documentation of versions. One such policy can be that only syntactically correct code can be part of a version. Another policy can be that builds are attempted (and should succeed) every week. Finally, the configuration management process includes policies for notifying relevant developers when new versions are created or when a build fails. Some configuration management systems enable developers to automate such work flows.

Traditionally, configuration management is seen as a management discipline, helping project managers with change control, status accounting, and auditing activities ([Bersoff et al., 1980] and [IEEE Std. 1042-1987]). More recently, however, configuration management has also been seen as a development support discipline, helping developers deal with the complexity associated with large numbers of changes, components, and variants [Babich, 1986]. In this chapter, we focus in more detail on the latter view and only briefly address the activities of change control and status accounting.

In our view, configuration management pervades the software life cycle. It begins with the identification of configuration items after the deliverables and principal components of the system have been defined. It continues throughout development as developers create versions of work products during analysis, system design, object design, and implementation. With rationale maintenance (see Chapter 8, *Rationale Management*), configuration management is the principal tool available to developers for dealing with change.

Next, let us focus in more detail on the concepts of configuration management.

10.3 Configuration Management Concepts

In this section, we present the main concepts of configuration management (Figure 10-1). As often as possible, we use the same terminology as the IEEE guidelines on configuration management [IEEE Std. 1042-1987]:

- A **configuration item** is a work product or a piece of software that is treated as a single entity for the purpose of configuration management. A composite of configuration items is defined as an **configuration management aggregate** (called CM aggregate for short). The fly-by-wire software of the A320 is a configuration item. The A320 is a CM aggregate. The serial port device driver is a configuration item. The Linux operating system is a CM aggregate.
- A **change request** is a formal report, issued by a user or a developer, requesting a modification in a configuration item. For example, the *Engineering Change Proposal*

[MIL Std. 480], the standard change request form in the United States government, is seven pages long. An informal change request can be a one-line E-mail message.

• A **version** identifies the state of a configuration item or a configuration at a well-defined point in time. Given a CM aggregate, a consistent set of versions of its configuration items is defined as a **configuration**. A configuration can be thought as a version of a CM aggregate.

• A **promotion** is a version that has been made available to other developers in the project. A **release** is a version that has been made available to the client or the users.

• A **repository** is a library of releases. A **workspace** is a library of promotions.

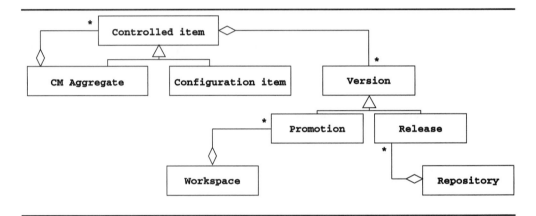

Figure 10-1   Configuration management concepts (UML class diagram).

10.3.1   Configuration Items and CM Aggregates

A **configuration item** is a work product or a component of a work product that is under configuration management and treated as a single entity for such purposes. For example, the fly-by-wire software of the A320 is a configuration item. During an upgrade, the complete software is replaced. The fly-by-wire software cannot be broken down into smaller components that can be installed independently. Similarly, the device driver for the serial port in any operating system is a configuration item. This component is simple enough that it cannot be broken down further as far as installation is concerned.

A CM aggregate is a composition of configuration items. The 747 is a CM aggregate of six million parts. The Linux[1] operating system is a CM aggregate that includes a process scheduler, a memory manager, many device drivers, network daemons, file systems, and many other subsystems.

---

1. Linux is a freely available POSIX [POSIX, 1990] operation system created by Linus Torwalds. For more information check http://www.linux.org/.

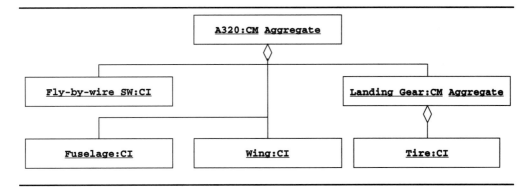

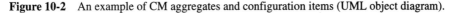

Figure 10-2   An example of CM aggregates and configuration items (UML object diagram).

10.3.2 Versions and Configurations

A **version** identifies the state of a configuration item at a well-defined point in time. Successive versions of a work product differ by one or more changes, such as the correction of a fault, the addition of new functionality, or the removal of unnecessary or obsolete functionality. A **configuration** identifies the state of a CM aggregate.

A **baseline** is a version of a configuration item that has been formally reviewed and agreed on, by management or the client, and which can be changed only through a change request. For example, each aircraft needs to go through a rigorous certification process by the governing agency (i.e., the FAA or the JAA) before it can be operated by an airline. Any change to the aircraft after certification requires a formal change process and recertification. This ensures that changes are made consistently with project goals (e.g., safety and reliability) and regulations, and that they are communicated to relevant developers and users (e.g., the airline passengers and the airline operator).

Versions that are intended to coexist are called **variants**. For example (Figure 10-3), the A319, the A320, and the A321 are variants of the same basic aircraft. The principal difference is their length, that is, the number of passenger and freight that they can carry. The A320-200, however, is a version of the A320 that replaced the initial version. In other words, an airline can buy both the A319 and the A320-200, but it cannot buy the older A320-100. In the case of a software system, the system can have a Macintosh variant, a Windows variant, and a Linux variant, each providing identical functionality. A system may also have a standard variant and a professional or deluxe variant, supporting a different range of functionality. Variants share a large amount of code that implements the core functionality, and differences are confined to a small number of lower level subsystems.

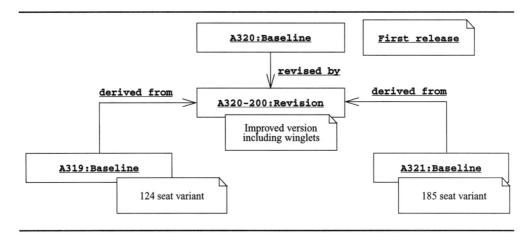

Figure 10-3   Examples of baselines, revisions, and variants (UML object diagram). The A319, A320, and the A321 are all based on the same design. They vary mostly by the length of their fuselage.

10.3.3 Change Requests

A **change request** is a formal step initiating the change process. A user, client, or developer discovers a fault in a work product and wants a new feature. The author of the change request specifies the configuration item to which the requests applies to, its version, the problem that needs to be solved, and a proposed solution. In the case of a formal change process, the costs and benefits of the change are then assessed before the change is approved or rejected. In both cases, the rationale of the decision is recorded with the change request.

For example, shortly after the A320 was certified in February 1988, a revised version, the A320-200, was recertified. The new version included a few modifications that yielded a longer range and larger take-off weight. One of these changes was the addition of winglets at the end of the wings that significantly reduced drag and thus reduced fuel consumption. Fuel consumption is a major cost for the airline operator and, thus, a strong selling argument for the airline manufacturer. During the A320 design, a change request was issued, describing the winglet change, its performance evaluation, and its estimated cost. The change was approved, implemented, and the A320-200 passed certification in November 1988. A change request for the Linux operating system kernel is an E-mail message to Linus Torwalds.

10.3.4 Promotions and Releases

A **promotion** is a version that is made available to other developers. A promotion denotes a configuration item that has reached a relatively stable state and that can be used or reviewed by other developers. For example, subsystems are promoted for other teams using that subsystem. Subsystems are then promoted for the quality control team to assess their quality. Later, as faults are discovered and repaired, revisions of the subsystem are promoted for reevaluation.

A **release** is a version that is made available to users. A release denotes that a configuration item has met the quality criteria set by the quality control team and can be used or reviewed by the users. For example, the system is released to beta testers for finding additional faults and assessing the perceived quality of the system. As faults are discovered and repaired, revisions of the subsystem are promoted for reevaluation by the quality control team and, when the quality criteria are met, released again to the users.

10.3.5 Repositories and Workspaces

Configuration management systems provide a **repository**, in which all configuration items are stored and tracked, and a **workspace**, in which the developer makes changes. Developers create new versions by checking in changes from their workspace to the repository.

A **software library**, as defined in [IEEE Std. 1042-1987], provides facilities to store, label, and identify versions of the configuration items (i.e., documentation, models, and code). A software library also provides functionality to track the status of changes to the configuration items. We distinguish between three types of libraries.

1. The **developer's workspace**, also known as the dynamic library, is used for everyday development by the developers. Change is not restricted and is controlled by the individual developer only.
2. The **master directory**, also known as the controlled library, tracks promotions. Change needs to be approved and versions need to meet certain project criteria (e.g., "Only code that can be compiled without errors may be checked in") before they are made available to the rest of the project.
3. The **software repository**, also known as the static library, tracks releases. Promotions need to meet certain quality control criteria (e.g., "All faults detected by regression tests must be repaired") before a promotion becomes a release.

10.3.6 Version Identification Schemes

Versions are uniquely identified by developers and systems using a **version identifier**, also called a version number. Some exotic examples include the following.

- The Ada specification went through five successive major versions, named Strawman, Woodenman, Tinman, Ironman, and Steelman [Steelman, 1978].
- The version identification scheme for T_EX, a typesetting program for technical texts [Knuth, 1986], is based on decimals of the number π: Each time a bug is found (which is rare) and repaired the version number of T_EX is incremented to add another digit. The current version is 3.14159.

In general, however, version numbers of a given configuration item can be quite large. In this case, developers and configuration management systems use version identification schemes that support automation more easily, such as sequential numbers with two or three decimals. For example, consider a UML editor, called MUE (for My UML Editor), which is built and released incrementally. We can use a three-digit scheme to distinguish between functional changes, small improvements, and bug fixes (Figure 10-4). The leftmost digit denotes a major version (e.g., overhaul of functionality or of the user interface), the second digit, the minor version (e.g., addition of limited functionality), and the third digit denotes revisions (e.g., corrections). By convention, versions before 1.0.0 denote versions released for the purpose of alpha or beta testing.

Such a simple sequential scheme, however, only works with a sequential series of versions. A **branch** identifies a concurrent development path requiring independent configuration management. Releases are seen by the user as an incremental and sequential development process. The development of different features, however, can be done by different teams concurrently and later merged into a single version. The sequence of versions created by each team is a branch, which is independent from the versions created by the other teams. When versions of different branches need to be reconciled, the versions are **merged**; that is, a new version is created containing selected elements from both ancestor versions.

For releases, the sequential identification scheme is usually sufficient, because the concept of branch is not visible to the users. For developers and configuration management systems, however, this is not sufficient, because branches are often used for supporting concurrent development. The version identification scheme used by CVS [Berliner, 1990], for example, explicitly represents branches and versions. Version numbers include a branch identifier

---

Three-digit version identification scheme

<version> ::= <configuration item name>.<major>.<minor>.<revision>
<major> ::= <nonnegative integer>
<minor> ::= <nonnegative integer>
<revision> ::= <nonnegative integer>

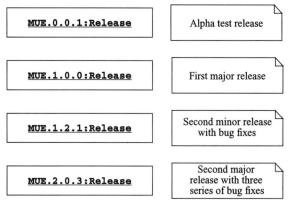

MUE.0.0.1:Release	Alpha test release
MUE.1.0.0:Release	First major release
MUE.1.2.1:Release	Second minor release with bug fixes
MUE.2.0.3:Release	Second major release with three series of bug fixes

---

Figure 10-4   Three digit version identification scheme (BNF and UML object diagram).

followed by a revision number. The branch identifier includes the version number from which the branch was started, followed by a unique number identifying the branch. This enables developers to identify to which branch a version belongs and in which order versions of one branch were produced.

In Figure 10-5, two branches are depicted: the main trunk (leftmost package) and the branch 1.2.1 derived from version 1.2 (rightmost package). In the MUE example, the branch may have been derived for the purpose of evaluating competing implementations of the same feature (e.g., support for UML interaction diagrams in MUE). Note that this identification scheme

CVS version identification scheme

\<version\> ::= \<configuration item name\>.\<version identifier\>

\<version identifier\> ::= \<branch\>.\<revision\>

\<branch\> ::= \<version identifier\>.\<branch number\> | \<branch number\>

\<branch number\> ::= \<nonnegative integer\>

\<revision\> ::= \<nonnegative integer\>

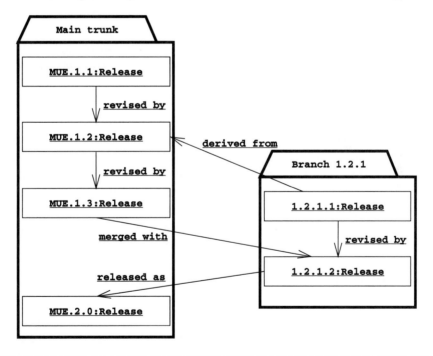

Figure 10-5 CVS version identification scheme (UML object diagram). Branches are identified with the version they were derived from followed by a unique number.

does not identify how versions are merged back onto a branch. In Figure 10-5, version `1.2.1.2` is merged with version `1.3` onto the main trunk to produce version `2.0`.

10.3.7 Changes and Change Sets

The evolution of a configuration item can be modeled in two ways.

- **State-based view**. As a series of versions, that is, as a series of states of the configuration item. Each state is identified by a version number (e.g., the A320-200, `MUE.1.0`). This is the view most often encountered in practice.

- **Changed-based view**. As a baseline followed by a series of **changes**, also called **deltas**. A change represents the difference between two successive versions, in terms of lines or paragraphs that have been added or removed from the configuration item. Often, repairing a fault or adding functionality to a system requires changes to several configuration items. All the changes to configuration items associated with a single revision of a configuration are grouped into a **change set**. If two change sets do not overlap (i.e., they apply to different and unrelated sets of configuration items), they can be applied to the same baseline in arbitrary order, thus providing more flexibility to the developer when selecting configurations.

Continuing the MUE example, assume that we revised the first baseline twice: `MUE.1.1` was released to fix a bug related to classes with no operations, and `MUE.1.2` was released to fix a bug related to drawing dashed lines. Each of these revisions corresponded to changes in a single subsystem. The change sets corresponding to each of these revisions is thus independent, and could be applied to the baseline in any order. For example, when the `emptyClassFix: ChangeSet` is applied to the `MUE.1.0:Release`, we derive the `MUE.1.1:Release`. Applying the `dashedLineFix:ChangeSet` next results in the `MUE.1.2:Release`. If instead, we apply the `dashedLineFix:ChangeSet` first, we would obtain the `MUE.1.1a:Release`. Applying the `emptyClassFix:ChangeSet` next, however, also results in the `MUE.1.2:Release`. The change set corresponding to the second baseline, however, depends on both of these revisions. Figure 10-6 illustrates the release history of MUE as a series of change sets and their dependencies.

The change-based view of configuration management is more general than the state-based view. It allows the developer to view related versions of different configuration items as one action. Moreover, when change sets do not overlap, they can be applied to more than one version. This approach is used for delivering bug fixes and minor improvements after a piece of software has been released; each change set is delivered as a separate patch that can be directly applied to the delivered base line or any derived version. As long as patches do not overlap, they can be applied in any order onto the baseline.

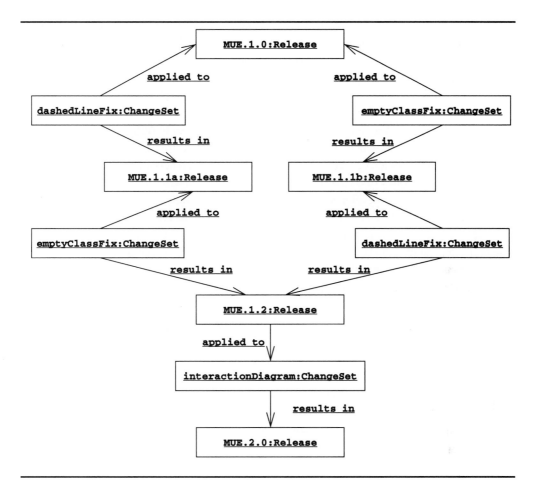

Figure 10-6 Change set representation of the MUE release history (UML object diagram). dashedLineFix:ChangeSet and emptyClassFix:ChangeSet can be applied to the MUE.1.0:Release in arbitrary order because they do not overlap.

10.3.8 Configuration Management Tools

Due to the importance of configuration management in software development, there are many configuration management and version management tools available to developers. In this section, we briefly describe four of them, RCS [Tichy, 1985], CVS [Berliner, 1990], Perforce [Perforce], and ClearCase [Leblang, 1994].

RCS (Revision Control System), a free tool, controls a repository storing all versions of the configuration items. To obtain a specific version, developers check out a version into their workspace by specifying a version number or a date. To change a configuration item, the developer needs to lock the item first, preventing all other developers from changing the item. When the change is completed, the developer checks the modified item back into the repository, simultaneously creating a new version and releasing the lock. To optimize storage, RCS only stores the latest version of each configuration item and the differences between each version. The concept of configuration can be realized by attaching a developer specified label to all versions that belong to the configuration. Developers can then check out a consistent set of versions by using the label. Note that this approach does not allow version control of the configuration itself. RCS does not support the concept of branch.

CVS (Concurrent Version System), also a free tool, extends RCS with the concept of branch. Instead of a sequence of differences, CVS stores a tree of differences for each configuration item. CVS also provides tools for merging two branches and detecting overlaps. The change control policy of CVS is also different from RCS. Instead of locking a configuration items, CVS considers each developer to be a separate branch. If only a single developer modified a configuration item between two check-ins, CVS automatically merges the branch onto the main trunk. If CVS detects a concurrent change, it first attempts to merge the two changes and then, in case of overlap, notifies the last developer to check in. With this policy, CVS can support a higher level of concurrent development than RCS.

Perforce is a commercial replacement for CVS. It is based on the same concept of central repository as CVS and RCS. Perforce, however, also supports the concept of change and change set, allowing the developer to more easily track the configuration items that were involved on a given change.

ClearCase, another commercial tool, supports also the concepts of CM aggregates and configurations. A CM aggregate is realized as a directory, which is managed as a configuration item by ClearCase. ClearCase also allows the specification of configurations with rules, selecting versions of each configuration item. A version can be specified with a static rule (i.e., refer to a specific version number) or with a dynamic rule (e.g., refer to the latest version of an item). ClearCase also provides access control mechanisms to define the ownership of each configuration item and configuration.

10.4 Configuration Management Activities

In the previous section, we described the main concepts of configuration management. In this section, we focus on the activities necessary to define and manage configuration items, promotions, and releases. We also describe activities related with the use of branches and variants for concurrent development. Configuration management activities described in this section include:

- configuration item and CM aggregate identification
- promotion management
- release management
- branch management
- variant management
- change management

For the basis of the examples in this section, we use a distributed car parts catalog called myCarParts. MyCarParts allows car dealers and car owners alike to browse and order parts from their computer. MyCarParts has a client/server architecture, with two types of clients: the EClient for expert users, such as car mechanics and part dealers, and the Nclient for novice users, including car owners who repair their own car. The system requires users to authenticate, which allows it to determine the list price of the parts given the particular user. A user who orders many parts is eligible for volume discounts, whereas an occasional client pays the full list price. The system also tracks the interests of each user, using this information to better optimize the network usage. The user is also sent customized notices about new products or new discount prices. Figure 10-7 displays the subsystem decomposition of myCarParts.

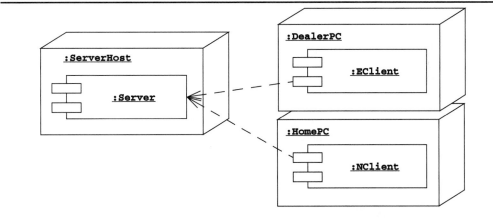

:DealerPC	The :DealerPC is the machine used by a dealer to order parts. The :DealerPC has often a higher bandwidth link to the server.
:EClient	The :EClient is located on the :DealerPC. It provides functionality to an expert user for finding parts by part identifier, vehicle make and year, and order history. The :EClient is designed for high-volume clients, such as car repair shops and part dealers.
:HomePC	The :HomePC is the machine used by a car owner to order parts. The :HomePC is connected to the server via a modem.
:NClient	The :NClient is located on the :HomePC. It provides functionality to the novice user for finding parts by description and, in subsequent releases, by clicking on a vehicle map. The :NClient is designed for the occasional client, such as a car hobbyist.
:ServerHost	The :ServerHost hosts the parts catalog server.
:Server	The :Server enables client to retrieve lists of parts by criteria and part entries, to order parts, and to track client activity.

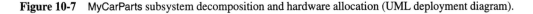

Figure 10-7   MyCarParts subsystem decomposition and hardware allocation (UML deployment diagram).

The development and evolution of the myCarParts system requires the coordinated release of several components.

- The protocol used by the clients and the server to exchange information is occasionally upgraded to support new client functionality and to improve response time and throughput. Because there is no guarantee that all users have the same version of the client, it is necessary for the server to maintain backward compatibility with older clients. Every new revision needs to be tested with older clients to validate this property.

- New client versions may implement functionality that is supported only in new versions of the server. Therefore, the server needs to be upgraded first, before the new client versions can be made available.

- When a new version of either client is available, the user can download a patch. The corresponding hardcopy manual, however, is sent via standard mail. In the event that several versions are released in a short time, a user needs to be able to identify which manual corresponds to which version.

For example, assume that the initial release of myCarParts allows users to browse the catalog using textual information only. Parts have a part identifier, a name, a description, the list of vehicles and years for which this part is manufactured, and cross references to other parts with which it can be assembled. The user can search the database using any of these fields. This can be problematic for novice users who do not know the name of the part they are looking for. In a second release, we address this problem by providing the user with a navigation map of parts. If the user knows what the part looks like and where it is located in the vehicle, he only needs to click on the corresponding part of the map. The change to introduce navigation maps and the releases of the components of myCarParts need to be carefully sequenced, considering the constraints we described before. The navigation map change requires the following sequence of steps.

1. The `Server` needs to be modified to support the storage and retrieval of subassembly maps.

2. The `Server` needs to be released and installed.

3. One map per vehicle and year needs to be created and stored in the database.

4. The `NClient` needs to be modified to use the navigation maps as a possible interface.

5. The `NClient` needs to be released and installed.

In the following sections, we use myCarParts and the navigation map change as the basis for the examples.

10.4.1 Configuration Item and CM Aggregate Identification

The identification of configuration items and CM aggregates occurs primarily after the project agreement, when a set of deliverables is agreed with the customer, and after system design, when most of the subsystems have been identified. The identification of configuration items and CM aggregates, however, continues throughout the development as the set of deliverables is redefined and as subsystems are added and removed from the subsystem decomposition.

Identifying configuration items and CM aggregates is similar to identifying objects during analysis. It is not algorithmic because some configuration items are trivial to identify (e.g., the RAD, the SDD), while others are more subtle (e.g., a client server protocol definition). Configuration items are self-contained documents or pieces of code whose evolution needs to be tracked and controlled. These include deliverable documents, work products, subsystems, off-the-shelf components that can evolve during the life cycle of the system, and interface descriptions. Usually, most configuration items have already been identified as objects of interest during project planning or system design.

In the myCarParts example, we identify each of the deliverable documents as a configuration item. In the myCarParts *Project Agreement*, the following were defined as deliverables:

- user level documents, including the RAD and the User's Manual (UM);
- system documents, including the SDD and the ODD
- the source code of the system, including its subsystems (depicted in Figure 10-7) and various installation programs

We identify, moreover, the interfaces between subsystems entities whose evolution should be carefully controlled, as changes to these can introduce major problems. We identify two components of the SDD, the *Client Server Protocol Specification* and the *Data Schema Description* as configuration items.

Figure 10-8 depicts the configuration items and the CM aggregates we identified for myCarParts. Because myCarParts subsystems can be released independently, we identify one CM aggregate for each subsystem that includes the configuration items relevant to the subsystem. For example, if we modify the NClient subsystem to include the navigation map functionality, we need to revise the RAD to specify the new use cases, change the NClient UM:CI to explain how this functionality is used, modify the NClient ODD:CI to include new classes for the map, and implement and test the changes in the source code.[2] The NClient:CM Aggregate is then revised to include the most recent versions of the configuration items related to the NClient, before it is released to the users. Note that this change can be done without modifying the

---

2. For brevity, the source code, test, and test manual are not depicted in Figure 10-8 .

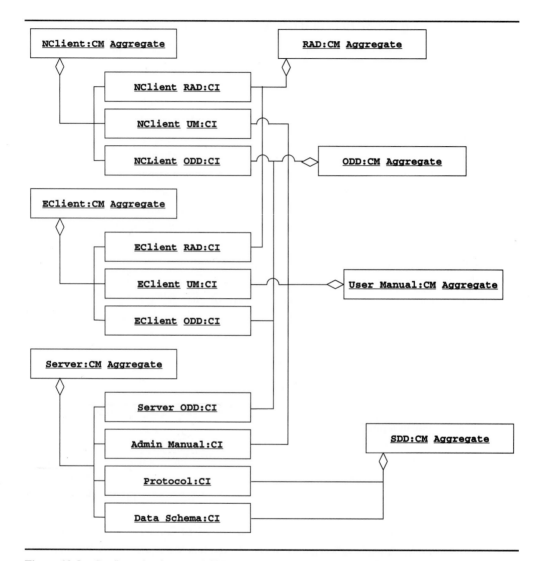

Figure 10-8   Configuration items and CM aggregates for myCarParts (UML object diagram).

EClient:CM Aggregate, and, thus, configuration items related to the EClient and the NClient subsystems are modeled as separate configuration items and CM aggregates.

The three subsystems constituting the myCarParts system, however, are not completely independent. Before we can add navigation maps to the NClient subsystem, we need first to provide functionality for storing and retrieving these tables in the Server subsystem. Although this functionality is realized and released separately, we still need to make sure that the releases of clients are coordinated with server releases (in the sense that servers need to be upgraded before clients are). For this purpose, we also identify system-level CM aggregates for each of the deliverables. The `RAD:CM Aggregate`, the `SDD:CM Aggregate`, and the `ODD:CM Aggregate` represent consistent versions of the deliverables. For example, the versions of the `ODD:CM Aggregate` with the `NClient ODD:CI` describing the navigation map classes also contains the `Server ODD:CI` describing how to store and retrieve these maps.

10.4.2 Promotion Management

Creating a new promotion for a configuration item occurs when a developer wants to share the configuration item with others. Developers create promotions to make the configuration item available for review, for the purpose of debugging another configuration item, or for a sanity check. Once the promotion is created and stored in the configuration management system, developers interested in the promotion check it out of the repository. Developers not interested in the promotion continue to work with earlier versions. Once a promotion is created, it cannot be modified. The developer who created the promotion can continue modifying the configuration item without interfering with the developers using the promotion. To distribute new changes, the developer needs to create a new promotion.

For example, consider the navigation map change in myCarParts (Figure 10-9). First, developers modify the analysis model to specify the navigation map use cases and its interaction with the existing use cases, resulting in the `NClient RAD.2.0:Promotion`. The system design model is then modified to accommodate the storage and downloading of maps, resulting in the `Protocol.2.0:Promotion` and `Data Schema.2.0:Promotion`. Then, a first implementation of the server side of the protocol is realized in the `Server.2.0:Promotion`, which is made available to the novice client team to test their implementation of the navigation map (`NClient 2.0:Promotion` and above). Several bugs are found in the server while testing the `NClient`. The server team identifies and addresses these bugs, resulting in the `Server.2.1:Promotion` and `Server.2.2:Promotion`. In the meantime, the documentation team revises the `NClient UM2.0:Promotion` based on the `NClient RAD.2.0:Promotion`. Note that during this time, the expert client team may be repairing bugs in the `EClient.1.5`, independently of the navigation map change. To test the `EClient`, the expert client team continues to use the former release of the server (i.e., `Server.1.4`). Figure 10-9 illustrates the above scenario by depicting a snapshot of each team's workspace. Even though teams are working toward a consistent system, they may all be working on different promotions of the same components until all components stabilize.

Promotions represent the state of a configuration item at the time it is made available for other developers. A project may usually require that code promotions do not contain compiler errors but make few other constraints to encourage the exchange of work products among teams. Once the quality of configuration items is improved and assessed by the quality control team, the promotion may become eligible for a release.

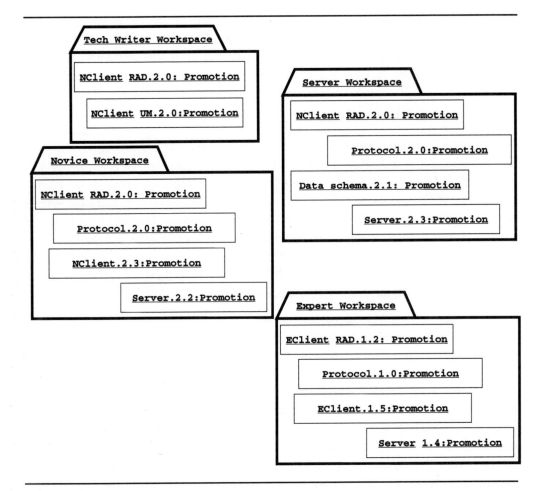

Figure 10-9   Snapshot of the workspaces used by myCarParts developers (UML object diagram). The Novice Workspace, the Tech Writer Workspace, and the Server Workspace contain promotions related to the navigation map functionality. The Expert Workspace, however, contains older and more stable versions. For all configuration items, version numbers of the form 1.x refer to the promotions without navigation maps functionality whereas version numbers of the form 2.x refer to the promotions containing partial or complete implementations of the navigation maps.

10.4.3 Release Management

The creation of a new release for a configuration item or an CM aggregate is a management decision, usually based on marketing and quality control advice. A release is made available to offer additional (or revised) functionality or to address critical bugs.

Although creating a release seems similar to creating a promotion, it is a much more complicated and expensive process. Developers deal with change as part of their work. If the new version of a component introduces more problems than it addresses, they can simply roll back to an earlier promotion. A user manual that is not up to date does not interfere with their work given that they know the product. Users, on the other hand, are not in the business of testing software. Discovering inconsistencies in the system and its documentation interferes with their work and can lead them to switch products or contractors. Releases, therefore, are created in a much more controlled process than promotions, attempting to ensure consistency and quality. The quality control team assesses the quality of the individual components of a release and coordinates revisions to defective components. This auditing process allows the quality control team to ensure the consistency of the release with minimal interference with the developer's work.

For example, consider the release of the navigation map functionality for myCarParts (Figure 10-10). We first create a stable promotion of the NClient.2.4 and the Server.2.3 that implements the new functionality. The quality control team tests these two promotions against the latest version of the RAD (i.e., NClient RAD.2.0). Quality control finds a bug, which is fixed in a subsequent promotion of the NClient.2.5. Quality control then tests the current version of the EClient (i.e., EClient.1.5) with the current version of the server. Satisfied with the state of the software, quality control decides to include NClient.2.5, EClient.1.5, and Server.2.3 in the next major release of myCarParts. Quality control then checks the user manual (NClient UM.2.0) for consistency against NClient.2.5. A few additional problems are found and addressed in the promotion NClient UM.2.1, which is then included in the release under construction. The release is then beta tested with a selected set of users. Two more problems with the NClient.2.5 and Server.2.3 are discovered by a beta tester and are addressed in NClient.2.6 and Server.2.4. The software is retested and released to the users as myCarParts.2.0.

The administrator of the myCarParts site first upgrades the Server and its database schema and observes, during a beta test, if any user discovers unforeseen compatibility problems with the older clients. After the beta test, the administrator then makes available the NClient.2.6 to the users who would like to use the navigation map functionality. Once the stability of the new release is validated in the field, all users are encouraged to upgrade and older versions of the server and the clients are discontinued. Any change to the documentation or subsystems of myCarParts will be delivered as a patch or as a third release.

The focus of the release process in the myCarParts example is on quality and consistency. The quality control team acts as a gatekeeper between the users and the developers. The assumption behind this process is that users are not interested in debugging the systems they use. They expect that these systems support their work. This assumption does not hold when the users are software developers. In this case, a substantial number of tools used by this group of users are also developed and maintained by them. These can range from simple scripts, making it more convenient to accomplish a repetitive task, to full-fledged programming languages,

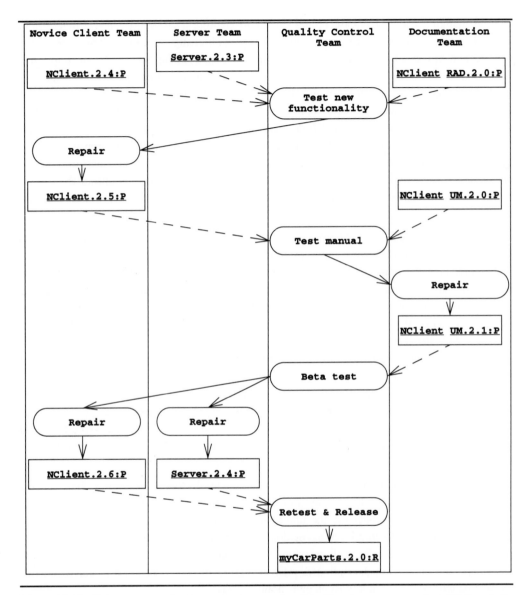

Figure 10-10   Release process for the navigation map functionality of `myCarParts.2.0` (UML activity diagram). `:P` denotes a promotion, `:R` denotes a release.

syntax editors, or configuration management systems. With the popularity of the Internet among software developers, an increasing number of these ad hoc tools are shared and distributed, especially those that address common problems. This leads to the availability of numerous freely available programs, ranging from simple scripts to operating systems (e.g., Linux). In this situation, users (who are software developers) are willing to test, debug, and send contributed code to the program author in exchange for early access to the piece of software. In this software development model, known as the bazaar model [Raymond, 1998], releases and promotions become much more similar than in the context of the controlled process we described above.

10.4.4 Branch Management

Until now, we have examined the management of promotions and releases in the context of a single change. Various configuration items are revised until the change is completed and then assessed by quality control. During this process, we have dealt with the complexity caused by the difficulty in maintaining consistency among related promotions and in minimizing the introduction of new faults. We have focused, however, only on a single thread of development.

Usually, developers work on multiple improvements concurrently. For example, while developers implement the navigation map functionality in the NClient and the Server, other developers may be improving the Server response time, while yet another group of developers may be extending the EClient to store the history of queries issued by the user. When threads of development focus on different subsystems of myCarParts (e.g., navigation maps in the NClient and the Server, query history in EClient), teams can be isolated by working on different configurations of the group same subsystems (e.g., the navigation map effort works with the most recent versions of the NClient and the Server, while the query history effort works with the most recent version of the EClient and an older, stable version of the Server). This approach works only if changes impact nonoverlapping sets of components and if subsystems interfaces remain backward compatible. However, when two changes require modifications to the same component, a different approach is required. Concurrent branches and subsequent merging can be used to coordinate changes.

For example, let us focus on two concurrent and overlapping changes: While developers implement the navigation map functionality (described in Section 10.4.2 and in Section 10.4.3), we assign another team the task of improving the response time of the Server. Both teams may change the Server, the NClient, and their interfaces to accomplish their respective goals.

These changes are assigned to different teams because of the difference in their associated risks. The navigation map improvement extends the functionality of myCarParts and is well defined. The response time improvement, however, requires experimental work and is open ended: The developers first need to identify performance bottlenecks and design heuristics to speed up common requests. The resulting improvement then needs to be measured and assessed against any loss of reliability and decrease in maintainability. Finally, separating both changes provides us with more flexibility during delivery: If the response time improvement is completed early, we can merge it with the functional improvement and release it at the same time. Otherwise, if the response time improvement takes more time to be completed, we can deliver it later as a patch.

To support both changes concurrently while keeping teams independent, we set up a branch, starting from the latest promotions of the subsystems at the time the changes are approved (see Figure 10-11).

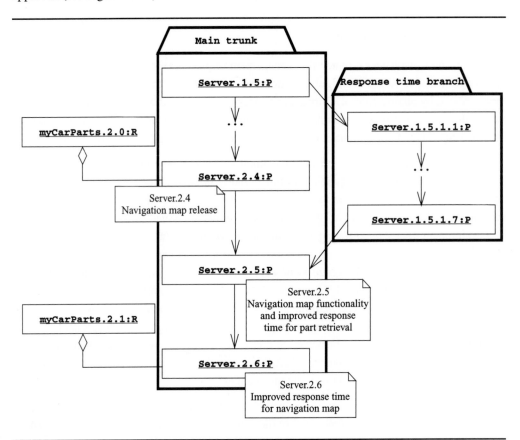

Figure 10-11   An example of branch (UML object diagram, some promotions were omitted for brevity, :P denotes a promotion, :R denotes a release). On the main trunk, developers add the navigation map functionality to myCarParts. On a concurrent branch, developers improve the response time of the server by integrating a cache between the server and the database. The response time improvement is completed after the release of the navigation map functionality and made available as a patch.

The teams working on functional improvements continue working on the main trunk (starting at `Server.1.5` and `NClient.1.6`). The team responsible for the response time improvement works on the branch (starting at `Server.1.5.1.1`).[3] The performance improvement team restricts its changes to the `Server` subsystem and decides to avoid

_____

3. We use the CVS identification scheme for identifying versions and branches [Berliner, 1990].

modifying the `Server` interface. Both teams then work independently until they complete their improvements. The navigation map improvement is completed first and made part of the second release of myCarParts, as we saw in Figure 10-10 (as `Server.2.4`). Soon after, the response time improvement is completed (`Server.1.5.1.7`, in Figure 10-11). The response time improvement is considered successful, yielding a fourfold decrease in response time for common requests, while marginally extending the client server protocol. At this point, we need to integrate this improvement with the main trunk, hoping to produce a version of `myCarParts` which has both the navigation map functionality and the fourfold improvement in response time.

Merges can usually be done with the help of the configuration management system, which attempts to merge the most recent parts of the versions to be merged. When conflicts are detected, that is, when both versions contain modifications to the same classes or methods, the configuration management tool reports the problem back to the developer. The developer then resolves the conflict manually. In our example, the tool reports a conflict in the `DBInterface` class which was modified by both teams (Figure 10-12).

The navigation map team added a method, `processMapRequest()`, to retrieve maps from the database. The response time improvement team modified the `processPartRequest()` which retrieves parts from the database given a part id. We construct a merged version of the `DBInterface` class by selecting the `processMapRequest()` from the main trunk and the `processPartRequest()` from the branch. We then test the revised `DBInterface` class to make sure we have dealt with all the conflicts, which results in the `Server.2.5:Promotion`. Later, we realize that the same caching mechanism can be used for the `processMapRequest()`, which can result in further response time improvements. We modify the `processMapRequest()` method, retest the server, and create the `Server.2.6:Promotion`.

Heuristics for branch management

As we saw in this example, merging two branches is a nontrivial operation. It usually needs to be supported by a configuration management tool and requires substantial intervention and testing by developers. In the `myCarParts` example, illustrating a very simple case, the response time improvement team was careful not to change the `Server` interface and limited their changes to the `Server` subsystem. These constraints minimized the likelihood of an overlap with the changes made by the navigation map team. In general, if no constraints are set, branches can diverge to the point where they cannot be merged. Although there are no reliable ways to address this problem, several heuristics can be used to mitigate the risk of divergent branches.

- **Identify likely overlaps**. Once the development branches are set up, but before design and implementation work starts, developers can anticipate where overlaps could occur. This information is then used to specify constraints for containing these overlaps. Examples of such constraints include not modifying the interface of classes involved in the overlap.

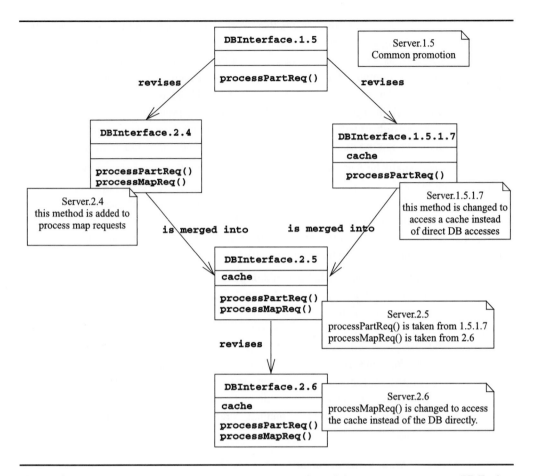

Figure 10-12   An example of merge for the `DBInterface` class of the `myCarParts` system (UML class diagram).

- **Merge frequently**. The configuration management policy can require developers working on a branch to frequently merge with the latest version of the main trunk (e.g., daily, weekly, or whenever a new promotion is created). The merges are only created on the branch and are not propagated back on the main trunk. The policy also may specify that such merges need only to ensure that the code still compiles; that is, the merges need not necessarily address all overlaps. This policy encourages developers to find overlaps early and think about how to address them before the actual merge.

- **Communicate likely conflicts**. Although teams working on different branches need to work independently, they should anticipate conflicts during the future merge and communicate them to the relevant teams. This also has the benefit of improving the design of both changes by taking into account constraints from both teams.

- **Minimize changes on the main trunk**. Minimizing the number of changes to one of the branches to be merged reduces the likelihood of conflicts. Although this constraint is not always acceptable, it is a good configuration management policy to restrict changes to the main branch to bug fixes and do all other changes on the development branch.

- **Minimize the number of branches**. Configuration management branches are complex mechanisms that should not be abused. Merge work caused by reckless branching may result into substantially more effort than if a single branch was used. Changes that may result in overlaps and conflicts usually depend on each other and can be addressed sequentially. Branches should be used only when concurrent development is required and when conflicts can be reconciled.

In all cases, creating a branch is a significant event in the development. It should require management approval and should be carefully planned.

10.4.5 Variant Management

Variants are versions that are intended to coexist. A system has multiple variants when it is supported on different operating systems and different hardware platforms. A system also has multiple variants when it is delivered with different levels of functionality (e.g., novice version vs. expert version, standard version vs. deluxe version). Two fundamental approaches are possible when dealing with variants (Figure 10-13).

- **Redundant teams**. A team is assigned to each variant. Each team is given the same requirements and is responsible for the complete design, implementation, and testing of the variant. A small number of configuration items are shared across variants, such as the user manual and the RAD.

- **Single project**. Design a subsystem decomposition that maximizes the amount of code shared across variants. For multiple platforms, confine variant specific code into low-level subsystems. For multiple levels of functionality, confine increments of functionality in individual and mostly independent subsystems.

The redundant-team option leads to multiple smaller projects that share a requirements specification. The single project option leads to a larger, single project with most teams sharing core subsystems. At first sight, the redundant team option leads to redundancies in the project as the core functionality of the system will be designed and implemented multiple times. The single project option seems more efficient, given that a potentially large amount of code can be reused across variants, given a good system design. Surprisingly, the redundant-team option is often chosen [Kemerer, 1997] in commercial developments to avoid organizational complexity.

Redundant team organization

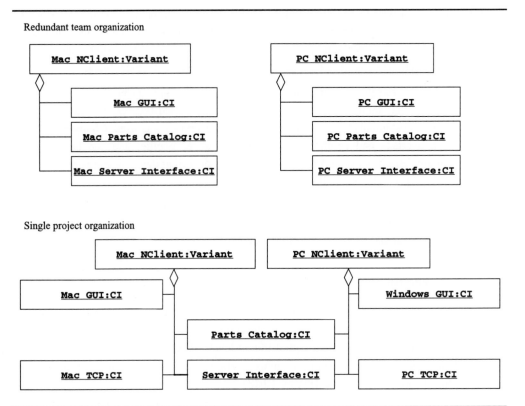

Figure 10-13 Examples of redundant variants and variants sharing configuration items (UML object diagram). In the redundant team organization, the myCarParts NClients for the Macintosh and the PC are realized independently. In the single project organization, the myCarParts NClients for the Macintosh and the PC differ in their UI.

Issues introduced by code sharing include:

- **Single supplier/multiple consumers**. Core subsystems are used by teams working on different variants, and, thus, with possibly diverging requirements. The core subsystem teams need to satisfy their requirements uniformly.
- **Long change request turnaround**. When one variant-specific team issues a change request for a core subsystem, the approval and implementation of the change can take longer than for other changes, given that the core subsystem team needs to ensure the change does not interfere with the other variant-specific teams.
- **Cross platform inconsistencies**. Core subsystems introduce constraints on variant specific subsystems that can interfere with platform constraints. For example, a core subsystem can be designed with a threaded control flow in mind, whereas the user interface toolkit of a specific variant assumes an event-driven flow of control.

Each of these issues can be perceived by variant-specific teams as a motivation to implement their own core subsystems. These issues can be addressed, however, by anticipating variant-specific issues during system design and through effective configuration management. A good system design is resilient to platform and variant-specific issues. This results in a subsystem decomposition that is identical for all variants, where each system variant differs by substituting one or more subsystems. For example in Figure 10-13, the Macintosh and PC variants of the NClient share the Parts Catalog and the Server Interface subsystem. The user interface and the network interface subsystems are different but have the same interface. This results in a subsystem decomposition where each subsystem is either variant independent (i.e., supporting all variants) or variant specific (i.e., supporting a small number of variants). The issues we raised before can then be addressed as follows.

- The *single supplier/multiple consumers* issue is addressed by careful change management: If a requested change is variant specific, it should not be addressed in a core subsystem. If the requested change benefits all variants, then it should be addressed only in the core subsystems.

- The *long change request turnaround* is shortened by involving the team that issued the change request during validation. The suggested change is implemented in a new promotion of the core subsystem and released to the team who requested the change. The team evaluates the solution and tests its implementation, whereas other teams continue using the former promotion. Once the change is validated, other variant teams may start using the revised subsystem. We described such a scenario with the Server side changes required by the navigation map (see Figure 10-9): The novice client team validated the new version of the server, while the EClient team continued working with a former (and more stable) release. Note that when variant teams require concurrent changes to the core subsystem, core developers can use branches to isolate the impact of each change until they reach a stable state.

- *Cross-platform inconsistencies* are avoided as much as possible during system design by focusing on a variant independent subsystem decomposition. Lower level cross-platform inconsistencies are addressed in variant-specific subsystems, at the cost of some glue objects or redundancy between core and variant-specific subsystems. If all else fails, independent development paths should be considered when the supported variants are substantially different.

Managing multiple variants with shared subsystems is complex, as we indicated earlier. After an upfront investment during system design, however, the shared code approach yields numerous advantages, such as increased quality and stability of the shared code, and greater consistency in quality across variants. Finally, when the number of variants is large, considering variant-specific issues early and designing configuration management mechanisms to meet them lead to substantial savings in time and cost.

10.4.6 Change management

The creation of new promotions and releases is driven by change requests. A team repairs a fault and creates a promotion for quality control to evaluate. Clients define new requirements or developers take advantage of a new implementation technology causing a new release of the system. Change requests can range from correcting a typo in a menu label to reimplementing a major subsystem to address performance issues. Change requests also vary in their timing: A request for additional functionality during the requirements review can lead to modifying the draft RAD, whereas the same request made during testing can additionally lead to major subsystem surgery. Change requests need to be handled differently depending on their scope and their timing. The handling of change requests, called change management, is part of configuration management.

Change management processes vary in their formality and complexity with the project goals. In the case of a complex system with high reliability requirements, for example, the change request form has several pages (e.g., [MIL Std. 480]), requires the approval of several managers, and takes several weeks to be processed. In the case of a simple tool written by one developer, informal communication is sufficient. In both cases, the change process includes the following steps (Figure 10-14).

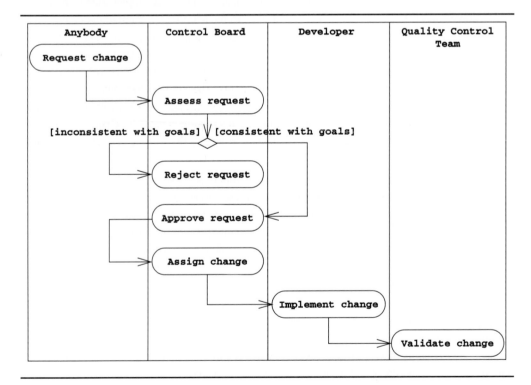

Figure 10-14   An example of change management process (UML activity diagram).

1. The change, identifying a fault or a new feature, is requested. This can be done by any one, including a user or a developer.

2. The request is assessed against project goals. In large projects, this is done by a control board. In smaller projects, this is done by the project manager. This may include a cost benefit analysis and an evaluation of impact of the change on the rest of the system.

3. Following the assessment, the request is either accepted or rejected.

4. If it is accepted, the change is planned, prioritized, and assigned to a developer and implemented.

5. The implemented change is audited. This is done by the quality control team or whoever is responsible for managing releases.

10.5 Managing Configuration Management

In this section, we address management issues related to configuration management. These include:

- documenting configuration management
- assigning configuration management responsibilities
- planning configuration management activities

10.5.1 Documenting Configuration Management

[IEEE Std. 828-1990] is a standard for writing *Software Configuration Management Plans* (SCMP). Such a plan documents all the relevant information to the configuration management activities of a specific project. The plan is generated during the planning phase, put under configuration management, and revised as necessary. The scope and the length of the plan may vary according to the needs of the project. A mission critical project with a formal change control process may require a 30-page document. A project developing a conceptual prototype may only require a five-page document.

An SCMP contains six types of information: introduction, management, activities, schedules, resources, and plan maintenance (see Figure 10-15).

The *Introduction* describes the scope and audience of the document, key terms, and references.

The *Management* section describes the organization of the project (which can be a reference to the corresponding section in the *Software Project Management Plan*, see Chapter 11, *Project Management*) and how the configuration management responsibilities are assigned within this organization.

The *Activities* section describes in detail the identification of configuration items, the change control process, the process for creating releases and for auditing, and the process for status accounting. Responsibilities for each of these activities are assigned to a role defined in the management section.

Software Configuration Management Plan

1. Introduction
   1.1 Purpose
   1.2 Scope
   1.3 Key terms
   1.4 References
2. Management
   2.1 Organization
   2.2 Responsibilities
3. Activities
4. Schedule
5. Resources
6. Plan Maintenance

Figure 10-15   An example of a template for the *Software Configuration Management Plan*.

The *Schedule* section describes when the configuration management activities take place and how they are coordinated. In particular, it defines at which point changes can be requested and approved through the formal change process.

The *Resources* section identifies the tools, techniques, equipment, personnel, and training necessary for accomplishing the software configuration activities.

Finally, the *Plan Maintenance* section defines how the SCMP, itself under configuration management, is maintained and revised. In particular, this section details the person responsible for its maintenance, the frequency of updates, and the change process for updating the plan.

The [IEEE Std. 828-1990] standard is defined such that the above outline can be applied to any project, from a reliable systems design to a freeware product.

10.5.2 Assigning Configuration Management Responsibilities

Configuration management is a project function that involves many different tasks and participants in the project. As in the case of system design, tasks that require consistency should be performed by a small number of persons. During system design, a small team of architects make decisions about the subsystem decomposition. Similarly, a small team of configuration managers identify the configuration items and CM aggregates that need to be controlled. As in the case of testing, quality control tasks such as release management should be performed by different participants than development tasks, such as object design and implementation.

Configuration management include the following roles.

- **Configuration manager.** This is the role responsible for identifying configuration items and CM aggregates. This role may also be responsible in defining the procedures for creating promotions and releases. This role is often combined with the role of architect.

- **Change control board member**. This role is responsible for approving or rejecting change requests based on project goals. Depending on the complexity of the change process, this role can also be involved in assessing the change and in planning accepted changes. This role is often combined with the role of team or project manager.
- **Developer**. This role creates promotions triggered by change requests or the normal activities of development. The main configuration management activity of developers is to check in changes and resolve merge conflicts.
- **Auditor**. This role is responsible for the selection and evaluation of promotions for release. The auditor is also responsible for ensuring the consistency and completeness of the release. This role is often accomplished by the quality control team.

The roles for configuration management are defined during project planning and assigned early, in order to ensure consistency. Reassigning configuration management roles too often can severely limit the benefits of configuration management and fail to control change.

10.5.3 Planning Configuration Management Activities

Project managers should plan configuration management activities during the project initiation phase. Most of the configuration management procedures can be defined before the project starts given that they do not depend on the system itself, but rather, on project goals and nonfunctional requirements such as safety and reliability.

The key elements in planning configuration management are:

- definition of the configuration management processes
- definition and assignment of roles
- definition of change criteria, that is, what attributes of the work products can be changed and how late in the process
- definition of release criteria, that is, which criteria should be evaluated when auditing promotions for a release

Moreover, configuration management procedures and tools need to be in place before changes start taking place, so that they can be recorded, approved, and tracked.

10.6 Exercises

1. RCS adopts a reverse delta approach for storing multiple versions of a file. For example, assume a file has three revisions, 1.1, 1.2, and 1.3, RCS stores the file as of version 1.3, then, the differences between 1.2 and 1.3, and the differences between 1.1 and 1.2. When a new version is created, say 1.4, the difference between 1.3 and 1.4 is computed and stored, and the 1.3 version is deleted and replaced by 1.4.

Explain why RCS does not simply store the initial version (in this case 1.1) and the differences between each successive version.

2. CVS uses a simple text-based rule to identify overlaps during a merge: There is an overlap if the same line was changed in both versions that are being merged. If no such line exists, then CVS decides there is no conflict and the versions are merged automatically. For example, assume a file contains a class with three methods, a(), b(), and c(). Two developers work independently on the file. If they both modify the same lines of code, say the first line of method a(), then CVS decides there is a conflict.

Explain why this approach will fail to detect certain types of conflict. Provide an example in your answer.

3. Configuration management systems such as RCS, CVS, and Perforce use file names and their paths to identify configuration items. Explain why this feature prevents the configuration management of CM aggregates, even in the presence of labels.

4. Explain how configuration management can be beneficial to developers, even in the absence of a change control or auditing process. List two scenarios illustrating your explanation.

5. In Chapter 8, *Rationale Management*, we described how rationale information can be represented using an issue model. Draw a UML class diagram for a problem tracking system that uses an issue model for the description and discussion of changes and their relationship with versions. Focus only on the domain objects of the system.

6. In Chapter 9, *Testing*, we described how the quality control team find faults in promotions created by subsystem teams. Draw a UML activity diagram including the change process activities and testing activities of a multiteam project.

References

[Babich, 1986]   W. A. Babich, *Software Configuration Management.* Addison-Wesley, Reading, MA, 1986.

[Berliner, 1990]   B. Berliner, "CVS II: parallelizing software development," *Proceedings of the 1990 USENIX Conference*, (Washington, DC,) pp. 22–26, Jan. 1990.

[Bersoff et al., 1980] E. H. Bersoff, V. D. Henderson, & S.G. Siegel, *Software Configuration Management: An Investment in Product Integrity.* Prentice Hall, Englewood Cliffs, 1980.

[Conradi et al., 1998] R. Conradi & B. Westfechtel, "Version models for software configuration management," *ACM Computing Surveys*, Vol. 30, No. 2, June 1998.

[Dart, 1991]   S. Dart, "Concepts in configuration management systems," *Third International Software Configuration Management Workshop*, June 1991.

[IEEE Std. 828-1990] *IEEE Standard for Software Configuration Management Plans*, IEEE Standards Board, Sept. 1990, in [IEEE 1997].

[IEEE Std. 1042-1987] *IEEE Guide to Software Configuration Management*, IEEE Standards Board, Sept. 1987 (Reaffirmed, Dec. 1993), in [IEEE 1997].

[IEEE, 1997]   *IEEE Standards Collection Software Engineering*, Piscataway, NJ, 1997.

[Kemerer, 1997]   C. F. Kemerer, "Case 7: Microsoft Corporation: Office Business Unit," *Software Project Management: Readings and Cases.* Irwin/McGraw-Hill, Boston, MA, 1997.

[Knuth, 1986]   D. E. Knuth, *The TeXbook.* Addison-Wesley, Reading, MA, 1986.

[Leblang, 1994]   D. Leblang, "The CM challenge: Configuration management that works," *Configuration Management*, W. F. Tichy (ed.), vol. 2 of *Trends in Software*, Wiley, New York, 1994.

[MIL Std. 480]   MIL Std. 480, U.S. Department of Defense, Washington, DC.

[Perforce]   Perforce, Inc., 2420 Santa Clara Ave., Alameda, CA.

[POSIX, 1990]   *Portable Operating System Interface for Computing Environments* in IEEE Std. 1003.1, 1990.

[Raymond, 1998]   E. Raymond, "The cathedral and the bazaar," Available at http://www.tuxedo.org/~esr/writings/cathedral-bazaar/cathedral-bazaar.html, 1998.

[Steelman, 1978]   *Requirements for high order computer programming languages: Steelman*, U.S. Department of Defense, Washington, DC, 1978.

[Tichy, 1985]   W. Tichy, "RCS - a system for version control," *Software Practice and Experience*. Vol. 15, No. 7, 1985.

11

11

Project Management

Take off your engineering hat and put on your management hat.
—Statement made during of the 51-L launch discussion

Managers do not generate a useful product of their own. Instead, they provide and coordinate resources so that others can generate useful products. Managing a software project requires a combination of managerial and social skills to foresee potentially damaging problems and to implement the appropriate response. Because of the lack of visible product and the reliance on nontechnical skills, management is usually the target of jokes by developers and others. Management, however, is a critical function for bringing a project to a successful end, given the complexity of current systems and the high rate of change during development.

Managers do not make technical decisions and often do not have the background to make such decisions. Instead, they are responsible for coordinating and administrating the project and ensuring that the high-quality system is delivered on time and within budget. The main tools of management are planning, monitoring, risk management, and contingency handling.

In this chapter, we describe the management activities that are visible to developers and the team leader. We assume a two-level management hierarchy, typical of many software industries today. Our goal is not to provide the reader with project management expertise but rather to give sufficient knowledge to be able to act as a team leader and effectively interact with project management. Consequently, we cover topics such as task plans, role assignments, risk management, and software project management plans; we leave out topics such as cost estimation, labor issues, and contract negotiation.

11.1 Introduction: The STS-51L Launch Decision

Consider the following example:

Example:[a] **The STS-51L launch decision**

On January 28, 1986, the Space Shuttle Challenger flying mission STS-51L exploded 73 seconds into flight, killing all seven crew members aboard. The Rogers Presidential Commission, formed to investigate the accident, determined that combustion gases leaking through a joint in the right solid rocket booster caused the ignition of hydrogen fuel from the external fuel tank. The Rogers Commission also determined that there were serious flaws in the decision-making process at NASA.

The main components of the Space Shuttle are the orbiter, the solid rocket boosters, and the external tank. The orbiter is the vehicle that transports cargo and astronauts. The solid rocket boosters provide most of the thrust necessary to put the orbiter in orbit. When they consume all their fuel, they are detached and fall back into the ocean. The external tank, providing fuel to the orbiter's engine, is also detached before reaching orbit. The solid booster rockets were built by a private contractor, Morton Thiokol. The solid booster rockets were built-in sections such that they could be easily transported. Once delivered to the launch site, the sections are assembled. Each section is connected by a joint. A design flaw of this joint was responsible for the combustion gas leak that caused the accident.

The Rogers Commission determined that the engineers at Thiokol, the contractor who built the solid rocket boosters, were aware of possible failure of the solid booster rocket joints. Solid booster rockets recovered from previous shuttle flights indicated that rubber gaskets, called O-rings, in the field joints had been eroded by combustion gases. This erosion seemed particular severe on flights that took place in cold temperatures. This erosion concerned engineers, because the O-rings had not been designed to come in contact with the combustion gases. Managers treated the joint problem as an acceptable risk, given that erosion had occurred in previous missions without causing an incident. Engineers at Thiokol had repeatedly and unsuccessfully attempted to communicate the severity of the problem to their management. In the days preceding the STS-51L launch, engineers were alarmed by the low temperatures at the launch site and attempted to convince their management to recommend against a launch. Thiokol initially recommended against the launch and then later reversed its position, at the urging of NASA.

Both NASA and Thiokol have hierarchical reporting structures, typical of public administration organizations. Moreover, the information flow through the organization is through the reporting structure. Engineers report to their group manager who then reports to the project manager and so on. Each level can choose to modify, distort, or suppress any information before sending it upward, based on its own objectives. The STS-51L mission had been delayed repeatedly and was already several months late. Management at both NASA and Thiokol wanted to meet the deadline. This situation resulted in a lack of communication, improper information dissemination, and inadequate risk evaluation at both NASA and Thiokol.

The Rogers Commission determined that the primary cause of the Challenger accident was a design flaw in the solid rocket booster joint. The Rogers Commission, however, also determined that the decision-making process and the communication structure at Thiokol and NASA were flawed and failed to assess the risks of launching the flawed vehicle.

---

a.   The Challenger accident has been summarized here as an example of project management failure. Both the mechanical and the administrative failures that caused the Challenger accident are much more complex than this summary suggests. For complete reference of the investigation, refer to the Rogers Commission report [Rogers et al., 1986] and related books on the subject [Vaughan, 1996].

Project management ensures the delivery of a quality system on time and within budget. The main components of this definition are quality, time, and money. Ensuring delivery within budget requires a manager to estimate and assign the resources required by the project in terms of participants, training, and tools. Ensuring on-time delivery requires a manager to plan work effort and to monitor the status of the project in terms of tasks and work products. Finally, ensuring quality requires a project manager to provide problem reporting mechanisms and monitor the status the product in terms of defects and risks. All three aspects of the project, quality, budget, and time, are essential and need to be addressed together for the project to succeed.

In this chapter, we describe the role of management in software projects. However, the material presented here is far from sufficient for learning to act as a project manager, on the Shuttle program or otherwise. This chapter is oriented toward developers who will become team leaders after some project experience. In this chapter, we assume a two-level management hierarchy, with the project manager at the top, the team leader at the middle, and developers at the bottom. This is large enough for experiencing the effects of complexity on management and small enough to be typical of today's software industry.

In Section 11.2, we provide a bird's eye view of management and its relationship to other development activities. In Section 11.3, we describe the models used for management, such as organizations, roles, work products, tasks, and schedules. In Section 11.4, we describe the management activities that manipulate these models and illustrate how these building blocks can be used together using an example from building facilities. In Section 11.5, we describe management issues related to project management.

11.2 An Overview of Project Management

Project management is concerned with planning and allocating resources to ensure the delivery of quality software system on time and within budget. Project management is subject to the same barriers as technical activities: complexity and change. Complex products require a large number of participants with diverse skills and backgrounds. Competitive markets and evolving requirements introduce change in the development, triggering frequent resource reallocation and making it difficult to track the status of the project. Managers deal with complexity and change the same way developers do: through modeling, communication, rationale, and configuration management. We have talked about the communication, rationale, and configuration aspects of management in previous chapters (Chapters 3, 8, and 10, respectively). In this chapter, we focus on the management models and the activities needed to create and maintain them.

Management models allow us to represent the resources available to the project, the constraints resources are subjected to, and the relationships among resources. In this chapter, we describe the following elements:

- **Teams** represent sets of participants who work on a common problem.
- **Roles** represent sets of responsibilities. Roles are used to distribute work to participants within a team.
- **Work products** represent the deliverables and intermediate products of the project. Work products are the visible results of work.
- **Tasks** represent work in terms of sequential steps necessary to generate one or more work products.
- **Schedules** represent the mapping of a task model onto a time line. A schedule represents work in terms of calendar time.

The project manager and team leaders construct and maintain these model elements throughout development. The management activities that concern a team leader are outlined in Figure 11-1.

Using these models, team leaders can communicate with managers and developers about status and responsibilities. If a substantial deviation occurs between the planned work and the actual work, the project manager reallocates resources or changes the project environment.

At the highest level of abstraction, the development life cycle can be decomposed into three major phases: **project initiation**, during which the project scope and resources are defined, **steady state**, during which the bulk of development work occurs, and **project termination**, during which the system is delivered and accepted.

Project initiation. During this phase, the project manager defines the scope of the system with the client and constructs the initial version of the management models. Initially, only the project manager, selected team leaders, and the client are involved. The project manager sets up the project environment, organizes teams, hires participants, and kicks off the project. Project initiation includes the following activities:

- **Problem statement definition**. During this activity, the client and the project manager define the scope of the system in terms of functionality, constraints, and deliverables. The client and the project manager agree on acceptance criteria and target dates.
- **Initial top-level design**. The project manager and the system architect decompose the system into subsystems for the purpose of team assignment. The project manager defines teams and work products in terms of subsystems. The system architect and the developers will revise the subsystem decomposition during system design.
- **Team formation**. The project manager assigns a team to each subsystem, defines cross-functional teams, and selects team leaders. The project manager and the team leaders together then assign roles and responsibilities to participants as a function of the skills of the participants. The team leaders establish training needs for the team during this phase.
- **Communication infrastructure setup**. The project manager and the team leaders set up the communication infrastructure of the project, including bulletin boards, Web sites,

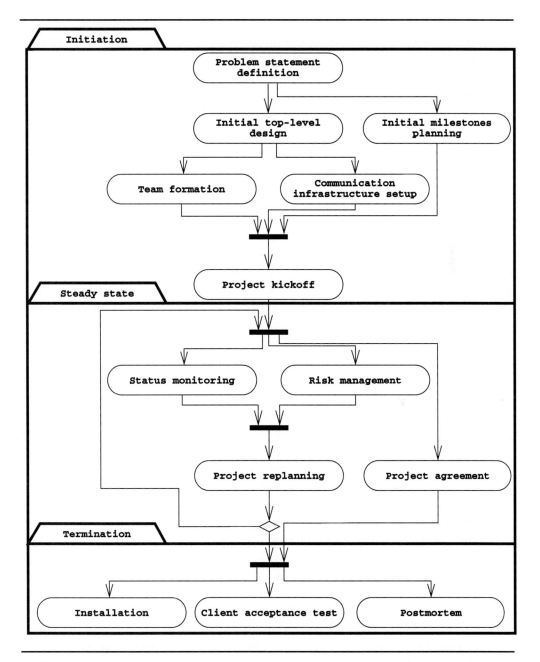

Figure 11-1 Management activities during initiation, steady state, and termination. (UML activity diagram).

configuration management tools, document templates, and meeting procedures. Project participants will use this infrastructure for distributing information and report problems in a timely manner.

- **Initial milestones planning**. The project manager schedules intermediate work products and external deliverables and assigns them to teams.

- **Project kickoff**. The project manager, the team leaders, and the client officially start the project. The purpose of the kickoff meetings is to explain to the project participants the scope of the project, the communication infrastructure, and the responsibilities of each team. After the kickoff, the project is in steady state.

Steady state.   During this phase, the role of team leader becomes critical. During project initiation, most decisions are made by the project manager. During steady state, team leaders are responsible for tracking the status of their team and identifying problems via team meetings. Team leaders report the status of their team to the project manager who then evaluates the status of the complete project. Team leaders respond to deviation from the plan by reallocating tasks to developers or obtaining additional resources from the project manager. The project manager is still responsible for the interaction with the client, obtaining formal agreement and renegotiating resources and deadlines. Steady state activities include the following:

- **Project agreement definition**. Once the analysis model is stable, the client and the project manager formally agree on the scope of the system and the delivery date. The *Project Agreement* document is derived from the problem statement and revised during analysis.

- **Status monitoring**. Throughout the project, team leaders and management monitor the status and compare it with the planned schedule. The team leaders are responsible for collecting status information through meetings, reviews, problem reports, and work product completion, and for summarizing it for the project manager.

- **Risk management**. During this activity, project participants identify the potential problems that could cause delays in the schedule and budget overruns. The project manager and the team leaders identify, analyze, and prioritize risks and prepare contingency plans for the important risks.

- **Project replanning**. When the project deviates from the schedule or when a contingency plan is activated, the project manager or the team leader revises the schedule and reallocates resources to meet the delivery deadline. The project manager can hire new staff, create new teams, or merge existing teams.

Project termination.   During this phase, the product is delivered and the project history is collected. Most of the developers' involvement with the project ends before this phase. A handful of key developers, the technical writers, and the team leaders are involved with wrapping up the system for installation and acceptance and collecting the project history for future use.

- **Client acceptance test**. The system is evaluated with the client according to the acceptance criteria set forth in the *Project Agreement*. Functional and nonfunctional requirements are demonstrated and tested using scenarios defined in the *Project Agreement*. The client formally accepts the product at this stage.

- **Installation**. The system is deployed in the target environment and documents are delivered. The installation may include user training and a roll out phase, during which data is moved from the previous system to the new system. Acceptance usually precedes installation.

- **Postmortem**. The project manager and the team leaders collect the history of the project for the organizational learning. By capturing the history of major and minor failures and by analyzing their causes, an organization can avoid repeating mistakes and improve its practice.

In all the above activities, timely and accurate communication between project management, the team leaders, and the developers is crucial for determining the status of a project and for making correct decisions. Several tools are available to the project participants, including the communication infrastructure, management documents, such as the *Software Project Management Plan* (SPMP), and, more generally, encouraging the free exchange of information. A team leader can substantially improve communication by rewarding accurate reporting instead of punishing the bearer of bad news, by releasing as much information as possible in a timely manner, and by responding constructively to problem reports.

Managers use models to deal with complexity and revise them to deal with change. In the next section, we describe the model elements used for management and represent them using UML class diagrams. In Section 11.4, we describe the activities during which these models are created and revised using object diagrams and activity diagrams.

11.3 Management Concepts

In this section, we describe the main concepts used during project management. Each element represents work from a different perspective (Figure 11-2).

- A **team** is a small group of people who work on the same subproblem (Section 11.3.1). The concept of team deals with the complexity associated with communicating among many persons. Instead of organizing and coordinating project participants as a large group, the project is divided into teams, each tackling a separate subproblem.

- A **role** represents a set of responsibilities assigned to a participant or a team (Section 11.3.2). The clear definition of roles enables unplanned tasks to be easily discovered and assigned. The role of a tester, for example, is to design and execute tests. If new unplanned testing activities are identified, they are assigned to the participant filling the tester role.

- A **work product** represents a concrete deliverable produced by a role (Section 11.3.3). Work products include technical and managerial documents, product features, test cases, test results, technology surveys, and usability reports.

- A **task** represents a work product in terms of an activity (Section 11.3.4). A task results in one or more work products, is assigned to a role, and consumes resources. Tasks are related to each other by dependencies. For example, *Database test planning* is the task of designing tests for the database subsystem. It requires the interface to the subsystem and results into a test plan and a test suite to be executed during the *Database test task*.

- A **schedule** represents tasks assigned to a time line (Section 11.3.5). The schedule is usually the most visible and evolving of all management models. The schedule is revised when estimates are refined, when constraints change, or when resources are reallocated.

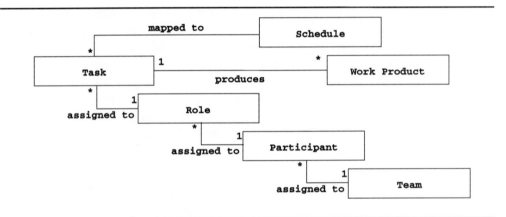

Figure 11-2 Relationships among participants, teams, roles, tasks, work products, and schedules (UML class diagram). `Participant` are assigned to `Teams` each responsible for a different subsystem. Each `Participant` is assigned a number of `Roles` each corresponding to a set of `Tasks`. `Tasks` result in one or more `Work Products`. A `Schedule` consists of a set of tasks mapped to a time line.

11.3.1 Teams

A **team** is a small group of people who work on the same subproblem. Instead of organizing and coordinating project participants as a large group of individuals, each cutting away the same problem, the system is divided into subsystems that are each assigned to a team. Each team is responsible for the analysis, design, and implementation of its subsystem. Each team negotiates with other teams the interfaces of the subsystems it needs. Such teams are called **subsystem teams**. Figure 11-3 represents a system architecture of three subsystems mapped to an organization of three subsystem teams.

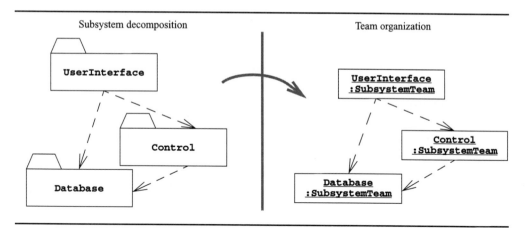

Figure 11-3 An example of a subsystem decomposition mapped onto a team organization (UML object diagram). The arrows represent dependencies among subsystems and among teams.

Each team is managed by a **team leader** who assigns responsibilities to its members, facilitates team meetings, and tracks status. The team leader is often an experienced developer who is familiar with the technical content of the subsystem. The team leader collects and summarizes status information for the project manager and reports open issues.

The hierarchical relationship between developers, team leaders, and the project manager represents the **reporting structure.** The developer, who has the most detailed knowledge of technical details, makes decisions locally and reports to the team leader. The team leader, who has an overview of the subsystem, can override decisions from the developers when necessary and reports to the project manager. The project manager, who has a global view of the objectives of the project and its status, can virtually override any decision. Decisions and guidelines from the project manager are implemented by the team leaders by assigning action items to specific developers. Figure 11-4 illustrates the information flow up and down the reporting structure of a three-subsystem-team organization.

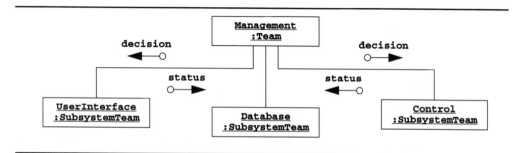

Figure 11-4 Example of reporting structure (UML collaboration diagram). Status information is reported to the project manager and corrective decisions are communicated back to the teams by the team leaders. The team leaders and the project manager are called the management team.

The reporting structure corresponds to the flow of status information and decision information. The reporting relationships, however, represent only a small part of the information flow in the project. Team leaders, for example, usually do not discuss details of the subsystem interface with the project manager. They need, however, to negotiate these details with the teams that depend on their subsystem. Sometimes, team leaders from dependent teams interact directly. Most often, however, a developer, called a **liaison**, is responsible for the task of communicating with another team and shuttling information back and forth. The documentation team, for example, has a liaison to the user interface team to facilitate information about recent changes made to appearance of the system. Teams that do not work directly on a subsystem, but rather, accomplish a project-wide function, are called **cross-functional teams**. Examples of cross-functional teams include the documentation team, the architecture team, and the testing team.

In every organization, there are three types of associations between teams:

- the reporting association, which is used for reporting status information
- the decision association, which is used for propagating decisions
- the communication association, which is used for exchanging other information needed for decisions (e.g., requirements, design models, issues)

In hierarchical organizations, such as a military or church organization, the reporting structure also serves for decision making and communication. In complex software projects, however, most technical decisions are made locally by developers. This requires much information to be exchanged and updated among the teams. This information cannot be exchanged via the reporting structure, given its complexity and volume. Instead, this information exchange is addressed by cross-functional teams and by liaisons. Figure 11-5 depicts an example of team organization with liaisons to cross-functional teams.

Figure 11-6 is an example of team organization for a system with three subsystems. The links between each team and the management team (displayed in thick lines for clarity) represent the reporting structure. All other associations represent communication. The links among the subsystem teams represent communication resulting from dependencies between subsystems.

The role of a team leader is to make sure that not only is the project manager aware of the status of the team, but also that team members have all the information they need from other teams. This requires the selection effective communicators as liaisons and to interact with other team leaders to ensure all necessary communication paths exist.

Other team organizations

In team-based projects, the organization changes over time. If new subsystems are identified in the software architecture, new subsystem teams are formed. If new cross functions are required, liaisons from the subsystem teams are selected and assembled into a new cross-functional teams. Similarly, teams are removed from the organization once their work is completed. The team model

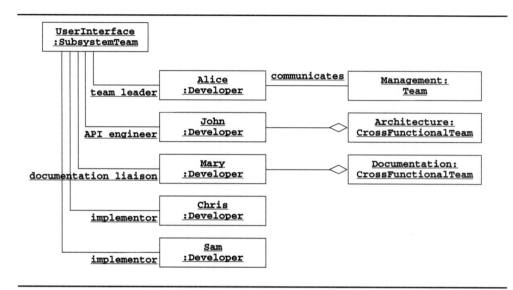

Figure 11-5 Examples of a team organization (UML object diagram). The team is composed of five developers. Alice is the team leader, also called the liaison to the management team. John is the API engineer, also called the liaison to the architecture team. Mary is the liaison to the documentation team. Chris and Sam are implementers and interact with other teams only informally.

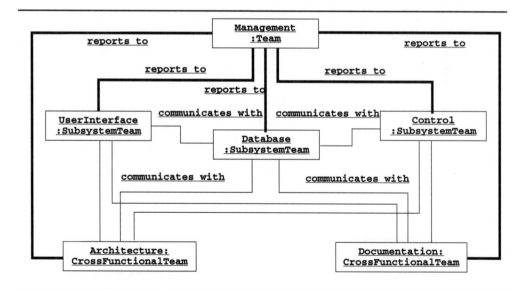

Figure 11-6 An example of a team-based organization with four subsystem teams and three cross-functional teams (UML object diagram). The links between all teams and the management team (drawn thick for clarity) represent the reporting structure. All other associations represent communication.

should be treated the same way as the system model: It is updated to reflect changes in the reality and constantly evolves according to the need of the system and of the project.

Software engineering introduces a trade-off in team organization. Developers have the most technical knowledge about the system and are best able to make decisions locally. However, they optimize only local criteria, which may result in suboptimal decisions at the project level, especially when interteam coordination is difficult. In addition to a team-based organization, different alternative team organizations have been proposed in the literature.

The **chief programmer organization** [Brooks, 1975] is a hierarchical organization that assigns all team decisions to the team leader, called the **chief programmer**. The chief programmer is responsible for the design and development of the subsystem and delegates programming tasks to a pool of specialists. The chief programmer is supported by an assistant chief programmer, who substitutes the chief when needed, and a librarian, responsible for documentation and all clerical functions. The chief programmer has the final say on everything.

Whereas the chief programmer organization takes a hierarchical position on management, **egoless programming** [Weinberg, 1971] takes a democratic one. Responsibility is assigned to the team instead of to the individuals. Results, not participants, are criticized. Issues are resolved by voting. The structure of the team is informal, and communication occurs spontaneously.

In general, there is a spectrum of organizations ranging from a strict hierarchy, such as a military organization, to a dynamic set of collaborating groups. Raymond [Raymond, 1998] refers to the former as the **cathedral model** and the latter as the **bazaar model**. Until recently, it was assumed that the bazaar model was only appropriate for simple systems developed by a team of experienced programmers. It was commonly thought that the cathedral model was necessary for dealing with system complexity. The Linux[1] operating system has provided a counterexample. Linux has been developed from scratch by thousands of developers, most of whom have never met face to face. Moreover, most of these developers are part-time contributors who are not receiving any financial reward for contributing code to Linux.

The complexity of the application domain, the experience of the developers and management, their location, and their communication infrastructure eventually determines where the team organization is located in the cathedral/bazaar spectrum. We might often find that a project's organization starts near the cathedral end of the spectrum and moves toward the bazaar end, once developers gain experience, get to know each other, and develop and communicate a shared model of the system.

Corporate organizations

The emphasis of this book is on software development projects and, consequently, we limit the scope of our discussion to roles up to and including the project manager. We need to recognize that every project occurs in the context of a broader organization, such as a

---

1. Linux is a freely available Unix operation system created by Linus Torwalds. For more information check http://www.linux.org/.

corporation or a university. A project is formed by selecting among the skills, experience, and tools available within the broader organization.

In the **functional organization**, participants are grouped by specialties into departments. A department of analysts constructs the analysis model, a department of designers transform it into a design model, quality assurance is handled by another department, and so on. The functional organization usually corresponds to a sequential order of the life cycle activities, that is, a waterfall model. Projects are pipelined through functional organizations, resulting in few participants being involved for the complete duration of the project. This type of organization is appropriate only for well-defined problems in which the rate of change is low.

The **project-based organization** is an organization in which participants are assigned to only one project at a time for the duration of the project. Participants are usually grouped by subsystems. The information flow between teams, however, is still low, as there are no cross-functional teams or liaisons. Communication and reporting are both done via the reporting structure. The project-based organization is better able to deal with change than the functional organization. The team-based organization we described is a refinement of the project-based organization, in which communication among teams is handled by cross-functional teams. A virtual company is a project-based organization. A set of heterogeneous groups is assembled under one umbrella for the duration of a single project.

The **matrix organization** is a combination of functional and project-based organization. Each participant belongs to a department and is assigned to a project. When the participant's involvement with the project ends, the participant is reassigned to another project. The matrix organization results in two overlapping reporting structures: The participant reports to the department head and to the project manager, with the department head taking precedence. Matrix organizations suffer from the "double-boss" problem when department interests and project interests conflict.

11.3.2 Roles

Once the project is organized into teams, we need to define how team members are assigned individual responsibilities. In this section, we define how to assign a set responsibilities by assigning a **role**. A role defines the types of technical and managerial tasks that are expected from a person. For example, the role of tester of a subsystem team carries the responsibility of defining test suites for the subsystem under development, for executing these tests, and for reporting discovered defects back to the developers.

We distinguish between five types of roles:

- **Management roles** are concerned with the organization and execution of the project within constraints. These roles include the project manager and the team leader.
- **Development roles** are concerned with specifying, designing, and constructing subsystems. These roles include the analyst, the system architect, the object designer, and the implementor.

- **Cross-functional roles** are concerned with coordinating more than one team.

- **Consultant roles** are concerned with providing temporary support in areas where the project participants lack expertise. The users and the client act in most projects as consultants on the problem domain. Technical consultants may also bring expertise on new technologies or methods.

- **Promoter roles** are concerned with promoting changes through an organization. Once the organization is set up, the task plan in place, and the project is running in steady state, it becomes increasingly difficult to introduce changes in the project. Promoters are roles for overcoming barriers to change.

We described the management roles in the previous section. We described development roles in Chapters 5, 6, and 7. Below, we describe in more detail cross-functional roles, consultant roles, and promoter roles.

Cross-functional roles

Cross-functional roles are concerned with coordination among teams. Developers filling these roles are responsible for exchanging information relevant to other teams and negotiating interface details.

The **liaison** is responsible for disseminating information from one team to another. In some cases (such as the API engineer), a liaison functions as a representative of a subsystem team and may be called to resolve interteam issues. There are six types of cross-functional roles:

- The **API engineer** is responsible for the interface definition of the assigned subsystem. The interface has to reflect the functionality already assigned to the subsystem and to accommodate the needs of the dependent subsystems. When functionality is traded off with other subsystems, resulting in subsystem changes, the API engineer is responsible for propagating changes back to the subsystem team.

- The **document editor** is responsible for integrating documents produced by a team. A document editor can be seen as a service provider to other teams that depend on a given subsystem team. A document editor also manages information released internally to the team, such as the meeting agendas and minutes.

- The **configuration manager** is responsible for managing different versions of documents, models, and code produced by a team. For simple configuration management policies (e.g., single hardware platform, single branch), this role may be taken over by the same person as the team leader.

- A **tester** is responsible for ensuring that each subsystem works as specified by the designer. Often, development projects have a separate team responsible only for testing. Separating the roles of designer, implementor, and tester leads to more effective testing.

Consultant roles

Consultant roles address critical short-term needs of knowledge. Consultants are usually not involved full-time with the project. There are three types of consultant roles.

- The **client** is responsible for the formulation of scenarios and the requirements. This includes functional and nonfunctional requirements as well as constraints. The client is expected to be able to interact with the other developers' roles. The client represents the end user of the system.

- The **application domain specialist** is responsible for providing domain knowledge about a specific functional area of the system. Whereas the client has a global view of the functionality of the system, the application domain specialist has detailed knowledge of the day-to-day operation of a specific part of the system.

- The **technical consultant** is responsible for providing missing know-how to developers on a specific topic. This topic can be related to the development method, the process, implementation technology, or the development environment.

Promoters

When the organization is in place, roles and tasks have been assigned to participants, and participants have been trained, it becomes increasingly difficult to introduce changes in the project. To deal with this problem, especially in hierarchical organizations and functional organizations, promoter roles are essential in pushing an organizational change [Hauschildt & Gemuenden, 1998]. Promoters are self-appointed individuals who identify themselves with the outcome of the project. They are members of the corporate organization and may not necessarily be directly involved with the project. Instead, they are interfaces to the rest of the corporate organization. Because of their power, knowledge of technology, or familiarity with the project's processes, they are able to promote and push specific changes through the organization. Promoters seem like revolutionaries: Their main job is to embody change by getting rid of the old organization. However, this view is incorrect. Promoters, unlike revolutionaries, stay within the structure of the current organization. To overcome the barriers, they even use hierarchical power to move to the new process. There are three key promoters for any change to occur: the power promoter, the knowledge promoter, and the process promoter.

The **power promoter**, also called the executive champion, pushes the change through the existing organizational hierarchy. The power promoter convinces, encourages, creates enthusiasm, punishes, and rewards. The power promoter is not necessary at or near the top of the organization, but must have protection from top-level management; otherwise, project opponents might be able to prevent the success of the project. However, the power promoter does not avoid confrontation with top-level management. He or she needs to constantly identify difficulties, resolve issues, and communicate with the project members, especially with the developers.

The **knowledge promoter**, also called the technologist, promotes change arising in the application domain or the solution domain. He or she is a specialist because of specific capabilities and is usually associated with the power promoter. The knowledge promoter acquires information iteratively, understands the benefits and limitations of new technologies, and argues its adoption with the other developers.

The **process promoter** has intimate knowledge of the project's processes and procedures. The process promoter is in constant interaction with the power promoter to get consensus on the overall goals. In addition, the process promoter has sufficient managerial and technical knowledge to provide a bridge between the power and knowledge promoters, who often do not speak or understand the same language. An example of process promoter is the development lead, which is sometimes found in development teams. This role, not covered in detailed in this chapter, is responsible for the administrative aspects of a project, including planning, milestones definition, budgeting, and communication infrastructure.

11.3.3 Work Products

Assigning a role to a participant usually translates into assigning the responsibility of a specific work product. A **work product** is an artifact that is produced during the development, such as an internal document for other project participants or a deliverable to the customer. An analyst is responsible for a section of the RAD describing the functionality of the system. A system architect is responsible for the SDD describing the system's high-level architecture. A project manager is responsible for the SPMP describing the development processes. Finally, the system and its accompanying documentation also constitute a set of work products that are delivered to the client. Complex work products, such as a RAD, can be treated as the composition of several smaller work products, such as the requirements for different types of users.

Work products are the result of tasks and are subject to deadlines. Work products are usually then fed into other tasks. For example, the test planning activity for the database subsystem results in a work product including a number of test suites and its expected results. The test suite is then fed to the testing activity of the given subsystem (Figure 11-7).

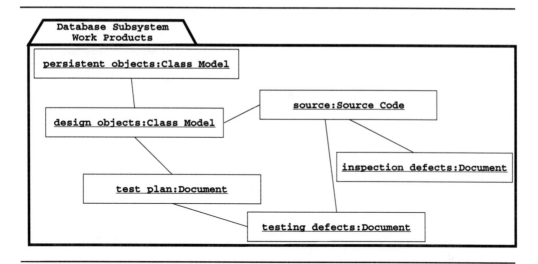

Figure 11-7 Work products for the a database subsystem team (UML object diagram). Associations represent dependencies among work products.

Work products are important management artifacts, because we can assess their delivery and the start of the tasks depending on specific work products. The late delivery of a testing suite for a subsystem, for example, will delay the start of its testing. Note, however, that focusing only on timely delivery is not sufficient: Rushing the delivery of test suites will meet the project schedule, but can also mean that critical faults are not discovered in time.

11.3.4 Tasks

A role describes work in terms of a set of tasks. A task includes a description, a duration, and is assigned to a role. A task represents an atomic unit of work that can be managed: A manager assigns it to a developer, the developer carries it out, and the manager monitors the progress and completion of the task. Tasks consume resources, result in a work products, and depend on work products produced by other tasks. Table 11-1 provides simple examples of tasks.

Table 11-1   Examples of tasks for the realization of the database subsystem

Task name	Assigned role	Task description	Task input	Task output
Database subsystem requirements elicitation	System designer	Elicits requirements from subsystem teams about their storage needs, including persistent objects, their attributes, and relationships	Team liaisons	Database subsystem API, persistent object analysis model (UML class diagram)
Database subsystem design	Subsystem design	Designs the database subsystem, including the possible selection of a commercial product	Subsystem API	Database subsystem design (UML diagram)
Database subsystem implementation	Implementor	Implements the database subsystem	Subsystem design	Database subsystem source code
Database subsystem inspection	Implementor	Conducts a code inspection of the database subsystem	Subsystem source code	List of discovered defects
Database subsystem test plan	Tester	Develops a test suite for the database subsystem	Subsystem design, subsystem source code	Tests and test plan
Database subsystem test	Tester	Executes the test suite for the database subsystem	Subsystem, test plan	Test results, list of discovered defects

Tasks are related by dependencies. For example, in Table 11-1, the `Database subsystem test` task cannot start before completion of the `Database subsystem implementation` task. Finding the dependencies between tasks enables us to find which tasks can be executed in parallel. For example, in Table 11-1, the `Database subsystem inspection` and the `Database subsystem test plan` can be assigned to two different developers and proceed at the same time. The set of tasks and their dependencies are called the task model. Figure 11-8 depicts in UML the task model corresponding to Table 11-1.

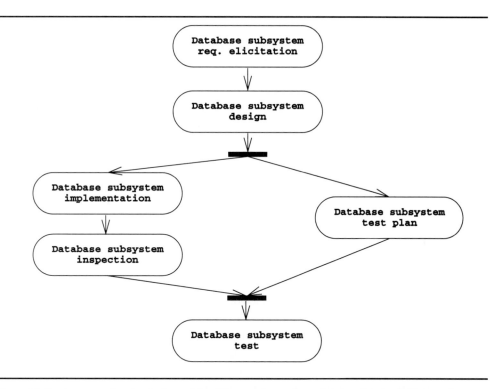

Figure 11-8 An example of a task model with precedence dependencies for the database subsystem example of Table 11-1 (UML activity diagram).

Task dependencies are relationships between individual tasks and time. Task constraints can be used to make sure a project is on schedule independent from the relationship of the task with other tasks. They usually represent an interaction with the client or the user. For example, if a task T has to start on a Monday, it has an MSO (see Table 11-2) constraint. If the system must be delivered in the first week of December, it has an MFO constraint. ASAP is the most commonly used constraint by people ordering tasks, (e.g., project managers), ALAP is the most commonly used constraint by people receiving tasks.

11.3.5 Schedule

The task model contains the tasks, their dependencies, their constraints, and their planned duration. Similar to object models, where objects and object dependencies are illustrated, there are many ways to represent task models. A schedule is the mapping of tasks onto time: Each task is assigned planned start and end times. This allows us to plan the deadlines for individual deliverables. The two most often used diagrammatic notations for schedules are PERT and Gantt charts [Hillier & Lieberman, 1967]. A **Gantt chart** is a compact way to present the schedule of a software project along the time axis. A Gantt chart is a bar graph, where the horizontal axis

Table 11-2   Task constraints

Constraint	Definition
ASAP	Start the task as soon as possible
ALAP	As late as possible
FNET	Finish no earlier than
SNET	Start no earlier than
FNLT	Finish no later than
SNLT	Start no later than
MFO	Must finish on
MSO	Must start on

represents time. The vertical axis represents the different tasks to be done. Tasks are represented as bars whose length correspond to the planned duration of the task. A schedule for the database subsystem example is represented as a Gantt chart in Figure 11-9.

A **PERT chart** represents a schedule as an acyclic graph of tasks. Figure 11-10 is a PERT chart for the database subsystem. The planned start and duration of the tasks are used to compute the critical path, which represents the shortest possible path through the graph. The length of the critical path corresponds to the shortest possible schedule, assuming sufficient resources to accomplish in parallel tasks that are independent. Moreover, tasks on the critical path are the most important, as a delay in any of these tasks will result in a delay in the overall project. The tasks and bars represented in thicker lines belong to the critical path.

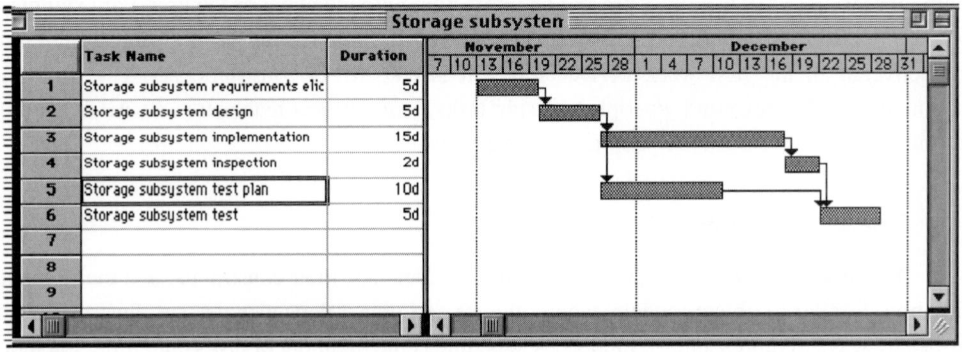

Figure 11-9   An example of schedule for the database subsystem (Gantt chart).

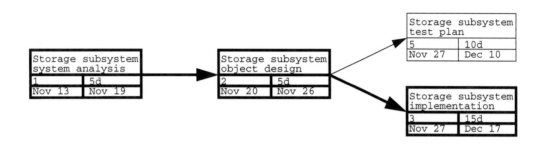

Figure 11-10   An example of schedule for the database subsystem (PERT chart). Tasks on the critical path are represented with thick lines.

PERT charts and Gantt charts are useful tools for planning a project and tracking its execution. Note, however, that these models are only as good as the estimations they represent. Accurate estimation of the duration of a task is difficult. Project managers use their experience, data from past projects, and their intuition to estimate the tasks required for the execution of the project and their duration. Inaccurate estimation, such as the omission of a key task or the underestimation of a task on the critical path, leads to substantial delays in the schedule. Unexpected events, such as change in requirements or the late discovery of design errors, disrupt the schedule, no matter how accurate the planning. A project manager must try to anticipate these unwanted situations by allowing error margins and leaving room for change in the schedule. A task dedicated to the periodic review and change of requirements during the project is one such example. In general, PERT and Gantt charts are of limited usefulness if the tasks are not known during planning or if the tasks change frequently.

In the next section, we describe how project management organizes participants into teams, assigns them roles, plans the project in terms of tasks, and most important, revises the organization, role assignment, and tasks as the project progresses and encounters unanticipated events.

11.4 Project Management Activities

In this section, we describe the activities of project management. These include all the activities necessary to define and revise the organization, roles, work products, tasks, and schedule of the project. Most of the team leader effort is spent in monitoring and managing a team during steady state. Team leaders should be aware, however, of the project initiation activities preceding their involvement with the project and of the interaction with the client.

We focus on the following management activities:

- **Project initiation** (Section 11.4.2), including defining the problem, identifying the initial task plan, and allocating resources to tasks

- **Steady state**, including project monitoring (Section 11.4.3), risk management (Section 11.4.4), and the project agreement (Section 11.4.5)

- **Project termination**, including the client acceptance test (Section 11.4.6), installation (Section 11.4.7), and project postmortem (Section 11.4.8)

We illustrate the project management activities using the OWL project as an example [Bruegge et al., 1997]. The goal of OWL is to provide a system for intelligent buildings, allowing workers to adjust their environment, facilities managers to rapidly detect faulty components, and companies to reconfigure the floor plan based on their evolving needs. OWL entails the use and integration of new technology, including sensors for monitoring work's environment, actuators for controlling the temperature, humidity, and lighting of the work environment, distributed real-time control kernels, and Web technology. The requirements of OWL have not yet stabilized, as different manufacturers are still being considered. These factors will cause in several changes late in the development and introduce significant risk into the project, and thus OWL serves as the basis of the examples in this section.

11.4.1 Intelligent Office Buildings

An intelligent office building aims at providing individualized services to its workers while optimizing resource consumption. Workers in intelligent buildings are able to adjust many parameters of their individual environment, such as light level, temperature, and speed and direction of airflow, similar to what they already do in their cars. Moreover, a modular design enables workspaces to be rapidly reconfigured to meet changing organization or technological needs. Adding a computer or a video conference unit to a workspace can be done with limited rewiring. Finally, control systems integrated with intelligent buildings make their maintenance easier: Burned out light bulbs or defective components are detected remotely and replaced with minimum latency.

A critical component of intelligent buildings is their control system. The control system is a distributed real-time system that:

- responds to worker specified parameters by controlling shades, individual heating and cooling units, and windows based on the current climate to adjust temperature and airflow

- records building data for future analysis

- performs diagnostics

- notifies facilities managers about any problems or emergencies

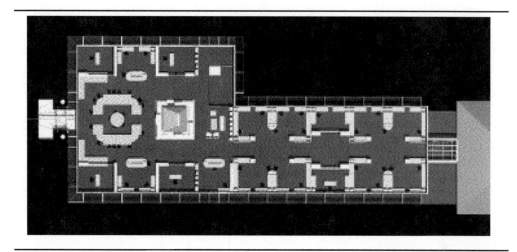

Figure 11-11 Floor plan for the Intelligent Workplace, an intelligent building in the Department of Architecture in Carnegie Mellon University.

Such control systems also need to be modular and modifiable to accommodate new components and equipment from a variety of manufacturers. Figure 11-11 displays the floor plan for the Intelligent Workplace, an intelligent building at Carnegie Mellon University [Hartkopf et al., 1997]. In this chapter, we describe project management examples from OWL, a control system for the Intelligent Workplace.

11.4.2 Initiating the Project

Project initiation focuses on defining the problem, planning a solution, and allocating resources. Project initiation results in the following work products (Figure 11-12):

- The **problem statement** is a short document describing the problem the system should address, the target environment, the client deliverables, and acceptance criteria. The problem statement is an initial description and is the seed for the *Project Agreement*, formalizing the common understanding of the project by the client and management, and for the RAD, a precise description of the system under development.
- The **top-level design** represents the initial decomposition of the system into subsystems. It is used to assign subsystems to individual teams. The top-level design is also the seed for the SDD, documenting the software architecture.
- The **organization** describes the initial teams of the project, their roles, and their communication paths. The **initial task plan** and the **initial schedule** are initial descriptions of how resources should be allocated. The organization, the initial task plan, and the initial schedule are the seeds for the SPMP, which documents all managerial aspects of the project.

During project initiation, management assembles the teams according to the top-level design and the selected organization, sets up the communication infrastructure, and then kicks off the project by organizing the first meeting. Once all participants are assigned tasks and status reporting mechanisms are in place, the project is considered to be in steady state.

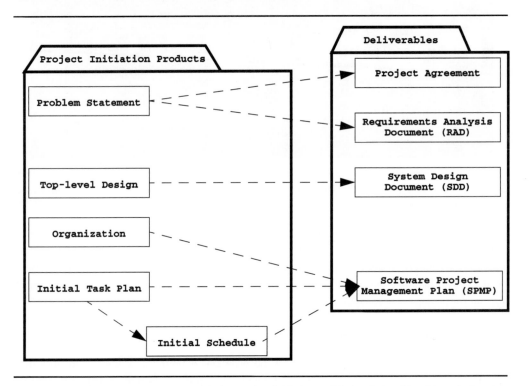

Figure 11-12   Work products generated during project initiation and their relationship with typical project deliverables (UML class diagram).

Developing the problem statement

The *Problem Statement* is developed by the project manager and the client as a mutual understanding of the problem to be addressed by the system. The problem statement describes the current situation, the functionality it should support, and environment in which the system will be deployed. It also defines the deliverables expected by the client, together with delivery dates and a set of acceptance criteria. The problem statement may also specify constraints on the development environment, such as the programming language to be used. The problem statement is not a precise or complete specification of the system. Instead, it is a high-level summary of two project documents yet to be developed: the RAD and the SPMP.

The problem statement is developed iteratively by the project manager and the client. Developing the problem statement is both a negotiation activity and an information gathering activity during which each party learns the expectations and constraints of the other. Whereas the project statement contains a high-level description of the functionality of the system, it should also provide concrete examples to ensure that both parties are sharing the same vision. This is best done by using scenarios (see Chapter 4, *Requirements Elicitation*) for describing the current situation and future functionality.

Figure 11-13 is an example outline for a problem statement. The first section describes the problem domain. Section 2 of the problem statement provides example scenarios describing the interaction between users and the system for the essential functionality. Scenarios are used both for describing the current situation and the future situation.

PROBLEM STATEMENT

1. Problem domain
2. Scenarios
3. Functional requirements
4. Nonfunctional requirements
5. Target environment
6. Deliverables & deadlines

Figure 11-13 Outline of problem statement document. Note that the sections 2, 3, and 4 are not a complete or precise specification of the system. They provide the basis for requirements elicitation. Section 6, however, describes contractual deliverables and their associated due dates.

Figure 11-14 provides examples of scenarios used in the OWL problem statement. Section 3 is a summary of the functional requirements of the system. Section 4 is a summary of the nonfunctional requirements, including client constraints such as programming language and component reuse. Section 5 is a description of the deployment environment, including platform, physical environment, users, and so on. Section 6 is a list of client deliverables and their associated deadlines.

Defining the top-level design

The top-level design describes the software architecture of the system. In a project- or team-based organization, the top-level design is used as basis of the organization: Each subsystem is assigned to a team that is responsible for its definition and realization. The subsystem decomposition is refined and modified later during system design (see Chapter 6, *System Design*). We only need, however, to identify the major subsystems and their services; we need not define their interfaces at this point. Teams who work on dependent subsystems will negotiate individual services and their interfaces as they are needed.

The top-level design of OWL includes five major subsystems, described in Figure 11-15. Note that this subsystem decomposition is high level and focuses on functionality. Other subsystems may be added later in the project, such as a communication layer for moving objects among nodes in the network and a notification subsystem for pushing notices to users. Once

---

OWL PROBLEM STATEMENT

1. Problem domain

A current trend in the building industry is to provide distributed services and control for the individual occupant as a strategy to correct the overreliance on large centralized systems that characterize office buildings built in the last 30 years. At the Intelligent Workplace workers will have more control over their environmental conditions—adjusting light level and temperature of their workspace, reducing glare, controlling speed and direction of air flow delivered to workspace. (You can do that in your car—why not in your office?) An energy-efficient facade will allow for fresh air ventilation from operable windows and incorporate movable shading devices that adjust to minimize glare and maximize natural lighting of the workspace.

It is desirable to adopt three forms of control in the Intelligent Workplace: responsive, scheduled, and user driven. Responsive control is when the system reacts to a change in sensor reading by actuating some components. Scheduled control can be adopted in the presence of predictable data that allows the components to be directly controlled by a carefully designed schedule. For example, because the position of the Sun is predictable, a schedule for the interior shades of the Intelligent Workplace can be adopted. Control system should be flexible enough to respond to the needs of the occupants. If they would like to change the temperature of their local environment, they should be given that opportunity.

In this project, you are asked to build a system called OWL (Object-Oriented Workplace Laboratory) that attempts to improve the way we deal with buildings.

[. . .]

2. Scenarios

2.1 Building control

The building occupant uses a Web browser to access his Personal Environment Module (PEM). He adjusts the temperature and airspeed to cool his workspace. The control information is sent to the PEM equipment. The control actions are logged in the database and the equipment adjusts the heater and the ventilation of the workspace. The system checks neighboring PEMs to check if cooling this particular workspace requires other workspaces heating to be increased.

[. . .]

2.5 Building maintenance

The system monitors the behavior of the controlled devices to detect faults in the system. Faulty light bulbs and unusual parameter readings are reported to the facilities manager who then plans inspections and repairs. The occurrences of device faults are logged and analyzed for trends, enabling the facilities manager to anticipate faults in the future.

[. . .]

Figure 11-14   Excerpts from the problem statement of OWL [OWL, 1996].

analysis produces a stable model and the subsystem decomposition is revisited during subsystem design, new subsystems can be created during the system design phase, and the organization might have to be changed to reflect the new design.

Identifying the initial tasks

The starting points for task identification are the problem statement (including deliverables and deadlines), the life cycle activities, and past experience. The client and the

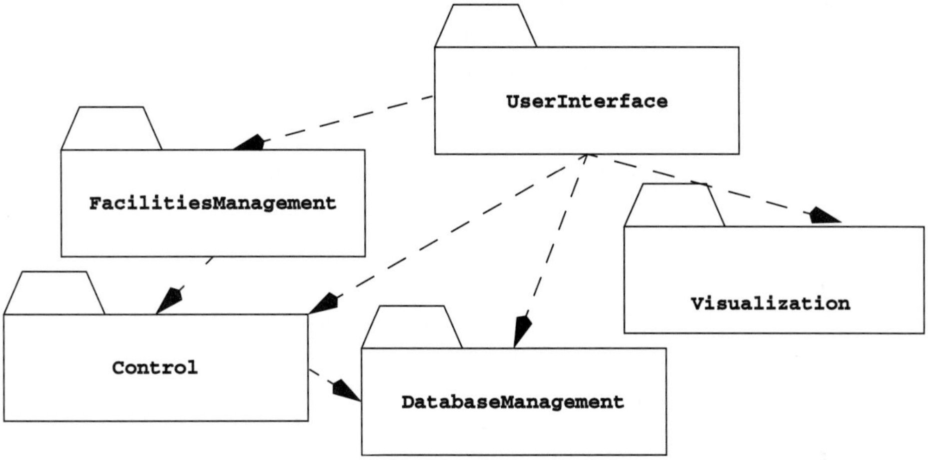

Subsystem	Services
Control	• Interface to sensors and actuators • Provide reactive algorithms to maintain temperature and humidity
DatabaseManagement	• Provide archival of building operation data (sensor and control) • Capture and store weather forecast data
FacilitiesManagement	• Maintain map of sensor, actuators, and rooms • Maintain cable schematic and network structure • Maintain a current map of the workspace configurations (e.g., furniture)
UserInterface	• Provide a Web browser interface for users to visualize and specify environmental parameters • Provide speech interface • Provide facilities manager interface
Visualization	• Provide navigation of a 3D model of the building • Provide 3D visualization of temperature and energy consumption • Provide 3D visualization of problems and emergencies

Figure 11-15   Top-level design of OWL (UML class diagram, packages collapsed).

project manager agree to a series of reviews whose purpose is to review the progress of the project. Each deliverable must be covered by least one task.

The planning activity identifies additional work products for the project's own consumption. These include management work products, such as the SPMP, development work products, such as preliminary interface definitions, rapid prototypes, and evaluations, such as summary sheets for tools, methods, or procedures.

The work is initially decomposed into tasks that are small enough to be estimated and assigned to a single person. This initial decomposition is often called the work breakdown structure (WBS) and resembles a large To Do list. Usually, the more specific the requirements and the deliverables, the easier it is to define precise tasks. When requirements are not well defined, the manager must allocate additional time for replanning and revising the task plan as the requirements stabilize.

For example, let us consider the design activities for the team who develops the `DatabaseManagement` subsystem of OWL. From the requirements, the team knows that the `DatabaseManagement` subsystem should reliably maintain the state of sensors and the actions issued to the actors. Moreover, the `DatabaseManagement` subsystem should support searches over historical data for trend analysis. Table 11-3 depicts an example of an initial work breakdown structure for such a subsystem. Estimated times are based on prior experience of the manager or the estimator.

The initial work breakdown structure should not be too detailed. Many project managers have a tendency to create detailed To Do lists at the beginning of the project. Even though a detailed model of work effort is desirable, it is difficult to create a meaningful detailed work breakdown structure initially. Refining the system definition during analysis and designing the software architecture during system design generate many changes to the original work breakdown structure, including new tasks to investigate recent technology, new subsystems, and additional functionality. Creating a detailed work breakdown structure only leads to additional work when the plan is revised. Instead, a manager details the work breakdown structure only for the short term while describing the longer term tasks in less detail. The manager revises and details the work breakdown structure only as the project progresses.

Identifying task dependencies

Once tasks have been identified, we need to find the dependencies among them. Identifying dependencies allows us to assign resources to tasks more efficiently. For example, two independent tasks can be assigned to different participants to be accomplished in parallel. We find dependencies among tasks by examining the work products each tasks requires. For example, a unit testing task requires the specification of the unit programmer interface, generated by the system design task. The system design task must then be completed before the testing task can be initiated. Figure 11-16 depicts the dependencies among the tasks identified in Table 11-3. The set of tasks and their dependencies constitute the task model. The next step is to map the task model to resources and time by creating a schedule.

Creating the initial schedule

The initial schedule is created by mapping the task model to time and resources. Task dependencies, estimated task durations, and the number of participants are used for creating the initial schedule. The initial schedule is used to plan dates for the primary interactions with the

Table 11-3   An example of initial work breakdown structure for `DatabaseManagement`

Task	Estimated time
1. Select database management system	2 weeks
2. Identify persistent objects and their attributes	1 week
3. Identify queries	1 week
4. Identify searchable attributes	1 day
5. Define schema	2 weeks
6. Build prototype for performance evaluation	2 weeks
7. Define API to other subsystems	3 days
8. Identify concurrency requirements	2 days
9. Implement database subsystem	2 weeks
10. Unit test database subsystem	3 weeks
11. Address remaining concurrency hazards	2 weeks

client and the users, including user interviews, client reviews, and deliveries. These dates are made part of the problem statement and represent deadlines mutually agreed on by the client and the project manager. These dates are planned such that, even in the event of change, the deadlines can still be met. Figure 11-17 depicts the initial schedule for OWL.

Similar to the task model, it is unrealistic to create a detailed schedule at the beginning of the project. The initial schedule should include deadlines for all client deliverables and detailed scheduling for the short term (e.g., the first two months). Detailed scheduling for the rest of the project is performed only as the project progresses. Also, once the project is underway, each team can contribute to the planning of its tasks, given that it has a more detailed view of the work to be accomplished. The overall scheduling is done as part of a continuing trade-off between resources, time, and implemented functionality and is updated constantly.

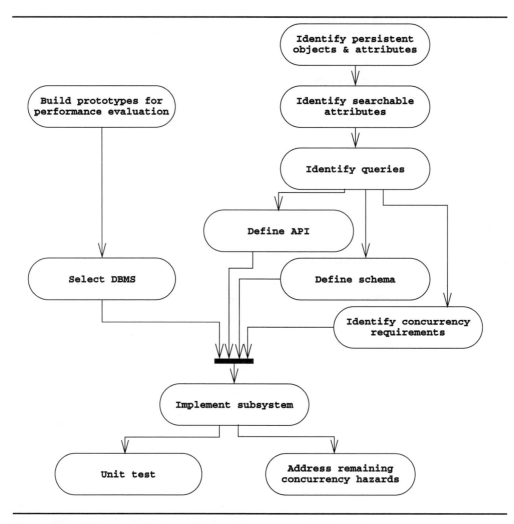

Figure 11-16   Task model for the work breakdown structure of Table 11-3.

Assembling the teams

The next step of project initiation is to assemble the teams who will produce the deliverables. Developers who will work for the project can be assigned to the project all at once (flat staffing), or the project can be gradually ramped up by hiring people as needed (gradual staffing). On the one hand, gradual staffing is motivated by saving resources in the early part of the project. Requirements elicitation and analysis do not require as many people as coding and testing do. Moreover, analyst and implementor are roles requiring different skills and thus should be assigned to different people. On the other hand, flat staffing has the advantage of establishing teams early and the social environment necessary for spontaneous communication.

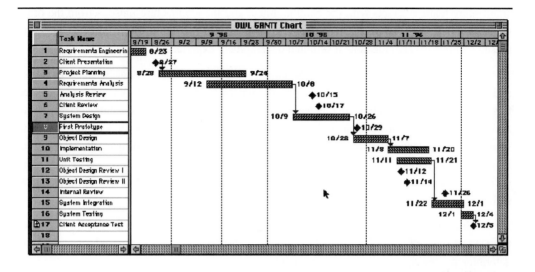

Figure 11-17   Initial project schedule for OWL (Gantt chart). The initial schedule serves to estimate the delivery dates and the interaction with the client. The schedule is detailed and revised as the project progresses.

Some of the developers can be assigned to the analysis activities with the analysts, while the others may already start other activities such as setting up the configuration management environment, technology survey and evaluation, and training. With shorter projects and market deadlines, flat staffing is becoming the preferred staffing scheme. The dilemma between gradual staffing and flat staffing has been discussed in length by Brooks [Brooks, 1975].

The project manager staffs teams by examining the top-level design and considering the skills required for each subsystem. Often, not enough developers with the required skills are available, in which case the project manager includes time in the task model for the technical training of new staff. The project manager distributes new staff across the project such that each team has at least one experienced developer. The experienced developer provides technical leadership and serves as a mentor for the new developers who then gain experience more quickly when putting their new training into practice. Formal training and learning by practice is a trade-off the project manager evaluates given project time constraints. Formal training enables developers to become more productive earlier; however, it is expensive and constitutes a longer term investment benefiting future projects.

The project manager selects the team leaders before the teams are formed. In addition to being capable of understanding the team status, the team leader needs to be able to communicate effectively, recognize pending crises (social or technical), and make trade-offs taking into account project level concerns. The start of the project is also an ideal time for training team leaders, for familiarizing them with project procedures and ground rules. The team leader role is distinct from the role of technical leader. The technical lead, usually the liaison to the architecture team, interacts with the chief architect and the architecture liaisons from the other teams and has final say on the technical decisions within the team. The role of architecture liaison requires excellent technical skill and development experience.

In a training context, the team leader can be split into two roles. A coach trains, explains, and advises the team. The coach also acts as the liaison to management. A team leader trainee fills all other responsibilities of the team leader, including facilitating status meetings and assigning tasks. In a course project, this role is filled by the instructor or the teaching assistant, whereas the architecture liaison is filled by a student. In a development project, the team leader is filled by a developer who has experience and knowledge with the organization's management procedures, whereas the architecture liaison is filled by a developer who has strong technical skills.

Table 11-4 depicts an example of role assignment to participants for the database team of the OWL project. The project manager and team leaders assign roles based on skills and determine the training needs for each participants.

Table 11-4   Role assignment, skills, and training needs for the database team of OWL

Participant	Roles	Skills	Training needs
Alice	Team leader	Management: team leader Programming: C Configuration management	UML Communication skills
John	Architecture liaison Implementor	Programming: C++ Modeling: UML	Java
Mary	Configuration manager Implementor	Programming: C++, Java Modeling: Entity relationship Databases: relational Configuration management	Object-oriented databases UML modeling
Chris	Implementor	Programming: C++, Java Modeling: Entity relationship Databases: object-oriented	UML modeling
Sam	Facilities management liaison Tester	Programming: C++ Testing: whitebox, black box	Inspections Java

Setting up the communication infrastructure

Clear and accurate communication is critical for the success of a development project. Moreover, communication becomes crucial when the number of project participants increases. Consequently, setting up the communication infrastructure for a project occurs as early as possible, that is, during project initiation. The project manager needs to address the following modes of communication, as described in Chapter 3, *Project Communication*:

- *Scheduled modes of communication.* These include planned milestones, such as client and project reviews, team status meetings, inspections, and so on. Scheduled modes of communication are the formal means through which project participants gather and share information. These are best supported by synchronous or face-to-face communication, such as meetings, formal presentations, video conferences, and telephone conference calls. The manager schedules dates and designates facilitators for each of these interactions.

- *Event-based modes of communication.* These include problem reports, change requests, issue discussion, and resolution. Event-based modes usually arise from unforeseen problems and crises. Asynchronous mechanisms such as E-mail, groupware, and problem databases need to be set up early, and participants need to be trained to use them. When the number of participants is large, centralized infrastructures, such as Web sites and bulletin boards are preferable as they make more information visible to more people than E-mail or bilateral conversations do. For example, Figure 11-18 is the home page of the OWL project, providing access to the project address book, bboards, documents, and source code. This infrastructure also has the advantage of being accessible with minimum software and platform requirements.

The project manager uses different mechanisms of communication with the client and the end users than with the developers. Developers, on the one hand, and clients and end users, on the other hand, have different terminology, information needs, and availability. The client and end users speak the application domain language and may not have much software engineering background. They need information about the status of the project and of the analysis model. Their involvement with the project is thus episodic and focuses on their own work. Developers speak the language of the solution domain and may not have much application domain knowledge. Their information need is technical and daily. A good heuristic is to conduct communication face to face several times during the project and to establish a client bulletin board for unscheduled communication needs (e.g., for clarification of requirements). This assumes that the client is familiar with the use of bulletin boards and on-line communication. Training or other mechanisms or communication are used otherwise. Note, however, that the communication channel between the client and the users has a low bandwidth and needs to be used efficiently.

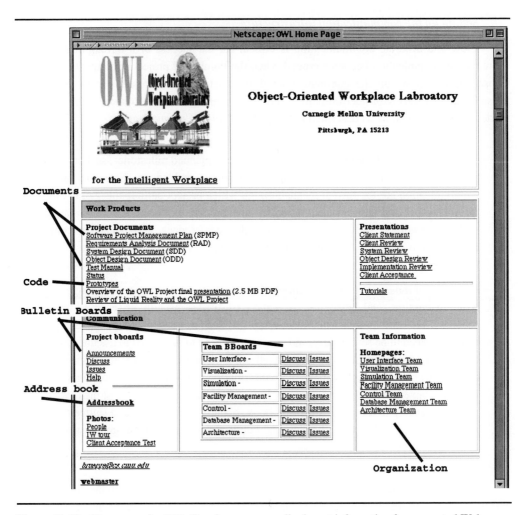

Figure 11-18   Home page for OWL. Developers access all relevant information from a central Web page.

Kicking off the project

The project kickoff meeting marks the end of the project initiation phase and the beginning of the development phase. The project manager has completed much of the initial planning and top-level design, selected an organization, hired developers, and designated team leaders. The project kickoff consists of three meetings.

- *The client presentation.* All project participants are included in this meeting. It includes a presentation by the client on the system requirements and a presentation by the manager on the initial organization and schedule.

- *The management kickoff meeting.* This meeting is facilitated by the project manager and includes all the team leaders. This meeting serves to define and train managerial procedures, such as meeting procedures, configuration management, and problem reporting.

- *Individual team kickoff meetings.* These meetings are facilitated by team leaders and includes the team members. Procedures defined during the management meeting are communicated to the participants. Team members are introduced to each other. This is where the involvement of a team leader begins. Figure 11-19 is an example of an agenda for the database team kickoff meeting.

The goal of the three kickoff meetings is for participants to get to know each other and to initiate communication. Participants become familiar with basic meeting procedures, the organization and the assignment of roles, and the general mechanisms of the project. Soon after, tasks are distributed and regular status meetings take place. After a small number of status meetings, the scheduled aspects of communication should be solidly in place.

Next, we describe the activities of project monitoring during steady state. The management activities during steady state focus mostly on unexpected events and contingency plans.

11.4.3 Project Monitoring

To make effective decisions, the project manager needs accurate status information. Unfortunately, collecting accurate status is difficult. While a complex system is difficult to understand in itself, the status of its components and its impact on future deliveries are even more difficult to understand. Developers will not report to their team leader any problem they believe they can address in time. However, small departures from the schedule, not worth reporting independently, aggregate and degenerate into large departures much later in the schedule. By the time team leaders discover and report a major problem to the project manager, it has already caused a substantial delay in the project.

Several tools are available to collect status information. Because none of them are accurate or reliable alone, team leaders and project managers need to use a combination of these. Below we review their advantages and disadvantages.

Meetings
- *Periodic status meetings.* Status meetings conducted at the team level have the best potential for reporting status and information required for corrective decisions. Status meetings, however, can also provide inaccurate status information if team members do not cooperate. Participants are naturally reluctant to report problems or mistakes. They cooperate only if they can trust a manager not to step into problems that they can resolve themselves. Managers need to make problem reporting beneficial to developers by intervening only when necessary.
- *Sharp milestones.* Progress can be measured by determining if developers deliver work products on time. Managers can increase the accuracy of this method by defining sharp milestones such that they can be accurately monitored. For example, the "coding completed" milestone is not a sharp milestone, because it does not take into account the

---

AGENDA: Database team kickoff meeting

When and Where	**Role**
Date: 11/13/1998	**Primary Facilitator**: Mary
Start: 4:30pm	**Timekeeper**: John
End: 5:30pm	**Minute Taker**: Chris
Building: AC Hall	**Room**: 3421

1. Purpose
Become familiar with project management roles for a medium-scale project with a 2-level hierarchy.

2. Desired outcome
- Group roles are assigned to people
- Meeting times are finalized
- First set of action items for next meeting

3. Information sharing [Allocated time: 25 minutes]
Meeting procedures
- guidelines
- agendas/minutes
- roles

Team roles
- Team leader
- Architecture Liaison
- Documentation Liaison
- Configuration Manager
- Toolsmith

Team tasks

Team schedule

Problem reporting

4. Discussion [Allocated time: 25 minutes]
Define ground rules

Initial role and task assignment

5. Wrap up [Allocated time: 5 minutes]
Review and assign new action items

Meeting critique

Figure 11-19   An example of an agenda for the database team kickoff meeting in the OWL project.

quality of the code delivered. The code could contain few or many defects and the milestone would be considered completed in either case. Conversely, defining a milestone as the completion of the test, demonstration, documentation, and integration of a specific feature yields better status information. When defining and monitoring sharp milestones, managers do not need the cooperation of developers.

- *Project reviews.* A project review is a means for all participants to exchange status and plan information about all the teams with formal presentation. Project reviews suffer from similar problems as status meetings: If participants are already reluctant to admit problems in front of their team leader, they definitively will not admit problems in a public forum.

- *Code inspections.* Formal peer reviews of code are an effective methods for discovering defects early. When performed frequently, their results can also be used as an indication of progress.

- *Prototype demonstrations.* Prototype demonstrations are partial implementations of the system for evaluating technology or functionality. They usually do not illustrate how border cases are dealt with or how robust the implementation is. They are good for measuring initial progress but are not sharp measures of completion.

Metrics

- *Defects to be resolved.* Once an initial version of the system exists, the number of defects to be resolved is an intuitive measure of how much effort needs to be expended before the system can be delivered. However, measuring the number of open defects encourages their quick resolution and triggers the introduction of new defects, thus defeating the original purpose of measuring the number of defects.

- *Source code metrics.* Various metrics on source code, ranging from the number of lines of code to ratios of the number of operators and operands and to function points, have been proposed for estimation. These metrics are sensitive to many factors in the environment, including the coding style of the implementers. Moreover, results do not seem transferable from one organization to the other. These measures should only be used if a systematic effort, across multiple projects, is organized within the organization.

Finally, independently of the methods used for determining status, the project manager, the team leaders, and the developers need to communicate status information in understandable terms. Next, we describe risk management as a method for controlling projects, communicating potential problems, and planning contingencies.

11.4.4 Risk Management

The focus of risk management is to identify possible problems in the project and address them before they can impact significantly the delivery date or the budget. The key element of risk management is to set up the appropriate information flows such that risks and problems are accurately reported in a timely manner. Many projects fail either because simple problems were reported too late or because the wrong problem was addressed. In this section, we focus on the activities of risk management for identifying, analyzing, and addressing risks. For more details on risk management in software engineering, we refer the reader to the specialized literature; for example, [Boehm, 1991] and [Charette, 1989].

Identifying risks

The first step of risk management is to identify risks. Risks are potential problems that result from an area of uncertainty. Risks can be managerial or technical. Managerial risks include any uncertainty related to the organization, work products, roles, or task plan. Technical risks include any uncertainty related to the system models, including changes of the functionality of the system, the nonfunctional requirements, the architecture, or the implementation of the system. In particular, technical risks include defects discovered late in the development. Table 11-5 depicts examples of risks in the OWL project.

Table 11-5   Examples of risks identified in the OWL project

Risk	Risk type
Manufacturer's Personal Environment Module (PEM) does not comply with published standard	Technical
Manufacturer's PEM delivery date is not later than planned	Managerial
Users are not willing to use Web browser to adjust temperature settings	Technical
Selected middleware too slow to meet performance requirement for data logging	Technical
Development of abstract PEM layer takes more time than scheduled	Managerial

Developers are often aware of the risks applicable to their tasks. The challenge is to encourage developers to report risks such that they can surface and be managed. This entails rewarding developers for reporting risks and problems and making the risk management activities directly beneficial to developers. Spontaneous risk reporting is usually not sufficient: Project participants, including the client, the developers, and the managers, are usually reluctant to communicate potential failures or shortcomings and are too optimistic about their outcome. A more-systematic approach to risk identification is to interview the project participants using a structured questionnaire: Participants are asked in group sessions to list the risks they anticipate with respect to specific tasks. Figure 11-20 depicts example questions from the Taxonomy-based Risk Identification process of the SEI [Carr et al., 1993]. In this example, the interviewer attempts to determine if there are any risks related to performance nonfunctional requirements. Depending on the answer to the first question, the interviewer can ask follow-up questions to make sure no other related risks are present. The rationale behind this questionnaire is to cover all the areas of development in which risks are typically found.

1. Requirements

. . .

d. Performance

. . .

[23] Has a performance analysis been done?

(Yes) (23.a) What is your level of confidence in the performance analysis?

(Yes) (23.b) Do you have a model to track performance through design and implementation?

Figure 11-20 Questions for eliciting performance risks in the Taxonomy-based Risk Identification process. If the question to question 23 is positive, questions 23.a and 23.b are asked of the developers [Carr et al., 1993].

Prioritizing risks

Systematic risk identification produces a large number of managerial and technical risks, some of them critical, others unimportant. Prioritizing risks allows managers to focus on the critical risks only. Risks are characterized by the likelihood they can become problems and by their potential impact to the project when they become problems. By using these two attributes, risks can be assigned to one of four categories:

- likely, high potential impact
- unlikely, high potential impact
- likely, low potential impact
- unlikely, low potential impact

The risks of the first category are those managers should worry about (likely, high potential impact). For these risks, developers and managers should draw contingency plans and monitor the risk carefully. If the likelihood of the risk increases, managers can activate the contingency plan and address the problem in time. Moreover, managers should monitor the risks of the second category (unlikely, high potential impact). Contingency plans do not need to be drawn for them unless their likelihood increases. Finally, the risks in the third and fourth categories can be ignored unless sufficient resources are available for monitoring them. Table 11-6 is the ordering of the risks presented in Table 11-5.

Table 11-6   Prioritized risks for the OWL project

Risk	Likelihood	Potential impact
Manufacturer's Personal Environment Module (PEM) does not comply with published standard	Not likely	High
Manufacturer's PEM delivery date is later than planned	Not likely	High
Users are not willing to use Web browser to adjust temperature settings	Likely for users spending less than 2 hours per day in front of a computer	High
Selected middleware too slow to meet performance requirement for data logging	Not likely, low sampling frequency	High
Development of abstract PEM layer takes more time than scheduled	Likely, first occurrence	High

Mitigating risks

Once risks have been identified and prioritized, mitigation strategies need to be designed for the critical risks. Mitigation strategies can include lowering the likelihood of the risk or decreasing its potential impact. Risks are usually caused by an area of uncertainty, such as missing information or lack of confidence in some information. Developers decrease the likelihood of a risk by further investigating the causes of the risk, by changing suppliers or components, or by selecting a redundant supplier or component. Similarly, developers reduce the impact of the risk on the project by developing an alternate or redundant solution. In most cases, however, mitigating a risk incurs additional resources and cost. Table 11-7 describes mitigation strategies for the risks presented in Table 11-5.

Table 11-7 Mitigation strategies for the OWL risks

Risk	Mitigation strategy
Manufacturer's Personal Environment Module (PEM) does not comply with published standard	• Run benchmarks to identify nonconformance • Investigate if nonconforming functions can be avoided
Manufacturer's PEM delivery date is later than planned	• Monitor risk by asking manufacturer for intermediate status reports
Users are not willing to use Web browser to adjust temperature settings	• Perform usability studies using mock-ups. • Develop alternate interface
Selected middleware too slow to meet performance requirement for data logging	• Monitor risk. Plan for a performance evaluation prototype
Development of abstract PEM layer takes more time than scheduled	• Increase the priority of this task with respect to other implementation tasks • Assign key developers to this task

Communicating risks

Once risks are identified, prioritized, and mitigated, the risk management plan needs to be communicated to all concerned. Risk management relies on timely communication. Spontaneous and timely reporting of potential problems needs to be encouraged. Risk management plans and technical documents are communicated using the same channels. Developers and other project participants review risks at the same time they review the technical content of the project. As mentioned earlier, communication is the most significant barrier when dealing with uncertainty.

11.4.5 Project Agreement

The *Project Agreement* is a document that formally defines the scope, duration, cost, and deliverables for the project. The form of a *Project Agreement* can be a contract, a statement of work, a business plan, or a project charter. The *Project Agreement* is typically finalized sometime after the analysis model is stabilized and the planning of the rest of the project is underway.

A *Project Agreement* should contain at least the following:

• list of deliverable documents

• criteria for demonstrations of functional requirements

• criteria for demonstrations of nonfunctional requirements, including accuracy, reliability, response time, and security
• criteria for acceptance

The *Project Agreement* represents the baseline of the client acceptance test. Any change in the functionality to be delivered, the nonfunctional requirements, the deadlines, or the budget of the project requires the renegotiation of the *Project Agreement*.

11.4.6 Client Acceptance Test

The purpose of the client acceptance test is the presentation of the system and the approval of the client according to acceptance criteria set forth in the *Project Agreement*. The result of the client acceptance test is the formal acceptance (or rejection) of the system by the client. Installation of the system and field tests by the client may already have occurred prior to this test. The client acceptance test constitute the visible end of the project.

The client acceptance test is conducted as a series of presentations of functionality and novel features of the system. Important scenarios from the *Problem Statement* are exercised and demonstrated by the developers or by future users. Additional demonstrations focus on the nonfunctional requirements of the system, such as accuracy, reliability, response time, or security. If installation and user evaluations occurred prior to the client acceptance test, their results are presented and summarized. Finally, the client acceptance test also serves as a discussion forum for subsequent activities such as maintenance, knowledge transfer, or system enhancement.

11.4.7 Installation

The installation phase of a project includes the field test of the system, the comparison of the system results with the legacy system, the rollout of the legacy system, and the training of users. The installation may be conducted by the supplier or by the client, depending on the *Project Agreement*.

To minimize risks, installation and field testing are usually done incrementally, with noncritical sites used as a field test environment. It is only when the client is convinced that the disruption to his business will be kept to a minimum that the delivered system enters full-scale operation. Replacement systems and upgrades are rarely introduced in a "big-bang" fashion, as the largest number of problems are discovered during the first few days of operation.

11.4.8 Postmortem

Every project uncovers new problems, unforeseen events, and unexpected failures. Each project, therefore, constitutes an opportunity for learning and anticipating new risks. Many software companies conduct a postmortem study of each project after its completion. The postmortem includes collecting data about the initial planned delivery dates and actual delivery dates, number of defects discovered, qualitative information about technical and managerial problems encountered, and suggestions for future projects. Although this phase is the least visible in the life cycle, the company depends on it the most for learning and improving its efficiency.

11.5 Managing Project Management Models and Activities

Project management activities, as technical activities, need to be documented, assigned, communicated, and revisited when unexpected events arise. In this section, we describe the management issues that apply to project management activities, including

- documenting management models (Section 11.5.1)
- assigning responsibilities for controlling and monitoring the project (Section 11.5.2)
- communicating about project management (Section 11.5.3)

11.5.1 Documenting Project Management

The management models described in Section 11.3 are documented in the SPMP [IEEE Std. 1058.1-1993]. The audience of the SPMP includes the management and the developers. The SPMP documents all issues related to client requirements (such as deliverables and acceptance criteria), the project goals, the project organization, the division of labor into tasks, and the allocation resources and responsibilities. Figure 11-21 depicts an example of outline for the SPMP.

The first section of the SPMP, *Introduction*, provides background information for the rest for the document. It briefly describes the project, the client deliverables, the project milestones, and the changes that the document can be expected to go through. This section contains the hard constraints found the *Project Agreement* that are relevant to the developers.

The second section of the SPMP describes the *Project organization*. The top-level design of the system is described, along with the subsystem and cross-functional teams that make up the project. The boundaries of each team and of the management are defined and responsibilities assigned. Communication roles, such as liaisons, are described in this section. By reading this section, developers are able to identify the participants in other teams they need to communicate with.

The third section of the SPMP, *Managerial process*, describes how management monitors project status and how it addresses unforeseen problems. Dependencies among teams and subsystems are described, anticipated risks and contingency plans are made public. Documenting what could go wrong makes it easier for the developers to report it when problems do occur. This section should be regularly updated to include newly identified risks.

The fourth section of the SPMP, *Technical process*, describes the technical standards that all teams are required to adopt. These range from the development methodology, to the configuration management policy of documents and code, to coding guidelines, and the selection of standard off-the-shelf components. Some might be imposed by companywide interests and others by the client.

Software Project Management Plan (SPMP)

1. Introduction
    1.1 Project overview
    1.2 Project deliverables
    1.3 Evolution of this document
    1.4 References
    1.5 Definitions and acronyms
2. Project organization
    2.1 Process model
    2.2 Organizational structure
    2.3 Organizational boundaries and interfaces
    2.4 Project responsibilities
3. Managerial process
    3.1 Management objectives and priorities
    3.2 Assumptions, dependencies and constraints
    3.3 Risk management
    3.4 Monitoring and controlling mechanisms
4. Technical process
    4.1 Methods, tools, and techniques
    4.2 Software documentation
    4.3 Project support functions
5. Work elements, schedule, and budget

Figure 11-21   An example of a template for the SPMP.

The fifth section of the SPMP, *Work elements, schedule, and budget,* represents the most visible product of management. This section details how work is to be carried out and who should carry it out. The first versions of the SPMP contains detailed plans only for the early phases of the project. Detailed plans for later phases are updated as the project progresses and important risks are better understood.

The SPMP is written early in the process, before the *Project Agreement* is finalized. It is reviewed both by management and by developers to ensure that the schedule is feasible and that important risks have not been omitted. The SPMP is then updated throughout the process when design decisions are made or problems are discovered. The SPMP, once published, is baselined and put under configuration management. The revision history section of the SPMP provides a history of changes as a list of changes, including author responsible for the change, date of change, and brief description of the change.

11.5.2 Assigning Responsibilities

Management assigns two types of roles to developers, management roles, such as team leader and liaison, and technical roles, such as architect, analyst, or tester. Management assigns these roles to an individual or to a team, depending on the effort requirements and the type of role assigned.

Assigning management roles

Management roles are assigned to individual participants. A role such as team leader cannot be filled effectively if shared by two or more participants. First, a team leader fills a communication function by acting as a liaison between higher level management and developers and thus must be able to communicate a consistent picture of status back and forth. Second, although a team leader makes usually decisions seeking the consensus of developers, he or she occasionally has to impose time-critical decisions. Other management roles, such as liaison between teams also require the same degree of consistency and thus are assigned to an individual.

Management seeks three qualities when assigning management roles: the ability to communicate, the ability to recognize risks early, and the discipline to separate management decisions from technical ones. Such qualities often come from experience in the project setting.

Assigning technical roles

Technical roles, unlike management roles, can be assigned to a team of participants. Complex projects have an architecture team and a testing team composed of only system architects and testers, respectively. Once management has defined the responsibilities of the team, the team leader assigns individual tasks to each team member based on availability or skill. Technical roles do not require the same level of consistency as management roles do, given that their tasks are better defined and that they rely on management and liaisons for coordination.

The skills required for each technical role vary significantly with the role. As design methods and implementation technology evolve rapidly, however, there is a greater shortage of technical skills than management skills, in which case, much training is required at the beginning of the project. Assigning technical roles to teams also allows mixing experts with novices, who can then complement their training with the availability of experienced mentors.

Selecting team sizes

Although technical roles can be assigned to teams, the size of a single team is constrained by management and communication overhead. The more participants in one team, the higher the communication overhead and the lower the effectiveness of the team. The observations below are adapted from [Kayser, 1990], who originally applied these heuristics to the formation of subgroups during meetings. Given that team meetings are a significant tool for collecting status, negotiation, and decision making, constraints on the number of participants in meetings are the upper limits on the team size.

- *Three members.* During meetings, every member has a chance to speak. Issues are discussed thoroughly and resolved easily. A possible problem with this team size is that one member can dominate the other two. Also, small teams suffer from the cumulation of multiple roles for each participant ("too many hats" syndrome).

- *Four members.* Starting with teams of this size allows the team to continue to function even if a participant drops out of the team. Reaching consensus with a team of even numbers can be problematic, however, as there can be a tie when voting. As a result, resolving issues can take a relatively long time.
- *Five and six members.* This is the ideal size for a software development team. Members can still meet face to face. Diverse perspectives, supported by a mix of ideas, opinions, and attitudes promotes creative thinking. Single roles can be assigned to each member, creating a miniorganization in which each member complements the others.
- *Seven members.* This is still a relatively effective team size, but team meetings tend to become long. Reviewing the status requires more than half an hour. If teams of seven are necessarily, it is advisable to form subteams during the formal team meetings, each having the task to discuss and resolve a subset of the open issues from the agenda.
- *Eight and more members.* Teams with this size become difficult to manage. The internal structure often starts to break down into subteams. Coalitions and side conversations often occur during formal meetings. Members have more opportunities to compete than to cooperate. Although results are usually satisfactory, the time to reach these results is longer than with a team of smaller size.

11.5.3 Communicating About Project Management

Communication about project management is difficult for several reasons. As in the case of analysis, management, developers, and the client have different backgrounds and do not discuss the system at the same level of abstraction. Management, developers, and the client each have a vested interest in the system, which creates a barrier during communication. The client strives for a useful system at the lowest cost. Management strives to respect time and budget constraints, either by asking a higher price from the client or by pressuring developers to develop faster in order to lower cost. Developers have the technical knowledge and take interventions by the client or the management as an intrusion in their territory. These factors, already present during analysis, become worse when communication is about management, including the allocation of resources and the review of status.

Below, we discuss heuristics for facilitating communication among all three parties.

Communicating with the client

The communication with the client is characterized by its episodic nature. The client is present at the kickoff, during external reviews, and during the acceptance test. Otherwise, the client is usually not available. This motivates a face-to-face communication for making decisions followed by short, written documents as a record of these decisions. These include the *Problem Statement*, used when kicking off the project, the *Project Agreement*, when the scope of the project is baselined, and the *Client Acceptance*, once the product is delivered. Detailed status information and partial drafts of technical information are usually not shared with the client.

Communicating with team leaders

The communication between project management and the team leaders determines the quality of the status information available to project management. If project management is seen reacting prematurely to status reports, a team leader will stop reporting the problems he believes he can handle alone. If the project manager believes the team leaders take too much initiative, he will withhold critical information. Setting up a weekly meeting with project management and team leaders, in which the information flows freely, is a critical element for addressing issues in time. The project manager can support this communication by separating status meetings from decision meetings. The project manager can, moreover, reward problem reporting by making available to the reporting team leader the appropriate resources to deal with the problem.

Communicating with developers

The project manager does not usually communicate directly with developers in the same way he meets with the team leaders. The main channel of communication are the SPMP, project reviews, and team leaders. Most often, team leaders act as a shield between project management and the developers filling the gap between the highest and the lowest level of abstraction. The communication between the team leader and developers is critical, as the team leader usually has the technical expertise to assess problems encountered by the developers.

11.6 Exercises

1. What are the relative advantages of flat staffing versus gradual staffing?
2. What is the difference between status meetings and decision meetings? Why should they be kept separate?
3. Why should the role of architect and team leader be assigned to distinct persons?
4. Draw a UML model of the team organization of the OWL project for each the three main phases (i.e., initiation, steady state, termination).
5. Draw a detailed task plan of the system design of the MyTrip system presented in Chapter 6, *System Design*.
6. Estimate the time to complete each task of the task model produced in Exercise 5 and determine the critical path.
7. Identify, prioritize, and plan for the top five risks related to the system design of MyTrip presented in Chapter 6, *System Design*.
8. Identify, prioritize, and plan for the top five risks related to the user interface subsystem of CTC presented in Chapter 8, *Rationale Management*.
9. Linux, developed using the bazaar model, is more reliable and more responsive than many operating systems running on Intel PCs. Discuss in some detail why the bazaar model should, however, not be used for the Space Shuttle control software.
10. Contrast the roles of project manager, development lead, and technical lead, as defined in Section 11.3.2. In particular, describe the tasks each lead is responsible for and which decisions they have final say on.

References

[Allen, 1985]   T. J. Allen, *Managing the Flow of Technology: Technology Transfer and the Dissemination of Technological Information within the R&D Organization,* 2nd ed. MIT Press, Cambridge, MA, 1995.

[Boehm, 1987]   B. Boehm, "A spiral model of software development and enhancement," *Software Engineering Project Management*, pp. 128–142, 1987.

[Boehm, 1991]   B. Boehm, "Software risk management: Principles and practices," *IEEE Software*, Vol. 1, pp. 32–41, 1991.

[Brooks, 1975]   F. P. Brooks, *The Mythical Man Month,* Addison-Wesley, Reading, MA, 1975.

[Bruegge et al., 1997]   B. Bruegge, S. Chang, T. Fenton, B. Fernandes, V. Hartkopf, T. Kim, R. Pravia, & A. Sharma, "Turning lightbulbs into objects," *OOPSLA'97* Experience paper. (Atlanta,) 1997.

[Carr et al., 1993]   M. J. Carr, S. L. Konda, I. Monarch, F. C. Ulrich, & C. F. Walker, "Taxonomy-based risk identification," *Technical Report CMU/SEI-93-TR-6*, Software Engineering Institute, Carnegie Mellon Univ., Pittsburgh, PA, 1993.

[Charette, 1989]   R. N. Charette, *Software Engineering Risk Analysis and Management*. McGraw-Hill, New York, 1989.

[Hartkopf et al., 1997]   V. Hartkopf, V. Loftness, A. Mahdavi, S. Lee, & J. Shankavarm, "An integrated approach to design and engineering of intelligent buildings—The Intelligent Workplace at Carnegie Mellon University," *Automation in Construction*, Vol. 6, pp. 401–415, 1997.

[Hauschildt & Gemuenden, 1998] J. Hauschildt & H. G. Gemuenden, *Promotoren*. Gabler, Wiesbaden, Germany, 1998.

[Hillier & Lieberman, 1967]   F. S. Hillier & G. J. Lieberman, *Introduction to Operation Research.* Holden-Day, San Francisco, 1967.

[IEEE Std. 1058.1-1993]   *IEEE Standard for Software Project Management Plans*, IEEE Computer Society, New York, 1993.

[Kayser, 1990]   T. A. Kayser, *Mining Group Gold*. Serif, El Segundo, CA, 1990.

[Kemerer, 1997]   C. F. Kemerer, *Software Project Management: Readings and Cases.* Irwin/McGraw-Hill, Boston, MA, 1997.

[OWL, 1996]   *OWL Project Documentation*, School of Computer Science, Carnegie Mellon Univ., Pittsburgh, PA, 1996.

[Raymond, 1998]   E. Raymond, "The cathedral and the bazaar," Available at http://www.tuxedo.org/ ~esr/writings/cathedral-bazaar/cathedral-bazaar.html, 1998.

[Rogers et al., 1986]   *The Presidential Commission on the Space Shuttle Challenger Accident Report*. Washington, DC, June 6, 1986.

[Vaughan, 1996]   D. Vaughan, *The Challenger Launch Decision: Risky Technology, Culture, and Deviance at NASA.* The University of Chicago, Chicago, 1996.

[Weinberg, 1971]   G. M. Weinberg, *The Psychology of Computer Programming*, Van Nostrand, New York, 1971.

PART IV
Starting Over

12

Software Life Cycle

*There must always be a discrepancy between
concepts and reality, because the former are static
while the latter is dynamic and flowing.*
—Robert Pirsig, in Lila

A software life cycle model represents all the activities and work products necessary to develop a software system. Life cycle models enable managers and developers to deal with the complexity of the process of developing software in the same way as an analysis model or a system design model enables developers to deal with the complexity of a software system. In the case of software systems, the reality being modeled includes phenomena such as watches, accidents, trains, sensors, and buildings. In the case of software development, the reality includes phenomena such as participants, teams, activities, and work products. Many life cycle models have been published in the literature in attempt to better understand, measure, and control the development process. Life cycle models make the software development activities and their dependencies visible and manageable.

In this chapter, we describe selected well-known life cycle models and revisit the activities described in previous chapters from the perspective of life cycle modeling. The modeling techniques we used for modeling software systems can also be used for representing life cycles. Whereas life cycle models are usually represented with ad-hoc notations, we use UML class diagrams and UML activity diagrams whenever possible. First, we describe the typical activities and work products of a software life cycle as defined by the IEEE standard 1074 [IEEE Std. 1074-1995]. Next, we introduce the Capability Maturity Model, a framework for assessing the maturity of organizations and their life cycles. Next, we discuss different life cycle models that have been proposed to deal with the development of complex software systems. We also introduce a new life cycle model called the issue-based model, where products and activities are modeled as a set of issues stored in a knowledge base. The issue-based model is an entity-centered view of the software life cycle that deals better with frequent changes within the duration of a project. We conclude with two examples of software life cycle models that can be used for a single semester or a two semester course project.

12.1 Introduction

In Chapter 2, *Modeling with UML*, we describe modeling as classifying real world phenomena into concepts. So far, we have been interested in phenomena related to watches, emergency handling, facility management, train traffic control, vehicle part catalogs, and environmental modeling. This chapter, however, treats the software development process as the reality of interest. The phenomena we want to model include all the activities necessary to build a software system and the work products produced during development. Models of the software development process are called **software life cycle models**. Modeling the software life cycle is a difficult undertaking, because it is a complex and changing system. As software systems, software life cycles can be described by several different models. Most proposed life cycle models have focused on the activities of software development and represented them explicitly as first class objects. This view of the software life cycle is called **activity-centered**. An alternative view of the software life cycle is to focus on the work products created by these activities. This alternate view is called **entity-centered**. The activity-centered view leads participants to focus on how work products are created. The entity-centered view leads participants to focus on the content and structure of the work products.

Figure 12-1 depicts a simple life cycle for software development using three activities: Problem definition, System development, and System operation.

Figure 12-2 shows an activity-centered view of this simplistic life cycle model. The associations between the activities show a linear time dependency, which is implied by the use of the activity diagram notation: The problem statement precedes system development, which in turn precedes system operation. Alternate time dependencies are possible.

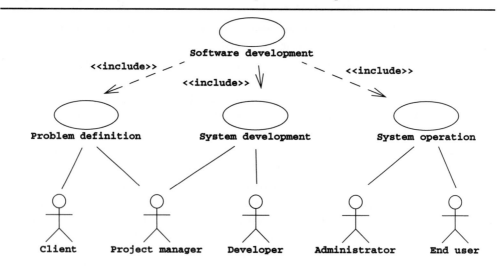

Figure 12-1   Simple life cycle for software development (UML use case diagram).

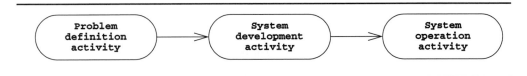

Figure 12-2 Simple life cycle for software development (UML activity diagram).

For example, in the software life cycle of Figure 12-3 the activities System development and Market creation can be done concurrently.

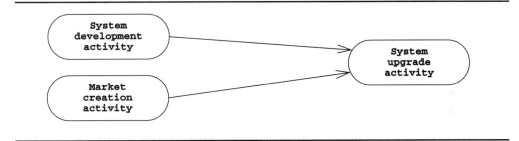

Figure 12-3 Another simple life cycle (UML activity diagram).

Figure 12-4 is an entity centered view of the model depicted by Figure 12-2. Software development produces four entities, a Market survey document, a System specification document, an Executable system and a Lessons learned document.

The activity-centered view and the entity-centered view are complementary, as illustrated by Figure 12-5. For every product there is one or more activity that generates it. The Problem definition activity uses a Market survey document as input and generates a System specification document. The System development activity takes the System specification document as input and produces an Executable system. System operation generates a Lessons learned document that could be used during the development of the next product. Alternatively, every activity generates one or more products.

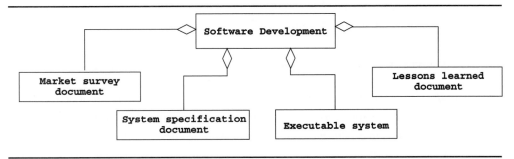

Figure 12-4 Entity-centered view of software development (UML class diagram).

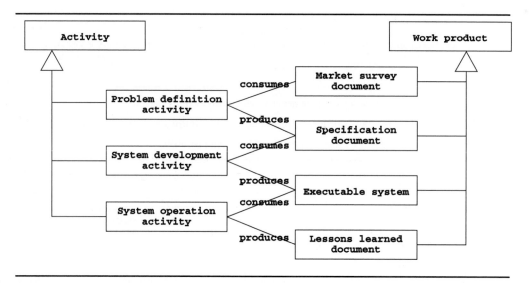

Figure 12-5   Activities and products of the simple life cycle of Figure 12-2 (UML class diagram).

In Section 12.2, we describe the life cycle activities defined by the IEEE 1074 standard [IEEE Std. 1074-1995]. This standard introduces precise definitions that enable project participants to understand and communicate effectively about the life cycle. In this section, we also describe the information flows between activities.

In Section 12.3, we describe the Capability Maturity Model, a framework for assessing the maturity of organizations and their life cycles. This framework enables organizations and projects to be compared, based on the activities of their life cycles.

In Section 12.4, we survey several activity-centered life cycle models that propose different ordering of activities. In particular, we discuss the waterfall model [Royse, 1970], the spiral model [Boehm, 1987], the V model [Jensen & Tonies, 1979], the sawtooth model [Rowen, 1990], and the Unified Software Process [Jacobson et al., 1999].

In Section 12.5, we describe two specific life cycle model instances for a team-based project, including its activities, products, and information flow.

12.2 IEEE 1074: Standard for Developing Life Cycle Processes

The *IEEE Standard for Software Life Cycle Processes* describes the set of activities and processes that are mandatory for the development and maintenance of software [IEEE Std. 1074-1995]. Its goal is to establish a common framework for developing life cycle models and provide examples for typical situations. In this section, we describe the main activities introduced by the standard and clarify its fundamental concepts using UML diagrams.

12.2.1 Processes and Activities

A **process** is a set of activities that is performed towards a specific purpose (e.g., requirements, management, delivery). The IEEE standard lists a total of 17 processes (Table 12-1). The processes are grouped into higher levels of abstractions called **process groups**. Examples of process groups are project management, pre-development, development, and post-development. Examples of processes in the development process group include:

- the *Requirements Process*, during which the developers develop the system models
- the *Design Process*, during which developers decompose the system into components
- the *Implementation Process*, during which developers realize each component

Table 12-1   Software processes in IEEE 1074

Process group	Processes
Life Cycle Modeling	Selection of a Life Cycle Model
Project Management	Project Initiation Project Monitoring and Control Software Quality Management
Pre-development	Concept Exploration System Allocation
Development	Requirements Design Implementation
Post-development	Installation Operation and Support Maintenance Retirement
Integral Processes	Verification and Validation Software Configuration Management Documentation Development Training

Each process is composed of activities. An **activity** is a task or group of sub activities that are assigned to a team or a project participant to achieve a specific purpose. The *Requirements Process*, for example, is composed of three activities:

- *Define and Develop Software Requirements*, during which the functionality of the system is defined precisely
- *Define Interface Requirements*, during which the interactions between the system and the user are precisely defined

• *Prioritize and Integrate Software Requirements*, during which all requirements are integrated for consistency, and prioritized by client preference

Tasks consume resources (e.g., personnel, time, money) and produce a work product. During planning, activities are decomposed into project specific tasks, are given a start and ending date and assigned to a team or a project participant (Figure 12-6). During the project, actual work is tracked against planned tasks, and resources are reallocated to respond to problems.

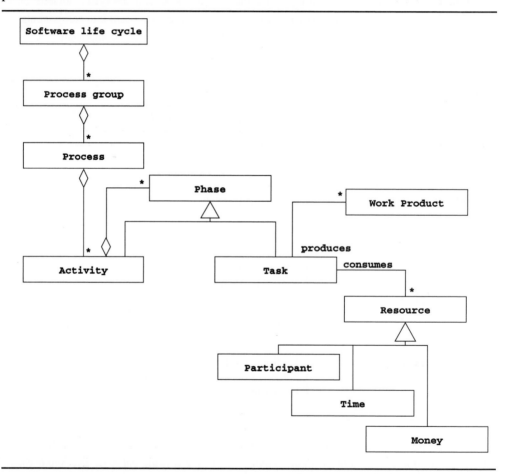

Figure 12-6   Model of the software life cycle (UML class diagram). A software life cycle consists of process groups, which in turn consist of processes. A process accomplishes a specific purpose (e.g., requirements, design, installation). A process consists of activities, which are in turn consists of subactivities or tasks. Tasks represent the smallest piece of work that is relevant to management. Tasks consume resources and produces one or more work products. A project is an instance of a software life cycle.

The processes required by IEEE 1074 are listed in Table 12-1. From the developers' point of view, the first six processes (i.e., the *Life Cycle Modeling Process*, the *Project Management Processes*, and the *Pre-development Processes*) have often already been initiated before their involvement with the project.

12.2.2 Life Cycle Modeling

During *Life Cycle Modeling*, the project manager customizes the activities defined in IEEE 1074 for a specific project (i.e., for an instance of a life cycle model). Not all projects require the same activities and the same sequencing of activities. For example, projects that do not deal with a persistent storage do not need to execute the activity *Design Data Base*. The selected life cycle model serves as input to the *Project Initiation Process* described in the next section. We provide two examples of *Life Cycle Modeling* in Section 12.5.

12.2.3 Project Management

During the *Project Management* group the project manager initiates, monitors, and controls the project throughout the software life cycle. *Project Management* consists of three processes (Table 12-2).

The *Project Initiation Process* creates the infrastructure for the project. During this process the task plan, schedule, budget, organization, and project environment are defined. The project environment includes project standards, communication infrastructure, meeting and reporting

Table 12-2   Project management processes

Process	Clause[a]	Activities
Project Initiation	3.1.3	Map Activities to Software Life Cycle Model
	3.1.4	Allocate Project Resources
	3.1.5	Establish Project Environment
	3.1.6	Plan Project Management
Project Monitoring and Control	3.2.3	Analyze Risks
	3.2.4	Perform Contingency Planning
	3.2.5	Manage the Project
	3.2.6	Retain Records
	3.2.7	Implement Problem Reporting Model
Software Quality Management	3.3.3	Plan Software Quality Management
	3.3.4	Define Metrics
	3.3.5	Manage Software Quality
	3.3.6	Identify Quality Improvement Needs

a.   The 'Clause' column in this table and the other tables in this chapter refers to a clause number in IEEE 1074. This is a cross reference to the standards document as published in [IEEE Std. 1074-1995]

procedures, development methodology, and development tools. Most of the information generated during this process is documented in the *Software Project Management Plan (SPMP)*. The *Project Initiation Process* is complete as soon as a stable environment for the project is established.

The *Project Monitoring and Control Process* ensures that the project is executed according to the task plan and budget. If the project manager observes any deviation from the schedule, she will take corrective action such as reallocating some of the resources, changing procedures, or replanning the schedule. The SPMP is updated to reflect any of these changes. The *Project Monitoring and Control Process* is active throughout the life cycle.

The *Software Quality Management Process* ensures that the system under construction meets the required quality standards (which were selected during Project Initiation). This process is executed by a separate quality management team to avoid conflicts of interest (i.e., the goal of the developers is to complete the system on time, the goal of the quality management team is to ensure that the system is not considered complete until it meets the required quality standard). The *Software Quality Management Process* is active throughout most of the life cycle.

We describe in Chapter 11, *Project Management*, the activities of *Project Initiation* and *Project Monitoring and Control* that are related to planning, organization, and tracking. The activity *Establish Project Environment* requires particular attention in the context of a team-based project. One of the critical parts of the project environment is the communication infrastructure that will support the dissemination of information among the participants. To be able to react rapidly to changes and report problems without introducing an unreasonable overhead, all project participants need to be aware of the information flow through the project and the mechanisms for disseminating information. We describe in Chapter 3, *Project Communication*, the activities related to defining and using the communication infrastructure. Note that in order to define the development team structure, and thus, the communication infrastructure, the initial system architecture (produced by the *System Allocation Process* described in the next section) needs to be defined.

12.2.4 Pre-Development

During *Pre-development,* management (or marketing) and a client identify an idea or a need. This can be addressed with a new development effort (greenfield engineering), or a change to the interface of an existing system (interface engineering) or software replacement of an existing business process (reengineering). The *System Allocation Process* establishes the initial system architecture and identifies the hardware, software and operational requirements. Note that the subsystem decomposition is the foundation of the communication infrastructure among the project members. The requirements, subsystem decomposition and communication infrastructure are described in the *Problem Statement*[1], which serves as input for the *Development* process. The pre-development processes are depicted in Table 12-3.

---

1. The *Statement of Need* mentioned in the IEEE 1074 standard is similar to the *Problem Statement*, but does not contain any project organization information.

Table 12-3   Pre-development processes

Process	Clause	Activities
Concept Exploration	4.1.3	Identify Ideas or Needs
	4.1.4	Formulate Potential Approaches
	4.1.5	Conduct Feasibility Studies
	4.1.6	Plan System Transition (If Applicable)
	4.1.7	Refine and Finalize the Idea or Need
System Allocation	4.2.3	Analyze Functions
	4.2.4	Develop System Architecture
	4.2.5	Decompose System Requirements

12.2.5 Development

Development consists of the processes directed toward the construction of the system.

The *Requirements Process* starts with the informal description of the requirements and defines the system requirements in terms of high-level functional requirements, producing a complete specification of the system and a prioritization of the requirements. We describe the *Requirements Process* in Chapter 4, *Requirements Elicitation*, and Chapter 5, *Analysis*.

The *Design Process* takes the architecture produced during the *System Allocation Process* and the specification from the *Requirements* and produces a coherent and well-organized representation of the system. The activities *Perform Architectural Design* and *Design Interfaces* activities result in a refinement of the subsystem decomposition. This also includes the allocation of requirements to hardware and software systems, the description of boundary conditions, the selection of off-the-shelf components, and the definition of design goals. The detailed design of each subsystem is done during the *Perform Detailed Design* activity. The *Design Process* results in the definition of design objects, their attributes and operations, and their organization into packages. By the end of this activity, all methods and their type signatures

Table 12-4   Development processes

Process	Clause	Activities
Requirements	5.1.3	Define and Develop Software Requirements
	5.1.4	Define Interface Requirements
	5.1.5	Prioritize and Integrate Software Requirements

Table 12-4   Development processes

Process	Clause	Activities
Design	5.2.3	Perform Architectural Design
	5.2.4	Design Data Base (If Applicable)
	5.2.5	Design Interfaces
	5.2.6	Select or Develop Algorithms (If Applicable)
	5.2.7	Perform Detailed Design
Implementation	5.3.3	Create Test Data
	5.3.4	Create Source
	5.3.5	Generate Object Code
	5.3.6	Create Operating Documentation
	5.3.7	Plan Integration
	5.3.8	Perform Integration

are defined. New classes are introduced to take into account nonfunctional requirements and component specific details. The *Design* process used in this book is described in Chapter 6, *System Design*. and Chapter 7, *Object Design*.

The *Implementation Process* takes the design model and produces an equivalent executable representation. The *Implementation Process* includes integration planning, and integration activities. Note that tests performed during this process are independent of those performed during quality control or *Verification and Validation*. We describe in Chapter 9, *Testing* the testing and integration aspects of the *Implementation*. The development processes are depicted in Table 12-4.

12.2.6 Post-Development

Post-development consists of the installation, maintenance, operation and support, and retirement processes (Table 12-5).

During *Installation* the system software is distributed and installed at the client site. The installation culminates with the client acceptance test according to the criteria defined in the *Project Agreement*. *Operation and Support* is concerned with user training and operation of the system. *Maintenance* is concerned with the resolution of software errors, faults and failures after the delivery of the system. *Maintenance* requires a ramping of the software life cycle processes and activities into a new project. *Retirement* removes an existing system terminating its operations or support. *Retirement* takes place when the system is upgraded or replaced by a new system. To ensure a smooth transition between the two systems, both systems are often run in parallel until the users have gotten used to the new system. Except for client delivery and acceptance, we do not address the post-development processes in this book.

Table 12-5   Post-development processes

Process	Clause	Activities
Installation	6.1.3	Plan Installation
	6.1.4	Distribution of Software
	6.1.5	Installation of Software
	6.1.7	Accept Software in Operational Environment
Operation and Support	6.2.3	Operate the System
	6.2.4	Provide Technical Assistance and Consulting
	6.2.5	Maintain Support Request Log
Maintenance	6.3.3	Reapply Software Life Cycle
Retirement	6.4.3	Notify Users
	6.4.4	Conduct Parallel Operations (If Applicable)
	6.4.5	Retire System

12.2.7 Integral Processes (Cross-Development)

Several processes take place during the complete duration of the project. These are called integral processes (we also use the term *cross-development processes*) and include *Validation and Verification*, *Software Configuration Management*, *Documentation Development*, and *Training* (Table 12-6).

Verification and Validation includes verification and validation tasks. Verification tasks focus on showing that the system models comply with the specification. Verification includes reviews, audits, and inspections. Validation tasks ensure that the system addresses the client's needs and include system testing, beta testing, and client acceptance testing. *Verification and Validation* activities occur throughout the life cycle with the intent of detecting anomalies as early as possible. For example, each model could be reviewed against a checklist at the end of the process that generated it. The review of a model, say the design model, may result in the modification of a model generated in other processes, say the analysis model. The activity *Collect and Analyze Metric Data* generates project data that can also serve for future projects and contribute to the knowledge of the organization. The activities *Plan Testing and Develop Test Requirements* can be initiated as early as after the completion of the requirements. In large projects, these tasks are performed by different participants than the developers. We describe mechanisms for reviews, audits and inspections in Chapter 3, *Project Communication*. We describe specific reviews associated with requirements elicitation, analysis, and system design in Chapters 4, 5, and 6, respectively. We describe testing activities in Chapter 9, *Testing*.

The *Configuration Management Process* focuses on the tracking and control of changes of work products. Items under configuration management include the source code for the system, all development models, the software project management plan, and all documents visible to the

Table 12-6   Integral processes (also called cross-development processes)

Process	Clause	Activities
Verification and Validation	7.1.3	Plan Verification and Validation
	7.1.4	Execute Verification and Validation Tasks
	7.1.5	Collect and Analyze Metric Data
	7.1.6	Plan Testing
	7.1.7	Develop Test Requirements
	7.1.8	Execute the Tests
Software Configuration Management	7.2.3	Plan Configuration Management
	7.2.4	Develop Configuration Identification
	7.2.5	Perform Configuration Control
	7.2.6	Perform Status Accounting
Documentation Development	7.3.3	Plan Documentation
	7.3.4	Implement Documentation
	7.3.5	Produce and Distribute Documentation
Training	7.4.3	Plan the Training Program
	7.4.4	Develop Training Materials
	7.4.5	Validate the Training Program
	7.4.6	Implement the Training Program

project participants. We describe configuration management in Chapter 10, *Software Configuration Management*.

The *Documentation Process* deals with the work products (excluding code) documenting the results produced by the other processes. Document templates are selected during this activity. The IEEE 1074 standard, however, does not prescribe any specific document or template. Development and cross-development specific documentation issues are discussed in chapters where documents are produced (e.g., Chapter 5, *Analysis*, discusses the *Requirements Analysis Document*; Chapter 10, *Software Configuration Management*, discusses the *Software Configuration Management Plan*).

12.3 Characterizing the Maturity of Software Life Cycle Models

In the previous section we introduced the set of activities and artifacts that constitute a software life cycle. Which of these activities and artifacts are chosen for a specific project is not defined by the standard. One of the goals of the Capability Maturity Model (CMM) is to provide guidelines for selecting life cycle activities. The CMM assumes that the development of software systems is made more predictable when an organization uses a well-structured life cycle process, visible to all project participants, and adapts to change. CMM uses the following five levels to characterize the maturity of an organization [Paulk et al., 1995].

Level 1: Initial. An organization on the initial level applies ad-hoc activities to develop software. Few of these activities are well-defined. The success of a project on this maturity level usually depends on the heroic efforts and skills of key individuals. From the client's point of view, the software life cycle model, if it exists at all, is a black box: After providing the problem statement and negotiating the project agreement, the client must wait until the end of the project to inspect the deliverables of the project. During the duration of the project, the client has effectively no way to interact with project management.

Level 2: Repeatable. Each project has a well-defined software life cycle model. Models, however, differ between projects, reducing the opportunity for teamwork and reuse of know how. Basic project management processes are used to track cost, and schedule. New projects are based on the experience of the organization with similar older projects and success is predictable for projects in similar application domains. The client interacts with the organization at well-defined points in time, such as client reviews and the client acceptance test, allowing some corrections before delivery.

Level 3: Defined. This level uses a documented software life cycle model for all managerial and technical activities across the organization. A customized version of the model is produced at the beginning of each project during the *Life Cycle Modeling* activity. The client knows the standard model and the model selected for a specific project.

Level 4: Managed. This level defines metrics for activities and deliverables. Data are constantly collected during the duration of the project. As a result, the software life cycle model can be quantitatively understood and analyzed. The client is informed about risks before the project begins and knows the measures used by organization.

Level 5: Optimized. The measurement data are used in a feedback mechanism to improve the software life cycle model over the lifetime of an organization.The client, project managers, and developers communicate and work together during the development of the project.

To be able to measure the maturity of an organization, a set of key process areas (KPA) has been defined by the SEI. To achieve a specific level of maturity, the organization must demonstrate that it addresses all the key process areas defined for that level. Some of these key process areas go beyond activities defined in the IEEE 1074 standard. Table 12-7 shows a mapping between maturity level and key process areas.

Table 12-7   Mapping process maturity level and key process areas

Maturity Level	Key Process Area
Initial	Not applicable
Repeatable	Focus: Establish basic project management controls. • **Requirements Management:** Requirements are baselined in a project agreement and maintained during the project • **Project Planning and Tracking**: A software project management plan is established at the beginning of the project and is tracked during the execution of the project. • **Subcontractor Management:** The organization selects and effectively manages qualified software subcontractors. • **Quality Assurance Management:** All deliverables and process activities are reviewed and audited to verify that they comply with standards and guidelines adopted by the organization. • **Configuration Management:** A set of configuration management items is defined and maintained throughout the entire project.
Defined	Focus: Establish an infrastructure that allows a single effective software life cycle model across all projects. • **Organization process focus:** The organization has a permanent team to constantly maintain and improve the software life cycle. • **Organization process definition:** A standard software life cycle model is used for all projects in the organization. A database is used for software life cycle-related information and documentation. • **Training program:** The organization identifies the needs for training for specific projects and develops training programs. • **Integrated Software management:** Each project has the possibility to tailor their specific process from the standard process. • **Software product engineering:** The software is built in accordance with the defined software life cycle, methods and tools. • **Intergroup coordination:** The project teams interact with other teams to address requirements and issues. • **Peer reviews:** Developer examine deliverables on a peer level to identify potential defects and areas where changes are needed.

Table 12-7 Mapping process maturity level and key process areas

Maturity Level	Key Process Area
Managed	Focus: Quantitative understanding of the software life cycle process and deliverables. • **Quantitative process management:** Productivity and quality metrics are defined and constantly measured across the project. It is critical that these data are not immediately used during the project, in particular to assess the performance of developers, but are stored in a database to allow for comparison with other projects. • **Quality management:** The organization has defined a set of quality goals for software products. It monitors and adjusts the goals and products to deliver high-quality products to the user.
Optimized	Focus: Keep track of technology and process changes that may cause change in the system model or deliverables even during the duration of a project. • **Defect prevention:** Failures in past projects are analyzed, using data from the metrics database. If necessary, specific actions are taken to prevent those defects to occur again. • **Technology change management:** Technology enablers and innovations are constantly investigated and shared throughout the organization. • **Process change management:** The software process is constantly refined and changed to deal with inefficiencies identified by the software process metrics. Constant change is the norm, not the exception.

12.4 Life Cycle Models

Figure 12-7 depicts the information flow among processes in the IEEE 1074 standard. The complexity of the standard is significant as can be seen in the many dependencies between the processes. Each association represents a work product that is generated by a process and consumed by another process. Each association also represents a formal communication channel between project participants supported by the exchange of documents, models, or code.

When selecting a life cycle model, a modeler has to address two questions: Is it necessary to model all these dependencies and in what order should they be scheduled? That is, which activities be left out and in what order should the remaining activities be performed and managed to deliver a high-quality system within budget and on time while change occurs during the duration of the project?

There is no single answer to these questions. First, different projects require different processes and different dependencies. For example, if the application domain is well known, as in the case of a business reengineering project, the ordering of the development activities may be sequential, especially if the developers require only minimum training. A first-of-a-kind project may require substantial prototyping in which case all the development processes should be executed concurrently. This, in turn, makes the management and configuration management processes much more complex.

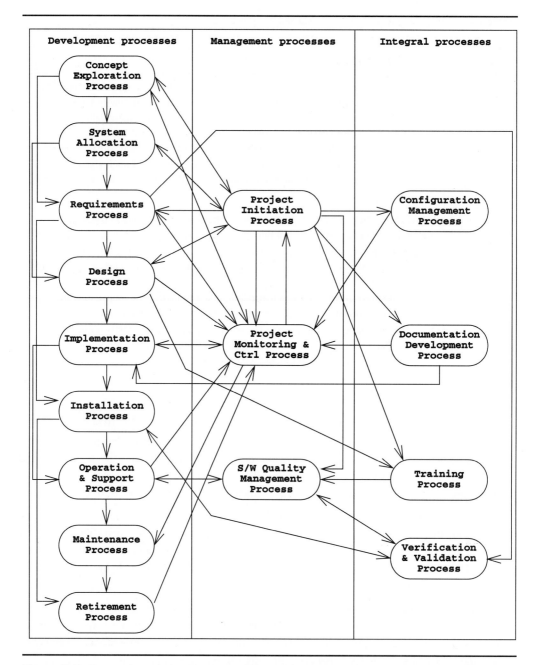

Figure 12-7   Process interrelationships in the IEEE 1074 standard (UML activity diagram, adapted from [IEEE Std. 1074-1995]]. As suggested by this picture, dependencies among processes and activities are complex and seldom allow a sequential execution of processes.

The selection of the life cycle model also depends on the system model. Reengineering a software system with existing use case and object models requires a different set of activities than building a system from scratch. In a project with experienced developers, good CASE tool support and a tight deadline, the project manager might select an entity-centered life cycle model instead of an activity-centered one.

For these reasons, IEEE 1074 does not dictate a specific life cycle model, but rather, provides a template that can be customized in many different ways. In this section we review selected life cycle models. Most of these models focus on the development processes exclusively.

12.4.1 Waterfall Model

The **waterfall model** was first described by Royse [Royse, 1970]. The waterfall model is an activity-centered life cycle model that prescribes a sequential execution of a subset of the development processes and management processes described in the last section (Figure 12-8).

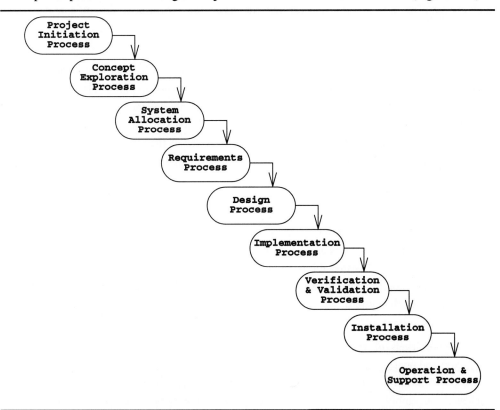

Figure 12-8 The waterfall model of software development is an activity-centered view of the software life cycle: Software development activities are performed in sequence (UML activity diagram adapted from [Royse, 1970] using IEEE 1074 names; project management and cross-development processes are omitted).

The requirements activities are all completed before the system design activity starts. The goal is to never turn back once an activity is completed. The key feature of his model is the constant verification activity (called "verification step" by Royse) that ensures that each development activity does not introduce unwanted or deletes mandatory requirements. This model provides a simple (or even simplistic) view of software development that measures progress by the number of tasks that have been completed. The model assumes that software development can be scheduled as a step-by-step process that transforms user needs into code.

Figure 12-9 shows a widely used waterfall model, the DOD 2167A standard life cycle model.

The main characteristic of this model is that each development activity is followed by a review. The starting point in this model is the system requirements analysis activity whose goal is to generate unambiguous system requirements. The first review is the *System Requirements Review*, during which the requirements are reviewed with respect to completeness, consistency, and clarity. The system requirements are the basis for the system design activity, which generates the system design. The system design is reviewed during the *System Design Review* activity.

The system design is baselined once the system design review is successfully completed. The functional baseline serves as the starting point for the software requirements analysis, which creates the software requirements. The software requirements are then reviewed and baselined before serving as a basis for implementation. Implementation starts with the preliminary design followed by the detailed design activity. An important review is the critical design review (CDR). Coding does not occur before the CDR completes successfully.

12.4.2 V-Model

The **V-model** is a variation of the waterfall model that makes explicit the dependency between development activities and verification activities. The difference between the waterfall model and the V model is that the latter makes explicit the notion of level of abstraction. All activities from requirements to implementation focus on building more and more detailed representation of the system, whereas all activities from implementation to operation focus on validating the system.

Higher levels of abstractions of the V-model deal with the requirements in terms of elicitation and operation. The middle-part of the V-model focuses on mapping the understanding of the problem into a software architecture. The lower level of the V-model focuses on details such as the assembly of software components and the coding of new ones. For example, the goal of the *Unit Test* activity is to validate units against their description in the detailed design. The *Component Integration and Test* activity validates functional components against the preliminary (or high-level) design.

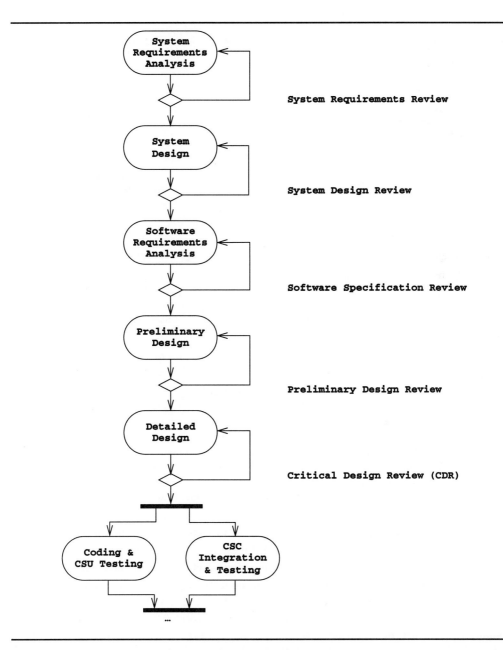

Figure 12-9 Waterfall model for the DOD Standard 2167A (UML activity diagram). Note activities specific to the DOD are used instead of IEEE 1074 activities. Decision points denote reviews: The subsequent activity is initiated only if the review is successful.

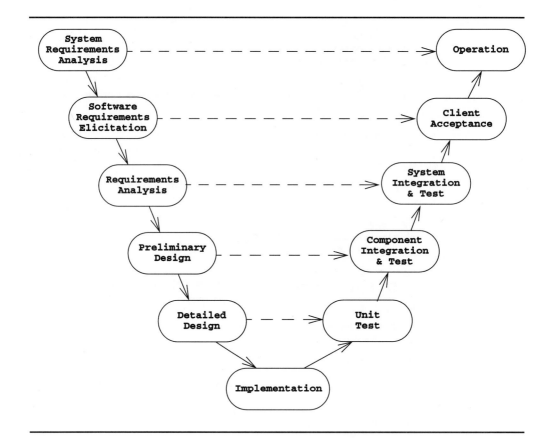

Figure 12-10   V-Model of software development (UML activity diagram; adapted from [Jensen & Tonies, 1979]). The horizontal object flow denotes the information flow between activities of same abstraction level (e.g., the system requirements analysis results are validated during system and integration test). The V-shape layout of the activities was conserved to reflect the original drawing. However, the layout of the activities has no semantics in UML.

In many aspects, the waterfall model and its variants are simplistic abstractions of the software development process. The weakness of these models is that they assume that after an activity is finished and reviewed the associated work product can be baselined. Such an idealized model is only appropriate if the specification of the requirements is of high level of assurance and does not change during development. In practice, system development rarely conforms to this ideal model. Changes during an activity often require work of a prior activity to be revisited. Figure 12-10 depicts the V-model.

12.4.3 Boehm's Spiral Model

Boehm's spiral model [Boehm, 1987] is an activity-centered life cycle model that was devised to address the source of weaknesses in the waterfall model, in particular, to accommodate infrequent change during the software development. It based on the same activities as the waterfall model, however, it adds several activities such as risk management, reuse, and prototyping to each activity. These extended activities are called **cycles** or **rounds**.

The spiral model focuses on addressing risks incrementally, in order of priority. Each round is composed of four phases (Figure 12-11). During the first phase (upper left quadrant), developers explore alternatives, define constraints, and identify objectives. During the second phase (upper right quadrant), developers manage risks associated with the solutions defined during the first phase. During the third phase (lower right quadrant), developers realize and validate a prototype or the part of the system associated with the risks addressed in this round. The fourth phase (lower left quadrant) focuses on the planning of the next round based on the results produced in the current round. The last phase of the round is usually conducted as a review involving the project participants, including developers, clients, and users. This review covers the products developed during the previous and current rounds and the plans for the next round. Boehm's spiral model distinguishes the following rounds: *Concept of Operation, Software Requirements, Software Product Design, Detailed Design, Code, Unit Test, Integration and Test, Acceptance Test, Implementation.*[2]

Each round follows the waterfall model and includes the following activities:

1. Determine objectives
2. Specify constraints
3. Generate alternatives
4. Identify risks
5. Resolve risks
6. Develop and verify next level product
7. Plan

The first two activities define the problem addressed by the current cycle. The third activity, *Generate alternatives*, defines the solution space. The activities *Identify risks* and *Resolve risks* serve to identify future problems that may result in high costs or in the cancellation of the project. The activity *Develop and verify next level product* is the realization of the cycle, The activity *Plan* is a management activity preparing for the next cycle.

These rounds can be viewed in a polar-coordinate system shown in Figure 12-11. The first round, *Concept of Operation*, starts in the upper left quadrant. Subsequent rounds are

---

2. Note that the figure illustrates only the first three activities (*Concept of Operation, Software Requirements* and *Software Product Design*). The rounds for the remaining activities–*Detailed Design, Code, Unit Test, Integration and Test, Acceptance Test*–are not shown in detail, but only as blocks at the end of the last layer of the spiral

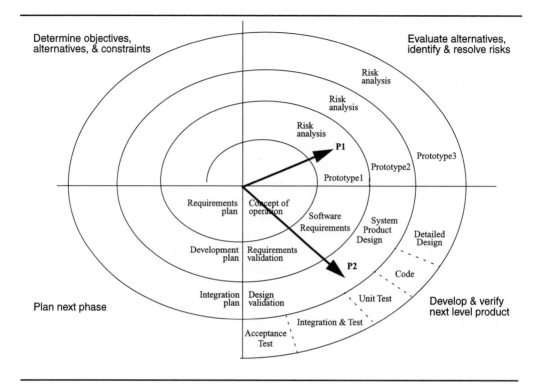

Figure 12-11   Boehm's spiral model (Adapted from [Boehm, 1987]). The distance from the origin represents the cost accumulated by the project. The angle from the horizontal represents the type of activity. For example, the project P1 is currently in the risk analysis activity associated with software requirements. The project P2 is in the development of the system product design.

represented as additional layers on the spiral. The notation allows easily to determine the status of the project over time. The distance from the origin is the cost accumulated by the project. The angular coordinate indicates the progress accomplished within each phase.

12.4.4 Sawtooth Model

The life cycle models we described until now emphasize the management of software developers. They do not address the needs of the customer or the user. The waterfall model, the V model, and the spiral model all assume that the software requirements will not change drastically during the duration of the project and that it is sufficient to show progress according to the development plan. The drawback of this approach is that the client and the user do not see a running system before the client acceptance test, and thus, cannot correct any requirement problems.

Users and implementors, however, have different needs when trying to understand software systems. The **sawtooth model** [Rowen, 1990] tries to solve this discrepancy by showing the user and software developer's perception of the system at different levels of abstractions over time.

At the beginning of a project, developers and the client are at the same level of abstraction, namely the requirements of the system as described in the problem statement. During development these points of view differ quite a bit. The user stays at the level of requirements, whereas the developers focus on feasibility. The software development process has to ensure that both points of view meet at the end of the project. The sawtooth model achieves this goal by introducing new activities. The span between these levels of abstractions corresponds to the gap between the user's perception of the system and the developer's perception of the system. To make sure that these meet at the end, checkpoints are introduced during development. This is usually done by getting the client involved *at their level of abstraction.*

For example, after the requirements and system design phase of an interactive software system, the developers can prototype the screen sequences in terms of the use cases describing the functional requirements. By demonstrating this prototype to the client, the client is able to evaluate quite early in the development whether the prototype satisfies the functional requirements. By repeating this process several times during the development, the manager makes sure that the trajectories intersect several times during the development. This makes it much more probable that they meet at the end of development.

The sawtooth model is a modified V-Model that includes these intersections. It is called the sawtooth model, because each prototype demonstration results in a "tooth." The tip of each tooth is an intersection with the client's level of abstraction. Figure 12-12 shows the sawtooth model for a development project with two prototypes, a revolutionary prototype, and an evolutionary prototype.

The revolutionary prototype is often an illustrative prototype because it needs to be built quickly for demonstrating the functionality of the system. There is little intent to deliver this prototype for production use.[3] No matter how realistic, this prototype is still only a model of the system. The scenarios demonstrated will be contrived and represent only a small fraction of the required functionality. The short cuts taken to develop a quick version would be a maintenance nightmare if this prototype was promoted to production use.

The second prototype is usually an evolutionary prototype. It is shown late in the development where some functionality has already been implemented. The primary distinction between the two types of prototyping is that the revolutionary prototype does not need an overall design whereas the evolutionary prototype does. It is in general counterproductive to insist on a complete subsystem decomposition when showing the first prototype to the user.

The tasks and activities of the prototype development process in the sawtooth model are shown in Table 12-8.

---

3. If the revolutionary prototyping environment is identical to the development environment, then it might be possible to reuse some parts of the revolutionary prototype during implementation. But reuse is not the goal when producing a revolutionary prototype.

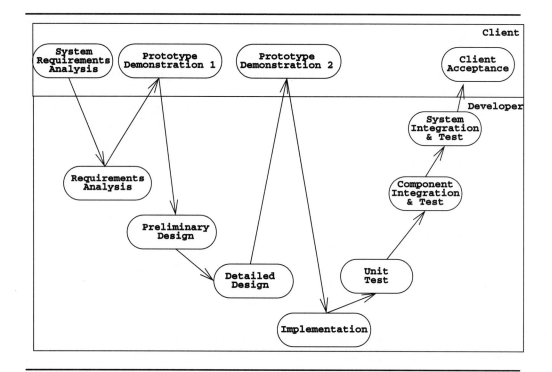

Figure 12-12   Sawtooth Model with two prototype demonstrations (UML activity diagram). The `Client` swimlane encloses the activities that are visible to the client, whereas the `Developer` swimlane encloses the activities that are at a lower abstraction level.

Table 12-8   Activities of the Prototype Development Process ("Tooth") in the Sawtooth Model

Activity	Task
Preparation	Select prototyping environment Select functionality to be demonstrated Develop prototype Develop agenda for prototype demonstration Notify client and review agenda
Demonstration	Install prototype Demonstrate selected functionality Record minutes
Evaluation of feedback	Review minutes from demonstration Identify issues Discuss issues
Project correction	Resolve open issues

12.4.5 Shark Tooth Model

The **shark tooth model** is a refinement of the sawtooth model. In addition to the client demonstrations, management reviews and demonstrations are introduced as well.

For example, large teeth can include a functional prototype and a user interface mock-up. The former demonstrates the feasibility of the functions that will be implemented in the system, whereas the latter illustrates the layout (or look and feel) of the user interface. Small teeth can include a system integration prototype that demonstrates the interaction between the components of the system. Such an integration prototype can be built as soon as the components are selected and need not implement any functionality. The client is not a good target for the demonstration of a system integration prototype. In general the project manager is targeted as the audience for the system integration prototype demonstration and we call the associated review an internal review. The system integration prototype can be demonstrated several times during the project, each of these demonstration leading to a small tooth. To describe the demonstrations for management, we add another swimlane to the sawtooth model that depicts the level of understanding of the project manager (see Figure 12-13).

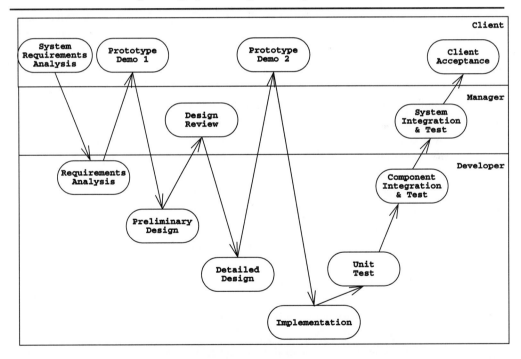

Figure 12-13 Shark tooth model with two prototype demonstrations and 1 review (UML activity diagram, levels of abstraction are represented with swimlanes). Small teeth reaching the management swimlane are internal reviews involving a prototype demo by the developers for the project manager. Large teeth reaching the client swimlane are prototype demonstrations to the client.

The project manager's swimlane is shown between the client and the developer swimlanes. Demonstrating the system integration prototype is a tooth involving the developers and the project manager. The shark tooth model assumes that the project manager is interested in system design and object design issues and thus wants to reach deeper level of system understanding than the client, and neither wants to follow the developer to the lowest levels of detail in the system. Small teeth are internal reviews involving a prototype demonstration for the project manager. Large teeth are prototype demonstrations for the client.

12.4.6 Unified Software Development Process

The **Unified Software Development Process** (also called the **Unified Process**) is a life cycle model proposed by Booch, Jacobson, and Rumbaugh [Jacobson et al., 1999]. Similar to Boehm's spiral model, a project consists of several cycles, each of which ends with the delivery of a product to the customer. Each cycle consists four phases: *Inception*, *Elaboration*, *Construction*, and *Transition*. Each phase itself consists of a number of iterations. Each iteration addresses a set of related use cases or mitigates some of the risks identified at the beginning of the iteration.

The inception phase corresponds to the IEEE 1074 *Concept Exploration* activity. During this phase, a need or an idea is defined and its feasibility is evaluated. The elaboration phase corresponds to the project initiation process, during which the project is planned, the system is defined and resources are allocated. The construction phase corresponds to the development processes. The transition phase corresponds to the installation and post-development processes.

The Unified Process emphasizes the staging of resources, an aspect of software development that is not captured in the other life cycle models. The Unified Process assumes that the activities *Requirements*, *Analysis*, *Design*, *Implementation,* and *Testing* participate in each of these iterations. However, these activities have differing phase-specific needs. For example, during the elaboration phase, the requirements and analysis activities are allocated most of the resources. During the construction phase, the resource requirements for requirements and analysis activities diminish, but the design and implementation activities are allocated more resources.

Figure 12-14 shows an entity-centered view of the Unified Process as a set of models. The requirements are captured in the use case model. The analysis model describes the system as a set of classes. The design model defines the structure of the system as a set of subsystems and interfaces and the deployment model defines the distribution across. The implementation model maps the classes to components and the test model verifies that the executable system provides the functionality described in the use case model.

All models are related to each other through traceability dependencies. A model element can be traced to at least one element in an associated model. For example, every use case has a traceable relationship with at least one class in the analysis model. Traceability allows us to understand the effect of change in one model on other models, in particular it allows to provide traceability in the requirements.

The maintenance of the dependencies between the models in Figure 12-14 can be done in different ways. During **forward engineering**, analysis and design models are established from the use case model, and the implementation model and test models are then generated from these models. During **reverse engineering** the analysis and design models are extracted or updated from existing code. **Round trip engineering** is a combination of reverse engineering and forward engineering. It allows the developer to switch between these development modes at any time, depending on which model is undergoing the most amount of change.

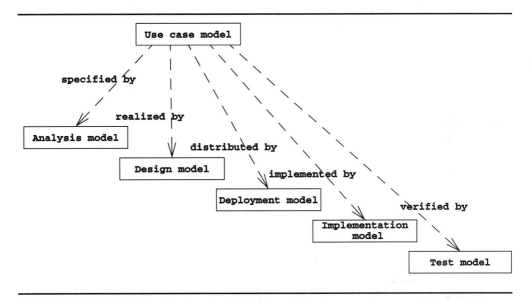

Figure 12-14 Entity-centered life cycle view of the models of the Unified Process (UML class diagram). the dependencies depict traceability. There are dependencies between all models. Only the dependencies between the use case model and the other models are shown [Jacobson et al., 1999].

12.4.7 Issue-Based Life Cycle Model

If the time between changes is significantly smaller than the duration of an activity, and if changes can occur in the application domain as well as in the solution domain, both the waterfall model and the spiral model exhibit problems. For example, assume the development team selects the hardware platform and that new platforms appear every three to four years. As long as the project time is significantly less than three years, the knowledge of the development team at the beginning of the project is usually sufficient to select a platform once during system design. However, if a new platform appears every three to four months and the duration of the project is also three or four months, there is a high probability that the platform decision will need to be reconsidered during the project.

In this section, we describe an entity-centered life cycle model, called the **issue-based life cycle model** that aims at dealing with frequent changes. This model is based on the rationale behind the system as an issue model (see Chapter 8, *Rationale Management)*. Each project starts with a set of issues. If the project starts from scratch, these issues are drawn from the project manager's experience or from a standard template. In a re-engineering or interface project, issues may be available from the issue model of the previous project. If the project has a long history, the rationale should be well populated. Examples of issues are "How do we set up the initial teams?", "Should the mechanic have access to driver-specific information", "What is the appropriate middleware?", "What software architecture shall we use?", and "What should we use as implementation language"? All issues are stored in an issue base that is accessible to all project participants.

The status of an issue can be closed or open. A closed issue is an issue that has been resolved. For example, a closed issue can be a decision about the platform on which the system should run (e.g., Solaris). Closed issues can be reopened, however, as changes occur in the application or solution domain. For example, if we need to support additional platforms (e.g., Linux and Windows NT), we reopen the issue, reevaluate the alternatives, and provide a new resolution. Open issues are resolved by discussion and negotiation among project participants (see Chapter 3, *Project Communication)*. An issue `i2` depends on another issue `i1` if the resolution of `i1` constrains the alternatives available for `i2`. Tracking the dependencies among issues enables developers to assess the impact of revisiting a given issue. The issue base also tracks dependencies among issues. Figure 12-15 shows a snapshot of the issue base of a project, depicting the issue status and dependencies.

Issues can be mapped to the activities of life cycle models described earlier. For example, assume the activities *Planning* and *System Design* are part of the selected life cycle model. "How do we set up the initial teams?" can be categorized as a planning issue and "What

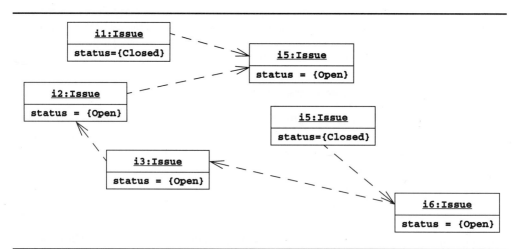

Figure 12-15   Snapshot of a project issue base (UML object diagram). Issues `i1` and `i5` have been resolved, whereas all other issues are still open. Dependencies among issues indicate that the resolution of an issue can constraint the alternatives for dependent issues.

software architecture shall we use?" can be categorized as a system design issue. The status of issues can then be used to track the status of each activity. If there are any system design issues still open, the *System Design* activity has not yet been completed. The life cycle models we described earlier can then be seen as special cases of the issue-based model. In the Waterfall model, for example, developers completely resolve the issues associated with an activity before moving to the next activity. Figure 12-16 depicts the state of a project during *System Design*.

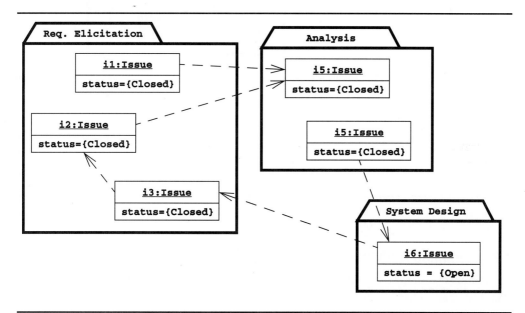

Figure 12-16   The waterfall model as a special case of the issue-based life cycle model (UML object diagram). All issues that belong to the same issue category are contained in the same UML package. In the project status shown in the figure, all the requirements elicitation and analysis issues have been closed; that is, the requirements elicitation and analysis activities have been completed.

In Boehm's spiral model, risks correspond to issues that are evaluated and reopened at the beginning of each round. Issues are resolved in the order of their priority as defined during risk analysis. Note, however, that "issue" is a more general concept than "risk." For example, the issue "Which access control model should we use?" is a design problem, not a risk.

In the general case (Figure 12-17), all activities still may have open issues associated with them, which means that all activities need to be managed concurrently. The goal of the project manager is to keep the number of open issues small and manageable without imposing time or activity-based constraints on the resolution of issues. Using issues and their dependencies for managing the life cycle activities allows all life cycle activities to proceed concurrently.

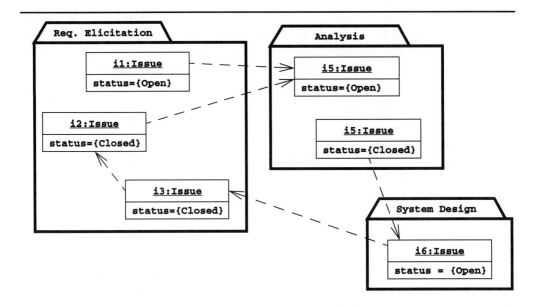

Figure 12-17   In a complex project state, all activities can still have some open issues, which means that all activities need to be managed concurrently.

12.5 Managing Activities and Products

In this section we describe the process of life cycle modeling for two example projects. The first example project, a four-month single-site prototype development, can be used for a single-semester project course. The second example project, an eight month two-site prototype development, can be used for a two-semester project course where each semester occurs at a different location.

12.5.1   Example 1: Four-Month One-Site Project

Project goals and constraints

One goal of the project is to develop a demonstration prototype of a software system. A second goal of the project is to expose its participants to state-of-the-art software engineering methods and tools. It has forty participants, most of which have not worked together before. The developers and technical writers involved in the project have strong technical background in writing programs and documentation but no large scale development experience. The application domain is new to all the participants. The delivery of the prototype must occur within four months. Given the short time span, flat staffing must be used.

Activities

We select a life cycle model consisting of three phases. During the first phase, called pre-development, preliminary requirements are formulated and an initial software architecture is developed for the purpose of allocating resources for the rest of the project. Infrastructure choices are also made during the preliminary phase. Only a subset of the project participants— the client, project manager and coaches—are involved. During the second phase, called development, a system exhibiting the core requirements is constructed following a waterfall model. All developers have been assigned to a team and are actively working towards the construction of the system. The goal of the development phase is to validate the architecture of the system and expose the participants to all aspects of the life cycle. During the third phase, called post-development, the optional functionality is added to the system. The goal of the third phase is to extend the functionality of the system while controlling risks. Functionality is added at all levels of abstractions: The requirements, design, implementation, and test cases are developed incrementally. The rationale for this approach is to deliver a functional system on time as opposed to delivering a complete system late. Table 12-9 describes each of these three phases in terms of objectives and IEEE 1074 activities and processes.

Table 12-9 Activities for example project 1.

Phase	Purpose	Activities	Corresponding IEEE 1074 activities
Pre-development	Initiate project	Project Initiation Concept Exploration Top-level Design	3.1. Project Initiation 4.1 Concept Exploration 4.2 System Allocation
Development	Validate architecture Train participants Demonstrate core requirements Demonstrate feasibility	Project Management Requirements Elicitation Analysis Analysis Review System Design System Design Review Object Design Object Design Review Implementation Unit Testing System Integration Testing System Testing (alpha test) Configuration Management Tutorials	3.2 Project Monitor & Control 5.1 Requirements 5.2 Design 5.2.7 Perform Detailed Design 5.3 Implementation 7.1 Verification & Validation 7.2 Software Configuration Management 7.4 Training
Post-development	Demonstrate optional requirements Deliver prototype Client acceptance	Project Management Refinement Install Software Client Acceptance Test Field Testing (beta test) Configuration Management	3.2 Project Monitor & Control 6.3 Maintenance 6.1.5 Install Software 6.1.6 Accept Software 7.1 Verification & Validation 7.2 Software Configuration Management

Note that this life cycle is not complete, it does not include operation and support activities given that the goal of the example project is to develop a demonstration prototype.

Work products

The project produces three kinds of information: *system information*, *management information*, and *rationale*. This information is represented by three kinds of models: Task models represent management information, system models describe the system (requirements, analysis, design, implementation), and issue models represent the rationale behind design and management decisions.

Task models are detailed, project specific, process models. They are constructed during project initiation by management and revised throughout the project. They are documented in the *Project Agreement*, *Software Project Management Plan*, and the *Top-level Design* document (Table 12-10). We describe task models in Chapter 11, *Project Management*.

Table 12-10   Management documents

Document	Purpose	Produced by
Problem Statement	Describes the needs, visionary scenarios, current system, target system, requirements and constraints	Concept Exploration
Initial Schedule	Describes major milestones	Project Initiation
Top-level Design	Describes preliminary system architecture, teams, constraints, communication infrastructure	Top-level Design
Software Project Management Plan	Controlling document for managing the project	Project Initiation Project Monitor and Control
Software Configuration Management Plan	Controlling document for software configuration management activities	Software Configuration Management

System models represent the system at different levels of abstraction and from different perspectives. The use case model describes the system from the user's point of view. The analysis model describes the application objects that the system manipulates. The system and object design models represent the solution objects. The use case and analysis models are documented in the *Requirements Analysis Document* (Table 12-11). The system design model is documented in the *System Design Document*. The object design model and sequence diagrams are documented in the *Object Design Document*. We describe the *System Design Document* and the *Object Design Document* in Chapters 6 and 7, respectively.

Table 12-11   System documents

Document	Purpose	Produced by
Requirements Analysis Document (RAD)	Describes the functional and global requirements of the system as well as 4 models: the use case model, the object model, the functional model, and the dynamic model	Requirements
User Manual	Describes the use of the system often in form of a tutorial	Requirements
System Design Document (SDD)	Describes the design goals, trade-offs made between design goals, the high-level decomposition of the system, concurrency identification, hardware/software platforms, data management, global resource handling, software control implementation, and boundary conditions	System Design
Object Design Document (ODD)	Describes the system in terms of refined object models, in particular the chosen data structures and algorithms as well as full signatures for all public methods. this document results in the detailed specification of each class used by the programmers during the implementation phase	Object Design
Test Manual	Describes testing strategy, the unit and system tests performed on the system along with expected and actual results	Testing
Administrator Manual	Describes the administrative procedures to install, operate and bring down the system. Also contains a list of error codes, failure and termination conditions	Install Software

The rationale of the system is represented with an issue model. Developers focus on the system, argue about different alternatives, have different design goals or base many decisions on prior experience. The motivation behind capturing the rationale is to facilitate communication and make design goals and constraints explicit throughout the project. System goals and constraints are described in the system design document. Issues are described in the *Issues Document* (Table 12-12). We describe issue models in Chapter 8, *Rationale Management*.

Table 12-12   Rationale documents

Document	Purpose	Produced by
Issues Document (ID)	Describes the open issues, possible options, arguments, and their resolution	All processes

12.5.2 Example 2: Eight-Month, Two-Site Project

Project goals and constraints

In this example, we describe a pilot project with two development phases occurring at two sites. The end of the first development phase overlaps with the beginning of the second phase, allowing some knowledge transfer to occur between both sites. Again, most participants are not involved with the pre-development and the post-development phase. Participants at one site have not yet worked with the participants of the other site prior to this project. The delivery of a prototype system must occur within eight months, with an intermediate demonstration of the prototype occurring at the end of the first four months.

Activities

We refine the life cycle of the first example project to include a second development phase and activities focused on transferring knowledge from one site to the other (Table 12-13). Both development phases are structured in the same way, such that the same documents, methods, and procedures can be used. The second development phase is an improvement iteration that produces a refined version of the *Requirements Analysis Document*, the *System Design Document*, the *Object Design Document*, and the prototype system. An additional work product, called the *Inventory Analysis Document*, is produced at the beginning of the second development phase to describe the current status of the system. It includes a list of components, documents, and models that have been constructed in the first phase and a list of issues describing problems in those items that need to be addressed.

Knowledge transfer between sites

Distributed software development can have several advantages. For example, a project can leverage off specific combinations of skills without relocating participants within the organization. Often, the system will also be deployed at different sites and the project manager may want developers to be geographically close to several user communities. Distribution, however, introduces new challenges, such as communicating asynchronously and transferring knowledge from one group of participants to another.

In example project 2, knowledge transfer needs to occur at the end of the first development phase and at the beginning of the second development phase. Since there is minimal overlap between both phases, participants of different sites do not know each other. Consequently, opportunities for spontaneous exchanges do not exist. Instead, we formalize this knowledge transfer with the Inventory Analysis activity. Participants from the second site first become familiar with the system by attending via video conference one or more reviews, such as the object design review or the client acceptance test. Then, participants of the second site reverse engineer the first prototype system to find inconsistencies and omissions with its accompanying documentation. Some of the participants of the first site stay with the project temporarily to wrap up the first development phase and answer questions from participants of the second site. The result of the Inventory Analysis is the *Inventory Analysis Document* describing the components of the first prototype and their status.

Table 12-13   Activities for example project 2. Differences from example 1 highlighted in *italics*.

Phase	Purpose	Activities	IEEE 1074 activities
Pre-development phase	Initiate project	Project Initiation Concept Exploration Top-level Design	3.1. Project Initiation 4.1 Concept Exploration 4.2 System Allocation
First development phase	Validate architecture Train participants of first site Demonstrate core requirements Demonstrate feasibility	Project Management Requirements Elicitation Analysis System Design Object Design Implementation Unit Testing System Integration Testing System Testing (alpha test) Configuration Management Lectures & Tutorials	3.2 Project Monitor & Control 5.1 Requirements 5.2 Design 5.2.7 Perform Detailed Design 5.3 Implementation 7.1 Verification & Validation 7.2 Software Configuration Management 7.4 Training
Second development phase	*Improve architecture* *Train participants of second site* *Demonstrate extensibility* *Demonstrate desirable requirements*	*Inventory Analysis* *Inventory Review* *Project Management* *Requirements Elicitation Analysis* *Requirements Analysis Review* *System Design* *System Design Review* *Object Design* *Object Design Review* *Implementation* *Unit Testing* *System Integration Testing* *System Testing (alpha test)* *Configuration Management* *Tutorials*	 *3.2 Project Monitor & Control* *5.1 Requirements* *5.2 Design* *5.2.7 Perform Detailed Design* *5.3 Implementation* *7.1 Verification & Validation* *7.2 Software Configuration Management* *7.4 Training*
Post-development phase	Demonstrate complete functionality Deliver prototype Client acceptance	Project Management Refinement Install Software Client Acceptance Test Field Testing (beta test) Configuration Management	3.2 Project Monitor & Control 6.3 Maintenance 6.1.5 Install Software 6.1.6 Accept Software 7.1 Verification & Validation 7.2 Software Configuration Management

The amount of overlap between both phases presents a critical project management trade-off. A short overlap prevents sufficient knowledge to be transferred. Participants from the second site will then have to reengineer most of the knowledge from work products only. The longer the overlap, the more opportunities there will be for knowledge transfer in the form of targeted questions and answers. If the second development phase starts too early, however, participants of the second site will interfere with the participants of the first site who are still in the process of creating the knowledge being transferred.

Documents

The documents created by this example are the same as in example project 1, in addition to the *Inventory Analysis Document* produced during Inventory Analysis (Table 12-14). The main different between these projects is that the major technical documents (i.e., *Requirements Analysis Document, System Design Document, Object Design Document, Issue Document*) are revised substantially during the second development phase, to account for the lessons learned during the first development phase.

Table 12-14   Inventory documents

Document	Purpose	Produced by
Inventory Analysis Document	Describes the components and models that have been realized, their status, and the problems associated with them	Inventory Analysis

12.6 Exercises

1. Assume you have to build a CASE tool for the IEEE 1074 standard life cycle model. Define the actors and use cases for the Design Process.

2. Adapt Figures 12-1, 12-3, and 12-4 to produce an integrated UML class diagram representing the activities and workproducts discussed in this chapter.

3. Assume that the waterfall model shown in Figure 12-8 has been derived from the IEEE standard model in Figure 12-7 during the activity Life Cycle Modeling. What processes and activities have been omitted in the waterfall model?

4. Map the names of the activities in the DOD 2167A standard in Figure 12-9 to the names of activities in the IEEE 1074 standard.

5. Redraw Boehm's spiral model in Figure 12-11 as a UML activity diagram. Compare the readability of the original figure with the activity diagram.

6. Draw a UML activity diagram describing the dependency between activities for a life cycle in which requirements, design, implementation, test, and maintenance occur concurrently. (This is called an evolutionary life cycle.)

7. Describe how testing activities can be initiated well before implementation activities. Explain why this is desirable.

8. Assume you are part of the IEEE committee that will revise the IEEE 1074 standard. You have been assigned the task of modeling communication as an explicit integral process. Make a case for the activities that would belong to this process.

References

[Boehm, 1987] B. Boehm, "A spiral model of software development and enhancement," *Software Engineering Project Management.* pp. 128-142, 1987.

[Humphrey, 1989] W. Humphrey, *Managing the Software Process.* Addison-Wesley, Reading, MA, 1989.

[IEEE, 1997] *IEEE Standards Collection Software Engineering.* IEEE, Piscataway, NJ, 1997.

[IEEE Std. 1074-1995] *IEEE Standard for Developing Software Life Cycle Processes*, IEEE Computer Society, New York, 1995, in [IEEE 1997].

[Jacobson et al., 1999] I. Jacobson, G. Booch, & J. Rumbaugh, *The Unified Software Development Process.* Addison-Wesley, Reading, MA, 1999.

[Jensen & Tonies, 1979] R. W. Jensen & C. C. Tonies, *Software Engineering,* Prentice Hall, Englewood Cliffs, NJ, 1979.

[Paulk et al., 1995] M. C. Paulk, C. V. Weber, & B. Curtis (eds.), *The Capability Maturity Mode: Guidelines for Improving the Software Process.* Addison-Wesley, Reading, MA, 1995.

[Rowen, 1990] R. B. Rowen, "Software project management under incomplete and ambiguous specifications," *IEEE Transactions on Engineering Management,* vol. 37, no. 1, 1990.

[Royse, 1970] W. W. Royse, "Managing the development of large software systems," in *Tutorial: Software Engineering Project Management*, IEEE Computer Society, Washington, DC, pp. 118–127, 1970.

PART V
Appendices

Design Patterns

Design patterns are partial solutions to common problems, such as separating an interface from a number of alternate implementations, wrapping around a set of legacy classes, protecting a caller from changes associated with specific platforms. A design pattern is composed of a small number of classes that, through delegation and inheritance, provide a robust and modifiable solution. These classes can be adapted and refined for the specific system under construction. In addition, design patterns provide examples of inheritance and delegation.

Since the publication of the first book on design patterns for software [Gamma et al., 1994], many additional patterns have been proposed for a broad variety of problems, including analysis [Fowler, 1997] [Larman, 1998], system design [Buschmann et al., 1996], middleware [Mowbray & Malveau, 1997], process modeling [Ambler, 1998], dependency management [Feiler et al., 1998], and configuration management [Brown et al., 1999]. The term itself has become a buzzword that is often attributed many different definitions. In this book, we focus only on the original catalog of design patterns, as it provides a concise set of elegant solutions to many common problems. This appendix summarizes the design patterns we use in this books. For each pattern, we provide pointers to the examples in the book that use them. Our goal is to provide a quick reference that can also be used as an index. We assume from the reader a basic knowledge of design patterns, object-oriented concepts, and UML class diagrams.

A.1 Abstract Factory: Encapsulating Platforms

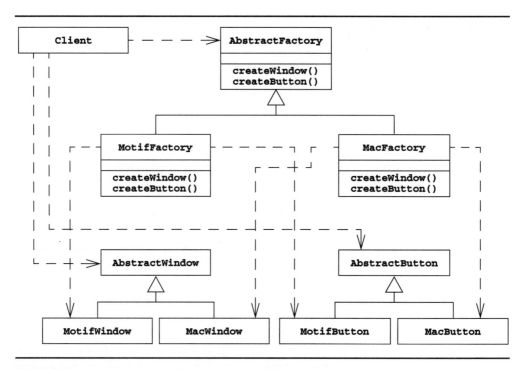

Figure A-1   `AbstractFactory` design pattern (UML class diagram).

Purpose   This pattern is used to shield an application from the concrete classes provided by a specific platform, such as a windowing style or an operating system. Consequently, by using this pattern, an application can be developed to run uniformly on a range of platforms.

Description   Each platform (e.g., a windowing style) is represented by a `Factory` class and a number of `ConcreteClasses` for each concept in the platform (e.g., window, button, dialog). The `Factory` class provides methods for creating instances of the `ConcreteClasses`. Porting an application to a new platform is then reduced to implementing a `Factory` and a `ConcreteClass` for each concept.

Examples
- statically encapsulating windowing styles (Figure 7-28 on page 267)
- dynamically encapsulating windowing styles (Swing, [JFC, 1999])

Related concepts   Increasing reuse (Section 7.4.9 on page 265), removing implementation dependencies (Section 7.4.10 on page 267).

A.2 Adapter: Wrapping Around Legacy Code

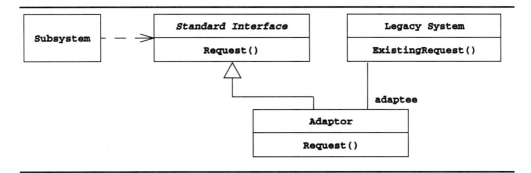

Figure A-2 Adapter pattern (UML class diagram). The Adapter pattern is used to provide a different interface (*New Interface*) to an existing component (Legacy System).

Purpose This pattern encapsulates a piece of legacy code that was not designed to work with the system. It also limits the impact of substituting the piece of legacy code for a different component.

Description Assume a Calling Subsystem needs to access functionality provided by an existing Legacy System. However, the Legacy System does not comply with a *Standard Interface* used by the Calling Subsystem. This gap is filled by creating an Adaptor class which implements the *Standard Interface* using methods from the Legacy System. When the caller only accesses the *Standard Interface*, the Legacy System can be later replaced with an alternate component.

Example
- Sorting instances of an existing String class with an existing sort() method (Figure 6-34 on page 202): MyStringComparator is an Adaptor for bridging the gap between the String class and the Comparator interface used by the Array.sort() method.

Related concepts The Bridge (Section A.3) fills the gap between an interface and its implementations.

A.3 Bridge: Allowing for Alternate Implementations

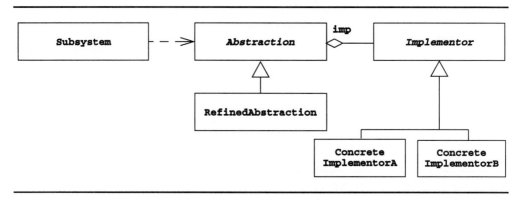

Figure A-3 `Bridge` pattern (UML class diagram).

Purpose This pattern decouples the interface of a class from its implementation. Unlike the `Adapter` pattern, the developer is not constrained by an existing piece of code. Both the interface and the implementation can be refined independently.

Description Assume we need to decouple an `Abstraction` from an `Implementor`, because we need to substitute different `Implementor`s for a given `Abstraction` without any impact on a calling `Subsystem`. This is realized by providing an `Abstraction` class that implements its services in terms of the methods of an `Implementor` interface. `Concrete Implementors` that need to be substituted refine the `Implementor` interface.

Examples
- Vendor independence (Figure 6-37 on page 206): The `ODBC` interface (the `Abstraction`) decouples a caller from a database management system. For each database management system, an `ODBC Driver` refines the `ODBC Implementation` (the `Implementor`). When the `Abstraction` makes no assumptions about the `Concrete Implementors`, `Concrete Implementors` can be switched without the calling `Subsystem` noticing, even at run-time.
- Unit testing (Figure 9-11 on page 342): the `Database Interface` (the `Abstraction`) decouples the `User Interface` (the `Subsystem`) from the `Database` (a `Concrete Implementor`), allowing the `User Interface` and the `Database` to be tested independently. When the `User Interface` is tested, a `Test Stub` (another `Concrete Implementor`) is substituted for the `Database`.

Related concepts The `Adapter` pattern (Section A.2) fills the gap between two interfaces.

A.4 Command: Encapsulating Control

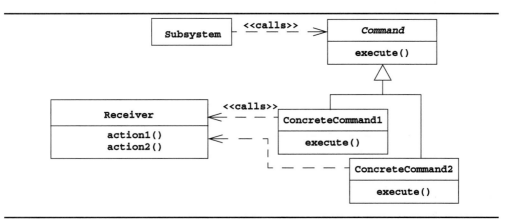

Figure A-4   Command pattern (UML class diagram).

Purpose   This pattern enables the encapsulation of control such that user requests can be treated uniformly, independent of the specific request. This pattern protects these objects from changes resulting from new functionality. Another advantage of this pattern is that control flow is centralized in the command objects as opposed to being distributed across interface objects.

Description   An abstract `Command` interface defines the common services that all `ConcreteCommands` should implement. `ConcreteCommands` collect data from the Client `Subsystem` and manipulate the entity objects (`Receivers`). `Subsystems` interested only in the general `Command` abstraction (e.g., an undo stack), only access the `Command` abstract class. Client `Subsystems` do not access directly the entity objects.

Examples
  • Providing an undo stack for user commands: All user-visible commands are refinements of the `Command` abstract class. Each command is required to implement the `do()`, `undo()`, and `redo()` methods. Once a command is executed, it is pushed onto an undo stack. If the user wishes to undo the last command, the `Command` object on the top of the stack is sent the message `undo()`.
  • Decoupling interface objects from control objects (Figure 6-45 on page 215, see also Swing `Actions`,[JFC, 1999]): All user visible commands are refinements of the `Command` abstract class. Interface objects, such as menu items and buttons, create and send messages to `Command` objects. Only `Command` objects modify entity objects. When the user interface is changed (e.g., a menu bar is replaced by a tool bar), only the interface objects are modified.

Related concepts   MVC architecture (Figure 6-15 on page 184).

A.5 Composite: Representing Recursive Hierarchies

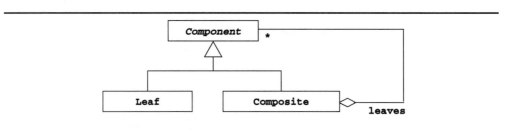

Figure A-5 Composite pattern (UML class diagram).

Purpose   This pattern represents a recursive hierarchy. The services related to the containment hierarchy are factored out using inheritance, allowing a system to treat a leaf or a composite uniformly. Leaf specific behavior can be modified without any impact on the containing hierarchy.

Description   The Component interface specifies the services that are shared among Leaf and Composite (e.g., move(x,y) for a graphic element). A Composite has an aggregation association with Components and implements each service by iterating over each contained Component (e.g., the Composite.move(x,y) method iteratively invokes the Component.move(x,y)). The Leaf services do the actual work (e.g., Leaf.move(x,y) modifies the coordinates of the Leaf and redraws it).

Examples
- Recursive access groups (Lotus Notes): A Lotus Notes access group can contain any number of users and access groups.
- Groups of drawable elements: Drawable elements can be organized in groups that can be moved and scaled uniformly. Groups can also contain other groups.
- Hierarchy of files and directories (Figure 5-7 on page 137): Directories can contain files and other directories. The same operations are available for moving, renaming, and uniformly removing files and directories.
- Describing subsystem decomposition (Figure 6-3 on page 173): We use a Composite pattern to describe subsystem decomposition. A subsystem is composed of classes and other subsystems. Note that subsystems are not actually implemented as Composites to which classes are dynamically added.
- Describing hierarchies of tasks (Figure 6-8 on page 177): We use a Composite pattern to describe the organizations of Tasks (Composites) into Subtasks (Components) and ActionItems (Leaves).We use a similar model to describe Phases, Activities, and Tasks (Figure 12-6 on page 462).

Related concepts   Facade pattern (Section A.6).

A.6 Facade: Encapsulating Subsystems

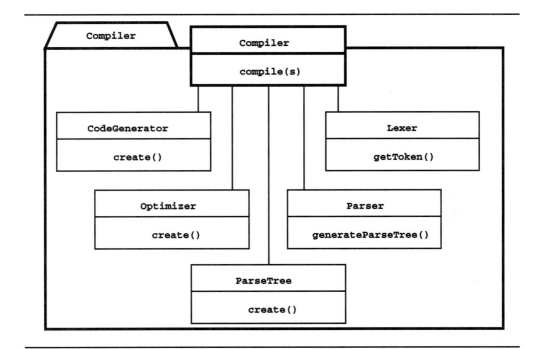

Figure A-6 An example of a `Facade` pattern (UML class diagram).

Purpose The `Facade` pattern reduces dependencies among classes by encapsulating a subsystem with a simple unified interface.

Description A single `Facade` class implements a high-level interface for a subsystem by invoking the methods of lower level classes. A `Facade` is opaque in the sense that a caller does not access the lower level classes directly. The use of `Facade` patterns recursively yields a layered system.

Example
- Subsystem encapsulation (Figure 6-30 on page 198):A `Compiler` is composed of `Lexer`, `Parser`, `ParseTree`, a `CodeGenerator`, and an `Optimizer`. When compiling a string into executable code, however, a caller only deals with the `Compiler` class, which invokes the appropriate methods on the contained classes.

Related concepts Coupling and coherence (Section 6.3.3 on page 174), layers and partitions (Section 6.3.4 on page 178), `Composite` pattern (Section A.5).

A.7 Observer: Decoupling Entities from Views

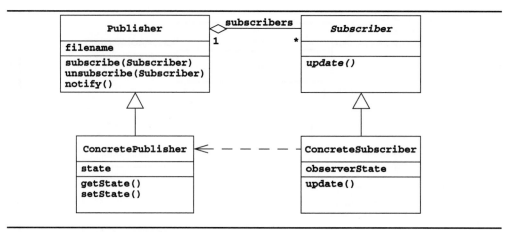

Figure A-7   The Observer pattern (UML class diagram).

Purpose   This pattern allows us to maintain consistency across the states of one Publisher and many *Subscribers*.

Description   A Publisher (called a Subject in [Gamma et al., 1994]) is an object whose primary function is to maintain some state; for example, a matrix. One or more *Subscribers* (called *Observers* in [Gamma et al., 1994]) use the state maintained by a Publisher; for example, to display a matrix as a table or a graph. This introduces redundancies between the state of the Publisher and the *Subscribers*. To address this issue, *Subscribers* invoke the subscribe() method to register with a Publisher. Each ConcreteSubscriber also defines an update() method to synchronize the state between the Publisher and the ConcreteSusbcriber. Whenever the state of the Publisher changes, the Publisher invokes its notify() method, which iteratively invoke each Subscriber.update() method.

Examples
- The Observer interface and Observable class are used in Java to realize an Observer pattern ([JFC, 1999]).
- The Observer pattern can be used for realizing subscription and notification in an Model/ View/Controller architecture (Figure 6-15 on page 184).

Related concepts   Entity, interface, control objects (Section 5.3.1 on page 134).

A.8 Proxy: Encapsulating Expensive Objects

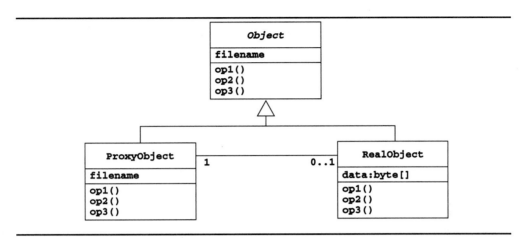

Figure A-8   The Proxy pattern (UML class diagram).

Purpose   This pattern improves the performance or the security of a system by delaying expensive computations, using memory only when needed or checking access before loading an object into memory.

Description   The ProxyObject class acts on behalf of a RealObject class. Both classes implement the same interface. The ProxyObject stores a subset of the attributes of the RealObject. The ProxyObject handles certain requests completely (e.g., determining the size of an image), whereas others are delegates to the RealObject. After delegation, the RealObject is created and loaded in memory.

Examples
- Protection proxy (Section 6-38 on page 210): An Access association class contains a set of operations that a Broker can use to access a Portfolio. Every operation in the PortfolioProxy first checks with isAccessible() if the invoking Broker has legitimate access. Once access has been granted, PortfolioProxy delegates the operation to the actual Portfolio object. If access is denied, the actual Portfolio object is not loaded into memory.
- Storage proxy (Section 7-31 on page 273): An ImageProxy object acts on behalf of an Image stored on disk. The ImageProxy contains the same information as the Image (e.g., width, height, position, resolution) except for the Image contents. The ImageProxy services all contents independent requests. Only when the Image contents need to be accessed (e.g., when it is drawn on the screen), the ImageProxy creates the RealImage object and loads its contents from disk.

Related concepts   Caching expensive computations (Section 7.4.13 on page 272).

A.9 Strategy: Encapsulating Algorithms

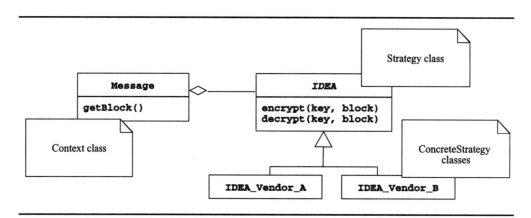

Figure A-9   An example of `Strategy` pattern encapsulating multiple implementation of the IDEA encryption algorithm (UML class diagram). The `Message` and *IDEA* classes cooperate to realize the encryption of plain text. The selection of an implementation can be done dynamically.

Purpose   This pattern decouples an algorithm from its implementation(s). It serves the same purpose than the adapter and bridge patterns except that the encapsulated unit is a behavior.

Description   An abstract `Algorithm` class provides methods for initializing, executing, and obtaining the results of an `Algorithm`. `ConcreteAlgorithm` classes refine `Algorithm` and provide alternate implementations of the same behavior. `ConcreteAlgorithms` can be switched without any impact on the caller.

Examples
  • Encryption algorithms (Figure 6-40 on page 212): Vendor-supplied encryption algorithms
    pose an interesting problem: How can we be sure that the supplied software does not
    include a trap door? Moreover, once a vulnerability is found in a widely used package,
    how do we protect the system until a patch is available? To address both issues, we can use
    redundant implementations of the same algorithm. To reduce the dependency on a specific
    vendor, we encapsulate these implementations with a single `Strategy` pattern.

Related concepts   `Adaptor` pattern (Section A.2) and `Bridge` pattern (Section A.3).

References

[Ambler, 1998]   S. W. Ambler, *Process Patterns: Building Large-Scale Systems Using Object Technology*, Cambridge University Press, New York, 1998.

[Brown et al., 1999]   W. J. Brown, H. W. McCormick, & S. W. Thomas, *AntiPatterns and Patterns in Software Configuration Management*, Wiley, New York, 1999.

[Buschmann et al., 1996] F. Buschmann, R. Meunier, H. Rohnert, P. Sommerlad, & M. Stal, *Pattern-Oriented Software Architecture: A System of Patterns*. Wiley, Chichester, U.K., 1996.

[Feiler et al., 1998]   P. Feiler & W. Tichy. "Propagator: A family of patterns," *Proceedings of TOOLS-23'97*, Jul. 28–Aug. 1 1997, Santa Barbara, CA.

[Fowler, 1997]   M. Fowler, *Analysis Patterns: Reusable Object Models*. Addison-Wesley, Reading, MA, 1997.

[Gamma et al., 1994]   E. Gamma, R. Helm, R. Johnson, & J. Vlissides, *Design Patters: Elements of Reusable Object-Oriented Software,* Addison-Wesley, Reading, MA, 1994.

[JFC, 1999]   *Java Foundation Classes*, JDK Documentation. Javasoft, 1999.

[Larman, 1998]   C. Larman, *Applying UML and Patterns: An Introduction to Object-Oriented Analysis and Design*. Prentice Hall, Upper Saddle River, NJ, 1998.

[Mowbray & Malveau, 1997] T. J. Mowbray & R. C. Malveau. *CORBA Design Patterns*. Wiley, New York, 1997.

Glossary

Abstract class   Superclass that is used only for generalization and that is never instantiated.

Abstract data type   A data type whose structure is encapsulated from the caller.

Abstract factory pattern   A design pattern encapsulating concrete classes provided by specific platforms, such as a windowing style or an operating system.

Abstraction   The classification of phenomena into concepts. *See also* modeling.

Acceptance testing   A system testing activity during which the client decides whether the system meets the acceptance criteria.

Access control list   A representation of access control in which legitimate rights are represented as a list of {actor, operation} pairs attached to each class that is controlled.

Action item   A task assigned to a participant with a completion date, usually as a result of an issue resolution.

Action state   A state whose outgoing transitions are triggered by the completion of an action associated with the state. Activities in UML activity diagrams are action states.

Activity   Set of tasks that is performed towards a specific purpose. Activities can include a few or many tasks, depending on the extent of their goal. Examples of activities include requirements elicitation, object identification, and unit testing. *See also* process.

Activity-centered software life cycle model   A software life cycle model which represents primarily the activities of development. *Contrast with*: entity-centered software life cycle model.

Activity diagram   UML notation representing the behavior of a system in terms of activities. An activity is a state which represents the execution of a set of operations. The completion of these operations then triggers a transition to another activity. Activity diagrams are used to illustrate combinations of control and data flow.

Actor   External entity that needs to exchange information with the system. An actor can represent either a user role or another system.

Adaptability   Quality of a system indicating how easily the system can be ported to different application domains.

Adapter pattern   A design pattern encapsulating an existing component that was not designed to work with the system.

Aggregation   An association denoting a whole part relationship between two classes. For example, a System is composed of Subsystems is an aggregation association.

Alternative   *See* proposal.

Ambiguity   Property of a model indicating whether a concept corresponds to two or more unrelated phenomena.

Analysis   An activity during which developers ensure that the system requirements are correct, complete, consistent, unambiguous, and realistic. Analysis produces the analysis model.

Analysis model   A model of the system that aims to be correct, complete, consistent, unambiguous, realistic, and verifiable. The analysis model consists of a functional model, an object model, and a dynamic model.

Analysis object model   The object model produced during analysis. The analysis object model describes the application domain concepts that the system manipulates and the user visible interfaces of the system.

Analyst   A role representing the developers who elicit application domain information from users and clients and constructs a use case model of the system to be developed.

API   *See* Application Programmer Interface.

API engineer   A role concerned with defining the API of a subsystem. This role is often combined with the role of architecture liaison.

Application domain   Represents all aspects of the user's problem. This includes the physical environment in which the system will run, the users, and their work processes. The application domain is represented by the analysis model during the requirements and analysis activities. The application domain is also called the problem domain. *Contrast with*: solution domain.

Application domain specialist   A consultant role responsible for providing application domain expertise to a project.

Application object   Object in the analysis model that represents an application domain concept. The application object is also called the application domain object.

Application Programmer Interface (API)   Set of fully specified operations provided by a subsystem.

Architect   A role representing the developers who make strategic system decisions and construct the system design model.

Architectural pattern   *See* architectural style.

Architectural style   A general system design model which can be used as a starting point for system design. Examples of architectural styles include client/server, peer to peer, pipe and filter, and model/view/controller.

Architecture   *See* system design model.

Architecture liaison   A role representing the developers who represent a subsystem team in the architecture team. They convey information from their team, negotiate interface changes, and ensure the consistency of APIs across the system.

Argument   Value passed along with a message.

Argumentation   The debate participants go through to resolve an issue.

Association   A relationship between two or more classes denoting the possible links between instances of the classes. An association has a name and can have multiplicity and role information attached to each of its ends.

Association class   An association which has attributes and operations.

Attribute   A named property of a class defining a range of values an object can contain. For example, `time` is an attribute of the class `Watch`.

Attribute visibility   Specifies whether the attribute can be accessed by other classes or not.

Auditing   Validation of versions before a release ensuring a consistent and complete delivery.

Auditor   A role responsible for the selection and evaluation of promotions for release.

Authentication   The process of associating a person with access rights.

Availability   Fraction of time the system can be used to accomplish normal tasks.

Baseline   A version of a configuration item that has been formally reviewed and agreed on.

Bazaar model   A project organization including a dynamic and distributed set of collaborating groups. *Contrast with*: cathedral model.

Big bang testing   An integration testing strategy in which all components are tested together immediately after the unit testing.

Blackbox framework   A framework which relies on well defined interfaces for extensibility. *Contrast with*: whitebox framework.

Blackbox test   A test which focuses on the input/output behavior of a component without considering its implementation. *Contrast with*: whitebox test.

Bottom–up testing   An integration testing strategy in which components are incrementally integrated together starting with the lower level components. Bottom–up testing does not require any test stubs.

Boundary object   An object that represents the interactions between the user and the system.

Boundary condition   A special condition the system must handle. Boundary conditions include startup, shutdown, and exceptions.

Brainstorming   A scheduled mode of communication during which participants generate a large number of alternatives.

Branch   A concurrent development path under configuration management.

Bridge pattern   A design pattern encapsulating existing and future implementations of an interface. A Bridge pattern allows implementations to be substituted at run time.

Build management   Tool support for automatically building the system when new versions are added to the system.

Bug   *See* fault.

Capability   A representation of access control in which legitimate rights are represented as {class, operation} pairs attached to an actor. Examples of capabilities include a door key, a smart card, and a theater ticket.

Capability Maturity Model (CMM)   Framework for assessing the maturity of organizations characterized by five levels of maturity.

Cathedral model   A project organization emphasizing planning, system architecture, and hierarchical control. The chief programmer team is an example of cathedral model. *Contrast with*: bazaar model.

Centralized traffic control (CTC)   Procedures and systems enabling dispatchers to monitor and control train traffic remotely from a central location.

Change   *See* delta.

Change control   Process approving or rejecting change request ensuring that the system is evolving consistently with project goals.

Change control board   Team approving change requests in the context of a formal change process.

Change request   An event-driven mode of communication during which a participant requests a modified or a new feature in a work product. In configuration management: a formal report requesting the modification of a configuration item.

Change set A set of deltas indicating the differences between two configurations.

Chief programmer team A hierarchical project organization in which the team leader makes all the critical technical decisions.

Class An abstraction of a set of objects which have the same attributes, operations, relationships and semantics. Classes are different than abstract data types in that a class can be defined by specializing another class. For example, programming languages such as Modula and Ada provide mechanisms for defining abstract data types; object-oriented languages such as Java, C++, or Smalltalk provide mechanisms for defining classes.

Class diagram UML notation representing the structure of the system in terms of objects, classes, attributes, operations, and associations. Class diagrams are used to represent object models during development.

Client A role representing the person or company paying for the development of the system.

Client review A scheduled mode of communication during which a client monitors the status of a project.

Client/server architecture A software architecture in which user interactions are managed by simple client programs and functionality is delivered by a central server program.

Closed architecture A layered system in which a layer can only depend on layers immediately below it. *Contrast with:* open architecture.

Closed issue An issue that has been resolved.

CM aggregate *See* configuration management aggregate.

CMM *See* Capability Maturity Model.

Coherence Strength of dependencies within a subsystem or a class. High coherence is desirable as it keeps related classes together so they can be modified consistently.

Command pattern A pattern encapsulating control objects such that they can be uniformly treated by the system.

Communication An activity during which developers exchange information, either synchronously or asynchronously, and either spontaneously or according to a schedule.

Communication mechanism A tool or a procedure that can be used to transmit and receive information. Communication mechanisms support one or more communication modes. Examples of communication mechanisms include telephone, fax, E-mail, and groupware. Communication mechanisms can be either synchronous or asynchronous, depending whether the sender and receiver need to be available at the same time or not.

Communication mode A type of information exchange that has a defined objective and scope. Examples of communication modes include client reviews, status reviews, and problem reports. A communication mode can be scheduled or event-driven.

Communication relationship   A type of relationship in a use case diagram denoting the flow of information between an actor and a use case.

Completeness   Property of a model indicating whether all relevant phenomena are modeled or not. A model is incomplete if one or more relevant phenomena do not have a corresponding concept in the model.

Complex transition   A transition with multiple source states or multiple target states. A transition represents the joining or splitting of multiple threads of control. Complex transitions are used in activity diagrams to denote the synchronization of activities.

Component   A physical and replaceable part of the system that complies to an interface. Examples of components include class libraries, frameworks, and binary programs.

Composite pattern   A design pattern for representing recursive hierarchies.

Concept   An abstraction of a set of phenomena which have common properties. For example, this book, my black watch, and the Valley Fisherman's Club are phenomena. Textbooks on object-oriented software engineering, black watches, and fisherman's clubs are concepts. *Contrast with*: Phenomenon.

Configuration   Version of a CM aggregate.

Configuration management aggregate   An aggregate of related configuration management items. Also called CM aggregate.

Configuration item   A work product which is treated as a single entity for the purpose of configuration management and that needs to be baselined. *See also* configuration management aggregate.

Configuration management   *See* software configuration management.

Configuration manager   A role representing the developers responsible for tracking, baselining, and archiving work products.

Constraint   Rule attached to a UML element restricting its semantics. Constraints can be depicted by a note containing natural language text or an expression in a formal language (e.g., OCL).

Consistency   Property of a model indicating whether it contradicts itself or not. A model is inconsistent if it provides several incompatible views of the system.

Consultant   Any role that is concerned with providing temporary and specialized support where project participants lack expertise. Consultant roles include the user, the client, the technical consultant, and the application domain specialist.

Contract   A set of constraints on a class or a component allowing the caller and the callee to share the same assumptions about the class or the component. *See also* invariant, precondition, and postcondition.

Control flow   The sequence of execution of operations in the system. *Contrast with*: data flow.

Control object   An object that represents a task performed by the user and supported by the system.

Correction   Change to a component with the purpose of repairing a fault.

Cost criterion   A design goal related to the cost of developing, operating, or installing the system.

Coupling   Strength of the dependencies between two subsystems or two classes. Low coupling results in subsystems that can be modified with minimal impact on other subsystems.

Criterion   A measure of goodness used when evaluating alternatives for an issue.

Cross development   A process group which includes the processes that occur throughout the project and that ensure the completion and quality of project functions. Examples of cross development processes include validation and verification, configuration management, documentation, and training. Also called integral processes.

Cross–functional role   Any role that is concerned with coordinating the work of more than one team. Examples of cross functional roles include the configuration manager, the architecture liaison, the tester, and the document editor.

Cross–functional team   A team responsible for supporting subsystem team during a cross functional activity such as configuration management, integration, or testing.

CTC   *See* centralized traffic control.

Data flow   The sequence in which data is transferred, used, and transformed in the system. Contrast: control flow.

Data type   An abstraction of a set of values in the context of a programming language. For example, int is the Java data type abstracting all the integer values.

Debugging   A fault detection technique that attempts to find a fault from an unplanned failure by stepping through successive states of the system.

Decision   In the context of activity diagrams: a branch in the control flow of an activity diagram. A decision denotes alternative transitions based on a condition. In the context of issue modeling: an issue resolution.

Decision Representation Language (DRL)   An issue model extending IBIS to represent the qualitative elements of decision making.

Defect   *See* fault.

Delegation   Mechanism for code reuse in which an operation merely resends (i.e., delegates) a message to another class to accomplish the desired behavior.

Deliverable   A work product destined for the client.

Delta   Set of differences between two successive versions. Also called change.

Dependability criterion   A design goal related to minimizing the number of system crashes and the consequences of a system crash. Examples of dependability criteria include robustness, reliability, availability, fault tolerance, security, and safety.

Deployment diagram   A UML diagram representing runtime components and their assignments to hardware nodes.

Design goal   Quality that the system should optimize. Design goals are often inferred from nonfunctional requirements and are used to guide design decisions. Examples of design goals include usability, reliability, security, and safety.

Developer   *See* development role.

Development role   Any role that is concerned with specifying, designing, and constructing subsystems. Examples of development roles include the analyst, the system architecture, the object designer, and the implementor.

Different time, different place groupware   See groupware.

Document editor   A role representing the person performing the integration of the documents.

DRL   See Decision Representation Language.

Dynamic access control   An access control policy that can be set at run-time. *Contrast with*: static access control.

Dynamic model   The dynamic model describes the components of the system that have interesting behavior. In this book, we represent the dynamic model with statechart diagrams, sequence diagrams, and activity diagrams.

Egoless programming   A project organization where responsibilities are assigned to a team instead of individuals. Roles within a team are interchangeable.

Encryption   A translation of a message, called plaintext, into an encrypted message, called ciphertext, such that it cannot be understood by unauthorized persons.

End user criterion   A design goal related to user visible attributes of the system not yet covered under a dependability or performance criterion.

Enterprise application framework   An application specific framework used for enterprise business activities.

Entity-centered software life cycle model   A software life cycle model which primarily represents the work products produced during development. *Contrast with*: activity-centered software life cycle model.

Entity object   An object which represents persistent or long lived information tracked by the system.

Error   State of the system such that further processing will lead to a failure.

Event-driven control   Control flow paradigm in which a main loop waits for an event and dispatches it to the appropriate object.

Extend relationship   A type of relationship in a use case diagram denoting that a use case extends the flow of events of another one. Extends relationships are typically used for modeling exceptional behavior, such as exception handling and help functionality.

Event   A relevant occurrence in the system. An event is an instance of an event class. Examples of events include a stimulus from an actor, a time-out, or the sending of a message between two objects.

Event class   An abstraction representing a set of events for which the system has a common response.

Exception   An unexpected event that occurs during the execution of the system.

Exception handling   A mechanism by which a system treats an exception.

Extensibility   Quality of a system indicating how easily the system can be changed to accommodate new functionality.

Facilitator   A meeting management role responsible for organizing and executing a meeting. The primary facilitator writes the meeting agenda, notifies the meeting participants, and ensures during the meeting that the agenda is followed. A secondary facilitator supports the primary facilitator's role in keeping the meeting on track.

Failure   Deviation of the observed behavior from the specified behavior.

Falsification   Process of explicitly trying to demonstrate that a model has faults (e.g., the model omits relevant details or represents relevant details incorrectly). Prototype and testing are examples of falsification.

Fault   Mechanical or algorithmic cause of an error. Also called a bug or a defect.

Fault avoidance   A method aimed at preventing the insertion of faults while building the system. Examples of fault avoidance techniques include development methodologies, configuration management, verification, and reviews.

Fault detection   A method aimed at discovering faults in the running system. Examples of fault detection techniques include debugging and testing.

Fault tolerance   A method aimed at constructing systems that do not fail in the presence of faults. Ability to withstand faults without failing.

Forward engineering   A model maintenance activity during which the implementation model is generated or updated from the analysis and design model. *Contrast with*: reverse engineering.

Framework   A set of classes providing a general solution that can be refined to provide an application or a subsystem.

FRIEND   A distributed incident management system developed at Carnegie Mellon University.

Functional model   Describes the functionality of the system from the user's point of view. In this book, we represent the functional model with use cases.

Functional organization   A project organization in which work is divided according to project activities (e.g., requirements elicitation, analysis, system design, object design, implementation, testing, configuration management).

Functional requirement   An area of functionality the system must support. The functional requirements describe the interactions between the actors and the system independent of the realization of the system.

Functional testing   A system testing activity during which developers find differences between the observed functionality and the use case model.

Generalization   A type of relationship between a general class and a more specialized class. The specialized class adds semantics and functionality to the general class. The specialized class is called the subclass and the general class is called the superclass.

Global access table   A representation of access rights in which every legitimate right is represented as an {`actor, class, operation`} tuple.

Goal   High level principle that is used to guide the project. Goals define the attributes of the system that are important. For a transportation vehicle, safety is a goal. For shrinkwrapped software, low cost is a goal.

Greenfield engineering   A development project which starts from scratch. *See also* re-engineering and interface engineering.

Groupware   Software tool supporting the exchange of information among a set of participants. Same time different place groupware support synchronous exchanges. Different time, different place groupware support asynchronous exchanges.

Hallway conversation   A synchronous mechanism of communication during which participants meet face to face accidentally.

Hook method   A method provided by a framework class that is meant to be overwritten in a subclass to specialize the framework.

Implementation   An activity during which developers translate the object model into code.

Implementation domain   *See* solution domain.

Implementation inheritance   Inheritance used solely as a mechanism for reuse.

Include relationship   A type of relationship in a use case diagram denoting that a use case invokes another use case. A use case inclusion is analog to a method invocation.

Infrastructure framework   A framework used to realize an infrastructure subsystem, such as a user interface or a storage subsystem.

Inheritance   Reusability technique in which a child class inherits all the attributes and operations of a parent class. Inheritance is a mechanism that can be used to realize a generalization relationship.

Inspection   A scheduled mode of communication during which developers formally peer review a work product.

Installation   An activity during which the system is installed and tested in its operating environment. Installation can also include the training of users.

Installation testing   A system testing activity during which developers and the client test the system in the operational environment.

Instance   Member of a specific data type. For example, 1291 is an instance of the data type int. 3.14 is an instance of the data type float.

Integral process group   *See* cross development.

Integration testing   A testing activity during which developers find faults by combining a small number of subsystems or objects.

Interface engineering   A development project in which the interface of a system is redesigned and reimplemented. The core functionality is left untouched. *See also* greenfield engineering and reengineering.

Interface inheritance   Inheritance used as a means of subtyping.

Internal work product   A work product destined only for the internal consumption of the project.

Invariant   A predicate that is always true for all instances of a class.

IBIS   See Issue-based information system.

Issue   A critical problem that has no clear solution.

Issue-based information system (IBIS)   An issue model proposed by Kunz Rittel composed of three types of nodes: Issue, Position, and Argument.

Issue-based life cycle model   An entity-based software life cycle model in which an issue model is used to monitor and control progress in the project.

Issue model   A model representing the rationale of one or more decisions as a graph. Nodes of an issue model typically includes issues, proposals, arguments, criteria, and resolutions.

Issue resolution   An event-driven mode of communication during which participants reach a consensus or a decision on an issue.

JAD   *See* Joint Application Design

JEWEL An emissions modeling environment realized at Carnegie Mellon University allowing users to run, manage, organize, and visualize emissions simulations.

Joint Application Design (JAD) A requirements elicitation technique involving the collaboration of clients, users, and developers in constructing a system specification, through a week–long working meeting.

KAT *See* Knowledge Analysis of Tasks.

Key process area (KPA) A set of activities that achieve a goal considered important for attaining a given level of process maturity. Examples of KPA includes configuration management, requirements change management, and risk management.

Kick-off meeting A meeting including all project participants marking the end of the project initiation phase and the beginning of steady state.

Knowledge acquisition The activity of collecting data, organizing it into information, and formalizing it into knowledge.

Knowledge Analysis of Tasks Application domain modeling technique based on the observation of users in action.

Knowledge promoter A promoter role concerned with pushing change through an organization using specialized knowledge about the benefits and limitations of technologies or methods.

KPA *See* key process area.

Questions, Options, and Criteria (QOC) (An issue model, proposed by McLean et al, extending IBIS to represent criterion and assessment information.

Questionnaire A synchronous mechanism of communication during which information is elicited from a participant with a structured set of questions.

Layer Subsystem in a hierarchical decomposition. A layer can only depend on lower level layers and has no knowledge of the layers above it.

Liaison A communication role responsible for the information flow between two teams. For example, an architecture liaison represents a subsystem team at the architecture team.

Life cycle *See* software life cycle.

Link An instance of an association. A link connects two objects.

Maintenance criterion A design goal related to the difficulty of changing or upgrading the system after it has been delivered.

Management role Any role that is concerned with the planning, monitoring, and controlling of the project. Examples of management roles include the project manager and the team leader.

Many-to-many association An association with $0..n$ or $1..n$ multiplicity on both ends.

Matrix organization A project organization combining the functional and project-based organization. Each participants reports to two managers, a division (or functional) manager and a project manager.

Meeting A synchronous mechanism of communication during which present, discuss, negotiate, and resolve issues, either face-to-face or via telephone or videoconferencing.

Message Mechanism by which a sending object requests the execution of an operation in the receiving object. A message is composed of a name and a number of arguments. The receiving object matches the name of the message to one or more operations and passes the arguments to the operation. The message send ends when the results of the operation are returned back to the sending object.

Method In the context of development: a repeatable technique for solving a specific problem. For example, a recipe is a method for cooking a specific dish. In the context of a class or an object: the implementation of an operation. For example, `SetTime(t)` is a method on the class `Watch`.

Methodology A collection of methods for solving a class of problems. A seafood cookbook is a methodology for preparing seafood. This book describes a methodology for dealing with complex and changing systems.

Middleware framework A framework used to integrate distributed applications and components.

Minute taker A meeting role responsible for recording a meeting, in particular, the resolutions that participants have agreed on and their implementation in terms of action items.

Model An abstraction of a system aimed at simplifying the reasoning about the system by omitting irrelevant details. For example, if the system of interest is a ticket distributor for a train, blue prints for the ticket distributor, schematics of its electrical wiring, object models of its software are models of the ticket distributor.

Model/View/Controller A three tier software architecture in which domain knowledge is maintained by model objects, displayed by view objects, and manipulated by control objects. In this book, model objects are called entity objects and view objects are called boundary objects.

Modeling An activity during which participants construct an abstraction of a system by focusing on interesting aspects and omitting irrelevant details. What is interesting or irrelevant depends on the task in which the model is used. *See also* abstraction.

Modifiability Quality of a system indicating how easily existing models can be modified.

Multiplicity A set of integers attached to an association end indicating the number of links that can legitimately originate from an instance of the class at the association end. For example, an association denoting that a `Car` has four `Wheels` has a multiplicity of 1 on the `Car` end and 4 on the `Wheel` end.

Nonfunctional requirement   A user visible constraint on the system. Nonfunctional requirements describe user visible aspects of the system that are not directly related with the functionality of the system. *See also* design goal.

Notation   A graphical or textual set of rules for representing a model. For example, the Roman alphabet is a notation for representing words. UML is a graphical notation for representing system models.

Note   Comment attached to a diagram.

Object   Instance of a class. An object has an identity and stores attribute values.

Object Constraint Language (OCL)   A formal language defined as part of the UML used for expressing constraints.

Object design   An activity during which developments define custom objects to bridge the gap between the analysis model and the hardware/software platform. This include specifying object and subsystem interfaces, selecting off-the-shelf components, restructuring the object model to attain design goals, and optimizing the object model for performance. Object design results in the object design model.

Object Design Document (ODD)   A document describing the object design model. The object design model is often generated from comments embedded in the source code.

Object design model   Detailed object model representing the solution objects which make up the system. The object design model includes detailed class specifications, including contracts, types, signatures, visibilities for all public operations.

Object designer   A role representing developers who refine and specify the interface of classes during object design.

Object diagram   A class diagram that includes only instances.

Object model   Describes the structure of a system in terms of objects, attributes, associations, and operations. The analysis object model represents the application domain, that is, the concepts that are visible to the user. The object design model represents the solution domain, that is, the custom and off-the-shelf objects that bridge the gap between the analysis model and the hardware/software platform.

Object-oriented analysis   An activity concerned with modeling the application domain with objects.

Object-oriented design   An activity concerned with modeling the solution domain with objects.

Organization   A set of teams, roles, communication paths, and reporting structure targeting at a specific project (project organization) or a class of projects (division or corporate organization).

Observer pattern   A design pattern that decouples entity objects from their views. Views subscribe to the entity objects they are interested in. Entity objects broadcast notifications to subscribers when they change their state.

OCL   *See* Object Constraint Language.

ODD   *See* Object Design Document.

One-to-many association   An association that has a 1 multiplicity on one end and a 0..n or a 1..n multiplicity on the other end.

One-to-one association   An association with multiplicity 1 on each end.

Open architecture   A layered architecture in which a layer make use of services in any layer below it (as opposed to only the layers immediately below it). *Contrast with*: closed architecture.

Open issue   An issue that has not yet been resolved.

Operation   An atomic piece of behavior that is provided by a class. A calling object triggers the execution of an operation by sending a message to the object on which the operation should be executed.

OWL   Facilities management system realized at Carnegie Mellon University allowing its users to control environmental parameters (e.g., temperature, air flow, light) via a web browser. OWL also enables a facilities manager to locate faulty components.

Package   A UML grouping concept denoting that a set of objects or classes are related. Packages are used in use case and class diagrams to deal with the complexity associated with large numbers of use cases or classes.

Participant   Person involved with a software development project.

Participating object   Analysis objects that are involved in a given use case.

Partition   A subsystem in a peer to peer architecture.

Peer-to-peer architecture   A generalization of the client/server architecture in which subsystems can act both as clients or servers.

Performance criterion   A design goal related to the speed or space attributes of a system. Examples of performance criteria include response time, throughput, and memory space.

Performance testing   A system testing activity during which developers find differences between nonfunctional requirements and the system performance.

Phase   Often used as a synonym for activity or process.

Phenomenon   An object of a reality as it is perceived by the modeler. Modeling consists of selecting the phenomena of a reality that are of interest, identifying their common properties, and abstracting them into concepts. *Contrast with*: concept.

Pipe and filter architecture   A software architecture in which subsystems sequentially process data from a set of inputs and send their results to other subsystems via a set of outputs. Associations between subsystems are called pipes. Subsystems are called filters. Filters do not depend on each other and can thus be rearranged in different order and configurations.

Portability   Quality of a system indicating how easily the system can be ported to different hardware/software platforms.

Postmortem review   A scheduled mode of communication during which participants capture the lessons they learned during the project.

Postcondition   A predicate that must be true after an operation is invoked.

Power promoter   A promoter role concerned with pushing change through an organization using knowledge of the chain of control.

Precondition   A predicate that must be true before an operation is invoked.

Problem definition   A scheduled mode of communication during which the client and manager define the scope of the system.

Problem domain   *See* application domain.

Problem solving   A search activity including the generation and evaluation of alternatives addressing a given problem, often by trial and error.

Problem Statement   A document cooperatively written by the client and project management briefly describing the scope of the system, including its high level requirements, its target environment, deliverables, and acceptance criteria.

Procedure-driven control   Control flow paradigm in which operations wait for input. The sequencing of operations is otherwise done explicitly through the sending of messages.

Process   A set of activities that is performed towards a specific purpose. Examples of processes include requirements elicitation, analysis, project management, and testing. A process is synonym for a high level activity. See also activity.

Process group   Grouping of related processes. Examples of process groups include management, pre-development, development, and post-development.

Process promoter   A promoter role concerned with pushing change through an organization using her knowledge of the organization's internal processes.

Project Agreement   A document that formally defines the scope, duration, cost, and deliverables of a project. Requirements are often categorized into core requirements (i.e., which the system must meet when delivered), desirable requirements (i.e., which must be satisfied eventually), and optional requirements (i.e., which may or may not be required in the future). The Project Agreement subsumes the Problem Statement.

Project initiation A project management activity during which the project scope and resources are defined.

Project management An activity during which managers plan, budget, monitor, and control the development process. Project management ensures that constraints and project goals are met.

Project-based organization A corporate organization in which work is divided according to projects, i.e., each participant works on exactly one project at any one time.

Project review A scheduled mode of communication during which a project manager monitors the status of a project.

Project steady state A management activity during which management monitors and controls the progress of the project.

Project termination A management activity during which the project is concluded: the system is delivered and accepted by the client.

Promoter role Any role that is concerned with promoting change through an organization. Examples of promoter roles include the knowledge promoter, the process promoter, and the power promoter.

Promotion A version that has been made available internally to other developers in the project. *See also* release.

Proposal A possible resolution of an issue.

Prototyping A process of designing and realizing a simplified version of the system for evaluation with the user or the manager. For example, a usability prototype evaluates the usability of different interfaces. A performance prototype assesses the performance of different alternatives.

Proxy pattern A design pattern encapsulating an expensive computation. For example, a Proxy pattern can be used to delay the loading of an image in memory until it needs to be displayed.

Pseudo requirement A constraint on the implementation of the system imposed by the client.

Qualified association An association with one end indexed by an attribute. For example, the association between `Directory` and `File` is a qualified association indexed by a filename on the `Directory` end. Qualification is a technique for reducing the multiplicity of associations.

RAD *See* Requirements Analysis Document.

Rationale The justification of decisions. For example, selecting myDBMS as a database management system is a system design decision. Stating that myDBMS is reliable and responsive enough to attain the project's goals is part of the rationale for this design decision. Also called design rationale.

Rationale editor A role responsible for collecting and organizing rationale information.

Rationale management   An activity during which developers create, capture, update, and access rationale information.

Readability   Quality of a system indicating how easily the system can be understood from its source code.

Realizability   Property of a model indicating whether the system it represents can be realized.

Reengineering   A development project in which a system and its accompanying business processes are redesigned and reimplemented. See also greenfield engineering and interface engineering.

Release   In communication: a scheduled mode of communication during which a developer makes available to the rest of the project a new version of a work product. In configuration management: a version that has been made available externally, that is, to the client or the users.

Reliability   Property of a system indicating the probability that its observed behavior conforms to the specification of its behavior.

Reporting structure   Structure representing the chain of control and status reporting.

Repository   In a repository architecture: the central subsystem which manages persistent data. In configuration management: a library of releases.

Repository architecture   Software architecture in which persistent data is managed and stored by a single subsystem. Peripheral subsystems are relatively independent and interact only through the central subsystem.

Request for change   *See* change request.

Request for clarification   An event-driven mode of communication during which a participant requests more information.

Requirement   A function that the system must have (a functional requirement) or a user visible constraint on the system (nonfunctional requirement).

Requirements Analysis Document (RAD)   A document describing the analysis model.

Requirements elicitation   An activity during which project participants define the purpose of the system. Requirements elicitation produces the functional model.

Requirements engineering   An activity that includes requirements elicitation and analysis.

Resolution   The alternative selected by participants to close an issue.

Resources   Assets that are used to accomplish work. Resources include time, equipment, and labor.

Reverse engineering   A model maintenance activity during which the analysis and design model are generated or updated from the implementation model. *Contrast with*: forward engineering.

Reviewer   A role representing the persons validating work products for quality criteria such as completeness, correctness, consistency, and clarity.

Risk   An area of uncertainty which can lead to a deviation in the project plan (e.g., late delivery, requirements not met, cost above budget), including the failure of the project.

Risk management   A management method for identifying and addressing areas of uncertainty before they negatively impact the schedule of the project or the quality of the system.

Robustness   Ability to withstand unexpected input. For example, a robust component detects and handles invalid arguments that are passed to its operations. A robust user interface checks and handles invalid user input.

Role   In the context of an organization: a set of responsibilities in the project assigned to a person or a team. A person can fill one or more roles. Examples of roles include analyst, system architect, tester, developer, manager, reviewer, and tester. In the context of an association end: a string indicating the role of the class at the association end with respect to the association.

Round trip engineering   A model maintenance activity that combines forward and reverse engineering. Changes to the implementation model are propagated to the analysis and design models through reverse engineering. Changes to the analysis and design models are propagated to the implementation model through forward engineering.

Safety   Property of a system indicating its ability to not endanger human lives, even in the presence of errors.

Same time, difference place groupware   See groupware

Sandwich testing   An integration testing strategy that combines top down and bottom up testing.

Sawtooth model   A software life cycle model in which developers show progress to the client with demonstrations of prototypes.

Scenario   Instance of a use case. A scenario represents a concrete sequence of interactions between one or more actors and the system.

Schedule   A mapping of a task model onto a time line. A schedule represents work in terms of calendar time.

SCMP   *See* Software Configuration Management Plan.

SDD   *See* System Design Document.

Security   Property of a system indicating its ability to protect the resources against unauthorized use, whether malicious or accidental.

Sequence diagram   UML notation representing the behavior of the system as a series of interactions among a group of objects. Each object is depicted as a column in the diagram. Each interaction is depicted as an arrow between two columns. Sequence diagrams are used during analysis to identify missing objects, attributes, relationships, or attributes. Sequence diagrams are used during object design to refine the specification of classes.

Service   A set of related operations offered by a class.

Shark tooth model   A variation of the sawtooth model in which developers show progress to both client and management with the demonstrations of prototypes.

Signature   Given an operation, the tuple made out of the types of its parameters and the type of the return value. Operation signatures are specified during object design.

Software architecture   *See* system design model.

Software configuration management   An activity during which developers monitor and control changes to the system or its models. Goals of configuration management include saving enough information such that it is possible to restore the system as of a prior version; preventing changes that are not consistent with project goals; managing concurrent development paths aimed at evaluating competing solutions.

Software Configuration Management Plan (SCMP)   A document defining the procedures and conventions associated with the configuration management of a project. These include the identification of configuration items, the accounting of their status, the process for approving change requests, and the auditing activities.

Software life cycle   All activities and work products necessary for the development of a software system.

Software life cycle model   An abstraction representing a software life cycle for the purpose of understanding, monitoring, or controlling a software life cycle. Examples of software life cycle models include the waterfall model, the V model, Boehm's spiral model, the Unified Process, and the issue-based life cycle model.

Software Project Management Plan   The controlling document of a software project. The SPMP defines the activities, work products, milestones, and resources allocated to the project. Also defined in the SPMP are the management procedures and conventions applicable to the project, such as status reporting, risk management, and contingency management.

Software reliability   Property of a software system indicating the probability that the software will not cause a failure of the system for a specified duration.

Solution domain   The space of all possible systems. The solution domain is the focus of the system design, object design, and implementation activities. *Contrast with*: application domain.

Solution object   An object in the system design or object design model that represents a solution domain concept.

Spiral model   An iterative and incremental software life cycle model centered around risk management.

SPMP   *See* Software Project Management Plan.

State   A condition that is satisfied by the attribute values of an object or a subsystem.

Statechart diagram   UML notation representing the behavior of an individual object as a number of states and transitions between these states. A state represents a particular set of values for an object. Given a state, a transition represents a future state the object can move to and the conditions associated with the change of state. Statechart diagrams are used during analysis to describe objects with nontrivial behavior.

Static access control   An access control policy that can be set only at compile time. *Contrast with*: dynamic access control.

Status accounting   In configuration management: the tracking of change requests, change approval, and rationale for change.

Status review   A scheduled mode of communication during which team leaders monitor the status of their team.

Stereotype   String enclosed in angle brackets attached to a UML element which enables modelers to create new building blocks. For example, the stereotype <<control>> attached to an object denotes a control object.

Stimulus   A message sent to an object or to the system by an actor or another object which usually results in the invocation of an operation. Examples of stimuli include clicking on a user interface button, selecting a menu item, typing a command, or sending a network packet.

Strategy pattern   A design pattern which encapsulates several implementations of the same algorithm.

Subclass   The specialized class in a generalization relationship. *See also* generalization.

Subsystem   In general, a smaller, simpler part of a larger system; in system design, a well defined software component that provides a number of services to other subsystems. Examples of subsystems include storage subsystems (managing persistent data), user interface subsystems (managing the interaction with the user), networking subsystems (managing the communication with other subsystems over a network).

Subsystem decomposition   Division of the system into subsystems. Each subsystem is described in terms of its services during system design and its API during object design. The subsystem decomposition is part of the system design model.

Subsystem team   A team responsible for the development of a subsystem. *Contrast with*: cross functional team.

Superclass   The general class in a generalization relationship. *See also* generalization.

Swimlane   A UML grouping concept denoting activities that are carried out by the same object or set of objects.

System   Organized set of communicating parts designed for a specific purpose. For example, a car, composed of four wheels, a chassis, a body, and an engine, is designed to transport people. A watch, composed of a battery, a circuit, wheels, and hands, is designed to measure time.

System design   An activity during which developers define the system design model, including the design goals of the project and decompose the system into smaller subsystems that can be realized by individual teams. System design also leads to the selection of the hardware/software platform, the persistent data management strategy, the global control flow, the access control policy, and the handling of boundary conditions.

System Design Document   A document describing the system design model.

System design model   High level description of the system, including design goals, subsystem decomposition, hardware/software platform, persistent storage strategy, global control flow, access control policy, and handling of boundary conditions. The system design model represents the strategic decisions made by the architecture team which allows subsystem teams to work concurrently and cooperate effectively.

System model   A model describing a system. Examples of system models include the analysis model, the system design model, the object design model, and the source code.

System specification   A complete and precise description of the system from the user's point of view. A system specification, unlike the analysis model, is understandable to the user. In UML, the system specification is represented with use cases.

System testing   A testing activity during which developers test all the subsystems as a single system. System testing includes functional testing, performance testing, acceptance testing, and installation testing.

Task   Atomic unit of work that can be managed. Tasks consume resources and produce one or more work products.

Task model   A model of work for a project represented as tasks and their interdependencies.

Team   A set of participants who work on a common problem in a project.

Team leader   A management role responsible for the planning, monitoring, and control of a single team.

Technical consultant   A consultant role concerned with providing solution domain expertise to the project.

Technical writer   *See* document editor.

Test case   A set of inputs and expected results that exercises a component with the purpose of causing failures.

Test driver   A partial implementation of a component that exercises the tested component. Test drivers are used during unit and integration testing.

Test Manual   A document describing the test cases used to test the system along with their results.

Test stub   A partial implementation of a component on which the tested component depends. Test stubs are used to isolate components during unit and integration testing and allow components to be tested even when their dependent components have not yet been implemented.

Tester   A role concerned with the planning, design, execution, and analysis of tests.

Testing   An activity during which developers find differences between the system and its models by executing the system (or parts of it) with sample input data sets. Testing includes unit testing, integration testing, system testing, and usability testing.

Thread   Control flow paradigm in which the system creates an arbitrary number of threads to handle an arbitrary number of input channels.

Time keeper   A meeting role responsible for tracking time such that the primary facilitator can accelerate the resolution of an issue (or table it) if necessary.

Top–down testing   An integration testing strategy in which components are incrementally integrated together starting with the highest level components. Top down testing does not require any test drivers.

Top–level design   Initial subsystem decomposition used for team organization and initial planning.

Traceability   Property of a model indicating whether a model element can be traced to the original requirement or rationale that motivated its existence.

Transition   A possible change of state associated with an event.

UML   *See* Unified Modeling Language.

Unified Modeling Language (UML)   A standard set of notations for representing models.

Unified Process   *See* Unified Software Development Process

Unified Software Development Process   An iterative software life cycle model characterized by cycles of four phases, called *Inception*, *Elaboration*, *Construction*, and *Transition*.

Unit testing   Testing of individual components.

Usability   Quality of a system that indicates how easily users can interact with the system.

Usability testing   The validation of a system or a model through the use of prototypes and simulations by a user.

Use case   A general sequence of interactions between one or more actors and the system. *See also* scenario.

Use case diagram   UML notation used during requirements elicitation and analysis to represent the functionality of the system. A use case describes a function of the system in terms of a sequence of interactions between an actor and the system. A use case also includes entry conditions that need to be true before executing the use case and the exit conditions that are true at the completion of the use case.

User   A role representing the persons who interact directly with the system when accomplishing their work.

User Manual   A document describing the user interface of the system such that a user unfamiliar with the system can use it.

V model   A variation of the waterfall model which makes explicit the dependencies between development processes and verification processes.

Variant   Versions that are intended to coexist. For example, if a system can be executed on different platforms, the system has a variant for each platform (e.g., a Windows variant, a Macintosh variant, a Linux variant).

Verifiability   Property of a model indicating whether it can be falsified or not.

Verification   A set of formal methods which attempt to detect faults without executing the system.

Version   A state of a configuration item or a CM aggregate at a well defined point in time. The version of a CM aggregate is called a configuration.

Version identifier   A number or a name that uniquely identifies a version.

View   Subset of a model. Views focus on only selected model elements to make it more understandable.

Waterfall model   A software life cycle model in which all development processes occur sequentially.

Whitebox framework   A framework which relies on inheritance and dynamic binding for extensibility. *Contrast with*: blackbox framework.

White box test   A test which focuses on the internal structure of a component. Contrast: black box test.

Work product   Artifact that is produced during the development. Examples of work products include the Requirements Analysis Document, the System Design Document, user interface prototypes, market surveys, and the delivered system.

Workspace   In configuration management: a library of promotions.

Bibliography

[Abbott, 1983] R. Abbott, "Program design by informal English descriptions," *Communications of the ACM*, Vol. 26, No 11, 1983.

[Allen, 1985] T. J. Allen, *Managing the Flow of Technology: Technology Transfer and the Dissemination of Technological Information within the R&D Organization,* 2nd ed. MIT Press, Cambridge, MA, 1995.

[Ambler, 1998] S. W. Ambler, *Process Patterns: Building Large-Scale Systems Using Object Technology.* Cambridge University Press, New York, 1998.

[Apple, 1989] Apple Computers, Inc., *Macintosh Programmers Workshop Pascal 3.0 Reference.* Apple Computers, Cupertino, CA, 1989.

[Babich, 1986] W. A. Babich, *Software Configuration Management.* Addison-Wesley, Reading, MA, 1986.

[Bass et al., 1999] L. Bass, P. Clements, & R. Kazman, *Software Architecture in Practice.* Addison-Wesley, Reading, MA, 1999.

[Berliner, 1990] B. Berliner, "CVS II: parallelizing software development," *Proceedings of the 1990 USENIX Conference.* pp. 22–26, Washington, DC , Jan. 1990.

[Bersoff et al., 1980] E. H. Bersoff, V. D. Henderson, & S. G. Siegel, *Software Configuration Management: An Investment in Product Integrity.* Prentice Hall, Englewood Cliffs, NJ, 1980.

[Bezier, 1990] B. Bezier, *Software Testing Techniques,* 2nd ed. Van Nostrand, New York, 1990.

[Binder, 1994] R. V. Binder, "Testing object-oriented systems: A status report," *American Programmer.* Apr. 1994.

[Birrer, 1993] E. T. Birrer, "Frameworks in the financial engineering domain: An experience report," *ECOOP'93 Proceedings.* Lecture Notes in Computer Science No. 707, 1993.

[Boehm, 1987]   B. Boehm, "A spiral model of software development and enhancement,"
                                 Software Engineering Project Management. pp. 128-142, 1987.

[Boehm, 1991]   B. Boehm, "Software risk management: Principles and practices," *IEEE
                                 Software*. Vol. 1, pp. 32-41, 1991.

[Boehm et al., 1995]   B. Boehm, P. Bose, E. Horowitz, & M. J. Lee, "Software requirements
                                 negotiation and renegotiation aids: A theory-W based spiral approach,"
                                 Proceedings of the ICSE-17. (Seattle, WA,) 1995.

[Booch, 1994]   G. Booch, *Object-Oriented Analysis and Design with Applications,* 2nd ed.,
                                 Benjamin/Cummings, Redwood City, CA, 1994.

[Booch et al., 1998]   G. Booch, J. Rumbaugh, & I. Jacobson, *The Unified Modeling Language User
                                 Guide*. Addison-Wesley, Reading, MA, 1998.

[Brooks, 1975]   F. P. Brooks, *The Mythical Man Month*. Addison-Wesley, Reading, MA, 1975.

[Brown et al., 1999]   W. J. Brown, H. W. McCormick, & S. W. Thomas, *AntiPatterns and Patterns in
                                 Software Configuration Management*. Wiley, New York, 1999.

[Bruegge, 1992]   B. Bruegge, "Teaching an Industry-oriented Software Engineering Course,"
                                 Software Enginering Education, SEI Conference, Lecture Notes in Computer
                                 Sciences, Vol. 640. Springer Verlag, San Diego, CA, pp. 65-87, Oct. 1992.

[Bruegge et al., 1992]   B. Bruegge, J. Blythe, J. Jackson, & J. Shufelt, "Object-oriented system
                                 modeling with OMT," *Conference Proceedings OOPSLA '92 (Object-Oriented
                                 Programming Systems, Languages, and Applications)*, pp. 359-376, Oct. 1992.

[Bruegge et al., 1993]   B. Bruegge, T. Gottschalk, & B. Luo, "A framework for dynamic program
                                 analyzers," *OOPSLA' 93 (Object-Oriented Programming Systems, Languages,
                                 and Applications)*, Washington, DC, pp. 65-82, Sept. 1993.

[Bruegge & Coyne, 1993]   B. Bruegge & R. Coyne, "Model-based software engineering in larger scale
                                 project courses," *IFIP Transactions on Computer Science and Technology,* Vol.
                                 A-40, pp. 273-287, 1993.

[Bruegge, 1994]   B. Bruegge, "From toy systems to real system development," *Improvements in
                                 Software Engineering Education*, Workshop of the German Chapter of the
                                 ACM. B.G. Teubner Verlag, Stuttgart, pp. 62- 72, Feb. 1994.

[Bruegge & Coyne, 1994]   B. Bruegge & R. Coyne, "Teaching iterative object-oriented development:
                                 Lessons and directions," *7th Conference on Software Engineering Education,*
                                 Lecture Notes in Computer Science, Vol. 750, Jorge L. Diaz-Herrera (ed.),
                                 Springer Verlag, pp. 413–427, Jan. 1994.

[Bruegge & Riedel, 1994]   B. Bruegge & E. Riedel, "A geographic environmental modeling system:
                                 Towards an object-oriented framework," *Proceedings of the European
                                 Conference on Object-Oriented Programming (ECOOP-94),* Bologna, Italy,
                                 Lecture Notes in Computer Science. Springer Verlag, July 1994.

[Bruegge et al., 1994]   B. Bruegge, K. O'Toole, & D. Rothenberger, "Design considerations for an
                                 accident management system," in M. Brodie, M. Jarke, M. Papazoglou (ed.),
                                 *Proceedings of the Second International Conference on Cooperative
                                 Information Systems*. Toronto: University of Toronto Press, pp. 90–100, May
                                 1994.

[Bruegge & Bennington, 1995]   B. Bruegge & B. Bennington, "Applications of mobile computing and communication," *IEEE Journal on Personal Communications, Special Issue on Mobile Computing*, pp. 64–71, Feb. 1996.

[Bruegge et al., 1995]   B. Bruegge, E. Riedel, G. McRae, & T. Russel, "GEMS: An Environmental Modeling System," *IEEE Journal for Computational Science and Engineering.* pp. 55–68, Sept. 1995.

[Bruegge et al., 1997]   B. Bruegge, S. Chang, T. Fenton, B. Fernandes, V. Hartkopf, T. Kim, R. Pravia, & A. Sharma, "Turning lightbulbs into objects," Experience paper presented at *OOPSLA'97.* Atlanta, 1997.

[Buckingham Shum & Hammond, 1994]   S. Buckingham Shum & N. Hammond, "Argumentation-based design rationale: What use at what cost?" *International Journal of Human-Computer Studies*, Vol. 40, pp. 603-652, 1994.

[Buschmann et al., 1996]   F. Buschmann, R. Meunier, H. Rohnert, P. Sommerlad, & M. Stal, *Pattern-Oriented Software Architecture: A System of Patterns.* Wiley, Chichester, U.K., 1996.

[Carr et al., 1993]   M. J. Carr, S. L. Konda, I. Monarch, F. C. Ulrich, & C. F. Walker, *Taxonomy-Based Risk Identification,* Technical Report CMU/SEI-93-TR-6, Software Engineering Institute, Carnegie Mellon Univ., Pittsburgh, PA, 1993.

[Carroll, 1995]   J. M. Carroll (ed.), *Scenario-Based Design: Envisioning Work and Technology in System Development.* Wiley, New York, 1995.

[Charette, 1989]   R. N. Charette, *Software Engineering Risk Analysis and Management.* McGraw-Hill, New York, 1989.

[Christel & Kang, 1992]   M. G. Christel & K.C. Kang, "Issues in requirements elicitation." Software Engineering Institute, Technical Report CMU/SEI-92-TR-12, Carnegie Mellon Univ., Pittsburgh, PA, 1992.

[Coad et al., 1995]   P. Coad, D. North, & M. Mayfield, *Object Models: Strategies, Patterns, & Applications.* Prentice Hall, Englewood Cliffs, NJ, 1995.

[Conklin & Burgess-Yakemovic, 1991]   J. Conklin & K. C. Burgess-Yakemovic, "A process-oriented approach to design rationale," *Human-Computer Interaction*, Vol. 6, pp. 357–391, 1991.

[Conradi & Westfechtel, 1998]   R. Conradi & B. Westfechtel, "Version models for software configuration management," *ACM Computing Surveys*, Vol. 30, No. 2, June 1998.

[Constantine & Lockwood, 1999]   L. L. Constantine & L.A.D. Lockwood, *Software for Use.* Addison-Wesley, Reading, MA, 1999.

[Coyne et al., 1995]   R. Coyne, B. Bruegge, A. Dutoit, & D. Rothenberger, "Teaching more comprehensive model-based software engineering: Experience with Objectory's use case approach," *8th Conference on Software Engineering Education*, Lecture Notes in Computer Science, Linda Ibraham (ed), Springer Verlag, Berlin, pp. 339–374, Apr. 1995.

[Dart, 1991]   S. Dart, "Concepts in configuration management systems," *Third International Software Configuration Management Workshop.* ACM, June 1991.

[Day & Zimmermann, 1983]   J. D. Day & H. Zimmermann, "The OSI Reference Model," *Proceedings of the IEEE*, Vol. 71, pp. 1334-1340, Dec. 1983.

[De Marco, 1978]   T. De Marco, *Structured Analysis and System Specification.* Yourdon, New
                                          York, 1978.

[DIAMOND, 1995]   *DIAMOND Project Documentation*, School of Computer Science, Carnegie
                                          Mellon Univ., Pittsburgh, PA, 1995–1996.

[D'Souza & Wills, 1999]   D.F. D'Souza & A. C. Wills, *Objects, Components, and Frameworks with
                                          UML: The Catalysis Approach.* The Addison-Wesley Object Technology
                                          Series. Addison-Wesley, Reading, MA, 1999.

[Dumas & Redish, 1998]   Dumas & Redish, *A Practical Guide to Usability Testing.* Ablex, NJ, 1993.

[Dutoit, 1996]   A. H. Dutoit, "The rôle of communication in team-based software engineering
                                          projects," Ph.D. dissertation, Carnegie Mellon Univ., Pittsburgh, PA, Dec.
                                          1996.

[Dutoit et al., 1996]   A. H. Dutoit, B. Bruegge, & R. F. Coyne, "The use of an issue-based model in
                                          a team-based software engineering course," *Conference Proceedings of
                                          Software Engineering: Education and Practice* (SEEP'96). Dunedin, NZ, Jan.
                                          1996.

[Dutoit & Bruegge, 1998]   A. H. Dutoit & B. Bruegge, "Communication metrics for software
                                          development," *IEEE Transactions on Software Engineering*, Aug. 1998.

[Erman et al., 1980]   L. D. Erman, F. Hayes-Roth, et al., "The Hearsay-II Speech-Understanding
                                          System: Integrating knowledge to resolve uncertainty." *ACM Computing
                                          Surveys*, Vol. 12, No. 2, pp. 213–253, 1980.

[Fagan, 1976]   M. E. Fagan, "Design and code inspections to reduce errors in program
                                          development," *IBM System Journal*, Vol. 15, No. 3, pp. 182–211, 1976.

[Fayad & Hamu, 1997]   M. E. Fayad & D. S. Hamu, "Object-oriented enterprise frameworks: Make vs.
                                          buy decisions and guidelines for selection," *The Communications of ACM*,
                                          1997.

[Feiler & Tichy, 1998]   P. Feiler & W. Tichy, "Propagator: A family of patterns," in *Proceedings of
                                          TOOLS-23'97*, Santa Barbara, CA, July 28–Aug. 1 1997.

[Feynman, 1988]   R. P. Feynman, "Personal observations on the reliability of the Shuttle," in
                                          [Rogers et al., 1986]. This article is also available at various locations on the
                                          Web, e.g.,http://www.virtualschool.edu/mon/SocialConstruction/
                                          FeynmanChallengerRpt.html.

[Fischer et al., 1991]   R. Fisher, W. Ury, & B. Patton, *Getting to Yes: Negotiating Agreement Without
                                          Giving In*, 2nd ed. Penguin Books, 1991.

[Fowler, 1997]   M. Fowler, *Analysis Patterns: Reusable Object Models.* Addison-Wesley,
                                          Reading, MA, 1997.

[FRIEND, 1994]   *FRIEND Project Documentation*, School of Computer Science, Carnegie
                                          Mellon University, Pittsburgh, PA 1994.

[Gamma et al., 1994]   E. Gamma, R. Helm, R. Johnson, & J. Vlissides, *Design Patters: Elements of
                                          Reusable Object-Oriented Software.* Addison-Wesley, Reading, MA, 1994.

[Grudin, 1988]   J. Grudin, "Why CSCW applications fail: Problems in design and evaluation of
                                          organization interfaces," *Proceedings of CSCW'88*, Portland, OR, 1988.

[Grudin, 1990]   J. Grudin, "Obstacles to user inVolvement in interface design in large product development organizations," *Proceeding IFIP INTERACT'90 Third International Conference on Human-Computer Interaction*, Cambridge, U.K., Aug. 1990.

[Hammer & Champy, 1993]   M. Hammer & J. Champy, *Reengineering The Corporation: A Manifesto for Business ReVolution.* Harper Business, New York, 1993.

[Harel, 1987]   D. Harel, "Statecharts: A visual formalism for complex systems," *Science of Computer Programming*, pp. 231–274, 1987.

[Hartkopf et al., 1997] V. Hartkopf, V. Loftness, A. Mahdavi, S. Lee, & J. Shankavarm, "An integrated approach to design and engineering of intelligent buildings—The Intelligent Workplace at Carnegie Mellon University, *Automation in Construction*, Vol. 6, pp. 401–415, 1997.

[Hauschildt & Gemuenden, 1998]   J. Hauschildt & H. G. Gemuenden, *Promotoren.* Gabler, Wiesbaden, Germany, 1998.

[Hillier & Lieberman, 1967]   F. S. Hillier & G. J. Lieberman, *Introduction to Operation Research.* Holden-Day, San Francisco, 1967.

[Horn, 1992]   B. Horn, "Constraint patterns as a basis for object-oriented programming," in *Proceedings of the OOPSLA'92*, Vancouver, Canada, 1992.

[Hueni et al., 1995]   H. Hueni, R. Johnson, & R. Engel, "A framework for network protocol software," *Proceedings of OOPSLA*, Austin, TX, Oct. 1995.

[Humphrey, 1989]   W. Humphrey, *Managing the Software Process.* Addison-Wesley, Reading, MA, 1989.

[iContract]   Java Design by Contract Tool, http://www.reliable-systems.com/tools/iContract/iContract.htm.

[IEEE, 1997]   *IEEE Standards Collection Software Engineering.* IEEE, Piscataway, NJ, 1997.

[IEEE Std. 1042-1987]   *IEEE Guide to Software Configuration Management*, IEEE Standards Board, Sept. 1987 (Reaffirmed, Dec. 1993), in [IEEE 1997].

[IEEE Std. 982-1989]   *IEEE Guide for the Use of IEEE Standard Dictionary of Measures to Produce Reliable Software*, IEEE Standards Board, July 1989, in [IEEE 1997].

[IEEE Std. 828-1990]   *IEEE Standard for Software Configuration Management Plans*, IEEE Standards Board, Sept. 1990, in [IEEE 1997].

[IEEE Std. 829-1991]   *IEEE Standard for Software Test Documentation*, IEEE Standards Board, Mar. 1991, in [IEEE 1997].

[IEEE Std. 1058.1-1993] *IEEE Standard for Software Project Management Plans*, IEEE Computer Society, New York, 1993, in [IEEE 1997].

[IEEE Std. 1074-1995]   *IEEE Standard for Developing Software Life Cycle Processes*, IEEE Computer Society, New York, 1995, in [IEEE 1997].

[Jackson, 1995]   M. Jackson, *Software Requirements & Specifications: A Lexicon of Practice, Principles and Prejudices*, Addison-Wesley, Reading, MA, 1995.

[Jacobson et al., 1992] I. Jacobson, M. Christerson, P. Jonsson, & G. Overgaard, *Object-Oriented Software Engineering—A Use Case Driven Approach.* Addison-Wesley, Reading, MA, 1992.

[Jacobson et al., 1999]	I. Jacobson, G. Booch, & J. Rumbaugh, *The Unified Software Development Process*. Addison-Wesley, Reading, MA, 1999.
[Javadoc, 1999a]	Sun Microsystems, Javadoc homepage, http://java.sun.com/products/jdk/javadoc/.
[Javadoc, 1999b]	Sun Microsystems, "How to write doc comments for Javadoc," http://java.sun.com/products/jdk/javadoc/writingdoccomments.html.
[JCA, 1998]	*Java Cryptography Architecture*, JDK Documentation. Javasoft, 1998.
[JDBC, 1998]	*JDBC^{TM}—Connecting Java and Databases*, JDK Documentation. Javasoft, 1998.
[Jensen & Tonies, 1979]	R. W. Jensen & C. C. Tonies, *Software Engineering.* Prentice Hall, Englewood Cliffs, NJ, 1979.
[JFC, 1999]	*Java Foundation Classes*, JDK Documentation. Javasoft, 1999.
[Johnson, 1992]	P. Johnson, *Human Computer Interaction: Psychology, Task Analysis and Software Engineering.* McGraw-Hill Int., London, 1992.
[Johnson & Foote, 1988]	R. Johnson & B. Foote, "Designing reusable classes," *Journal of Object-Oriented Programming.* Vol. 1, No. 5, pp. 22–35, 1988.
[Jones, 1977]	T. C. Jones, "Programmer quality and programmer productivity," IBM Technical Report TR–02.764, 1977.
[Kayser, 1990]	T. A. Kayser, *Mining Group Gold.* Serif, El Segundo, CA, 1990.
[Kemerer, 1997]	C. F. Kemerer, *Software Project Management: Readings and Cases.* Irwin/McGraw-Hill, Boston, MA 1997.
[Knuth, 1986]	D.E. Knuth. *The TeXbook.* Addison-Wesley, Reading, MA, 1986.
[Kompanek et al., 1996]	A. Kompanek, A. Houghton, H. Karatassos, A. Wetmore, & B. Bruegge, "JEWEL: A distributed system for emissions modeling," *Proceedings of the Conference for Air and Waste Management*, Nashville, TN, June 1996.
[Kunz & Rittel, 1970]	W. Kunz & H. Rittel, "Issues as elements of information systems," Working Paper No. 131, Institut für Grundlagen der Plannung, Universität Stuttgart, Germany, 1970.
[Larman, 1998]	C. Larman, *Applying UML and Patterns: An Introduction to Object-Oriented Analysis and Design.* Prentice Hall, Upper Saddle River, NJ, 1998.
[Leblang, 1994]	D. Leblang, "The CM challenge: Configuration management that works," in *Configuration Management*, W.F. Tichy (ed.), Vol. 2, *Trends in Software.* Wiley, New York.
[Lee, 1990]	J. Lee, "A qualitative decision management system," in P.H Winston & S. Shellard (eds.), *Artificial Intelligence at MIT: Expanding Frontiers.* MIT Press, Cambridge, MA, Vol. 1, pp. 104–33, 1990.
[Lee, 1997]	J. Lee, "Design rationale systems: Understanding the issues," *IEEE Expert*, May/June 1997.
[Lions, 1996]	J.-L. Lions, *ARIANE 5 Flight 501 Failure: Report by the Inquiry Board,* http://www.esrin.esa.it/htdocs/tidc/Press/Press96/ariane5rep.html, 1996.
[Liskov & Guttag, 1986]	B. Liskov & J. Guttag, *Abstraction and Specification in Program Development.* MIT Press, McGraw-Hill, New York, 1986.

[Macaulay, 1996]   L. Macaulay, *Requirements Engineering*. Springer Verlag, London, 1996.

[MacLean et al., 1991]   A. MacLean, R. M. Young, V. Bellotti, & T. Moran, "Questions, options, and criteria: Elements of design space analysis," *Human-Computer Interaction*, Vol. 6, pp. 201–250, 1996.

[McCabe, 1976]   T. McCabe, "A software complexity measure," *IEEE Transactions on Software Engineering*, Vol. 2, No. 12, Dec. 1976.

[Martin & Odell, 1992]   J. Martin & J. J. Odell, *Object-Oriented Analysis and Design*. Prentice Hall, Englewood Cliffs, NJ, 1992.

[Mellor & Shlaer, 1998]   S. Mellor & S. Shlaer, *Recursive Design Approach*. Prentice Hall, Upper Saddle River, NJ, 1998.

[Meyer, 1997]   B. Meyer, *Object-Oriented Software Construction*, 2nd ed. Prentice Hall, Upper Saddle River, NJ, 1997.

[Microsoft, 1995]   Microsoft, "Chapter 9: Open Database Connectivity (ODBC) 2.0 fundamentals," *Microsoft Windows Operating Systems and Services Architecture,* Microsoft Corp., 1995.

[MIL Std. 480]   MIL Std. 480, U.S. Department of Defense, Washington, DC.

[Miller, 1956]   G. A. Miller, "The magical number seven, plus or minus two: Some limits on our capacity for processing information." *Psychological Review*, Vol. 63, pp. 81–97, 1956.

[Moran & Carroll, 1996]   T. P. Moran & J. M. Carroll (eds.), *Design Rationale: Concepts, Techniques, and Use*. Lawrence Erlbaum Associates, Mahwah, NJ, 1996.

[Mowbray & Malveau, 1997] T. J. Mowbray & R. C. Malveau, *CORBA Design Patterns*. Wiley, New York, 1997.

[Myers, 1979]   G. J. Myers, *The Art of Software Testing*, Wiley, New York, 1979.

[Neumann, 1995]   P. G. Neumann, *Computer-Related Risks*. Addison-Wesley, Reading, MA, 1995.

[Nielsen, 1993]   J. Nielsen, *Usability Engineering*, Academic, New York, 1993.

[Nielsen & Mack, 1994]   J. Nielsen & R. L. Mack (eds.), *Usability Inspection Methods*. Wiley, New York, 1994.

[Nye & O'Reilly, 1992]   A. Nye & T. O'Reilly, *X Toolkit Intrinsics Programming Manual: OSF/Motif 1.1 Edition for X11 Release 5—The Definitive Guides to the X Windows Systems,* Vol. 4. O'Reilly & Associates, Sebastopol, CA, 1992.

[OMG, 1995]   Object Management Group, *The Common Object Request Broker: Architecture and Specification*. Wiley, New York, 1995.

[OMG, 1998]   Object Management Group, *OMG Unified Modeling Language Specification*. Framingham, MA, 1998, http://www.omg.org.

[Orlikowski, 1992]   W.J. Orlikowski, "Learning from Notes: Organizational issues in groupware implementation," in *Conference on Computer-Supported Cooperative Work Proceedings*, Toronto, Canada, 1992.

[OWL, 1996]   *OWL Project Documentation*, School of Computer Science, Carnegie Mellon Univ., Pittsburgh, PA, 1996.

[Paech, 1998]   B. Paech, "The four levels of use case description," *Proceedings of the 4th International Workshop on Requirements Engineering: Foundations for Software Quality*, Pisa, Italy, June 1998.

[Parnas & Weiss, 1985]   D. L. Parnas & D. M. Weiss, "Active design reviews: principles and practice," *Proceedings of the Eight International Conference on Software Engineering.* London, England. pp 132–136, Aug. 1985.

[Paulk et al., 1995]   M. C. Paulk, C. V. Weber, & B. Curtis (eds.), *The Capability Maturity Mode: Guidelines for Improving the Software Process.* Addison-Wesley, Reading, MA, 1995.

[Perforce]   Perforce, Inc., 2420 Santa Clara Ave., Alameda, CA.

[Pfleeger, 1991]   S. L. Pfleeger, *Software Engineering: The Production of Quality Software*, 2nd ed. Macmillan, 1991.

[Popper, 1992]   K. Popper, *Objective Knowledge: An EVolutionary Approach.* Clarendon, Oxford, 1992.

[POSIX, 1990]   *Portable Operating System Interface for Computing Environments* IEEE Std. 1003.1, IEEE, 1990.

[Potts, 1996]   C. Potts, "Supporting software design: Integrating design methods and design rationale," in T.P. Moran & J.M. Carroll (eds.) *Design Rationale: Concepts, Techniques, and Use.* Lawrence Erlbaum Associates, Mahwah, NJ, 1996.

[Potts & Bruns, 1988]   C. Potts & G. Bruns, "Recording the Reasons for Design Decisions," in *Proceedings of the 10th International Conference on Software Engineering*, pp. 418–427, 1988.

[Potts et al., 1994]   C. Potts, K. Tkahashi, & A. I. Anton, "Inquiry-based requirements analysis," *IEEE Software*, Vol. 11, No. 2, pp. 21–32, 1994.

[Purvis et al, 1996]   M. Purvis, M. Purvis, & P. Jones, "A group collaboration tool for software engineering projects," *Conference Proceedings of Software Engineering: Education and Practice (SEEP'96)*, Dunedin, NZ. Jan. 1996.

[Rational, 1998]   *Rationale Rose 98: Using Rose.* Rational Software Corp., Cupertino, CA, 1998.

[Raymond, 1998]   E. Raymond, "The cathedral and the bazaar," available at http://www.tuxedo.org/~esr/writings/cathedral-bazaar/cathedral-bazaar.html, 1998.

[Reeves et al., 1992]   B. Reeves & F. Shipman, "Supporting communication between designers with artifact-centered eVolving information spaces," in *Conference on Computer-Supported Cooperative Work Proceedings*, Toronto, Canada, 1992.

[RMI, 1998]   *Java Remote Method Invocation*, JDK Documentation. Javasoft, 1998.

[Rogers et al., 1986]   *The Presidential Commission on the Space Shuttle Challenger Accident Report.* Washington, DC, June 1986.

[Rowen, 1990]   R. B. Rowen, "Software project management under incomplete and ambiguous specifications," *IEEE Transactions on Engineering Management,* Vol. 37, No. 1, 1990.

[Royse, 1970]   W. W. Royse, "Managing the development of large software systems," in *Tutorial: Software Engineering Project Management*, IEEE Computer Society, Washington, DC, pp. 118–127, 1970.

[Rubin, 1994]	J. Rubin, *Handbook of Usability Testing*. Wiley, New York, 1994.
[Rumbaugh et al., 1991]	J. Rumbaugh, M. Blaha, W. Premerlani, F. Eddy, & W. Lorensen, *Object-Oriented Modeling and Design*. Prentice Hall, Englewood Cliffs, NJ, 1991.
[Saeki, 1995]	M. Saeki, "Communication, collaboration, and cooperation in software development—How should we support group work in software development?" in *Asia-Pacific Software Engineering Conference Proceedings,* Brisbane, Australia, 1995.
[Schmidt, 1997]	D. C. Schmidt, "Applying design patterns and frameworks to develop object-oriented communication software," *Handbook of Programming Languages*, Vol. 1, Peter Salus (ed.), MacMillan Computer, 1997.
[Seaman & Basili, 1997]	C. B. Seaman & V. R. Basili, "An empirical study of communication in code inspections," in *Proceedings of the 19th International Conference on Software Engineering,* Boston, MA, 1997.
[Shaw & Garlan, 1996]	M. Shaw & D. Garlan, *Software Architecture: Perspectives on an Emerging Discipline*. Prentice Hall, Upper Saddle River, NJ, 1996.
[Shipman & McCall, 1997]	F. M. Shipman III & R. J. McCall, "Integrating Different Perspectives on Design Rationale: Supporting the Emergence of Design Rationale from Design Communication," *Artificial Intelligence in Engineering Design, Analysis, and Manufacturing*, Vol. 11, No. 2, 1997.
[Siewiorek & Swarz, 1992]	D. P. Siewiorek & R. S. Swarz, *Reliable Computer Systems: Design and Evaluation*. 2nd ed. Digital, Burlington, MA, 1992.
[Silberschatz et al, 1991]	A. Silberschatz, J. Peterson, & P. Galvin, *Operating System Concepts*. 3rd ed. Addison-Wesley, Reading, MA, 1991.
[Simon, 1970]	H. A. Simon, *The Sciences of the Artificial*. MIT Press, Cambridge, MA, 1970.
[Spivey, 1989]	J. M. Spivey, *The Z Notation, A Reference Manual*. Prentice Hall Int., Hertfordshire, U.K., 1989.
[Steelman, 1978]	*Requirements for High Order Computer Programming Languages: Steelman*. U.S. Department of Defense, Washington, DC, 1978.
[Subrahmanian et al., 1997]	E. Subrahmanian, Y. Reich, S. L. Konda, A. Dutoit, D. Cunningham, R. Patrick, M. Thomas, & A. W. Westerberg, "The *n*-dim approach to building design support systems," *Proceedings of ASME Design Theory and Methodology DTM '97*, ASME, New York, 1997.
[Szyperski, 1998]	C. Szyperski, Component Software: Beyond Object-Oriented Programming, ACM Press, New York, Addison-Wesley, 1998.
[Tanenbaum, 1996]	A. S. Tanenbaum, *Computer Networks,* 3rd ed. Prentice Hall, Upper Saddle River, NJ, 1996.
[Teamwave, 1997]	Teamwave Inc., http://www.teamwave.com, 1997.
[Tichy, 1985]	W. Tichy, "RCS—a system for version control," *Software Practice and Experience*. Vol. 15, No. 7, 1985.
[Turner & Robson, 1993]	C. D. Turner & D. J. Robson, "The state-based testing of object-oriented programs," *Conference on Software Maintenance*. pp. 302–310, Sept. 1993.

[Vaughan, 1996]   D. Vaughan, *The Challenger Launch Decision: Risky Technology, Culture, and Deviance at NASA*. The University of Chicago Press, Chicago, IL, 1996.

[Walker et al., 1980]   B. J. Walker, R. A. Kemmerer, & G. J. Popek, "Specification and verification of the UCLA Unix security kernel." *Communications of the ACM*, Vol. 23, No. 2, pp. 118–131, 1980.

[Wilson & Ostrem, 1999]   G. Wilson & J. Ostrem, *WebObjects Developer's Guide*. Apple Computers, Cupertino, CA, 1998.

[Weinand et al., 1988]   A. Weinand, E. Gamma, & R. Marty, "ET++—An object-oriented application framework in C++," in *Object-Oriented Programming Systems, Languages, and Applications Conference Proceedings*, San Diego, CA, Sept. 1988.

[Weinberg, 1971]   G. M. Weinberg, *The Psychology of Computer Programming*, Van Nostrand, New York, 1971.

[Wirfs-Brock, 1995]   R. Wirfs-Brock, "Design objects and their interactions: A brief look at responsibility-driven design," in *Scenario-Based Design: Envisioning Work and Technology in System Development,* J. M. Carroll (ed.), Wiley, New York, 1995.

[Wirfs-Brock et al., 1990]   R. Wirfs-Brock, B. Wilkerson, & L. Wiener, *Designing Object-Oriented Software.* Prentice Hall, Englewood Cliffs, NJ, 1990.

[Wood & Silver, 1989]   J. Wood & D. Silver, *Joint Application Design®*. Wiley, New York, 1989.

[Wordsworth, 1992]   J. B. Wordsworth, *Software Development with Z: A Practical Approach to Formal Methods in Software Engineering,* Addison-Wesley, Reading, MA, 1992.

[Zultner, 1993]   R. E. Zultner, "TQM for technical teams," *Communications of the ACM,* Vol. 36, No. 10, pp. 79–91, 1993.

Index

Design Patterns

Abstract Factory (267, 498) this pattern is used to shield an application from the concret classes provided by a specific platform, such as a windowing style or an operating system.

Adapter(202, 499) This pattern encapsulates a piece of legacy code that was not designed to work with the system. It also limits the impact of substituting the piece of legacy code for a different component.

Bridge (206, 342, 500) This pattern decouples the interface of a class from its implementation. Unlike the Adapter pattern, the developer is not constrained by an existing piece of code.

Command (215, 501) This pattern enables the encapsulation of control such that user requests can be treated uniformly, independent of the specific request. This pattern protects these objects from changes due to new functionality.

Composite (137, 173, 177, 502) This pattern represents a recursive hierarchy. The services related to the containment hierarchy are factored out using inheritance, allowing a system to treat a leaf or a composite uniformly.

Facade (198, 503) The `Facade` pattern reduces dependencies among classes by encapsulating a subsystem with a simple unified interface.

Observer (184, 504) This pattern allows to maintain consistency across the states of one `Publisher` and many `Subscribers`.

Proxy (210, 273, 505) This pattern improves the performance or the security of a system by delaying expensive computations, using memory only when needed, or checking access before loading an object into memory.

Strategy (212, 506) This pattern decouples an algorithm from its implementations. It serve the same purpose than the adapter and bridge patterns except that the encapsulated unit is a behavior.

Notations

UML use case diagrams (25, 39) Use case diagrams are used to represent the functionality of the system, as seen by an actor.

UML class diagrams (25, 45, 135, 137) Class diagrams are used to represent the structure of the system, in terms of subsystems, objects, their attributes, and their operations.

UML sequence diagrams (26, 50) Sequence diagrams represent behavior in terms of a series of interactions among a set of objects.

UML statechart diagrams (26, 52) Statechart diagrams represent behavior as a state machine in terms of events and transitions.

Activity diagrams (28, 54) Activity diagrams are flow diagrams which represent behavior as a set of activities and transitions.

UML deployment diagrams (188) Deployment diagrams represent the mapping of software components to hardware nodes.

Issue models (290) Issue models represent the justification of decisions in terms of issues, proposals, arguments, criteria, and resolutions.

PERT charts (425) PERT charts represent the division of work into tasks and ordering constraints.